D0203319

PASCAL

Exploring Problem-Solving and Program Design

PASCAL

Exploring Problem-Solving and Program Design

Dennis Corliss
Corvallis High School

Kathleen Seagraves Higdon
Oregon State University

West Publishing Company
St. Paul   New York   Los Angeles   San Francisco

Copyediting: Janet Hunter
Composition: Carlisle Communications
Cover Design: Studio West, Inc.

Chapter opening quotes reprinted from *Through the Looking Glass* by Lewis Carroll; courtesy of Random House, Inc.

Permission granted to use the name UCSD PASCAL™ by the Regents of the University of California on behalf of the San Diego Campus.

Turbo Pascal® developed by Borland, Inc.

Apple® is a registered trademark of Apple Computer, Inc.

COPYRIGHT © 1988 by WEST PUBLISHING COMPANY
                  50 W. Kellogg Boulevard
                  P.O. Box 64526
                  St. Paul, MN 55164-1003

All rights reserved

Printed in the United States of America

Library of Congress Cataloging-in-Publication Data

Corliss, Dennis.
    Pascal : exploring problem solving and program design.

    Includes index.
    1. Pascal (Computer program language)   I. Seagraves
Higdon, Kathy. II. Title.
QA76.73.P2C69 1988   005.13′3   87-25440
ISBN 0-314-59361-6
ISBN 0-314-59360-8 (soft)

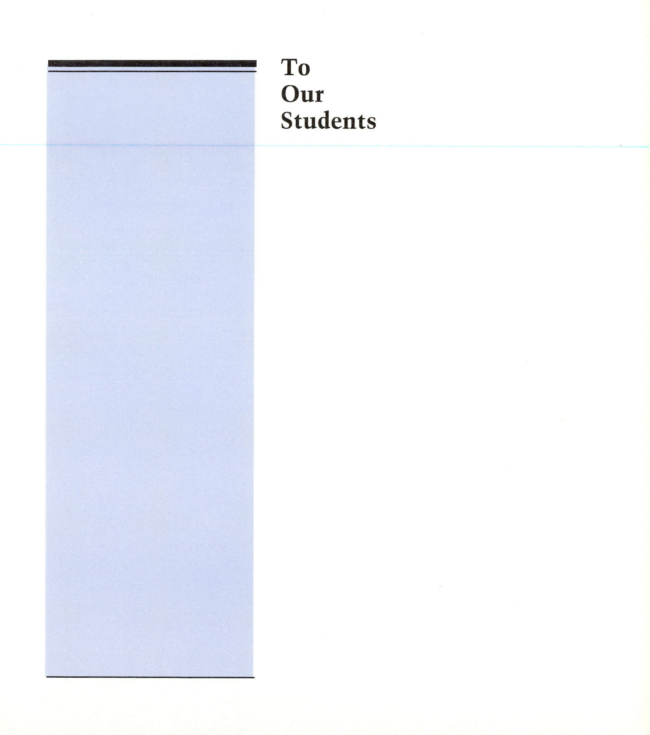

To
Our
Students

Contents

Chapter 15   Records   399

Chapter 16   Files   425

Chapter 17   Linked Lists   451

Programmer's Handbook

Preface

Computer programming involves a great deal more than the syntax of a particular language. Perhaps the most essential ingredient of computer programming is the ability to solve problems. These abilities allow us to take the available information and tools, and manipulate them to solve a problem. The problem-solving skills developed through studying a programming language are far more important than the language itself. Combining a strong problem solving base with a complete knowledge of the programming language and system used, along with an appropriate programming style, can produce effective and understandable programs.

With this in mind, the intent of this book is to provide students and teachers with a tool that will not only illustrate Pascal, a programming language, but will also develop good problem-solving techniques and programming style. Practice with problem-solving techniques in a variety of exercises will enhance the learner's abilities. In this textbook the heuristics of problem-solving and elements of programming style are introduced gradually, so the learner can practice the techniques in the order they are developed. Thus, problem solving and programming style should be a major emphasis throughout a course that uses this textbook.

Organization

This book assumes no previous programming experience. The early chapters emphasize the rudiments of Pascal and develop problem-solving techniques and programming style. Procedures are introduced early in their simplest form (Chapter 4), so that the structure of Pascal programming begins right away. Students then practice modular programming and gain experience with this concept before tackling procedures with parameters (Chapter 8). This method of introducing procedures has proven extremely effective, especially for students with little experience in structured programming and the passing of parameters. The looping structures (Chapters 5 and 6) are introduced before the conditional statements (Chapter 7) in order to encourage their use.

The data structures of Pascal are developed in Chapters 11-18, starting with programmer-defined types and sets. Chapter 13 presents the structure of arrays and Chapter 14 develops numerous applications of arrays. These chapters are followed by chapters introducing records, files, linked lists, and trees. The previously learned data structures are used with each of these developments.

Some chapters or parts of chapters can be introduced earlier, if desired. For example, it may be helpful to introduce files (Chapter 16) early to allow easy storage and retrieval of larger sets of data. The string and graphics chapters (Chapter 19 and Chapter 20) can also be introduced earlier. These chapters are not essential for most Pascal courses, but provide useful tools and enrichment activities.

Features

Several features are included in the textbook to assist the learner and the teacher in developing programming skills.

- Perspectives introduce the material covered in each chapter and establish an appropriate framework for learning.
- Lessons introduce topics in a concise manner. They are short enough to be easily manageable, yet provide complete coverage of the topics. Clear examples illustrate key concepts and are presented throughout the lessons.
- Problem-solving techniques are discussed and used throughout the textbook.
- Complete programs allow the learner to enter the program and study how the new concept works.
- Highlighted statements and boldface terms provide the learner with helpful guides. New terms are boldfaced the first time they are introduced.
- Boxed information provides a summary of important points.
- Lesson Checks follow each lesson to allow for the review of important points. Answers to the Lesson Checks are provided at the end of each chapter.
- Programming Tips provide the students with numerous ideas on problem solving and program design. These tips build techniques in the early chapters that are practiced and expanded during the later chapters.
- Summary and Key Terms provide a review of the chapter material.
- Exercises give the students the opportunity to solve problems. The exercises are presented in three levels of difficulty and offer great variety. Answers to selected exercises are provided at the back of the textbook.
- Programmer's Handbook provides reference material, tutorials, and sample programs for selected topics. Some of the sections will be an integral part in most courses, such as the tutorials on editing, whereas others will be used for enrichment.

■ Glossary provides definitions of key terms used throughout the textbook.

Acknowledgments

Many individuals have given valuable input regarding improvements to this textbook. This text was tested extensively at both the high school and the college level. It began as a packet of materials written by K. Seagraves Higdon for a Pascal course for prospective teachers. A very special thank you to the students of this first class. These first materials were soon being used by other teachers at the high school and college level.

We wish to thank the high school and college teachers who used the preliminary versions of the book and provided us with helpful feedback: Asa Daly, South Albany High School, Albany, Oregon; Alan Dunn, Oregon City High School, Oregon City, Oregon; James Ellis, West Albany High School, Albany, Oregon; Margaret Moore Niess, Oregon State University, Corvallis, Oregon; Carla Randall, Division of Continuing Education, Portland State University, Portland, Oregon; Wallace Rogelstad, Rex Putnam High School, Milwaukie, Oregon; Joan Winter, Oregon State University, Corvallis, Oregon.

We would also like to thank the following individuals for their reviews of the manuscript.

Reza Ahmadnia	LouAnne Laurance
Kathy Beard	William Leprere
Andrew Bernat	James L. Lyle
Don Cochran	Robert Macartney
Wayne Cole	Gloria Musgnug
Leslie Conery	Richard O'Lander
Sister Victoria Commins	Michael Owens
Richard Easton	Judith A. Palagallo
John Ekstrom	John E. Parnell
Mary Enox	Early Roddy
Bill Goodyear	Naomi R. Salaman
Linda Hardman	Harlie Smith
John D. Holt	Charlene Wagstaff
Joseph B. Klerlein	Paul Weber
Mary Lanard	Melanie Wolf-Greenburg
Richard G. Larson	Henderson Yeung

We would like to thank the people at West Publishing Company for their efforts and encouragement. A special thanks to Richard Jones for his constant support and many constructive comments.

Additionally, we would like to thank our many high school and college students who motivated this book. In particular, Peter Ernie and Conan Witzel should be thanked for specific contributions.

A very special thanks goes to Laurie Corliss for her extensive editing, proofreading, and writing of numerous exercises. Her diligent work, suggestions, and encouragement were crucial to the success of this project.

And finally, we thank our spouses, Laurie and Bob, for their constant encouragement and support, and our children, David, Daniel, Leanna, and Lauren for understanding.

PASCAL

Exploring Problem-Solving and Program Design

1

A Computer Science Perspective

Thus grew the tale of Wonderland:

Thus slowly, one by one,

Its quaint events were hammered out—

—Lewis Carroll

Overview

Gaining a Perspective

Computers play a significant role in modern society. Today's changing lifestyle bears dramatic witness to the impact of computers on society, often referred to as the Computer Revolution.

Computers have allowed business and industry to expand, and have opened new frontiers in research and development. In business, computers are commonly used to record transactions and keep track of inventories. For example, grocery stores often use the Universal Product Code (UPC), the vertical bars printed on most items, to record sales and inventory information. Business offices keep track of appointments, and booking agencies (such as travel agencies) schedule travel plans using the computer. Financial services provide up-to-date quotes on stocks, bonds, and commodity prices. The automated teller provided by most banks allows computerized deposits and withdrawals. In industry, parts are checked for defects, and designs for new products are drawn using a computer. Industrial robots are excellent for repetitive tasks and for jobs that could be dangerous to humans, such as working with radioactive material. Computers are also used in science to record data, make predictions, and interpret results. Many current medical advances utilize computer technology.

Computers have also presented some difficulties. Use of computers in business now requires extra security measures and programs to thwart computer fraud. In some cases, computers that have helped automate work have put human workers out of their jobs either because the same number of workers were no longer necessary or because they were replaced with robots. Information on individuals—ranging from personal data, to financial worth, to medical history—is increasingly stored in data bases. Medical diagnosis can be very accurate and medical research can include enormous amounts of data, but might such use impinge upon the patients' privacy? Laws have been written to protect individual privacy threatened by the information storage made possible by computers. New laws will continue to be necessary as computer capability expands.

The computers available today are changing rapidly in size, speed, capability, and cost. Keeping up with these changes is a difficult task at best. To better appreciate the capabilities of today's computers, a look at the history of computing is in order. This chapter will take a look at computers both past and present, and the means by which today's computers are used.

Lesson 1.1 History of Computing

The history of computers actually begins with human interest in finding easier methods of counting objects and tabulating results. Counting on fingers was simple and transportable; it accounts for the base-10 numbering system we use everyday. But as the number of objects to be counted increased, other counting techniques became necessary.

Early shepherds kept track of the number of sheep in their herds by using a stone to represent each sheep. An extra stone meant there was a sheep missing. But think how cumbersome that method must have been for the shepherd with many sheep or with only large, heavy stones. In this lesson, we will describe some of the early computing techniques and devices used to simplify and speed up the process of counting. As we will see, these developments eventually led to today's computers.

Computers' Precursors

A calculating device called the **abacus,** used in many early civilizations, is still used today in parts of China and Japan. The early abacus consisted of beads strung on wires. In the present-day abacus, each wire has a different place value; that is, one wire represents the one's digit; the next wire, the ten's digit; and so on. Addition and subtraction can be performed using the abacus. A slightly different abacus was devised by the Romans. This abacus consisted of a grooved tablet with stones in each groove. The Romans called the stones calculi, from which the word *calculate* originates.

A variety of inventors contributed greatly to the development of computing. John Napier (1550–1617), a sixteenth century Scottish mathematician and theologian, advanced the ideas of his day. In his writings, he described a tank, a submarine, and a machine gun. Napier invented **logarithms** to simplify computations. Logarithms may be used to turn multiplication and division problems into easier problems.

Napier also invented a mechanical device, called **Napier's bones,** to simplify multiplication problems. Napier's bones consisted of nine rods; for this reason, the device is sometimes referred to as Napier's rods. Each rod is divided into nine equal squares, each with a number and diagonal line inscribed. The squares on the first rod are numbered 1 through 9; those on the

Figure 1.1
Multiplying Using
Napier's Bones

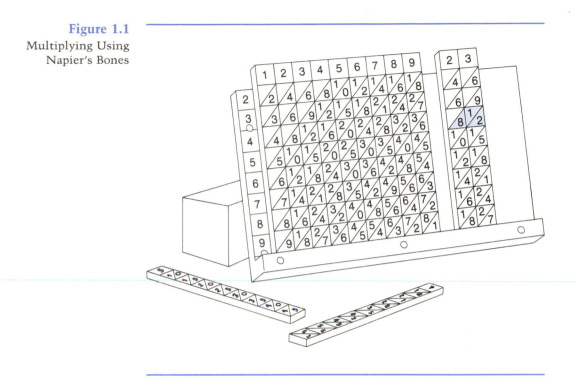

second rod, 2 through 18 (multiples of two); those on the third rod, 3 through 27 (multiples of 3); and so on through all nine rods. As an example, to multiply 23 by 4, use rods 2 and 3. Next find row 4 on both rods. The digits of the answer are obtained by adding the numbers between the diagonal lines of row 4, as shown in Figure 1.1. This device led to the development of the slide rule by William Oughtred, an English mathematician and clergyman.

In 1623, William Stickard invented the first calculating machine to help with astronomical calculations. Stickard used the ideas of clockmakers to make a gear-driven calculator that could add and subtract automatically, and multiply and divide with some intermediate help from the user. Stickard and his entire family died in a plague resulting from the Thirty Years War so knowledge of his calculator was not widespread.

Soon after, in 1643, Blaise Pascal (1623–1662), a French mathematician and philosopher, independently invented a mechanical calculator that could add and subtract automatically and convert among the various French coinages. Pascal developed the calculator to help his father with the calculations involved in revising the tax structure in their French province. The machine, called the **Pascaline,** was a mechanical device using gears; it is illustrated in Figure 1.2. Pascal, like Stickard, realized how to make a machine that could carry and borrow. Each of the wheels of the machine had ten cogs. When a ten-cogged wheel turned one complete revolution, one cog turned on a second ten-cogged wheel (making one-tenth of a revolution). Pascal and Stickard had in-

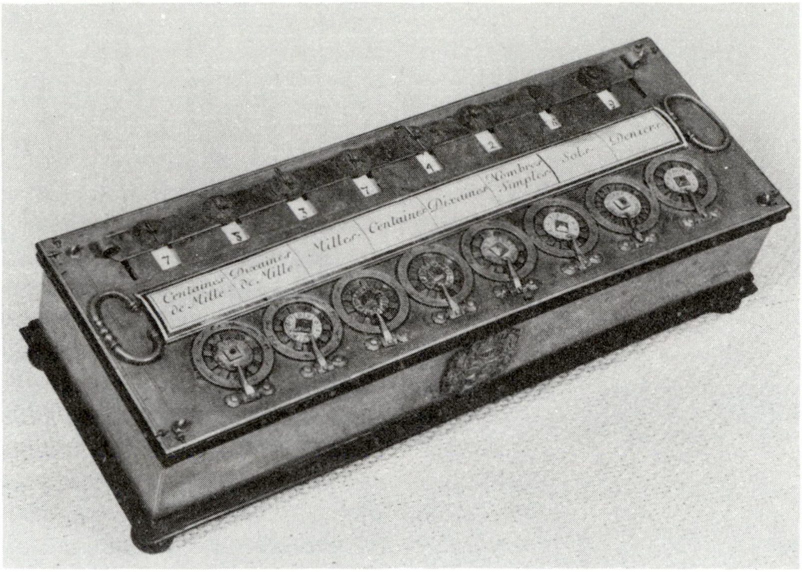

Figure 1.2
The Pascaline
(*Courtesy IBM
Corporation*)

vented a mechanical representation of base-10 place value. Blaise Pascal, for whom the computer language **Pascal** was named, was a mathematical genius. His most famous work was devising Pascal's Triangle, useful in algebra and probability.

Thirty years later, Gottfried Wilhelm Leibniz (1646–1716), a German historian, jurist, mathematician, philosopher, and scientist, devised a calculator that could perform the four basic operations (addition, subtraction, multiplication, and division) and extract square roots. This calculator used two main sets of wheels, one for input and the other for output. These same wheels were used in all operations. Multiplication and division required an additional wheel, called the stepping wheel. Leibniz, known as a universal genius, also suggested that all reasoning could be represented by a language. His ideas helped lead to the development of **Boolean algebra,** the logic of computers today.

As indicated earlier, accounting and calculations of astronomical numbers played significant roles in the development of computing devices. During the Industrial Revolution, the changing technology and demands of the growing population also created a need for better mechanization.

One technological advancement that aided computer development was the **Jacquard loom.** In 1801, Joseph-Marie Jacquard (1752–1834), a French silk-weaver, invented a loom that used punched cards to control the woven patterns in cloth. Jacquard's card consisted of patterns of punched holes, which were used to determine the pattern of the weave. The loom contained a series of threaded needles or rods. The punched card would allow the needle corresponding to a hole to drop through and block the needles not corresponding to a hole. The pattern of the punched holes created the pattern in the woven cloth. The woven pattern could be altered by using different punched cards. Jacquard's punched cards worked on a similar principle to the computer punched cards used today.

Charles Babbage (1792–1871), an English inventor and mathematician, is known as "the Father of Computing." Babbage often noticed errors in published mathematical tables, especially logarithmic tables. The tables were computed by hand and a small error in the table could cause a larger error in a final result. These computational errors led Babbage to design the **Difference Engine,** (see Figure 1.3), a machine that could solve polynomial equations. His dream was to invent a machine that could calculate tables more accurately and efficiently than humans could. The development of Babbage's Difference Engine was plagued by many difficulties. Imperfections in the components caused serious complications. Babbage's ideas were one hundred years ahead of the current technology and the workers were eventually forced to stop work on this project, but Babbage did not stop creating. His next venture was the **Analytical Engine,** a description of a programmable computer. The Analytical Engine consisted of input devices, output devices, an arithmetical unit (called the *mill*), a control unit, and a storage unit; thus, Babbage described the five main parts of modern computers. The Analytical Engine was designed to be programmed using machined cards and was to be powered by steam.

Figure 1.3
Babbage's Difference
Engine (*Courtesy IBM
Corporation*)

Ada Augusta Byron (1815–1852), Countess of Lovelace, was the daughter of Lord Byron (an early nineteenth century British poet) and a contemporary of Charles Babbage. She studied his designs for the Analytical Engine and greatly encouraged his work. According to Ada Byron, the Analytical Engine wove number patterns just as the Jacquard loom wove cloth. She corrected some serious errors in Babbage's work and wrote of some limitations of his machine. She described the idea of a computer program and touched upon the realm of **artificial intelligence,** the forefront of much of today's research in computers. In the mid-1970s, a new computer language called **Ada,** named after Ada Byron, was introduced.

In the late nineteenth century, Dorr E. Felt (1862–1930) and W. S. Burroughs (1855–1898) developed machines that eased business-related calculations. Felt invented the **Comptometer** in 1885. The first version of the Comptometer consisted of a macaroni box, metal staples, rubber bands, and meat skewers. Felt's machine became the main desktop calculator commercially sold for over 15 years. Later, Burroughs invented the Adding and Listing Machine, which was key driven and hand cranked, and which listed the results of its calculations.

The government also had hopes of increasing productivity by using calculating machines. Tabulation of the results of the United States census of 1880 took seven-and-a-half years. For the 1890 census, the United States Census Bureau initiated a contest to find the fastest census tabulator. The winner of the contest was Herman Hollerith (1860–1929), a Census Bureau worker. Hollerith's system used punched cards to represent census information. Using this system, the 1890 census was tabulated in two-and-a-half years and the total population of the United States was tallied in one month. Hollerith's coding scheme is still used. Later, Hollerith started his own company, which eventually became IBM (International Business Machines Corp.).

During the 1930s and 1940s, computer development was rapid due to the world wars. A variety of military problems involving ballistics and equipment design required improved computing devices. From 1937 to 1944, Howard Aiken (1900–1973) of Harvard University supervised a team of scientists who completed the **Mark I,** the first automatic computer. The machine, shown in Figure 1.4, was an electromechanical digital computer controlled by punched cards and paper tape. The Mark I could multiply 10-digit numbers in three seconds. The machine could also compute logarithms, exponentials, sines, and cosines.

In 1945, John Mauchly (1908–1980) and J. Presper Eckert (1919–   ) both of the University of Pennsylvania completed the **ENIAC** (Electronic Numerical Integrator And Calculator), which was the first electronic digital computer. Although ENIAC was built for military purposes, it was flexible enough to be used for other scientific purposes, such as weather prediction. An enormous machine 80 feet long by 8 feet high by 3 feet deep, ENIAC

Figure 1.4   The Mark I (*Courtesy IBM Corporation*)

contained 18,000 vacuum tubes and could perform up to 5,000 additions per second.

Generations of Computers

ENIAC touched off an era of computer development, from the 1950s to the present, that can be categorized according to the technological advances that affected the speed, size, and cost of the machines. The machines of this era may be grouped into four generations.

Vacuum tubes, which controlled the internal operations of the computers, characterize the first generation of computers (1951–1958). (ENIAC was a first generation computer.) The **EDVAC** (Electronic Discrete Variable Automatic Computer) and **EDSAC** (Electronic Delay Storage Automatic Computer) both used vacuum tubes. EDVAC and EDSAC were also the first computers to store instructions (or programs) in the computer, encoded electronically. EDVAC actually stored the programs in a binary code. Prior to these computers, the machines were rewired for each new program; the idea of storing instructions in the computer was developed by John Von Neumann (1903–1957). The **UNIVAC** (UNIVersal Automatic Computer) was the first commercial electronic computer. During this era, the speed of the machines changed dramatically. The UNIVAC I could perform 2,000 additions per second, whereas the UNIVAC III performed 33,000 additions per second. In general, first generation computers were unreliable; they were very large, used a large amount of electricity, and the heat generated by their vacuum tubes caused serious breakdowns. The machines used mercury tubes for memory.

In second generation computers (1959–1964), transistors replaced the vacuum tubes to control the internal operations of the computer. Transistors were more reliable; they were smaller, used less electricity, and generated less heat than vacuum tubes. Magnetic tapes provided a means for external storage of information for second generation computers. Internal storage consisted of magnetic core memory.

Third generation computers (1965–1970) used integrated circuits (ICs), which were tiny transistors placed on pieces of silicon called chips. The machines were faster than first and second generation computers and could perform up to 50 million additions in one second. Third generation computers used semiconductor memory. The development of minicomputers during this era allowed businesses to acquire computing devices at relatively low cost.

Fourth generation computers (1971–198?) use large-scale integrated circuits (LSI) and very-large-scale integrated circuits (VLSI). These circuits are smaller, with more transistors placed on a chip. Microcomputers were developed during this era. Experts disagree as to the end of this generation. Some say the fourth generation is over and the fifth is well underway. They point to superchips that are essentially computers in themselves, large amounts of memory in smaller packages, and increased speed as signs of a fifth generation. Others say these are just extensions of fourth generation technology and that a major change in technology is needed to mark a new generation. No matter who is correct, computers are obviously getting smaller, faster, and less expensive. With current research delving into alternatives to the silicon chip for storing information, as well as predictable advances in technology, the trend toward more power at less cost is bound to continue.

Lesson Check 1.1

1. Match the statement on the left with the correct individual on the right.
   a. Inventor of a mechanical calculator   Babbage
   b. Father of computing   Hollerith
   c. Worked with the 1890 census   Lovelace
   d. Invented logarithms   Napier
   e. Created the idea of a stored program   Von Neumann
                                                   Pascal

2. Describe the internal circuitry that characterized each generation of computers.

Lesson 1.2   Hardware and Software

A **computer** is an information-processing machine that is controlled by a set of instructions. Computers vary greatly in size, memory capabilities, and speed of calculations.

Hardware Components

The machinery or physical components of a computer are called **hardware.** A computer usually consists of four main types of hardware components: input devices, output devices, a processor, and memory. These components are diagrammed in Figure 1.5.

Input devices allow entry of data or instructions into the computer. Examples of input devices include the keyboard, disk drive, tape recorder, card reader, light pen, mouse, joy stick and paddles, and optical character readers. **Output devices** allow the computer to communicate its information to the outside. Examples of output devices are a printer, a CRT (cathode ray tube) or a monitor, and a plotter. Output from a printer is called a **hard copy.** All input and output (**I/O**) devices are called **peripherals.** Peripherals are external devices that communicate with the main computer.

Information that is entered into the computer is changed or processed by the computer. The central processing unit (**CPU**) consists of three units: the arithmetic/logic unit, the control unit, and registers. The arithmetic/logic unit (**ALU**) performs all arithmetic computations and determines the outcome of logic statements or comparisons. The **control unit** controls all activity of a computer system. The control unit interprets each instruction and signals other units when they are needed. For example, the control unit communicates with the input and output devices, when the storage or retrieval of data is specified, and monitors the activity of the arithmetic/logic unit. The **registers** hold the instruction and data currently being used and store the intermediate results of all calculations. The storage of data in registers is temporary. The two most important registers are the **program counter,** which points to the next instruction and the **instruction**

Figure 1.5
Main Components of
a Computer

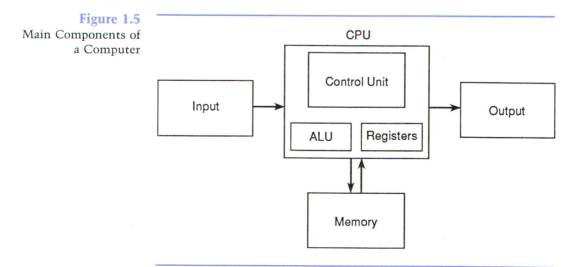

register, which holds the current instruction. There is also a **memory address register** that holds the addresses of information stored in main memory. In a microcomputer, the entire CPU is a chip made on a tiny wafer of silicon and is called the **microprocessor.**

Main **memory** stores data and instructions. There are primarily two types of memory chips: ROM and RAM. **ROM,** which stands for Read-Only Memory, cannot be altered by the programmer. **RAM,** which stands for Random-Access Memory, can be written to and read from, thereby giving the programmer temporary storage of instructions and data.

As mentioned earlier, the registers of the computer temporarily hold program instructions and data, and are a part of the main computer. In contrast, secondary memory is commonly a peripheral of the computer system. Examples of secondary storage devices are magnetic tapes and disks. A magnetic tape consists of a plastic film, much like a cassette tape. Magnetic tapes and disks serve as both output and input devices. A tape drive magnetizes certain spots on the tape surface when writing information and detects the spots when reading information. For small computer systems, cassette tapes are used, whereas larger systems use reels. The data stored on tape must be located sequentially; that is, to locate specific data, the tape must be read in order. Mass storage devices, such as cartridge tapes, are used to store larger amounts of data. Both storage and retrieval of information is slower with tape drives than with magnetic disks. Magnetic disks, which are circular or record-shaped, also have magnetized surfaces. As information is stored on the disk, the location of the data is recorded in a directory; thus, direct access of data is possible. Microcomputers generally use **floppy disks,** which are each made of a thin piece of plastic. Larger systems store information on a hard disk pack, which consists of disks stacked one on top of another. An access arm can search for data by first locating the appropriate disk and then the particular track on the disk.

Hardware that has been set up in a particular way is called the **system configuration.** Examples of system configurations range from a microcomputer, with perhaps a monitor, disk drive, and printer, to a much larger system. One possibility is a **network,** which consists of a group of computers that can communicate with one another over special cables. Computers can also be connected to a mainframe computer. The computing time of the main computer can be shared by all users of the system. This setup is often called **time-sharing.**

Systems and Applications Software

Software consists of the sets of instructions, or programs, that are written for the computer. There are two types of software: systems and application software.

Systems software are programs that are used by other programs. For example, **operating systems** and programming languages, such as Pascal or FORTRAN, are systems software. Closely related to systems software are firmware. **Firmware** are programs that are actually part of the hardware of a system.

Systems software in the form of **programming languages** have been written at many levels and for a wide variety of reasons. **High-level languages** use English-like commands and meet many of the needs of programmers in specific areas of application, the most common being business, education, or science. Examples of high-level languages are BASIC, COBOL, FORTRAN, LISP and Pascal. **BASIC** (Beginner's All-purpose Symbolic Instruction Code) is an easily-learned language developed at Dartmouth in the mid-1960s and available on nearly all computers. On many computers, BASIC is built-in or a part of the firmware of the system. **COBOL** (COmmon Business-Oriented Language) was developed to closely fit the format of business applications that utilize file processing and record keeping. **FORTRAN,** (FORmula TRANslator), is primarily used for scientific computations. **LISP** (LISt Processing) was developed as a tool for designing artificial intelligence programs. (We will discuss the Pascal language in depth later.) There are also **low-level languages** which operate at the machine level. Programs written in **machine language** run much faster than those written in a high-level language, but are usually much more difficult to write and read.

Applications software are programs that are written or used by the user, such as a spreadsheet, data base, or word processor. Also, modeling or simulation programs (designed to indicate what may happen given certain conditions) are applications software.

It should be noted that the actual categories of software are blurred, since the categories reflect the user's perspective. To the Pascal programmer, the two categories just described are accurate; however, to an individual who writes the actual higher-level language, Pascal is categorized as applications software.

Data Representation

Computers interpret information entered by the user by translating high-level programs into a form the machine can use. Computers represent data using the two possible states of digital circuitry—off or on—which correspond to the binary numbers, 0 and 1, respectively.

Binary numbers, also called base-2 numbers, are represented with the digits 0 and 1, just as base-10 numbers are represented with the digits 0 to 9. Counting in base-2 and base-10 requires carrying when all of the possible digits have been used. For instance, the third binary number, 10_2, is formed by carrying 1. In binary, this number is read "one, zero." (The subscript 2 indicates the base.)

By way of example, let's expand a longer binary number

1101_2 (read "one, one, zero, one")

to find its base-10 equivalent. We can write each digit of the binary number as a power of 2. Then we need only multiply and add to find the base-10 equivalent.

$$1101_2 = (1 \times 2^3) + (1 \times 2^2) + (0 \times 2^1) + (1 \times 2^0)$$
$$ 8 + 4 + 0 + 1 = 13_{10}$$

Thus, $1101_2 = 13_{10}$.

We can use this same process, but in reverse, to convert a base-10 number to its base-2 representation. As shown in Figure 1.6, we divide by 2 and keep track of the remainder, until a quotient of 0 is reached. Thus, $13_{10} = 1101_2$. The digits of the base-2 answer are the remainders, listed from last to first (in this example, 1101_2). When the ALU performs arithmetic and logic operations, it uses binary representations for both the problem and the answer.

The contents of memory locations in the computer are also represented in binary. When many computers display the data stored in various memory locations, the binary representation is converted to a **hexadecimal** (base-16) form, which is easier to read. (Some computers display memory locations in octal (base-8) or decimal (base-10) form.) The hexadecimal number system consists of 16 symbols, which are 0, 1, 2, 3, 4, 5, 6, 7, 8, 9, A, B, C, D, E, and F. Table 1.1 shows the binary (base-2), decimal (base-10), and hexadecimal (base-16) equivalents for hexadecimal values 0 to 11_{16}.

Converting hexadecimal numbers to base-2 or base-10 is similar to earlier conversion methods. For example, the hexadecimal value $A1F_{16}$ is equivalent to 2591_{10}, since each digit is a power of 16.

$$A1F_{16} = (A \times 16^2) + (1 \times 16^1) + (F \times 16^0)$$
$$\phantom{A1F_{16} = } (10 \times 256) + (1 \times 16) + (15 \times 1)$$
$$\phantom{A1F_{16} = } 2560 + 16 + 15 = 2591_{10}$$

Figure 1.6

Conversion of a Base-10 Number to Base-2

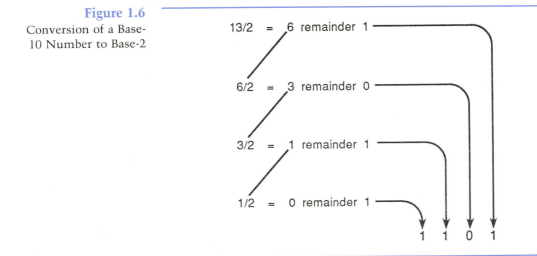

Table 1.1
Base-2, Base-10, and
Base-16 Numbers

Base 2	Base 10	Base 16
0000	0	0
0001	1	1
0010	2	2
0011	3	3
0100	4	4
0101	5	5
0110	6	6
0111	7	7
1000	8	8
1001	9	9
1010	10	A
1011	11	B
1100	12	C
1101	13	D
1110	14	E
1111	15	F
10000	16	10
10001	17	11

Like the base-10 to base-2 method, a base-10 number may be converted to hexadecimal by dividing by 16 and keeping track of the remainders.

As mentioned earlier, hexadecimal numbers are easier for the programmer to read than binary numbers. Converting between base-2 and base-16 is much easier than base-10 conversions. Notice in Table 1.1 that four binary digits are represented by one hexadecimal digit. We can easily convert base-2 to base-16 and vice versa by selecting groups of four binary digits (starting at the right). In the following example, we convert a base-16 number to base-2:

$$A1F_{16} = 1010 / 0001 / 1111 = 101000011111_2$$
$$A \quad 1 \quad F$$

In the next example, we convert a base-2 number to base-16.

$$11011010010_2 = 0110 / 1101 / 0010 = 6D2_{16}$$
$$6 \quad D \quad 2$$

Each binary digit is called a **bit** (Binary digIT). Computers input or output characters (letters, numbers, punctuation, and so on) by using a numeric code for each character. The numbers are changed by the computer to a binary representation called the **bit code.** Today's computers use 6-, 7-, 8-, or 9-bit codes. **EBCDIC** (pronounced "EBB see dick"), the Extended Binary Coded Decimal

Interchange Code, is an 8-bit code. **ASCII** (pronounced "AS key"), the American Standard Code for Information Interchange, is a 7-bit code. A 7-bit code allows 128 (2^7) characters to be represented. When the letter A is pressed by the user, an ASCII code machine converts the A to a 7-bit code. The binary code for the letter A is 1000001, which has the decimal value 65. (See Programmer's Handbook, Section A for additional information).

Lesson
Check
1.2

1. What are the four main components of a computer?

2. What are the three units of the central processing unit?

3. What is the function of the arithmetic/logic unit?

4. What are the two main categories of software? Specify examples of each type of software.

5. What is a high-level programming language? List some examples.

6. Count in base-2, starting at 0 and listing the next 20 values.

7. Count in base-16, starting at 0 and listing the next 20 values.

8. Convert 26_{10} to base-2.

9. Convert 26_{10} to base-16.

Lesson 1.3 Algorithms and Programs

An **algorithm** refers to a sequence of the steps to solve a given problem. An algorithm may be developed prior to writing a program in a particular language.

To illustrate an algorithm, we will take an example that may be familiar to you from camping. We need to show someone how to make a s'more. But rather than just demonstrate, we need to outline the steps necessary to make these treats. The following is a possible algorithm for making s'mores:

1. Roast marshmallows over a campfire.
2. Place a graham cracker on a paper plate.
3. Place a chocolate bar on top of the graham cracker.
4. Place roasted marshmallow on top of chocolate bar.
5. Place another graham cracker on top of roasted marshmallow.

We could have added additional steps to this algorithm. For example, we could have specified the quantity needed of each ingredient or we could have elaborated instructions for building the campfire. The set of instructions and syntax for using them form a language for writing recipes.

A **program** is a precise set of instructions that tells the computer what steps to perform to solve a particular problem and to produce a desired output. Computer programs can be written to solve routine arithmetic computations, or complex problems in specific areas, such as business, engineering, and science.

In 1971, Niklaus Wirth (1934–   ), a computer science professor of the Technical University in Zurich, Switzerland, developed a programming language called Pascal. Wirth named Pascal as a tribute to the seventeenth century French mathematician and philosopher, Blaise Pascal.

Wirth wanted programmers to learn to code—that is, to learn to write programs—in a manner that could be understood by others, as well as be easily maintained and improved by the programmer. With these goals in mind, Wirth developed the Pascal language as a teaching tool to help programmers learn aspects of good programming. Pascal's greatest strengths are its structure, legibility, ease of **documentation** (explanations accompanying the program to enhance understanding) and ease of alteration (especially important in larger, more involved programs). Pascal gives programmers a tool to clearly organize the solution to a problem.

Pascal Versions

Today, many different versions of Pascal exist. **Standard Pascal** refers to the Pascal developed by the International Standards Organization, (ISO). **UCSD Pascal** is a version of Pascal that was developed at the University of California at San Diego to allow users to run Pascal programs on microcomputers. It has special extensions of Standard Pascal, such as additional graphics and sound capabilities. UCSD Pascal is the main subject of this text. Where possible, we also indicate major differences from Standard Pascal.

UCSD Pascal is a compiled language. This means that Pascal programs are translated by another program, the **compiler,** into machine code prior to executing the program. When a program is compiled, it is checked for **syntax errors.** The programmer must remove any syntax errors and compile the program again before it can be stored as a code file. The code file can then be executed many times without recompiling.

In contrast to compiled languages, some languages (such as BASIC) use an **interpreter.** An interpreter reads and executes a program line-by-line. When an interpreter reads a line, it checks for language errors, and then immediately performs the instruction. The next time the program is run, each instruction is again read and checked for errors. This repeated error checking causes the interpreted program to run more slowly than the compiled program.

Lesson Check 1.3

1. Identify each statement as true or false.
   a. An algorithm is an outline of a solution to a problem.
   b. Blaise Pascal invented Pascal, the computer language.

2. Why was Pascal developed?

3. What are some of the advantages of Pascal?

Lesson 1.4   Programming Tip— Problem Solving Hints

The ability to solve problems is the essence of computer programming, as well as other endeavors. Unfortunately, problem solving is not something that comes easily to everyone. The process of problem solving is difficult to capsulize into an easy-to-swallow form. Problem solving can, however, be broken into fairly universal and discernible steps. Adhering to the following steps— each of which we will address in this text—can lead to quicker and better solutions:

1. Understand the problem.
2. Identify and analyze information needed to solve the problem.
3. Devise a plan to solve the problem.
4. Carry out the plan.
5. Check the solution for accuracy or improvement.

Far too often a programmer will start at the third step (Devise a plan to solve the problem.) or, worse yet, at the fourth step (Carry out the plan.). Few problems have an instant, correct solution. If you skip or slight the initial steps of problem solving, your final solution may be inadequate or unattainable. Remember that the time you spend in the early phase of solving a problem will pay off with a correct, high-quality solution.

Good problem-solving techniques go a long way toward making a good programmer. Supplementing these skills with a sound knowledge of the programming language being used and an effective programming style will lead to an ability to attack and solve challenging problems in a systematic manner.

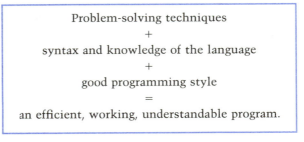

Problem-solving techniques
+
syntax and knowledge of the language
+
good programming style
=
an efficient, working, understandable program.

Summary

Today's computers vary greatly in capability and size, from the self-contained microcomputer system to the nationwide network of terminals and peripheral devices that may be connected to a mainframe computer system.

Hardware, the physical components of a computer, consists of four types of components: input devices, output devices, the processor, and memory. Any program written for the computer is called software. Systems and applications software are the two main types of computer software. An example of systems software is the programming language, Pascal. Pascal is a high-level language developed to help programmers learn to write programs. The structure of Pascal encourages the development of clearly-organized and easy-to-read programs. In contrast to systems software, applications software consist of word processors, data bases, spreadsheets, games, simulations, and drill and practice programs.

The historical development of computing devices dates back thousands of years. Calculations related to accounting, astronomy, and other sciences encouraged the development of machines to simplify computational tasks. Inventions in other areas of study, such as clockmaking and science, advanced the development of computers.

Over the past 50 years, the development of computers has been characterized by the devices used for their internal operations. First generation computers used vacuum tubes; second generation computers had transistors; third generation computers contained integrated circuits; and fourth generation computers used large-scale integrated circuits. The capabilities of computers have changed dramatically over the past few years and will, in all likelihood, continue to do so. Whether the fifth generation has arrived or is due soon, it is clear that computers will continue to have an equally dramatic effect on daily human lives.

Key Terms

abacus	computer	interpreter
Ada	control unit	I/O device
algorithm	CPU	Jacquard loom
ALU	Difference Engine	LISP
Analytical Engine	documentation	logarithm
applications software	EBCDIC	low-level language
artificial intelligence	EDSAC	machine language
ASCII	EDVAC	Mark I
BASIC	ENIAC	memory
binary numbers	firmware	memory address register
bit	floppy disk	microprocessor
bit code	FORTRAN	Napier's bones
Boolean algebra	hard copy	network
COBOL	hardware	operating system
compiler	hexadecimal	output device
Comptometer	high-level language	Pascal
	input device	Pascaline
	instruction register	

peripheral	RAM	system configuration
problem solving	register	systems software
program	ROM	time-sharing
program counter	software	UCSD Pascal
programming language	Standard Pascal	UNIVAC
	syntax error	

Answers to Lesson Checks

Lesson 1.1

1. **a.** Pascal
   b. Babbage
   c. Hollerith
   d. Napier
   e. Von Neumann

2. The first generation is characterized by vacuum tubes and mercury tube memory. The second generation is characterized by transistors and magnetic core memory. The third generation is characterized by integrated circuits (chips) and semiconductor memory. The fourth generation is characterized by large-scale (LSI) and very-large-scale (VLSI) integrated circuits and superchips.

Lesson 1.2

1. The four main components of a computer are the CPU, main memory, input devices, and output devices.

2. The control unit, ALU, and registers are the three units of the central processing unit.

3. The ALU performs all arithmetic computations and logic comparisons.

4. Software can be categorized as applications software and systems software. Spreadsheets, data bases, and word processors are examples of applications software; operating systems and programming languages are examples of systems software.

5. A high-level programming language uses English-like commands to give instructions to the computer. Examples of high-level languages are Pascal, FORTRAN, and BASIC.

6. 0, 1, 10, 11, 100, 101, 110, 111, 1000, 1001, 1010, 1011, 1100, 1101, 1110, 1111, 10000, 10001, 10010, 10011, 10100

7. 0, 1, 2, 3, 4, 5, 6, 7, 8, 9, A, B, C, D, E, F, 10, 11, 12, 13, 14

8. 11010_2

9. $1A_{16}$

Lesson 1.3

1. **a.** True.
   b. False.

2. Pascal was developed as a teaching tool to encourage good programming and problem-solving skills.

3. Pascal's advantages include its structure, readability, and the fact that it is a compiled language (making it much faster than languages which use an interpreter).

Exercises   ## Set I. Comprehension

For Exercises 1–4, select the item that best completes the sentence.

1. The author of the Pascal language was _____.
   a. Babbage
   b. Leibniz
   c. Pascal
   d. Wirth

2. The three controlling parts that perform all the functions of a computer are known collectively as the _____.
   a. arithmetic/logic unit
   b. central processing unit
   c. control unit
   d. registers

3. A computer language that was developed as a teaching tool is _____.
   a. Ada
   b. COBOL
   c. FORTRAN
   d. Pascal

4. A set of instructions written in a computer language is called a(n) _____.
   a. algorithm
   b. formula
   c. list
   d. program

5. Match the general term in Column A with the device(s) in Column B. Each device in Column B may be used once, more than once, or not at all.

Column A	**Column B**
a. Secondary Memory	Card Reader
b. Central Processing Unit	Disk Drive
c. Input	Keyboard
d. Output	Microprocessor
	Modem
	Monitor
	Printer
	Tape Recorder

6. Identify each statement as true or false.
   a. The arithmetic/logic unit is part of the CPU.
   b. The registers coordinate all computer activities.
   c. Pascal is an unstructured programming language.
   d. Firmware refers to built-in software.

7. Convert each binary value to a decimal number.
   a. 11010_2
   b. 1001110_2
   c. 11111111_2

8. Convert each binary value to a decimal number.
   a. 1111000_2
   b. 10101111_2
   c. 11000111011_2

9. Convert each decimal number to a binary value.
   a. 27_{10}
   b. 152_{10}
   c. 87_{10}

10. Convert each decimal number to a binary value.
    a. 36_{10}
    b. 123_{10}
    c. 76_{10}

11. Convert each binary value to a hexadecimal value.
    a. 11100011_2
    b. 10100111100_2
    c. 111110000100_2

12. Convert each binary value to a hexadecimal value.
    a. 10011111_2
    b. 1011001111_2
    c. 111001100101_2

13. Convert each hexadecimal value to a binary value.
    a. $AD3_{16}$
    b. $2B4E_{16}$
    c. $AA1FF_{16}$

14. Convert each hexadecimal value to a binary value.
    a. ABC_{16}
    b. 229_{16}
    c. $B21F_{16}$

Set II. Application

15. Devise an algorithm for changing a tire.

16. Devise an algorithm for changing a light bulb.

17. Devise an algorithm for sorting socks.

18. Devise an algorithm to determine which person in a room is the tallest.

Set III. Synthesis

19. Research three historical events that contributed to the development of the computer.

20. Select an area of study, such as business, education, industry, or science, and research the effects computers have had in this area.

21. Produce a poster or timechart of the historical development of the computer, and the people and events that figured prominently in this development.

22. Select an individual who has contributed significantly to the development of computers. Study that person's work in-depth.

23. Study and report on the latest developments in the realm of artificial intelligence.

2

Input and Output in Pascal

"R ead them," said
the King.

*The White Rabbit put
on his spectacles.*

*"Where shall I begin,
please your Majesty?"
he asked.*

*"Begin at the
beginning," the King
said, very gravely, "and
go on till you come to
the end; then stop."*

—Lewis Carroll

Overview

Gaining a Perspective

The main ingredients of a program usually include the input and processing of data, and the output of the results. These ingredients correspond to the devices or parts of the computer used to enter, process, and output information.

Input consists of the instructions or data entered into the computer and can be thought of as the raw material used in the program. The input may be entered by the program user at the keyboard or may come from a data storage device, such as a disk drive.

Processing requires acting upon the instructions or data. This might necessitate finding the product of two numbers, alphabetizing a list of names, or determining the next move in computer chess. As discussed in Chapter 1, the Central Processing Unit (CPU) of the computer handles all computer processing.

Output involves displaying the results of the processing and can be thought of as the finished product of a computer program. Formatting and printing meaningful output often requires a great deal of a programmer's effort. Output is usually seen on the screen or monitor, but is often sent to a printer or a data storage device.

The components of a program must be put together according to the specific rules of syntax and structure of the programming language. The **syntax** of a programming language, like rules of grammar, is the way statements must be written to be accepted by the computer. The Pascal language has definite rules. In Chapter 2 we will cover the syntax of input and output and the basic structure of a Pascal program.

Lesson 2.1   Program Structure

Program 2.1

```
PROGRAM HELLO. (OUTPUT);

BEGIN

   WRITELN('WELCOME TO PASCAL')

END.
```

The first line of Program 2.1

```
PROGRAM HELLO (OUTPUT);
```

is called the **program heading.** Program headings include the word **PROGRAM,** a program name, a list of the external environments used in the program, and a semicolon.

All Pascal programs begin with the word PROGRAM. The word PROGRAM is a reserved word. A **reserved word** is a part of the Pascal language that cannot be used for any other purpose in the program. You will find a complete list of Pascal reserved words at the end of this book in the Programmer's Handbook, Section R.

Program names in Pascal are called **identifiers.** Identifiers are primarily names chosen by the programmer. In Program 2.1, the program name is the identifier HELLO. The program name should be a word that describes what the program will accomplish. Usually this name will not be used in other parts of the program.

Identifiers have additional uses in a program, so their form is important to understand.

Identifier Form

Letter   followed by $\begin{cases} \text{Letters} \\ \text{Digits} \\ \text{Underline character (\_), in some} \\ \text{versions of Pascal} \end{cases}$

Here are some examples of legal and illegal Pascal identifiers.

Legal Identifiers	Illegal Identifiers
CO2	2BE
GOODPROGRAM	BOB'S
ENDWHEN	BEGIN
AVERAGE	PERCENT%
SALES_TAX	SALES-TAX
WRITELN	PROGRAM
TOTALSALARY	TOTAL SALARY

Pascal identifiers must meet four requirements, as shown in the following list.

■ All identifiers must begin with an alphabetic character, a letter.

■ All the characters after the first may be letters or numbers, but not spaces. (UCSD Pascal compilers allow the underscore (_) in identifiers.) Single-letter identifiers are acceptable, but are usually not descriptive of the identifier's role in the program.

- An identifier cannot be a reserved word; however, a part of an identifier may be a reserved word (as, for example, GOODPROGRAM).

- A **pre-defined identifier,** that is, an identifier that has already been defined in Pascal, may be used in a program for a purpose other than the reason for which it was already defined. The original intent of the identifier, however, is lost for that program. (WRITELN is a predefined identifier in Pascal. For a complete list of predefined identifiers, see Programmer's Handbook, Section R.)

- All identifiers in UCSD Pascal have what is called *eight-character significance.* This means that only the first eight characters are recognized by the computer. If the identifier has more than eight characters, the computer will display the entire identifier, but will actually use only the first eight characters. Thus, TOTALSALARY is treated internally as TOTALSAL and another identifier having the same first eight characters (TOTALSALE, for example) would be the same identifier, as far as Pascal is concerned. (Note: The eight-character significance is system dependent.)

In Program 2.1, the word **OUTPUT** (in parentheses following the program name) signals the computer to expect output. Specifying the expected external environments in the program heading is not essential in UCSD Pascal, but we recommend it for purposes of documentation. Another external environment that may be indicated in the program heading is **INPUT,** which signals the computer to expect input.

Program Heading Form

```
PROGRAM program name (external environments);
```

Notice the semicolon (;) following the program heading. Semicolons are used to separate Pascal statements. We will discuss the use of semicolons in more depth later in this lesson.

In program HELLO (Program 2.1), the reserved words **BEGIN** and **END** specify the beginning and the end of the **program body** (the location of the program **statements**), and are therefore called **delimiters.** BEGIN tells the computer that a set of instructions is to follow and END designates the conclusion of the instructions. END is followed by a period (.) signifying the end of the program. As will be seen, more than one END can be used in a program. The statements enclosed by a BEGIN-END pair are called **compound statements.** The program heading, BEGIN, and END form the basic shell of a Pascal program.

The third line of Program 2.1,

```
WRITELN('WELCOME TO PASCAL')
```

uses the built-in procedure **WRITELN** to print a message. (A **procedure** is a routine that accomplishes a particular task. More on this in Chapter 4.) WRITELN (pronounced "write line") is the most common method of obtaining program output. The desired output follows the word WRITELN, and is always enclosed in parentheses. Single quotation marks are used to print a message or text; they specify the beginning and end of the text to be printed. The text output ('WELCOME TO PASCAL') is called a **literal string constant.** The output of Program 2.1 is

```
WELCOME TO PASCAL
```

The structure of a Pascal program serves to make the program more readable. While writing a program, you should add **comments** to describe the purpose of the program and to provide additional clarification where needed.

Comments in a program are enclosed by braces; for example, { COMMENT }. A comment may be a word, sentence or paragraph and may be included anywhere in a program. Comments are ignored when a program is compiled or run. The open brace ({) must be followed by a matching closing brace (}). Since brace keys do not exist on some keyboards, an alternative is the open parenthesis and an asterisk, for the left brace and asterisk and the close parenthesis for the right brace; for example, (* COMMENT *).

Program 2.2
```
PROGRAM COMMENT (OUTPUT);

     { PURPOSE: TO ILLUSTRATE THE USE OF COMMENTS }

BEGIN

   WRITELN('MUST YOU CONSTANTLY COMMENT');
   WRITELN('WITHOUT END')

END.   { END OF PROGRAM COMMENT }
```

The first comment in this program describes the purpose of the program. The last comment denotes the end of the program.

Notice the semicolon at the end of the first WRITELN. This semicolon separates consecutive statements of the program. There is no semicolon following the WRITELN just before the END. This may seem contradictory. A semicolon is not needed immediately before an END, since END is a part of the BEGIN-END pair and it is not a complete statement. You could include a semicolon immediately before the END statement if you wanted. It is not necessary, but it is acceptable.

Lesson Check 2.1

1. Name the essential parts of the program heading. What part of the program heading is optional?

2. Which of the following names are legal Pascal identifiers? If the identifier is not legal, explain why.
   a. PRODUCT
   b. GET INFO
   c. NUMBER1
   d. 24TEA
   e. END
   f. GRADE%
   g. BEGINEND
   h. TOTAL_COST

3. Identify and correct the errors in the following program:

```
PROGRAM TO ERR (OUTPUT)

        { COMMENT: CATCH ME IF YOU CAN!

    BEING

        (WRITLEN 'IS.HUMAN')
        PRINT(CONGRATULATIONS')

    END.
```

4. Enter and run the following program:

```
PROGRAM COUNT (OUTPUT);

        { PURPOSE: TO PRACTICE }

    BEGIN

        WRITELN('THE ROSE IS RED');
        WRITELN('THE VIOLET IS BLUE');
        WRITELN('SUGAR IS SWEET');
        WRITELN('AND SO ARE YOU');
        WRITELN('IF YOU LOVE ME AS I LOVE YOU,');
        WRITELN('NO KNIFE CAN CUT OUR LOVE IN TWO.')

    END.
```

Lesson 2.2 Variables and Input

Programs usually require more than just the ability to print messages. Information from the keyboard or another input device may be desired. This information may then be used in the program. The input of information from the keyboard allows the user to interact with the program as it is in progress.

Program 2.3

```
PROGRAM BIRTHDAY (INPUT,OUTPUT);

     { PURPOSE: TO DEMONSTRATE VARIABLES AND INPUT }

VAR
    YEAR : INTEGER;

BEGIN

    WRITELN('ENTER YEAR OF BIRTH.');
    READLN(YEAR);
    WRITELN('YOU WERE BORN IN ',YEAR,'.')

END.
```

In Program 2.3, the program name BIRTHDAY suggests that this program will have something to do with birthdays. Both input and output are expected in the program, as indicated in the program heading.

The **variable declaration,** just before BEGIN in the program, declares the name and the data type of any **variable(s)** used in the program. A variable must always be declared before it is used.

Variable Declaration

```
VAR variable identifier : data type;
```

VAR is a reserved word and the variable identifier, like the program name, is an identifier chosen by the programmer. The **data type** of the variable tells what kind of values can be assigned to that variable. There are predefined variable types called **simple data types,** which are BOOLEAN, CHAR (for CHARacter), INTEGER, and REAL. These are also called **scalar types.** (Scalar means that they are described by a single quantity). Simple data types may be further categorized as ordinal types or **REAL. Ordinal data types** are variables with unique values before and after each element of that type. For example, each element of the set of integers has an integer that precedes and an integer that follows it. The categories of possible data types are outlined in Table 2.1. STRING and long INTEGER variables are available in UCSD Pascal, but not in Standard Pascal.

Table 2.1
Data Types

Simple Data Types		Non-Standard Data Types
Ordinal Types[*]	REAL	STRING
		Long INTEGER
BOOLEAN		
CHAR		
INTEGER		

[*]We will introduce other ordinal types in Chapter 11.

A detailed look at the variety of data types is in order before further discussion of variable declarations.

Types of data may be categorized into **numeric** (INTEGER and REAL), **symbolic** (CHAR and STRING), and **logical data types** (BOOLEAN). In UCSD Pascal, there are two versions of integers that are useful, **INTEGER** and **long INTEGER.** Integers consist of zero, the natural numbers, and their opposites.

$$\ldots -5, -4, -3, -2, -1, 0, 1, 2, 3, 4, 5, \ldots$$

Pascal places a limit on the size of the integers. INTEGER values can range from −32768 to 32767. The maximum integer that the computer can handle is often called **MAXINT.** (MAXINT is a **predefined constant** equal to 32767 in UCSD Pascal.) Here are some legal INTEGER values.

Legal INTEGER Values

−32768

0

3456

−345

32767

A comma is not used in any numeric value; for example, 32,767 is not a legal numeric value. The declaration of the variable in Program 2.3 is an example of an INTEGER declaration. Here is another INTEGER variable declaration.

```
VAR
    POINTS : INTEGER;
```

If an integer is less than or greater than the minimum and maximum values, either the values wrap around (the next integer after 32767 will be −32768) or an integer error may occur, depending on the system. You must therefore be aware of the range of integer values that will be entered or used in a program.

If you will need larger integers, you must specify the length or number of digits. These long INTEGER values may have up to 36 digits. The number of digits of a long INTEGER is indicated in square brackets. For example, integers entered with the variable POPULATION, according to the following declaration, may have up to 29 digits:

```
VAR
    POPULATION : INTEGER[29];
```

(You should be aware that several limitations exist in the use of long INTEGER values. We will discuss these limitations in Chapter 3.)

Real numbers form a numeric data type that includes both rational and irrational numbers. Rational numbers are numbers that can be written as the ratio of two integers, p and q, when q

Figure 2.1
Numeric Data Types

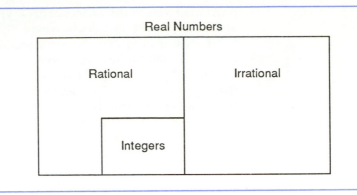

is not zero. Rational numbers can be written as terminating or non-terminating repeating decimals. Irrational numbers are non-repeating, non-terminating decimals and must be approximated by rational values on a computer. Figure 2.1 distinguishes between the numeric data types. The smallest legal value for a REAL number is -3.40282×10^{38}, the largest legal value is 3.40282×10^{38}, and the smallest possible positive REAL value is 1.17549×10^{-38}. Some examples of real numbers follow:

Pascal REAL	Mathematics Real
5.0	5
8.76000	8.76
0.0	0
2.89345E-3	.00289345
3.43256E6	3.43255665×10^6
0.6	.6
3.60000E2	360
1.414	$\sqrt{2}$

Notice that the Pascal REAL values are written in what is called **E-notation** (exponential notation) or as decimal numbers (**fixed notation**). In Pascal, REAL numbers may have up to six significant decimal places and must have at least one digit on each side of the decimal point. Values with more than six decimal places are rounded. A form of floating-point notation, E-notation, is used to represent the powers of 10. (It is often called scientific notation in mathematics.) This notation means to multiply the decimal written before the letter E by the power of 10 indicated by the integer following the letter E. The following examples should help familiarize you with E-notation:

Pascal E-Notation	Mathematics Scientific Notation	Pascal Fixed Notation
4.35430E2	4.35430×10^2	435.43
2.89345E-3	2.89345×10^{-3}	0.00289345
-3.10000E6	-3.10000×10^6	-3100000

Symbolic data types consist of single characters (CHAR) and characters grouped together (STRING). **CHAR** values may be single letters, numbers, or punctuation; they may be any of the ASCII representations. Examples of CHAR are

Legal CHAR values

'A'

'b'

'3'

';'

'+'

'%'

' '   (space)

The single quotation marks surrounding the characters indicate that the data is of a symbolic data type. These single quotation marks are needed to distinguish values; for instance, they are needed to distinguish between the value 3 as CHAR and the value 3 as INTEGER.

STRING values are a sequence of characters; these may be letters, digits, or special symbols. STRING is a data type in UCSD Pascal, and is not available as a predefined type in Standard Pascal. Here are some examples of STRING values.

Legal STRING values

'Hi there'

'A'

'56'

'$4.50'

'80%'

'Now is the time for all great people!'

An example of a STRING variable declaration is

```
VAR
   WORD : STRING;
```

STRING variables declared in this way may have up to 80 characters. If the maximum length of the STRING is longer, the length must be specified in square brackets.

```
VAR
    PHRASE : STRING[81];
```

All STRING lengths must be less than or equal to 255 characters. Where practical, the maximum length of STRING variables should be specified for documentation purposes. Also, if the maximum length of the STRING value is always significantly less than 80 characters, specifying the length will enable you to save space in memory. (This would be true in the case of a STRING variable designed to hold the name of a state, for example.)

BOOLEAN variables have one of two values, TRUE or FALSE. **BOOLEAN** is a variable type that was named after George Boole, a famous nineteenth century mathematician.

BOOLEAN values are   {   TRUE or FALSE

We will provide a more detailed discussion of BOOLEAN variables in Chapter 6.

The colon (:) between the variable name and data type tells the computer that the variable is of the type indicated. Variables of the same data type may be separated by a comma and grouped together. Variables of different data types must be separated by a semicolon.

```
VAR
    NAME,
    ADDRESS  : STRING;
    NUMBER1,
    NUMBER2  : INTEGER;
    COMPLETE : BOOLEAN;
    ANSWER   : CHAR;
```

The spacing used in our variable declarations is for readability and allows us to add comments for each variable to give further descriptions of their use. The declaration could have been grouped as follows or in many other forms:

```
VAR NAME, ADDRESS : STRING;
    NUMBER1, NUMBER2 : INTEGER;
    COMPLETE : BOOLEAN;
    ANSWER : CHAR;
```

Each variable name may be associated with a single type and may be declared only once in a given program block. In this chapter and the next, there will be one program block consisting of the program body. We will explain program blocks more thoroughly in Chapter 4.

Now, look back at Program 2.3. The first statement (WRITELN) will print the message that is written between the single quotation marks.

`ENTER YEAR OF BIRTH.`

Program 2.3 also contains the command **READLN** (pronounced "read line"). READLN tells the computer to wait until a value is entered from the keyboard and followed by a return; then it is to assign this value to the variable. Here are some input examples for the READLN of Program 2.3.

Input	Result
`1975`	This is a correct input.
`SEVENTY-FIVE`	This results in an error message, since this input is a STRING, not an INTEGER.

The last WRITELN of Program 2.3 will print the message contained in single quotation marks followed by the contents of the variable YEAR. Commas separate kinds of output (here, they separate text and the value of a variable). If we use 1975 as the input for YEAR, the output is

`YOU WERE BORN IN 1975.`

We have named Program 2.4 BIRTHDAY2 since it builds on program BIRTHDAY (of Program 2.3); we have also declared additional variables. Take a look at the program indentation, which has been formatted for readability.

Program 2.4

```
PROGRAM BIRTHDAY2 (INPUT,OUTPUT);

    { PURPOSE: TO DEMONSTRATE PROGRAM INPUT }

VAR
    YEAR,
    DAY   : INTEGER;
    MONTH : STRING;

BEGIN

    WRITELN('ENTER MONTH OF BIRTH.');
    READLN(MONTH);
    WRITELN('ENTER DAY AND YEAR OF BIRTH,');
    WRITELN('SEPARATED BY A SPACE.');
    READLN(DAY,YEAR);
    WRITELN('BORN ',MONTH,' ',DAY,', ',YEAR)

    { COMMAS SEPARATE DIFFERENT KINDS OF OUTPUT }

END.
```

Program 2.4 shows that a READLN may contain more than one variable. (MONTH required a separate READLN because it is a STRING variable.) Possible output for this program follows:

```
ENTER MONTH OF BIRTH.
JUNE             (entered by user)
ENTER DAY AND YEAR OF BIRTH,
SEPARATED BY A SPACE.
11 1975          (entered by user)
BORN JUNE 11, 1975
```

Commas are used to separate variables declared of the same type, to separate different variables in the same READLN, and to separate kinds of output in a WRITELN.

READLN is the primary method of obtaining input from the external environment into the computer.

> **READLN Form**
>
> ```
> READLN(variable name, ..., variable name);
> ```

READLN assigns to each variable name in parentheses the values entered in sequence from the keyboard. After all of the values requested in the READLN have been entered, the program continues. (INTEGER and REAL values may be separated by a carriage return or spaces. STRING values must be separated by a carriage return.) For example, the following READLN requests the input of three numbers. Assume NUMBER1, NUMBER2, and NUMBER3 have been declared of type INTEGER.

```
READLN(NUMBER1, NUMBER2, NUMBER3);
```

The numbers may be entered all on one line (separated by spaces) or on separate lines. The numbers could be entered as follows:

```
23 43 45 <RETURN>
```

or

```
23 <RETURN>
43 <RETURN>
45 <RETURN>
```

The result of the entries is that NUMBER1 is assigned the value 23; NUMBER2 is assigned the value 43; and NUMBER3 is assigned the value 45.

The **READ** statement is another way to allow data input of characters or numbers. READ assigns values to the variables in parentheses in sequence as the values are entered from the keyboard. For data type CHAR, READ grabs each character that is entered from the keyboard, including spaces and returns. In the following example, if LETTER1 and LETTER2 are of data type CHAR, then LETTER1 will be the first character entered from the keyboard; LETTER2 will be the next, and LETTER3, the last.

```
READ(LETTER1, LETTER2);
READ(LETTER3);
```

abc   (entered by the user)

As a result of the user's entry; LETTER1 is assigned a; LETTER2 is assigned b; and LETTER3 is assigned c.

No returns or spaces are expected in the input. If either a return or space is entered, then one of the variables will be assigned a carriage return. Suppose the user enters

ab   <RETURN>
c

In this case, LETTER1 is assigned a; LETTER2 is assigned b; and LETTER3 is assigned <RETURN>.

The following two program segments contrast READ and READLN for the data type INTEGER. In Program Segment 2.5, READ looks for the next integer entered.

Program Segment 2.5
```
READ(FIRST, SECOND);
READ(THIRD);
WRITELN(FIRST, SECOND, THIRD);
```

Input	Output
1 2 3	1 2 3
1	
2	
3	1 2 3
1 2	
3	1 2 3

In Program Segment 2.6, READLN is used. Notice that for the first line of input, two values are read using READLN. The pair of READLN statements assign the first two integers on the first line to FIRST and SECOND, respectively, and then assign the first value on the next line to THIRD.

Program Segment 2.6
```
READLN(FIRST, SECOND);
READLN(THIRD);
WRITELN(FIRST, SECOND, THIRD);
```

Input	Output	
1 2 *3*	1 2 3	
1 2 3 *4*	1 2 4	(The 3 is ignored since the first READLN requested two input values. After the request is met, the program continues with the next line.)
1 *2* *3*	1 2 3	(The input of SECOND does not occur on the first line, so the program waits for the next INTEGER input.)

READLN can also be used alone (without variable names in parentheses).

```
READLN;
```

By using READLN this way, you can hold information on the screen until you press the return key.

What happens if the value of the variable entered is not the correct data type? Take a look at the following program segment:

Program Segment 2.7
```
VAR
     NUMBER : INTEGER;

BEGIN

    READLN(NUMBER);
```

Suppose the user enters a value other than an integer for the variable NUMBER. The program execution will stop and an error message will be printed. (See Programmer's Handbook, Section E for error messages.) If a real number is entered, the decimals are ignored. On the other hand, NUMBER could be declared as a REAL and an integer may be entered with no problem, since integers are a part of reals.

Lesson Check 2.2

For Problems 1–5, match the value in Column A with the variable type in Column B. Each variable type in Column B may be used once, more than once, or not at all.

Column A	Column B
1. 5678	**a.** BOOLEAN
2. 'Z'	**b.** CHAR
3. 68.72	**c.** INTEGER
4. FALSE	**d.** REAL
5. 'HELLO'	**e.** STRING

6. Assume the data type of A, B, and C in the following program segment is INTEGER. Using the data that follow, determine the output.

```
READLN(A);
READLN(B,C);
WRITELN(A,B,C);

2 3
4 5 6
```

7. Assume the data type of A, B, and C in the following program segment is INTEGER. Using the data that follow, determine the output.

```
READ(A);
READ(B,C);
WRITELN(A,B,C);

2 3
4 5 6
```

8. Rework problems 6 and 7, assuming that the data type for A, B, and C is CHAR. What is the output of each, given the following input?

```
x34
y56
z78
```

Lesson 2.3 Output

In Lesson 2.1 and 2.2, we introduced the WRITELN statement as the primary method of obtaining output in a Pascal program. WRITELN prints a message enclosed in single quotation marks or a value indicated within the parentheses. A return follows the output.

WRITELN Form

```
WRITELN(expression, expression, ... ,
        expression);
```

The **expression** may be a literal string constant in single quotation marks, a numeric value, a variable, or an expression involving both numeric values and variables. A WRITELN statement may include a return after a comma, but not within an expression.

Another output statement, **WRITE,** may also contain expressions like that of WRITELN but there is no return following its output. Program 2.8 uses both WRITE and WRITELN.

Program 2.8
```
PROGRAM JACK (OUTPUT);

     { PURPOSE: TO DEMONSTRATE WRITE }

BEGIN

    WRITE('JACK');
    WRITE(' BE NIMBLE,');
    WRITELN;
    WRITE('JACK');
    WRITE(' BE QUICK,');
    WRITELN;
    WRITE('JACK JUMP OVER THE');
    WRITELN(' CANDLESTICK.')

END.
```

Output
```
JACK BE NIMBLE,
JACK BE QUICK,
JACK JUMP OVER THE CANDLESTICK.
```

The WRITE statement is almost the same as WRITELN, except WRITE does not return at the end of its output; the next line of print is therefore on the same line. A WRITELN followed only by a semicolon,

```
WRITELN;
```

will either leave a blank line or provide a return for a preceding READ or WRITE.

WRITE has several uses, including prompting for READLN as shown in Program 2.9. A **prompt** is usually a message specifying information about input that follows. It is a good programming practice to make programs user-friendly and interactive. Prompting all input from the user in an appropriate manner is a part of this practice.

Program 2.9
```
PROGRAM PROMPT (INPUT,OUTPUT);

     { PURPOSE: USE WRITE TO PROMPT A READLN }

VAR
    NUMBER : INTEGER;

BEGIN

    WRITE('ENTER AN INTEGER BETWEEN 1 AND 100: ');
    READLN(NUMBER)

END.
```

The number will be entered on the same line as the prompt, as

```
ENTER AN INTEGER BETWEEN 1 AND 100: (enter here)
```

What happens when the message to be printed contains an apostrophe? For example, suppose the message to be output is

```
DON'T PANIC
```

To print this message, enclose the message in single quotation marks and use two single quotation marks where you want the apostrophe.

```
WRITELN('DON''T PANIC');
```

Another consideration in data output is appropriate formatting. **Field widths** allow the programmer to specify the width or the spacing of printed items. The widths of the field are indicated within a WRITE or WRITELN, as

---

WRITELN Form Specifying Field Width

```
WRITELN(expression:fieldwidth, ... ,
        expression:fieldwidth);
```

The following program statements have field widths that allow a field of 20 spaces for the output.

```
WRITELN('USE' : 20);
WRITELN('FIELD' : 20);
WRITELN('WIDTHS' : 20);
```

Output

```
                 USE
               FIELD
              WIDTHS
```

```
- - - - - - - - - - - - - - - - - - - -
```
            (20 spaces)

Here is an example of printing three integers with a field width of 10 each.

```
WRITELN(47:10, 29:10, 213:10);
```

Output

```
        47        29       213
```

```
- - - - - - - - - - - - - - - - - - - - - - - - - - - - - -
```
(10 spaces)   (10 spaces)   (10 spaces)

If the field width specified is larger than the number of spaces used for the output, then the output is right-justified, leaving blank spaces to the left of the output. If the field width specified is less than the number of spaces used for the output, then the field is expanded to accommodate the output—essentially ignoring the field width—except for STRING values. (STRING output that is longer than the specified field width is truncated.)

For variables of data type REAL, the number of digits shown after the decimal point may be specified, as follows:

WRITELN Form Specifying Digits

```
WRITELN(expression : field width : digits);
```

Rounding will occur. For example, given

```
WRITELN(3.14159 : 10 : 2);
```

the computer will print

```
      3.14
```

```
- - - - - - - - - -
```
     (10 spaces)

and for

```
WRITELN(3.14159 : 10 : 4);
```

the computer will print

```
3.1416
```

(10 spaces)

The field width includes the sign, whole number digits, a decimal point, and the decimal digits. If the number of decimal places desired is not specified in the formatting of a real, the output will be in E-notation. Both the field width and the number of digits after the decimal place must be positive integer values or expressions. This technique for specifying the number of digits after the decimal place works only if a field width is also specified.

A special output command, **GOTOXY,** allows the programmer to specify the position of the output on the screen. This command is shown in Program 2.10.

Program 2.10

```
PROGRAM PRACTICE (OUTPUT);

    { PURPOSE: TO DEMONSTRATE GOTOXY }

BEGIN

    GOTOXY(0,20);
    WRITELN('HERE I AM!')

END.
```

Execution of Program 2.10 places the message "HERE I AM!" on the left margin, 21 lines down. The first value in the parentheses following GOTOXY is the horizontal component, the column; the second value is the vertical component, the row. As shown in Figure 2.2, text screen positions use coordinates of 0,0 for the upper-left corner of the screen; 0,23 for the lower-left;

Figure 2.2
Text Screen

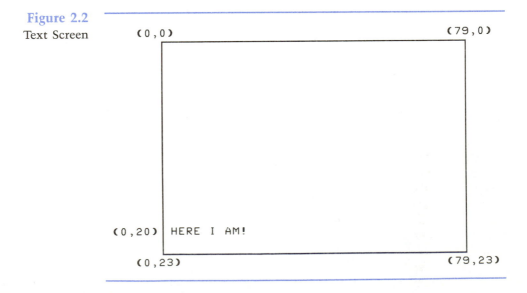

79,23 for the lower-right; and 79,0 for the upper-right. UCSD Pascal assumes an 80-column text screen, although it also works fine on a 40-column screen.

Another special output statement, **PAGE(OUTPUT),** clears the screen and moves the cursor to the top-left corner of the screen. We will use this statement in sample programs in later chapters.

Lesson Check 2.3

1. Determine the output of the following program segment.

```
WRITE('HELLO ');
WRITELN('THERE');
WRITELN;
WRITE('HOW');
WRITELN;
WRITELN(' ARE');
WRITE('YOU?')
```

2. Is the following statement true or false?

GOTOXY is a programming statement that allows jumping from one statement of a Pascal program to an earlier or later statement in the program.

3. Specify the exact output of each program statement. Indicate each space with a dash.
   a. `WRITELN('TEN':10);`
   b. `WRITELN('TWENTY':20);`
   c. `WRITELN(5.467:5:2);`
   d. `WRITELN(2.3:10, 3.567:10, 5.123456789:10);`

Lesson 2.4   Programming Tip—Style

Programs should be written to be understandable by the programmer, as well as by others reading the program. Descriptive identifiers and indentation are important ways of self-documenting a Pascal program, that is, making it easier to read. Select identifiers that are meaningful. For example, a program with the program heading

```
PROGRAM AVERAGE;
```

undoubtedly computes the average of some numbers. Identifiers should reflect what they represent, without being so long as to detract from the readability of the program. Pascal identifiers have eight-character significance, which is a good approximate length for identifiers. In addition, you can use the underline (_) character to improve the recognition of identifiers, as in SALES_TAX and CIRCLE_AREA.

Throughout this book, we provide suggestions about indentation. For a start, indenting two to four spaces within a BEGIN ... END block and leaving blank lines between program parts clarifies program structure.

```
Program Shell
PROGRAM heading;
    { comment concerning purpose of program }
VAR
    variable declarations;
BEGIN
    program body        (to be indented 2 to 4 spaces)
END.
```

In general, use indentation to indicate levels of a program and to show what statements belong to a given block. Pascal provides an environment that allows for creation of easy-to-read and understandable programs. **Debugging** (correcting) or adapting a program can be made much easier if you select identifiers carefully and use indentation to emphasize program parts.

In addition, strategically placed comments can further clarify the meaning of a program or its parts. Comments can make the difference not only in understanding the program, but also in debugging. A good practice is to have a comment at the beginning of the program and each procedure. (We'll discuss this at more length in Chapter 4.) Also, we encourage you to provide comments for unique statements or routines that need clarification. A comment at the beginning of the main program helps show program structure. Comments on END statements, and other program blocks, keep confusion to a minimum and help in debugging.

Summary

Chapter 2 introduced the basic Pascal program structure. The program heading, like the title to a paper, briefly indicates what the program will do. The program heading consists of the reserved word PROGRAM followed by a program name. Reserved words are part of the Pascal language that may not be used for other purposes in the program. On the other hand, an identifier, such as the program name, is a word that is determined by the programmer or may be a part of the Pascal language (for example, WRITELN). Identifiers must begin with a letter and may be followed by letters, digits, or the underscore (_), but may not contain spaces or punctuation. The program parameters (most often INPUT and OUTPUT) used to communicate with the external environment are an optional portion of the heading in UCSD Pascal.

Variables are also identifiers and must be declared as a data type. The standard types are INTEGER, REAL, CHAR, and

BOOLEAN. In addition, variables in UCSD Pascal may be declared as long INTEGER or STRING.

Data Type Summary

Numeric Data Types	INTEGER
	Long INTEGER
	REAL
Symbolic Data Types	CHAR
	STRING
Logical Data Types	BOOLEAN

Program input may be obtained by using the built-in procedures READ and READLN. Both of these procedures assign the values entered by the user in sequence to the variables of the READ or READLN. READLN requires a return at the end of its input. READ does not require a return when CHAR values are being entered.

WRITE and WRITELN are built-in procedures that result in program output. The output, indicated within parentheses, may be text or variables. Text or literal output must be enclosed in single quotation marks and commas are used to separate items of output. WRITELN has a built-in return, whereas WRITE does not. Field width parameters and GOTOXY allow formatting of the output. PAGE provides a way for clearing the screen.

Beyond simple syntax, writing good programs in Pascal involves developing a style that makes them easily understood. The environment provided by Pascal for entering readable programs is one of its main strengths.

Key Terms

BEGIN	expression	MAXINT
BOOLEAN	field width	numeric data type
CHAR	fixed notation	ordinal data type
comment	GOTOXY	OUTPUT
compound statement	identifier	PAGE(OUTPUT)
data type	INPUT	predefined constant
debugging	INTEGER	predefined identifier
delimiter	literal string constant	procedure
END	logical data type	PROGRAM
E-notation	long INTEGER	

program body	scalar type	VAR
program heading	simple data type	variable
prompt	statement	variable declaration
READ	STRING	
READLN	symbolic data type	WRITE
REAL	syntax	WRITELN
reserved word		

Answers to Lesson Checks

Lesson 2.1

1. The word PROGRAM, the program name, and a semicolon are essential parts of the program heading. The list of the external environments is optional.

2. The names given in **a, c, g,** and **h** are legal Pascal identifiers.
   b is not legal because it contains a space.
   d is not legal because it begins with a number.
   e is a reserved word and is therefore not a legal Pascal identifier.
   f is not legal because it contains the percent (%) symbol.

3. PROGRAM TOERR (OUTPUT);   (No spaces in program name; semicolon at end of line.)

   { COMMENT: CATCH ME IF YOU CAN! } (Need closing brace.)

   BEGIN   (BEGIN, not BEING)

   WRITELN('IS HUMAN');   (Move opening parenthesis; WRITELN, not WRITLEN; semicolon needed at end of line.)

   WRITELN('CONGRATULATIONS')   (WRITELN, not PRINT; opening single quotation mark missing.)

   END.

Lesson 2.2

1. **c, d**

2. **b, e**

3. **d**

4. **a**

5. **e**

6. 245

7. 234

8. The output for Problem 6, as reworked, is xy5
   The output for Problem 7, as reworked, is x34

Lesson 2.3

1. HELLO THERE

HOW
  ARE
YOU?

2. False.

3. a. - - - - - - -TEN
   b. - - - - - - - - - - - - -TWENTY
   c. -5.47
   d. - - -2.30000- - -3.56700- - -5.12346

Exercises   Set I. Comprehension

1. Which of the following are legal Pascal identifiers? If the name is not a legal identifier, explain why it is not.
   a. 2NDPLAYER
   b. NAME5
   c. MAGIC SQUARE
   d. LIBRARY
   e. OUTPUT
   f. NUMBERS$
   g. MAGIC_SQUARE

2. Which of the following are legal Pascal identifiers? If the name is not a legal identifier, explain why it is not.
   a. WRITELINE
   b. A23B
   c. 123BUCKLEMYSHOE
   d. SUM
   e. TOTAL WAGE
   f. PER%
   g. INTEREST-RATE

3. Compare the following pair of identifiers. Does each represent a distinct Pascal identifier? If the identifiers are not distinct, state the reason.
   COMPUTE
   COMPUTATIONS

4. Compare the following pair of identifiers. Does each represent a distinct Pascal identifier? If the identifiers are not distinct, state the reason.

   CALCULATION
   CALCULATE

5. Classify each of the following as a reserved word, a predefined identifier, or neither:
   a. READLN
   b. PROGRAM
   c. AREA
   d. GOTOXY
   e. END

6. Classify each of the following as a reserved word, a predefined identifier, or neither:
   a. WRITELN
   b. BEGIN
   c. VAR
   d. PAGE
   e. READLINE

7. Specify the errors in the following program headings:
   a. PROGRAM AVERAGE (OUTPUT)
   b. PROGRAM BEGIN;

8. Specify the errors in the following program headings:
   a. PROGRAM NAME (INPUT; OUTPUT);
   b. PROGRAM WRITELN (OUTPUT);

9. What punctuation is used to separate Pascal statements?

10. What punctuation is used to separate the expressions in a WRITELN?

11. Which of the following are valid Pascal INTEGER values? If any are not valid, explain why.
    a. 23.7
    b. 3,567
    c. −32768
    d. 2

12. Which of the following are valid Pascal INTEGER values? If any are not valid, explain why.
    a. 5,678,888
    b. 32767
    c. 54.
    d. 0

13. Which of the following are valid Pascal REAL values? If any are not valid, explain why.
    a. .56
    b. −456.0
    c. 5.4E2
    d. 75E−3

14. Which of the following are valid Pascal REAL values? If any are not valid, explain why.
    a. 5.62E.5
    b. .43E−2
    c. 23.
    d. 5.48E50

15. Write each of the following numbers in decimal notation:
    a. 5.8543E6
    b. 9.7544E−2
    c. 0.4323E−3
    d. −0.022E4

16. Write each of the following numbers in decimal notation:
    a. 3.45600E7
    b. −2.34000E−2
    c. 0.23400E−4
    d. 0.03334E5

17. Write each of the following numbers in E-notation:
    a. 63000
    b. −8980000
    c. −0.0002
    d. 0.0000014

18. Write each of the following numbers in E-notation:
    a. 36000
    b. −3456000
    c. −51.7268
    d. 0.0000029

19. Write a variable declaration for the following variables and their types:

Variable	Data Type
a. VALUE	INTEGER
b. QUOTIENT	REAL
c. FIRSTNAME	STRING
d. SYMBOL	CHAR

20. Write a variable declaration for the following variables and their types:

Variable	Data Type
a. NUMBER	REAL
b. COUNTER	INTEGER
c. WORD	STRING
d. LETTER	CHAR

21. Identify the following statement as true or false:

    A variable may be read before it has been declared.

22. Identify the following statement as true or false:

    Identifiers are always variables.

For Exercises 23 and 24, suppose the following variable declaration was made:

```
VAR
    WORD   : STRING;
    LETTER : CHAR;
    NUMBER : INTEGER;
```

23. To which variable(s) could each of the following values be assigned?
    a. 45
    b. 'A'
    c. 'HELLO'

24. To which variable(s) could each of the following values be assigned?
    a. 2
    b. 'ABC'
    c. '2'

For Exercises 25 and 26, suppose the following variable declaration was made:

```
VAR
    WHOLE    : INTEGER;
    FRACTION : REAL;
```

25. To which variable(s) could each of the following values be assigned?
    a. 3.4
    b. -3
    c. 34

26. To which variable(s) could each of the following values be assigned?
    a. 0.7
    b. -2.3
    c. -14

27. Identify and correct the errors in the following program:

```
PROGAM ADVERTISEMENT (INPUT,)

BEGIN

VAR TITLE : WORD;

WRITELN('ENTER THE NAME OF YOUR COMPANY);
READLN(TITLE, ITEM),
WRITLN(BUY'; ITEM; ' FROM ';TITLE)

END
```

28. Identify and correct the errors in the following program:

```
PROGRAM FIRST (INPUT, OUTPUT)

VAR LETTER : CHARACTER;

BEGIN

    WRITE('ENTER A LETTER':);
    READ(LETTER);
    WRITELN('THE LETTER ENTERED WAS ,LETTER')

END;
```

29. List several ways in which you can clarify the purpose and structure of a program.

30. Specify the output of each program segment.

    a. ```
       WRITE('FIRST');
       WRITE('SECOND');
       WRITELN('THIRD');
       ```

    b. ```
       WRITE('FIRST');
       WRITELN;
       WRITE('SECOND');
       WRITELN;
       WRITE('THIRD');
       ```

    c. ```
       WRITELN('FIRST');
       WRITE('SECOND');
       WRITELN('THIRD');
       ```

    d. ```
       WRITELN('FIRST');
       WRITELN;
       WRITELN('SECOND');
       WRITELN;
       WRITELN('THIRD');
       ```

31. Specify the output of each program segment, using the input provided. Assume the variables C1, C2, C3, and C4 are of type CHAR.

Input

```
A B C
D E
```

   a. `READ(C1,C2);`
      `READ(C3,C4);`
      `WRITELN;`
      `WRITELN(C1,C2,C3,C4);`
   b. `READLN(C1,C2);`
      `READLN(C3,C4);`
      `WRITELN(C1,C2,C3,C4);`

32. Specify the output of the following program statements:
   a. `WRITELN(5.89:10, 6.7888:10);`
   b. `WRITELN('HELLO THERE':20);`
   c. `WRITELN('ABRACADABRA':20,`
         `'MAGICAL HAPPENINGS':25);`
   d. `WRITELN(3:8, 2:8, 6:8);`
   e. `WRITELN('IT''S ALICE''S TURN.');`

33. Specify the output of the following program statements:
   a. `WRITELN(43.551:10:2);`
   b. `WRITELN(5.334:5:2);`
   c. `WRITELN(6.2343:5:2, 8.6544:5:2);`
   d. `WRITELN(23.54383:8:1, 23.54383:8:2,`
         `23.54383:8:3);`
   e. `WRITELN('YOU''RE SURE TO WIN!');`

34. Rewrite the following program using appropriate indentation and inserting comments:

```
PROGRAM SAYHI (INPUT, OUTPUT);VAR NAME:STRING;
BEGIN WRITELN('ENTER THE NAME OF THE PERSON');
WRITELN('THAT YOU WOULD LIKE TO SAY HELLO TO');
READLN(NAME);WRITE('HELLO ');WRITELN(NAME) END.
```

35. Rewrite the following program using appropriate indentation and inserting comments:

```
PROGRAM ADDNUMBERS (INPUT, OUTPUT); VAR
NUMBER1, NUMBER2 : INTEGER; BEGIN WRITE
('ENTER TWO NUMBERS: '); READLN(NUMBER1,
NUMBER2); WRITELN('THE SUM OF ',NUMBER1,
' AND ',NUMBER2,' IS ',NUMBER1 + NUMBER2) END.
```

Set II. Application

36. Write a program that will request a person's name and age, and then print a message including the name and age.

37. Write a program that will request today's date and print the date in the form mm–dd–yy.

38. Write a program that will print a form letter, using the first and last name, title (Ms. or Mr.), and address entered by the user. For example, the name *John Doe* would be referred to in several places throughout the letter as *John* or *Mr. Doe*.

39. Write a program that will print the following design:

```
COMPUTER
COMPUTE
COMPUT
COMPU
COMP
COM
CO
C
```

40. Write a program that will print and center your initials on the screen. For example,

```
XXXXXXX      X             X        X
X     X      X             X        X
X     X      X             X        X
XXXXXX       X             XXXXXXXX
X     X      X             X        X
X     X      X             X        X
X     X      XXXXXXXX      X        X
```

41. Write a program that will draw the following text picture on the screen:

```
           T
         T T T
        R R R R
       E E E E E
      E E E E E E
         X X X
         X X X
GRASSGRASSGRASSGRASSGRASSGRASS
```

42. Write a program that "draws" an object on the screen using the words that describe the object, as in Exercise 41.

43. Write a program that allows the user to enter a noun and a verb and then prints a sentence using this noun and verb.

44. Write a program that will print a Mad-Lib. A Mad-Lib consists of a paragraph, written by the programmer, from which a few words have been left out. The user is asked to supply the missing words. The program might ask the user to enter a noun, a verb, an adverb, and an adjective, or enter a favorite animal, color, or food. After the user enters the requested information, the paragraph created by the programmer and the user is printed.

45. Write a program that will print the following table of grade point averages:

STUDENT	HIGH-SCHOOL GPA	COLLEGE GPA
1	3.4	2.5
2	2.3	2.0
3	4.0	3.9
4	3.1	3.5

Use field width parameters for this exercise.

3 Computation

"I couldn't afford to learn it," said the Mock Turtle with a sigh. "I only took the regular course."

"What was that?" inquired Alice.

"Reeling and Writhing, of course, to begin with," the Mock Turtle replied; "and then the different branches of Arithmetic—Ambition, Distraction, Uglification, and Derision."

—Lewis Carroll

Overview

Gaining a Perspective

The ability to process data is one of the most important features of the computer. The central processing unit (CPU) coordinates all of the computer's activities, including both program execution and arithmetic and logic computations. The CPU can be thought of as the brain of the computer. The arithmetic operators and functions introduced in this chapter are performed in the arithmetic/logic unit (ALU) of the CPU.

Many of the Pascal arithmetic operators and functions are similar to their mathematical counterparts. Expressions are formed by combining values with operators such as add, subtract, multiply, or divide; or functions such as absolute value or square root. In addition, several special operations and functions exist in Pascal to enhance programming.

Lesson 3.1 Assigning Values

In Chapter 2, READ and READLN were introduced as a means of allowing program input from an external device, such as the keyboard. The variables specified in these statements were assigned the values entered from the keyboard. An **assignment statement** provides a way to assign values to variables internally.

Assignment Statement Form

```
variable := expression;
```

The := means that the variable is assigned or replaced with the value of the expression; it may be read "becomes." A variable or identifier is always on the left side of the assignment symbol and an expression is always on the right side. The value of the variable is found by evaluating the expression. For example, if the variable DATE were declared INTEGER, then DATE can be assigned an integer value or an expression that simplifies to an integer.

```
DATE := 1988;
NEWDATE := DATE + 1;
```

The first statement could be read "DATE is or becomes 1988." The second statement assigns to NEWDATE (also declared IN-TEGER) the value of DATE plus 1, or 1989.

Caution: Do not confuse the assignment symbol (:=) with the equality symbol (=). Program 3.1 shows assignment statements for several different data types.

Program 3.1

```
PROGRAM ASSIGN (OUTPUT);

    { PURPOSE: TO DEMONSTRATE ASSIGNMENT }

VAR
    LETTER1,
    LETTER2,
    LETTER3   : CHAR;
    WORD      : STRING[5];
    IVALUE    : INTEGER;
    RVALUE    : REAL;

BEGIN

    LETTER1 := 'N';
    LETTER2 := 'I';
    LETTER3 := 'E';
    WORD       := 'NINE';
    IVALUE   := 9;
    RVALUE  := 9.0;
    WRITELN('FOUR DIFFERENT WAYS OF WRITING NINE.');
    WRITELN(LETTER1, LETTER2, LETTER1, LETTER3);
    WRITELN(WORD);
    WRITELN(IVALUE);
    WRITELN(RVALUE)

END.
```

The output of Program 3.1 is

```
FOUR DIFFERENT WAYS OF WRITING NINE.
NINE
NINE
9
9.00000
```

Expressions that are of the type CHAR or STRING must be enclosed in single quotation marks. These quotation marks denote the beginning and the end of the string and also differentiate an INTEGER 9 from a CHAR '9'.

The assignment statement is not like an algebraic equation. The assignment statement always consists of a single variable name on the left side which is assigned the value of the expression on the right side. For example, the following sequence of assignment statements lets NUMBER start at 1 and then increases it by 2. Assume NUMBER is of type INTEGER.

Figure 3.1
Change in Memory
Location NUMBER

Memory after first assignment statement:

NUMBER

1

Memory after second assignment statement:

NUMBER

3

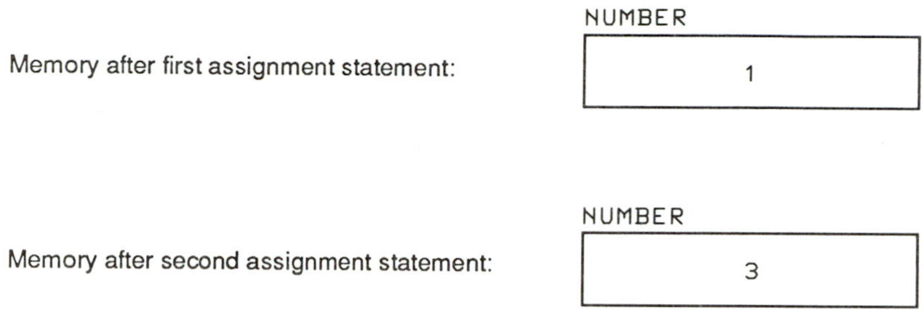

```
NUMBER := 1;
NUMBER := NUMBER + 2;
```

The first statement **initializes** or sets the value of the variable NUMBER to 1. The second assignment statement adds 2 to the current value stored in **memory location** NUMBER. Figure 3.1 shows the change in the value stored in memory location NUMBER.

All variables should be initialized before they are used in an expression (on the right side of the assignment statement). There are two ways to initialize a variable: by use of READ (or READLN) or by an assignment statement.

Caution: Variables that are not initialized may lead to unpredictable results.

Lesson Check 3.1

1. Classify each of the following assignment statements as valid or invalid. Assume the following declarations:

```
VAR
     AVERAGE         : REAL;
     WORD            : STRING[10];
     CHARACTER       : CHAR;
```

   a. AVERAGE := 4.5;
   b. WORD := KATHY;
   c. CHARACTER := ',';
   d. WORD := 'HELLO';
   e. 'HI' := WORD;

2. Write program segments that will do each of the following. Include a variable declaration in each segment.
   a. Assign 8 to the INTEGER variable NUM.
   b. Assign to the STRING variable WORD1 the value 'GOODBYE'.

Lesson 3.2 Arithmetic Operators

The **arithmetic operators** in Pascal are similar to the arithmetic operators used in mathematics. The most common operators used in calculations and expressions are shown in Table 3.1.

Table 3.1
Operator Symbols

Operator	Description
+	Addition
−	Subtraction
*	Multiplication
/	Division (Real division)

An asterisk (*) is the symbol for multiplication and a slash (/) is used for division, as in many other programming languages. The operands of division done with the / may be either INTEGER or REAL values, but the result will always be REAL. For example,

60 * 5 / 6

yields 5.00000E1, a REAL number. In this example, 60 and 5 are the operands of the multiplication (the values that are operated on). (The spaces before and after the operators are for readability.)

Two other operators, **DIV** and **MOD,** may be used to avoid the E-notation of REAL division (see Table 3.2). The operator DIV results in the quotient, the integer portion of the answer when two integers are divided; whereas the operator MOD gives the remainder of the division. DIV and MOD are abbreviations for divide and modulus, respectively.

The following example indicates the relationship between the DIV and MOD operators and division:

```
        25      (The answer to 605 DIV 24 is 25)
   24)605
       48
      ───
      125
      120
      ───
        5      (The answer to 605 MOD 24 is 5)
```

Here are additional examples.

Expression	Result	Expression	Result
16 DIV 5	3	16 MOD 5	1
5 DIV 20	0	5 MOD 20	5
15 DIV 3	5	15 MOD 3	0

Table 3.2
Integer DIV and MOD

Operator	Description
DIV	The quotient (whole number) when INTEGER and/or long INTEGER values are divided.
MOD	The remainder when two INTEGER values (not long INTEGER) are divided.

Caution: When using DIV and MOD, the right operand must not be equal to zero. For example, 4 DIV 0 and 4 MOD 0 will both result in error messages. Division by zero using either the REAL division operator (/) or DIV (or MOD) is not allowed.

Program 3.2

```
PROGRAM DIVISION (INPUT,OUTPUT);

    { PURPOSE: DEMONSTRATE DIV AND MOD OPERATORS }

VAR
   DIVIDEND,
   DIVISOR    : INTEGER;

BEGIN

   WRITE('ENTER TWO INTEGERS TO DIVIDE, ');
   WRITELN('SEPARATED BY A SPACE');
   READLN(DIVIDEND,DIVISOR);
   WRITELN('THE QUOTIENT IS ',DIVIDEND DIV DIVISOR);
   WRITELN('THE REMAINDER IS ',DIVIDEND MOD DIVISOR)

END.
```

Program 3.2 will print the quotient and the remainder when two integers are divided.

```
ENTER TWO INTEGERS TO DIVIDE, SEPARATED BY A SPACE
15 2
THE QUOTIENT IS 7
THE REMAINDER IS 1
```

The operators DIV and MOD are closely related. The MOD operator can be rewritten in terms of DIV as follows:

x MOD y is equivalent to $x - ((x$ DIV $y) * y)$

Substituting integers for x and y may help in understanding this statement.

20 MOD 3 is equivalent to $20 - ((20$ DIV $3) * 3)$

    2   is equivalent to $20 - (6 * 3)$

That is, the remainder of a division problem is the difference between the dividend and the divisor times the quotient.

Program 3.3 identifies each digit of a three-digit integer by using the DIV and MOD operators to break apart the integer.

Program 3.3

```
PROGRAM PLACEVALUE (INPUT, OUTPUT);

    { PURPOSE: TO FIND INDIVIDUAL DIGITS }

VAR
    ONES,
    TENS,
    HUNDREDS,
    NUMBER        : INTEGER;

BEGIN

    WRITE('ENTER A THREE-DIGIT INTEGER: ');
    READLN(NUMBER);
    HUNDREDS := NUMBER DIV 100;
    TENS := (NUMBER MOD 100) DIV 10;
    ONES := NUMBER MOD 10;
    WRITELN('THE ONES DIGIT IS ', ONES);
    WRITELN('THE TENS DIGIT IS ', TENS);
    WRITELN('THE HUNDREDS DIGIT IS ', HUNDREDS)

END.
```

Program 3.3 prints the ones, tens, and hundreds place of a three-digit integer. If the NUMBER entered is 739, then the output is:

```
THE ONES DIGIT IS 9
THE TENS DIGIT IS 3
THE HUNDREDS DIGIT IS 7
```

One of the most important considerations when evaluating an expression is the **order of operations,** or the order in which operations are performed. Correct analysis of an expression depends on the order shown in Table 3.3. All arithmetic operations are performed in the order of these three categories. Operators within each category are evaluated from left to right as they occur in the expression. For example, to evaluate

$$15 - 3 * 6 / 2$$

first scan the problem for parentheses. Next perform the multiplication and division from left to right (perform the leftmost multiplication or division first).

$$15 - \underbrace{18 / 2}$$
$$\underline{15 - 9.00000}$$
$$6.00000$$

Table 3.3
Order of Operation Categories

Order	Operation
1.	Take care of operations in parentheses.
2.	Perform all *, /, DIV, and MOD, left to right.
3.	Perform all + and −, left to right.

Although the subtraction is the first operation to appear in the expression, it is done last according to the order of operations.
Here are a few more examples.

$$16 - \underbrace{12 / 4} + 5$$
$$\underbrace{16 - 3.00000} + 5$$
$$\underbrace{1.30000E1 + 5}$$
$$1.80000E1$$

In contrast, if the subtraction and addition were to be performed before the division, the problem would be written as follows:

$$\underbrace{(16 - 12)} / \underbrace{(4 + 5)}$$

$$\underbrace{4 \qquad / \qquad 9}$$

$$4.44444E - 1$$

More difficult examples might involve additional parentheses. In an expression, the total number of left parentheses must equal the total number of right parentheses. Operations are performed starting with the innermost parentheses and working outward.

For numeric operations, the operands may be of different types. Table 3.4 summarizes what the resulting type will be, given the operator and the types of the operands.

Caution: Notice that an INTEGER result can be assigned to a REAL variable, but a REAL result cannot be assigned to an INTEGER variable. Also, notice the limitations on long INTEGER values.

Table 3.4   Results of Operations on Variable Types

Type of First Operand	Type of Second Operand	Result of Operation					
		+	−	*	/	MOD	DIV
REAL	REAL	REAL	REAL	REAL	REAL	ERROR	ERROR
REAL	INTEGER	REAL	REAL	REAL	REAL	ERROR	ERROR
REAL	LONGINT	ERROR	ERROR	ERROR	ERROR	ERROR	ERROR
INTEGER	INTEGER	INTEGER	INTEGER	INTEGER	REAL	INTEGER	INTEGER
INTEGER	LONGINT	LONGINT	LONGINT	LONGINT	ERROR	ERROR	LONGINT
LONGINT	LONGINT	LONGINT	LONGINT	LONGINT	ERROR	ERROR	LONGINT

The operations introduced in this lesson can be used in the expression part—the right side—of the assignment statement. For example,

```
NUMBER := 3 * 72 DIV 10;
```

Or the operations can be used as a part of a WRITE or WRITELN statement.

```
WRITELN(5 * 4 + 3);
WRITELN('THE SUM OF 5 + 12 IS ', 5 + 12);
```

Note that in these WRITELN statements, no assignment is made but the expressions are evaluated and their results printed. The results are

```
23
THE SUM OF 5 + 12 IS 17
```

Lesson Check 3.2

1. Evaluate each of the following expressions:
   a. 9 − 15 / 3
   b. 66 * 4 + 5
   c. 14 DIV 3
   d. 15 MOD 4
   e. (18 − 3) / 3 + 7

2. Given the following expression:

   60 + 5 DIV 5 * 6

   choose the proper order in which the operations would be performed.
   a. +, DIV, *
   b. DIV, *, +
   c. *, DIV, +
   d. +, *, DIV

3. The following program segment converts Fahrenheit degrees to Celsius. What is the Celsius equivalent of 78 degrees Fahrenheit? Assume C and F are of type REAL.

```
READ(F);
C := (F - 32) * 5 / 9;
WRITELN('CELSIUS IS ', C);
```

   a. 1.07778E1
   b. 2.55556E1
   c. 5.92222E1
   d. 1.70600E2

4. Identify the following statements as true or false.
   a. The operations DIV and MOD may be used with REAL operands.
   b. Long INTEGER values may be divided using the DIV operator.
   c. A REAL result may be assigned to an INTEGER variable.

Lesson 3.3   Standard Functions

Many applications of the computer involve manipulating numbers, characters, and strings. Pascal contains predefined functions to aid with these computations. These functions are called **standard functions;** that is, functions that are built-in and are a part of the Pascal language. (Do not confuse this use of the word *standard* with the use in the phrase *Standard Pascal*.) Most functions studied in this lesson will be familiar from mathematics.

Functions consist of a function name, followed by an argument enclosed in parentheses. The function names used for built-in functions are predefined identifiers. The **argument** of the function is the value acted upon by the function. A function returns a value based on the value of the argument.

The following statement is referred to as a **function call:**

Function Call Form

```
function name (argument)
```

Function calls may be part of expressions. Figure 3.2 shows a function machine that takes the function of an argument and returns a result. There are many types of functions, including algebraic, transcendental, transfer, and miscellaneous functions.

Algebraic Functions

Algebraic functions must have numeric values for both the argument and the result. Table 3.5 sets forth information concerning algebraic functions.

Figure 3.2
Function Diagram

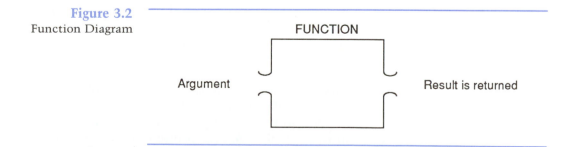

Table 3.5
Algebraic Functions

Function	Description	Argument	Result
ABS(NUMBER)	Absolute value of NUMBER	INTEGER REAL	INTEGER REAL
SQR(NUMBER)	Square of NUMBER	INTEGER REAL	INTEGER REAL
PWROFTEN(NUMBER)	Base of 10 raised to power NUMBER	Positive INTEGER	REAL

PWROFTEN (an abbreviation for PoWeR OF TEN) is a UCSD Pascal function only, whereas ABS and SQR are Standard Pascal functions. Here are some expressions using these functions.

Expression	Result
ABS(−9)	9
ABS(0)	0
ABS(7.8)	7.80000
SQR(5)	25
SQR(−9)	81
PWROFTEN(2)	1.00000E2 (10^2)

Assuming that POSITIVE and NUMBER are INTEGER variables, then the following assignment could be made:

```
POSITIVE := ABS(NUMBER);
```

Algebraic functions can also be used in output statements.

```
WRITELN('THE SQUARE OF ',VALUE,' IS ',SQR(VALUE));
WRITELN('THE ABSOLUTE VALUE OF ',-8,' IS ',ABS(-8));
```

The variable VALUE could be declared as type INTEGER or REAL.

Transcendental Functions

Transcendental functions are functions that cannot be written in an algebraic form; that is, they transcend or go beyond algebraic functions.

In Standard Pascal, many transcendental functions are built-in. In order to use any transcendental functions in UCSD Pascal, the programmer must make a special declaration, USES, just below the program heading.

```
USES TRANSCEND;
```

This declaration calls a portion of the SYSTEM.LIBRARY (see the Programmer's Handbook, Section L) that stores the routines for these functions. Any of the transcendental functions (all of which are set forth in Table 3.6) can be used after this statement is executed.

Table 3.6
Transcendental
Functions

Function	Description	Argument	Result
SQRT(NUMBER)	Square root of NUMBER	Positive INTEGER or REAL	Positive REAL
LN(NUMBER)	Natural logarithm of NUMBER	Positive INTEGER or REAL	REAL
LOG(NUMBER)	Common logarithm of NUMBER	Positive INTEGER or REAL	REAL
EXP(NUMBER)	Power of e to NUMBER	INTEGER or REAL	REAL
SIN(ANGLE)	Sine of ANGLE in radians	INTEGER or REAL	REAL
COS(ANGLE)	Cosine of ANGLE in radians	INTEGER or REAL	REAL
ATAN(NUMBER)	Arc tangent in radians of NUMBER	INTEGER or REAL	REAL

Here are some examples of the square root function.

Expression	Result
SQRT(4.0)	2.00000
SQRT(8)	2.82843

Program 3.4 uses the square root function to print the square root of any positive integer or real number.

Program 3.4

```
PROGRAM ROOT (INPUT,OUTPUT);

    { PURPOSE: TO DEMONSTRATE TRANSCEND }

USES
    TRANSCEND;

VAR
    NUMBER : REAL;

BEGIN

    WRITELN('ENTER A POSITIVE NUMBER');
    READLN(NUMBER);
    WRITE('THE SQUARE ROOT OF ',NUMBER);
    WRITELN(' IS ',SQRT(NUMBER):10:2)

END.
```

If the REAL variable VALUE had been declared in Program 3.4, an assignment statement could be added.

```
VALUE := SQRT(NUMBER);
WRITELN('THE SQUARE ROOT OF ',NUMBER,
        ' IS ',VALUE:10:2)
```

In Pascal, there is no single function that will compute a general power of a number. In order to compute a real number raised to a power, two transcendental functions—EXP and LN—must be used. The general mathematical formula used to calculate a given number to a power follows:

```
NUMBERᴾᴼᵂᴱᴿ := EXP(POWER * LN(NUMBER))
```

where both NUMBER and POWER are of type REAL or INTEGER. NUMBER must be positive. The resulting type is REAL. For example,

Mathematical Expression	Pascal Expression	Result
2^3	EXP(3 * LN(2))	8.00000
$16^{1/4}$	EXP(1 / 4 * LN(16))	2.00000
2^{-3}	EXP(-3 * LN(2))	$1.25000E-1$

The argument of the trigonometric functions, SIN and COS, must be in radians. The value returned is REAL. Remember that 180 degrees is approximately 3.1416 radians; to convert degrees to radians, multiply by 0.017453 (pi/180). For ATAN, the number returned is in radians. For example,

Expression	Result
SIN(3.1416)	$-7.23993E-6$
COS(3.1416)	-1.00000
ATAN(-1)	$-7.85398E-1$

The other trigonometric functions can be defined in terms of these functions, as shown in Program Segment 3.5. For example, the tangent ratio can be computed by dividing the SIN function by the COS function.

Program Segment 3.5

```
VAR
    NUMBER,
    TAN      : REAL;

BEGIN

    READLN(NUMBER);
    TAN := SIN(NUMBER) / COS(NUMBER);
    .
    .
    .

END.
```

Transfer Functions

Transfer functions convert certain data types. For example, the function TRUNC takes a REAL or INTEGER argument and returns an INTEGER result. Table 3.7 summarizes the transfer functions.

TRUNC essentially chops off (TRUNCates) the decimal part of a real number, keeping only an INTEGER value, as shown in Program Segment 3.6.

Program Segment 3.6

```
VAR
      BEFORE : REAL;
      AFTER  : INTEGER;

BEGIN

      WRITELN('ENTER A REAL NUMBER');
      READLN(BEFORE);
      AFTER := TRUNC(BEFORE);
      WRITELN('THE TRUNCATED NUMBER IS ',AFTER);
```

Suppose the user entered 28.64 when the program was executed. The result would be the integer 28. An input of −28.64 would result in −28 output.

The function ROUND rounds a real number to the nearest integer. That is, if the tenths digit of the argument is greater than or equal to 5, then the number is rounded to the next higher integer; and if the tenths digit is less than 5, the number is rounded down.

Expression	Result
ROUND(28.64)	29
ROUND(28.45)	28
ROUND(−2.67)	−3
ROUND(−3.2)	−3

Table 3.7 Transfer Functions

Function	Description	Argument	Result
TRUNC(NUMBER)	Integer part of NUMBER	INTEGER or REAL	INTEGER
ROUND(NUMBER)	Round NUMBER to nearest integer	INTEGER or REAL	INTEGER
ORD(CHARACTER)	Ordinal position of CHARACTER in ASCII set	CHAR	INTEGER
CHR(NUMBER)	Character with NUMBER's ordinal ASCII position	INTEGER	CHAR

Programs 3.7 rounds a real number to the specified digit. For negative arguments, ROUND rounds the absolute value of the argument and then applies the negative sign.

Program 3.7

```
PROGRAM ROUNDING (INPUT,OUTPUT);

    { PURPOSE: TO DEMONSTRATE ROUNDING }

VAR
    ANSWER,
    NUMBER,
    PLACE : REAL;

BEGIN

    WRITE('ENTER THE NUMBER TO ROUND: ');
    READLN(NUMBER);
    WRITE('ENTER THE  DECIMAL PLACE TO ROUND: ');
    READLN(PLACE);
    ANSWER := ROUND(NUMBER / PLACE) * PLACE;
    WRITELN('ROUNDED VALUE IS ',ANSWER)

END.
```

A sample program run looks like this:

```
ENTER THE NUMBER TO ROUND: 29.26
ENTER THE DECIMAL PLACE TO ROUND: 0.1
ROUNDED VALUE IS 2.93000E1
```

The use of the CHR and ORD functions directly involves the ASCII character set. (Remember ASCII, pronounced "AS key," stands for American Standard Code for Information Interchange.) The ASCII character set consists of all the keyboard characters—the letters, symbols, numbers, and codes that can be entered from the keyboard and have meaning to the computer. Each ASCII character has a corresponding ordinal value. For the complete ASCII character set see the Programmer's Handbook, Section A.

The ORD function yields the ordinal value of the argument in the ASCII character set. The CHR function results in the character that corresponds to a particular ordinal value. ORD and CHR are inverse (or complementary) functions. For example,

Expression	Result
ORD('A')	65
CHR(65)	A
ORD(CHR(65))	65
CHR(ORD('A'))	A

Miscellaneous Functions

Two other functions, SUCC and PRED, are useful in a variety of situations. These functions relate to the ORD function and can be used on any ordered values (see Table 3.8).

Table 3.8
SUCC and PRED
Functions

Function	Description	Argument	Result
SUCC(*value*)	Returns the value that follows the given value	INTEGER BOOLEAN or CHAR	Same as argument
PRED(*value*)	Returns the value that precedes the given value	INTEGER BOOLEAN or CHAR	Same as argument

Here are some examples of these functions.

Expression	Result
SUCC('B')	'C'
PRED(TRUE)	FALSE
SUCC(17)	18

Lesson Check 3.3

1. Give the result of each assignment statement. (Assume correct variable declarations.)
   a. NUMBER := TRUNC(54.67);
   b. VALUE := ROUND(54.67);
   c. LETTER := CHR(70);
   d. VALUE := ORD('C');
   e. NUMBER := ABS(-68);
   f. VALUE := SQR(25);
   g. NEXT := SUCC(21);

2. Write an expression that will find each of the following:
   a. The ordinal value of the symbol ⟨.
   b. The absolute value of −72.5.
   c. The character whose ordinal value is 37.
   d. The square of 67.
   e. The tangent of 1.57 radians.
   f. The character that precedes 'M'.

Lesson 3.4 Constant Definitions

Constants are values that do not change in a program and are defined above the declaration of variables (VAR) using the reserved word **CONST**.

> **Constant Form**
>
> CONST *constant identifier* = *value*;

An equal sign (=) separates the constant name and its value. Constants must be values or previously defined constants, not variables or expressions. Notice that the data type of the constant is not declared as in the variable block. The type is implied by the definition. For example, the following are CONST definitions:

```
CONST
    PI = 3.1416;            ( REAL CONSTANT )
    FREEZING = 32;          ( INTEGER CONSTANT )
    BOILING = 212.0;        ( REAL CONSTANT — Note the .0 )
    ALTITUDE = 54926;       ( LONG INTEGER CONSTANT )

CONST
    LETTER = 'A';           ( CHAR OR STRING CONSTANT )
    BLANK = ' ';            ( CHAR OR STRING CONSTANT )
    NAME = 'JANE DOE';      ( STRING CONSTANT )

CONST
    DONE = TRUE;            ( BOOLEAN CONSTANT )
```

The equal sign may be read "is equal to." The values of constants of type CHAR or STRING are enclosed in single quotation marks.

Program 3.8 uses a constant to find the actual price of a sales item in a store.

Program 3.8
```
PROGRAM STORE (INPUT,OUTPUT);

        { PURPOSE: TO DEMONSTRATE USE OF CONSTANTS }

CONST
    RATE = 0.25;

VAR
    PRICE,
    DISCOUNT,
    ACTUALPRICE  : REAL;

BEGIN

    WRITE('ENTER THE PRICE BEFORE THE DISCOUNT: ');
    READLN(PRICE);
    DISCOUNT := RATE * PRICE;
    ACTUALPRICE := PRICE - DISCOUNT;
    WRITELN('THE DISCOUNT IS $',DISCOUNT:5:2);
    WRITELN('THE ACTUAL PRICE IS $',ACTUALPRICE:5:2)

END.
```

Sample Output

```
ENTER THE PRICE BEFORE THE DISCOUNT: 12.65
THE DISCOUNT IS $ 3.16
THE ACTUAL PRICE IS $ 9.49
```

Constants are used for documentation purposes and for easy program alteration. If a value that does not change is used in a program, that value should be specified under a descriptive name as a constant. For example, suppose a program for computing taxes was written when the tax rate was 10 percent, and a few years later the tax rate increased to 12 percent. Using a constant for the tax rate allows for simple changes in this value.

Caution: It is illegal to make an assignment to a constant.

Lesson Check 3.4

1. Rearrange the following program statements to form a valid Pascal program. Write the corresponding letters in the correct order.
   a. `VAR CIRCUM, RADIUS : REAL;`
   b. `BEGIN`
   c. `READLN(RADIUS);`
   d. `END.`
   e. `PROGRAM CIRCLE (INPUT, OUTPUT);`
   f. `CONST PI = 3.1416;`
   g. `CIRCUM := 2 * PI * RADIUS;`
   h. `WRITELN('THE CIRCUMFERENCE IS ', CIRCUM);`
   i. `WRITE('ENTER THE RADIUS OF A CIRCLE: ');`

2. Identify the errors in each of the following constant definitions:
   a. `CONST`
        `TAX : 0.85;`
   b. `CONST`
        `PI = REAL;`
   c. `CONST`
        `R = .7;`

Lesson 3.5 Programming Tip— Understanding the Problem

This may sound simple, but many bad solutions to a problem occur because the problem solver didn't completely understand what outcome was desired. The problem solver is not always to blame. Often problems are presented in unclear terms and with information not necessary to solve the problem. Suppose someone was asked to

> Assist in implementing initial sanitary procedures in the food preparation area of the living quarters by removing debris previously placed in a collecting receptacle.

Would that person automatically know to take out the kitchen garbage? Probably not. Many problems are presented in this manner or worse. Some problems can become surprisingly easy once their intent is understood.

An individual faced with a possibly unfamiliar problem needs to first spend some time understanding what exactly is expected in the solution. A problem might be made more clear by taking the following steps:

- State the problem in simpler terms.
- Identify relevant facts.
- Eliminate unnecessary facts.
- Create a diagram to help visualize the problem.
- Break the problem into its main parts.

A problem should be stated in the simplest terms possible. This includes taking out irrelevant information, and possibly, rewording the problem—without changing its intent. A diagram or picture may show the problem from a different perspective and shed new light on a possible solution. Finally, looking at a problem as several smaller problems simplifies the entire process. (In addition, a reasonable amount of certainty that a solution to the problem exists should be established during this first step.)

Can the following problem be restated in clear, concise terms? Can it be solved using the computer?

> Jeff and Bob both work for a pencil manufacturing company. Jeff, who is 36, works in the eraser department; Bob, who is 34, works, in the lead department. They have both been working there for five years. They each work 40 hours per week, but Jeff works four 10-hour shifts and Bob works five 8-hour shifts. Bob's wages are $240 per week and so are Jeff's. Bob is thinking about leaving his job for another one that pays $5.95 per hour. The other job is also a 40-hour week, but it is at a paper manufacturing company. Bob wonders if his hourly wage at the pencil manufacturing company is as good as that of the job at the paper manufacturing company.

A more precise statement of the problem might be

> Find the hourly wage for a job that pays $240 for 40 hours of work.

Much wheel-spinning can be avoided and total solution time reduced by taking a few minutes to become familiar with the problem, what data are available, and what outcome is expected.

Summary

The assignment statement, operations, functions, and the constant definition were introduced in this chapter.

The assignment statement allows the assignment of values of expressions to variables within a Pascal program. The statement consists of the assignment symbol (: =) separating a variable on the left and an expression on the right. The variable is a Pascal identifier and the expression can be previously initialized variables and constants brought together with operations and functions.

The Pascal operators for addition, subtraction, multiplication, and division may be the most familiar. The INTEGER operators DIV and MOD produce the quotient and remainder of a division problem and are useful programming tools. A function changes some value, the argument, into another value, the result. The functions introduced include algebraic functions (absolute value and squaring), transcendental functions (square root, logarithmic, and trigonometric functions), and transfer functions (TRUNC, ROUND, ORD, and CHR). Two other functions, SUCC and PRED, involve ordered values; that is, BOOLEAN, CHAR, INTEGER, or programmer-defined types.

Constants represent values that do not change in a program and should be declared in the constant definition portion of the program. The constant definition provides a good source of documentation.

Key Terms

ABS	DIV	PWROFTEN
algebraic functions	EXP	ROUND
argument	function call	SIN
arithmetic	initialize	SQR
operators	LN	SQRT
assignment	LOG	standard functions
statement	memory location	SUCC
ATAN	MOD	transcendental
CHR	ORD	functions
CONST	order of operations	transfer functions
constants	PRED	TRUNC
COS		

Answers to Lesson Checks

Lesson 3.1

1. **a, c,** and **d** are valid assignment statements.

2. **a.**
```
VAR
    NUM : INTEGER;

BEGIN
    NUM := 8;
```
b.
```
VAR
    WORD1 : STRING;

BEGIN
    WORD1 := 'GOODBYE';
```

Lesson 3.2

1. **a.** 4.00000
   b. 2.69
   c. 4
   d. 3
   e. 1.20000E1

2. **b** presents the proper order.

3. **b** is the Celsius equivalent.

4. **a.** False.
   b. True.
   c. False.

Lesson 3.3

1. **a.** 54
   b. 55
   c. F
   d. 67
   e. 68
   f. 625
   g. 22

2. **a.** ORD('<')
   b. ABS(-72.5)
   c. CHR(37)
   d. SQR(67)
   e. SIN(1.57) / COS(1.57)
   f. PRED('M')

Lesson 3.4

1. To write a valid Pascal program, rearrange the lines to be in order as follows: **e, f, a, b, i, c, g, h**, and **d**.

2. **a.** CONST
         TAX = 0.85;   (= not :)
   b. CONST
         PI = 3.14159;   (REAL is a data TYPE. CONST
                              expects specific value.)
   c. CONST
         R = 0.7;   (A number cannot start with a
                              decimal.)

Exercises   Set I. Comprehension

1. Give the result of each of the following expressions:
   a. 7 + 9
   b. 66 - 32
   c. 8 * 10
   d. 15 DIV 4
   e. 20 DIV 5
   f. 24 MOD 7

2. Give the result of each of the following expressions:
   a. 9 + 4
   b. 4 - 13
   c. 19 * 6
   d. 16 DIV 3
   e. -21 DIV 3
   f. 32 MOD 4

3. Here are some problems that give practice with order of operations. Answer them first by working the problems on paper. Then check them on the computer.
   a. 2 + 6 DIV 2
   b. (9 + 6) MOD 8
   c. (7 + 4) * (5 - 2 * 3)
   d. 9 DIV 3 * -3
   e. 8 MOD 4 * 5

    f. `(9 + 7) DIV 3`
    g. `6 + 7 * 8 / 4`
    h. `7 - 8 * 5 + 6 / (2 + 4)`
    i. `3 * (5 + 2 * (7 - 4) + 5)`
    j. `81 MOD (2 * 5 - 3 * (4 + 6 * (5 DIV 2))) DIV 10`

4. Work each of the following problems, first on paper and then
   check each on the computer:
     a. `6 DIV 4 - 3`
     b. `(4 + 5) MOD 2`
     c. `8 * 7 - 2 * (3 + 15)`
     d. `12 DIV 5 * 6`
     e. `35 MOD 3 * -4`
     f. `(4 * 3 + 2) DIV 5`
     g. `(35 + 31) / 3 - 1`
     h. `(35 + 31) / (3 - 1)`
     i. `2 * (5 + (2 - 3) * 6 - 3 / 3)`
     j. `65 DIV ((3 * 6 + 4 * -2) * (12 - 8)) MOD 4`

5. Identify the data type of the resulting value in each of the
   following expressions:
     a. `72 / 9`
     b. `35 DIV 3`
     c. `2.0 * 5`
     d. `8 - 6`
     e. `67 MOD 2`

6. Identify the data type of the resulting value in each of the
   following expressions:
     a. `65 / 5`
     b. `2 DIV 3`
     c. `12 * 6`
     d. `73 MOD 2`
     e. `54 - 38`

7. Evaluate each of the following expressions:
     a. `TRUNC(322.14)`
     b. `ROUND(0.45)`
     c. `SQRT(64)`
     d. `SQR(4)`
     e. `TRUNC(7.98)`
     f. `PWROFTEN(2)`
     g. `ABS(ROUND(-7.94))`
     h. `SQRT(4 * 4 + 3 * 3)`
     i. `ABS(-34.8)`
     j. `PRED('R')`

8. Evaluate each of the following expressions:
     a. `ROUND(6.5)`
     b. `TRUNC(6.88)`
     c. `SQR(-4)`
     d. `SQR(7)`
     e. `SQRT(81)`
     f. `PWROFTEN(3)`
     g. `ABS(ROUND(-9.22))`
     h. `SQRT(24 * 6)`
     i. `ABS(-12.5)`
     j. `SUCC(3 * 5)`

9. Evaluate each of the following expressions:
   a. `ROUND(23.67 * 10.0) / 10`
   b. `ABS(-TRUNC(23.4) - 56 MOD 16)`
   c. `ABS(ROUND(72.46) - ROUND(72.67))`
   d. `SQRT(SQR(4))`
   e. `ABS(TRUNC(2.34 - 12 MOD 5) - 2)`

10. Evaluate each of the following expressions:
   a. `ROUND(25.456 / 10) * 10`
   b. `TRUNC(ABS(45.6 - SQR(5) * 30))`
   c. `SQR(35 MOD 4 * 6)`
   d. `ROUND((34 DIV 7) / 2)`
   e. `TRUNC(3246 / 10) - 100 * TRUNC(3246 / 1000)`

11. Find the value of X, Y, and Z after each of the following assignment statements. Assume the initial values for each problem are

   `X := 2; Y := 5; Z := -1;`

   and that X, Y, and Z are REAL.
   a. `X := Y * Z;`
   b. `Z := X + Y * X;`
   c. `Y := Y + 5;`
   d. `Z := X + Y / Y + Z;`
   e. `Z := (X + Y) / (Y + Z);`

12. Rework Exercise 11, assuming the initial values for each problem are

   `X := -4; Y := -3; Z := 5;`

13. Identify the errors in each of the following assignment statements. Assume that VALUE, NUMBER, and QUOTIENT are of type REAL.
   a. `VALUE = 5 * 6 + 7;`
   b. `NUMBER := (5 * 9 + 6 / ) 5 + 3 / 7;`
   c. `7 DIV 9 := QUOTIENT;`

14. Identify the errors in each of the following assignment statements. Assume that A, B, and C are of type REAL.
   a. `A := 5 + 3 MULT 2`
   b. `B = 4 / (3 + 6) DIV 2`
   c. `C := A + B = 2`

15. Write each of the following mathematical expressions in Pascal:
   a. $\dfrac{x + y}{z}$

   b. $\dfrac{x + y}{w + z}$

   c. $x - \dfrac{y + w}{x + z}$

16. Write each of the following mathematical expressions in Pascal:
   a. $xy + wz$

   b. $x + \dfrac{y}{w} + z$

   c. $a(b + c)$

17. Write each of the following mathematical expressions in Pascal:
   a. $a^2 + b^2$
   b. $5a^2$
   c. $b^{1/4}$

18. Write each of the following mathematical expressions in Pascal:
   a. $a^2 - b^2$
   b. a^3
   c. $a^{1/3}$

19. Write a Pascal assignment statement for each of the following mathematical expressions:
   a. $c = \dfrac{1}{2}(a^2 + b^2)$
   b. $y = j - k^2 + 3$
   c. $z = r^3 + 2st + w(d + 5)$

20. Write a Pascal assignment statement for each of the following mathematical expressions:
   a. $f = \sqrt{4ab}$
   b. $g = |j^3|$
   c. $h = (x^y)^2$

21. Which of the following are valid ways to represent the value 16?
   a. ROUND(15.6)
   b. ORD('P')
   c. ORD('V') - 70
   d. SQRT(SQR(SQR(4)))
   e. ORD(16)
   f. SUCC(17)

22. Which of the following are valid ways to represent the value -5?
   a. ROUND(-5.6)
   b. TRUNC(-5.2)
   c. ORD('-5')
   d. SQRT(SQR(-5))
   e. CHR('-5')
   f. PRED(-6)

23. Identify the correct assignment statements, given the following declarations:

```
VAR
      A      : INTEGER;
      L      : REAL;
      X      : STRING;
      H, I  : CHAR;
```

   a. A := 18.5;
   b. X := HI;
   c. H := '1';
   d. I := 0;
   e. L := 15;

24. Identify the correct assignment statements, given the following declarations:

```
VAR
      INTVALUE   :  INTEGER;
      REALVALUE  :  REAL;
      WORD       :  STRING;
      CHARACTER  :  CHAR;
```

   a. `CHARACTER := 'H';`
   b. `INTVALUE := 5.0;`
   c. `WORD := '1';`
   d. `REALVALUE := 67;`
   e. `CHARACTER := 7;`

25. Write a single assignment statement for each of the following sets of statements:

   a.
```
B := A + 2;
B := B - 3;
```
   b.
```
X := 2 * Y;
X := X + 4;
```
   c.
```
A := 3 * B;
B := C + 4;
C := A / B;
```

26. Write a single assignment statement for each of the following sets of statements:

   a.
```
C := A + 3;
C := C - 5;
```
   b.
```
A := 4 - B;
A := 5 * A;
```
   c.
```
A := -3 * B;
B := C - 2;
C := A / B;
```

For Exercises 27 and 28, provide variable declarations and an assignment statement for each mathematical formula. Use a constant definition for pi (π).

27. $A = \pi R^2$ (AREA OF CIRCLE)

28. $T = \dfrac{1}{2} H(A + B)$ (AREA OF A TRAPEZOID)

Set II. Application

29. Write a program that will do the following arithmetic problems. The program should print both the problems and the answers.

$$425 + 64$$
$$85 - 123$$
$$98 * 34$$
$$245 / 22$$

30. Write a program that will request four real numbers and which will then print the sum of the four numbers and their average.

31. Write a program that will convert Celsius degrees into the Fahrenheit equivalent. Use real numbers. Results should be

accurate to the nearest tenth. Revise the formula from Lesson Check 3.2, Problem 3.

32. Write a program that asks the user to enter a number and which then prints the number and the square of the number.

33. Write a program that asks the user to enter a number and which then prints the number and the cube of the number.

34. Write a program that will compute the cube root of a given number.

35. Write a program that will compute the fourth root of a given number.

36. Write a program that will accept the height of an object in feet and then print the height in inches. For example, suppose the height of the object is four feet. The output would be 48 inches.

37. Suppose the user enters the total number of hours and minutes it takes to walk to the park. Write a program that will convert the total number of hours and minutes entered to minutes. For example, suppose the total number of hours and minutes entered is 2 hours, 15 minutes. The output would be 135 minutes.

38. Write a program that will convert a height entered in inches to yards, feet, and inches. For example, suppose a height of 68 inches is entered. The output would be 1 yard, 2 feet, 8 inches. Use DIV and MOD.

39. Write a program that will convert a time entered in minutes to hours and minutes. For example, suppose 78 minutes is the time entered. The output would be 1 hour, 18 minutes. Use DIV and MOD.

40. Write a program that requests the input of a letter and then prints a number corresponding to that letter. The letter A corresponds to 5; B, to 10; C, to 15; D, to 20; and so on, with Z corresponding to 130. Use the ORD function.

41. Write a program that asks for the price of an item and the amount given to the sales clerk by the customer and which then computes the sales tax and the change. Use constants. Assume the sales tax rate is 4.5 percent.

42. Write a program that will compute the commission received for the sale of a home by a real estate agent. The program should request the price of the home, the rate of the commission (5.5 percent), and print out the total commission received. Use constants.

43. Write a program that computes both the surface area and volume of a rectangular box. The dimensions should be entered by the user when the program is executed.

44. Write a program that computes the surface area and volume of a sphere. The radius of the sphere should be entered by the user when the program is executed. Use a constant for pi (π).

$$\text{Surface Area} = 4\pi R^2$$
$$\text{Volume} = \frac{4}{3}\pi R^3$$

Set III. Synthesis

45. Write a program that computes the cost to carpet a room. The dimensions of the room, length and width in feet, and the cost of the carpet per square yard should be entered. The output of the program will be the total area of the room in square yards and the total cost of the carpet.

46. Write a program that computes the cost of drapes for a given window. The dimensions of the window and the cost of the drapes per square yard should be entered. The program will compute the total square yardage and money needed to make the drapes.

47. Write programs to evaluate the following expressions. Allow the user to enter the value for x.

   a. $(x^2 + 1)^2 (x - 1)^5 x^3 \dfrac{4x}{x^2+1} + \dfrac{5}{x-1} + \dfrac{3}{x}$

   b. $\dfrac{1}{2} \sqrt{\dfrac{(x-1)(x-2)}{(x-3)(x-4)}} \left(\dfrac{1}{x-1} + \dfrac{1}{x-2} - \dfrac{1}{x-3} - \dfrac{1}{x-4} \right)$

   c. $2xe^{x^2-1}$

   d. $e^x \cos x + e^x \sin x$

   e. $\dfrac{x - (1 + x^2) \operatorname{atan} x}{x^2(1 + x^2)}$

   f. $\dfrac{1}{2} e^{\sqrt{x}} \left(\dfrac{1}{x} + \dfrac{\log \sqrt{x}}{\sqrt{x}} \right)$

   g. $(\cos \pi x)^x(-\pi x \tan \pi x + \log (\cos \pi x))$

Procedures and Program Design

"*How queer it seems,*" *Alice said to herself, "to be going messages for a rabbit! I suppose Dinah'll be sending me on messages next!*"

—*Lewis Carroll*

Overview

Structure of Procedures
    Built-in versus Programmer-defined
    Procedure Call
Programming with Procedures
    Procedure Block
    Global and Local Variables
    Scope of Identifiers
Programming Tip
    Program Design

Gaining a Perspective

Most problems, whether solved by a computer or not, have the property of being made up of several parts. Solving a problem by breaking it into its parts is both natural and convenient. Each of the parts can then be thought of as a problem that is easier to understand than the original problem. Also, each of these subproblems can, if necessary, be broken into parts to make each one easier to understand. The process can be repeated until each part is manageable and can be solved.

Problems may appear overwhelming when first attempted. Take, for example, the problem of cleaning a house. Initially it is an enormous task; however, no one actually attacks this as a single problem. Most commonly, the problem of cleaning a house is broken down room-by-room (living room, bedroom, kitchen, and so on). Cleaning a room is certainly more manageable than cleaning the entire house and when all the rooms are clean, the original problem will be done. Also, the smaller problem of cleaning a room can be broken down further into smaller tasks: dusting, vacuuming, mopping, polishing, washing, and so on. These subtasks are much more manageable than the ones before them and they, in turn, can be further broken down. Eventually, the problems are small enough to easily be solved.

Figure 4.1 presents a diagram of one method for solving the problem of cleaning the house. It illustrates how a very difficult problem can be turned into a number of easier problems. Notice that some of the subproblems are repeated (for example, vacuuming and cleaning the floor); thus, once a solution is devised, it can be repeated when needed. There is no need to resolve that part of the problem.

This method of solving a problem by breaking it into its logical parts and then repeating the process for each part is referred to as **top-down design.** The main strategy involves breaking a problem down into smaller, easier parts. Pascal provides a structure called a **procedure** that readily lends itself to this type of problem solution. Procedures give the programmer a natural tool for breaking a problem into its parts and allow for a direct implementation of the problem's designed solution to the actual Pascal program.

Figure 4.1
Cleaning the House

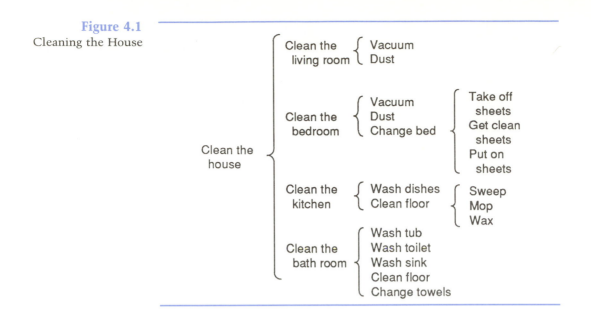

Lesson 4.1   Structure of Procedures

Procedures are subprograms or routines whose main purpose is to perform a specific task for the program. Pascal provides for built-in as well as programmer-defined procedures. Built-in procedures are a part of the Pascal operating system, such as READLN and WRITELN. Programmer-defined procedures are written by programmers. The structure of a procedure is similar to the structure of the main program. Procedures are used in order to make programs easier to write and understand. Procedures also provide an easy way of using a series of statements anywhere in a program without having to repeat the statements each time.

Program 4.1 has three procedures. GETINFO allows the user to enter certain information about an employee. COMPUTE-SALARY computes the employee's salary and PRINTINFO prints out this information. This program illustrates the three steps commonly encountered when solving problems on the computer.

- Input (get the information needed to solve the problem).
- Process (perform the necessary calculations).
- Output (print the desired results).

When Program 4.1 is executed, the first statement in the main program calls the procedure GETINFO. The procedure name written in the main program (or a subprogram) invokes (or calls) the procedure. After completing that procedure, control is returned to the **calling block** to the statement following the completed **procedure call.** Thus, when GETINFO is finished, procedure

Program 4.1

```
PROGRAM EMPLOYEESALARY (INPUT,OUTPUT);

    { PURPOSE: THIS PROGRAM CALCULATES AN EMPLOYEE'S
              SALARY FROM INFORMATION TYPED IN BY
              THE USER }

CONST
   WAGE = 7.50;

VAR
   NAME        : STRING[20];
   IDNUM       : INTEGER;
   HOURSWORKED,
   SALARY      : REAL;

PROCEDURE GETINFO;

    { ENTER REQUIRED INFORMATION }

   BEGIN

      WRITELN('ENTER THE INFORMATION REQUESTED');
      WRITE('NAME: ');
      READLN(NAME);
      WRITE('ID NUMBER: ');
      READLN(IDNUM);
      WRITE('HOURS WORKED: ');
      READLN(HOURSWORKED)

   END; { GETINFO }

PROCEDURE COMPUTESALARY;

    { FIND THE SALARY }

   BEGIN

      SALARY := WAGE * HOURSWORKED

   END; { COMPUTESALARY }

PROCEDURE PRINTINFO;

    { PRINT THE RESULTS }

   BEGIN

      WRITELN('NAME: ',NAME);
      WRITELN('ID NUMBER: ',IDNUM);
      WRITELN('HOURS WORKED: ',HOURSWORKED);
      WRITELN;
      WRITELN('SALARY: $',SALARY:6:2)

   END; { PRINTINFO }

BEGIN    { MAIN PROGRAM }

   GETINFO;
   COMPUTESALARY;
   PRINTINFO

END.
```

COMPUTESALARY is executed, followed by procedure PRINT-INFO. This program shows how a problem can be broken down into smaller parts to make it easier to understand and solve. The variables in this program were declared after the program heading and are used by all of the procedures. As will be seen, a better programming practice is to have each procedure declare and use its own variables, making them independent of the main program and other procedures and more readily used in different situations.

Lesson Check 4.1

1. Identify each statement as true or false.
   a. READLN is an example of a programmer-defined procedure.
   b. Three common uses of procedures are for entering data, processing data, and printing results.
   c. Procedures are only used when a set of steps must be done once.

2. What happens after a procedure has been completed in a program?

Lesson 4.2 Programming with Procedures

Procedures are declared between the variable declaration and the BEGIN statement of the main program. A procedure has almost the same form as the main program, except the word **PROCEDURE** is used instead of the word PROGRAM. Also, the INPUT,OUTPUT information in the main program is not a part of the procedure heading. The entire procedure, from its heading to the END statement of the procedure, is called a **procedure block**. Unlike the main program, the END statement of a procedure block is followed by a semicolon. Remember, semicolons in Pascal are used to separate

- consecutive statements within a block of a program.
- consecutive blocks of a program.

Constants may be defined and variables may be declared in a procedure. Special names are given to constants or variables (identifiers) that are defined or declared in the main program versus those defined or declared in a procedure. The identifiers that are used in the main program are called **global identifiers.** In Program 4.1, NAME, IDNUM, HOURSWORKED, and SALARY are global variables. Global variables may be used anywhere in the program, including any of the procedures.

Caution: Declaring all variables as global to avoid worrying about which procedure uses them might seem easiest; however, this defeats the purpose of procedures. Procedures should be self-contained blocks that can be used and understood independently. Declaring variables or constants at the main program level that are used in a procedure makes the procedure difficult to understand, prevents its use in other programs (transportability), and

leads to confusion in the general structure of the program. When-
ever possible, constants and variables should be declared in the
procedure in which they are used. In Chapter 8 we will learn how
to add more flexibility to this process.

An identifier that is used *only* within a procedure is called a
local identifier. In Program 4.1, there are no local variables. Parts
of this program are dependent on the variable declaration at the
beginning of the program and are not very adaptable to other
situations. In this program, keeping the parts separate may not
have been that important. In general, however, the use of local
variables is preferable for structured program design.

Caution: A local identifier has meaning only within the procedure
in which it is declared and can be used only within that procedure.
When an identifier is used in only one procedure, it should be
declared locally.

The placement of procedures within a program follows:

Placement for Procedures

```
program heading

constant definitions of the main program

variable declaration of the main program

procedure declarations

        .

        .

        .

main program
```

The general form of a procedure block, where the compound
statement is a series of Pascal statements starting with BEGIN
and ending with END, follows:

Procedure Form

```
PROCEDURE identifier;

CONST
    local constants;

VAR
    local variables;

    compound statement;
```

```
PROGRAM SCOPEONE;

VAR

     { GLOBAL VARIABLES DECLARED FOR SCOPEONE }


     PROCEDURE P1;

        VAR

           { LOCAL VARIABLES FOR PROCEDURE P1 }

        BEGIN

           .
           .
           .

        END; { P1 }



     PROCEDURE P2;

        VAR

           { LOCAL VARIABLES FOR PROCEDURE P2 }

        BEGIN

           .
           .
           .

        END; { P2 }


  BEGIN { MAIN PROGRAM }

     .
     .
     .

  END.
```

The **scope** of an identifier is the part or block of the program in which the identifier has meaning. Figure 4.2 shows the scope of constants and variables in a program called SCOPEONE. Assume that global constants or variables have been defined or declared in the main program and that each procedure has local constants or variables.

For this program, global constants or variables are accessible throughout the program, including procedures P1 and P2. Constants or variables local to either procedure—that is, constants or variables declared under the procedure heading—are known only to that procedure. Thus, a variable declared in procedure P1 would only be known to P1 and has no meaning in P2 or in the main program.

Figure 4.3 gives a more complicated example of scope. Again, global identifiers are known in all parts of the program. The identifiers of procedure T1 are known to its subprocedures, procedure T2 and procedure T3. (In effect, a local variable in T1 is global to T2 and T3.) The identifiers of procedures T2, T3, and T4 are known only to their respective procedures. Notice that procedure T1 mimics the main program; its statements follow the subprocedure definitions.

The funnel-like entrance to each procedure shows that identifiers from outside the procedure are known to that block or subprogram, but identifiers declared in the procedure are not known outside of that procedure. In other words, subprograms of the main program may use the main program's global identifiers, while subprocedures of a particular procedure may use identifiers of that procedure. In Chapter 8, more options concerning procedures and their relationship to the main program and other procedures will be introduced.

A procedure may call another procedure if the latter has been declared earlier in the same block. (For example, in Figure 4.2, procedure P2 can call procedure P1.) If an identifier (constant or variable) has been declared more than once, the most local value will be used at that level.

Caution: Declaring an identifier more than once is legal but can cause some confusion. Program 4.2 illustrates the confusion that can result from declaring an identifier more than once. In this program, the identifier DISPLAY is declared as both a global and local variable. The output shows that the most local variable takes precedence.

Figure 4.3
Scope of Identifiers

```
PROGRAM SCOPETWO;
VAR
    { GLOBAL VARIABLES FOR SCOPETWO }

   PROCEDURE T1;
      VAR
         { LOCAL VARIABLES FOR T1 }

        PROCEDURE T2;
           VAR
              { LOCAL VARIABLES FOR T2 }
           BEGIN
              .
              .
              .
           END; { T2 }


        PROCEDURE T3;
           VAR
              { LOCAL VARIABLES FOR T3 }
           BEGIN
              .
              .
              .
           END; { T3 }

      BEGIN
         .
         .
         .
      END; { T1 }


   PROCEDURE T4;
      VAR
         { LOCAL VARIABLES FOR T4 }
      BEGIN
         .
         .
         .
      END; { T4 }

BEGIN { MAIN PROGRAM }
   .
   .
   .
END.
```

Program 4.2

```
PROGRAM SKETCH(INPUT,OUTPUT);

    { PURPOSE: ILLUSTRATE GLOBAL, LOCAL VARIABLES }

VAR
    DISPLAY : STRING[10];

PROCEDURE DRAW;

    { DRAWS PART OF PATTERN }

    VAR
        DISPLAY : STRING[10];

    BEGIN

        DISPLAY := '   * *';
        WRITELN(DISPLAY);
        WRITELN(DISPLAY)

    END; { DRAW }

BEGIN { MAIN PROGRAM }

    DISPLAY := '* * * * *';
    WRITELN(DISPLAY);
    DRAW;
    WRITELN(DISPLAY);
    DRAW;
    WRITELN(DISPLAY)

END.
```

The output of this program is

```
* * * * *
    * *
    * *
* * * * *
    * *
    * *
* * * * *
```

Program 4.2 illustrates how a local variable takes precedence and is used only within its procedure. Changing the variable DISPLAY in procedure DRAW does not alter its meaning in the main program. Notice that DRAW is called more than once, reducing the number of statements necessary to complete the diagram.

Program 4.3 gives a final example of the use of procedures. As illustrated earlier, problems are broken into parts and each part is in turn broken into smaller parts. In Pascal, procedures represent these parts nicely and allow for construction of well-designed problem solutions. Program 4.3 shows how one procedure may be declared within another (nested) and called as many times as needed. The procedure (DRAWLINE) is unknown to the main program so an error results if DRAWLINE is called from the main program.

Program 4.3

```
PROGRAM PROC_TEST(OUTPUT);

    { PURPOSE: TO ILLUSTRATE NESTED PROCEDURES }

PROCEDURE PRINTSCREEN;

    { INTRODUCE PROGRAM }

    PROCEDURE DRAWLINE;

        { DRAW HORIZONTAL LINE }

        BEGIN

            WRITELN('=================================')

        END; { DRAWLINE }

    BEGIN

        DRAWLINE;
        DRAWLINE;
        WRITELN('This program illustrates the');
        WRITELN('use of a procedure within a');
        WRITELN('procedure. The procedure');
        WRITELN('DRAWLINE has meaning only in');
        WRITELN('this procedure (PRINTSCREEN).');
        WRITELN;
        DRAWLINE;
        WRITELN;
        WRITELN('If DRAWLINE were invoked from');
        WRITELN('the main program, it would be');
        WRITELN('an undeclared identifier and');
        WRITELN('an error would result.');
        WRITELN;
        DRAWLINE;
        DRAWLINE

    END;  { PRINTSCREEN }

BEGIN  { MAIN PROGRAM }

    PAGE(OUTPUT);        { CLEARS THE SCREEN }
    GOTOXY(0,3);         { POSITIONS CURSOR ON SCREEN }
    PRINTSCREEN;
    WRITELN;
    WRITELN('PRESS <RETURN> TO EXIT.');
    READLN

END.
```

Lesson
Check
4.2

1. Identify each statement as true or false.
   a. Procedures are declared between the program heading and the variable declaration of the main program.
   b. The END statement of a procedure is followed by a period.
   c. An identifier that is declared in a procedure is called a local identifier.
   d. When an identifier is declared more than once, the most local value of the identifier is used.

2. What is meant by the scope of an identifier?

3. Why should a variable that is used only in a procedure be declared in that procedure and not in the main program?

Lesson 4.3   Programming Tip— Program Design

Designing the solution to a problem, once the problem is understood, has many facets and can be approached in a variety of ways. The final design can be extremely complex and detailed. The initial design, however, can be general in nature and more like an outline of the solution.

The diagram at the beginning of this chapter (Figure 4.1) outlined the steps needed to clean a house. The problem (cleaning a house) was broken into several smaller programs. These smaller problems were easier to handle. In turn, these smaller problems were broken down into even simpler tasks. The process can continue until each subproblem becomes manageable. Then a solution for each of the smaller problems can be implemented. This technique of outlining horizontally is called a **logic diagram.** Logic diagrams give the programmer a systematic way to attack a complex problem.

The process of starting with a large problem and breaking it into smaller ones is referred to as top-down design. Logic diagrams fit nicely with this technique. In addition, the use of procedures can directly follow the logic diagram. Logic diagrams often define the procedures needed to solve the problem.

One concern in using logic diagrams is how far to break the problem down before attempting to write solutions for the individual parts. In general, the individual parts should have a straightforward solution and be of a manageable size. When working with procedures, the ideal is for each procedure to be no longer than one full screen (so that the entire procedure may be viewed at once on the monitor). Actually, this is somewhat unrealistic, especially when procedures are formatted for proper readability. Every attempt should be made, however, to keep procedure size small— perhaps less than two full screens. Most Pascal systems limit the size of individual procedures to encourage smaller parts.

A Detailed Look

The problem solving and programming techniques discussed so far can now be used to develop the solution to a particular problem.

Problem Statement: The Adams family is planning a trip across the United States in their motor home. They would like to take along their portable computer to help determine the miles per gallon (mpg) of gas at each gas stop. Write a program to allow the Adams family to enter the miles traveled since the last gas stop and the number of gallons of gas. The values to be entered and the desired output follow:

Input

Miles traveled from the last gas stop.
Gallons of gas.

Output

Miles per gallon of gas.

The next step in solving the problem is to devise a plan of attack. The plan should include a rough outline of the subtasks used to write the program. Here is a rough plan for the problem.

1. Obtain the miles traveled and the gallons of gas used.
2. Compute the miles per gallon.
3. Print the miles per gallon.

The logic diagram shown in Figure 4.4 corresponds to this rough plan. Logic diagrams usually provide more detail than a preliminary outline.

Program TRIP uses three procedures that correspond to the three main parts of the logic diagram. Procedure GETINFO obtains the miles traveled and the gallons of gas used. Procedure COMPUTE calculates the miles per gallon and procedure PRINTRESULTS prints the miles per gallon. Notice that all three procedures are called from the main program.

Figure 4.4
Logic Diagram for
Trip

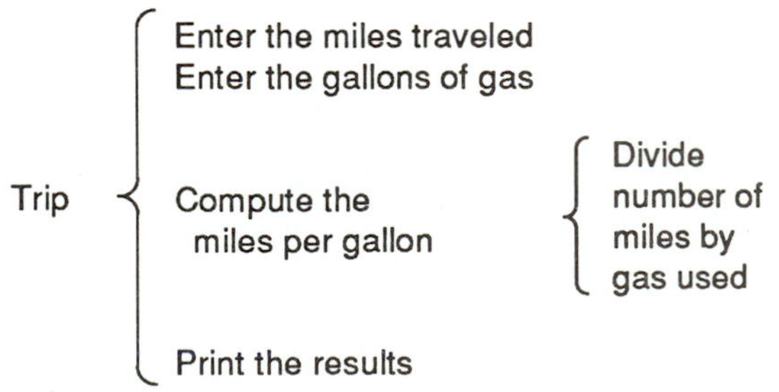

Program 4.4

```
PROGRAM TRIP (INPUT, OUTPUT);

    { PURPOSE: FIND THE MILES PER GALLON ON
               THE FAMILY VACATION }

VAR
    MILES,
    GAS,
    MPG   : REAL;

PROCEDURE GETINFO;

    { OBTAIN ALL NECESSARY INFORMATION }

    BEGIN

        WRITE('MILES TRAVELED FROM LAST GAS STOP: ');
        READLN(MILES);
        WRITE('GALLONS OF GAS FOR THIS FILL-UP: ');
        READLN(GAS)

    END;     { GETINFO }

PROCEDURE COMPUTE;

    { COMPUTE THE MILES PER GALLON }

    BEGIN

        MPG := MILES/GAS

    END;      { COMPUTE }

PROCEDURE PRINTRESULTS;

    { PRINT THE MILES PER GALLON }

    BEGIN

        GOTOXY(0,10);
        WRITELN('********************************');
        WRITELN('*    THE MILES PER GALLON      *');
        WRITELN('*    SINCE THE LAST STOP IS    *');
        WRITELN('*         ',MPG:5:2,'          *');
        WRITELN('********************************')

    END;  { PRINTRESULTS }

BEGIN  { MAIN PROGRAM }

    GETINFO;
    COMPUTE;
    PRINTRESULTS

END.
```

In Chapter 8 this problem will be revised and a new program will be written that uses the material to be introduced in the intervening chapters.

Summary

Solving a problem often looks like an enormous task, but can be simplified by breaking the problem into smaller parts and solving the parts first. Procedures are an integral part of program design and aid in problem solving. Each distinct part of a program should be represented by a procedure called from the main program or another procedure. Procedures are declared after variable declarations in the main program. They often fall into the general categories of input, process, and output.

Global identifiers are declared in the main program's declaration block and are known to all procedures in the program. Local identifiers are declared within a procedure and are known only within that procedure. The scope of an identifier refers to the parts of the program in which the identifier has meaning.

Key Terms

calling block	logic diagram	procedure call
global identifier	PROCEDURE	scope
local identifier	procedure block	top-down design

Answers to Lesson Checks

Lesson 4.1

1. **a.** False.
   b. True.
   c. False.

2. The control returns to the statement following the procedure call.

Lesson 4.2

1. **a.** False.
   b. False.
   c. True.
   d. True.

2. The scope is the portion of the program that recognizes the identifier.

3. Variables should be declared locally for transportability, so that blocks are self-contained, so that the main program is independent, and to make the procedure more understandable.

Exercises

Set I. Comprehension

Use the following program segment for Exercises 1 and 2.

```
PROGRAM A;

    PROCEDURE B;
        BEGIN
            .
            .
            .
        END;
```

```
        PROCEDURE C;

            PROCEDURE D;
                BEGIN
                    B
                END;
            BEGIN
                D;
                D
            END;

BEGIN
    C
END.
```

1. A variable that has been declared only in procedure C can be used
   a. anywhere in the program.
   b. in procedure C only.
   c. in procedures C and D.
   d. in procedures B, C, and D.
   e. in none of the above.

2. What is the order in which the procedures are called?
   a. C, D, D, B, C
   b. C, D, B, D, B
   c. B, C, D, B, D, D, C
   d. C, D, B, D, D
   e. None of the above.

(Note: For Exercises 3, 4, 5, and 6, use of the same identifier for both global and local variables is generally not a good practice.)

3. Specify the output of the following program, assuming input of DAVID, DANIEL:

```
PROGRAM WHODONEIT(INPUT,OUTPUT);

VAR
    WHO : STRING;

PROCEDURE FIND;

    VAR
      WHO : STRING;

    BEGIN
        READLN(WHO);
        WRITELN(WHO,' MIGHT HAVE DONE IT')
    END;   { FIND }

BEGIN   { MAIN PROGRAM }

    READLN(WHO);
    FIND;
    WRITELN(WHO,' DEFINITELY DID IT')

END.
```

4. Specify the output of the following program:

```
PROGRAM HOW(OUTPUT);

VAR
    WHO : INTEGER;

PROCEDURE HOWWHO;

    VAR
        WHO : INTEGER;

    BEGIN
        WHO := 56
    END; { HOWWHO }

BEGIN  { MAIN PROGRAM }

    WHO := 20;
    HOWWHO;
    WRITELN(WHO)

END.
```

5. Specify the output of the following program:

```
PROGRAM TEST(OUTPUT);

VAR
    WHAT : CHAR;

PROCEDURE TESTWHAT;

    VAR
        WHAT : CHAR;

    BEGIN
        WHAT := 'B';
        WRITELN(WHAT);
        WHAT := 'A';
        WRITELN(WHAT)
    END;  { TESTWHAT }

BEGIN  { MAIN PROGRAM }

    WHAT := 'Z';
    WRITELN(WHAT);
    TESTWHAT;
    WRITELN(WHAT)

END.
```

6. Specify the output of the following program:

```
PROGRAM AGAIN(OUTPUT);

VAR
    WHERE : INTEGER;

PROCEDURE AGAINWHERE;

    VAR
        WHERE : INTEGER;

    BEGIN
        WHERE := 3;
        WRITELN(WHERE);
        WHERE := -3
    END;

BEGIN  { MAIN PROGRAM }

    WHERE := 2;
    AGAINWHERE;
    WRITELN(WHERE)

END.
```

7. Is the following program structure valid? Why or why not?

```
PROGRAM COMPUTE(INPUT,OUTPUT);
PROCEDURE COMP;
VAR local variables;
BEGIN
    .
    .
    .
END;
VAR global variables;
BEGIN  { MAIN PROGRAM }
    .
    .
    .
END.
```

8. Is the following program structure valid? Why or why not?

```
PROGRAM SAMPLE(INPUT,OUTPUT);
VAR X : INTEGER;
PROCEDURE SAMP;
VAR X : CHAR;
BEGIN
    .
    .
    .
END;
BEGIN  { MAIN PROGRAM }
    .
    .
    .
END.
```

Use the following program structure to complete Exercises 9–12.

```
PROGRAM SCOPE(INPUT,OUTPUT);

VAR X, Y1, Z1 : INTEGER;

PROCEDURE P1;
    VAR Y2, X1 :   INTEGER;

    PROCEDURE P5;
        VAR L, J, C : INTEGER;
        BEGIN
            .
            .
            .
        END; { P5 }

    PROCEDURE P2;
        VAR L3 : INTEGER;
        BEGIN
            .
            .
            .
        END; { P2 }

    BEGIN
        .
        .
        .
    END; { P1 }

PROCEDURE P4;
    VAR X2, Y4 :  INTEGER;

    PROCEDURE P3;
        VAR Y3, L1, C2 : INTEGER;
        BEGIN
            .
            .
            .
        END; { P3 }

    BEGIN
        .
        .
        .
    END; { P4 }

BEGIN   { MAIN PROGRAM }
    P1;
    P4
END.
```

9. Classify each of the following variables, with respect to the block specified, as either local, global, or unknown. (Reproduce the table on paper.)

Variable	Block	Local	Global	Unknown
X	P4	_____	_____	_____
L3	P2	_____	_____	_____
L3	P5	_____	_____	_____
L3	SCOPE	_____	_____	_____

10. Classify each of the following variables, with respect to the block specified, as either local, global, or unknown. (Reproduce the table on paper.)

Variable	Block	Local	Global	Unknown
C2	P4	_____	_____	_____
Y4	P3	_____	_____	_____
X1	P2	_____	_____	_____
J	P5	_____	_____	_____
X2	P3	_____	_____	_____

11. Identify each of the following statements as true or false:
    a. Procedure P2 can be called only by procedure P1.
    b. Procedure P4 will be called before procedure P5.
    c. Procedures P2 and P5 can be called by the main program.

12. Identify each of the following statements as true or false:
    a. Procedure P4 may be called before procedure P1 in the main program.
    b. X1 := 5; is a valid statement in the main program.
    c. Y3 := X2; is a valid statement in procedure P3.

13. From the following problem description, which of the statements (a–e) best represents the actual problem? (Do not try to write the program at this time.)

    Problem Description: Computers can be used in breaking codes. Clues to coded messages may be found by determining how often each letter of the alphabet occurs in a passage. After this initial step, these frequencies can be compared to known letter frequencies for the language in question and a good guess may be made as to the content. Use the computer to assist in the first step of code breaking.

    a. Write a program to break codes based on a relationship in the frequency of coded letters and the frequency of actual letters in the given language.

    b. Write a program to determine the structure of a coded message based on the letter frequency of the characters in the message and the letter frequency of the characters in the English language.

    c. Write a program to determine how often each letter of the alphabet occurs in a given passage.

    d. Write a letter-frequency program.

    e. Write a code-breaking program.

Set II. Application

For the problem descriptions given in Exercises 14 and 15,

    a. Restate the problem in clear, concise terms.

    b. Break the problem into parts by writing descriptive procedure names.

    c. Write a program to solve the problem.

14. **Problem Description:** When Mr. Pham first came to the United States, he did not know anything about the English language or alphabet. He soon learned several spoken English words, but still has difficulty learning the specific letters. One way he thinks might help him would be to learn the ABC song. The problem with this plan is that he can't always remember the order. He needs some way to remind himself of the number location of a particular letter in the alphabet (for example, that letter *A* is number 1 in the alphabet, or that letter *M* is at number location 13). Use the computer to help Mr. Pham learn the numerical location of the letters in the English alphabet.

15. **Problem Description:** Bonnie works on a ranch for Mr. Sirkle. Mr. Sirkle likes his corrals fenced in circles. On a square area of land with 57,600 square feet, he has four circular corrals of equal size. The distance from one side of a corral straight across to the other side is 120 feet. Mr. Sirkle got tired of this arrangement and so he tore down all the fences and built one large circular corral that reaches all four sides of the square land. Mr. Sirkle believes that he got more area of land fenced in this way than he had before. Bonnie thinks it does look big; but she doesn't think he has more space than before. Who is right?

16. Write a procedure that will take two integer variables, ALPHA and BETA, and switch their contents.

17. Write a procedure that will compute the reciprocal of a nonzero number entered by the user. (The reciprocal of *x* is $1/x$.)

18. Write a procedure that will take a three-digit apartment number and print the floor number on which the apartment is located. For example, apartment 241 is located on floor 2 and apartment 679 is located on floor 6.

19. Write a procedure to compute the sale price of an item given its original price and the percent of discount. (This problem was introduced in Chapter 3.)

20. Write programs using procedures to print each of the following patterns:

```
a.  X X X X X      b.  X           c.  X           d.  X
    X       X          X               X X             O
    X       X          X               X X X           X
    X       X          X               X X             O O
    X X X X X          X X X X X        X               X
                                                        O O O
                                                        X
```

21. Write a program that prints a tic-tack-toe board. Assuming the procedures have only one line of output each, what is the minimum number of procedures needed to print the board? The program should use procedures that are called more than once to draw the board.

Set III. Synthesis

22. Write a program that will take an integer entered by the user, find its square root, then square the result. Theoretically, the square of the square root of 25 should be 25. Does the computer give this result? Why or why not?

Use the following procedures:

```
GETNUMBER
SQUAREROOT   { USE REAL VARIABLE }
SQUARE
PRINTRESULT
```

23. Write a program to approximate the Julian date for a given calendar date. The program should ask the user for the month number and the day of the month. The Julian date may be approximated by the following formula:

$$(month - 1) \times 30 + day$$

Find the Julian equivalents for March 11, August 4, November 30, and December 31.

For example, November 4 has an approximate Julian date of

$$(11 - 1) \times 30 + 4 = 304$$

Procedures used:

```
GETDATE
FINDJULIAN
PRINTRESULT
```

24. Write a program that will draw a text picture or pattern on the screen. The program should use at least one procedure that is called more than once to draw a part of the picture.

25. Write a program that will find the cost of building a deck. Use the following procedures:

```
GETDECKDIMENSIONS
GETCOSTPERSQFOOT
FINDAREA
CALCULATECOST
```

26. Linda was standing on a bridge one day, dropping rocks into the water below. She noted that it took approximately five seconds for each rock to reach the water. Write a program to find the height of the bridge, given the following formula:

$$\text{DISTANCE} = \frac{1}{2} \text{GT}^2$$

where DISTANCE is the height of the bridge in meters; G is a constant (gravity 9.81 meters/second^2), and T is the time in seconds. Use the following procedures:

```
GETTIME
FINDHEIGHT
PRINTRESULT
```

Printed decimal amounts should be rounded to the hundredths place using field widths.

27. Write a program that will take an integer variable, PERCENT, and convert its value to a decimal number, stored in DECIMAL. Allow the user to enter the value for PERCENT. The program should perform decimal conversion to two decimal places and print the value followed by the percent symbol (%).
Use the following procedures:

```
GETPERCENT
FINDDECIMAL
PRINTRESULT
```

28. The following recipe makes eight pancakes:

1.25	cups flour
3	tsp. baking soda
1	Tbsp. sugar
1	egg
1	cup milk
2	Tbsp. vegetable oil

Write a program to convert this pancake recipe, given the desired number of servings. For example, if the user enters 16, then the recipe is doubled. If the user enters 10, then each ingredient in the recipe is multiplied by 10/8. Use the following structure and procedures:

```
PROGRAM PANCAKES(INPUT,OUTPUT);
    .
    .
    .
BEGIN
    SETUPRECIPE;        { DEFINE VARIABLE VALUES }
    PRINTRECIPE;
    GETSERVINGS;        { ENTER SERVINGS DESIRED }
    CONVERTRECIPE;
    PRINTRECIPE
END.
```

Printed decimal amounts should be rounded to the hundredths place using field widths.

29. Write a program that will accept a measurement in feet and inches and print the amount in inches. The program should then convert the inches to centimeters (centimeters = inches × 0.3937) and print the result. Use the following main program:

```
BEGIN
    GETMEASURE;
    FINDINCHES;
    PRINTRESULT;
    FINDCENTIMETERS;
    PRINTRESULT
END.
```

Printed decimal amounts should be rounded to the hundredths place using field widths.

30. Rewrite the program from Exercise 29 to include output of the measurement in meters and centimeters. (Some of the standard functions may be helpful here.)

31. Write a program to find the difference between two long-jump attempts. The jumps are given in feet and inches. Procedure FINDINCHES from Exercise 29 might prove helpful. The program should output the difference in feet and inches.

32. Write a program that will "guess" the serial number on a dollar bill. The program should ask the user to look at a dollar bill and give the sum of the first two digits, the sum of the second and third digits, the sum of the third and fourth digits, and so on through all the digits. For an eighth and final sum, the user should give the sum of the last and second digits.

    The program should then print the serial number using the following method:

```
PAIRSUMS :=    SUM2 - SUM3 + SUM4 - SUM5 + SUM6 -
               SUM7 + SUM8;
SECONDDIGIT := PAIRSUMS / 2;
```

The remaining digits can be found by subtractions:

    1st digit = SUM1 - SECONDDIGIT
    2nd digit = SECONDDIGIT
    3rd digit = SUM2 − 2nd digit
    4th digit = SUM3 − 3rd digit
    5th digit = SUM4 − 4th digit
    and so on.

The program should use the following procedures:

```
GETSUMS
COMPUTEDIGITS
PRINTSERIALNUM
```

Repetition: FOR

"And how many hours a day did you do lessons?" said Alice. . . .

"Ten hours the first day," said the Mock Turtle: "nine the next, and so on."

"What a curious plan!" exclaimed Alice.

"That's the reason they're called lessons," the Gryphon remarked: "because they lessen from day to day."

—Lewis Carroll

Overview

The FOR Structure
    Definite Iteration
    Rules for Using FOR Loops
Programming Using the FOR Structure
    Accumulating
    Nested Loops
Programming Tip
    Collecting Information

Gaining a Perspective

Very often during the solution of a problem there is a need to repeat a number of steps. Programming would be extremely time-consuming if there weren't some structure for repetition—performing a particular task a number of times. Pascal provides several ways to handle repetition or looping. If the number of desired repetitions is known, the FOR structure lends itself readily to a quick solution to the problem. With a FOR loop, any process can be repeated a specified number of times.

Lesson 5.1   The FOR Structure

The **FOR loop** is a structure that is useful when the exact number of times a task is repeated is known. This loop results in what is called **definite iteration,** where iteration means looping or repeating.

The FOR loop might be useful to a schoolboy or schoolgirl who got in trouble for talking too much in class and was assigned to write the phrase "I will not talk in class" one hundred times. In Pascal, the FOR structure allows an easy solution to this time-consuming assignment, assuming the teacher accepts computer-generated solutions.

Program 5.1

```
PROGRAM TALK(OUTPUT);

      { PURPOSE: TO DEMONSTRATE THE FOR LOOP }

VAR
     COUNTER : INTEGER;

BEGIN    { MAIN PROGRAM }

    FOR COUNTER := 1 TO 100 DO
       WRITELN('I WILL NOT TALK IN CLASS.')

END.
```

Of course, if the student created more of a disturbance, the work for the assignment could easily be adjusted. The number of times the message must be written, or the message itself, could be altered.

The FOR Structure

```
FOR counter := initial TO final DO
    statement;
```

or (for counting backwards)

```
FOR counter := initial DOWNTO final DO
    statement;
```

The counter must be a declared variable of any ordinal type: INTEGER, CHAR, BOOLEAN, or a programmer-defined type (see Chapter 11). The initial and final values (the limits of the loop) are expressions of the same type as the counter variable. The TO in the first structure means to **increment** (increase) the counter by 1 and the DOWNTO in the second structure means to **decrement** (decrease) the counter by 1. The statement part of the FOR structure is either

1. A single statement: a statement that allows input, output, an assignment statement, a procedure call, an **empty statement** (a semicolon only), or any other statement (including another FOR statement); or
2. A compound statement: several statements placed between a BEGIN and an END that work together to perform a given task.

If the counter is an INTEGER, the number of times the FOR loop is executed is equal to the absolute value of the difference between the initial and final values, plus 1. Program 5.1 is executed one hundred times.

$$\text{Number of executions} = |\text{ final } - \text{ initial }| + 1$$
$$= |\text{ }100 - 1\text{ }| + 1$$
$$= 100$$

The $|\ \ |$ is the mathematical symbol for absolute value. In Pascal, the expression would be written

```
ABS(final - initial) + 1
```

The following programs illustrate the use of each type of statement with a FOR loop. Program 5.2 uses a FOR loop with a single Pascal statement and a counter (CHARACTER) of type CHAR.

Program 5.2
```
PROGRAM DEMO1(OUTPUT);

      { PURPOSE: EXAMPLE OF CHAR AS LOOP VALUES }

VAR
   CHARACTER : CHAR;

BEGIN  { MAIN PROGRAM }

   FOR CHARACTER := 'A' TO 'Z' DO
      WRITE(CHARACTER,' ');
   WRITELN

END.
```

Program 5.2 prints the letters of the alphabet in a row across the screen, with a space between each letter.

Program 5.3 uses a procedure call as the statement in the FOR loop and an INTEGER counter. The procedure is executed three times.

Program 5.3
```
PROGRAM DEMO2(OUTPUT);

      { PURPOSE: EXAMPLE OF A PROCEDURE CALL }

VAR
   COUNTER : INTEGER;

PROCEDURE PRINTHELLO;

   BEGIN

      WRITELN('HELLO')

   END;  { PRINTHELLO }

BEGIN  { MAIN PROGRAM }

   WRITELN;
   FOR COUNTER := 3 TO 5 DO { LOOP EXECUTED 3 TIMES }
      PRINTHELLO;              { PROCEDURE CALL }
   WRITELN

END.
```

The output of Program 5.3 is
```
HELLO
HELLO
HELLO
```

Program 5.4 uses the FOR structure to create a **timing loop,** which causes a delay in the program. An empty statement is used for the statement of the loop.

Program 5.4

```
PROGRAM DEMO3(OUTPUT);

     { PURPOSE: EXAMPLE OF AN EMPTY STATEMENT }

VAR
    COUNTER : INTEGER;

BEGIN  { MAIN PROGRAM }

    WRITELN('THERE WILL BE A SHORT DELAY');
    FOR COUNTER := 1 TO 15000 DO;
    WRITELN('DONE')

END.
```

The semicolon after the DO ends the FOR statement. Thus, the FOR loop simply counts to 15,000, taking several seconds to do so. This empty loop is a useful programming tool if a delay is desired in a program while information is presented on the screen.

Program 5.5 uses an assignment statement within a FOR loop. The statement in the FOR loop is a compound statement, as delimited by BEGIN and END.

Program 5.5

```
PROGRAM DEMO4(OUTPUT);

     { PURPOSE: EXAMPLE OF A COMPOUND STATEMENT }

VAR
    COUNTER,
    EVEN     : INTEGER;

BEGIN  { MAIN PROGRAM }

    FOR COUNTER := 10 DOWNTO 1 DO
       BEGIN
          EVEN := 2 * COUNTER;
          WRITE(EVEN,' ')
       END;  { FOR COUNTER }
    WRITELN

END.
```

Program 5.5 prints the even numbers from 20 down to 2. The output is

```
20 18 16 14 12 10 8 6 4 2
```

Program 5.5 illustrates that, while a loop counter may only increase or decrease by 1, the counter may be used in an expression and assigned to a different variable within the loop. This allows for a variety of results from the loop.

Here are some rules to follow with regard to the FOR loop.

■ The initial and final expressions are evaluated upon entering the loop. If the initial value is greater than the final value (or less, in the case of DOWNTO) upon entering the loop, the statement in the loop is not executed and the program moves on to the statement immediately following the loop. If the initial value equals the final value upon entering the loop, the loop is executed once; that is,

$$| \text{ final } - \text{ initial } | + 1 = 1$$

- The counter variable must be of the same type as the initial and final value. The choice of types for these variables is INTEGER, CHAR, BOOLEAN or programmer-defined types (introduced in Chapter 11).

- The value of the counter variable should not be changed from within the loop. Instead, another variable should be declared on which to make the changes. For example, Program 5.5 uses a descriptive variable (EVEN) whose value is determined by the counter variable.

- The value of the counter variable after leaving the loop is one more (or less, if DOWNTO is used) than the final loop value. For example, in Program 5.5, COUNTER is 0 after the loop is completed. If the value of the counter variable will be needed later, it should be stored in a different variable. (The value of the counter variable upon completion of the loop varies according to the version of Pascal. In Standard Pascal, it is undefined.)

- If a FOR loop is used within a procedure, the counter variable should be declared locally in that procedure.

Program 5.6 illustrates a few of the rules just set forth. Procedure SHOULDNOTDO is an example of changing the counter within the loop. There should never be a need to do this. Notice that in the second procedure, NOTMUCH, COUNTER is not altered by the assignment statements within the loop, since the initial and final expressions are evaluated upon loop entry. The desired output of procedure WORLDFAMOUSMISTAKE is HELLO printed five times, but HELLO is printed only once due to a misplaced semicolon. Even though the indentation implies that the WRITELN is in the FOR loop and should be done five times, the semicolon changes the program segment from what was intended.

Program 5.6

```
PROGRAM TESTRULES(INPUT,OUTPUT);

PROCEDURE SHOULDNOTDO;

    { PURPOSE: SHOW AN EXAMPLE OF CHANGING THE
               COUNTER WITHIN THE LOOP }
```

```
VAR
   COUNTER,
   NUM1,
   NUM2     : INTEGER;

BEGIN
   NUM1 := 1;
   NUM2 := 5;
   WRITELN('PROCEDURE SHOULDNOTDO');
   FOR COUNTER := NUM1 TO NUM2 DO
      BEGIN
         WRITELN(COUNTER);
         COUNTER := COUNTER + 1
      END  { FOR COUNTER }
END;  { SHOULDNOTDO }

PROCEDURE NOTMUCH;

      { PURPOSE: TO SHOW THAT THE INITIAL AND FINAL
                 VALUES ARE EVALUATED UPON ENTRY INTO
                 THE LOOP }

   VAR
      COUNTER,
      NUM1,
      NUM2     : INTEGER;

   BEGIN
      NUM1 := 1;
      NUM2 := 6;
      WRITELN('PROCEDURE NOTMUCH');
      FOR COUNTER := NUM2 DOWNTO NUM1 DO
         BEGIN
            NUM1 := 100;
            NUM2 := 1000;
            WRITELN('THESE ASSIGNMENT STATEMENTS DO');
            WRITELN('NOT ALTER THE INITIAL AND FINAL');
            WRITELN('VALUES OF THE LOOP.')
         END  { FOR COUNTER }
   END;  { NOTMUCH }

PROCEDURE WORLDFAMOUSMISTAKE;

      { PURPOSE: TO SHOW HOW A MISPLACED SEMICOLON CAN
                 CAUSE AN UNINTENTIONAL ERROR.  THE FOR
                 LOOP HAS A SEMICOLON FOLLOWING THE DO,
                 MEANING THAT THE STATEMENT IS AN EMPTY
                 STATEMENT. }

   VAR
      COUNTER : INTEGER;

   BEGIN
      WRITELN('PROCEDURE WORLDFAMOUSMISTAKE');
      FOR COUNTER := 1 TO 5 DO;
         WRITELN('HELLO')
   END;  { WORLDFAMOUSMISTAKE }
```

```
BEGIN  { MAIN PROGRAM }

   SHOULDNOTDO;
   NOTMUCH;
   WORLDFAMOUSMISTAKE

END.
```

The output of Program 5.6 is

```
   PROCEDURE SHOULDNOTDO
1
3
5
PROCEDURE NOTMUCH
THESE ASSIGNMENT STATEMENTS DO
NOT ALTER THE INITIAL AND FINAL
VALUES OF THE LOOP.
THESE ASSIGNMENT STATEMENTS DO
NOT ALTER THE INITIAL AND FINAL
VALUES OF THE LOOP.
THESE ASSIGNMENT STATEMENTS DO
NOT ALTER THE INITIAL AND FINAL
VALUES OF THE LOOP.
THESE ASSIGNMENT STATEMENTS DO
NOT ALTER THE INITIAL AND FINAL
VALUES OF THE LOOP.
THESE ASSIGNMENT STATEMENTS DO
NOT ALTER THE INITIAL AND FINAL
VALUES OF THE LOOP.
THESE ASSIGNMENT STATEMENTS DO
NOT ALTER THE INITIAL AND FINAL
VALUES OF THE LOOP.
PROCEDURE WORLDFAMOUSMISTAKE
HELLO
```

Lesson Check 5.1

1. What is meant by definite iteration?

2. How many times are each of the following loops executed?
   a. FOR NUM := 5 TO 17 DO
   b. FOR COUNT := 2 TO 2 DO
   c. FOR NUMBER := 100 DOWNTO 49 DO

3. What will happen if the following limits are used in a FOR loop?

   FOR COUNTER := 5 TO 1 DO

Lesson 5.2 Programming Using the FOR Structure

Karl Friedrich Gauss (1777–1855), a famous German mathematician, was presented with a mathematics problem when he was a boy. His teacher asked the pupils of his class to find the sum of an arithmetic series of numbers, such as the integers from 1 to 100. Within a few short moments, Gauss gave the answer, having worked out a formula to compute the arithmetic series. Had he the use of a computer, Gauss's work could have been accomplished by a program such as Program 5.7, which shows the use of a FOR loop to find the sum of the numbers from 1 to 100.

Program 5.7

```
PROGRAM SUM(OUTPUT);

    { PURPOSE: TO FIND THE SUM OF THE NUMBERS
               FROM 1 TO 100 }

CONST
    ENDCOUNT = 100;

VAR
    COUNTER,
    SUM      : INTEGER;

BEGIN  { MAIN PROGRAM }

    SUM := 0;
    FOR COUNTER := 1 TO ENDCOUNT DO
       SUM := SUM + COUNTER;
    WRITE('SUM OF NUMBERS FROM 1 TO ',ENDCOUNT,' = ');
    WRITELN(SUM)

END.
```

First, SUM is set (initialized) to zero to avoid unpredictable results. Within the FOR loop, COUNTER is added to SUM as it changes from 1 to 100. SUM is used to **accumulate** the total of the numbers. After the loop is complete, the sum of the numbers from 1 to 100 is printed. The output is

```
SUM OF NUMBERS FROM 1 TO 100 = 5050
```

The content of the variables for Program 5.7 is outlined in the following table:

COUNTER	SUM + COUNTER		SUM
---	---	---	0
1	0 +	1	1
2	1 +	2	3
3	3 +	3	6
4	6 +	4	10
.		.	.
.		.	.
.		.	.
99	4851 +	99	4950
100	4950 +	100	5050

In Program 5.8 the statement within the outer loop is a compound statement. This is also called a **nested loop.** An entire inner loop occurs during one count of the outer loop.

Program 5.8
```
PROGRAM NUMBERSHAPE(OUTPUT);

    { PURPOSE: TO DEMONSTRATE NESTED LOOPS }

VAR
    LOOP1,
    LOOP2  : INTEGER;

BEGIN  { MAIN PROGRAM }

    FOR LOOP1 := 1 TO 9 DO
        BEGIN
            FOR LOOP2 := LOOP1 TO 9 DO
                WRITE(LOOP2,' ');
            WRITELN
        END  { FOR LOOP1 }

END.
```

The outer loop causes the inner loop to be done nine times. The inner loop counts from the current value of LOOP1 to 9. A trace of the contents of the variables LOOP1 and LOOP2 follows:

LOOP1	LOOP2	Output
1	1 . . . 9	1 2 3 4 5 6 7 8 9
2	2 . . . 9	2 3 4 5 6 7 8 9
3	3 . . . 9	3 4 5 6 7 8 9
4	4 . . . 9	4 5 6 7 8 9
5	5 . . . 9	5 6 7 8 9
6	6 . . . 9	6 7 8 9
7	7 . . . 9	7 8 9
8	8 . . . 9	8 9
9	9 . . . 9	9

Program 5.9 presents another example of nested loops. The innermost statement is a FOR loop.

Program 5.9
```
PROGRAM NESTEDFORS(OUTPUT);

    { PURPOSE: TO DEMONSTRATE NESTED FOR LOOPS }

VAR
    ONE,
    TWO,
    THREE : INTEGER;

BEGIN  { MAIN PROGRAM }

    FOR ONE := 1 TO 3 DO
        BEGIN
            FOR TWO := 1 TO 3 DO
                FOR THREE := 1 TO 3 DO
                    WRITE(ONE,TWO,THREE,'/');
            WRITELN
        END  { FOR ONE }

END.
```

Program 5.9 outputs the following:

```
111/112/113/121/122/123/131/132/133/
211/212/213/221/222/223/231/232/233/
311/312/313/321/322/323/331/332/333/
```

The following partial trace of Program 5.9 illustrates how the output was obtained:

ONE	TWO	THREE	Portion of Output
1	1	1 . . . 3	111/112/113/
1	2	1 . . . 3	121/122/123/
1	3	1 . . . 3	131/132/133/
2	1	1 . . . 3	211/212/213/
2	2	1 . . . 3	221/222/223/

The loops of Program 5.9 are nested three deep. Loop THREE is done three times every time the program executes loop TWO, and loop TWO is done three times every time the program executes loop ONE. Thus, the WRITE in loop THREE will be done twenty-seven times. Notice loops TWO and THREE do not contain compound statements; therefore, BEGIN . . . END blocks for these loops are unnecessary.

Lesson Check 5.2

1. How many times will

   HAPPY BIRTHDAY!

   be printed in the following program segment?

   ```
   FOR COUNT1 := 1 TO 3 DO
      FOR COUNT2 := 1 TO 5 DO
         WRITELN('HAPPY BIRTHDAY!');
   ```

2. Rewrite the main program block of Program 5.7 to include output of the sum after each addition.

Lesson 5.3   Programming Tip— Collecting Information

After understanding the problem, the next step in the solution of a problem is to identify the information (or data) available, select the information that is relevant in the given situation, and analyze the information to see how it relates to the problem. This task can be simplified by employing some of the following techniques:

- Clarify the expected outcome of the problem.
- Identify information needed to arrive at the desired outcome.
- Eliminate unnecessary information.
- Gather information from sources other than the problem.
- Classify (organize) the information.
- Represent the data with a diagram, graph, or table.
- Look for patterns in the data.
- Represent the information symbolically (in mathematical terms).

Knowing what is and isn't necessary to the solution of a problem is the key. These steps can help the programmer a great deal in making decisions about the information related to the problem.

Given the problem of determining the cost per acre of a lot, which of the following data would be needed in order to solve the problem?

1. Price of the lot.
2. Cost per square yard of a similar lot.
3. Slope of the land.
4. Length of the lot in yards.
5. Width of the lot in yards.
6. Appraised value of the lot.
7. Number of square yards in an acre.

Items **1, 4, 5,** and **7** are needed in order to find the cost per acre of the lot. The other items may be of some importance to a prospective buyer, but are not necessary to the solution of the problem at hand. Once the information is collected, the programmer is ready to plan a solution to the problem.

Summary

The FOR loop is a Pascal structure used for repeating a statement when the desired number of repetitions is known. A FOR loop represents definite iteration since the number of repetitions is specified in advance. The counter used in a FOR loop should be of any ordinal type (INTEGER, CHAR, BOOLEAN, or programmer-defined). The limits of the loop must be of the same type as the counter. Any legal Pascal statement, including a compound statement, may be used in a FOR structure.

The limits of a FOR loop are evaluated upon entry into the loop. Thus, changing the limits in the loop doesn't affect how many times the loop is executed. Although it is legal in many versions of Pascal, attempting to change the loop counter from within the loop, is not a good idea and can lead to much confusion.

FOR loops may be nested: one loop may occur inside another. This causes the inner loop to be executed the specified number of times every time through the outer loop. Thus, the effect is multiplied.

Key Terms

accumulate   FOR   loop

decrement   increment   nested loop

definite iteration

Answers to Lesson Checks

Lesson 5.1

1. Definite iteration is a process of repeating something a specific number of times.

2. a. 13
   b. 1
   c. 52

3. The loop will not be executed. The FOR loop should use DOWNTO in place of TO.

Lesson 5.2

1. HAPPY BIRTHDAY!
will be printed fifteen times.

2.
```
BEGIN
    SUM := 0;
    FOR COUNTER := 1 TO ENDCOUNT DO
        BEGIN
            SUM := SUM + COUNTER;
            WRITE(SUM : 6)
        END;
    WRITELN;
    WRITE('SUM OF NUMBERS FROM 1 TO ',
          ENDCOUNT,' = ');
    WRITELN(SUM)
END.
```

Exercises

Set I. Comprehension

1. Assume correct variable declarations and input of 10, 25, 4, and −50. What is the output of the following program segment?

```
BIG := 100;
FOR COUNT := 1 TO 4 DO
    BEGIN
        READLN(TAKEAWAY);
        BIG := BIG - TAKEAWAY
    END;
WRITELN(BIG);
```

2. Assume correct variable declarations for the following program segment. What is the output?

```
FOR ARGUE := 1 TO 2 DO
   BEGIN
      WRITELN('NO YOU CAN''T!');
      WRITELN('YES I CAN!')
   END;
FOR YELL := 1 TO 3 DO
   WRITELN('YES I CAN!!');
```

3. Which of the following will print the alphabet in order from A to Z? (There may be more than one correct answer.) Assume that LETTER has been appropriately declared in each example.

   a.
```
FOR LETTER := 'A' TO 'Z' DO
   WRITELN(LETTER);
```
   b.
```
FOR LETTER := 'Z' DOWNTO 'A' DO
   WRITELN(LETTER);
```
   c.
```
FOR LETTER := 65 TO 90 DO
   WRITELN(CHR(LETTER));
```
   d.
```
FOR LETTER := 'B' TO '[' DO
   WRITELN(SUCC(LETTER));
```

4. Which of the following program segments will print even numbers from 2 through 50? (There may be more than one correct answer.) Assume that NUMBER has been appropriately declared in each segment.

   a.
```
FOR NUMBER := 1 TO 25 DO
   WRITELN(2 * NUMBER);
```
   b.
```
FOR NUMBER := 1 TO 50 DO
   BEGIN
      EVEN := 2 * NUMBER;
      WRITELN(NUMBER)
   END;
```
   c.
```
FOR NUMBER := 2 TO 50 DO
   WRITELN(NUMBER);
```
   d.
```
FOR NUMBER := 1 TO 50 DO
   BEGIN
      NUMBER := NUMBER + 1;
      WRITELN(NUMBER)
   END;
```

5. Describe the output of the following program segment. Assume the loop counters have been appropriately declared.

```
FOR ALOOP := 1 TO 5 DO
   FOR BLOOP := 'A' TO 'E' DO
      FOR CLOOP := 1 TO 5 DO
         WRITELN(ALOOP,BLOOP,CLOOP);
```

6. What is the output of Exercise 5, if the third line is changed to

```
FOR CLOOP := 5 DOWNTO 1 DO
```

7. Find the number of times each of the following loops will be executed:

   a. `FOR COUNT := 1 TO 50 DO`
   b. `FOR COUNT := 100 DOWNTO 20 DO`
   c. `FOR X := 2 TO SQR(2) DO`
   d. `FOR Y := -20 TO 10 DO`
   e. `FOR Z := -1 DOWNTO -3 DO`

8. Find the number of times each of the following loops will be executed:
   a. FOR NUMBER := 3 TO 60 DO
   b. FOR COUNT := 45 DOWNTO 2 DO
   c. FOR X := 20 TO 20 DO
   d. FOR Y := 4 TO 3 DO
   e. FOR Z := -9 DOWNTO -20 DO

9. Describe what will be printed on the screen when each of the following program segments is executed:
   a. FOR COUNT := 1 TO 10 DO
       WRITELN(3*COUNT);
   b. FOR NUMBER := 3 TO 20 DO
       WRITELN(NUMBER,(20-NUMBER+3));

10. Describe what will be printed on the screen when each of the following program segments is executed:
    a. FOR COUNTER := 2 TO 200 DO
        WRITELN(3 * COUNTER);
    b. FOR COUNTER := 1 TO 25 DO
        WRITELN(COUNTER, (25 - COUNTER + 1));

11. Correct the errors in the following program so that it will find the sum of the even numbers from 2 to 100:

```
PROGRAM EVENSUM (OUTPUT);

VAR
    COUNT,
    ECOUNT,
    SUM      : INTEGER;

BEGIN

    SUM := 0;
    FOR COUNT = 1 TO 50 DO;
       ECOUNT := COUNT * 2;
       SUM := SUM + COUNT;
    WRITE('SUM OF EVEN NUMBERS FROM 2 TO 100 =');
    WRITELN(SUM)

END.
```

12. Correct the errors in the following program so that it will find the product of the odd numbers from 1 to 30:

```
PROGRAM PRODUCT (OUTPUT);

VAR
    COUNT,
    PRODUCT : INTEGER;

BEGIN

    PRODUCT := 0;
    FOR COUNT := 1 DOWNTO 10 DO;
       ODDCOUNT := COUNT * 2 + 1;
       PRODUCT := PRODUCT * ODDCOUNT;
    WRITE('PRODUCT OF THE ODD NUMBERS ');
    WRITE('FROM 1 TO 30 = ');
    WRITELN(PRODUCT)

END.
```

13. How many times will the procedure PROCESS be called in the following program segment?

```
FOR LOOPX := 1 TO 7 DO
   FOR LOOPY := 8 TO 10 DO
      FOR LOOPZ := 11 TO 15 DO
         PROCESS;
```

14. How many times will the procedure LOOPDELOO be called in the following program segment?

```
FOR LOOP1 := 2 TO 5 DO
   FOR LOOP2 := 9 TO 11 DO
      FOR LOOP3 := 3 DOWNTO 1 DO
         LOOPDELOO;
```

15. What data would be necessary to find the volume of a cube?
    a. The weight of the cube.
    b. The length of one side of the cube.
    c. The area of one face of the cube.
    d. The formula for finding the volume of a cube.
    e. The mass of the cube.
    f. The composition of the cube.

16. What data would be necessary in order to compute the amount of time a bicyclist needs to complete 50 laps on a track?
    a. The speed of the bicycle (MPH).
    b. The brand of the bicycle.
    c. The length of one lap in feet.
    d. The shape of the track.
    e. The weight of the bicyclist.
    f. The number of feet in a mile.

17. What data might be necessary in order to find the cost of electricity to operate an appliance?

18. What data might be necessary in order to estimate the cost of gasoline for an automobile trip?

Set II. Application

19. Write a FOR loop to replace the following segment:

```
WRITELN('5');
WRITELN('4');
WRITELN('3');
WRITELN('2');
WRITELN('1');
WRITELN('0');
WRITELN('BLASTOFF!!!');
```

20. Write a FOR loop to print the answers to the following multiplication problems:

```
 3 * 23469
 6 * 23469
 9 * 23469
12 * 23469
15 * 23469
18 * 23469
```

21. Write a program segment to print the odd numbers from 1 to 99. Use a FOR loop.

22. Write a program segment that will print the following sequence:

```
$  5.75
$  5.25
$  4.75
$  4.25
      .
      .
      .
$   .25
```

23. Write a FOR loop that will add .01 to itself, one hundred times.

24. Write a FOR loop that will find the sum of the squares of five numbers entered by the user.

25. For each of the following, write a FOR loop to find the sum of the series:
    a. 1/2 + 2/3 + 3/4 + ... + 99/100
    b. $1^3 + 2^3 + 3^3 + ... + 9^3$
    c. 1 + 1/2 + 1/3 + ... + 1/100

26. Write a program segment to find
        1/2/3/ ... N
    where N is entered by the user.

27. Write programs using FOR loops that will print each of the following patterns:

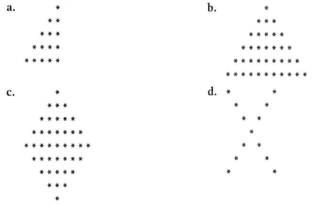

28. Write a program that will compute the average of 25 numbers entered by the user.

29. Rewrite the program from Exercise 28 to allow for any number of values. The program should prompt the user for the number of values to be entered.

30. Write a program that will create a multiplication table up to 9 x 9, as follows:

```
X   0   1   2   3   4   5   6   7   8   9
0   0   0   0   0   0   0   0   0   0   0
1   0   1   2   3   4   5   6   7   8   9
2   0   2   4   6   8  10  12  14  16  18
3   0   3   6   9  12  15  18  21  24  27
4   0   4   8  12  16  20  24  28  32  36
5   0   5  10  15  20  25  30  35  40  45
6   0   6  12  18  24  30  36  42  48  54
7   0   7  14  21  28  35  42  49  56  63
8   0   8  16  24  32  40  48  56  64  72
9   0   9  18  27  36  45  54  63  72  81
```

31. Write a procedure that will output a table with the numbers from 1 to 20, their squares, and their cubes.

32. Given the exponential function
$$y = 5^x$$
Write a procedure that will print a table of x and y values, with x ranging from 1 to 4, using increments of .25. Printed values should be rounded to the hundredths place.

33. The height of a rocket at a particular time, T, can be described by the expression

$$4T^2 + 3T + 2$$

For $T = 3$ seconds, the rocket's height is

$$= 4(3)^2 + 3(3) + 2$$
$$= 36 + 9 + 2$$
$$= 47 \text{ feet}$$

Write a program that will print the rocket height in feet for each second during the first 10 seconds of its flight. The output from your program should begin as follows:

```
TIME        HEIGHT
 1              9
 2             24
 3             47
```

Set III. Synthesis

34. A factorial is the product of all the positive integers from 1 to a given number. Write a program to print a table of factorials. Prompt the user for the upper limit of the table.
For example, the table for 4! (or $4! = 4 \times 3 \times 2 \times 1$) might be

```
n       n!
1        1
2        2
3        6
4       24
```

35. The sequence of numbers

    0, 1, 1, 2, 3, 5, 8, 13, . . .

    is called a Fibonacci number sequence. Fibonacci numbers are generated by starting the sequence with 0 and 1 and continuing the sequence by adding the two previous numbers. Write a program to print any number of terms of the Fibonacci sequence.

36. Write a program using nested loops to create each of the following designs:

```
a. 987654321        b. 987654321        c. 123456789
    87654321            98765432            12345678
     7654321            9876543              1234567
      654321            987654                123456
       54321            98765                  12345
        4321            9876                     1234
         321            987                       123
          21            98                         12
           1            9                           1

d. 987654321        e.         1        f.          1
    87654321                  21                   12
     7654321                 321                  123
      654321                4321                 1234
       54321               54321
        4321              654321
         321             7654321               1234
          21            87654321               123
           1           987654321                12
                                                 1
```

37. Write a program that uses a timing loop. (A stopwatch is needed for this problem.) Experiment with the FINAL value to find a loop that will run
    a. one second.
    b. three seconds.

    Assuming INTEGER counters, what is the maximum amount of time taken in a single timing loop? What is the maximum amount of time taken in a nested loop (two FOR loops)?

38. In the song "The Twelve Days of Christmas," gifts are bestowed upon the singer in the following pattern: the first day, she received a partridge in a pear tree; the second day, two turtledoves and a partridge in a pear tree; the third day, three french hens, two turtledoves, and a partridge in a pear tree. This continued for a total of 12 days. On the 12th day, she received

    12 + 11 + 10 + . . . + 2 + 1

    gifts. Write a program to print the number of gifts presented on each of the 12 days and the total up to that day.

39. Carrie entered a fishing contest that lasted one week. Two points were given for each fish caught. Write a program to produce a horizontal bar graph of Carrie's daily catch of fish and print her total points at the bottom of the graph. The program should prompt the user for each day's catch and then, on the same line of input, print a series of asterisks (*) to indicate the number caught that day. The output should look something like the following:

```
DAY      CATCH
 1         4       *   *   *   *
 2         7       *   *   *   *   *   *   *
 3         5       *   *   *   *   *
 .         .                   .
 .         .                   .
 .         .                   .
 8         8       *   *   *   *   *   *   *   *
TOTAL POINTS = 72
```

40. Andy was having trouble finding a job; it seemed that employers weren't ready to pay him the $2,000 per month that he required. When he went for an interview with a rich miser, he asked to be paid one cent on the first day, two cents on the second day, four cents on the third day, eight cents on the fourth, and so on for 30 days. The idea appealed to the miser and Andy was hired. Write a program to find how much Andy was paid on each day and his total accumulated wages each day.

41. Grandma is making a quilt and using four colors of material. She would like a list of all the possible ways to arrange the colors in blocks of four. Some possible arrangements include 1142, 4321, and 1234. (A color may be used more than once in an arrangement.) Write a program to print the ordered arrangements of the four colors.

42. Mark works in a bakery where one of his tasks is to develop food colors for decorator frosting. He has three food dyes—A, B and C—and would like to know the possible ways he can combine three drops taken from the three dyes. Write a program to help Mark find all the mixtures of dyes A, B, and C using three drops. (In this exercise, repetitions are allowed, but the order in which the dyes are mixed does not matter. For example, a mixture of AAB is valid, but listing both AAB and ABA is not.)

6

Repetition: REPEAT and WHILE

. . . the Mock Turtle repeated thoughtfully. "I should like to hear her try and repeat something now. . . ."

"Stand up and repeat ' 'Tis the voice of the sluggard,' " said the Gryphon.

"How the creatures order one about, and make one repeat lessons!" thought Alice.

—Lewis Carroll

Overview

BOOLEAN Expressions and Operators
    Indefinite Iteration
    Declaration of BOOLEAN
      Variables
    BOOLEAN Expressions and
      Relational Operators
    Assignments to BOOLEAN
      Variables
    BOOLEAN Operators
    Order of Operations
    Evaluation of BOOLEAN
      Expressions
The REPEAT Structure
    Form and Body of REPEAT
      Structure
    Infinite Loops
    Rules of REPEAT Structure
The WHILE Structure
    Form and Body of WHILE
      Structure
    Rules of WHILE Structure
Using WHILE and REPEAT
    BOOLEAN Functions
      ODD Function
      EOLN Function
      EOF Function
    Nested Loops
Programming Tip
    Style

Gaining a Perspective

In the previous chapter, the FOR structure was introduced as a means of repeating a process a specific number of times. The FOR structure is appropriate as long as the number of repetitions is known in advance. More often, however, a programmer will need to have some statements executed as long as some condition (or some conditions) is or is not met. That is, there might be a need to perform some process while certain conditions are in effect or until some condition comes into being. In the housecleaning example from Chapter 4, vacuuming would continue until done, not for an arbitrary length of time. Pascal provides two structures that take care of these cases: WHILE and REPEAT. This chapter will describe these structures, along with the methods for checking various conditions using BOOLEAN expressions.

Lesson 6.1   BOOLEAN Expressions and Operators

In Chapter 2, five data types were introduced: INTEGER, CHAR, REAL, STRING, and BOOLEAN. The first four were discussed in detail. The fifth data type, BOOLEAN, named after the famous logician and mathematician George Boole, will now be explained more thoroughly. BOOLEAN variables are logic variables that have a value of TRUE or FALSE. In this chapter, BOOLEAN variables are used to control **indefinite iteration** (iteration without a predetermined number of executions). BOOLEAN expressions determine the number of iterations of a loop.

BOOLEAN variables are declared in the variable declaration portion of a program or procedure as follows:

```
VAR
   FIRST,
   SECOND : BOOLEAN;
```

Also, BOOLEAN constants may be defined as

```
CONST
   TEST = TRUE;
   DONE = FALSE;
```

Expressions with BOOLEAN values are needed to determine whether **conditional statements** are TRUE or FALSE. **BOOLEAN expressions** can be created using relational operators similar to those found in mathematics (see Table 6.1). For example, the following expressions:

```
NUMBER > 0                    (NUMBER is declared INTEGER)
FIRSTNAME <= SECONDNAME       (FIRSTNAME and SECONDNAME
                               are both declared STRING)
FINISHED = 'YES'              (FINISHED is declared STRING)
```

are BOOLEAN expressions; that is, expressions that are either TRUE or FALSE. In the first example, the BOOLEAN expression is TRUE if NUMBER is greater than zero; otherwise, it is FALSE. In the second example, if FIRSTNAME alphabetically precedes or is the same as SECONDNAME, then the BOOLEAN expression is TRUE; otherwise, it is FALSE. In the final example, if the value stored in FINISHED is equal to the word YES, the expression will evaluate to TRUE; otherwise, it will be FALSE.

BOOLEAN variables or expressions may be used in assignment statements. A BOOLEAN variable is on the left side of the assignment statement, while the right side contains a BOOLEAN expression that evaluates to TRUE or FALSE.

> **BOOLEAN Assignment Form**
>
> `BOOLEAN variable := BOOLEAN expression;`

In the following examples, RESPONSE, FINISHED, RICH, and POOR are all declared as BOOLEAN variables:

```
RESPONSE := TRUE;

FINISHED := RESPONSE;

RICH := (BALANCE >= 100000);

POOR := (ASSETS - LIABILITIES) < 0;
```

In the first example, RESPONSE is a BOOLEAN variable and TRUE is a BOOLEAN value. The second example shows a BOOLEAN variable being assigned to another BOOLEAN variable. Finally, the last two examples show how an expression that evaluates to TRUE or FALSE may be assigned to a BOOLEAN variable. Notice that in these two expressions, the variables on the right side of the assignment (BALANCE, ASSETS, and LIABILITIES) could be

Table 6.1
Relational Operators

Mathematical Symbol	Pascal Symbol	Meaning
=	=	Equal to
≠	< >	Not equal to
<	<	Less than
>	>	Greater than
≤	< =	Less than or equal to
≥	> =	Greater than or equal to

of any numeric type as long as they are used in expressions that are evaluated to TRUE or FALSE.

Additional operators exist for testing more than one condition in an expression. BOOLEAN expressions have three operators: NOT, AND, and OR. The **NOT** operator negates the BOOLEAN value that follows it. **AND** and **OR** join two or more expressions into a single expression. Each expression is evaluated as TRUE or FALSE, and these results are then combined to get a final BOOLEAN value for the entire expression. Some examples of BOOLEAN expressions follow:

```
(LOWER < UPPER) AND (LOWER = 5)

(SMALL = 2) OR (LARGE = 12)

NOT(SMALL = 5)

(SIZE = 8) AND (COLOR = 'BLUE') AND (COST < 20)
```

When the BOOLEAN operators NOT, AND, and OR are used with relational operators parentheses are necessary. In the hierarchy of operations, BOOLEAN operators are dealt with before relational operators. In expressions that combine operators, an order of operations has been established for the arithmetic, relational, and BOOLEAN operators. The order of operations, listed from highest to lowest priority, is shown in Table 6.2. All expressions are evaluated from left to right within the order of operations. The following tables summarize the evaluation of expressions using

Table 6.2
Order of Operation Categories

Order	Operation
1.	( )
2.	NOT
3.	* / DIV MOD AND
4.	+ − OR
5.	= < > < <= > >=

NOT, AND, and OR. Assume that P and Q are BOOLEAN expressions.

NOT means to take the opposite state of the BOOLEAN expression. For example, if the BOOLEAN expression P were TRUE, then the expression NOT P would be FALSE, as shown in the following table:

P	NOT P
TRUE	FALSE
FALSE	TRUE

AND means both BOOLEAN expressions (P and Q) must be TRUE for the entire expression to be TRUE. In the example

```
(SIZE = 8) AND (COLOR = 'BLUE') AND (COST < 20)
```

the first two expressions

```
(SIZE = 8) AND (COLOR = 'BLUE')
```

are evaluated and the result is used with the third expression

```
(result) AND (COST < 20)
```

The AND operator is shown in the following table:

P	Q	P AND Q
TRUE	TRUE	TRUE
TRUE	FALSE	FALSE
FALSE	TRUE	FALSE
FALSE	FALSE	FALSE

OR means that at least one of the BOOLEAN expressions (P or Q) must be TRUE for the entire expression to be TRUE. The OR operator is shown in the following table:

P	Q	P OR Q
TRUE	TRUE	TRUE
TRUE	FALSE	TRUE
FALSE	TRUE	TRUE
FALSE	FALSE	FALSE

Given the initializations of

```
DONE := TRUE;
TEST := FALSE;
NUMBER := 7;
NAME := 'SAM';
LETTER := 'Q';
COST := 17.95;
```

the following expressions evaluate as indicated:

Expression	BOOLEAN Value
`NOT(DONE)`	FALSE
`(NUMBER = 7) AND (NAME = 'SAM')`	TRUE
`NOT(DONE) AND TEST`	FALSE
`(LETTER = 'Z') OR (COST > 20)`	FALSE
`(LETTER = 'Z') OR (COST < 20) AND DONE`	TRUE
`(LETTER = 'Q') OR (COST = 25) AND TEST`	TRUE
`((LETTER = 'Q') OR (COST = 25)) AND TEST`	FALSE
`NOT(DONE OR TEST) AND (NUMBER > 3)`	FALSE

The following example illustrates how to evaluate the final expression.

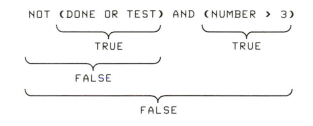

Lesson Check 6.1

1. What is indefinite iteration?

2. How many different values can BOOLEAN variables have?

3. Evaluate the following BOOLEAN expressions for TEST1 = TRUE and TEST2 = FALSE.

    a. `TEST1 AND TEST2`
    b. `TEST1 OR TEST2`
    c. `NOT(TEST2)`
    d. `TEST1 OR NOT(TEST1)`
    e. `NOT(TEST1 OR TEST2) AND TEST1`

Lesson 6.2 The REPEAT Structure

REPEAT provides a method for executing a number of statements until some condition is met. The REPEAT structure is a form of indefinite iteration, since the number of times the statements will be executed is undetermined.

Program 6.1 uses the REPEAT structure to find the sum of the numbers from 1 to 100.

Program 6.1

```
PROGRAM REPEATSUM(OUTPUT);

    { PURPOSE: TO FIND THE SUM OF THE NUMBERS
                FROM 1 TO 100 }

CONST
    ENDCOUNT = 100;

VAR
    COUNTER,
    SUM      : INTEGER;

BEGIN   { MAIN PROGRAM }

    SUM := 0;       { INITIALIZE SUM }
    COUNTER := 0;   { INITIALIZE COUNTER }
    REPEAT
        COUNTER := COUNTER + 1;
        SUM := SUM + COUNTER
    UNTIL COUNTER = ENDCOUNT;   { COUNTER = 100 }
    WRITELN(SUM)

END.
```

The REPEAT structure is a looping mechanism that first completes some process and then evaluates an **exit condition.** This structure has no built-in counter, as with the FOR structure. The process is repeated until the exit condition is TRUE. The exit condition may or may not involve a counter. The form of the REPEAT structure is

---

REPEAT Form

```
REPEAT

    statement

UNTIL BOOLEAN expression;
```

The statement of the REPEAT structure can be any of those discussed earlier. The possibilities follow:

1. A single statement: this can be a procedure call, an assignment statement, an empty statement, and so on.
2. A compound statement: the BEGIN . . . END block is not needed. The REPEAT and UNTIL mark the beginning and end of a compound statement.

Caution: The BOOLEAN expression must contain a variable whose value may be altered by a statement within the loop. If the BOOLEAN expression is never TRUE, the loop would be infinite, as shown in Program Segment 6.2.

Program Segment 6.2

```
{ FOREVER }

COUNT := 0;
REPEAT
   WRITELN(COUNT)
UNTIL COUNT = 50;
```

COUNT will never be equal to 50, so Program Segment 6.2 will print 0 an infinite (never-ending) number of times. Since COUNT is not changed within the loop, the exit condition is never met. This is known as an **infinite loop**.

The next program segment provides an example using RE-PEAT to check for correct input in a READLN.

Program Segment 6.3

```
REPEAT
   WRITELN('ENTER A NUMBER BETWEEN 1 AND 5');
   READLN(NUM)
UNTIL (NUM>=1) AND (NUM<=5);
```

The BOOLEAN exit condition will be TRUE when the number entered is between 1 and 5, inclusive.

When working with a REPEAT loop, remember the following:

- A REPEAT loop is always completed at least one time, since it is tested using a BOOLEAN exit condition.
- The loop stops when the exit condition is TRUE and then executes the statement following the UNTIL.
- The exit condition must contain a variable whose value is changed within the loop.
- No BEGIN or END is needed, although use of a BEGIN . . . END block is legal. The REPEAT and UNTIL are the delimiters of the loop.

Program 6.4 uses a REPEAT loop to print the sum of two numbers entered by the user. The user controls the program and can exit when desired by setting both numbers to zero.

Program 6.4

```
PROGRAM ADDNUMBERS(INPUT,OUTPUT);

   { PURPOSE: THE PROGRAM WORKS AS A SIMPLE
              CALCULATOR TO ADD NUMBERS ENTERED
              BY THE USER }

PROCEDURE ADD;

   VAR
      SUM,
      NUM1,
      NUM2 : INTEGER;
```

```
                    BEGIN
                      WRITELN('USE 0 FOR BOTH INTEGERS TO END.');
                      REPEAT
                        WRITE('FIRST NUMBER: ');
                        READLN(NUM1);
                        WRITE('SECOND NUMBER: ');
                        READLN(NUM2);
                        SUM := NUM1 + NUM2;
                        WRITELN('THE SUM OF ');
                        WRITELN(NUM1,' AND ',NUM2,' IS ',SUM)
                      UNTIL (NUM1 = 0) AND (NUM2 = 0)    { EXIT }
                    END;   { ADD }

              BEGIN   { MAIN PROGRAM }

                PAGE(OUTPUT);
                WRITELN('ENTER INTEGERS AS INSTRUCTED AND THE');
                WRITELN('PROGRAM WILL GIVE THE SUM.');
                WRITELN;
                ADD;
                WRITELN('PRESS <RETURN> TO EXIT');
                READLN   { HOLDS THE SCREEN FOR THE USER }

              END.
```

This program shows exit from the REPEAT . . . UNTIL loop on some condition other than a counter. Any expression that can be evaluated as TRUE or FALSE may be used for the exit condition.

Lesson Check 6.2

1. What is an infinite loop?

2. Identify each statement as true or false.
   a. REPEAT loops require a BEGIN and END.
   b. The statement within a REPEAT loop is executed until an exit condition is evaluated as TRUE.
   c. The REPEAT structure does not contain a built-in counter.

Lesson 6.3   The WHILE Structure

The other indefinite iteration method, the **WHILE** structure, performs some process while a condition is TRUE. For example, Program 6.5 uses a WHILE loop to find the sum of the numbers from 1 to 100.

Program 6.5
```
PROGRAM WHILESUM(OUTPUT);

        { PURPOSE: TO FIND THE SUM OF THE NUMBERS
                   FROM 1 TO 100 }

CONST
   ENDCOUNT = 100;

VAR
   COUNTER,
   SUM      : INTEGER;
```

```
BEGIN    { MAIN PROGRAM }

    SUM := 0;
    COUNTER := 0;
    WHILE COUNTER <> ENDCOUNT DO
        BEGIN
            COUNTER := COUNTER + 1;
            SUM := SUM + COUNTER
        END;
    WRITELN(SUM)

END.
```

Similarities exist between the WHILE structure and the RE-PEAT structure. For example, the BOOLEAN expression must contain a variable whose value is altered within the loop. The condition of the WHILE structure, however, is evaluated upon entry to the loop. This means the statement in a WHILE loop may not be executed at all, whereas a REPEAT loop is always executed at least once. The location of the loop condition is the main consideration when making a choice between these two structures.

WHILE Form

```
WHILE BOOLEAN expression DO
    statement;
```

The statement of the WHILE structure can be any of the statements discussed earlier (single or compound). The BOOLEAN expression determines

1. If the loop will be entered.
2. When the loop will be completed.

Remember, in contrast to the REPEAT loop, the WHILE loop may be completely skipped (if the condition is FALSE on entry). Program Segment 6.6 illustrates this situation.

Program Segment 6.6
```
COUNT := 10;
WHILE COUNT < 10 DO
    COUNT := COUNT + 1;
```

The WHILE condition is tested on entry and the loop stops when the condition is FALSE. For compound statements, the WHILE loop needs a BEGIN and an END. Program 6.7 uses a compound statement within a WHILE loop to compute a class average.

Program 6.7

```
PROGRAM GRADES(INPUT,OUTPUT);

      { PURPOSE: COMPUTE AVERAGE GRADE }

CONST
   FINISHED = 0;

VAR
   STUDENTNUMBER,
   MARK,
   COUNT,
   SUM            : INTEGER;

BEGIN  { MAIN PROGRAM }

   SUM := 0;
   COUNT := 0;
   WRITELN('ENTER THE STUDENT''S NUMBER AND GRADE.');
   WRITELN('   (USE 0 FOR BOTH WHEN FINISHED)'');
   WRITE('STUDENT NUMBER: ');
   READLN(STUDENTNUMBER);
   WRITE('GRADE: ');
   READLN(MARK);
   WHILE STUDENTNUMBER <> FINISHED DO   { EXIT }
      BEGIN
         SUM := SUM + MARK;
         COUNT := COUNT + 1;
         WRITE('STUDENT NUMBER: ');
         READLN(STUDENTNUMBER);
         WRITE('GRADE:   ');
         READLN(MARK)
      END; { WHILE }
   WRITELN;
   WRITELN('AVERAGE = ',ROUND(SUM / COUNT))

END.
```

When working with a WHILE loop, remember the following:

- The loop condition is tested upon entry.
- The statement of a WHILE loop may not be executed, since the loop condition may be FALSE upon entry.
- The value of the loop condition must be changed within the loop.
- For compound statements, the loop needs a BEGIN and an END.

Lesson Check 6.3

1. What is the main consideration when choosing between WHILE and REPEAT?

2. What happens in a WHILE loop if the condition is evaluated as FALSE upon entering the loop?

Lesson 6.4   Using WHILE and REPEAT

BOOLEAN Functions with WHILE and REPEAT

Three built-in BOOLEAN functions are worth mentioning here. The functions ODD, EOLN, and EOF are useful in WHILE and REPEAT structures.

The BOOLEAN function **ODD** returns a value of TRUE if the argument is an odd number. For example,

Function	Value Returned
ODD(7)	TRUE
ODD(22)	FALSE

This function can be used in a WHILE or REPEAT loop, as in the following examples:

```
WHILE ODD(X) DO              REPEAT
   BEGIN                        .
      .                         .
      .                         .
      .                      UNTIL NOT(ODD(X));
   END;    { WHILE }
```

EOLN stands for end-of-line and is used to test whether or not the end of a line of input has been reached. This will be especially useful when processing and manipulating text files (Chapter 16), but can come in handy here as well.

EOLN will be TRUE if the end of a line is reached. EOLN is usually associated with a carriage return. Program Segment 6.8 shows how EOLN can be used to accept characters from the keyboard until <RETURN> is pressed.

Program Segment 6.8

```
PROCEDURE GETCHARACTERS;

VAR
   CH : CHAR;

BEGIN
   WRITELN('ENTER SOME CHARACTERS.');
   WRITELN('PRESS <RETURN> WHEN FINISHED.');
   WHILE NOT(EOLN) DO
      BEGIN
         READ(CH);
         WRITE(CH)
      END;
   WRITELN
END;   { GETCHARACTERS }
```

The last of the three built-in BOOLEAN functions, **EOF,** stands for end-of-file. It is used almost exclusively in reading files to check for the end of the file. Since the end of a file is marked with a character (CTRL-C), the EOF function can be used to stop any input, including input from the keyboard. (This may be system dependent.) Program Segment 6.9 shows how this can be done. (CH is of type CHAR.)

Program Segment 6.9
```
WRITELN('ENTER SOME CHARACTERS.');
WRITELN('USE CONTROL-C TO EXIT.');
WRITE('ENTER CHARACTERS: ');
WHILE NOT(EOF) DO
   READ(CH);
```

This technique could be used in input procedures designed to handle specific types of data entry, such as entering lines of data where <RETURN> indicates the end of a line but not the end of the entire entry process.

Nested Loops

WHILE and REPEAT loops may be nested (one or more inside another) much as the FOR loops discussed in Chapter 5. When loops are nested, the inner loop is done to completion before continuing with the outer loop. Program 6.10 uses nested loops to produce a pattern of numbers similar to that of Program 5.8.

Program 6.10
```
PROGRAM NESTED(OUTPUT);

   { PURPOSE: NESTED WHILE AND REPEAT }

VAR
   COUNT1,
   COUNT2  : INTEGER;

BEGIN

   COUNT1 := 1;
   WHILE COUNT1 < 10 DO
      BEGIN
         COUNT2 := COUNT1;
         REPEAT
            WRITE(COUNT2,' ');
            COUNT2 := COUNT2 + 1
         UNTIL COUNT2 = 10;
         WRITELN;
         COUNT1 := COUNT1 + 1
      END  { WHILE }

END.
```

The output for Program 6.10 is

```
1 2 3 4 5 6 7 8 9
2 3 4 5 6 7 8 9
3 4 5 6 7 8 9
4 5 6 7 8 9
5 6 7 8 9
6 7 8 9
7 8 9
8 9
9
```

Lesson Check 6.4

1. How does EOLN differ from EOF?

2. Using input of

   12, 13, 10, 4, 5, 4, 2, 3, 2, 2, 1, 0

   give the output for the following program segment:

```
DONE := FALSE;
WHILE NOT(DONE) DO
    BEGIN
        REPEAT
            WRITE('ENTER NUMBER: ');
            READLN(NUMBER);
            DONE := (NUMBER = 0)
        UNTIL ODD(NUMBER) OR DONE;
        WRITELN(NUMBER)
    END;
```

3. Write a program segment that will wait for the user to enter an even integer.

4. In Program 6.10, how many times is the REPEAT loop executed?

5. What would be the output of Program 6.10 if COUNT1 were initialized to 5 instead of 1?

Lesson 6.5 Programming Tip—Style

Carefully chosen BOOLEAN variables can lead to a better understanding of the intent of a particular program segment. Compare these two REPEAT loops.

1.
```
CHECK := FALSE;
REPEAT
    WRITELN('ENTER A NUMBER');
    READLN(NUMBER);
    CHECK := (NUMBER = 0)
UNTIL CHECK = TRUE;
```

2.
```
ENDOFDATA := FALSE;
REPEAT
    WRITELN('ENTER A NUMBER');
    READLN(NUMBER);
    ENDOFDATA := (NUMBER = 0)
UNTIL ENDOFDATA;
```

Both loops accomplish the task and are correct. The reason for leaving the first loop, however, is unclear. What is being checked? The exit condition of the first loop does not give a clear picture as to what must happen to cause the loop to end. As routines become more complex, this type of BOOLEAN test becomes more difficult to understand.

The second example uses a descriptive BOOLEAN identifier. The loop will be done until there are no more data entered. Notice that

```
ENDOFDATA = TRUE
```

would have been acceptable as the exit condition.

The more readable a program is, the easier it is to understand. Using expressions like the following can improve the understanding of a program:

```
REPEAT                          REPEAT
    .                               .
    .                               .
    .                               .
UNTIL NOMOREDATA                UNTIL NOT(TODAY)


WHILE NOT(ENDOFDATA) DO         WHILE DAY_IS_FRIDAY DO
```

Summary

Indefinite iteration allows for repetition of a process when the number of iterations is not known in advance. WHILE and RE-PEAT give the programmer tools for creating loop structures in many different situations.

BOOLEAN expressions are used to determine if a loop is to continue or terminate. Relational operators (such as =, <>, <, and >) are used to determine whether expressions are TRUE or FALSE. The BOOLEAN operators NOT, AND, and OR can be used for more complex expressions. Parentheses are necessary in complex BOOLEAN expressions to establish the order of evaluation.

The REPEAT structure is used to execute a single or compound statement until some condition becomes TRUE. A REPEAT loop is tested using an exit condition and the statement of the loop is done at least once. The exit condition should contain a variable whose value is changed in the loop. A BEGIN . . . END block is not needed for a compound statement within a REPEAT loop, since REPEAT begins the loop and UNTIL ends the loop.

The WHILE structure gives an alternative method for looping. A WHILE loop is tested upon entry, meaning that the statement in a WHILE loop may not be executed at all. A BEGIN . . . END block is necessary for a compound statement within the WHILE loop.

EOLN and EOF are built-in BOOLEAN functions that test for the end of a series of input. The BOOLEAN function ODD is used to determine if a numeric value is odd.

WHILE and/or REPEAT loops may be nested to produce varied results. The inner loop is completed before control returns to the outer loop.

Key Terms   AND   EOLN   ODD

BOOLEAN   exit condition   OR
  expression   indefinite iteration   REPEAT
conditional   infinite loop   WHILE
  statement   NOT

EOF

Answers to   ## Lesson 6.1
Lesson Checks
1. Indefinite iteration means repeating a process an unknown number of times.

2. BOOLEAN variables have two possible values: FALSE or TRUE.

3. **a.** FALSE
   b. TRUE
   c. TRUE
   d. TRUE
   e. FALSE

Lesson 6.2

1. An infinite loop is one that theoretically never stops.

2. **a.** False.
   b. True.
   c. True.

Lesson 6.3

1. The main consideration when choosing between WHILE and REPEAT is whether the exit condition should be tested before or after the statement of the loop.

2. If the condition of a WHILE loop is FALSE upon entry, the statement within the loop is not executed.

Lesson 6.4

1. EOLN determines whether the end of a line of input has been reached. EOF tests for the end of an entire file or group of input, which could consist of many EOLN characters.

2. 13   5   3   1   0

3. ```
REPEAT
    READLN(NUMBER)
UNTIL NOT ODD(NUMBER);
```

4. The REPEAT loop is executed 45 times.

5. ```
5 6 7 8 9
  6 7 8 9
  7 8 9
  8 9
  9
```

Exercises **Set I. Comprehension**

1. Decide which of the following apply to a REPEAT structure, a WHILE structure, to both, or neither:
   a. The loop never requires a BEGIN and an END.
   b. The statement within the loop is always executed at least once.
   c. The loop must include a counter variable.

2. Decide which of the following apply to a REPEAT structure, a WHILE structure, to both, or neither:
   a. The BOOLEAN expression is evaluated upon entry.
   b. The loop can be infinite.
   c. The BOOLEAN expression is evaluated after the statement.

3. Which of the listed REPEAT loops is (are) equivalent to the following FOR statement:

```
FOR COUNT := 1 TO 50 DO
```

   a. ```
COUNT := 1;
REPEAT
      .
      .
      .
      COUNT := COUNT + 1
UNTIL COUNT = 50;
```

   b. ```
COUNT := 1;
REPEAT
      .
      .
      .
      COUNT := COUNT + 1
UNTIL COUNT > 50;
```

   c. ```
COUNT := 1;
REPEAT
      .
      .
      .
      COUNT := COUNT + 1
UNTIL COUNT >= 50;
```

4. Which of the listed WHILE loops is (are) equivalent to the following FOR statement:

```
FOR COUNT := 100 DOWNTO 1 DO
```

   a. ```
COUNT := 100;
WHILE COUNT > 1 DO
   BEGIN
      .
      .
      .
      COUNT := COUNT - 1
   END;
```

```
b. COUNT := 100;
   WHILE COUNT >= 1 DO
       BEGIN
           .
           .
           .
           COUNT := COUNT - 1
       END;

c. COUNT := 100;
   WHILE COUNT >= 0 DO
       BEGIN
           .
           .
           .
           COUNT := COUNT - 1
       END;
```

5. Write each English statement or phrase as a BOOLEAN expression.
   a. *Jump* is not equal to *High*.
   b. *Bankrupt* is less than *Balance* and zero.
   c. The opposite of *Done*.

6. Write each English statement as a BOOLEAN expression.
   a. *Score* is larger than *Quiz 1* and *Quiz 2*.
   b. *Number* is greater than zero.
   c. *Jane* is younger than *Don* or older than *Michelle*.

7. Assume that A is TRUE and B is FALSE. What is the value of each of the following expressions?
   a. `A AND B`
   b. `A OR B`
   c. `NOT B`

8. Assume that both A and B are FALSE. What is the value of each of the following expressions?
   a. `A AND B`
   b. `A OR B`
   c. `NOT B`

9. Evaluate each of the following expressions for all possible values of the BOOLEAN variables P and Q:
   a. `P OR NOT(Q)`
   b. `P AND NOT(Q)`
   c. `NOT(P AND NOT(P))`
   d. `P OR NOT(P)`

10. Given the following values for BOOLEAN variables A, B, C, and D

    A = TRUE   B = FALSE   C = FALSE   D = TRUE

    evaluate each of the following BOOLEAN expressions:
    a. `(A AND B) OR (A AND D)`
    b. `NOT C AND D AND A`
    c. `NOT(A AND D) OR (C OR D)`
    d. `(A OR B) AND NOT(C OR D)`

11. Using these assignments

```
HEIGHT := 6;  NAME := 'JUDY';  REALVALUE := 5.67;
```

evaluate each of the following expressions:
a. `REALVALUE <= 5E+00`
b. `HEIGHT <> REALVALUE / 4 + 4`
c. `NAME <> 'PAUL'`

12. Using these assignments

```
A := 10;  B := 2;  C := 5;  ANSWER := 'DONE';
```

evaluate each of the following expressions:
a. `(A > 5) AND (B = 2)`
b. `(ANSWER = 'FINAL') OR (C < 4)`
c. `(A < 10) OR ((B < 5) AND (C = 5))`

13. The following program segment was designed to find the sum of the odd numbers and the sum of the even numbers from 1 to 10. It contains a logic error. Which two lines need to be switched to correct the error?

```
 1   COUNT := 0;
 2   ODDSUM := 0;
 3   EVENSUM := 0;
 4   WHILE COUNT <= 10 DO
 5      BEGIN
 6         COUNT := COUNT + 1;
 7         ODDSUM := ODDSUM + COUNT;
 8         EVENSUM := EVENSUM + COUNT;
 9         COUNT := COUNT + 1
10      END;
11   WRITELN('EVEN SUM = ',EVENSUM);
12   WRITELN('ODD SUM = ',ODDSUM);
```

14. Determine which of the program segments given in **a–d** is (are) functionally equivalent to the following:

```
S := 0;
N := 0;
WHILE N < 100 DO
   BEGIN
      N := N + 1;
      S := S + N
   END;
WRITELN('SUM = ',S);
```

a.
```
   S := 0;
   FOR N := 1 TO 100 DO
      S := S + N;
   WRITELN('SUM = ',S);
```
b.
```
   S := 0;
   N := 0;
   REPEAT
      S := S + N;
      N := N + 1
   UNTIL N = 100;
   WRITELN('SUM = ',S);
```

```
c. S := 0;
   N := 1;
   REPEAT
       S := S + N;
       N := N + 1
   UNTIL N = 101;
   WRITELN('SUM = ',S);
d. S := 0;
   N := 1;
   WHILE N < 101 DO
       BEGIN
           N := N + 1;
           S := S + N
       END;
   WRITELN('SUM = ',S);
```

Set II. Application

15. Suppose the BOOLEAN operators included an XOR, or Exclusive-OR. A XOR B would be considered TRUE if A were TRUE or B were TRUE, but FALSE if both or neither were TRUE. That is,

A	B	A XOR B
TRUE	TRUE	FALSE
TRUE	FALSE	TRUE
FALSE	TRUE	TRUE
FALSE	FALSE	FALSE

Write a BOOLEAN expression to simulate A XOR B using the available Pascal BOOLEAN operators. Assume A and B are BOOLEAN variables.

16. What is the difference between counting and accumulating? Write a program segment to count the number of positive integer values entered by the user. Write another program segment to accumulate 10 values entered by the user.

17. Write an input segment using the REPEAT structure that will require the user to enter a number between 1 and 10 before continuing on in the program.

18. Write a program segment that will allow the user to enter a set of numbers to be added. The loop should continue accepting numbers until a sum of 100 is reached or a negative number is entered. The negative number should not be included in the sum.

19. Write a REPEAT loop that is equivalent to the following FOR statement:

```
FOR COUNT := 1 TO 25 DO
    BEGIN
        WRITE(COUNT,' IS ');
        WRITELN(CHR(COUNT))
    END;
```

20. Write a WHILE loop that is equivalent to the following FOR statement:

```
FOR ALPHA := 'Z' DOWNTO 'A' DO
   WRITELN(ALPHA, ORD(ALPHA));
```

21. Write a program that uses a WHILE loop to compute the sum of the odd numbers from a given starting odd value to an end value.

22. Repeat Exercise 21, except compute the sum of the even numbers from a given starting even value to an end value. Use a REPEAT loop.

Set III. Synthesis

23. In a certain ancient kingdom, the game of chess was invented by a mathematician. The king insisted a reward was in order and so the mathematician made the following request: He asked to be given one grain of wheat for the first square on the chessboard, two grains for the second square, four grains for the third, eight for the fourth, and so on, doubling the amount for each square. The king wondered if he had enough grains of wheat to fulfill the mathematician's request.

    Write a program to determine the number of squares that can be filled with a given amount of wheat (input by the user). There are 64 squares on a chessboard.

24. Write a program that will count the number of letters in a word entered by the user. Use a CHAR variable for input and EOLN to see when the word has been completely entered.

25. Write a program that will find the average number of letters in a list of names. Allow the user to enter the names, pressing <RETURN> after each name. Instruct the user to press <CTRL-C> when all the names have been entered.
    Hint: Use CHAR variable for input, and the BOOLEAN functions EOLN and EOF.

26. Given that the population of Marysville is 7,500 and the population grows at a rate of 2 percent each year, write a program to find the number of years it takes to exceed a population of 10,000.

27. Carla opened a savings account at the beginning of 1987 with $200. Her account earns interest at a rate of 5 percent, compounded quarterly. She deposits an additional $50 at the beginning of each quarter, beginning with the second quarter of 1987. Write a program to find how many years it will take for her balance to exceed $5,000.

28. Rewrite the program from Chapter 5, Exercise 33 (rocket height) using a WHILE or a REPEAT loop. Print the rocket's height in feet for each second of its flight until a height of MAX feet or more is reached. Let the value for MAX be entered by the user. The formula for rocket height at time T is

$$height = 4T^2 + 3T + 2$$

29. Write a program to find the greatest common divisor (GCD) for two integers using the Euclidean algorithm:

    a. Enter two integers, X and Y.
      If negative, convert to positive.
    b. Find R (the remainder) when X is divided by Y.
    c. If R = 0 then GCD = Y
      else X := Y
        Y := R
        go back to step **b.**

30. Write a program to keep track of a day's calorie intake. The program should allow the user to enter his or her maximum daily calorie intake. As the user enters the caloric content of foods consumed, the program should print the cumulative calorie intake and the amount of calories the user has left for the day. The program should continue until the user enters 0, or the maximum daily calorie intake has been met or exceeded.

31. A dartboard contains concentric circles with the following point values (starting with the outer circle and moving inward): 10, 25, 50, 75, and 100. A player is given three darts at a time and the object is to hit the bull's-eye (the center circle). Write a program that will allow the user to enter dart scores until the user gets a bull's-eye (100 points). After every three consecutive dart scores are entered, the program should print the total score for that round. When the user enters 100 to signal a bull's-eye has been hit, the program should print the total number of darts thrown and the average of all dart scores.

32. Write a program to find the arithmetic mean (average) and standard deviation of a sample of ungrouped data. Use the following formula to calculate the standard deviation:

$$s^2 = \frac{1}{n-1}\left[\Sigma x_i^2 - \frac{1}{n}(\Sigma x_i)^2\right]$$

where

  n = number of values entered.

  Σx_i^2 = sum of the square of each value.

  Σx_i = sum of the values.

(s^2 is known as the variance; s is the standard deviation.)

  The user should enter n, followed by the values. The following values may be used:

    12, 24, 13, 27, 32, 31, 20, 11, 9, 26, 28, 27,
    32, 32, 34, 30, 8, 19, 18, 29, 24, 38, 41, 25

where

    $n = 24$.

7 Selection

> "Cheshire-Puss," she began. . . . "Would you tell me, please, which way I ought to go from here?"
>
> "That depends a good deal on where you want to get to," said the Cat.
>
> "I don't much care where—" said Alice.
>
> "Then it doesn't matter which way you go," said the Cat.
>
> —Lewis Carroll

Overview

Gaining a Perspective

Examine the following three numbers:

5   13   14

Could these numbers represent the lengths of the sides of a triangle? What statements could be used in a program to determine whether a triangle can be formed; and, if a triangle can be formed, to determine whether it will be equilateral, isosceles, or scalene?

A Pascal statement that allows decision-making is needed to program this problem. In order for three given numbers to be lengths of the sides of a triangle, the sum of any two of the side lengths must be greater than the third length. In a program, the sum of the lengths of any two sides must be compared to the length of the third side. This problem will be programmed later in this chapter (see Program 7.11).

The need to perform an action based on a condition is a common aspect of most programming languages. That is, if some condition is met, then something will happen, otherwise something else will happen. This process is called **selection** and is accomplished in Pascal with the IF . . . THEN . . . ELSE or the CASE structure. These structures add decision-making power to a program.

Lesson 7.1   IF . . . THEN . . . ELSE Structure

The Pascal structure, **IF . . . THEN . . . ELSE,** allows choice and decision-making ability in programming. The structure consists of a condition followed by two statements. If a given condition is TRUE, then the first statement is completed; otherwise, the condition is FALSE and the other statement is completed.

The following statement prints a message depending on whether the given condition

```
CHECKBALANCE  >= 0.0
```

is TRUE or FALSE. For this example, assume CHECKBALANCE is a REAL variable.

```
IF CHECKBALANCE >= 0.0
   THEN WRITELN('ACCOUNT OK')
   ELSE WRITELN('ACCOUNT OVERDRAWN');
```

If CHECKBALANCE is 500.0, then the condition is TRUE and the output is

```
ACCOUNT OK
```

On the other hand, if CHECKBALANCE is −27.50, then the condition is FALSE and the output is

```
ACCOUNT OVERDRAWN
```

The IF . . . THEN . . . ELSE statement contains three distinct parts. In general, the IF . . . THEN . . . ELSE statement looks like

---

IF . . . THEN . . . ELSE Form

```
IF  BOOLEAN expression
    THEN  statement
    ELSE  other  statement;
```

The BOOLEAN expression yields a BOOLEAN value of TRUE or FALSE. The statements are either single or compound statements, which have been discussed earlier. IF . . . THEN . . . ELSE is often called two-way selection, for reasons illustrated in Figure 7.1.

Figure 7.1
Two-Way Selection

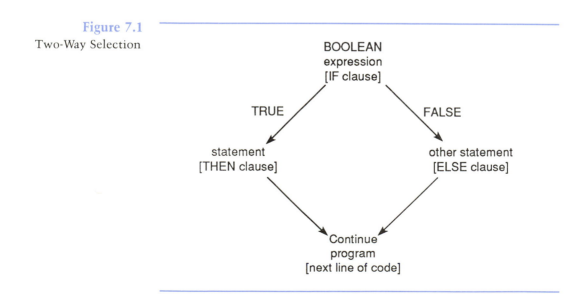

For two-way selection, once the BOOLEAN expression is evaluated, one of two paths is taken. If the BOOLEAN expression is TRUE, execute the statement following THEN (the **THEN clause**); otherwise (if it is FALSE), execute the other statement (the **ELSE clause**). After either clause has been executed, the program continues with the next line of code following the ELSE clause.

If there is no alternative or other statement, the selection statement simplifies to **IF . . . THEN,** as follows:

IF . . . THEN Form

```
IF  BOOLEAN  expression
    THEN  statement;
```

This structure is actually a special case of the IF . . . THEN . . . ELSE statement; in this case, the ELSE clause does not exist. Again, the BOOLEAN expression is any expression that evaluates to a BOOLEAN value (TRUE or FALSE) and the statement is either a single or compound statement. The structure uses what is called one-way selection, which is shown in Figure 7.2. For one-way selection, if the BOOLEAN expression is TRUE, the statement is executed and the program continues. If the BOOLEAN expression is FALSE, the program skips the THEN clause and continues with the next statement.

Program 7.1 is an example of one-way selection. This program computes the balance of a checking account and prints a message if the account is overdrawn.

Figure 7.2
One-Way Selection

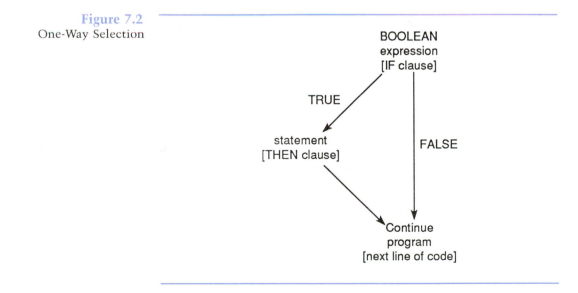

Program 7.1
```
PROGRAM CHECKING (INPUT,OUTPUT);

      { PURPOSE: TO DEMONSTRATE IF...THEN }

VAR
   FINISHED     : BOOLEAN;
   TRANSACTION,
   BALANCE      : REAL;

BEGIN    { MAIN PROGRAM }

   WRITE('ENTER THE BEGINNING BALANCE: ');
   READLN(BALANCE);
   WRITE('ENTER FIRST TRANSACTION: ');
   READLN(TRANSACTION);
   FINISHED := (TRANSACTION = 0.0);
   WHILE NOT(FINISHED) DO
      BEGIN
         BALANCE := BALANCE + TRANSACTION;
         IF BALANCE < 0.0 THEN WRITELN('OVERDRAWN');
         WRITE('ENTER NEXT TRANSACTION: ');
         READLN(TRANSACTION);
         FINISHED := (TRANSACTION = 0.0)
      END;    { WHILE }
   WRITELN('BALANCE = ',BALANCE:8:2)

END.
```

Sample Output

```
ENTER THE BEGINNING BALANCE: 500.00
ENTER FIRST TRANSACTION: -25.99
ENTER NEXT TRANSACTION: -13.42
ENTER NEXT TRANSACTION: 125.00
ENTER NEXT TRANSACTION: -80.38
ENTER NEXT TRANSACTION: 0.0
BALANCE = 505.21
```

In Program 7.1, the assignment

```
FINISHED := (TRANSACTION = 0.0);
```

means that the BOOLEAN variable FINISHED is TRUE when
TRANSACTION is zero; otherwise, it is FALSE. The WHILE loop
will continue as long as the transaction is not zero.

Two-way selection is an important statement in programming
for logic development. Program 7.2 compares the values of two
integers that have been entered from the keyboard. When the
program is executed, the integers are printed on the screen, the
largest integer first.

Program 7.2
```
PROGRAM ORDER (INPUT,OUTPUT);

      { PURPOSE: TO DEMONSTRATE IF...THEN...ELSE }

VAR
   FIRST,
   SECOND : INTEGER;
```

```
BEGIN      { MAIN PROGRAM }
    WRITELN('ENTER TWO NUMBERS.');
    READLN(FIRST, SECOND);
    IF FIRST > SECOND
        THEN WRITELN('ORDER IS ',FIRST:6,SECOND:6)
        ELSE WRITELN('ORDER IS ',SECOND:6,FIRST:6)
END.
```

Notice that the ELSE clause in Program 7.2 is not preceded by a semicolon. The ELSE is a part of the IF . . . THEN . . . ELSE statement.

Caution: If a semicolon had been placed after the statement associated with the THEN clause, the IF . . . THEN statement would have ended and left an ELSE "hanging," as if the ELSE were a statement by itself. This would cause an error when compiling. For example, the following statement would result in a compiler error:

```
IF FIRST > SECOND
    THEN WRITELN('ORDER IS ',FIRST:6,SECOND:6);
    ELSE WRITELN('ORDER IS ',SECOND:6,FIRST:6);
```

Placing a semicolon after the THEN, as in the following example, is also incorrect:

```
IF FIRST > SECOND THEN;
    WRITELN('ORDER IS ',FIRST:6,SECOND:6)
    ELSE WRITELN('ORDER IS ',SECOND:6,FIRST:6);
```

In this example, the IF . . . THEN becomes a condition with an empty THEN clause. The semicolon following the THEN marks the end of the statement; thus, the THEN clause and the ELSE clause do not match up. This statement would result in a compiler error indicating that there is no semicolon after the WRITELN statement. In addition, if the ELSE clause of this statement were deleted, the program would compile, but the THEN clause would still be empty, and the WRITELN following the IF . . . THEN would always be executed regardless of the condition.

A good use of the IF . . . THEN . . . ELSE structure is to check errors in input, as demonstrated in Program 7.3. This program calculates the quotient and the remainder when dividing two numbers. If the user selects a divisor of zero, an error message is printed.

Program 7.3

```
PROGRAM DIVISION (INPUT,OUTPUT);

    { PURPOSE: FIND QUOTIENT AND REMAINDER }

VAR
    DIVISOR,
    DIVIDEND,
    QUOTIENT,
    REMAINDER : INTEGER;
```

```
BEGIN    { MAIN PROGRAM }

    WRITELN('THIS PROGRAM WILL DIVIDE TWO INTEGERS.');
    WRITE('FIRST ENTER THE DIVIDEND ');
    WRITELN('AND THEN THE DIVISOR.');
    WRITELN('SEPARATE THE NUMBERS WITH A SPACE.');
    WRITE('WHEN FINISHED ENTER 999 ');
    WRITELN('FOR THE DIVIDEND.');
    WRITELN;
    WRITE('ENTER TWO NUMBERS: ');
    READLN(DIVIDEND,DIVISOR);
    WHILE DIVIDEND <> 999 DO

        BEGIN
            IF DIVISOR = 0
                THEN
                    BEGIN
                        WRITELN;
                        WRITELN('CANNOT DIVIDE BY ZERO!')
                    END     { THEN }
                ELSE
                    BEGIN
                        QUOTIENT := DIVIDEND DIV DIVISOR;
                        REMAINDER := DIVIDEND MOD DIVISOR;
                        WRITELN;
                        WRITELN(' QUOTIENT OF ',DIVIDEND);
                        WRITELN('  DIVIDED BY ',DIVISOR);
                        WRITELN('         IS ',QUOTIENT);
                        WRITELN('     AND THE');
                        WRITELN('REMAINDER IS ',REMAINDER);
                        WRITELN
                    END;     { ELSE }
            WRITELN;
            WRITE('ENTER TWO NUMBERS: ');
            READLN(DIVIDEND,DIVISOR)
        END     { WHILE }

END.
```

Sample Output

```
THIS PROGRAM WILL DIVIDE TWO INTEGERS.
FIRST ENTER THE DIVIDEND AND THEN THE DIVISOR.
SEPARATE THE NUMBERS WITH A SPACE.
WHEN FINISHED ENTER 999 FOR THE DIVIDEND.

ENTER TWO NUMBERS: 7 2

  QUOTIENT OF 7
  DIVIDED BY 2
          IS 3
      AND THE
REMAINDER IS 1

ENTER TWO NUMBERS: 5 0

CANNOT DIVIDE BY ZERO!

ENTER TWO NUMBERS: 999 1
```

A way of further increasing the decision-making ability of a program is to nest IF . . . THEN . . . ELSE statements; that is, to place one inside the other, as shown in Figure 7.3. Lining up the THEN and the ELSE clauses makes the nested IF . . . THEN . . . ELSE structure less confusing. When executing a program with nested IF . . . THEN . . . ELSE statements, each ELSE is matched with the closest unused THEN. Remember, ELSE is never preceded by a semicolon. If the structure gets very complex, comments should be used to clarify the THEN . . . ELSE matches.

Nesting IF . . . THEN . . . ELSE statements gives the programmer more control, as demonstrated in Program 7.4, which prints certain messages with regard to a height entered by the user.

Program 7.4

```
PROGRAM HEIGHTCLASS (INPUT,OUTPUT);

     { PURPOSE: TO DEMONSTRATE NESTED
                IF...THEN...ELSE }

VAR
    HEIGHT : REAL;

BEGIN      { MAIN PROGRAM }

    WRITE('ENTER YOUR HEIGHT IN INCHES: ');
    READLN(HEIGHT);
    IF HEIGHT > 60.0
       THEN IF HEIGHT >= 72.0
               THEN IF HEIGHT >= 84.0
                       THEN WRITELN('7 FEET OR OVER')
                       ELSE WRITELN('6 - 7 FEET')
                    ELSE WRITELN('5 - 6 FEET')
            ELSE WRITELN('5 FEET OR UNDER')

END.
```

Sample Output

```
ENTER YOUR HEIGHT IN INCHES: 74.0
6 - 7 FEET
```

Figure 7.3

Nested IF . . . THEN . . . ELSE Statements

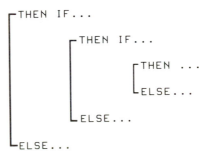

Looking at what occurs when each condition of a nested IF . . . THEN . . . ELSE structure is FALSE provides a quick understanding of the structure. In Program 7.4, if the height is less than or equal to 60.0, the first condition is FALSE, and the last ELSE is completed. If the height is between 60.0 and 72.0, the second condition is FALSE, so the second from the last ELSE is completed. If the height is between 72.0 and 84.0, the third condition is FALSE and the third from the last ELSE is completed. If the height is greater than or equal to 84.0, the third condition is TRUE.

The format of IF . . . THEN . . . ELSE statements can greatly enhance their readability. Some nested IF . . . THEN . . . ELSE statements cause a syntactic ambiguity. For example,

```
IF X > 0 THEN IF X > 100 THEN
    WRITELN('X IS LARGER THAN 100')
    ELSE WRITELN('X IS BETWEEN 0 AND 100');
```

The indentation of this program segment is confusing. To which IF . . . THEN does the ELSE belong? This question was answered earlier. The ELSE is matched up with the closest unmatched THEN. The program segment may be rewritten as follows:

```
IF X > 0
    THEN IF X > 100
            THEN WRITELN('X IS LARGER THAN 100')
            ELSE WRITELN('X IS BETWEEN 0 AND 100');
```

Without the indentation, this statement would be syntactically correct; however, the meaning would not be as clear. Clarity should be as important a consideration as technical correctness.

Program 7.5 provides another example of nested IF . . . THEN . . . ELSE statements. The program allows three integers to be entered and then prints the integers in decreasing order.

Program 7.5
```
PROGRAM MOREORDER (INPUT,OUTPUT);

    { PURPOSE: FIND DECREASING ORDER }

VAR
    INT1,
    INT2,
    INT3   : INTEGER;

BEGIN     { MAIN PROGRAM }

    WRITE('ENTER THREE INTEGERS,');
    WRITELN('EACH SEPARATED BY A SPACE.');
    READLN(INT1, INT2, INT3);
    WRITE('DECREASING ORDER IS ');
```

```
IF INT1 > INT2
   THEN IF INT2 > INT3
           THEN WRITELN(INT1,INT2,INT3)
           ELSE IF INT1 > INT3
                   THEN WRITELN(INT1,INT3,INT2)
                   ELSE WRITELN(INT3,INT1,INT2)
   ELSE IF INT1 > INT3
           THEN WRITELN(INT2,INT1,INT3)
           ELSE IF INT2 > INT3
                   THEN WRITELN(INT2,INT3,INT1)
                   ELSE WRITELN(INT3,INT2,INT1)

END.
```

Sample Output

```
ENTER THREE INTEGERS, EACH SEPARATED BY A SPACE.
6 9 7
DECREASING ORDER IS 976
```

In both Program 7.4 and 7.5 there was an equally likely chance that any of the conditions would be TRUE. (Lesson 7.2 will introduce a new programming statement called CASE, which is useful for nested conditions that are equally likely to occur.) If one condition is more likely to occur than any of the others, then the most efficient way to write the IF portion of the program is to start with the most likely condition.

For example, suppose a programmer knew that the user would enter integers ranging between 0 and 100, and that the probabilities of each number would be as follows:

Number Range	Probability
0–25	10 percent
26–75	40 percent
76–100	50 percent

The most efficient order for the nested IF . . . THEN . . . ELSE statements would be the most likely condition first, followed by the second most likely, followed by the third most likely.

```
IF X >= 76
   THEN WRITELN('LARGEST NUMBER GROUP')
   ELSE IF X >= 26
           THEN WRITELN('NEXT LARGEST NUMBER GROUP')
           ELSE WRITELN('SMALLEST NUMBER GROUP')
```

This is the most efficient order for these conditions. When the first condition is TRUE, the other statements are not executed.

Lesson
Check
7.1

1. Identify each statement as true or false.
   a. In one-way selection, there is no ELSE clause.
   b. Nesting IF . . . THEN . . . ELSE statements produces a loop structure.
   c. Error checking is a good use of the IF . . . THEN . . . ELSE structure.
   d. Each ELSE in a nested IF . . . THEN . . . ELSE structure is matched up with the closest unmatched THEN.

Lesson 7.2   Multiple Choice—The CASE Structure

If there are more than two alternatives in a selection statement, the CASE structure may be desirable. The **CASE** structure allows for many alternatives; think of it as a multiple choice structure. Program 7.6 uses an old nursery rhyme to demonstrate this aspect of the CASE statement.

Program 7.6

```
PROGRAM LITTLEPIGS (INPUT,OUTPUT);

     { PURPOSE: TO DEMONSTRATE THE CASE STATEMENT }

VAR
   TOE : INTEGER;

BEGIN     { MAIN PROGRAM }

   WRITELN('ENTER CHOICE OF TOE, 1-5:');
   READLN(TOE);
   CASE TOE OF
       1 : WRITELN('THIS LITTLE PIG WENT TO MARKET;');
       2 : WRITELN('THIS LITTLE PIG STAYED HOME;');
       3 : WRITELN('THIS LITTLE PIG HAD ROAST BEEF;');
       4 : WRITELN('THIS LITTLE PIG HAD NONE;');
       5 : BEGIN
             WRITE('AND THIS LITTLE PIG CRIED, ');
             WRITELN('WEE, WEE, WEE!');
             WRITELN('ALL THE WAY HOME.')
           END
   END     { CASE }

END.
```

The output of Program 7.6 depends on the value entered for the variable TOE.

Input	Output
1	THIS LITTLE PIG WENT TO MARKET;
2	THIS LITTLE PIG STAYED HOME;
3	THIS LITTLE PIG HAD ROAST BEEF;
4	THIS LITTLE PIG HAD NONE;
5	AND THIS LITTLE PIG CRIED, WEE, WEE, WEE!
	ALL THE WAY HOME.

In general, the CASE structure is as follows:

CASE Form

```
CASE expression OF
      constant1     : statement;
      constant2,
      constant3     : statement;
      constant4,
      constant5     : statement;
      constant6     : statement;
        .
        .
        .
      constantN     : statement
END;       { CASE }
```

The expression is an ordinal type; that is, it has a value of the type INTEGER, CHAR, or BOOLEAN (excluding REAL and STRING, but including types to be introduced in Chapter 11). The **CASE constants** (1 to N) are the possible values for the expression, and the statements are any of the possible statements discussed earlier—single statements, including the empty statement (which is written as ";"), and compound statements. The constants may be one value or a list of values separated by commas.

The CASE statement selects the constant that is equal to the given expression and then executes the statement corresponding to that constant. After that statement has been executed, the program continues with the next line following the END of the CASE statement. The list of constants should include all of the values of the expression. If the value of the expression is not among the list of constants, then the program skips the CASE statement and continues with the rest of the program. (For some Pascal compilers, all of the possible values must be in the list of constants.) Figure 7.4 illustrates the CASE structure.

Figure 7.4
CASE Structure

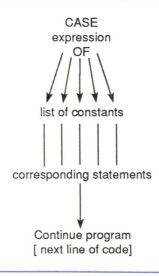

The following example shows two ways of listing INTEGER constants in a CASE statement:

```
CASE VALUE OF

    1     :  WRITELN('GRAND TROPHY');
    2     :  WRITELN('HONORS CERTIFICATE');
    3, 4  :  WRITELN('SPECIAL CERTIFICATE')

END;     { CASE }
```

In this example, VALUE is an INTEGER variable. Constants can be single values or values specified in any order separated by a comma. Notice that no semicolon is needed before the END of the CASE structure and that there is no BEGIN to the CASE structure. CASE marks the beginning of the structure and is matched with an END. This can make matching the BEGINs and ENDs in a program confusing. Putting a comment after the END of a CASE statement helps ease this confusion.

Program 7.7 uses the CASE statement to solve the same problem presented in Program 7.4. (Another height category has been added to this version.) The expression in the CASE statement

```
TRUNC(HEIGHT/12)*12
```

has been carefully formulated so that for each interval, the correct statement is executed.

Program 7.7

```
PROGRAM HEIGHTAGAIN (INPUT,OUTPUT);

        { PURPOSE: TO CLASSIFY HEIGHTS }

VAR
    HEIGHT : REAL;

BEGIN     { MAIN PROGRAM }

    WRITE('ENTER YOUR HEIGHT IN INCHES: ');
    READLN(HEIGHT);
    IF HEIGHT <= 60.0
        THEN WRITELN('5 FEET OR UNDER')
        ELSE IF HEIGHT >= 96.0
            THEN WRITELN('8 FEET OR OVER')
            ELSE
                BEGIN

                    CASE (TRUNC(HEIGHT/12) * 12) OF

                        60 : WRITELN('5 TO 6 FEET');
                        72 : WRITELN('6 TO 7 FEET');
                        84 : WRITELN('7 TO 8 FEET')

                    END     { CASE }

                END     { ELSE }

END.
```

Notice that all of the possible values of the CASE expression are listed as constants in the CASE statement. The IF statements handle input that is outside the range of values of the CASE statement.

Program Segment 7.8 shows the use of a CASE statement with BOOLEAN constants. Since BOOLEAN values are ordered (FALSE, TRUE) they may be used as constants in a CASE statement. (The corresponding statements of the CASE constants are procedure calls.) Assume SCORE is of type INTEGER.

Program Segment 7.8

```
WRITE('ENTER EXAM SCORE: ');
READLN(SCORE);
CASE SCORE >= 70 OF
    TRUE  : PASS;      { CALL TO PROCEDURE PASS }
    FALSE : FAIL       { CALL TO PROCEDURE FAIL }
END;    { CASE }
```

This program segment could have been written using an IF . . . THEN . . . ELSE statement, as follows:

```
IF SCORE >= 70
    THEN PASS      { CALL TO PROCEDURE PASS }
    ELSE FAIL;     { CALL TO PROCEDURE FAIL }
```

Program 7.9 uses CHAR as the constant type. This program prints the pronunciation for the letters of the alphabet.

Program 7.9

```
PROGRAM ALPHABET (INPUT,OUTPUT);

    { PURPOSE: LETTER PRONUNCIATION }

VAR
    LETTER : CHAR;

BEGIN      { MAIN PROGRAM }

    WRITE('ENTER A LETTER OF THE ALPHABET: ');
    READLN(LETTER);
    CASE LETTER OF

        'J','K'          : BEGIN
                              WRITE(LETTER);
                              WRITELN('A')
                           END;
        'B','D','P',
        'T','V','Z'      : BEGIN
                              WRITE(LETTER);
                              WRITELN('E')
                           END;
        'F','L','M',
        'N','S'          : BEGIN
                              WRITE('E');
                              WRITELN(LETTER)
                           END;
```

```
            'A','E',
            'I','O'          : WRITELN(LETTER);
            'C'              : WRITELN('SE');
            'G'              : WRITELN('JE');
            'H'              : WRITELN('ACH');
            'Q'              : WRITELN('KYOO');
            'R'              : WRITELN('AR');
            'U'              : WRITELN('YOO');
            'W'              : WRITELN('DUB''L YOO');
            'X'              : WRITELN('EKS');
            'Y'              : WRITELN('WI')

        END      { CASE }

    END.
```

Sample Output

```
ENTER A LETTER OF THE ALPHABET: M
EM
```

Notice that the user may enter data that is not included among the CASE constants. In Lesson 7.3, a new relational operator, IN, will be introduced to perform additional error checking.

Caution: Remember that the constants in a CASE statement must be ordinal types—INTEGER, CHAR, or BOOLEAN, or a programmer-defined type (introduced in Chapter 11). For example, the following program segments are incorrect:

```
CASE NUMBER OF

    1 <= NUMBER < 2 : WRITELN('1-2');
    2 <= NUMBER < 3 : WRITELN('2-3')   ( Cannot be interval )

END;

CASE WORD OF

    'TOM'   : WRITELN('HELLO');
    'SALLY' : WRITELN('GOOD-BYE')       ( Cannot be STRING )

END;

CASE VALUE OF

    3.14 : WRITELN('PI');
    2.71 : WRITELN('E')            ( Cannot be REAL )

END;

CASE VALUE OF

    1..5  : LOW;
    6..10 : HIGH       ( Cannot be specified as a range of values )

END;
```

Lesson
Check
7.2

1. What are the possible types of values of the constant list of a CASE statement?

2. What are the possible types of values of the expression of a CASE statement?

3. Describe the two ways that constants may be specified in the constant list of a CASE statement.

4. What happens in UCSD Pascal if the constant list does not contain the value of the expression of the CASE statement?

Lesson 7.3   BOOLEAN and Relational Operators

BOOLEAN operators, introduced in Chapter 6, allow greater control in programming. The operators NOT, AND, and OR will be used in this lesson to combine BOOLEAN expressions in the selection statements. Also, a new relational operator, IN, will be introduced. (IN is part of the study of Pascal sets, which will be covered in Chapter 12.)

The BOOLEAN expression of an IF . . . THEN . . . ELSE statement may also contain BOOLEAN operators. For example,

```
IF (AGE > 15) AND (GRADE >= 70)
   THEN WRITELN('YOU ARE NOW A LICENSED DRIVER.');

IF (AGE < 16) OR NOT(GRADE >= 70)
   THEN WRITELN('SORRY, TRY AGAIN LATER.');

IF NOT(AGE > 16)
   THEN WRITELN('UNDERAGE')
   ELSE WRITELN('YOU ARE ELIGIBLE.');
```

The parentheses enclosing each of the relations are necessary, since NOT, AND, and OR come before the relational operators in order of precedence. Without the parentheses, the first example would result in a compiler error.

```
IF AGE > 15 AND GRADE >= 70
   THEN WRITELN('YOU ARE NOW A LICENSED DRIVER.');
```

In this example, the BOOLEAN operator AND would be performed first. The INTEGER values 15 and GRADE would be compared using the BOOLEAN operator AND, which is not possible since AND requires BOOLEAN operands.

IN

The relational operator **IN** tells whether or not a value is an element of a given set of values. If the value is in the set, then the BOOLEAN expression is TRUE, otherwise it is FALSE. This BOOLEAN expression is written as follows:

> **IN Form**
>
> *value* IN [*list of values*]

The value and the list of values are of the same ordinal type (INTEGER, CHAR, BOOLEAN or programmer-defined type). In Pascal, square brackets, [ ], are used to enclose a set of values. (Brackets also indicate the maximum number of digits or characters in a long INTEGER or STRING declaration, and—as we will see in Chapter 13—are used for specifying the size of an array.) The list of values may be written in any order. For example,

Expression	Result
12 IN [2,4,6,8,10,12,14,16]	TRUE
5 IN [1,2,6,8]	FALSE
'a' IN ['a','b','c']	TRUE
3 IN [3,2,1]	TRUE

A good use of the IN operator is in error checking. If a user is asked to enter a number from 1 to 5, the IN operator checks to make sure the input is within the range, as shown in Program 7.10.

Program 7.10

```
PROGRAM PLACE (INPUT,OUTPUT);

     { PURPOSE: TO DEMONSTRATE IN }

VAR
   NUMBER : INTEGER;

BEGIN    { MAIN PROGRAM }

   WRITE('ENTER FINISHING PLACE, 1 TO 5: ');
   READLN(NUMBER);
   IF (NUMBER IN [1,2,3,4,5])
      THEN

         CASE NUMBER OF

            1   : WRITELN('YOU ARE NUMBER ONE!');
            2   : WRITELN('YOU CAME IN SECOND!');
            3   : WRITELN('YOU CAME IN THIRD!');
            4,5 : WRITELN('SORRY, NO TROPHY!')

         END { CASE }

      ELSE WRITELN('NOT EVEN POSSIBLE!')

END.
```

To test if a value is not in a given set, the BOOLEAN operator NOT can be used, as shown in the following statement:

```
IF NOT(VALUE IN [0,1,2,3,4,5,6,7,8,9])
   THEN WRITELN('NUMBER IS NOT BETWEEN 0 AND 9');
```

A different way of writing this statement would be to use a loop that will wait for a value to be entered within the desired range, such as

```
REPEAT
   WRITE('ENTER AN INTEGER BETWEEN 0-9: ');
   READ(VALUE)
UNTIL VALUE IN [0,1,2,3,4,5,6,7,8,9];
```

Table 7.1 lists the hierarchy for precedence of the arithmetic, BOOLEAN, and relational operators, including IN. In an expression, each of these operations are performed starting from left to right within each category.

The following examples show some common errors made when using the relational operator IN:

```
IF (ITEM NOT IN [0,1,2,3,4,5,6,7,8,9]) THEN ...
```

```
IF NOT ITEM IN [0,1,2,3,4,5,6,7,8,9] THEN ...
```

Due to the order of operations, the first example attempts to combine an INTEGER (ITEM) with the relational operator IN using the BOOLEAN operator NOT. The second example needs parentheses around the BOOLEAN value determined by

```
ITEM IN [0,1,2,3,4,5,6,7,8,9]
```

since the relational operator IN has last priority. The correct version is

```
IF NOT(ITEM IN [0,1,2,3,4,5,6,7,8,9])
   THEN WRITELN('THIS IS CORRECT');
```

If the values in brackets are in the order of their collating sequence, they can be specified by separating the first term and the last term of the sequence by two periods. For example,

Expression	Result
`3 IN [0..9]`	TRUE
`'b' IN ['A'..'Z']`	FALSE
`'b' IN ['a'..'z','A'..'Z']`	TRUE
`15 IN [0..10,100..200]`	FALSE

This provides a way for abbreviating a list of values.

Table 7.1
Order of Operation
Categories

Order	Operation
1.	( )
2.	NOT
3.	* / DIV MOD AND
4.	+ − OR
5.	= <> < <= > >= IN

Recall the problem first presented in this chapter: determine if three lengths entered by the user can be the lengths of the sides of a triangle, and if they can be, determine the type of triangle. Remember that a triangle is scalene if none of the sides are equal in length, isosceles if at least two sides are equal in length, or equilateral if all sides are equal in length.

Program 7.11

```
PROGRAM TRIANGLE (INPUT,OUTPUT);

    { PURPOSE: TO CLASSIFY TRIANGLES }

VAR A,
    B,
    C          : INTEGER;
    FINISHED : BOOLEAN;

BEGIN      { MAIN PROGRAM }
   FINISHED : = FALSE;
   WHILE NOT(FINISHED) DO
      BEGIN
         REPEAT
            WRITELN('ENTER THREE LENGTHS (1 - 50)');
            READLN(A, B, C);
            FINISHED := (A = 0)
         UNTIL (A IN [0..50]) AND (B IN [0..50]) AND
             (C IN [0..50]);
         IF NOT FINISHED
            THEN
               IF (A+B>C) AND (B+C>A) AND (A+C>B)
                  THEN
                     IF (A=B) AND (B=C)
                        THEN WRITELN('EQUILATERAL')
                        ELSE
                           IF (A=B) OR (B=C) OR (A=C)
                              THEN WRITELN('ISOSCELES')
                              ELSE WRITELN('SCALENE')
                  ELSE WRITELN('NOT A TRIANGLE')
      END        { WHILE }
END.
```

Sample Output

```
ENTER THREE LENGTHS (1 - 50)
45 45 45
EQUILATERAL
ENTER THREE LENGTHS (1 - 50)
20 10 40
NOT A TRIANGLE
ENTER THREE LENGTHS (1 - 50)
0 0 0
```

Lesson Check 7.3

1. Identify each statement as true or false. If the statement is false, explain why. (Assume A and B are INTEGER, FINISH is BOOLEAN, and that all variables have been initialized.)
   a. All relational and BOOLEAN operators have equal priority in a BOOLEAN expression.

b. The BOOLEAN expression
```
5 IN [1,2,3,4,5,7]
```
is TRUE.

c. The following is a valid BOOLEAN expression:
```
15 < A < 67
```

d. The following is a valid BOOLEAN expression:
```
A > 9 AND B < -7
```

e. The following is a valid BOOLEAN expression:
```
(B < 7) AND NOT FINISHED
```

Lesson 7.4   Programming Tip— Devising a Plan

Once the information given in a problem is identified and analyzed, the next step is to devise a plan to solve the problem using the data collected. In Lesson 4.3, logic diagrams were discussed as a straightforward method for breaking a problem into smaller, easy-to-handle parts. This is the first step in planning a solution to a problem and is especially important as problems become more complex. The smaller parts help the programmer come up with a solution, since each part should be easier to accomplish than the entire problem as a whole. Solving these mini-problems, however, can still be difficult and can involve false starts and dead ends. Several attempts may be made from varied angles before the light comes on and a plan is finalized. The failures, as well as the partial solutions obtained in these early stages, should all be considered part of the problem-solving process, as they will undoubtedly give hints or insight into the final plan. Some techniques that might assist in coming up with a plan for solving a problem follow:

- Look at the problem from different points of view (in a different light).
- Solve one condition at a time.
- Determine any limits of the possible solution.
- Eliminate possible approaches to the problem.
- Make predictions or estimates based on the data.
- Change the problem into a simpler problem or problems.
- Relate the problem to a previously solved problem.
- Work backwards.
- Leave the problem for a short time (allow it to incubate).

Designing a solution to a problem can involve hard work, inspiration, and luck. A programmer can overlook the obvious and spend hours on the wrong track, or be inspired and visualize the solution nearly instantly. If the solution is coming too slowly, the best approach may be to leave the problem for a short time. The human mind is amazing in that it will continue to work on the problem. This period of incubation should be used as an accepted part of the problem-solving process.

Once an approach to a problem is determined, time should be taken to make sure it is the best approach. Looking at the alternatives and sketching the steps needed to solve the problem can help verify the correctness of the approach. The time spent in these preliminary stages will be more than made up in the latter stages of the problem solution. Less time will be needed for making corrections, and possible backtracking may be avoided entirely. A good plan will lead to a good final product.

Summary

IF... THEN ... ELSE and CASE, the Pascal structures that allow selection or decision-making, were introduced in this chapter.

The IF... THEN ... ELSE structure has two forms: one-way and two-way selection. One-way selection allows for one alternative that will be executed if the condition of the IF clause is TRUE. It does not have an ELSE clause. Two-way selection provides two alternatives: the THEN clause is completed if the BOOLEAN expression of the IF clause is TRUE; otherwise, the ELSE clause is completed. BOOLEAN and relational operators, including IN, may be used as a part of the BOOLEAN expression of the IF clause. The IF... THEN ... ELSE structure is useful for error checking and the structure may be nested to enhance programmer control.

The CASE structure is useful when there are multiple alternatives or possible answers to an expression. The answers to the expression are listed as the constants of the CASE statement. The expression and the constants must be of the same ordinal type.

Key Terms

CASE	IF...THEN	selection
CASE constant	IF...THEN...ELSE	THEN clause
ELSE clause	IN	

Answers to Lesson Checks

Lesson 7.1

1. **a.** True.
   b. False.
   c. True.
   d. True.

Lesson 7.2

1. INTEGER, CHAR, and BOOLEAN (and programmer-defined) values may be in the constant list of a CASE statement.

2. INTEGER, CHAR, and BOOLEAN (and programmer-defined) values may be in the expression in a CASE statement.

3. Constants may be specified singly or grouped (separated by commas).

4. If the constant is not in the list, the CASE statement is skipped.

Lesson 7.3

1. **a.** False. See the order of operations presented in Table 7.1.
   b. True.
   c. False. The expression should be divided using AND, as

   ```
   (15 < A) AND (A < 67)
   ```

   d. False. Parentheses are needed for relational comparisons, as

   ```
   (A > 9) AND (B < -7)
   ```

   e. True.

Exercises   Set I. Comprehension

1. Write an IF . . . THEN statement for the following decision: if X is equal to 0, then print the message

   ```
   CANNOT DIVIDE BY ZERO.
   ```

2. Write an IF . . . THEN . . . ELSE statement for the following decision: if X is greater than 5, then print

   ```
   X IS GREATER THAN 5
   ```

   otherwise, print

   ```
   X IS LESS THAN OR EQUAL TO 5
   ```

3. Write an IF . . . THEN . . . ELSE statement that will assign female students to dorm 1 and male students to dorm 2.

4. Rewrite Exercise 3 to check if the student wants a roommate. Female students with roommates should be assigned to dorm 3; male students with roommates, to dorm 4.

5. Evaluate the program segment for each of the following values of X:
   a. 69
   b. 94
   c. 75
   d. 87

   ```
   IF X > 70
      THEN IF X > 80
              THEN IF X > 90
                      THEN WRITELN('EXCELLENT')
                      ELSE WRITELN('GOOD')
              ELSE WRITELN('O.K.')
      ELSE WRITELN('POOR');
   ```

6. Specify the output of the program segment for each of the following values of N:
   a. 1, 2, 3, 4
   b. 4, 3, 2, 1

c. 50, 23, 31, 35

```
L  := 9999;
H  := 0;
S  := 0;
I  := 0;
C  := 4;
WHILE I <= C DO
    BEGIN
        READLN(N);
        S := S + N;
        IF N < L THEN L := N;
        IF N > H THEN H := N;
        I := I + 1
    END;
A := S / C;
WRITELN(L, H, A);
```

7. What value of X will cause PRESSURE to exceed MAX in the following program segment?

```
A := 200;
MAX := 1520;
DANGER := FALSE;
WHILE NOT DANGER DO
    BEGIN
        READLN(X);
        PRESSURE := X / A;
        IF PRESSURE > MAX THEN DANGER := TRUE
    END;
```

8. The program segment in Exercise 7 would be most useful for which of the following applications?
   a. Averaging blood pressure readings.
   b. Monitoring a pressure cooker.
   c. Computing barometric pressure.
   d. Sorting oil pressure readings.

9. Evaluate each of the following expressions for A = 4 and B = 7:
   a. `(A < 3) AND (B > 8)`
   b. `(A <= 3) OR (A > 6)`
   c. `(A = 4) AND (B <> 6)`
   d. `NOT(A = 5)`

10. Evaluate each of the following expressions for X = −2 and Y = 3:
    a. `(X > 5) AND (Y < 6)`
    b. `(X <= -2) OR (Y < 2)`
    c. `(X = -2) AND (Y <> 9)`
    d. `NOT(Y < 2)`

11. Evaluate each of the following expressions:
    a. `2 IN [3,4,5]`
    b. `'B' IN ['A'..'Z']`
    c. `NOT(7 IN [2..6])`

12. Evaluate each of the following expressions:
    a. `3 IN [1,2,3]`
    b. `NOT('S' IN ['A'..'M'])`
    c. `-1 IN [1..10]`

13. Identify each of the following as valid or invalid IF statements. Assume that A, B, C, and D are INTEGER variables and that X and Y are BOOLEAN variables.

   a. `IF A = B THEN B := C;`

   b. `IF (D = A) OR X THEN WRITE('TRUE');`
      `ELSE WRITE('FALSE');`

   c. `IF NOT(Y) AND X THEN D := 2;`

   d. `IF X THEN Y := FALSE ELSE Y := TRUE;`

14. Identify each of the following as valid or invalid IF statements. Assume that A, B, C, and D are INTEGER variables and that X and Y are BOOLEAN variables.

   a. `IF A > B THEN B < D;`

   b. `IF X AND Y THEN WRITE(A) ELSE`
      `WRITE(B) ELSE WRITE(C);`

   c. `IF (A > B) OR (C > D) THEN BEGIN`
      `X := A > B; Y := C > D END;`

   d. `IF X AND ((A + B + C + D)/4 = 1)`
      `THEN A := 1;`

15. Which of the following statements will determine if the INTEGER variables X, Y, and Z are equal to 1? There may be more than one correct answer.

   a. `IF X AND Y AND Z = 1 THEN WRITELN`
      `('ALL EQUAL 1');`

   b. `IF X = 1 AND IF Y = 1 AND IF Z = 1 THEN`
      `WRITELN('ALL EQUAL 1');`

   c. `IF X = Y = Z = 1 THEN WRITELN`
      `('ALL EQUAL 1');`

   d. `IF (X = 1) AND (Y = 1) AND (Z = 1)THEN`
      `WRITELN('ALL EQUAL 1');`

   e. `IF (X = 1) OR (Y = 1) OR (Z = 1) THEN`
      `WRITELN('ALL EQUAL 1');`

   f. `IF X = 1 THEN IF Y = 1 THEN IF Z = 1 THEN`
      `WRITELN('ALL EQUAL 1');`

   g. `IF NOT(X = 1) THEN ELSE NOT(Y = 1)`
      `THEN ELSE IF Z = 1 THEN WRITELN('ALL EQUAL 1');`

16. Explain the circumstances by which each of the following WRITE statements will be executed. Assume that A and B are BOOLEAN variables, and that X and Y are INTEGER variables.

   a. `IF A OR B THEN WRITE('DONE');`

   b. `IF (A AND NOT B) OR (B AND NOT A)`
      `THEN WRITE('DONE');`

   c. `IF (X = Y) AND A THEN WRITE('DONE');`

17. Explain the circumstances by which each of the following WRITE statements will be executed. Assume that A and B are BOOLEAN variables, and that X and Y are INTEGER variables.

   a. `IF (X > Y) AND NOT A THEN WRITE`
      `('FINISHED');`

   b. `IF (X = Y - 1) OR (X = Y) OR (X - 1 = Y)`
      `THEN WRITE('DONE');`

   c. `IF B AND (X < Y) OR A THEN WRITE('DONE');`

18. Specify the output of the program segment using each of the following sets of input:
    a. A = 1 and B = −1
    b. A = 1 and B = 1
    c. A = −1 and B = 1
    d. A = −1 and B = −1

```
IF A > 0
   THEN IF B > 0
              THEN WRITE('ONE')
              ELSE WRITE('TWO');
```

19. What is the output of the following program segment if the numbers 1 through 4 are entered in ascending order?

```
FOR I := 1 TO 4 DO
   BEGIN
      READ(N);
      CASE N OF
         1 : ANSWER := N + I;
         2 : ANSWER := N - I;
         3 : ANSWER := N * I;
         4 : ANSWER := N / I
      END;
      WRITELN(ANSWER)
   END;
```

20. Write a CASE statement for the following:

    if x = 1 or 2, output "BUCKLE MY SHOE"
    if x = 3 or 4, output "SHUT THE DOOR"
    if x = 5 or 6, output "PICK UP STICKS"
    if x = 7 or 8, output "LAY THEM STRAIGHT"
    if x = 9 or 10, output "BIG FAT HEN"

21. Convert the following IF . . . THEN . . . ELSE statement to a CASE statement:

```
IF I = 1
   THEN A := A + 1
   ELSE IF I = 2
      THEN B := B + 1
      ELSE IF (I = 3) OR (I = 4)
         THEN C := C + 1
         ELSE IF I = 5
            THEN D := D + 1
```

22. Convert the following IF . . . THEN . . . ELSE statement to a CASE statement:

```
IF (X < 0) OR (X > 5)
   THEN WRITELN('INVALID')
   ELSE IF X = 0
      THEN WRITELN('NONE')
      ELSE IF X = 1
         THEN WRITELN('1/2')
         ELSE IF (X = 2) OR (X = 4)
            THEN WRITELN(S DIV 2)
            ELSE WRITELN(S DIV 2,' AND 1/2');
```

23. Rewrite the following IF statements using the relational operator IN. Assume that X, Y, and Z are INTEGER variables.
    a.
    ```
    IF (X = 1) OR (X = 2) OR (X = 3) OR (X = 4)
    THEN CASE X OF...
    ```
    b.
    ```
    IF (Z = 1) OR (Z = 2) OR (Z = 3) OR (Z = 51)
    OR (Z = 52) OR (Z = 53) THEN CASE Z OF...
    ```
    c.
    ```
    IF (Y < 0) OR (Y > 10) THEN WRITE ('TRY AGAIN')
    ELSE CASE Y OF...
    ```

24. Rewrite the following IF statements using the relational operator IN. Assume that A and B are INTEGER variables.
    a.
    ```
    IF (A = 5) OR (A = 4) OR (A = 3) OR
    (A = 2) OR (A = 1) THEN CASE A OF . . .
    ```
    b.
    ```
    IF (B = 4) OR (B = 5) OR (B = 6) OR
    (B = 1) OR (B = 2) THEN CASE B OF . . .
    ```
    c.
    ```
    IF (A < 100) OR (A > 50)
    THEN CASE A OF . . .
    ELSE WRITE('NOT IN SET');
    ```

25. Write an IF statement that will check for input errors in the following program segment:

    ```
    READLN(G);

    { insert IF statement here }

    CASE G OF
        'A' : S := 4;
        'B' : S := 3;
        'C' : S := 2;
        'D' : S := 1;
        'F' : S := 0
    END; { CASE }
    ```

Set II. Application

26. Write a program segment that allows the user to enter a temperature and then prints an appropriate message regarding the temperature entered. Use the information provided in the following table:

Temperature (Degrees Celsius)	Message
T <= 0	Freezing
0 < T <= 20	Cold
20 < T <= 40	Average
40 < T <= 60	Hot

27. Write a program segment that allows the user to enter an age and then prints an appropriate message regarding the age entered. Use the information provided in the following table:

Age	Message
A <= 13	Child
13 <= A < 20	Teenager
20 <= A < 40	Young Adult
40 <= A < 60	Middle Age
A >= 60	Senior

28. Write a program segment that will find the slope of the line that passes through two points, (A,B) and (C,D). The formula used to calculate slope is

$$M = (B - D) / (A - C)$$

When the denominator is equal to zero, the slope of the line is undefined.

29. Write a program segment that prints an appropriate message after allowing the user to enter the time (HOURS, MINUTES). For example,

Input	Output
12,0	12 O'CLOCK
3,15	QUARTER PAST 3
2,30	HALF PAST 2
10,45	QUARTER TO 11

For times in which the minutes are not a multiple of 15, write the time in the standard format HH:MM, as for instance

12:05

30. Write a CASE statement to create the following design:

```
      *        *
      *        *
* * * * * * * * * * * * * * * *
      *        *
      *        *
* * * * * * * * * * * * * * * *
      *        *
      *        *
```

31. Write a CASE statement to create the following design:

```
   *
* * * * *
  * * *
* * * * *
  * * *
* * * * *
   *
* * * * *
* * * * *
* * * * *
```

32. A track meet gives a ribbon for the top six finishers in a race. Write a CASE statement that will print "1st place" if RANK is 1, "2nd place" if RANK is 2, and so on through 6th place.

33. Write a program segment that will allow the user to enter a number between 1 and 7, where the numbers 1 to 7 represent the days of the week. (1 represents MONDAY, 2 represents TUESDAY, and so on.) The segment should print the actual day of the week for an input of 1 to 5, the weekdays, and the message WEEKEND for an input of 6 or 7. Be sure to check input for errors.

34. Write a program that will allow the user to enter an operation (+, −, *, or /) and two real numbers. The program should compute the indicated operation and print the result.

35. Write a program that will request that a number between 1 and 12 be entered, where 1 through 12 represent the months of the year. (1 represents JANUARY, 2 represents FEBRUARY, and so on.) If the number is greater than 12 or less than 1, an error message is printed; otherwise, the month is printed. For example, if the number 3 is typed in, MARCH is printed on the screen.

36. Write a program that will allow the user to enter the first three letters of a month. The program will print the rest of the letters that make up the spelling of that month. For example, if the user enters MAR, the computer prints CH. (Use a nested IF . . . THEN . . . ELSE structure.)

37. Write a program to compute an electric bill given the kilowatt-hour (KWH) usage. There is a basic charge of $3.00, plus usage billed at the following rates:

KWH	Rate
0–300 KWH	$ 0.04237 per KWH
301–1200 KWH	$ 0.05241 per KWH
over 1200 KWH	$ 0.06113 per KWH

For example, a customer who has used 1248 KWH will be charged the basic charge of $3.00, plus 300 KWH at $0.04237, 900 KWH at $0.05241, and 48 KWH at $0.06113, for a total of $65.81. (Round answers to the nearest hundredth.)

38. Suppose Rose Proper is selling primroses on a base rate plus commission basis. The base rate is $50.00 and the commission depends on the quantity of items she sells. The following table indicates Rose's commission for selling various quantities.

Quantity	Commission
1000 or more	$0.15 per primrose
500 to 999	$0.12 per primrose
250 to 499	$0.10 per primrose
100 to 249	$0.08 per primrose
0 to 99	$0.05 per primrose

Write a program that will allow the user to enter the number of primroses sold and which then prints the amount Rose earned.

39. A department store is having a red, white, and blue tag sale. Colored tags are attached to each item that is on sale. The color of the tag indicates the percent of discount on the item, as shown in the following table:

Color of Tag	Discount
Red	30 percent
White	20 percent
Blue	10 percent
No tag	0 percent

Write a program that will allow the user to enter the original price of the item, followed by the color of the tag. The program should then print the discount price.

40. Write a program that will allow the user to enter a number. The program should then state if the number is in the interval from -10 to 10 or that the number is not in the interval. The program should continue until the user enters 999.

41. Write a program that will accept only integers between 20 and 40. Count the number of integers accepted and those rejected. Output these amounts. Rewrite your program so that the minimum and maximum legal values are specified at the keyboard.

Set III. Synthesis

42. Write a program that will ask for the input of a Hindu-Arabic number between 1 and 2000 and which will then print the corresponding Roman numeral. For example, if 1988 were entered, the output would be MCMLXXXVIII. The following table specifies the Roman numerals corresponding to Hindu-Arabic numbers:

Hindu-Arabic	Roman
1	I
5	V
10	X
50	L
100	C
500	D
1000	M

43. A speaker would like to know a little about the age distribution of her audience. Write a program that will allow her to enter the ages and then find the oldest person in attendance, the youngest, how many are of voting age, how many are senior citizens (63 or older), and the total number of people in attendance. Use an age of 0 to indicate when all ages have been entered.

44. Write a program that will accept a student's five quiz scores and compute the average score. If the student missed a quiz, enter -1 for the score and print an asterisk (*) for each missed quiz next to the student's average. The missing score should not be included in

the average. For example, for quiz scores of 96, 93, 84, -1, 87, the program should write

```
AVERAGE IS 90 *
```

Assume each score is based on a 100-point quiz.

45. Create a menu for a restaurant using the following categories:

> Appetizers
> Entrees
> Vegetables
> Desserts
> Beverages

Include at least two or three items from which to choose in each category. Write a program that will print the menu and then accept as input a person's menu choices (in the form #X where # is the category number and X is the letter corresponding to the item chosen). The program should write a list of the items chosen. Be sure to allow for more than one entry per category, except for Entrees, which should be limited to one item.

46. Write a program that will allow the user to enter a date (MM/DD/ YY) and then print the day of the week that date occurred or will occur. (Assume the year is in the twentieth century.)

47. Write a program that will act as a calculator. Use the following operations:

> +
> —
> *
> /
> =
> CLEAR

For example, if the user enters

```
5  4  +
6  -
8  /
5  *
=
```

The answer

```
(5 + 4 - 6) / 8 * 5 = 1.875
```

is printed on the screen. The user may wish to CLEAR the memory or may continue.

Draw the calculator on the screen using text and format the output so that the numbers entered appear in the calculator window. (This problem is an extension of Exercise 34.)

Procedures with Parameters

"Who are you?" said the Caterpillar.

. . . Alice replied, rather shyly, "I—I hardly know, Sir, just at present—at least I know who I was when I got up this morning, but I think I must have been changed several times since then."

—Lewis Carroll

Overview

Gaining a Perspective

Procedures provide a way to organize a program by refining programming steps into subroutines or modules, as introduced in Chapter 4. This process is often called modularizing a program. Splitting an idea into easily manageable parts is a common practice in solving problems in many areas.

Coding with procedures offers many advantages over programs written without subprograms. Procedures may be called repeatedly during the program execution, which saves both programmer time (a procedure that is called repeatedly needs to be entered only once) and memory space, since the code is stored once and the space used for the local variables is used only when the procedure is called. Also, procedures may be easily repeated with a different set of arguments, as we will see in this chapter. Other advantages of procedures include increased readability and ease of transporting a procedure to other programs.

As mentioned earlier, the declaration of variables in Pascal provides a means of further documenting a program. The variables may be declared globally (known to the entire program) or locally (known only to a procedure). Global variables may be referenced throughout the program, whereas local variables may be referenced only in the procedure where they are declared. So far, global variables have been used throughout most of the chapters. In Chapter 4, local variables declared under the procedure heading were discussed. In this chapter, two additional types of local variables will be introduced: **value** and **variable parameters.** These parameters are enclosed in parentheses as a part of the procedure call. Value and variable parameters allow the programmer to write each procedure as a self-contained unit. Each procedure can receive what it needs from different parts of the program, go through the designated process, and then return any desired results to the calling block.

Lesson 8.1   Value and Variable Parameters

There are three ways that variables may be declared in a procedure, as shown in the following example:

```
PROCEDURE WHEREVER (WHO : STRING; VAR WHAT : REAL);

    VAR
        WHEN : INTEGER;
```

Variables can be declared below the procedure heading, as well as in parentheses after the procedure heading.

In Chapter 4, variables declared under the procedure heading were introduced as local variables. For example,

```
PROCEDURE COUNT;

    VAR
        NUMBER : INTEGER;    { LOCAL VARIABLE }
    .
    .
    .

BEGIN { MAIN PROGRAM }

    COUNT;    { PROCEDURE CALL}
    .
    .
    .

END.
```

The variable NUMBER is a local variable. Notice that both the variable identifier and its type are indicated. The declaration of a local variable under the procedure heading is similar to the global variable declaration in the main program. The memory space that is required for variable NUMBER is local to the procedure; that is, it is needed only when the procedure is called. After the procedure has been executed, the memory space needed for a local variable can be reused for other purposes. Local constants can be declared between the procedure heading and the local variable declaration and are known only to the procedure in which they have been declared.

Formal parameters are enclosed in parentheses in the procedure heading directly after the procedure identifier. These parameters are values or variables that come from a calling block and specify what, if anything, will be sent back to the calling block. (Recall that the calling block is the program block containing the procedure call.) The declaration of formal parameters is similar to other variable declarations in that both the variable identifier and its type are included in the declaration. There are two kinds of formal parameters:

1. value parameters.
2. variable parameters.

Value Parameters

An example of a predefined or built-in procedure that uses value parameters is the procedure WRITELN. When the machine executes the statement

```
WRITELN(NUMBER);
```

NUMBER is passed to the WRITELN procedure. The procedure WRITELN consists of the commands necessary for output in Pascal. WRITELN outputs the desired parameters and then returns control to the calling block; it does not alter the value of any variables.

Procedures with value parameters can also be written by the Pascal programmer, as shown in Program 8.1. This program computes the simple annual interest for a given principal and interest rate.

Program 8.1

```
PROGRAM COMPUTEINTEREST (INPUT,OUTPUT);

    { PURPOSE: TO COMPUTE SIMPLE ANNUAL INTEREST
               USING VALUE PARAMETERS }

VAR
    PRINCIPAL,
    RATE      : REAL;
    ANSWER    : STRING;

PROCEDURE SIMPLEANNUAL (P, R : REAL);

    VAR
        INTEREST : REAL;

    BEGIN

        INTEREST := P * R;
        WRITE('THE SIMPLE ANNUAL INTEREST WOULD BE ');
        WRITELN(INTEREST:9:2)

    END;   { SIMPLEANNUAL }

BEGIN     { MAIN PROGRAM }

    REPEAT

        WRITE('ENTER THE PRINCIPAL AND RATE: ');
        READLN(PRINCIPAL, RATE);
        SIMPLEANNUAL(PRINCIPAL, RATE);
        WRITELN;
        WRITE('DO YOU WISH TO ENTER ANOTHER ');
        WRITELN('SET OF DATA? (YES/NO)');
        READLN(ANSWER)

    UNTIL ANSWER = 'NO'

END.
```

Sample Output

```
ENTER THE PRINCIPAL AND RATE: 5000 .07
THE SIMPLE ANNUAL INTEREST WOULD BE    350.00

DO YOU WISH TO ENTER ANOTHER SET OF DATA? (YES/NO)
NO
```

Program 8.1 passes the global variables PRINCIPAL and RATE to procedure SIMPLEANNUAL as value parameters and declares these variables in the procedure heading as P and R. The variables are passed in the same order they are listed in the procedure call. The local value parameters used in the procedure heading, P and R, are the formal parameters, and the global variables used in the procedure call, PRINCIPAL and RATE, are called **actual parameters.** Variable INTEREST is local to the procedure.

Value parameters allow input to a procedure from the calling block. The values of these variables are passed from the procedure call to the procedure, and then used by the procedure. When value parameters are involved, the values of the global variables cor-

Figure 8.1

Parameters are Listed in Procedure Call in Same Order as in Procedure Heading

```
PROCEDURE SIMPLEANNUAL   (P, R : INTEGER);      {LOCAL}

    VAR

        INTEREST : REAL;                        {LOCAL}

        .
        .
        .

BEGIN   ( MAIN PROGRAM )

        .
        .
        .

    SIMPLEANNUAL  (PRINCIPAL, RATE);            {GLOBAL}

        ( ACTUAL PARAMETERS IN THE PROCEDURE CALL )

        ( THIS BLOCK OF THE PROGRAM IS CALLED THE

            CALLING BLOCK )

        .
        .
        .

END.
```

responding to the value parameters are not altered by the completion of the procedure call. Using value parameters is often referred to as "calling by value," "passing by value," or "using input parameters."

Value Parameter Form in Procedure Heading

```
PROCEDURE identifier (identifier : type);
```

or

```
PROCEDURE identifier (identifier1 : type1;
                      identifier2 : type2;
                      identifier3,
                      identifier4 : type3);
```

Value parameters are local variables with local scope. A global identifier with the same name would not be affected by changes in the value parameter.

Here is a summary of passing value parameters. In order to pass value parameters to a procedure, the programmer must write a procedure call and a procedure heading as follows:

Call

Write a procedure call, which includes the procedure identifier and the names of the parameters that are to be passed in parentheses. The parameters must be values or variables that have been previously assigned a value. The variable names used as parameters also must be declared in the variable declaration portion of the calling block. These values or variables are the actual parameters in the procedure call.

Heading

Declare the variables in parentheses after the procedure identifier. These formal parameters are written in parentheses as a part of the procedure heading and are the variable identifiers that are used in the procedure. They represent the actual parameters that were passed to the procedure.

Program 8.2 shows how value parameters obtain a value from the procedure call and are independent of the main program.

Program 8.2
```
PROGRAM VALUEDEMO (OUTPUT);

    { PURPOSE: TO DEMONSTRATE VALUE PARAMETERS }

VAR

    GLOBALA,
    GLOBALB : INTEGER;
```

```
PROCEDURE CHANGE (VALUEA, VALUEB : INTEGER);

    BEGIN

        WRITELN;
        WRITELN('ENTER PROCEDURE CHANGE');
        WRITELN;
        WRITE('VALUEA : ',VALUEA);
        WRITELN('   VALUEB : ', VALUEB);
        VALUEA := 6;
        VALUEB := 2;
        WRITE('VALUEA : ',VALUEA);
        WRITELN('   VALUEB : ', VALUEB);
        WRITELN;
        WRITELN('EXIT PROCEDURE CHANGE');
        WRITELN

    END;  { CHANGE}

BEGIN  { MAIN PROGRAM }

    GLOBALA := 2;
    GLOBALB := 6;
    WRITE('GLOBALA: ',GLOBALA);
    WRITELN('   GLOBALB: ', GLOBALB);
    CHANGE(GLOBALA, GLOBALB);
    WRITE('GLOBALA: ',GLOBALA);
    WRITELN('   GLOBALB: ', GLOBALB)

END.
```

When Program 8.2 is executed, the following values will be printed
on the screen:

```
GLOBALA: 2    GLOBALB: 6

ENTER PROCEDURE CHANGE

VALUEA : 2    VALUEB : 6
VALUEA : 6    VALUEB : 2

EXIT PROCEDURE CHANGE

GLOBALA: 2    GLOBALB: 6
```

The values of the global variables, GLOBALA and GLOBALB, were
not altered by procedure CHANGE. Four different spaces in memory are allocated for the variables used in Program 8.2; this is
shown in Figure 8.2. Once CHANGE has been completed, the
spaces in memory needed for VALUEA and VALUEB, the value
parameters, may be reused, thus conserving memory space. Value
parameters are used by the procedure, but forgotten upon return
to the calling block; that is, they are not passed back to the calling
block.

What would happen in Program 8.2 if the following statement
were added as the last statement of the main program?

```
WRITELN(VALUEA, VALUEB);
```

Figure 8.2

Memory Spaces Used
in Program 8.2

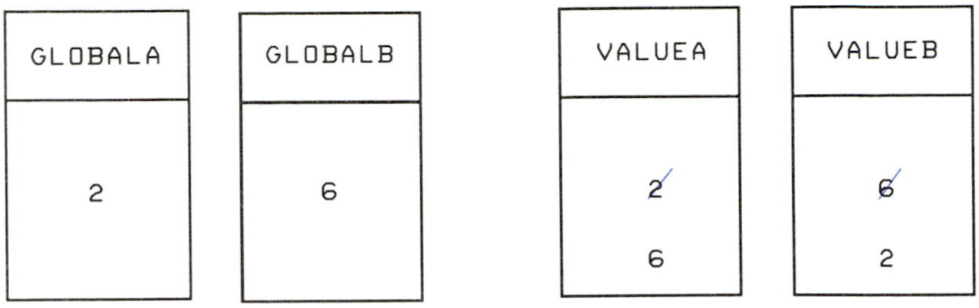

GLOBALA	GLOBALB	VALUEA	VALUEB
2	6	2̸ 6	6̸ 2

This statement would result in an error message, since VALUEA and VALUEB are local to procedure CHANGE and are not known globally; that is, they are unknown to the main program.

Value parameters are passed as expressions (INTEGER, STRING, REAL, and so on) or as variables that have been assigned a value prior to the procedure call. For example, the procedure call of Program 8.2 could be rewritten as

```
CHANGE(2,6);
```

This statement could replace CHANGE(GLOBALA, GLOBALB) and the global variables GLOBALA and GLOBALB would not need to be declared or initialized.

Variable Parameters

Variable parameters, often called input/output parameters, allow another way to communicate between the calling block and a procedure. Variable parameters allow procedures to both use and return a value to the calling block, thus altering the value of the global variable that was sent to the procedure. These parameters are said to be passed by VAR, since the word VAR is a part of the declaration of a variable parameter. The variables are also said to be "called by address" (called by reference), since the address of memory locations of variable parameters is known by their corresponding global variables.

READLN is an example of a predefined procedure that uses a variable parameter. The procedure call

```
READLN(NUMBER);
```

calls the built-in procedure READLN that waits for the user to enter a value. The procedure then returns the value entered through the variable NUMBER to the calling block. The value stored in the location NUMBER may then be used in the program.

Variable parameters receive the variable sent to a procedure and then allow for the return of a value to the main program. This return provides a means for variable input and output of a procedure. When variable parameters are used, no new memory location is created: variable parameters share memory (an address) with the global variables of the calling block. Thus, variable parameters are named locally in the procedure heading, but are global in effect. When the value of the variable parameter is changed, the value of its associated global variable changes also. Variable parameters must be passed as a variable, not as an expression.

Variable Parameter Form in Procedure Heading

PROCEDURE *identifier*(VAR *identifier* : *type*);

or

PROCEDURE *identifier* (VAR *identifier1* : *type1*;
                           VAR *identifier2* : *type2*);

Here is a summary of passing variable parameters. In order to pass variable parameters to a procedure, the programmer must write a procedure call and heading as follows:

Call

   Write a procedure call, which includes the procedure identifier and the names of the parameters that are to be passed in parentheses. These variable names must be declared as global variables and sent to the procedure as variables, not expressions. The variables written in the procedure call are the actual parameters. The difference between value and variable parameters in the procedure call is that value parameters must be assigned a value and variable parameters must be variables (which may or may not have been initialized).

Heading

   Declare variables (representing the actual parameters passed to the procedure) in parentheses after the procedure identifier. These variables listed in the procedure heading are formal parameters. Any changes in variable parameters will be sent back to the calling block through these names. Variable parameters are declared in the procedure heading using the word VAR to distinguish them from value parameters.

Program 8.3 shows how the value of the global variable that corresponds to a variable parameter is changed by the statements in a procedure.

Program 8.3

```
PROGRAM VARDEMO (OUTPUT);

    { PURPOSE: TO DEMONSTRATE VAR PARAMETERS }

VAR
    GLOBALA,
    GLOBALB  : INTEGER;
```

```
PROCEDURE CHANGE (VAR VARA, VARB : INTEGER);

    BEGIN
        WRITELN;
        WRITELN('ENTER PROCEDURE CHANGE');
        WRITELN;
        WRITELN('VARA: ',VARA,'   VARB: ',VARB);
        VARA := 6;
        VARB := 2;
        WRITELN('VARA: ',VARA,'   VARB: ',VARB);
        WRITELN;
        WRITELN('EXIT PROCEDURE CHANGE');
        WRITELN
    END;    { CHANGE }

BEGIN  { MAIN PROGRAM }

    GLOBALA := 2;
    GLOBALB := 6;
    WRITE('GLOBALA: ',GLOBALA);
    WRITELN('   GLOBALB: ', GLOBALB);
    CHANGE(GLOBALA, GLOBALB);
    WRITE('GLOBALA: ',GLOBALA);
    WRITELN('GLOBALB: ', GLOBALB)

END.
```

The results of the execution of Program 8.3 would be

```
GLOBALA: 2    GLOBALB: 6

ENTER PROCEDURE CHANGE

VARA: 2    VARB: 6
VARA: 6    VARB: 2

EXIT PROCEDURE CHANGE

GLOBALA: 6    GLOBALB: 2
```

In Program 8.3, GLOBALA and GLOBALB are given the same address as VARA and VARB, respectively. That is, the values of GLOBALA and GLOBALB are changed when the corresponding variable parameters in procedure CHANGE are altered within the procedure. Figure 8.3 shows that the spaces in memory allocated for the global variables and variable parameters of Program 8.3 are shared. GLOBALA and VARA have the same address in memory, as do GLOBALB and VARB.

Figure 8.3

Memory Spaces Used in Program 8.3

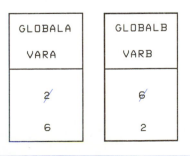

Program 8.4 uses both value and variable parameters, and contrasts the uses of the two parameters.

Program 8.4

```
PROGRAM EXCHANGE (INPUT,OUTPUT);
      { PURPOSE: TO SWITCH TWO NUMBERS }
VAR
     FIRST,
     SECOND : INTEGER;

PROCEDURE GETVALUES (VAR F, S : INTEGER);

    BEGIN

       WRITE('ENTER TWO INTEGERS:   ');
       READLN(F, S)

    END;

PROCEDURE SWITCH (VAR F, S : INTEGER);

    VAR
       TEMP : INTEGER;

    BEGIN

       WRITELN('SWITCH');
       TEMP := F;
       F    := S;
       S    := TEMP

    END;

PROCEDURE FALSESWITCH (F, S : INTEGER);

    VAR
       TEMP : INTEGER;

    BEGIN

       WRITELN('FALSE SWITCH');
       TEMP := F;
       F    := S;
       S    := TEMP

    END;

PROCEDURE PRINTOUT (F, S : INTEGER);

    BEGIN

       WRITELN('FIRST IS ',F,' AND SECOND IS ',S)

    END;
```

```
BEGIN   { MAIN PROGRAM }

   GETVALUES(FIRST, SECOND);
   PRINTOUT(FIRST, SECOND);
   SWITCH(FIRST, SECOND);
   PRINTOUT(FIRST, SECOND);
   FALSESWITCH(FIRST, SECOND);
   PRINTOUT(FIRST, SECOND)

END.
```

Program 8.4 passes actual parameters, FIRST and SECOND, to procedure GETVALUES as variable parameters (by VAR). This procedure requests that the user enter two integers. The integers entered are assigned to F and S, which share memory locations with global variables FIRST and SECOND. Upon return to the main program, FIRST and SECOND are passed to procedure SWITCH, again by VAR. SWITCH accepts FIRST and SECOND as F and S (variable parameters), and then switches the contents of the memory locations of F and S. SWITCH then passes the change back to the main program through global variables, FIRST and SECOND. FIRST and SECOND are passed to procedure PRINTOUT by value and PRINTOUT prints the switch. FIRST and SECOND are then passed to procedure FALSESWITCH by value. The values of the variables, F and S, are switched in FALSESWITCH; the switch is not known by the main program, however, since the variables were passed by value. PRINTOUT then prints the result of FALSESWITCH. The output of Program 8.4 follows:

```
ENTER TWO INTEGERS: 5 8
FIRST IS 5 AND SECOND IS 8
SWITCH
FIRST IS 8 AND SECOND IS 5
FALSE SWITCH
FIRST IS 8 AND SECOND IS 5
```

Figure 8.4 shows a schematic diagram of the use of value and variable parameters in Program 8.4. Notice that variable parameters both enter and exit the procedures (variables enter and any changes exit). Value parameters, on the other hand, enter the procedure, but have no exit.

Figure 8.4
Value and Variable
Parameters in
Program 8.4

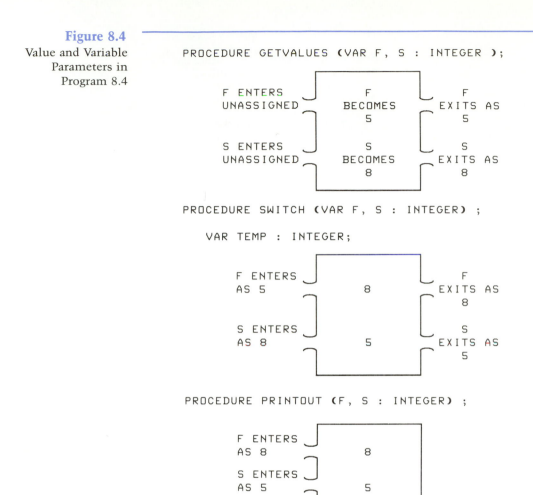

PROCEDURE GETVALUES (VAR F, S : INTEGER);

| F ENTERS UNASSIGNED | F BECOMES 5 | F EXITS AS 5 |
| S ENTERS UNASSIGNED | S BECOMES 8 | S EXITS AS 8 |

PROCEDURE SWITCH (VAR F, S : INTEGER) ;

VAR TEMP : INTEGER;

| F ENTERS AS 5 | 8 | F EXITS AS 8 |
| S ENTERS AS 8 | 5 | S EXITS AS 5 |

PROCEDURE PRINTOUT (F, S : INTEGER) ;

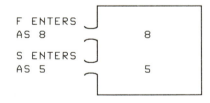

| F ENTERS AS 8 | 8 |
| S ENTERS AS 5 | 5 |

PROCEDURE FALSESWITCH (F, S : INTEGER);

| F ENTERS AS 8 | 8 |
| S ENTERS AS 5 | 5 |

PROCEDURE PRINTOUT (F, S : INTEGER):

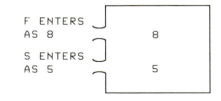

| F ENTERS AS 8 | 8 |
| S ENTERS AS 5 | 5 |

Lesson Check 8.1

1. Given the following program segment:

```
PROGRAM TEST;

VAR
    RESULT,
    A,
    B,
    C      : REAL;

PROCEDURE GETVALUES (VAR L, M, N : REAL);

    VAR
       COUNT : INTEGER;
    .
    .
    .

PROCEDURE COMPUTE (VAR ANSWER : REAL;
                       X, Y, Z : REAL);

    VAR
       COUNT : INTEGER;
    .
    .
    .

BEGIN   { MAIN PROGRAM }

    GETVALUES(A,B,C);
    COMPUTE(RESULT,A,B,C);
    .
    .
    .

END.
```

identify the
   a. actual parameters.
   b. formal parameters.
   c. global variables.
   d. local variables.
   e. value parameters.
   f. variable parameters.

2. What is the difference between each of the following:
   a. Global and local variables?
   b. Actual and formal parameters?
   c. Value and variable parameters?

Lesson 8.2 Using Value and Variable Parameters

A parameter list may include both value and variable parameters. If the headings are mixed, a semicolon is used to separate the value from the variable parameters, as well as parameters of different data types. In the following examples, WHO, WHAT, WHEN, and HOW are variable parameters. WHERE is a value parameter.

```
PROCEDURE ROGER (VAR WHO,WHAT:STRING; WHERE:STRING);

PROCEDURE TEN (VAR WHO:STRING; WHERE:STRING;
               VAR WHAT:STRING);

PROCEDURE FOUR (VAR WHEN:INTEGER; VAR HOW:STRING);
```

In procedure ROGER, two variable parameters (WHO and WHAT) are declared of type STRING and a value parameter (WHERE) is declared of type STRING. Procedure TEN is the same declaration as ROGER, in a different order. The order is only important when considering the order in which the variables are sent from the calling block. Procedure FOUR declares two variable parameters of different types.

When should value parameters be used instead of variable parameters? A variable should be declared as a value parameter if the procedure receives and uses the variable, but does not return its value to the calling block. The parameter should be declared as a variable parameter if the procedure receives and uses it, possibly changing it, and returns its value to the calling block.

Program 8.5 uses both value and variable parameters to find the sum of the integers between two numbers.

Program 8.5

```
PROGRAM GENERATESUM (INPUT,OUTPUT);

    { PURPOSE: TO FIND THE SUM OF THE INTEGERS
               BETWEEN TWO INTEGERS }

VAR
    NUMBER1,
    NUMBER2,
    SUM      : INTEGER;

PROCEDURE FINDSUM (NUM1, NUM2 : INTEGER;
                   VAR ACCUMULATE : INTEGER);

    VAR
       COUNT : INTEGER;

    BEGIN
       FOR COUNT := NUM1 TO NUM2 DO
          ACCUMULATE := ACCUMULATE + COUNT
    END;  { FINDSUM }
```

```
BEGIN   { MAIN PROGRAM }

   SUM := 0;
   WRITE('ENTER TWO NUMBERS:   ');
   READLN(NUMBER1, NUMBER2);
   IF NUMBER1 < NUMBER2
      THEN FINDSUM(NUMBER1, NUMBER2, SUM)
      ELSE FINDSUM(NUMBER2, NUMBER1, SUM);
   WRITE('THE SUM OF THE NUMBERS FROM ',NUMBER1);
   WRITELN(' TO ',NUMBER2,' IS ',SUM)

END.
```

Here is a sample run of Program 8.5.

```
ENTER TWO NUMBERS:   1 10
THE SUM OF ALL THE NUMBERS FROM 1 TO 10 IS 55
```

Notice that NUMBER1 and NUMBER2 are passed by value and are declared in procedure FINDSUM as NUM1 and NUM2. SUM is passed by VAR and declared in FINDSUM as ACCUMULATE. The procedure finds the sum of the numbers between (and including) NUM1 and NUM2 and stores the value in ACCU-MULATE. Upon completion of FINDSUM, the value of ACCU-MULATE is passed back to the main program as SUM. The spaces allocated in memory for the variables are shown in Figure 8.5.

Figure 8.5
Memory Allocation of Program 8.5

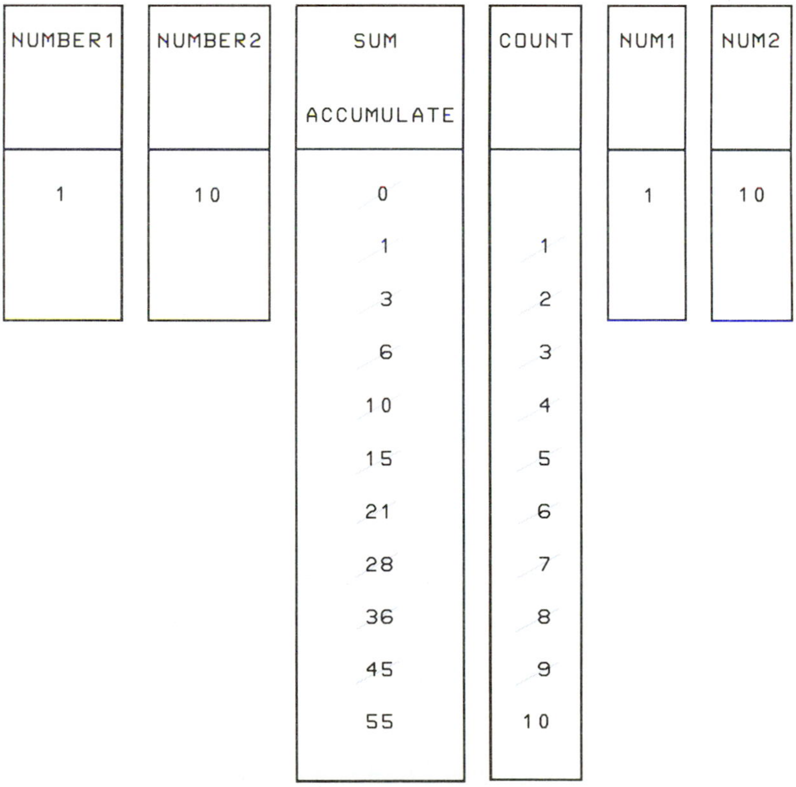

FORWARD Declaration

What happens at compile time if a procedure is called before it has been defined? As the computer compiles the program, a table is set up that indicates the procedures and variables used in the program or subprogram. If the compiler encounters a call to a procedure that has not been declared, as in Program Segment 8.6, it will give an error message: Undeclared Identifier.

Program Segment 8.6

```
{ CALLING PROCEDURE TWO BEFORE IT HAS BEEN READ
  WILL CAUSE AN ERROR MESSAGE }

PROCEDURE ONE (HOW : INTEGER);

   BEGIN
     statement part;
     TWO(parameter list)
   END;

PROCEDURE TWO (VAR WHAT : INTEGER);

   BEGIN
     ONE(parameter list);
     statement part
   END;

BEGIN  { MAIN PROGRAM }

   .
   .
   .

END.
```

In Program Segment 8.6, procedure ONE calls procedure TWO, which in turn calls ONE. As is, Program Segment 8.6 will result in an error message. Procedures should be declared before they are called; sometimes, however, this is not possible.

A **FORWARD declaration** solves this dilemma by providing a way to announce a procedure beforehand. This declaration tells the computer that the subprogram identifier is valid. To accomplish a FORWARD declaration, add the word FORWARD to the end of the procedure heading, as shown in Program Segment 8.7.

Caution: The parameter list cannot be repeated when the procedure is defined. The parameter list may be written as a comment following the procedure identifier, as with procedure TWO.

**Program
Segment 8.7**

```
{ A FORWARD DECLARATION MEANS THAT THIS
    PROCEDURE IS VALID AND WILL BE READ LATER }

PROCEDURE TWO (VAR WHAT : INTEGER); FORWARD;

PROCEDURE ONE (HOW : INTEGER);

    BEGIN
        statements;
        TWO(parameter list)
    END;

PROCEDURE TWO;          { VAR WHAT : INTEGER }

    BEGIN
        ONE(parameter list);
        statements
    END;
```

A need for FORWARD declarations will become clear in Chapter 10, when recursion is discussed.

*Lesson
Check
8.2*

1. Identify the value and variable parameters in each of the following procedure headings:
   a. PROCEDURE FIRST (VAR ONE,TWO:INTEGER;
                            THREE:INTEGER);
   b. PROCEDURE SECOND (ONE:INTEGER; VAR TWO:INTEGER;
                            THREE:INTEGER);
   c. PROCEDURE THIRD (ONE,TWO:REAL; THREE:INTEGER;
                            VAR FOUR:REAL);

2. Correct the errors in each of the following procedure headings:
   a. PROCEDURE GOOD (INTEGER);
   b. PROCEDURE BETTER (A:REAL, B:INTEGER);
   c. PROCEDURE BEST (VAR B, VAR C:STRING, A; D:REAL);

3. Identify each of the following statements as true or false:
   a. A procedure block must be defined before it is called.
   b. Formal variable parameters share memory space with their actual parameter counterparts.

Lesson 8.3 Programming Tip— Data Flow Analysis

Logic diagrams allow the programmer to outline a solution to a problem and determine what procedures are needed. This is a great first step toward solving the problem. It could be a big mistake, however, to attempt to write specific procedures without doing a little more preparation to determine how the procedures will work together. One good method to analyze how procedures will interact is to use **data flow diagrams.**

Data flow diagrams can be used to

- Specify what information is needed by each procedure to do the particular task.
- Specify what information is produced by each procedure for use elsewhere in the program or for output.
- Show how information moves through the procedures in a program.

For example, look at the fairly simple problem of computing collision insurance claims based on one of three types of coverage. The logic diagram might look like that shown in Figure 8.6.

Notice that the logic diagram need not set forth the specific numbers involved in the problem. This diagram shows what needs to be input to the program, what process will be done on the input, and what will be produced as a result of the program. The procedures can then be tied together using a data flow diagram, as shown in Figure 8.7.

From this analysis, the programmer should be able to write procedures to perform each of the separate jobs. The parameter list for each procedure should follow directly from the data flow diagram.

```
PROCEDURE GET_TYPE_CLAIM (VAR T,D : INTEGER);

PROCEDURE CALCULATE_AWARD (T, D : INTEGER;
                           VAR P : REAL);

PROCEDURE SHOW_AWARD (P : REAL);
```

Likewise, the procedure calls in the main program are straightforward.

```
GET_TYPE_CLAIM(TYPEPOLICY, DAMAGE);
CALCULATE_AWARD(TYPEPOLICY, DAMAGE, PAYMENT);
SHOW_AWARD(PAYMENT);
```

Remember that this is a simple illustration of an extremely powerful tool to use in planning the solution to a problem. The true power of data flow analysis will become more apparent as problems become more complex.

Figure 8.6
Logic Diagram for Computing Claims

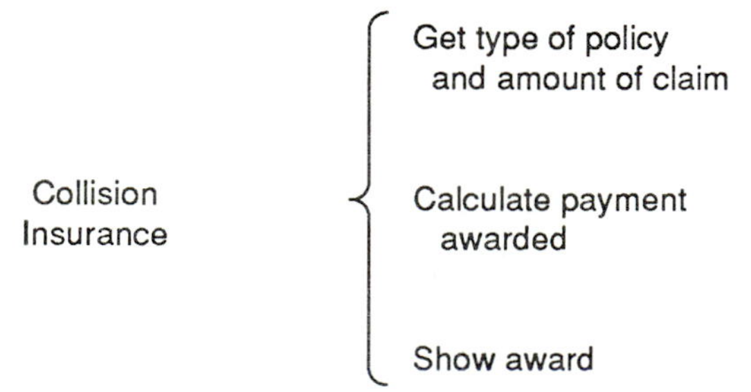

Collision Insurance

Get type of policy and amount of claim

Calculate payment awarded

Show award

Figure 8.7 Data Flow Diagram for Computing Claims

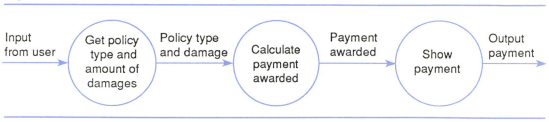

A Detailed Look

At the end of Chapter 4, the Adams family's travel situation was introduced. The programmed solution used the tools learned up to that point. The problem will now be revised slightly and a new program will be written that uses many of the features of Pascal and problem solving discussed in Chapters 5–8.

Problem Statement: Recall that the Adams family is traveling across the United States in their motor home. At each gas stop, they enter the miles traveled since the last stop and the gallons of gas. The program then computes the miles per gallon (mpg).

Revise the program to keep track of the total miles traveled to date, the mpg (for the day and to date), the average miles traveled per day, and the lowest and highest daily miles traveled to date. (Assume the family fills the gas tank once a day, at the end of the day.)

Aside from the revisions that will require the additional Pascal features introduced in Chapters 5–8, some enhancements can now be made to the original program. For example, the family can now enter the odometer reading and have the computer determine the number of miles traveled since the last gas stop. Also, with the addition of loop structures, the family need not rerun the program each day; they simply leave the program on throughout the trip. (Files, to be introduced in Chapter 16, would allow the family to quit the program without losing any previously entered data.)

One way to get a better understanding of the revisions to be made would be to list the new input and output requirements and revise the rough plan.

Input

> Initial odometer reading.
> Odometer reading for the day.
> Gallons of gas.

Output

> Miles per gallon for day.
> Miles traveled for day.
> Miles per gallon to date.
> Total mileage to date.

Average daily mileage.
Lowest daily mileage to date.
Highest daily mileage to date.

The revised rough plan follows:

1. Obtain the initial odometer reading.
2. Obtain the odometer reading and gallons of gas for the day.
3. Compute miles traveled and miles per gallon for day.
4. Compute total mileage and miles per gallon to date.
5. Compute average daily mileage.
6. Compute lowest and highest daily mileage to date.
7. Print results.
8. Repeat Steps 2–7.

The revised logic diagram is shown in Figure 8.8.

A data flow diagram illustrates relationships between the procedures and variables of a program. A data flow diagram for this problem is shown in Figure 8.9. The figure shows the variables needed for each procedure. The figure also indicates the three main procedures GETINFO, COMPUTE, and PRINTRESULTS, and the subprocedures MPG and TESTDAY of procedure COMPUTE.

Program 8.8 consists of the same three main procedures as Program 4.4 from Chapter 4. Procedure GETINFO is similar to the earlier procedure, except for the parameter passing. Procedure COMPUTE has changed considerably. This procedure also keeps a running total of the miles traveled and gas used, calls a subprocedure to determine the miles per gallon (once for the day and once for the miles per gallon to date), calls another subprocedure to determine if the new mileage is a low or a high for the trip, and computes the average miles traveled each day on the trip. As

Figure 8.8

Revised Logic
Diagram for Trip

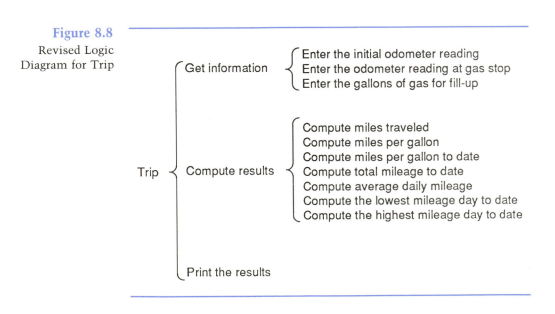

Figure 8.9 Data Flow Diagram for Trip

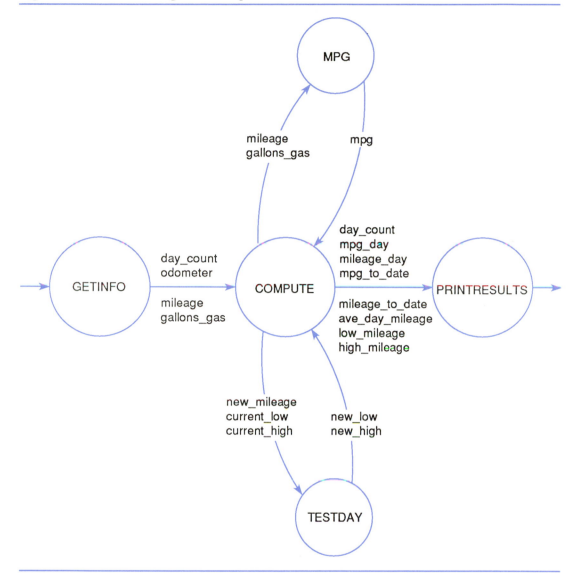

before, procedure PRINTRESULTS outputs the desired information.

The technique used for determining the low and high mileage for the trip first involves initializing the low and high to some extreme values for comparison. Each time a new mileage is entered, it is compared to these high and low mileages in procedure TESTDAY. If the mileage is a new high or low for the trip, then the appropriate variable is reassigned the new value.

The data flow analysis displays the parameter passing that occurs in this program. Notice that the global variables (prefixed by the letter G) are used in the main program only. In the procedures, local variables with similar names are used.

Program 8.8

```
PROGRAM TRIP (INPUT, OUTPUT);

    { PURPOSE: DETERMINE MILEAGE AND MPG
                INFORMATION FOR A TRIP }

VAR
    GMILES,
    GGAS,
    GMPG,
    GMPGTODATE,
    GMILESTODATE,
    GGASTODATE,
    GAVGMILES,
    GLOW,
    GHIGH,
    GODOMETER      : REAL;
    GDAYS          : INTEGER;
    GDONE          : BOOLEAN;

PROCEDURE GETINFO(VAR DAYS : INTEGER;
                  VAR PREVODOM, MILES, GAS : REAL);

    VAR
        NEWODOM : REAL;

    BEGIN

        IF DAYS = 0
            THEN
                BEGIN
                    WRITE('INITIAL ODOMETER READING: ');
                    READLN(PREVODOM)
                END;
            WRITE('ENTER NEW ODOMETER READING: ');
            READLN(NEWODOM);
            MILES := NEWODOM - PREVODOM;
            PREVODOM := NEWODOM;
            WRITE('GALLONS OF GAS FOR THIS FILL-UP: ');
            READLN(GAS);
            DAYS := DAYS + 1

    END;    { GETINFO }

PROCEDURE COMPUTE(DAYS, MILES, GAS : REAL;
                  VAR MPG, MPGTODATE, MILESTODATE,
                  GASTODATE, AVGMILES, LOW,
                  HIGH : REAL);

    { COMPUTE THE MPGS, MILEAGES, AVERAGE MILEAGE,
      LOWEST MILEAGE DAY, HIGHEST MILEAGE DAY }

    PROCEDURE MILESPERGAL(MMILES, MGAS : REAL;
                          VAR MMPG : REAL);

        { PURPOSE: FIND THE MILES PER GALLON OF GAS }

        BEGIN

            MMPG := MMILES / MGAS

        END;  { MILESPERGAL }
```

```
              PROCEDURE TESTDAY(TMILES : REAL; VAR TLOW,
                               THIGH : REAL);

                 { PURPOSE: FIND THE LOWEST AND HIGHEST
                           DAILY MILEAGE }

              BEGIN

                 IF TMILES > THIGH THEN THIGH := TMILES;
                 IF TMILES < TLOW THEN TLOW := TMILES

              END;   { TESTDAY }

           BEGIN

              MILESTODATE := MILESTODATE + MILES;
              GASTODATE := GASTODATE + GAS;
              MILESPERGAL(MILES, GAS, MPG);
              MILESPERGAL(MILESTODATE, GASTODATE, MPGTODATE);
              AVGMILES := MILESTODATE / DAYS;
              TESTDAY(MILES, LOW, HIGH)

           END;   { COMPUTE }

        PROCEDURE PRINTRESULTS(DAYS : INTEGER; MPG,
                              MPGTODATE, MILES, MILESTODATE,
                              AVGMILES, LOW, HIGH : REAL);

           BEGIN

              WRITELN;
              WRITELN('INFORMATION FOR DAY ',DAYS);
              WRITELN('*****************************');
              WRITELN('MPG FOR TODAY',MPG:15:2);
              WRITELN('MILEAGE FOR TODAY',MILES:11:2);
              WRITELN('CUMULATIVE MPG',MPGTODATE:14:2);
              WRITELN('CUMULATIVE MILEAGE',MILESTODATE:10:2);
              WRITELN('AVERAGE DAILY MILEAGE',AVGMILES:7:2);
              WRITELN('LOWEST DAILY MILEAGE',LOW:8:2);
              WRITELN('HIGHEST DAILY MILEAGE',HIGH:7:2);
              WRITELN('*****************************');
              WRITELN

           END;    { PRINTRESULTS }

        PROCEDURE CONTINUE (VAR DONE : BOOLEAN);

            { PURPOSE: OPTION TO CONTINUE PROGRAM }

           VAR
              ANSWER : CHAR;

           BEGIN

              WRITE('ENTER A NEW DAY? (Y/N): ');
              READLN(ANSWER);
              IF ANSWER = 'N'
                 THEN DONE := TRUE
                 ELSE DONE := FALSE

           END;  { CONTINUE }
```

```
BEGIN    { MAIN PROGRAM }

   GMPG := 0;
   GMPGTODATE := 0;
   GMILESTODATE := 0;
   GGASTODATE := 0;
   GDAYS := 0;
   GLOW := MAXINT;
   GHIGH := -1;
   GDONE := FALSE;
   REPEAT
      GETINFO(GDAYS, GODOMETER, GMILES, GGAS);
      COMPUTE(GDAYS, GMILES, GGAS, GMPG, GMPGTODATE,
              GMILESTODATE, GGASTODATE, GAVGMILES,
              GLOW, GHIGH);
      PRINTRESULTS(GDAYS, GMPG, GMPGTODATE, GMILES,
                   GMILESTODATE, GAVGMILES, GLOW,
                   GHIGH);
      CONTINUE(GDONE)
   UNTIL GDONE

END.
```

Summary

This chapter discussed the syntax and use of the three types of local variables. In addition to the local variables declared under the procedure heading, there are formal parameters declared in parentheses after the procedure identifier. The two types of formal parameters, value and variable parameters, each have a particular use in programming.

Value parameters are used for procedure input from a calling block. The procedure heading indicates the order and type of parameters that the procedure will accept. Value parameters do not return any information to the calling block.

Variable parameters allow both variable input and output in a procedure. The arguments passed must be variables and are listed in the procedure call. This list corresponds to the parameter list of the procedure heading, which lists variable parameters with the word VAR preceding the declaration.

A procedure identifier that must be used before the procedure is defined may be declared in advance using the FORWARD declaration.

Key Terms

actual parameters   FORWARD
data flow diagram   value parameters
formal parameters   variable parameters

Answers to Lesson Checks

Lesson 8.1

1. **a.** A, B, C, and RESULT are actual parameters.
   b. X, Y, Z, ANSWER, L, M, and N are formal parameters.
   c. A, B, C, and RESULT are global variables.
   d. COUNT, X, Y, Z, ANSWER, L, M, and N are local variables.
   e. X, Y, and Z are value parameters.
   f. L, M, N, and ANSWER are variable parameters.

2. **a.** Global variables are known to the entire program. Local variables are known only to the block where they are declared.
   b. Actual parameters are listed in the procedure call. Formal parameters are listed in the procedure heading.
   c. Value parameters are sent to a procedure with a predefined value, but do not return a value to the calling block. Variable parameters are sent to a procedure with or without a predefined value; they return a value to the calling block.

Lesson 8.2

1. **a.** ONE and TWO are variable parameters. THREE is a value parameter.
   b. TWO is a variable parameter. ONE and THREE are value parameters.
   c. FOUR is a variable parameter. ONE, TWO, and THREE are value parameters.

2. **a.** PROCEDURE GOOD (IDENTIFIERNAME : INTEGER);
      (Missing identifier)
   b. PROCEDURE BETTER (A : REAL; B : INTEGER);
      (Semicolon replaces comma)
   c. PROCEDURE BEST (VAR B, C : STRING; A, D : REAL);
      (Extra VAR removed. Comma and semicolon switched.)

3. **a.** False.
   b. True.

Exercises

Set I. Comprehension

Use the following declarations for Exercises 1 and 2.

```
PROGRAM S (INPUT  OUTPUT);

VAR
   DISTANCE,
   RATE,
   TIME      : REAL;

PROCEDURE COMPUTE (D, T : REAL; VAR R : REAL);

   VAR
      N : INTEGER;

      .
      .
      .

PROCEDURE OUT (SPEED : REAL; NUM : INTEGER);
```

1. Classify each of the following variables as local or global:
   a. DISTANCE
   b. RATE
   c. TIME
   d. D
   e. T
   f. R
   g. N
   h. SPEED
   i. NUM

2. Classify each of the following as a value or variable parameter:
   a. D
   b. R
   c. T
   d. SPEED
   e. NUM

3. Assume the following declarations (and that variables have been initialized):

```
PROGRAM FINAL (INPUT, OUTPUT);

VAR
    N    : INTEGER;
    V,
    A    : REAL;
    PASS : BOOLEAN;

PROCEDURE TEST (NUM : INTEGER; SCORE : REAL;
                VAR AVE : REAL; FLAG : BOOLEAN);
```

   Which of the following statements are valid in the main program block?
   a. TEST(N,V,A,PASS);
   b. TEST(N);
   c. TEST(N,V,PASS,A);
   d. TEST(5,A,V,PASS);
   e. PASS := TEST(N,V,A,PASS);
   f. TEST(N+1,V,A,NOT(PASS));

4. Assume the following declarations (and that variables have been initialized):

```
PROGRAM TEST (INPUT, OUTPUT);

VAR
    ONE    : INTEGER;
    TWO,
    THREE : REAL;
    FOUR  : STRING;

PROCEDURE PTEST (VAR O : INTEGER; T : REAL;
                 VAR TH : REAL; FOUR : STRING);
```

Which of the following statements are valid in the main program block?

a. `PTEST(0, T, TH, F);`
b. `PTEST(ONE, 6.5, THREE, 'BOB');`
c. `PTEST(ONE, TWO + 1, THREE, FOUR);`
d. `PTEST(1, 2.0, 3.0, 'FOUR');`
e. `NUMBER := PTEST(ONE, TWO, THREE, FOUR);`
f. `PTEST(ONE, 2);`

5. Write a procedure heading for procedure FIVE that declares A to be a REAL value parameter, FLAG to be a BOOLEAN variable parameter, and NUM to be an INTEGER variable parameter.

6. Write a procedure heading for procedure SIX that declares LETTER to be a STRING variable parameter, PASS to be a BOOLEAN value parameter, and NUMBER1 and NUMBER2 to be INTEGER value parameters.

7. What output is produced by the following program?

```
PROGRAM DEF(OUTPUT);

VAR
    A,
    B : INTEGER;

PROCEDURE ADD (VAR A : INTEGER; B : INTEGER);

    BEGIN
        B := B + 1;
        A := A + 1
    END;

BEGIN
    A := 0;
    B := 0;
    ADD(A, B);
    WRITE(A, B)
END.
```

8. What output is produced by the following program?

```
PROGRAM PASS(OUTPUT);

VAR
    NUM : INTEGER;

PROCEDURE INCREMENT (VAR ANUM,BNUM : INTEGER);

    BEGIN
        ANUM := ANUM + 1;
        BNUM := BNUM + 1
    END;

BEGIN
    NUM := 3;
    INCREMENT(NUM, NUM);
    WRITE(NUM)
END.
```

9. Correct the errors in the following program. The program should count the number of dice rolls needed to reach a total of 20 or more.

```
PROGRAM DICE (INPUT, OUTPUT);

VAR TOTAL,
    NUMBER,
    COUNT  : INTEGER;

PROCEDURE GETROLL (ROLL : INTEGER);

    WRITELN('ENTER VALUE OF DICE ROLL (1-6)');
    READLN(ROLL);

PROCEDURE ADD (VAR N, C : INTEGER; SUM : INTEGER);

    BEGIN
      REPEAT
        C := C + 1;
        SUM := SUM + C;
        GETROLL(N)
      UNTIL SUM >= 20
    END;

BEGIN  { MAIN PROGRAM }

    COUNT := 0;
    TOTAL := 20;
    GETROLL(NUMBER);
    ADD(NUMBER, COUNT, TOTAL);
    WRITELN('NUMBER OF ROLLS: ', COUNT)

END.
```

10. What will be the contents of the variables J, K, DIFF, and SUM after the following program is executed?

```
PROGRAM CHANGE (OUTPUT);

VAR
    J,
    K,
    DIFF,
    SUM   : INTEGER;

PROCEDURE DIFFERENCE (NUM1, NUM2 : INTEGER;
                      VAR DELTA : INTEGER);

    BEGIN
       DELTA := NUM1 - NUM2;
       WRITELN('THE DIFFERENCE IS ', DELTA)
    END;
```

```
BEGIN   { MAIN PROGRAM }

    SUM := 0;
    FOR J := 1 TO 4 DO
        BEGIN
            K := J * J;
            DIFFERENCE(K, J, DIFF);
            SUM := SUM + DIFF
        END;
    WRITE('SUM OF (X SQUARED - X) ');
    WRITELN('FOR X = 1,2,3,4 IS ', SUM)

END.
```

11. What will be the contents of the variables S, FLAG, Q, and P after the following program is executed?

```
PROGRAM TEST (OUTPUT);

VAR
    FLAG : BOOLEAN;
    P,
    Q,
    S    : INTEGER;

PROCEDURE A (J : INTEGER;
             VAR FLAGA : BOOLEAN); FORWARD;

PROCEDURE B (VAR K : INTEGER;
             VAR FLAGB : BOOLEAN);

    BEGIN
      K := K * 2;
      FLAGB := (K < 10);
      IF NOT FLAGB THEN A(K,FLAGB)
    END;

PROCEDURE A;  {J : INTEGER; VAR FLAGA : BOOLEAN }

    BEGIN
        FLAGA := (J IN [1..10])
    END;

BEGIN   { MAIN PROGRAM }

    S := 0;
    FLAG := TRUE;
    FOR Q := 1 TO 5 DO
        BEGIN
            P := Q;
            IF (P = 2) OR (P = 4)
                THEN A(P, FLAG)
                ELSE B(P, FLAG);
            S := S + P
        END;
    WRITELN(S)

END.
```

12. Trace the value of the global variables in the following program:

```
PROGRAM MULT (OUTPUT);

VAR
    SUM,
    J,
    K      : INTEGER;

PROCEDURE SQCU (VAR NUM : INTEGER);

    BEGIN
        IF ODD(NUM)
            THEN NUM := NUM * NUM
            ELSE NUM := NUM * NUM * NUM
        END;

BEGIN  { MAIN PROGRAM }

    SUM := 0;
    FOR J := 1 TO 5 DO
        BEGIN
            K := J;
            SQCU(K);
            SUM := SUM + K;
            WRITE('J = ',J,'  K = ',K);
            WRITELN(' SUM = ',SUM)
        END

END.
```

Set II. Application

13. Complete the following procedure. The variable CODE indicates the type of transaction, AMOUNT is the amount deposited or withdrawn, and NET is the current amount in the account.

```
PROCEDURE BANKACCOUNT (CODE : CHAR; AMOUNT : REAL;
                            VAR NET : REAL);

{ THIS PROCEDURE WILL DETERMINE IF A TRANSACTION
    IS A DEPOSIT (OR CHECK) AND ADD (SUBTRACT) THE
    AMOUNT TO (FROM) THE NET BALANCE. }
```

14. Given the following program, write procedure BILL. The procedure computes the running total of a grocery bill.

```
PROGRAM GROCERIES (INPUT, OUTPUT);

VAR
    MORE  : BOOLEAN;
    TOTAL,
    PRICE : REAL;
    NUM   : INTEGER;

{ PROCEDURE BILL here. }
```

```
BEGIN

    TOTAL := 0;
    MORE := TRUE;
    WRITELN('THIS PROGRAM FINDS THE TOTAL BILL');
    WRITELN('FROM A VISIT TO THE SUPERMARKET.');
    WRITELN('FIRST ENTER THE PRICE OF AN ITEM,');
    WRITELN('THEN THE NUMBER OF ITEMS PURCHASED');
    WRITELN('AT THAT PRICE.');
    WRITELN('ENTER 0 FOR PRICE WHEN FINISHED.');
    WRITELN;
    WHILE MORE DO
        BEGIN
            WRITELN('ENTER PRICE AND QUANTITY');
            READLN(PRICE, NUM);
            IF PRICE <> 0
                THEN BILL(PRICE, NUM, TOTAL)
                ELSE MORE := FALSE
        END;
    WRITELN('THE TOTAL AMOUNT DUE IS ', TOTAL)

END.
```

15. Given the following program, write procedures SUE, MIKE, and TOM.

```
PROGRAM ANSWERSERVICE (INPUT, OUTPUT);

{ THIS PROGRAM KEEPS TRACK OF A DAY'S TELEPHONE
  CALLS ACCORDING TO A CLIENT'S SPECIFIC NEEDS. }

VAR
    CODE                 : CHAR;
    MIKETOTAL, SUETOTAL,
    TOMTOT1, TOMTOT2     : INTEGER;
    PHONE                : INTEGER[7];

{ PROCEDURE SUE here. Sue wants the total
  number of calls. }

{ PROCEDURE MIKE here. Mike wants the total
  number of calls from out of town; that is,
  numbers not beginning with 754, 752, or 753. }

{ PROCEDURE TOM here. Tom wants separate totals
  for numbers beginning with 486 and 487. }
```

```
BEGIN { MAIN PROGRAM }

   MIKETOTAL := 0;
   SUETOTAL := 0;
   TOMTOT1 := 0;
   TOMTOT2 := 0;
   WRITELN('ENTER 7-DIGIT PHONE NUMBER AND CODE');
   WRITELN('S = SUE, M = MIKE, T = TOM');
   WRITELN('ENTER 0 FOR PHONE NUMBER WHEN DONE');
   WRITELN;
   REPEAT
      WRITELN('NUMBER AND CODE');
      READLN(PHONE, CODE);
      IF (PHONE > 0) AND (CODE IN ['M','S','T'])
         THEN CASE CODE OF
                  'M' : MIKE(PHONE,MIKETOTAL);
                  'S' : SUE(PHONE,SUETOTAL);
                  'T' : TOM(PHONE,TOMTOT1,TOMTOT2)
              END { CASE }
   UNTIL PHONE = 0;
   WRITELN('CALLS FOR SUE: ', SUETOTAL);
   WRITELN('CALLS FOR MIKE: ', MIKETOTAL);
   WRITELN('486-CALLS FOR TOM: ', TOMTOT1);
   WRITELN('487-CALLS FOR TOM: ', TOMTOT2)

END.
```

16. Given the following program, write procedures GETDATA, PROCESSDATA, and PRINTDATA.

```
PROGRAM AREARCT (INPUT, OUTPUT);

{ PROGRAM FINDS THE AREA OF A RECTANGLE, CIRCLE
  OR TRIANGLE. }

VAR
   AREA,
   SIDE,
   HEIGHT : REAL;
   SHAPE  : CHAR;

{ PROCEDURE GETDATA here. It should ask if shape
  is rectangle, circle, or triangle and get
  appropriate data. }

{ PROCEDURE PROCESSDATA here. It should find area
  using
        area of rectangle = side × height
        area of circle = 3.14159 × side × side
        (use side for radius and a constant pi)
        area of triangle = .5 × side × height
        (use side for base) }

{ PROCEDURE PRINTDATA here. It should print type
  of shape and area. }
```

```
BEGIN   { MAIN PROGRAM }

   GETDATA(SHAPE, SIDE, HEIGHT);
   PROCESSDATA(SHAPE, SIDE, HEIGHT, AREA);
   PRINTDATA(SHAPE, AREA)

END.
```

17. Write a program that averages a sequence of consecutive numbers. The length of the sequence of numbers and the starting number should be passed as value parameters. The average should be passed as a variable parameter.

18. Write a program to determine the measure of the hypotenuse (C) of a right triangle, if the measures of the legs (A and B) are given; use the Pythagorean Theorem:

$$C^2 = A^2 + B^2$$

A procedure should be written that will solve for the measure of the hypotenuse. The measures of the legs should be passed by value and the variable name representing the hypotenuse should be a variable parameter.

Extension: Write a program to solve for any side of a right triangle, if the other two sides are given.

19. No Problems Insurance Company has three types of collision insurance policies. Type 1 pays 90 percent with $400 deductible (that is, the company pays nothing if the damage is $400 or less and (damage amount − 400) × .9 if the damage exceeds $400). Type 2 pays 70 percent with $200 deductible. Type 3 pays 65 percent with $100 deductible. Write a program to compute the total awarded to each policy type using the 10 following claims:

Amount	Policy
500	1
300	1
350	3
200	1
320	2
150	2
600	3
50	3
250	2
900	2

(For some help in solving this exercise, look back to Figures 8.6 and 8.7 in Lesson 8.3.)

Set III. Synthesis

20. Write a program to compute the score for the first frame of a
bowling game. The score for a frame is found by adding the
number of pins knocked down by two rolls of a ball. If the player
knocks down all of the pins on the first roll, it is called a strike
(X) and the player skips the second roll. If the player does not get a
strike, but knocks down the rest of the pins with the second roll,
it is called a spare (/). A spare is counted as 10 plus the number of
pins knocked down on the first roll of the next frame. A strike is
counted as 10 plus the number of pins knocked down on the next
two rolls.

   If the user enters 10 for the first ball (a strike), the program
should ask for two more values (the number of pins knocked
down by each of the next two rolls). If the user enters a total of 10
for the first and second ball (a spare), the program should ask for
one more value.

   Here are some samples of program interaction.

```
ENTER ROLL 1: 4
ENTER ROLL 2: 6
ENTER ROLL 3: 5
SCORE FOR FRAME IS 15

ENTER ROLL 1: 7
ENTER ROLL 2: 2
SCORE FOR FRAME IS 9

ENTER ROLL 1: 10
ENTER ROLL 2: 9
ENTER ROLL 3: 0
SCORE FOR FRAME IS 19
```

21. The Law of Sines and Cosines allows computation of missing
angles or sides in a triangle when certain information about the
triangle is provided. Write a program to calculate three unknown
parts of a triangle when three parts are given. The program should
pass three value parameters (three positive (known) values) to a
procedure and three variable parameters (unknown). There are five
possibilities:

   1. Angle, side, angle.
   2. Side, angle, side.
   3. Angle, angle, side.
   4. Side, side, angle. (This is the ambiguous case. Include only as
       an extension.)
   5. Side, side, side.

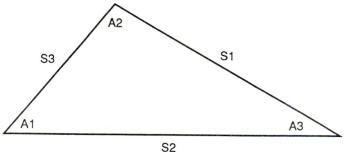

The data must be entered in the order that it appears in the triangle, clockwise or counterclockwise. For example, in the following triangle, the remaining parts may be found by entering the values for A1, A2, and S1 using the third possibility listed (angle, angle, side). (Angles should be entered in radians.)

Extension: For the ambiguous case (the fourth possibility), the given information can result in 0, 1, or 2 triangles being formed. Revise the program to account for these possibilities.

22. In order to find the time for a high or low ocean tide in a particular area, tide tables include a positive or negative time adjustment factor. For example, a Boston Tide Table says the morning high tide for a particular date is at 6:00 A.M. The tide correction table lists a time difference of -1 hour, 33 minutes for Los Angeles. Find the time for the morning high tide in Los Angeles by

$$
\begin{array}{r}
6 \text{ hours} \quad 0 \text{ minutes} \\
-1 \text{ hour} \quad 33 \text{ minutes} \\
\hline
\end{array}
$$

To perform the calculations, rewrite 6 hours to include minutes, as

$$
\begin{array}{r}
5 \text{ hours} \quad 60 \text{ minutes} \\
-1 \text{ hour} \quad 33 \text{ minutes} \\
\hline
\end{array}
$$

or

4:27 A.M.

Write a program that will add two times and print the answer in the form hh:mm.

23. Write a program to find a player's total score for five hands in a pinochle game. For each hand, the user should enter the bid (if any), points for meld and points for play of the hand. If the player did not take a bid, the score for the hand is equal to the points for meld plus the points for play of the hand. If the player took a bid, the score is
   a. Meld plus play of hand, if this sum is greater than or equal to the bid amount.
   b. $-$ Bid amount, if the meld plus play of hand is less than the bid amount.
   For example,

   Bid = 20   Meld = 4   Play of hand = 17
   $4 + 17 \geq 20$, so score for hand is 21.

   Bid = 0   Meld = 5   Play of hand = 4
   Score for hand is 9.

   Bid = 21   Meld = 11   Play of hand = 5
   $11 + 5 < 21$, so score for hand is -21.

The program should print each score as points for a hand are entered, then print the total score for the five hands.

24. Permutations involve all the arrangements of n distinct things taken r at a time

$$(1 \leq r \leq n)$$

Repetitions are not allowed. For example, the letters A, B, and C have possible permutations of ABC, ACB, BCA, BAC, CAB, and CBA when taken three at a time. ABA is not a permutation of the letters A, B, and C since a letter is repeated. If the letters were to be taken two at a time, the permutations would be AB, AC, BA, BC, CA, CB. The number of possible permutations of n distinct things taken r at a time can be computed by

$$_nP_r = \frac{n!}{(n-r)!}$$

For $n = 3$ and $r = 2$, the number of permutations $_3P_2$ is

$$\frac{3!}{(3-2)!} = \frac{6}{1} = 6$$

For $n = 3$ and $r = 3$, $_3P_3$ is

$$\frac{3!}{(3-3)!} = \frac{6}{1} = 6$$

(0! is defined as 1.)

If there are seven horses in a race, designated by the letters A through G, how many ways can three finish first, second, and third? Write a program to count and list all the permutations ($n = 7$, $r = 3$) and use the permutation formula to double-check the number of permutations.

Writing Functions

"I must be growing small again." She got up and went to the table to measure herself by it, and found that, as nearly as she could guess, she was now about two feet high, and was going on shrinking rapidly: she soon found out that the cause of this was the fan she was holding, and she dropped it hastily, just in time to save herself from shrinking away altogether.

—Lewis Carroll

Overview

Gaining a Perspective

Pascal functions are similar in many ways to procedures. There are many built-in functions, like SQRT or EXP, as well as built-in procedures, like READLN and WRITELN. In addition to these built-in functions and procedures, the programmer may write functions or procedures which are tailor-made to meet specific needs. The programmer-defined functions and procedures are located in the same position in a program: after the global variable declaration and before the main program. Both functions and procedures can be written to perform tasks that must be done several times in a program.

The differences between functions and procedures are also important to recognize. Procedures may accept either value or variable parameters and return a single value, many values, or no value to the calling block. Functions, on the other hand, generally accept only expressions (value parameters) and usually return a single value to the function call. The main purpose of a function is to represent a single value. The syntax of a function also differs somewhat from procedures and will be introduced in this chapter.

Lesson 9.1 Functions

To begin, Program 9.1 uses a function, BIGGER, to find the larger of two numbers entered by the user. The reserved word **FUNCTION** denotes the beginning of a function.

Program 9.1

```
PROGRAM LARGEST (INPUT,OUTPUT);

      { PURPOSE: TO FIND THE LARGER OF TWO NUMBERS
        USING A FUNCTION }

VAR
    NUMBER1,
    NUMBER2  : INTEGER;
    ANSWER   : STRING;

FUNCTION BIGGER (FIRST, SECOND : INTEGER) : INTEGER;

      { PURPOSE: FIND LARGER OF TWO INTEGERS }
```

```
        BEGIN

            IF FIRST > SECOND
                THEN BIGGER := FIRST
                ELSE BIGGER := SECOND

            END;   { BIGGER }

    BEGIN   { MAIN PROGRAM }

        REPEAT

            WRITE('ENTER TWO INTEGERS:  ');
            READLN(NUMBER1, NUMBER2);
            WRITE('THE LARGER IS ');
            WRITELN(BIGGER(NUMBER1, NUMBER2));
            WRITE('DO YOU WISH TO ENTER NEW VALUES?');
            WRITELN(' (YES/NO)');
            READLN(ANSWER)

        UNTIL ANSWER = 'NO'

    END.
```

In Program 9.1, BIGGER is called in the main program by the **function call**, BIGGER(NUMBER1, NUMBER2). The local variables of BIGGER (FIRST and SECOND) are INTEGER value parameters and the global variables, NUMBER1 and NUMBER2, are the INTEGER values sent to BIGGER. Within the body of the function a **function assignment** must be made; that is, the function identifier (BIGGER) is assigned a value, by

```
IF FIRST > SECOND
    THEN BIGGER := FIRST
    ELSE BIGGER := SECOND
```

Although there are two assignments to BIGGER, only one assignment will be made (the condition is either TRUE or FALSE). The value of BIGGER is sent back to the function call and is of type INTEGER, as indicated at the end of the function heading.

Caution: The assignment to a function identifier is not legal outside of the function portion of the program. For example, in Program 9.1, the assignment to the name of the function can only occur in function BIGGER. A function generally returns a single value whose type is indicated at the end of the function heading, as shown in Figure 9.1.

A function is called by using the function identifier in an expression. The function is evaluated when it is called as is a procedure call. During the execution of the function, a value is assigned to the function identifier. Upon completion, this value is returned to the function call through the function identifier. Here are some variations on the function call of Program 9.1.

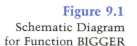

Figure 9.1
Schematic Diagram
for Function BIGGER

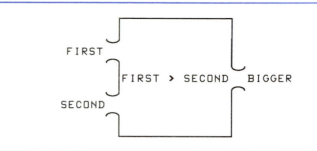

```
WRITELN('THE LARGER IS ', BIGGER(NUMBER2, NUMBER1));

IF BIGGER(NUMBER1, NUMBER2) > 100 THEN statement;

REPEAT
    statement
UNTIL BIGGER(NUMBER1, NUMBER2) = 0;

WHILE BIGGER(NUMBER1, NUMBER2) <> 0 DO
    statement;

LARGE := BIGGER(NUMBER1, NUMBER2);
{ LARGE MUST BE DECLARED AN INTEGER }
```

In each example, the function call is used as an expression and never alone.

The function heading and body may be written as follows:

FUNCTION Heading and Body Form

```
FUNCTION identifier(parameters:type):functiontype;

    const or var list

    BEGIN
        .
        .
        .

        identifier := expression;
        .
        .
        .

    END;
```

The parameters of a function usually consist of value parameters of a simple data type, which includes BOOLEAN, CHAR, INTEGER, REAL, or STRING. The function type is the type of the returning or resulting value of the function, and must be a simple data type (that is, BOOLEAN, CHAR, INTEGER, or REAL), a subrange (see Chapter 11), or a pointer type (see Chapter 17).

Notice that the punctuation of the function heading is a little different than the punctuation of a procedure heading. As shown in the following examples, a colon separates the parameters of the function and the function type:

```
FUNCTION QUADRATIC (NUMBER : REAL) : REAL;

FUNCTION ANSWER (NUMBER : INTEGER) : BOOLEAN;

FUNCTION LETTER (WORD1, WORD2 : STRING;
                 NUMBER : INTEGER) : CHAR;
```

Function QUADRATIC is passed a value parameter, NUMBER, and returns a REAL value to its calling statement. Function ANSWER is passed NUMBER (an INTEGER) and returns a BOOLEAN value. Function LETTER is passed two STRING values and an INTEGER, and returns a CHAR value.

Usually a function returns a single value. Although the use of variable parameters is permitted in functions (to return more than one value), it is not advised. If a calculation requires the return of more than a single value, a procedure should be used. If you are in doubt regarding the choice of function versus procedure, then use a procedure.

Pascal programmers can think of functions as subroutines that answer a single question (represent a single value) and procedures as accomplishing a more general task. The following examples and explanations clarify the differences between functions and procedures:

Calls

Function and procedure calls are similar in that both include the identifier followed by the parameters, if any, that are sent. A function call must be part of an expression, whereas a procedure call is a Pascal statement.

Headings

```
FUNCTION identifier(parameters):functiontype;

PROCEDURE identifier (parameters);
```

A function must return a value to the calling block, as specified at the end of the function heading; a procedure may or may not return any desired values to the calling block through variable parameters.

Assignment of a Value

The function identifier must be assigned a value within the function block. In contrast, the procedure identifier is never assigned a value.

As indicated, functions are handy to use if a calculation returns a single value and the calculation is repeated many times. For example, suppose a rancher has 540 feet of fencing. What are the dimensions of the largest field that the rancher can fence? Program 9.2 uses a function, called AREA, to compute the area of a rectangle. The program then tests possible lengths and widths until it finds the dimensions of the rectangular field that would provide the largest area.

Program 9.2

```
PROGRAM CALCULATE (OUTPUT);

    { PURPOSE: TO DEMONSTRATE FUNCTIONS }

CONST
    PERIMETER = 540;

VAR
    LENGTH,
    MAXLEN,
    WIDTH,
    MAXWID,
    MAXAREA,
    TEMPAREA    : REAL;

FUNCTION AREA (L, W : REAL): REAL;

    BEGIN

        AREA := L * W  { FUNCTION ASSIGNMENT }

    END;

BEGIN   { MAIN PROGRAM }
    WIDTH := 1;
    MAXAREA := 1;
    WRITELN('LENGTH', 'WIDTH':7, 'AREA':8);
    REPEAT
        LENGTH := (PERIMETER - 2 * WIDTH)/2;
        TEMPAREA := AREA(LENGTH, WIDTH);
        WRITELN(LENGTH:5:1, WIDTH:7:1, TEMPAREA:8:1);
        IF MAXAREA < TEMPAREA
            THEN
                BEGIN
                    MAXAREA := TEMPAREA;
                    MAXLEN := LENGTH;
                    MAXWID := WIDTH
                END;
        WIDTH := WIDTH + 1
    UNTIL (WIDTH >= PERIMETER/2) OR (WIDTH >= LENGTH);
    WRITELN('THE MAXIMUM DIMENSIONS ARE: ');
    WRITELN('    LENGTH = ', MAXLEN:5:1);
    WRITELN('    WIDTH  = ', MAXWID:5:1);
    WRITELN('    AREA   = ', MAXAREA:5:1)
END.
```

In Program 9.2, AREA is called in the main program by the function call AREA(LENGTH,WIDTH). The local variables of AREA, L and W, are value parameters. The global variables, LENGTH and WIDTH, are the values of the length and width that are sent to AREA. The value of AREA is sent back to the main program and is of type REAL, as indicated at the end of the function heading. Note the use of the variable, TEMPAREA, to store the value of function AREA. This allows the function value to be used in several places without calling the function again.

Caution: Although a function identifier is used like a variable in the assignment to the function, it is not a variable. The function identifier is used like a variable only within the function to make an assignment to the function. In Program 9.2, for example, the function identifier, AREA, will never be on the left side of an assignment statement outside of the function portion of the program.

Program Segment 9.3 shows possible errors caused by using a function identifier as if it were a variable. Function identifiers cannot be read, written, or tested without their parameter lists. Remember: If used in an expression such as a conditional or in a WRITELN, make sure to include the parameter list of the function.

Program Segment 9.3

```
FUNCTION AREA (L, W : REAL) : REAL;

     { PURPOSE: TO WARN OF ERROR}

BEGIN

    READLN(AREA);                    {ILLEGAL}

    IF AREA < 0                      {ILLEGAL}
       THEN WRITELN('MUST ENTER POSITIVE VALUES');

    AREA : = AREA(L, W) + L * W;    {LEGAL}

    WRITELN(AREA)                    {ILLEGAL}

END;
```

A function call must include its parameter list. A function call cannot be used in a READLN, but can be used as the expression of an IF . . . THEN or WRITELN statement, if the parameter list is included. The statement

```
AREA : = AREA(L, W) + L * W;
```

which uses the function identifier AREA on both sides of the assignment statement within a function, is a legal statement. On the right side of the assignment statement, the function is called again within the function itself. As we will see in Chapter 10, this process is called recursion.

Lesson Check 9.1

1. Correct each of the following function headings:
   a. FUNCTION TIME (HOURS, MINUTES,
                     SECONDS : INTEGER); REAL;
   b. FUNCTION CUBEROOT (NUMBER : REAL);

2. Identify each of the following statements as true or false:
   a. A function may be assigned a value anywhere in the body of a program.
   b. The use of variable parameters in a function is legal, but not recommended.

3. How do function calls differ from procedure calls?

Lesson 9.2   Using Functions

Functions can be nested within a procedure or function. The scope rules apply equally to functions and procedures. As shown in Program 9.4, the most local variables have precedence.

Program 9.4

```
PROGRAM INTEREST (INPUT, OUTPUT);

     { PURPOSE: TO CALCULATE COMPOUND INTEREST }

VAR
    PRINCIPAL,
    RATE          : REAL;
    TIME,
    NUMOFPERIODS : INTEGER;

PROCEDURE GETINFO (VAR P,R:REAL; VAR T,N:INTEGER);

    BEGIN

        WRITELN('COMPOUND INTEREST COMPUTATIONS');
        WRITE('ENTER THE PRINCIPAL: ');
        READLN(P);
        WRITE('ENTER THE RATE: ');
        READLN(R);
        WRITE('ENTER THE TIME OF THE INVESTMENT: ');
        READLN(T);
        WRITE('ENTER THE NUMBER OF PERIODS PER YEAR: ');
        READLN(N)

    END;  { GETINFO }

PROCEDURE TABLE (P, R : REAL; T, N : INTEGER);

    FUNCTION COMPOUND (P,R:REAL; T,N:INTEGER):REAL;

        VAR
            COUNT : INTEGER;
            AMT   : REAL;

        BEGIN
            COUNT := 0;
            AMT := 1;
            WHILE COUNT <> T * N DO
                BEGIN
                    AMT := AMT * (1 + R);
                    COUNT := COUNT + 1
                END;
            COMPOUND := P * AMT
        END;  { COMPOUND }
```

```
      BEGIN

         WRITELN('PRINCIPAL                    : ',P:5:2);
         WRITELN('RATE                         : ',R:5:2);
         WRITELN('TIME                         : ',T:5);
         WRITELN('NUMBER OF TIMES COMPOUNDED: ',N:5);
         WRITE('AMOUNT                        : ');
         WRITELN(COMPOUND(P,R,T,N):5:2)

      END;    { TABLE }

   BEGIN    { MAIN PROGRAM }

      GETINFO(PRINCIPAL, RATE, TIME, NUMOFPERIODS);
      TABLE(PRINCIPAL, RATE, TIME, NUMOFPERIODS)

   END.
```

The procedure GETINFO requests that the user enter the principal, rate, time, and the number of periods to be compounded. Procedure TABLE prints the information and the new principal. Function COMPOUND is nested within TABLE and known only to that procedure.

The RANDOM Function

Another use of functions is to generate random values. Random integers are often needed in games or simulations. UCSD Pascal has a built-in function and a procedure that aid the programmer in generating random values. **RANDOMIZE** is a special procedure that selects a random starting value or seed. (This procedure is a part of Apple Pascal and is stored in the SYSTEM.LIBRARY under the name APPLESTUFF. Other versions of Pascal vary in their approach.) The random function, **RANDOM** (also a part of Apple Pascal), returns an integer from 0 to 32767. The procedure RANDOMIZE is used once at the beginning of a program requiring random numbers and the function RANDOM is used each time a random number is desired.

The integer operator MOD (the remainder when integers are divided) may be used with RANDOM to generate various ranges of random values. The examples presented in Figures 9.2 to 9.5 generate random numbers within a given range of values. These examples are expressions, not complete Pascal statements.

In Figure 9.2, the word RANDOM calls the function and returns an integer between 0 and 32767, inclusive. The MOD operation gives the remainder after each random integer has been divided by 100. The possible remainders, when dividing by 100, are between 0 and 99, inclusive.

The MOD divisor selected for each problem equals the number of random numbers desired (the difference between the highest and lowest value plus one, if the numbers are consecutive). If, for example, 21 random numbers are needed—as in Figure 9.5—the expression RANDOM MOD 21 is used. Other operations are used to adjust the final random values.

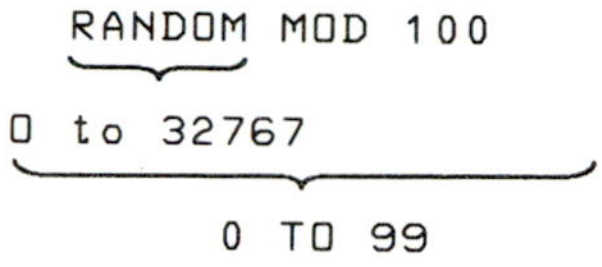

Figure 9.2
Random Integers
between 0 and 99

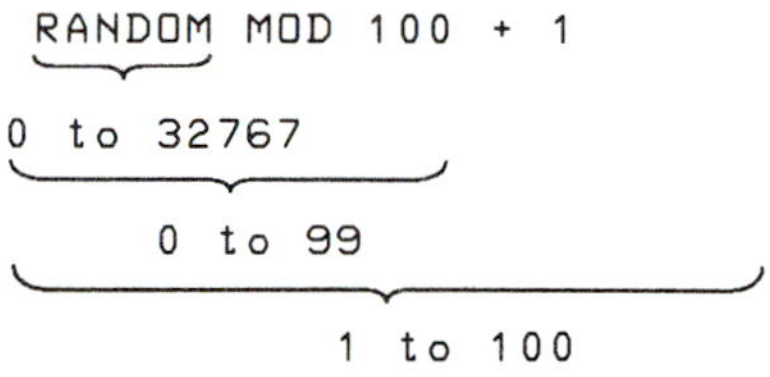

```
          RANDOM MOD 100
          ‿‿‿‿‿‿

     0 to 32767
     ‿‿‿‿‿‿‿‿‿

          0 TO 99
```

Figure 9.3
Random Integers
between 1 and 100

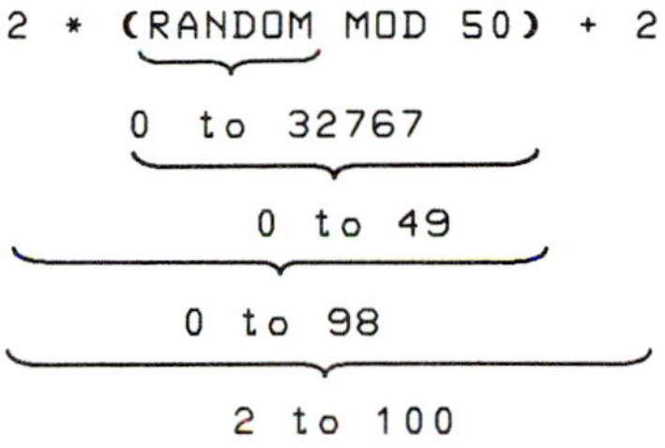

```
        RANDOM MOD 100 + 1
        ‿‿‿‿‿‿

     0 to 32767
     ‿‿‿‿‿‿‿‿‿

          0 to 99
          ‿‿‿‿‿‿‿‿‿

               1 to 100
```

Figure 9.4
Random Even Integers
between 2 and 100

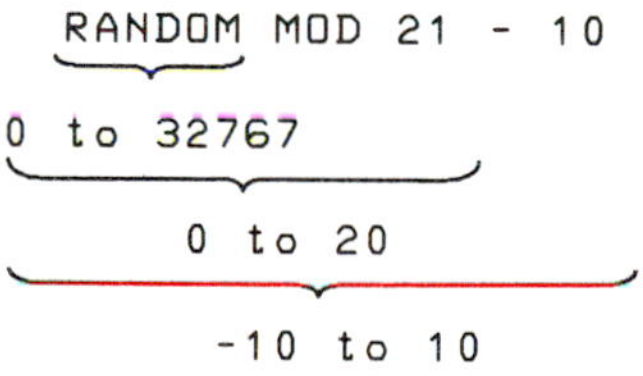

```
     2 * (RANDOM MOD 50) + 2
            ‿‿‿‿‿‿

          0 to 32767
          ‿‿‿‿‿‿‿‿

               0 to 49
          ‿‿‿‿‿‿‿‿‿

               0 to 98
               ‿‿‿‿‿‿‿‿‿

               2 to 100
```

Figure 9.5
Random Integers
between −10 and 10

```
          RANDOM MOD 21 - 10
          ‿‿‿‿‿‿

     0 to 32767
     ‿‿‿‿‿‿‿‿

          0 to 20
     ‿‿‿‿‿‿‿‿‿

          -10 to 10
```

The technique for generating random integers is demonstrated by Program 9.5. (This program and Program 9.6 specify, via the statement USES APPLESTUFF, that a unit from the Apple SYSTEM.LIBRARY is used.) In the main program, RANDOMIZE is called once to establish a random starting value. The programmer-defined function RND is called, sending the minimum and maximum random number desired. Function RND will return a value within the range of values, minimum to maximum, selected by the user. RND contains the following formula for generating random integers within the range of LOW to HIGH:

```
RANDOM MOD (HIGH - LOW + 1) + LOW
```

Program 9.5 generates random integers between a user-selected minimum and maximum value.

Program 9.5

```
PROGRAM SELECTRANDOM (INPUT,OUTPUT);

USES APPLESTUFF;

VAR
    MINIMUM,
    MAXIMUM,
    ANSWER    : INTEGER;

FUNCTION RND(LOW, HIGH : INTEGER) : INTEGER;

    { GENERATE A RANDOM NUMBER }

    BEGIN

        RND := RANDOM MOD (HIGH - LOW + 1) + LOW

    END;   { RND }

BEGIN   { MAIN PROGRAM }

    RANDOMIZE;
    WRITELN('ENTER THE MINIMUM AND MAXIMUM NUMBERS.');
    READLN(MINIMUM, MAXIMUM);
    ANSWER := RND(MINIMUM, MAXIMUM);
    WRITELN('THE RANDOM NUMBER SELECTED IS ',ANSWER)

END.
```

As mentioned earlier, random numbers play an important role in games. Bagels is a number-guessing game that provides the player with hints as the game progresses. First the computer randomly generates a three-digit number and then requests that the user guess the number in seven or fewer guesses. After the user makes a guess, the computer provides the user with some information about the guess. For example, the program prints BAGELS if the user's guess is entirely incorrect (that is, it contains no correct digits of the actual number). The computer prints PICO if a digit of the guess is a correct digit of the actual number, but in an incorrect place; and FERMI if a digit of the guess is a correct digit and is in the correct place. For example, if the computer-generated number is 574, the computer prints the following for each user guess:

Number	User Guess	Computer Message
1	123	BAGELS
2	456	PICO PICO
3	647	PICO PICO
4	564	FERMI FERMI
5	574	YOU ARE CORRECT

Program 9.6 uses the function RANDOM to generate a random three-digit integer from 100 to 999.

Program 9.6

```
PROGRAM BAGELS (INPUT, OUTPUT);

    { PURPOSE: TO PLAY THE GAME BAGELS USING
      FUNCTIONS AND PROCEDURES }

USES APPLESTUFF;    { APPLE LIBRARY UNIT }

VAR
    NUMBER,
    UNITS,
    TENS,
    HUNDREDS,
    GUESS,
    TRIES            : INTEGER;
    PLAY             : BOOLEAN;
    ANSWER           : STRING;

PROCEDURE INSTRUCTIONS;

    BEGIN

        WRITELN('BAGELS IS A NUMBER GUESSING GAME.');
        WRITELN('THE COMPUTER THINKS OF A THREE-');
        WRITELN('DIGIT NUMBER AND THE PLAYER TRIES');
        WRITELN('TO GUESS THE NUMBER. THE DIGITS');
        WRITELN('OF THE NUMBER ARE UNIQUE. IF THE');
        WRITELN('GUESS IS INCORRECT, CLUES ARE');
        WRITELN('PROVIDED. PICO MEANS A DIGIT');
        WRITELN('IS CORRECT BUT IN THE WRONG');
        WRITELN('POSITION. FERMI MEANS A DIGIT IS');
        WRITELN('CORRECT AND IN THE CORRECT POSITION.');
        WRITELN('BAGELS MEANS DIGITS IN THE GUESS');
        WRITELN('ARE WRONG. MULTIPLE PICOS AND FERMIS');
        WRITELN('INDICATE THE NUMBER OF DIGITS CORRECT');
        WRITELN('AND THE NUMBER OF DIGITS IN THE');
        WRITELN('CORRECT LOCATION. THE PLAYER WILL');
        WRITELN('HAVE SEVEN CHANCES TO GUESS THE');
        WRITELN('CORRECT NUMBER. GOOD LUCK!')

    END;   {INSTRUCTIONS }
```

```
PROCEDURE SELECTNUMBER (VAR N, U, T, H : INTEGER);

    { COMPUTER GENERATES A RANDOM
      THREE-DIGIT NUMBER }

  FUNCTION RND (LOW, HIGH : INTEGER) : INTEGER;

      { FUNCTION GENERATES A RANDOM DIGIT }

    BEGIN
       RND := RANDOM MOD (HIGH - LOW + 1) + LOW
    END;   { RND }

  BEGIN    { SELECTNUMBER }

    REPEAT
       U := RND(0, 9);
       T := RND(0, 9);
       H := RND(1, 9)
    UNTIL (U <> T) AND (U <> H) AND (T <> H);
    N := 100 * H + 10 * T + U

  END;   { SELECTNUMBER }

PROCEDURE USERGUESS (VAR GUESS : INTEGER;
                      TRIES : INTEGER);

  BEGIN

    WRITE('ENTER GUESS NUMBER ', TRIES, ': ');
    READLN(GUESS)

  END;   { USERGUESS }

PROCEDURE CHECK (GUESS, TRIES, N, U, T, H : INTEGER);

  { CHECKS USER GUESS BY COMPARING DIGITS OF GUESS
    WITH DIGITS OF RANDOM NUMBER }

  PROCEDURE HINTS (GUESS, N, U, T, H : INTEGER);

      { PROVIDES USER WITH HINTS AS TO THE
        CORRECT DIGITS AND POSITIONS }

    VAR
       COUNT,
       UNITGUESS,
       TENGUESS,
       HUNDREDGUESS,
       NUMPICO,
       NUMFERMI      : INTEGER;

    BEGIN

       NUMPICO := 0;
       NUMFERMI := 0;
       UNITGUESS := GUESS MOD 10;
       TENGUESS := (GUESS DIV 10) MOD 10;
       HUNDREDGUESS := GUESS DIV 100;
```

```
            IF  U  =  UNITGUESS
               THEN NUMFERMI := NUMFERMI + 1
               ELSE IF (U=TENGUESS) OR (U=HUNDREDGUESS)
                     THEN NUMPICO := NUMPICO + 1;
            IF  T  =  TENGUESS
               THEN NUMFERMI := NUMFERMI + 1
               ELSE IF (T=UNITGUESS) OR (T=HUNDREDGUESS)
                     THEN NUMPICO := NUMPICO + 1;
            IF  H  =  HUNDREDGUESS
               THEN NUMFERMI := NUMFERMI + 1
               ELSE IF (H=UNITGUESS) OR (H=TENGUESS)
                     THEN NUMPICO := NUMPICO + 1;
            IF (NUMPICO = 0) AND (NUMFERMI = 0)
               THEN WRITE('BAGELS')
               ELSE
                  BEGIN
                     FOR COUNT := 1 TO NUMPICO DO
                        WRITE('PICO ');
                     FOR COUNT := 1 TO NUMFERMI DO
                        WRITE('FERMI ')
                  END;
               WRITELN

      END;  { HINTS }

   BEGIN

      WHILE (GUESS <> N) AND (TRIES < 7) DO
         BEGIN
            HINTS(GUESS, N, U, T, H);
            TRIES := TRIES + 1;
            USERGUESS(GUESS, TRIES);
            IF TRIES = 7
               THEN WRITELN('THE NUMBER IS ', N)
         END;
      IF GUESS = N
         THEN WRITELN('YOU ARE CORRECT')

   END;  { CHECK }

BEGIN   { MAIN PROGRAM }

   INSTRUCTIONS;
   PLAY := TRUE;
   RANDOMIZE;    { TO GENERATE RANDOM SEED }
   WHILE PLAY DO
      BEGIN
         SELECTNUMBER(NUMBER, UNITS, TENS, HUNDREDS);
         TRIES := 1;
         USERGUESS(GUESS, TRIES);
         CHECK(GUESS, TRIES, NUMBER, UNITS,
               TENS, HUNDREDS);
         WRITELN('PLAY AGAIN? (YES/NO) ');
         READLN(ANSWER);
         IF ANSWER = 'NO'
            THEN PLAY := FALSE
      END

END.
```

FORWARD Declaration

As with procedures, a FORWARD declaration of a function may be necessary if the function is called by another subprogram prior to its declaration.

```
FORWARD Declaration Form

FUNCTION F1(parameters):functiontype; FORWARD;

PROCEDURE P1(parameters);

   BEGIN
      { STATEMENTS AND A CALL OF FUNCTION F1 }
   END;

FUNCTION F1;  { (parameters) }

   BEGIN
      { STATEMENTS OF FUNCTION F1 }
   END;
```

Notice that the first occurrence of the function heading includes the parameter list. When a function has been FORWARD declared, the second occurrence of the function heading does not include the parameter list. The parameter list may be added as a comment to the second occurrence of the function heading.

Lesson Check 9.2

1. Describe the integers generated by each of the following Pascal statements:
   a. RANDOM MOD 58 - 2
   b. RANDOM MOD (16 - 3 + 1) + 3
   c. 3 * RANDOM MOD 50 + 3

2. Identify each of the following statements as true or false. If false, explain.
   a. A function cannot be called before it has been defined.
   b. A function may be nested within another function or procedure.

Lesson 9.3   Programming Tip—Using Functions and Procedures

Now that functions and procedures (subprograms) are available for programming, several considerations must be taken about their use. The programmer needs to determine when subprograms should be used, how they will be used, and which is most appropriate for a given situation.

Knowing when to use a subprogram is an important skill for a programmer to master. There are times when adding a few lines to the main program is better than creating a new subprogram. Three things should be considered when deciding to use a subprogram; if any of these conditions exist, then a function or procedure is appropriate.

- Does the complexity of the problem require breaking it into more manageable parts? Breaking a problem into smaller parts is basic to the idea of problem solving. The solution is easier to understand and, if necessary, to revise.
- Does a process need to be repeated in various parts of the program? Rather than typing the same lines over again, creating a subprogram that can be called from wherever it is needed saves time as well as memory.
- Do the statements form an independent process that can be used with little knowledge of its inner workings? The use of subprograms is especially desirable if they can be used in various situations, given the information needed to complete each process (via parameters).

The choice between a function and a procedure is fairly easy to resolve. A procedure can be used in nearly every situation, since it is more flexible in its implementation. A function can be preferable, however, if a single value is to be returned.

The last question is the relationship of variables to subprograms. In general, all subprograms should communicate via parameters. The use of parameters eliminates the need for each subprogram to have direct access to global variables. The subprogram is then an independent block that can be used outside the original program and is understandable without inspecting the main program. Although making each subprogram self-contained seems like extra work, much confusion is avoided, especially as programs become larger. The programmer need only be concerned with the small number of identifiers in a particular subprogram rather than the larger number of global variables. As far as subprogram parameters are concerned, value parameters should be used unless a value must be returned to the calling block. Even though variable parameters require less memory, using them inappropriately can produce disastrous results, since the contents of a global variable may be unintentionally altered.

Summary

Programmer-defined functions are located after the global variable declaration and before the main program. The function call is identical to the call to a built-in function. The call must occur in an expression and list the parameters, if any, to be sent to the function in parentheses after the function identifier. The function heading consists of the reserved word FUNCTION followed by the function identifier, the list of parameters used within the function, and the type to be returned to the function call. Within the function, the function identifier must be assigned a value.

Functions should be used if a program needs a subprogram that returns a single value to the calling block. A subprogram should be written either if the routine adds to the clarity of the program or if the routine is needed many times in the program, or both.

Key Terms

FUNCTION   function call   RANDOMIZE
function assignment   RANDOM

Answers to
Lesson Checks

Lesson 9.1

1. a. FUNCTION TIME (HOURS, MINUTES,
                    SECONDS : INTEGER) : REAL;
(Replace semicolon preceding type.)
b. FUNCTION CUBEROOT (NUMBER : REAL) : REAL;
(Add function type.)

2. a. False.
b. True.

3. A function call is not a statement in itself, as is a procedure call. The function call must appear as part of an expression.

Lesson 9.2

1. a. -2 to 55
b. 3 to 16
c. 3 to 150 (in multiples of 3)

2. a. False. A function may be called before it has been defined by the use of the FORWARD declaration.
b. True.

Exercises

Set I. Comprehension

1. Identify each of the following statements as true or false. If false, explain.
   a. A function returns a value to the function call through a variable parameter.
   b. A function call is just like a procedure call.

2. Write a function for each of the following equations:
   a. $C = \sqrt{(A^2 + B^2)}$
   b. $Z = 5XY - 1$
   c. $S = \dfrac{2N}{.5} + 6(D - .3)$
   d. $A = 2PRH + 2PR^2$

3. Write a function for each of the following equations:
   a. $P = 2L + 2W$
   b. $A = \sqrt{(X^2 + Y^2 + Z^2)}$
   c. $R = \dfrac{1}{S} + \dfrac{1}{T}$
   d. $A = (P(1 + R))^T$

4. Assuming the function definition

   ```
   FUNCTION DAY (A,B : INTEGER) : INTEGER;
   ```

   which of the following statements is a valid Pascal statement? There may be more than one correct answer. (Assume LENGTH is of type INTEGER.)
   a. `DAY;`
   b. `DAY(1,3);`
   c. `READ(DAY(1,3));`
   d. `WRITELN(DAY(65, LENGTH));`
   e. `LENGTH := DAY(5, 7);`

5. Write a Pascal statement that will generate a random integer between the following inclusive values:
   a. 1 and 50.
   b. 2 and 100, even integers.
   c. 50 and 250, multiples of 5.
   d. -50 and 50, multiples of 10.

6. Write a Pascal statement that will generate a random integer between the following inclusive values:
   a. 1 and 200.
   b. 2 and 200, even integers.
   c. 12 and 200, multiples of 4.
   d. -200 and 200, multiples of 10.

7. Write a Pascal statement that will simulate
   a. the flipping of a single coin.
   b. the flipping of two coins.

8. Write a Pascal statement that will simulate
   a. the roll of a single die.
   b. the roll of a pair of dice.

Set II. Application

9. Write a function that will convert Fahrenheit to Celsius. Use the following formula:

   ```
   CELSIUS := 5.0/9.0 * (FAHRENHEIT - 32.0)
   ```

   Make a table of Fahrenheit and Celsius temperatures, ranging from 0° F to 100° F, with 10-degree increments. Round values in the table to the nearest tenth.

10. Write a function that will find the largest of three REAL values. For example, if the user enters

    5.6, 0.7, 9.6

    the function will compare these three values and return 9.6 to the calling block.

11. Write a function that will convert a length expressed in miles, yards, feet, and inches to total inches.

12. Write a function to find the sum of the integers from 1 to a number passed to the function.

13. Write a Boolean function to test input validity. The function should set VALIDDATA to TRUE if the input is valid. Use the following program segment:

```
{ insert function here }

BEGIN

    VALIDDATA := FALSE;
    REPEAT
       WRITELN('ENTER NUMBER 1-10');
       READLN(NUM);
       { insert function call here }
    UNTIL VALIDDATA;
```

14. Write a program that will find the area of a regular polygon. Use function AREA, as shown here.

```
FUNCTION AREA (SIDES, LEN : INTEGER) : REAL;
            { SIDES REPRESENTS THE NUMBER OF SIDES OF
              THE POLYGON AND LEN REPRESENTS THE LENGTH
              OF EACH SIDE OF THE POLYGON }
VAR
    ANGLE,
    PERPENDICULAR : REAL;

BEGIN

    ANGLE := PI / SIDES;
    PERPENDICULAR := SQRT(SQR(LEN/(2*SIN(ANGLE)))
                     - SQR(LEN/2));
    AREA := 1/2 * PERPENDICULAR * SIDES * LEN

END;   { AREA }
```

15. Assume that Pascal does not include the standard function ODD. Write a BOOLEAN function to determine if an integer is odd. The operator MOD may be helpful.

16. Write a function to calculate each of the following series:
    a. $X = 1^2 + 2^2 + 3^2 + \ldots + n^2$
    b. $X = 1/1 + 1/2 + 1/3 + \ldots + 1/n$
    c. $X = 1^1 + 2^2 + 3^3 + \ldots + n^n$
    d. $X = 1^3 + 2^3 - 3^3 + 4^3 - 5^3 + \ldots (+ \text{ or } -) n^3$

17. Write a program to convert Russian currency to U.S. dollars. The conversion factors are

    1 ruble = $1.50
    100 kopeks = 1 ruble

18. Write a program that will convert fractions to decimals; for example, $4\frac{3}{4}$ becomes 4.75. Have the user enter the whole number and the numerator and denominator of the fraction separately (there should be three inputs).

19. Write a program that will generate two random numbers and then calculate the sum and product of these numbers. The user can select the range of the random numbers. The program should continue as long as the user desires.

20. Write a program that will simulate flipping a coin 50 times. Report the number of heads and tails and the percentage of each.

21. Write a program to test what might be called the honesty of the random number function. Generate 1000 random whole numbers from 1 to 10 (inclusive) and compute the number and percentage of occurrences of each number. Print the results in a table.

Set III. Synthesis

22. Write a program to calculate the future value of an investment when interest is a factor. The program should include a function using the following formula (assuming no additional deposits and no withdrawals):

$$T = P(1 + i/N)^{NY}$$

where

T = total future value after Y years
P = initial investment
i = nominal interest rate per year
N = number of compounding periods per year
Y = number of years

23. Rewrite the program of Exercise 22 to include an option to compute the future value of an annuity (investment with regular deposits). This will require a separate function (or a variation on the previous function) using the following formula:

$$T = R(((1 + i/N)^{NY} - 1)/(i/N))$$

where

T = total future value after Y years
R = amount of regular deposits
N = number of deposits per year
i = nominal interest rate per year
Y = number of years

24. Write a program which includes a single Pascal function that will accept an angle in radians, along with a code indicating the desired trigonometric function to be performed, and return the result. SIN (sine) and COS (cosine) are standard built-in functions; other trigonometric functions may be derived using the following conversions:

Tangent
$$\tan t = \frac{\text{SIN } t}{\text{COS } t}$$

Cotangent
$$\cot t = \frac{\text{COS } t}{\text{SIN } t}$$

Secant
$$\sec t = \frac{1}{\text{COS } t}$$

Cosecant
$$\csc t = \frac{1}{\text{SIN } t}$$

25. Have the computer select a random number from 1 to 100 and challenge the user to guess the number. After each guess, the computer should output an appropriate message, for instance,

`TOO HIGH`

or

`TOO LOW`

or

`CORRECT!!!`

   Allow the user six chances to guess the correct number. If the correct guess is not given by the sixth try, reveal the correct number. Allow the user to continue the game for as long as desired.

26. Write a program to simulate a craps game. A 7 or 11 on the first roll wins, and 2, 3, or 12 on the first roll loses. Any other number becomes the point. The player continues rolling the dice until the point is rolled again (win) or a 7 is rolled (lose). Include an option to allow for betting.

27. Assume that Isaac, who was dazed by a bump to the head, is standing in the center of a seldom-traveled highway overpass. The overpass is 50 paces long and spans a busy freeway. Isaac staggers first in one direction and then another. The direction he will stagger next is unpredictable. He is lucky, however, and every time he takes a step, it will either be toward the left side of the freeway or toward the right side. He will not fall off the overpass.

   Write a program that will simulate Isaac staggering on the overpass. Determine the number of steps taken and the side (left or right) of the freeway to which he eventually staggers. Represent Isaac's movement using GOTOXY.

28. Write a program to calculate the amount of regular payments on a loan, given the term (time period) of the loan, the amount of the loan (principal), the annual interest rate charged, and the frequency of payments (number of payments per year). Use the following formula:

$$R = \frac{i\,(P/N)}{1 - \dfrac{1}{(i/N + 1)^{NY}}}$$

where

R = amount of regular payment
i = annual interest rate
P = principal
N = number of payments per year
Y = number of years

Y may be entered in years and months if the following conversion is included prior to computing R:

`Y := (12 * YEARS + MONTHS)/12;`

29. The brokerage fees for a particular real estate company are figured on a sliding scale, according to the value of the property. Write a program to find the brokerage fee for a property value entered by the user. The brokerage rate is as shown in the following table:

Property Value	Brokerage Rate (in percent)
up to $40,000	7.00
$40,001 to $55,000	6.75
$55,001 to $75,000	6.50
$75,001 to $100,000	6.00
$100,001 to $150,000	5.34
$150,001 and up	4.50

30. Write a program to convert between binary and decimal number representations. Convert decimal to binary by dividing the number by 2 and keeping track of the quotient and remainders until a quotient of 0 is reached. Each remainder is a digit of the binary number (from right to left). For example, the conversion 36_{10} to binary (100100_2) follows:

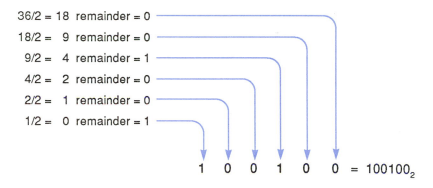

Convert binary to decimal by expanding powers of 2. For example, the conversion of 100100_2 to decimal (36_{10}) follows:

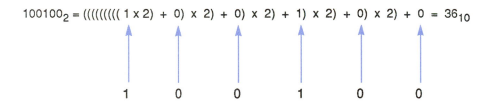

Limit the decimal input to 255_{10} and the binary input to 11111111_2.

31. While Kerry worked in a variety store, he learned that the price tags on all merchandise included a code from the purchasing department. The code consisted of letters corresponding to certain numbers which, when deciphered, would reveal the wholesale cost of the item. After some trial and error, Kerry discovered the code

key was MONEYTALKS, with M corresponding to 0 (zero), O corresponding to 1, N corresponding to 2, and so on, with S corresponding to 9. There were also special letters with the following meanings:

Q means to repeat the next character.
X means to double the value of the next character.
Z is a dummy letter; it is to be ignored.

A code of NTS meant the wholesale cost of the item was $2.59, while a code of ZQEXA meant the item actually cost the store $33.12.

Write a program to allow the user to enter a price code and find the wholesale cost of the item. The answer should be printed with a dollar sign and a decimal point.

32. Write a program to approximate the value of pi. Use each of the four following methods and compare the results:

a. $$\frac{pi}{4} = 1 - \frac{1}{3} + \frac{1}{5} - \frac{1}{7} + \frac{1}{9} - \frac{1}{11} + \ldots$$

b. $$\frac{pi^2}{4} = 1 + \frac{1}{2^2} + \frac{1}{3^2} + \frac{1}{4^2} + \ldots$$

c. $$\frac{pi}{2} = \frac{2}{1} \times \frac{2}{3} \times \frac{4}{3} \times \frac{4}{5} \times \frac{6}{5} \times \frac{6}{7} \times \frac{8}{7} \times \ldots$$

d. Find random points (X, Y) in a unit circle (a circle with a radius equal to 1) inscribed within a square, with each coordinate ranging from -1 to 1. The circle is determined by the formula

$$X^2 + Y^2 = 1$$

Since pi is equal to the area of the unit circle, the formula for calculating pi uses a percentage of these random points.

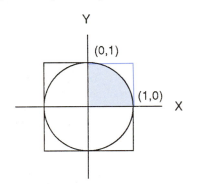

The shaded region represents one-fourth of the circle area, or pi/4. By working with the smaller square and the quarter-circle, the program need only be concerned with positive values for X and Y; that is, X and Y each ranging from 0 to 1.

$$pi = \frac{4 \times \text{number of points falling within the quarter circle}}{\text{(number of total points, or trials)}}$$

The accuracy of this approximation depends on the number of trials.

10 Recursion

I gave her one,
they gave him two, you
gave us three or more;
they all returned from
him to you, though
they were mine before.

—Lewis Carroll

Overview

Recursion with Procedures
   Limit versus Infinite
   Direct versus Indirect
   End versus Pending
   Stack
   FORWARD Declaration
Recursion with Functions
Programming Tip
   Iteration versus Recursion

Gaining a Perspective

Sometimes what appears to be the obvious way of attacking a problem doesn't always turn out to be the easiest or best. Take, for example, an office that is having trouble handling all of the phone calls it receives. The most obvious solution might be to add more phones; enough additional phones would certainly handle the phone traffic. The office staff, however, would either be run ragged trying to keep up with answering the phones or driven crazy by the constant ringing. So, even though that solution may work in some fashion, it certainly is not the best way to manage phone calls. A better solution might be to get phones that have a hold option, allowing employees to take more than one call at a time. An employee can then put calls on hold as new calls occur and retrieve them as needed. This solution takes less space (since only one phone per desk is needed) and requires less effort from the employees.

In the world of computer programming, like the example of the telephone system, the first and most obvious solution may not be the best choice. The tendency of programmers is to use the crunching power of the computer to beat a problem into submission. Up to a point, that works. Iteration—using FOR, WHILE, and REPEAT, as seen in earlier chapters—is appropriate for many problem solutions. Some problems, however, don't readily lend themselves to iterative processes. The programmer may try to force the problem into an iterative structure, causing the end result to become nearly indecipherable and increasing the effort needed to complete the program. In this chapter, an alternative to iteration will be introduced. This alternative gives an option to the programmer when iterative methods don't fit or when they appear too messy. The process, called **recursion**, allows a procedure or function to call itself. Initially, the recursive process is a bit difficult to follow; it is an unfamiliar way of thinking. After a little practice, however, you will find that recursion is a powerful tool that is useful in solving many advanced problems.

Lesson 10.1 Recursion with Procedures

Recursion can be used with functions or procedures and takes on various forms. This lesson discusses recursive procedures. Nearly any process that can be written using iteration can also be written with recursion. Recursion can simplify a messy problem and produce a more elegant solution. Since recursion is best suited to advanced applications, many of the examples presented in this lesson may not be typical uses of recursion; they will, however, serve to illustrate recursion in its many forms, using familiar problems that are easy to understand. In addition, some problems that are more easily solved using recursion will be presented.

Program Segment 10.1 shows a procedure that writes the numbers from a starting number (COUNT) to an ending number (FINISH). A WHILE loop is used to count iteratively. This procedure should be familiar from past chapters.

Program Segment 10.1

```
PROCEDURE COUNTITER(COUNT,FINISH : INTEGER);

     { COUNTS ITERATIVELY }

  BEGIN

    WHILE COUNT <= FINISH DO
       BEGIN
          WRITELN(COUNT);
          COUNT := COUNT + 1
       END   { WHILE }

  END;   { COUNTITER }
```

Program Segment 10.2 produces the same results as Program Segment 10.1, but does so recursively.

Program Segment 10.2

```
PROCEDURE COUNTREC(COUNT,FINISH : INTEGER);

     { COUNTS RECURSIVELY }

  BEGIN

     WRITELN(COUNT);
     IF COUNT < FINISH
        THEN COUNTREC(COUNT + 1,FINISH)
            { RECURSIVE CALL }

  END;   { COUNTREC }
```

Assume the following procedure call:

```
COUNTREC(1,10);
```

for Program Segment 10.2. In Table 10.1, we walk through procedure COUNTREC to help in understanding this, the simplest of recursive processes.

Table 10.1 Tracing a Recursive Procedure

Calling Statement	COUNT	FINISH	Output	COUNT + 1	COUNT < FINISH
COUNTREC(1,10)	1	10	1	2	TRUE
COUNTREC(2,10)	2	10	2	3	TRUE
COUNTREC(3,10)	3	10	3	4	TRUE
.	.	.	.	.	.
.	.	.	.	.	.
.	.	.	.	.	.
COUNTREC(9,10)	9	10	9	10	TRUE
COUNTREC(10,10)	10	10	10	--	FALSE

During the first call of the procedure, the initial value of COUNT is 1. The WRITELN prints 1, as in the iterative procedure. The procedure would end, however (since there is no looping structure), if not for the next statement. If COUNT is less than FINISH, COUNTREC is invoked again; this time with COUNT + 1. The output this time is 2. Since COUNT is less than 10, the procedure is called again. The process continues until COUNT is equal to FINISH.

The recursion shown in Program Segment 10.2 has a **limit.** The program will stop when some exit condition is met (for example, when COUNT becomes greater than or equal to FINISH). If the statement

```
IF COUNT < FINISH
   THEN COUNTREC(COUNT + 1,FINISH)
```

were replaced with

```
COUNTREC(COUNT + 1,FINISH)
```

the recursion would be **infinite;** that is, the loop (procedure calls) would go on forever because there is no stopping mechanism. Actually, the limits of the computer would likely cause the procedure to stop, either by surpassing the limit for representing numbers (a value range error) or by running out of memory to keep track of the continuing calls to COUNTREC (a stack overflow).

The recursion in Program Segment 10.2 is brought about by the procedure calling itself. Recursion in which a procedure calls itself is known as **direct recursion.** (As we will see, recursion may also occur between two different procedures.) Also, in procedure COUNTREC, the recursion occurs at the end of the procedure. **End recursion** occurs when the **recursive call** is the last statement of the procedure; that is, when there are no statements following the recursive call.

To summarize, there are three aspects to the recursion illustrated in Program Segment 10.2.

■ The recursion is limited: it will stop when some condition is met.
■ The recursion is direct: the procedure calls itself.
■ The recursive call is at the end of the procedure.

The recursive procedure in Program Segment 10.2 can be referred to as limit-direct-end recursion. Often recursions occur based on these three aspects. Understanding the differences in these aspects is essential to understanding recursion.

Pending recursion occurs when the recursive call is not the last statement of the recursive procedure; that is, there are still statements to complete after the exit condition of the recursion becomes true.

Limit-direct-pending recursion has an exit condition, calls itself, and has pending statements after the recursive call; Program 10.3 is an example of this type of recursion.

Program 10.3

```
PROGRAM REVERSE(INPUT,OUTPUT);

    { PURPOSE: TO REVERSE ORDER OF CHARACTERS }

PROCEDURE BACKWARDS;

    VAR
        CH : CHAR;

    BEGIN

        READ(CH);
        IF NOT EOLN
            THEN BACKWARDS;    { RECURSIVE CALL }
        WRITE(CH)

    END; { BACKWARDS }

BEGIN   { MAIN PROGRAM }

    WRITELN('ENTER A WORD');
    BACKWARDS;
    WRITELN

END.
```

Suppose the user entered the word *PASCAL*, followed by a carriage return. The computer would print:

```
ENTER A WORD
PASCAL <RETURN>
 LACSAP
```

Upon execution, procedure BACKWARDS accepts the letter P, since READ is used and the variable type is CHAR. Next the procedure checks if end-of-line (EOLN) has been reached (if the carriage return has been pressed). The IF condition is TRUE, since a carriage return has not been pressed (NOT EOLN). Procedure

BACKWARDS is called again, leaving a command (WRITE(CH)) unexecuted. That command is pending; it has not been executed and needs to be retained for execution when the recursion is complete. The next letter is A. Again, the exit condition (EOLN) has not been met so BACKWARDS is called again, leaving another WRITE(CH) to be executed. This command is retained as before. Each time the procedure is called, the remaining statements are remembered so that they can be performed upon the completion of the procedure calls. The statements are placed in memory one after another, much like dishes might be placed in a cupboard. The last dish placed on the stack of dishes is the first one removed. This is the same with pending statements of recursive calls. The arrangement of the statements to be executed is called a **stack.** Figure 10.1 illustrates how the stack operates after each procedure call in Program 10.3.

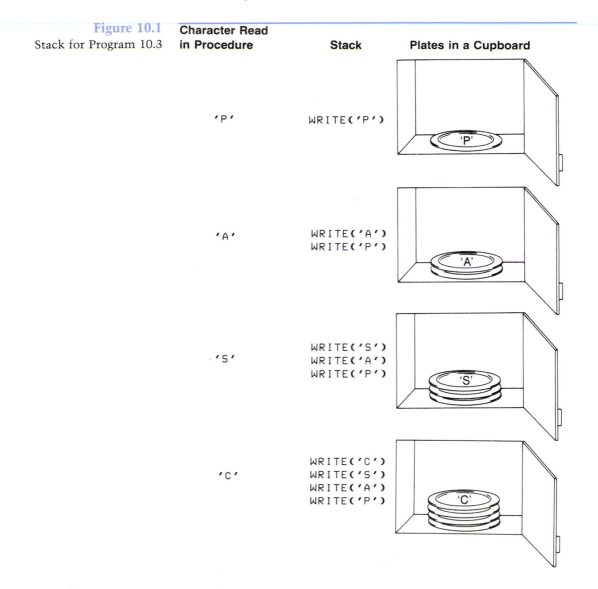

Figure 10.1
Stack for Program 10.3

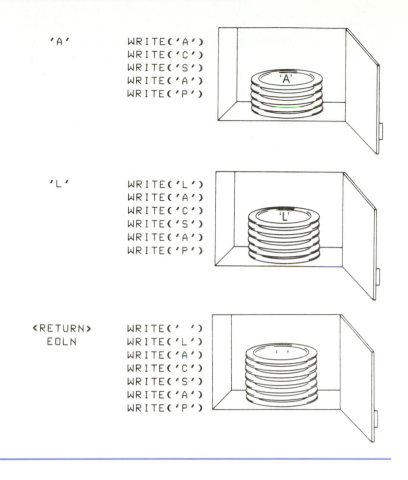

'A'   WRITE('A')
             WRITE('C')
             WRITE('S')
             WRITE('A')
             WRITE('P')

'L'   WRITE('L')
             WRITE('A')
             WRITE('C')
             WRITE('S')
             WRITE('A')
             WRITE('P')

<RETURN>   WRITE(' ')
  EOLN   WRITE('L')
             WRITE('A')
             WRITE('C')
             WRITE('S')
             WRITE('A')
             WRITE('P')

The pending statements are removed from the stack in the opposite order that they were put in; this order is called **Last-In First-Out** (**LIFO**). The top of the stack is removed first, just like removing the top plate from a stack in the cupboard. (*Note:* the space at the beginning of LACSAP is caused by the RETURN key, since UCSD Pascal treats RETURN as a space in a READ command.)

Recursion may also be **indirect** (or **mutual**) as opposed to direct. For example, procedure A may call procedure B, which in turn may call procedure A. Indirect recursion involves a procedure calling itself indirectly by calling another procedure.

Program 10.4 is an example of indirect recursion. The program approximates pi using the series

$$\mathrm{pi} = 4 \times \left(1 - \frac{1}{3} + \frac{1}{5} - \frac{1}{7} + \frac{1}{9} - \frac{1}{11} + \frac{1}{13} \cdots \right)$$

The process illustrates mutual recursion in a straightforward manner. The two procedures (PIADD and PISUBTR) add or subtract the appropriate number in the series. The exit condition is based on the number of terms desired (and thus the accuracy of the approximation). The program could also be easily written using an iterative process.

Program 10.4

```
PROGRAM MUTUAL(INPUT,OUTPUT);

    { PURPOSE: TO CALCULATE PI USING
                MUTUAL RECURSION }

VAR
    NUMBEROFTERMS,
    COUNT          : INTEGER;
    PI             : REAL;

PROCEDURE PIADD(NUMBER, C, NOFTERMS : INTEGER;
                VAR P : REAL); FORWARD;

PROCEDURE PISUBTR(NUMBER, C, NOFTERMS : INTEGER;
                  VAR P : REAL);

    BEGIN

        C := C + 1;
        IF C <= NOFTERMS
            THEN
                BEGIN
                    P := P - 1 / NUMBER;
                    PIADD(NUMBER + 2, C, NOFTERMS, P)
                END

    END;    { PISUBTR }

PROCEDURE PIADD;    { (NUMBER, C, NOFTERMS : INTEGER;
                       VAR P : REAL) }

    BEGIN

        C := C + 1;
        IF C <= NOFTERMS
            THEN
                BEGIN
                    P := P + 1 / NUMBER;
                    PISUBTR(NUMBER + 2, C, NOFTERMS, P)
                END

    END;    { PIADD }

BEGIN  { MAIN PROGRAM }

    PAGE(OUTPUT);
    WRITELN;
    WRITELN('HOW MANY TERMS?');
    READLN(NUMBEROFTERMS);
    PI := 0;
    COUNT := 0;
    PIADD(1, COUNT, NUMBEROFTERMS, PI);
    WRITELN('PI IS APPROXIMATELY ',4 * PI)

END.
```

Table 10.2
Approximations of pi
Using Mutual
Recursion

Number of Terms	Approximation of pi
10	3.04184
11	3.23232
12	3.05840
13	3.21840
14	3.07025
15	3.20819
50	3.12159
100	3.13159
200	3.13659
500	3.13959
1000	3.14059
1500	3.14092
2000	3.14109
2200	3.14114

In Program 10.4, procedure PIADD is declared FORWARD since it is to be called in procedure PISUBTR. In the FORWARD declaration, the procedure heading includes the parameter list. When procedure PIADD is actually defined, the heading is not included, although a comment showing the heading is helpful as a reminder. Procedures PIADD and PISUBTR continue calling each other until the desired number of terms is reached.

Table 10.2 shows the resulting approximations for several choices for the number of terms. The approximation gets more accurate as the number of terms increases.

Caution: There is one difficulty with using recursion to solve this problem; this difficulty is one which must be addressed in most recursive exercises. Since recursion takes extra memory (to store the recursive calls on a stack), there is always a danger of running out of memory. In fact, for Program 10.4, a number of terms much larger than 2200 may cause an error due to stack overflow. (This number will vary depending on the memory available and the machine being used.) One consideration when choosing between iterative and recursive solutions should therefore be memory requirements.

Lesson Check 10.1

1. Identify each of the following as true or false.
   a. Writing a program using recursion is always easier than using iteration.
   b. Most problems that can be solved using recursion can also be solved using iteration.
   c. Mutual recursion occurs when a procedure calls itself.
   d. Pending statements in a recursive procedure are put on a stack for execution at a later time.

Lesson 10.2 Recursion with Functions

Functions can also be recursive and are extremely useful in situations involving repetitive calculations. Program 10.5 shows how recursion can be used to calculate powers of numbers.

Program 10.5

```
PROGRAM EXPONENT(INPUT,OUTPUT);

    { PURPOSE: TO PERFORM EXPONENTIATION }

VAR
    BASE,
    EXPON : INTEGER;

FUNCTION POWER(B, E : INTEGER) : REAL;

    BEGIN

        IF E = 1
            THEN POWER := B
            ELSE POWER := B * POWER(B, E - 1)

    END; { POWER }

BEGIN { MAIN PROGRAM }

    WRITELN('ENTER THE BASE AND THE EXPONENT');
    READLN(BASE, EXPON);
    WRITELN(POWER(BASE, EXPON))

END.
```

Program 10.5 illustrates limit-direct-end recursion. Suppose the user entered 2 and 3 for the base and exponent, respectively. Figure 10.2 traces the recursive function. The first call to POWER says to multiply 2 times the result of POWER(2,2). The recursive call is in the assignment statement. The second call says to multiply 2 times the result of POWER(2,1). The third time the function is

Figure 10.2 Trace of Recursive Function in Program 10.5

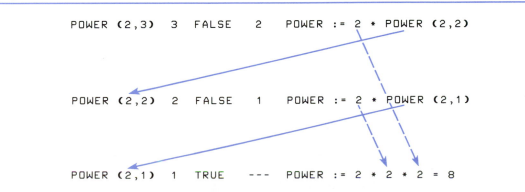

called, E = 1 so POWER := 2. Thus, the entire process results in multiplying 2 times 2 times 2. Since

$$2 \times 2 \times 2 = 8$$

the function has calculated 2 to the third power (2^3).

Program 10.6 uses a recursive function. This program has part of a statement (+ NUM) pending. Figure 10.3 illustrates how the sum is computed.

Program 10.6

```
PROGRAM EVENSUM(OUTPUT);

    { PURPOSE: TO FIND THE SUM OF THE EVEN NUMBERS
                UP TO 100 USING PENDING RECURSION }

FUNCTION SUM(NUM : INTEGER) : INTEGER;

    BEGIN

        IF NUM = 2
            THEN SUM := 2
            ELSE SUM := SUM(NUM - 2) + NUM

    END; { SUM }

BEGIN { MAIN PROGRAM }

    WRITE('THE SUM OF THE EVEN NUMBERS TO 100 ');
    WRITELN('IS ',SUM(100))

END.
```

The structure of Programs 10.5 and 10.6 is common to recursive functions. An exit condition is tested and, if TRUE, a final value is assigned; otherwise, the function is used recursively in an assignment statement.

Figure 10.3

Trace of Program 10.6

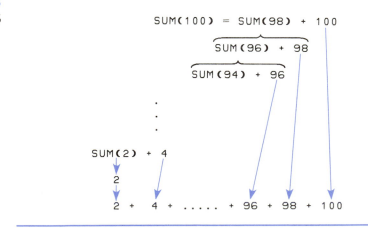

Lesson
Check
10.2
1. Identify each of the following as true or false.
   a. Repetitive calculations can often be accomplished using recursive functions.
   b. An exit condition is not needed in limit recursion.
   c. In end recursion, the recursive call is at the end of the function or procedure.

Lesson 10.3 A Final Example: Permutations

The examples presented in this chapter have used recursion, but they could have been solved without recursion, and may have then been easier to understand. If recursion is only an interesting alternative to iteration, is it worth the effort? There is more to this technique. Many of the uses of recursion come into play only in the most advanced stages of programming; some of these will be discussed later. For now, however, we can illustrate one example of the power of recursion.

Suppose a list of all the permutations of a set of objects is desired. To keep this example manageable, all permutations of three characters taken three at a time will be found. There are several valid approaches to the problem; some elegant and some very messy. Program 10.7 presents a recursive approach. It is a bit oversimplified at this point. A generalized version for producing permutations will be given as Exercise 41 in Chapter 13.

Program 10.7
```
PROGRAM PERMUTATIONS (INPUT,OUTPUT);

   { PURPOSE: PERMUTATIONS OF THREE CHARACTERS }

VAR
    CH1,
    CH2,
    CH3   : CHAR;
    COUNT : INTEGER;

PROCEDURE PERMUTE (C1,C2,C3 : CHAR; C : INTEGER);

    VAR
       CH : CHAR;

    BEGIN

       IF C < 6
          THEN
             BEGIN
                WRITELN(C1,C2,C3);
                IF ODD(C)
                   THEN
```

```
                        BEGIN
                            CH := C1;
                            C1 := C2;
                            C2 := CH
                        END
                    ELSE
                        BEGIN
                            CH := C2;
                            C2 := C3;
                            C3 := CH
                        END;
                    PERMUTE(C1,C2,C3,C + 1)
                END { IF }

        END; { PERMUTE }

    BEGIN { MAIN PROGRAM }

        COUNT := 0;
        WRITE('ENTER THREE CHARACTERS: ');
        READLN(CH1,CH2,CH3);
        PERMUTE(CH1,CH2,CH3,COUNT)

    END.
```

For characters A, B, and C, the result would be

```
ABC
ACB
CAB
CBA
BCA
BAC
```

As we will see in Chapter 13, the process can be written in a general form using arrays. In contrast, attempting a generalized program using iteration is extremely messy and difficult to understand.

Lesson Check 10.3

1. Using input of ABC trace Program 10.7 to determine how the output was obtained.

Lesson 10.4 Programming Tip— Iteration versus Recursion

Once the programmer becomes comfortable enough with recursion to consider it a viable alternative in problem solving, a pressing question still remains: When should recursion be used? The decision to use recursion instead of iteration is difficult for someone new to the recursion concept. The question is compounded by the fact that nearly all problems can be solved using either method. So, the question is then this: Which method is best in a given situation? A few guidelines may be in order.

A major consideration in devising an algorithm is to use an approach that will be as understandable as possible. This benefits the programmer in writing and debugging the routine, and allows other programmers to examine, use, or improve the routine. Because of its extensive use and possible relationship to other human processes, iteration may have an initial edge (with regard to simplicity), especially on problems with a straightforward solution. Looking for an iterative approach first may not be a bad idea; however, recursion should not be passed over for a messy iterative solution. The permutation problem in Lesson 10.3 is a good example. An iterative implementation, especially for the general case, gets difficult quickly.

The second consideration is related to the first, and involves ease of implementation by the programmer. The amount of time available to complete the project, as well as reasonableness of programming, come into play. The programmer must weigh programming effort (which may be translated into cost) versus other factors before deciding on an algorithm. Recursive solutions are often shorter than their iterative counterparts, thereby paying for any extra advance planning that may be required.

One final factor may not be important to some, but is often one for the programmer to consider. Occasionally, a programmer will devise a solution that is far more creative or interesting than any other. The solution may take a little more effort to understand, and may not be any easier to implement. The elegance of the solution, however, may make up for some slight shortcomings in other areas. Recursion can often be more elegant than the brute force associated with iteration. The programmer should look at all options before deciding between iteration and recursion.

When looking at possible situations in which to use recursion, a few suggestions may help.

- If iteration starts to get messy, look at recursion as an alternative.
- Watch for problems that are similar to those previously solved using recursion. There is a common look to the recursive problem.
- The number of problems in which recursion is nearly a requirement is limited. Become aware of these typical recursive problems.
- If the problem is readily broken down into a sequence of similar subproblems, try a recursive solution.
- Many advanced algorithms are much better suited to recursion. Some of these will be introduced in later chapters.

Summary

Recursion has a definite place in the programmer's bag of tricks, and may change the way the programmer thinks about problem solving. Nearly all problems are approached in an iterative manner, since iteration is stressed so much in early stages of programming. Most iterative processes, however, can be accomplished using recursion, and several advanced topics are better suited to this method.

A summary of the aspects of recursion follows:

> ■ Limit versus infinite. In limit recursion, there is an exit condition that will cause the process to stop. If this exit condition did not exist, the recursion would be infinite and would continue until the program was interrupted by the user or until an error occurred.
>
> ■ Direct versus indirect (mutual). Direct recursion occurs when a subprogram (a procedure or function) calls itself. In indirect recursion, a subprogram calls another subprogram which in turn calls the original subprogram. The FORWARD declaration is used in indirect recursion.
>
> ■ End versus pending. With end recursion, the recursive call occurs at the end of the subprogram. No statements are left to execute after the call. In pending recursion, there are statements after the recursive call. These statements are placed on the stack and executed after the recursion is finished, in a Last-In First-Out (LIFO) manner.

Recursion can simplify many problems, often making them shorter and more efficient. The uses of recursion will become even more apparent in future chapters.

Key Terms

direct recursion
end recursion
indirect (mutual) recursion
infinite recursion
Last-In First-Out (LIFO)

limit recursion
pending recursion
recursion
recursive call
stack

Answers to Lesson Checks

Lesson 10.1

1. **a.** False.
   b. True.
   c. False.
   d. True.

Lesson 10.2

1. **a.** True.
   b. False.
   c. True.

Lesson 10.3

1. C1, C2, C3 enter function as A, B, and C, respectively.

C	C < 6	Output	ODD(C)	C1	C2	C3
0	TRUE	ABC	FALSE	A	C	B
1	TRUE	ACB	TRUE	C	A	B
2	TRUE	CAB	FALSE	C	B	A
3	TRUE	CBA	TRUE	B	C	A
4	TRUE	BCA	FALSE	B	A	C
5	TRUE	BAC	TRUE	A	B	C
6	FALSE					

When the count (C) is odd, the contents of C1 and C2 are switched; otherwise (when C is even), the contents of C2 and C3 are switched.

Exercises   Set I. Comprehension

1. Match each statement on the left with an appropriate answer on the right. The phrases at the top of each column may be used to complete a sentence pertaining to each type of recursion.

Recursion that	is called
a. continues forever	**A.** end recursion.
b. has no statements or partial statements following the recursive call	**B.** pending recursion.
	C. direct recursion.
c. has procedures that call each other	**D.** indirect recursion.
d. stops when a condition is satisfied	**E.** limit recursion.
e. contains statements following the recursive call	**F.** infinite recursion.
f. has a procedure that calls itself	

2. Describe the recursion that occurs when the integers from 1 to 100 are listed.

3. Describe the recursion that occurs when the even integers from 2 to 500 are added together.

Actual programming for recursive designs will be discussed in Chapter 20. For now, describe—in English—the recursions in Exercises 4–6.

4. Describe the recursion in each of the following patterns:

5. Describe the recursion in each of the following patterns:

a.   b.

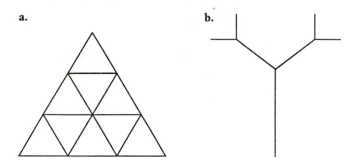

6. Describe the recursion in the following pattern of golden rectangles. In the drawing, ABCD, CEFG and so on are squares.

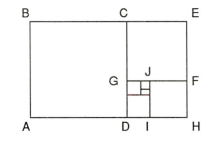

7. Given this function definition,

```
FUNCTION WHAT (ONE : INTEGER; TWO : REAL) : REAL;

BEGIN
   IF  ONE = 0
      THEN WHAT := TWO
      ELSE WHAT := WHAT(ONE - 1, TWO * 5.0)
END;
```

what is the value of X after each of the following function calls?
a. X := WHAT(1, 2.0);
b. X := WHAT(2, 2.0);
c. X := WHAT(-1, 3.0);

8. Given this function definition,

```
FUNCTION ADD (N : INTEGER) : INTEGER;

BEGIN
   IF N = 0
      THEN ADD := 1
      ELSE ADD := ADD(N-1) + N
END;
```

what is the value of Z after each of the following function calls?
a. Z := ADD(1);
b. Z := ADD(0);
c. Z := ADD(10);

9. In Exercise 7, how many times will the function be called recursively for an initial call of

```
X := WHAT(40,0.02);
```

10. In Exercise 8, how many times will the function be called recursively for an initial call of

```
Z := ADD(100);
```

11. Given this procedure definition,

```
PROCEDURE TALK (START, FINISH : INTEGER);

BEGIN
   IF START = FINISH
      THEN WRITELN('DONE')
      ELSE BEGIN
              TALK(START + 1, FINISH);
              WRITELN('WHAT IS HAPPENING?')
           END;
```

what is the output after each of the following procedure calls?
a. TALK(1, 1);
b. TALK(1, 2);
c. TALK(0, 5);

12. Given this procedure definition,

```
PROCEDURE LETTERS (CH : CHAR);

BEGIN
   IF CH < 'Z'
      THEN LETTERS(CHR(ORD(CH) + 1))
      ELSE WRITELN(CH);
   WRITE(CH)
END;
```

what is the output after each of the following procedure calls?
a. LETTERS('A');
b. LETTERS('N');
c. LETTERS('Z');

13. Find the errors in the following recursive function:

```
FUNCTION TRY (A,B : INTEGER);

BEGIN
   IF A > B
      THEN TRY := A
      ELSE TRYAGAIN := TRY(A + 1, B)
END;
```

14. Find the errors in the following recursive procedure:

```
PROCEDURE RECUR (A, B, C : INTEGER);

BEGIN
   WHILE A > B DO
      BEGIN
         WRITE(A + B);
         C := RECUR(A - 1, B)
      END;
   WRITELN(A - B)
END;
```

Set II. Application

15. Write a recursive function to compute the following sum:

$$1 + 9 + 25 + \ldots + (2n - 1)^2$$

16. Suppose a chessboard contains a single rook placed in one corner. Since the rook cannot travel in a diagonal direction, the shortest possible path from that corner to the opposite corner is over 14 squares. As shown in the following illustration, there are several different paths to take, each traveling over 14 squares.

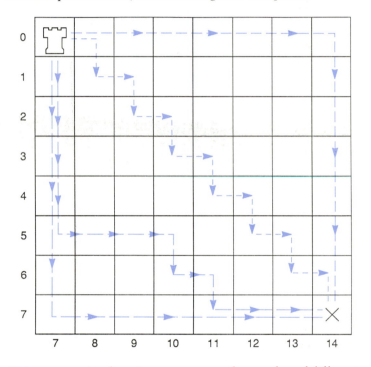

Write a recursive function to compute the number of different shortest paths, given the parameters N (total number of squares to travel—14) and R (the number of squares traveled from one corner to an adjacent corner—7). Use the following formula:

Number of shortest paths =

$$\frac{N \times (N - 1) \times (N - 2) \times \ldots \times (N - R + 1)}{1 \times 2 \times 3 \times \ldots \times R}$$

Hint:

$$f(N,R) = \frac{N}{R} \times f(N - 1, R - 1)$$

17. The following program is designed to produce random rolls of three dice. Complete the recursive procedure, ROLL, whose purpose is to continue rolling (and printing the numbers on) the dice until all three dice show the same number; for example, until all three dice show a 2. When a roll produces three of the same number, return the number on the dice (DIE) and the total number of rolls taken (COUNT).

```
PROGRAM DICE (OUTPUT);

USES APPLESTUFF;

PROCEDURE ROLL(VAR C, D : INTEGER);

    VAR
        DIE1,
        DIE2,
        DIE3 : INTEGER;

    FUNCTION RND (LOW, HIGH : INTEGER): INTEGER;

        BEGIN
            RND := RANDOM MOD (HIGH - LOW + 1) + LOW
        END;

    BEGIN  { ROLL }

        { Place procedure here }

    END;

BEGIN   { MAIN PROGRAM }

    RANDOMIZE;
    COUNT := 0;
    DIE := 0;
    ROLL(COUNT, DIE);
    WRITELN('NUMBER ON DICE IS ',DIE);
    WRITELN('TOTAL ROLLS: ',COUNT)

END.
```

18. Write a program that utilizes a recursive function to output a specific factorial. For example, the program should print

    `5! = 120`

    where 5 is the input and 120 is the output. Use

    `FACTORIAL := N * FACTORIAL(N - 1);`

    where N is the number input.

19. Write a function, SUM, that will generate the sum of the numbers from 1 to 100. Use

    `SUM := SUM + ADD(COUNT + 1);`

20. Write a program using recursion that will find the sum of the squares of integers between INTA and INTB (inclusive). Let the values for INTA and INTB be entered by the user.

21. Write a program with a recursive procedure that will reverse the digits of an integer input by the user. For example, if 456 is input, 654 is output.

Set III. Synthesis

22. Write a program to find the sum of the following series:

$$1 + \frac{1}{2} + \frac{1}{4} + \frac{1}{8} + \dots$$

Let the user enter the number of terms in the series.

23. Write a program using recursion that will determine if a series of positive numbers entered by the user is in ascending order. Allow the user to continue entering numbers until the series fails the ascending order test or until a value of -1 is entered.

24. Write a program to find an approximation (accurate to three decimal places) for the following continued fraction:

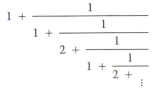

25. Write a program using recursion to print a complete pyramid of digits, as started (and ended) here.

```
              1
            1 2 1
          1 2 3 2 1
        1 2 3 4 3 2 1
              .
              .
              .
1 2 3 4 5 6 7 8 9 8 7 6 5 4 3 2 1
```

26. Write a program with a recursive procedure that will print the Fibonacci numbers. Fibonacci numbers are a sequence of numbers such that each consecutive number of the sequence is equal to the sum of the two preceding numbers. The sequence begins as follows:

0, 1, 1, 2, 3, 5, 8, 13, . . .

Use

```
F(N) := F(N - 1) + F(N - 2);
```

where N is the number of the terms in the sequence.

27. Write a program using recursion to find the greatest common divisor (GCD) for two positive integers using the Euclidean algorithm (defined in Chapter 6, Exercise 29).

28. Rewrite the program from Exercise 27 to find the GCD of three positive integers.

29. The least common multiple (LCM) of two positive integers, A and B, is the smallest integer that is a multiple of both A and B. For example, the LCM of 16 and 24 is 48. Write a program to find the LCM of two positive integers entered by the user.

30. Imagine dividing a square into smaller and smaller squares. Start with a simple square and make the first division by cutting the sides in half (using horizontal and vertical lines). How many squares are there? Now try cutting the simple square into thirds. Then fourths, and so on.

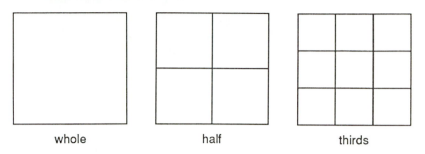

whole   half   thirds

Write a program using recursion that will output the number of divisions (up to a number entered by the user), the number of small squares, and the total number of squares. Your output should look something like the following:

Division	Small Squares	Total Squares
1	1	1
2	4	5
3	9	14
4	16	30
.	.	.
.	.	.
.	.	.

31. Write a program to convert decimal numbers to binary numbers, using recursion. (See Chapter 9, Exercise 30.)

32. Write a program to convert binary numbers to decimal numbers, using recursion. (See Chapter 9, Exercise 30.)

33. A certain club has a rule that requires all people attending a meeting to shake hands with each other. If two people meet, then one handshake occurs. If three people meet, then three handshakes occur, and so on, as outlined in the following table:

Number of People	Number of Handshakes
1	0
2	1
3	3
4	6
5	10
.	.
.	.
.	.

Write a program using recursion that will compute and output the number of handshakes. Allow the user to enter the number of people present.

34. The Towers of Hanoi is a problem involving three pegs and three disks of varying size, as shown here.

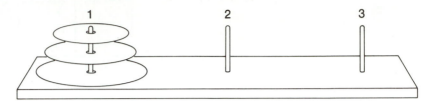

The idea is to move the disks from peg 1 to peg 3. This sounds simple enough. There are, however, a few rules to follow. Only one disk may be moved at a time (the top disk), and a larger disk cannot be placed over a smaller disk. Write a procedure to show how this problem may be solved.

11
Programmer-Defined Ordinal Types and Subranges

"It's a mineral, I think," said Alice.

"Of course it is," said the Duchess, who seemed ready to agree to everything that Alice said. . . .

"Oh, I know!" exclaimed Alice, . . . "It's a vegetable. It doesn't look like one, but it is."

—Lewis Carroll

Overview

Gaining a Perspective

In the past few chapters, procedures and functions have been written to meet particular needs. These subprograms were similar in many respects to the built-in procedures and functions of Pascal, yet allowed the programmer greater programming flexibility. The programmer can also create data types. These data types are called **programmer-defined ordinal types.** For example, the programmer might create a data type consisting of the days of the week. This data type could be used in a program that computes the weekly salaries of workers. Instead of looping from 1 to the number of days worked, the programmer could use a programmer-defined data type as the initial and final values of the loop (making the intent of the loop obvious). That is, the programmer can define a data type to represent the words MONDAY, TUESDAY, WEDNESDAY, THURSDAY, FRIDAY, SATURDAY, and SUNDAY, and then use a loop with an initial value of MONDAY and a final value of SUNDAY. This data type consists of the seven days of the week, just as the predefined data type BOOLEAN consists of the possible values FALSE or TRUE. Once a data type has been defined, the order of the values of the data type is established by the sequence given in its definition.

One drawback to programmer-defined ordinal types is that their values are not readable or printable in some versions of Pascal. In these versions, a procedure must be written to handle reading and writing programmer-defined ordinal types. Despite this, programmer-defined ordinal types add greatly to program readability and self-documentation. The programmer can also specify **subranges** or parts of already existing types. Subranges conserve memory space, since they specify what portion of a given data type will be used.

Lesson 11.1 Programmer-Defined Ordinal Types

Earlier, predefined data types (BOOLEAN, CHAR, INTEGER, REAL, and STRING) were introduced. These data types are a part of the Pascal language. The range of values of these types is dependent on the particular machine implementation. For example, the possible value of MAXINT (for data type INTEGER) varies depending on the version of Pascal and on the machine.

The programmer can also define data types to meet particular needs. A programmer-defined ordinal type is an ordered list of items specified or enumerated by the programmer. Ordinal means that each value in the list has a unique predecessor and successor. In particular, BOOLEAN, CHAR, and INTEGER are predefined ordinal data types. REAL and STRING are not ordinal, since each value does not have a unique predecessor or successor. For the most part, the programmer-defined ordinal types can be used much as the predefined types. The similarities and differences will be presented in this lesson.

The definition of a programmer-defined ordinal type begins with the reserved word **TYPE** followed by the **type identifier,** an equal sign, and a list of **type constants.** The constants consist of a list of identifiers separated by commas and enclosed in parentheses. The order of the type constants in the list is determined by the programmer. For example, the programmer can define some of the colors in the spectrum as follows:

```
TYPE
    SPECTRUM = (VIOLET,BLUE,GREEN,YELLOW,ORANGE,RED);
```

The type SPECTRUM consists of an ordered list, with each type constant having an ordinal value (ORD). The first constant will always have an ordinal value 0. For example, VIOLET has an ordinal value of 0 and RED, an ordinal value of 5. Each type constant in the list has a unique predecessor and successor. (The first type constant has no predecessor and the last type constant has no successor. For type SPECTRUM, the predecessor of VIOLET and the successor of RED are undefined.)

In a program, the type definition is placed after the constant (CONST) definitions and before the variable declaration.

Type Definition Form

```
PROGRAM program identifier;

CONST constant identifier = constant;

TYPE type identifier = (type constants);
VAR variable identifier : type identifier;

PROCEDURE ...
```

After the type identifier has been defined, a variable of that type must be declared prior to use in a program; for instance,

```
VAR
    COLOR : SPECTRUM;
```

In UCSD Pascal, global constant definitions cannot be of a programmer-defined ordinal type (since global constants are defined prior to the global type declaration). A procedure, however, can include a local constant definition of a programmer-defined ordinal type. A local constant can be defined to be of type SPECTRUM as follows:

```
PROCEDURE SUBPROGRAM;

    CONST
        LAWN = GREEN;
```

Programmer-Defined Ordinal Type Form

```
TYPE
    type identifier = (constantidentifier1,
                       constantidentifier2,
                           .
                           .
                           .
                       constantidentifierN);
VAR
    variable identifier : type identifier;
```

The following example contains additional type definitions and their accompanying variable declarations. In this example, type MONTH consists of the months of the year and type DAY, the days of the week. A new name can be given to a predefined type, as shown by type PAY, which is REAL. Also, more than one variable can be declared of a particular data type.

```
TYPE
    MONTH = (JANUARY,FEBRUARY,MARCH,APRIL,MAY,JUNE,
             JULY,AUGUST,SEPTEMBER,OCTOBER,NOVEMBER,
             DECEMBER);
    DAY   = (MONDAY,TUESDAY,WEDNESDAY,THURSDAY,
             FRIDAY,SATURDAY,SUNDAY);
    PAY   = REAL;

VAR
    FALL,
    WINTER,
    SPRING,
    SUMMER  : MONTH;
    WEEKDAY,
    WEEKEND : DAY;
    SALARY  : PAY;
```

Type definitions can be shortcutted by specifying the constants in the variable declaration portion of the program, as follows:

```
VAR
    FAMILY : (LISA, SARA, RON, CINDY);
```

FAMILY is a programmer-defined data type that consists of the four names listed. Since the programmer-defined type (FAMILY, in this instance) may be needed elsewhere in the program (such as in a procedure heading where the type must be specified), this technique is not recommended. Another reason for not recommending it is that the intent is not as clear as when the type is defined separately.

Some care should be taken when defining new data types. Defining overlapping or identical types is not valid. This also means that elements of the predefined ordinal types (BOOLEAN, CHAR, and INTEGER) cannot be listed as programmer-defined ordinal type constants. The following examples show these illegal uses:

```
TYPE
    TREES = (FIR, PINE, DOGWOOD);
    FLOWERS = (ROSE, TULIP, DOGWOOD);

TYPE
    DIGIT = (1, 2, 3);
    LETTER = ('A', 'B', 'C');

VAR
    VOWEL : ('A', 'E', 'I', 'O', 'U');
```

In the first example, type FLOWERS is invalid since the constant DOGWOOD is ambiguous; that is, DOGWOOD is included in two type definitions (TREES and FLOWERS). The values listed in the other examples are elements of predefined types. Programmer-defined ordinal types should be used when creating a data type that is not a part of a predefined type (except if the programmer changes the name of a predefined type, such as by defining PAY as REAL).

Variables declared as programmer-defined ordinal types can be assigned values of those types, and can be used with relational operators and built-in functions. These variables can also be used with many of the programming structures introduced earlier. The next series of examples will illustrate some uses of programmer-defined ordinal types.

A programmer-defined ordinal value can be assigned to a variable that has been previously declared of that type. This example assumes the earlier type definition of SPECTRUM (with a declaration of the variable COLOR).

```
COLOR := RED; { VALID }
COLOR := PINK; { INVALID }
```

First, the variable COLOR is assigned the value RED. RED is not a string or a variable, but is a value of type SPECTRUM. Assigning PINK to COLOR would result in an error message, since PINK is not an element of type SPECTRUM.

Programmer-defined ordinal type identifiers can also be used in expressions. The relational operators (=, >, <, >=, <=, <>, IN) and some built-in functions (such as ORD, PRED and SUCC) can be used with programmer-defined ordinal types. The ordinal value (ORD) of the type constant is determined by its position in the definition. (Recall that the ordinal value of a constant in a list is the constant's position counting from left to right, starting with 0. Thus, the ordinal value of the first element of a programmer-defined type is always 0.) The predecessor function (PRED) yields the previous constant in the type definition and the successor function (SUCC) yields the next constant in the type definition. The predecessor of the first item in a list and the successor of the last element in a list do not exist. In Standard Pascal, an error message will result if the predecessor of the first constant or the successor of the last constant is requested. In UCSD Pascal, however, the ordinal value of the predecessor of the first constant is -1 and the ordinal value of the successor of the last constant is one more than the ordinal value of the last constant in the list. The following table gives examples of programmer-defined types with relational operators and some built-in functions.

Expression	Result
VIOLET < BLUE	TRUE
BLUE > YELLOW	FALSE
PRED(BLUE)	VIOLET
SUCC(GREEN)	YELLOW
ORD(MONDAY)	0
ORD(FRIDAY)	4

Programmer-defined ordinal types can also be used in expressions with any of the programming structures studied earlier. For example, these data types could be the initial and final values of a FOR structure, or used in the BOOLEAN expression of a REPEAT loop, WHILE loop, or an IF . . . THEN . . . ELSE statement.

For the following program statements, assume the earlier declarations of the variables WEEKDAY, WEEKEND, and SALARY, and REAL declarations for HOURSWORKED and TOTAL.

```
TOTAL := 0;
FOR WEEKDAY := MONDAY TO FRIDAY DO
    BEGIN
        WRITE('ENTER HOURS WORKED: ');
        READLN(HOURSWORKED);
        TOTAL := TOTAL + HOURSWORKED
    END;
```

The FOR loop is indexed from MONDAY to FRIDAY, using the sequence of constants provided by the type definition, DAY. The computer merely assigns an ordinal value to each constant in a type definition. Although the program specified that the loop runs from MONDAY to FRIDAY, the computer is actually counting from 0 to 4. (A loop incremented from SUNDAY to SATURDAY would result in an error message, since SUNDAY is listed after SATURDAY in the type definition of DAY.)

Loops can also be decremented, as shown in the following example:

```
FOR WEEKDAY := SUNDAY DOWNTO MONDAY DO
```

The following program statements show that variables of the same type can be compared.

```
SPRING := JUNE;
SUMMER := JUNE;
IF SPRING = SUMMER
    THEN WRITELN('BOTH SPRING AND SUMMER');
```

Remember: The expressions compared in the BOOLEAN expression of an IF . . . THEN . . . ELSE, WHILE, or REPEAT statement must be of the same type.

As stated earlier, programmer-defined ordinal types can be used like predefined types, with some exceptions. Programmer-defined ordinal types are similar in most ways to BOOLEAN, but similar only in part to CHAR and INTEGER. BOOLEAN consists of the ordered values FALSE and TRUE, where FALSE is the predecessor of TRUE. BOOLEAN and programmer-defined ordinal type constants have no readable or printable representations in some versions of Pascal; that is, they cannot be used for input or output. This places severe restrictions on the use of variables declared of programmer-defined ordinal types. For those versions with this limitation, a procedure can be written to handle input or output involving programmer-defined ordinal types. Program Segment 11.1 simulates the output of constants of a programmer-defined ordinal type.

Program Segment 11.1

```
TYPE
    NAMETYPE = (ALICE, ASA, JIM, MAGGIE, WALLY);

PROCEDURE PRINTOUT;

    VAR
        LOOP : NAMETYPE;

    BEGIN
        FOR LOOP := ALICE TO WALLY DO
            BEGIN
                CASE LOOP OF
                    ALICE  : WRITE('ALICE':10);
                    ASA    : WRITE('ASA':10);
                    JIM    : WRITE('JIM':10);
                    MAGGIE : WRITE('MAGGIE':10);
                    WALLY  : WRITE('WALLY':10)
                END;   { CASE }
                WRITELN
            END
    END; { PRINTOUT }
```

Using a CASE statement allows for a reasonable approach to the input and output of these type constants. Program Segment 11.2 presents a means of entering the value of a variable declared as a programmer-defined ordinal type.

Program Segment 11.2

```
READ(CH);
CASE CH OF
    'V' : COLOR := VIOLET;
    'B' : COLOR := BLUE;
    'G' : COLOR := GREEN;
    'Y' : COLOR := YELLOW;
    'O' : COLOR := ORANGE;
    'R' : COLOR := RED
END;
```

The technique used in Program Segment 11.2 depends on the first letter of each constant of type COLOR being different. If the first letter is not unique, then an additional CASE or IF . . . THEN . . . ELSE statement can be added.

Variables of a programmer-defined ordinal type can be passed to functions or procedures as either value or variable parameters. Before these variables are passed, the data type must be defined globally. (The shortcut method of declaring a variable type—listing the constants in the variable declaration—cannot be used, since a formal parameter must be defined as a global type.)

Programmer-defined ordinal type variables can be declared locally within the function or procedure, and can be the result of a function. Program Segment 11.3 shows a programmer-defined ordinal type as the result of a function.

Program Segment 11.3

```
TYPE PLACE = (FIRST, SECOND, THIRD);

FUNCTION WINNER (TOTALPOINTS : REAL) : PLACE;

   BEGIN
      IF TOTALPOINTS > 500
         THEN WINNER := FIRST
         ELSE IF TOTALPOINTS > 300
                 THEN WINNER := SECOND
                 ELSE WINNER := THIRD
   END;  { WINNER }
```

Lesson Check 11.1

1. Identify each statement or group of statements as valid or invalid. If invalid, explain.
   a. ```
      TYPE
         NUMBERS = (1, 2, 3, 4);
      ```
   b. ```
      TYPE
         DOGBREEDS = (TERRIER, BASSET,
                      BEAGLE, SCHNAUZER);
      ```
   c. ```
      TYPE
         SALADS = (LETTUCE, MACARONI, FRUIT);
      CONST
         GREENSALAD = LETTUCE; { GLOBAL CONSTANT }
      ```
   d. ```
      VAR
         STUDENT : (FRESHMAN, SOPHOMORE,
                    JUNIOR, SENIOR);
      ```
   e. ```
      TYPE
         TEST = BOOLEAN;
      ```

2. Given these definitions,
   ```
   TYPE
      ANIMALTYPE = (APE, BEAR, CAT, DOG, ELEPHANT,
                    FOX, GOAT, HARE, IMPALA,
                    JAGUAR, KANGAROO);
      TREETYPE   = (FIR, PINE, HEMLOCK);

   VAR
      TWOLEGGED,
      FOURLEGGED : ANIMALTYPE;
      TREE   : TREETYPE;
   ```
   ```

identify each of the following statements as valid or invalid. If the statement is invalid, explain why.

a. IF TWOLEGGED = FOURLEGGED
    THEN WRITELN('TWO OR FOUR LEGS');
b. IF TWOLEGGED = TREE
    THEN WRITELN('THE ANIMAL LIVES IN A TREE');
c. FOR FOURLEGGED := CAT TO DOG DO
    WRITELN(ORD(FOURLEGGED));

Lesson 11.2   Subrange Types

A subrange specifies a portion (or range) of a predefined or pro-grammer-defined ordinal type. A subrange type further specifies an existing type. Subranges of the programmer-defined ordinal types used in Lesson 11.1 can be written as in the following ex-ample. FALL and MIX are subranges of MONTH and SPECTRUM, respectively. Subranges can also be declared using the shortcut method.

```
TYPE
    SPECTRUM=(VIOLET,BLUE,GREEN,YELLOW,ORANGE,RED);
    MONTH   =(JANUARY,FEBRUARY,MARCH,APRIL,MAY,JUNE,
             JULY,AUGUST,SEPTEMBER,OCTOBER,
             NOVEMBER,DECEMBER);
    FALL    =SEPTEMBER..NOVEMBER;
    MIX     =BLUE..YELLOW;

VAR
    DARK    : VIOLET..GREEN; { SUBRANGE OF SPECTRUM }
    SUMMER  : JUNE..AUGUST;  { SUBRANGE OF MONTH }
```

The predefined ordinal types (BOOLEAN, CHAR, and INTEGER) can also be declared in a subrange.

```
VAR
    COUNT     : 1..10;
    UPPERCASE : 'A'..'Z';
    LOWERCASE : 'a'..'z';
```

The lower limit of a subrange is always less than or equal to that of the upper limit. The lower and upper limits of the sub-ranges are determined at the time the program is compiled and cannot be changed during the execution of the program. Also, there must be at least one item in each subrange.

Subrange Definition Form

```
TYPE
    type identifier = (list of constants);
    type identifier = lowerlimit..upperlimit;
```

Shortcut Subrange Declaration

```
VAR
    variable identifier : lowerlimit..upperlimit;
```

In contrast to type definitions, subranges can involve an overlap in the definitions and declarations. For example, suppose the programmer defined the following subranges of INTEGER:

```
TYPE
    POSINT = 1..100;
    INT    = -100..100;

VAR
    INT1,
    INT2   : POSINT;
    INT3   : 1..100;
    INT4   : INT;
```

The variables INT1 and INT2 are of an **identical type.** INT3 is not identical to INT1 and INT2 (even though they consist of the same possible range of values) because they were not defined as the same type. However, since they are of **compatible types,** they can be assigned to each other. The following assignments are always legal:

```
INT3 := INT1;
INT2 := INT3;
```

INT4 is also of a compatible type. Since type INT includes all possible values of type POSINT, the following assignment statement is always legal:

```
INT4 := INT1;
```

On the other hand, the type POSINT does not include all of the possible values of type INT; thus, the following assignment is not always legal:

```
INT1 := INT4;
```

It would, for instance, not be legal if INT4 $\leq$ 0. Depending on the value of INT1 this last assignment could result in a value-range error at run-time.

Program Segment 11.4 (a calendar-watch simulation) uses programmer-defined ordinal types and subranges of predefined types. The program segment prints the day of the week, along with the hours, minutes, and seconds.

Program Segment 11.4

```
CONST
    DELAY = 100;

TYPE
    WEEK        = (MONDAY, TUESDAY, WEDNESDAY,
                    THURSDAY, FRIDAY, SATURDAY, SUNDAY);
    HOURTYPE    = 0..23;
    MINSECTYPE  = 0..59;
```

```
        PROCEDURE PRINTDAY (D : WEEK);

           BEGIN

              CASE D OF
                 MONDAY     : WRITE('MONDAY':10);
                 TUESDAY    : WRITE('TUESDAY':10);
                 WEDNESDAY  : WRITE('WEDNESDAY':10);
                 THURSDAY   : WRITE('THURSDAY':10);
                 FRIDAY     : WRITE('FRIDAY':10);
                 SATURDAY   : WRITE('SATURDAY':10);
                 SUNDAY     : WRITE('SUNDAY':10)
              END  { CASE D }

           END;  { PRINTDAY }

        PROCEDURE CLOCK;

           VAR
              DAY    : WEEK;
              HOUR   : HOURTYPE;
              MINUTE,
              SECOND : MINSECTYPE;
              WAIT   : INTEGER;

           BEGIN

              FOR DAY := MONDAY TO SUNDAY DO
                 FOR HOUR := 0 TO 23 DO
                    FOR MINUTE := 0 TO 59 DO
                       FOR SECOND := 0 TO 59 DO
                          BEGIN
                             PRINTDAY(DAY);
                             WRITE(HOUR : 10);
                             WRITE(MINUTE : 10);
                             WRITELN(SECOND : 10);
                             FOR WAIT := 1 TO DELAY DO
                          END

           END;  { CLOCK }
```

Lesson Check 11.2

1. Identify each subrange as valid or invalid. If invalid, explain why.
   a. TYPE
   ```
        NUMBERS = 1..10;
   ```
   b. VAR
   ```
        COUNT : 9..1;
   ```
   c. TYPE
   ```
        VEGETABLE = (CARROT, BROCCOLI, SPINACH,
                     PEAS, CORN);
        GREENVEGIE = BROCCOLI..PEAS;
   ```
   d. VAR
   ```
        FIRSTFIVE : ('A'..'E');
   ```

2. Assume the following type definition and variable declaration.
   ```
   TYPE
        PLACE = (FIRST, SECOND, THIRD);

   VAR
        NUMBERS : 1..10;
        POSITION : PLACE;
   ```

a. What would happen if NUMBERS were assigned the value 100?
b. What would happen if the following assignments were made to the variable POSITION?

```
POSITION := FIRST;
POSITION := POSITION + 1;
```

Lesson 11.3   Programming Tip— Using Programmer-Defined Types and Subranges

Programmer-defined ordinal types and subranges can be useful to Pascal programmers. Even though, at first glance, they may appear to just produce more work, these two structures add to the clarity of the program and can help in debugging.

Subranges provide a natural way to document a program as well as a method for error trapping. Consider a program in which bowling scores for a single game are to be stored. The final score is to be stored in a variable called SCORE. Two possible declarations for SCORE are

Option 1	Option 2
```VAR SCORE : INTEGER;```	```TYPE BOWLSCORE : 0..300; VAR SCORE : BOWLSCORE;```

The first option is certainly the shortest, but the second has some advantages that make it preferable and justify typing a few extra lines. If score is defined as just an INTEGER, it can take on any value from -32768 to 32767. By declaring SCORE as a subrange, the intent is clear. A person reading the program will quickly understand the use of SCORE. Even without the obvious type name (BOWLSCORE), the reader might be able to figure out that SCORE meant a bowling score.

In addition, setting the range can aid the programmer in detecting bad input. Depending on the Pascal system being used, a range error will occur if SCORE is outside the range 0 to 300. This can be a valuable tool when it is time to test the program.

Programmer-defined ordinal types are similar in their documenting nature. Using values that have specific meaning helps to clarify the intent of a program segment. Program Segments 11.5 and 11.6 contrast the use of obscure variables and programmer-defined ordinal types.

**Program
Segment 11.5**

```
VAR
    COUNT : INTEGER;

BEGIN
    .
    .
    .
    FOR COUNT := 1 TO 7 DO
        BEGIN
            .
            .
            .
            END;
    .
    .
    .
END.
```

**Program
Segment 11.6**

```
TYPE
    DAYS = (MONDAY,TUESDAY,WEDNESDAY,THURSDAY,
            FRIDAY,SATURDAY,SUNDAY);

VAR
    DAYCOUNT : DAYS;

BEGIN
    .
    .
    .
    FOR DAYCOUNT := MONDAY TO SUNDAY DO
        BEGIN
            .
            .
            .
            END;
    .
    .
    .
END.
```

While the FOR loop in Program Segment 11.5 may accomplish the task of going through the days of the week, its meaning would not be as clear without further investigation. The purpose of the FOR loop in Program Segment 11.6 is clear from the start, making the entire segment easier to understand.

Another advantage of programmer-defined ordinal types is that they are ordered values and, therefore, can be compared with each other to determine their relative position in the list of type constants. An example that might utilize this feature is a program to analyze poker hands. A type definition of poker hands can be written with the names of the hands in the order of their rank.

```
TYPE
    HANDS = (ONEPAIR, TWOPAIR, THREEOFKIND, STRAIGHT,
             FLUSH, FULLHOUSE, FOUROFKIND,
             STRAIGHTFLUSH);

VAR
    HAND1,
    HAND2 : HANDS;
```

By using a programmer-defined type, the task of comparing hands to determine a winner is simply a matter of comparing their rank in the original definition. The following program segment gives a simplified but straightforward illustration of how programmer-defined type variables can be compared.

```
BEGIN

    HAND1 := STRAIGHT;
    HAND2 := FULLHOUSE;
    IF HAND1 > HAND2
        THEN WRITELN('HAND 1 WINS')
        ELSE WRITELN('HAND 2 WINS')

END.
```

Proper use of programmer-defined ordinal types and subranges is more than a nicety; their use can make programs much easier to read and understand. Programmers can help themselves—as well as others examining their programs—by making their intent clear from the outset. Debugging can be simplified and the final problem solution made more elegant by exercising these options.

Summary

Programmer-defined ordinal types each consist of a list of constants ordered by the programmer. In the type definition, the reserved word TYPE indicates that new data types follow. An equal sign separates the type identifier and the ordered list of constants. The ordered list is enclosed in parentheses and each value is separated by a comma. An identifier of that type must be declared in the variable portion of the program before the type values are used in the program. A shortcut to defining a new data type is to declare a variable and then list the constants of that type in parentheses following the variable identifier.

While constant lists of programmer-defined ordinal types cannot list elements of previously defined types, subranges of existing data types can be specified. A subrange is the portion of a data type that is of special use to the programmer. Unlike programmer-defined ordinal types, subranges can overlap; that is, one subrange can contain some elements that are also included in another subrange. The specification of a subrange can be part of the type definition or part of a variable declaration. Defining or declaring a subrange limits the possible values of the data type and thus saves memory space.

Key Terms

compatible types	subrange
identical types	TYPE
programmer-defined	type constant
ordinal type	type identifier

Answers to Lesson Checks

Lesson 11.1

1. **a.** Invalid. Type constants cannot be of an existing type.
   b. Valid.
   c. Invalid. A global CONST definition must come before the TYPE definitions in a program; global constants cannot be programmer-defined types.
   d. Valid.
   e. Valid.

2. **a.** Valid.
   b. Invalid. This will result in a type-mismatch error.
   c. Valid.

Lesson 11.2

1. **a.** Valid.
   b. Invalid. The lower limit must be given first.
   c. Valid.
   d. Invalid. Subrange definitions do not include parentheses.

2. **a.** An out-of-range error would occur if NUMBERS were assigned a value of 100.
   b. A type-mismatch error would occur since the statement is attempting to combine a programmer-defined type with an integer.

Exercises

Set I. Comprehension

1. Write a programmer-defined ordinal type definition for each of the following:
   a. Five favorite foods.
   b. Pieces in a chess game.
   c. Four main arithmetic operations.

2. Write a programmer-defined ordinal type definition for each of the following:
   a. Three favorite sports.
   b. Positions on a baseball team.
   c. Suits in a deck of playing cards.

3. Write a subrange type definition for each of the following:
   a. Integers from −20 to 20, inclusive.
   b. Characters from M to Z, inclusive.
   c. The first three foods of the type defined in Part **a** of Exercise 1.

4. Write a subrange type definition for each of the following:
   a. Integers from −50 to 45, inclusive.
   b. Characters from a to z, inclusive.
   c. The last two positions of the type defined in Part **b** of Exercise 2.

5. Identify the following definitions as valid or invalid. If invalid, explain why.
   a. `TYPE NUMBER = INTEGER;`
   b. `TYPE DIGITS = 9..0;`
   c. `TYPE ALPHABET = 'A'..'Z';`
   d. `TYPE GOODGRADES = A..C;`
   e. `TYPE ODDDIGITS = (1,3,5,7);`
   f. `TYPE BADGRADES = 'D'..'I';`
      `VAR LETTERGRADE : BADGRADES;`
   g. `TYPE`
      `    WORKDAY = (MONDAY, TUESDAY, WEDNESDAY,`
      `              SATURDAY, SUNDAY);`

6. Identify the following definitions as valid or invalid. If invalid, explain why.
   a. `TYPE I = -MAXINT...0;`
   b. `TYPE R = 1.0..10.0;`
   c. `TYPE CHARACTERS = CHAR;`
   d. `TYPE CH = 'A'..'Z';`
   e. `TYPE R = REAL;`
   f. `TYPE LETTER = ('A', 'B');`
   g. `TYPE LETTER = (A, B);`
   h. `TYPE DEPT = (DAIRY, DRUGS, MEAT, PRODUCE);`
   i. `TYPE DIRECTIONS = NORTH, SOUTH, EAST, WEST;`

7. Assuming these definitions,

   ```
   TYPE
       FRUIT = (APPLE, PEAR, ORANGE, LEMON, LIME);
       LETTER = 'A'..'Z';
   ```

   evaluate each of the following expressions:
   a. `ORD(ORANGE)`
   b. `CHR(ORD(PEAR))`
   c. `ORD('A')`
   d. `PRED(ORANGE)`
   e. `SUCC(LEMON)`
   f. `SUCC(LIME)`

8. Assuming these definitions,

   ```
   TYPE
       STUDENT = (FRESHMAN, SOPHOMORE,
                  JUNIOR, SENIOR);
       GRADE   = (A, B, C, D, F);
       LETTER  = 'A'..'Z';
   ```

   evaluate each of the following expressions:
   a. `ORD(FRESHMAN)`
   b. `CHR(ORD(B))`
   c. `ORD('Z')`
   d. `PRED(JUNIOR)`
   e. `SUCC(C)`
   f. `PRED(A)`

9. Identify each statement as true or false. If false, explain why.
   a. A type constant cannot be a reserved word.
   b. Identical types can be declared.

10. Identify each statement as true or false. If false, explain why.
   a. REAL is a predefined ordinal type.
   b. A type definition can include an identifier defined of type REAL.

11. Identify the errors in the following program segment:

```
TYPE
    TREE = (FIR, PINE, SPRUCE, DOGWOOD,
            APPLE, CHERRY);
VAR
    CONIFER = TREE;

PROCEDURE PRINTOUT(FIR : TREE);

    VAR
       LOOP : TREE;
    BEGIN
       FOR TREE := FIR TO SPRUCE DO
       WRITELN(TREE);
    END;
```

12. Identify the errors in the following program:

```
PROGRAM WORKING(OUTPUT);

TYPE
    DAYS = MONDAY, TUESDAY, WEDNESDAY, THURSDAY,
           SATURDAY, SUNDAY;

VAR
    WEEKDAY : MONDAY..FRIDAY;
    WEEKEND : SATURDAY..SUNDAY;

PROCEDURE WORK (DAY : MONDAY..FRIDAY);

        BEGIN
          IF DAY >= "MONDAY" AND DAY <= "FRIDAY"
             THEN WRITELN('YOU MUST WORK TODAY.')
             ELSE WRITELN('THIS IS YOUR DAY OFF.')
        END;

BEGIN
    FOR WEEKDAY := MONDAY TO SUNDAY DO
       WORK(WEEKDAY);
       WORK(WEEKEND);
       WORK(SUNDAY);
       WORK(LABORDAY)
END.
```

13. Given

```
TYPE
    NUMBERS = -20..20;
```

classify each of the following type definitions as identical, compatible, or neither:

a. TYPE A = 0..20;
b. TYPE B = -60..-30;
c. TYPE C = -18..20;
d. TYPE D = NUMBERS;

14. Given

TYPE
    LETTERS = 'A'..'Z';

classify each of the following type definitions as identical, compatible, or neither:
a. TYPE A = 'A'..'B';
b. TYPE B = 'A'..'Z';
c. TYPE C = 'A'..'z';
d. TYPE D = CHAR;

Set II. Application

15. Write a procedure to return the predecessor and successor of a given month of the year. If the month and year is January 1973, then the procedure would return December 1972 (the predecessor) and February 1973 (the successor).

16. The game of chess consists of six kinds of playing pieces: Pawn, Knight, Bishop, Rook, Queen, and King. Write a function that will take an integer ranging from 0 to 5 and return the chess piece with the corresponding ordinal number.

17. Assume a four-digit integer code consists of information for a small high school as shown in the following table:

Digit Place	Integer	Explanation
First on left	1–4	Represents a grade level (Freshman, Sophomore, Junior, Senior)
Second from left	1–4	Represents a bus route (North, South, East, West)
Third and fourth from left	01–99	Represents a student's ID number

For example, a code of 3247 would represent a junior, riding the south bus route, with an ID number of 47.

Write a procedure to accept the integer and return the grade level (programmer-defined type), the bus route direction (programmer-defined type), and the ID number (INTEGER).

18. Write a function that will take a positive integer (in the subrange 1 to 1000) and return the Roman numeral corresponding to that number. If the integer does not exactly correspond to a single Roman numeral, return NONE. (For example, the number 5 would return V, but 6 would return NONE.) Assume the following definitions:

TYPE
    ROMAN = (I, V, X, L, C, D, M, NONE);

19. Assume the following type definitions for the organisms in a food chain:

```
TYPE
    FOODCHAIN  = (CHEESE,MOUSE,SNAKE,OWL,BOBCAT);
    OCCUPATION = (PREDATOR, PREY);
    DISTANCE   = 0..4;
```

Write a procedure to accept two members of the food chain and determine if the first is a predator or prey of the second and how far apart they are in the chain. For example, given input of MOUSE and BOBCAT, the output should be as follows:

```
FIRST IS PREY
SECOND IS PREDATOR
DISTANCE APART IS 3
```

Set III. Synthesis

20. Write a program that allows the user to enter a month number and which then prints the season of the year. Use the following information:

Month	Season
March, April, May	Spring
June, July, August	Summer
September, October, November	Fall
December, January, February	Winter

Option: Allow the user to enter the name of the month.

21. Write a program that allows the user to enter a season of the year and which then prints the months that occur during that season. Use the information from Exercise 20.

22. Write a program that will allow the daily input of an employee's hours worked and hourly rate. The program should compute the total wages for each day and output the total wages for the week. Use the days of the week as a programmer-defined ordinal type.

23. A comparison is being made between Hyde Park in London, England, and Central Park in New York City. Write a program that will find the total attendance of each park for one week. The user should be asked to enter the daily attendance for each park. For each park, report the total weekday attendance, the total weekend attendance, and the total attendance for the week. Also, report the total combined attendance of both parks.

24. Using the function from Exercise 18, write a program to convert a Roman numeral into its integer equivalent. The ordinal functions may be useful in this problem.

25. Write a program to accept the name of a course and report the number of periods (and the course titles) until the end of school. Include the following definitions:

```
TYPE
    CLASSES     = (HISTORY, BIOLOGY, DRAMA, ART,
                   LUNCH, MATH, ENGLISH, PE);
    NEXTPERIODS = BIOLOGY..PE;
```

For example, if the input is DRAMA, the output is

```
5
ART, LUNCH, MATH, ENGLISH, PE.
```

Sets

Alice ventured to
. . .taste it, and,
finding it very nice (it
had, in fact, a sort of
mixed flavour of
cherry-tart, custard,
pineapple, roast turkey,
toffy, and hot buttered
toast), she very soon
finished it off.

—Lewis Carroll

Overview

Gaining a Perspective

A set in mathematics consists of a collection of objects or **elements** enclosed in braces, { }. For example, the integers from 1 to 5, inclusive, can be defined as a mathematical set as follows:

   {1,2,3,4,5}

Similarly, a Pascal **set** is a collection of elements. A Pascal set is also a structured data type. Unlike a mathematical set, the elements of a Pascal set are enclosed in square brackets, [ ]. For example,

[1,2,3,4,5]

The elements of a Pascal set must all be of the same ordinal or subrange type.

   There are many other similarities and differences between mathematical and Pascal sets. In both kinds of sets, the order of the elements is not important. For example, the Pascal set

[1,2,3,4,5]

represents the same set as

[4,2,5,3,1]

Additionally, the operations of intersection, union, and set difference performed on sets in mathematics and Pascal are similar.

   A mathematical set can be of any size, whereas the size of a Pascal set is limited, depending on the machine implementation. In UCSD Pascal, for example, sets cannot contain more than 512 elements.

   This chapter will develop the definition and declaration of sets and illustrate some of their uses.

Lesson 12.1   Set Definition and Declaration

Pascal sets are defined in the type definition portion of a program, as shown in the following examples:

```
TYPE
   CHARACTERS = SET OF CHAR;

   CAPITALS    = 'A'..'Z';
   LETTERS     = SET OF CAPITALS;

   NUMBERS     = SET OF 1..20;

   WESTSTATES = (ALASKA,ARIZONA,CALIFORNIA,COLORADO,
                 HAWAII,IDAHO,MONTANA,NEW MEXICO,
                 OREGON,WASHINGTON,WYOMING);
   WESTSET     = SET OF WESTSTATES;

   COLORSET    = SET OF (RED, ORANGE, YELLOW, WHITE,
                         GREEN, BLUE, VIOLET);
```

The first identifier, CHARACTERS, consists of the set of all elements of CHAR (the elements of CHAR are machine dependent). CAPITALS is a subrange of CHAR consisting of the capital letters of the alphabet, not a set definition. The type identifier LETTERS is a set whose elements are of the type CAPITALS. NUMBERS is a set consisting of a subrange of INTEGER. WESTSTATES is a programmer-defined ordinal type, and not a set definition. (Note the parentheses around the elements.) WESTSET, the identifier following WESTSTATES, is a set definition. The type COLORSET defines a set consisting of programmer-defined ordinal elements and shows a shorter form of the set definition and the enumeration of a programmer-defined ordinal type. The use of each item in (RED, . . . , VIOLET) is limited to COLORSET, since there is no specific type definition, such as

```
COLORTYPE = (RED,ORANGE,YELLOW,GREEN,BLUE,VIOLET);
```

Variables can be declared as in the following examples, using some of the earlier set and type definitions. (These identifiers will be referenced throughout this lesson.)

```
VAR
   LETTER1,
   LETTER2,
   LETTER3,
   LETTER4,
   ALLCAPS    : LETTERS;
   EMPTY,
   ALL,
   EVEN,
   ODD,
   CODE       : NUMBERS;
   ONEDIGIT   : SET OF 0..9;
   FIRSTA     : WESTSET;
   PATRIOTIC  : COLORSET;
```

LETTER1, LETTER2, LETTER3, LETTER4, and ALLCAPS are variables of type LETTERS and thus can contain only elements of type LETTERS. The identifier ONEDIGIT combines a set definition and declaration in the variable declaration portion of a program. (ONEDIGIT was not defined earlier.)

> **Set Definition and Declaration Form**
>
> ```
> TYPE
>     type identifier = SET OF base type;
>
> VAR
>     identifier : type identifier;
> ```
>
> **Definition and Declaration, Shorter Form**
>
> ```
> VAR
>     identifier : SET OF base type;
> ```

The base type must be BOOLEAN, CHAR, a programmer-defined ordinal type, or a subrange type (for example, a subrange of INTEGER). The base type can also be an ordered list of programmer-defined elements, as in the example of COLORSET mentioned earlier. (Sets that are passed as formal parameters must be both defined and declared using the longer form). The base type cannot be a structured type; that is, a set of sets is illegal. In the following example, the type definition of WORDS is not a valid set definition.

```
TYPE
    ALPHABET = SET OF 'A'..'Z';
    WORDS    = SET OF ALPHABET;   { INVALID }
```

After a set type has been defined and variables have been declared of that type, a set can be constructed from the possible elements of that type. Like all other variables, the variables of a set type must be initialized before they are used in a program. Since all Pascal variables are undefined until initialized, a set is constructed (initialized) by assigning elements to the set. Each set assignment is enclosed in square brackets and each element is separated by a comma. Here are possible set assignments for LETTER1 and LETTER2:

```
LETTER1 := ['A','B','C','D'];

LETTER2 := ['B','C','D','E','F','G'];
```

LETTER1 and LETTER2 each contain a portion of the possible values of their type. The assignment of elements to LETTER2 could also be written as

```
LETTER2 := ['B'..'G'];
```

Although the order of elements of a set does not matter, the order of subrange elements assigned to a set does make a difference. The subrange listing of LETTER2 could not be reversed; for instance, in the example just given, ['G'..'B'] would be illegal.

Set assignments consist of the variable name, the assignment symbol, and the list of elements of the set enclosed in square brackets.

> **Set Assignment Form**
>
> ```
> variable identifier := [elements of the set];
> ```

Here are some additional examples of set construction using earlier declarations.

```
LETTER3 := ['H'];
LETTER4 := LETTER3;
EVEN := [2,4,6,8,10,12,14,16,18,20];
ODD  := [19,17,15,13,11,9,7,5,3,1];
ALL  := [1..20];
CODE := [1..5, 15..17]
FIRSTA := [ALASKA, ARIZONA];
PATRIOTIC := [RED, WHITE, BLUE];
EMPTY := [];
ALLCAPS := ['A'..'Z'];
```

Notice that sets contain part, all, or none of the base type. Variables, such as LETTER4, can be assigned the elements of an existing set. The identifier CODE specifies nonconsecutive parts of the base type. Variables can be initialized to the empty set, a set containing no elements. The identifier EMPTY is initialized to the empty set, denoted by empty square brackets.

One set is a subset of another set if each element of the first is an element of the second. Figure 12.1 illustrates the relationship between the various subsets of type LETTERS. The representation shown is called a Venn diagram in mathematics. A Venn diagram is a collection of closed curves whose interior points represent the elements of a set. In this diagram, LETTERS is called the

Figure 12.1

Venn Diagram of Sets of Type LETTERS

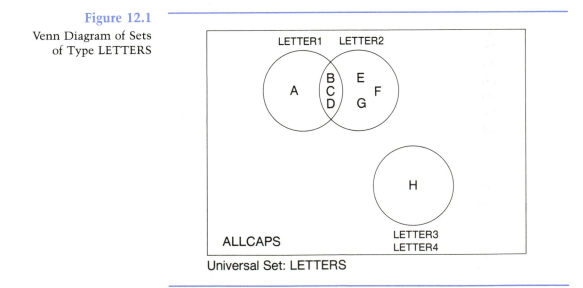

Universal Set: LETTERS

universal set (the set of all possible values of the set); ALLCAPS is the set containing all of the possible elements of LETTERS; and LETTER1, LETTER2, LETTER3, and LETTER4 are variables that represent subsets of LETTERS.

Lesson Check 12.1

1. Identify the legal set definitions. If the set definition is not legal, explain why.

   a. TYPE
   ```
        YEARS = SET OF 1977..1987;
   ```
   b. TYPE
   ```
        VEGETABLES = SET OF [PEAS, CORN,
                            BEANS, CARROTS];
   ```
   c. TYPE
   ```
       FLAVORS = (CHOCOLATE, VANILLA, STRAWBERRY);
       ICECREAM = SET OF FLAVORS;
   ```
   d. TYPE
   ```
        SHIRTS = SET OF (COWBOY,DRESS,POLO,JERSEY);
        SPORTSHIRTS = SET OF POLO..JERSEY;
   ```

2. Write the assignment statements needed to make EVEN the set of even integers from 2 to 10 and ODD the set of odd integers from 1 to 9. Assume the following set definition and declarations:

```
TYPE
    NUMBERS = SET OF [1..50];

VAR
    EVEN,
    ODD   : NUMBERS;
```

Lesson 12.2   Set Operators

Pascal **set operators** allow manipulation of sets of the same type. Table 12.1 summarizes the operations on sets and gives the corresponding mathematical set operators. The explanations use set A and set B, which represent any two sets of the same type that meet the size limitations of the Pascal compiler.

The next examples further illustrate the set operators. Program Segment 12.1 gives the variable initializations used in these examples.

Program Segment 12.1

```
TYPE
    LETTERS = SET OF 'A'..'Z';

VAR
    LETTER1,
    LETTER2,
    LETTER3,
    LETTER4 : LETTERS;
```

```
BEGIN

    { INITIALIZATIONS }

    LETTER1 := ['A','B','C','D'];
    LETTER2 := ['B'..'G'];
```

Table 12.1
Set Operators

Operation	Mathematical Symbol	Pascal Symbol	Definition
Union	A ∪ B	A + B	The set consisting of all elements from set A and set B.
Intersection	A ∩ B	A * B	The set consisting of elements that belong to both set A and set B.
Difference	A − B	A − B	The set consisting of all elements of set A that are not elements of set B.
Equal	A = B	A = B	Returns TRUE if set A and set B have identical elements.
Inequality	A ≠ B	A <> B	Returns TRUE if set A and set B do not have the same elements.
Subset	A ⊆ B	A <= B	Returns TRUE if all elements of set A are contained in set B.
	A ⊇ B	A >= B	Returns TRUE if all elements of set B are contained in set A.
Proper Subset	A ⊂ B	A < B	Returns TRUE if set A and set B do not have exactly the same elements and all elements of set A are contained in set B.
	A ⊃ B	A > B	Returns TRUE if set A and set B do not have exactly the same elements and all of the elements of set B are contained in set A.
Set Membership	E ∈ B	E IN B	Returns TRUE if the element E is a member of set B.

Reconstructing Sets

The **union** of two set variables is a set consisting of all the elements of both sets. For example, the union of LETTER1 and LETTER2 (using the set operator +) is the set containing the elements of LETTER1 and the elements of LETTER2.

```
LETTER3 := LETTER1 + LETTER2;
```

LETTER3 now contains the following elements:

```
['A','B','C','D','E','F','G']
```

Figure 12.2 illustrates this set union. The shaded region represents the set LETTER3.

The union operator can be used to add any variables or elements of the same base type. The following assignment adds the element 'Z' to LETTER1:

```
LETTER1 := LETTER1 + ['Z'];
```

LETTER1 now consists of the elements

```
['A','B','C','D','Z']
```

Here are some additional examples of the results obtained from set union.

Expression	Result
[2] + [2]	[2]
[] + [2,3]	[2,3]
[2] + [2,3]	[2,3]

Figure 12.2
Set Union of
LETTER1 and
LETTER2

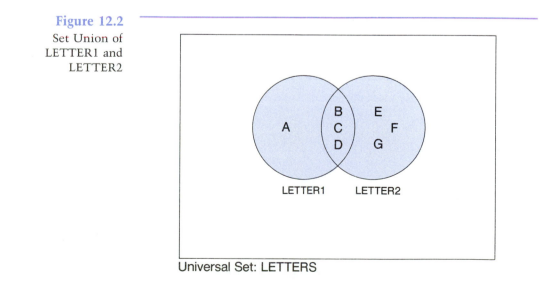

Universal Set: LETTERS

These examples show that the union set operator combines all of the elements of two sets. If a set is contained in another set (for example, [2] is a subset of [2,3]), the union of these sets is made up of the elements of the larger set.

As a final example, assume that MULT3 and MULT5 are variables of type NUMBERS, as defined in Lesson 12.1, and are initialized as follows:

```
MULT3 := [3,6,9,12,15,18];
MULT5 := [5,10,15,20];
```

Then the expression

```
MULT3 + MULT5
```

results in the following:

```
[3,5,6,9,10,12,15,18,20]
```

The **intersection** of sets (*) consists of the elements that both sets have in common. For example, the intersection of LETTER1 and LETTER2 (as shown in Figure 12.2) is the set made up of the letters B, C, and D.

```
LETTER4 := LETTER1 * LETTER2;
```

Now LETTER4 contains the elements 'B', 'C', and 'D'. The shaded region of Figure 12.3 shows this set intersection.

Assume EVEN and ODD were declared of type NUMBERS and initialized in Lesson 12.1. That is,

```
EVEN := [2,4,6,8,10,12,14,16,18,20];
ODD := [19,17,15,13,11,9,7,5,3,1];
```

Figure 12.3

Set Intersection of
LETTER1 and
LETTER2

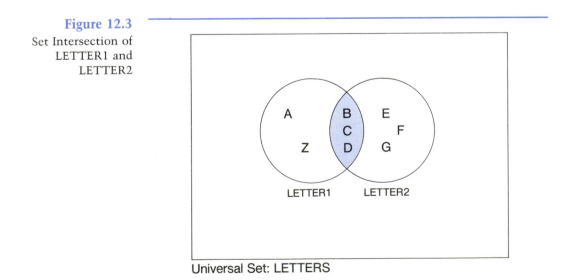

Universal Set: LETTERS

Also assume MULT3 and MULT5 are initialized as earlier in this lesson. The following are additional examples of set intersection:

Expression	Result
[2] * [2]	[2]
LETTER2 * ['B','H','E']	['B','E']
[] * [2,3]	[]
[1,2] * [3,4]	[]
EVEN * ODD	[]
[2] * [2,3]	[2]
MULT3 * MULT5	[15]

Set **difference** (−) allows elements to be removed from a set. In the following example, LETTER1 consists of the elements 'A', 'B', 'C', 'D', and 'Z', and LETTER2 consists of 'B'. . 'G'.

```
LETTER3 := LETTER2 - LETTER1;
```

LETTER3 is assigned ['E', 'F', 'G'], since all of the elements of LETTER1 that are also in LETTER2 are removed from LETTER2. Figure 12.4 shows the contents of LETTER3 in the shaded area.

In contrast to set union and intersection, set difference (like subtraction) is not commutative. For example,

(LETTER2 - LETTER1) does not equal (LETTER1 - LETTER2)

['E','F','G']   ['A','Z']

A single element can be removed from a set using the set difference operator. For instance,

```
LETTER1 := LETTER1 - ['D'];
```

Figure 12.4
Set Difference of
LETTER1 and
LETTER2

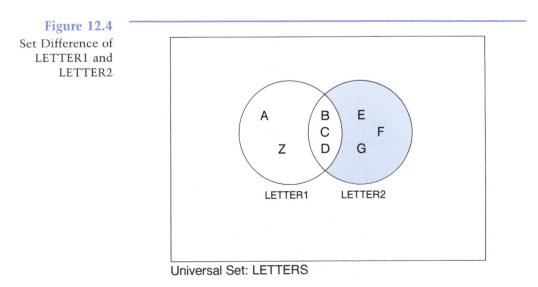

Universal Set: LETTERS

Now LETTER1 is

```
['A','B','C','Z']
```

Given the following assumptions:

```
MULT3 := [3, 6, 9, 12, 15, 18];
MULT5 := [5, 10, 15, 20];
```

here are some more examples of set difference.

Expression	Result
[2,3,4] - [2,3,4]	[]
[2,3] - [4,5]	[2,3]
[2,3] - []	[2,3]
MULT3 - MULT5	[3,6,9,12,18]
MULT5 - MULT3	[5,10,20]
[] - [2,3]	[]

Notice that set difference of identical sets is the empty set, and that common elements of two sets can be removed from one set using the difference operator. If the two sets do not have any elements in common (for example, [2,3] − [4,5] and [ ] − [2,3]), then the set difference is the first set.

If a subset must be constructed from a larger set, then set difference may be useful. In Program Segment 12.2, set difference is used to assign all consonants to the set CONSONANTS.

Program Segment 12.2

```
TYPE
    LETTERS = SET OF 'A'..'Z';

VAR
    ALPHABET,
    VOWELS,
    CONSONANTS : LETTERS;

BEGIN

    ALPHABET := ['A'..'Z'];
    VOWELS := ['A', 'E', 'I', 'O', 'U'];
    CONSONANTS := ALPHABET - VOWELS;
```

Notice that the set of consonants is obtained by using set difference; that is, by removing the vowels from all possible letters.

Relational Operators

The relational operators are useful for comparing two sets. Any of the examples to follow could be used as a BOOLEAN condition in a selection or looping structure.

Using earlier set definitions, the following examples illustrate the test for **equality** (=):

Expression	Result
MULT5 = [5,10,15,20]	TRUE
['A'..'Z'] = ['a'..'z']	FALSE
ODD = [3,15,9,17,19,9,7,13,1,5,11]	TRUE
[FALSE] = [TRUE]	FALSE
[3,2,1] = [1,2,3]	TRUE
[1..3] = []	FALSE
[3..1] = []	TRUE
EVEN + ODD = ALL	TRUE

The order of the set elements is not important. Note that in the next-to-last example, the subrange is listed in decreasing order. (No compiler error will occur, but listing the set elements in this manner may produce an unexpected result.) All of the elements of the set [3 .. 1] are ignored, so the empty set and the set [3 .. 1] are equal.

Similarly, the **inequality** (<>) of sets can also be determined, as in the following examples:

Expression	Result
MULT3 <> MULT5	TRUE
EVEN - ODD <> []	TRUE
EVEN <> [1,3]	TRUE
[3,2,1] <> [1,2,3]	FALSE
[3..1] <> []	FALSE
[] <> ['']	TRUE

The first three examples are rather straightforward once the elements of each set are known. The last example is a little tricky. The empty set is not equal to the set containing empty quotation marks since the latter set contains an element.

The following examples illustrate the various **subset** operators (<=, >=, <, >):

Expression	Result
[] <= MULT5	TRUE
EVEN <= ODD	FALSE
MULT3 < ALL	TRUE
MULT5 >= ALL	FALSE
[''] >= []	TRUE
[1,2,3] > [1,2,3]	FALSE
[1,2,3] >= [1,2,3]	TRUE
[1,2,3] < [1,2,3,4]	TRUE

The first example would be read as "Is the empty set a subset of the set containing multiples of 5?" Since the empty set is a subset of all sets, this expression is TRUE. Notice the differences between the results of the subset operators (<= and >=) and the proper subset operators (< and >).

Set **membership** (IN) is illustrated in the following examples. Recall from Chapter 7 that the IN operator is used to check whether a particular element is in a given list of values.

Expression	Result
3 IN MULT3	TRUE
5 IN [1..5]	TRUE
2 IN ODD	FALSE

The IN operator accompanying an IF . . . THEN statement or a REPEAT loop is useful for error-checking data. The following statements test to make sure that NUMBER is an integer between 1 and 5, inclusive:

```
IF (NUMBER = 1) OR (NUMBER = 2) OR (NUMBER = 3) OR
   (NUMBER = 4) OR (NUMBER = 5)
   THEN...

IF NUMBER IN [1..5]
   THEN...

REPEAT
   READ(NUMBER)
UNTIL NUMBER IN [1..5];
```

The IN operator can also provide a shortcut expression for an inequality, as shown by comparing the following pairs of IF . . . THEN statements:

```
IF (NUMBER >= 50) AND (NUMBER <= 100)
   THEN...

IF NUMBER IN [50..100]
   THEN...


IF (NUMBER > 10) OR (NUMBER < 1)
   THEN...

IF NOT(NUMBER IN [1..10])
   THEN...
```

The order in which set operations are performed is similar to the order of arithmetic operations, as shown in Table 12.2. All of these operations are performed starting from left to right within each category.

Table 12.2
Order of Operations
for Sets

Order	Operation
1. Perform all operations within parentheses.	( )
2. Perform set intersection.	*
3. Perform set union and difference.	+ −
4. Perform all relational operators.	< <= > >= = <> IN

The following examples show the application of this order on expressions involving more than one operator.

Expression	Result
`[1,2,3] + [4,5] * [5,6,7]`	`[1,2,3,5]`
`[4..9] - ([2..9] - [2..4])`	`[4]`
`['h'] <= ['a'..'z'] * ['h']`	`TRUE`
`[] - [4..7] + [4..7] = []`	`FALSE`

Lesson Check 12.2

1. Assume that sets A, B, and C have been declared appropriately and that the following assignments are made to sets A and B:

```
A := [1..9];
B := [1,3,5];
```

What elements does set C contain after each of the following operations has been performed?
   a. `C := A + B;`
   b. `C := A * B;`
   c. `C := A - B;`
   d. `C := A - B * [2,4,6,8];`
   e. `C := A * [6..10] - (B + [4..7]);`

2. Determine the BOOLEAN value of each of the following expressions, using the initialization of A and B provided in Problem 1.
   a. `B < A`
   b. `B = [1..5]`
   c. `A <> B`
   d. `1 IN B`
   e. `A <= B`

Lesson 12.3   Programming with Sets

Program 12.3 generates a set of the prime numbers between 1 and 100. Recall that a prime number is a positive integer that has exactly two factors: 1 and the number itself. For example, 5 is prime since it is divisible by 1 and 5; whereas 6 is composite since it is divisible by 1, 2, 3, and 6. The Sieve of Eratosthenes, an ancient method for finding prime numbers, involves listing all of the numbers in the set for which primes are to be found and then crossing out all multiples of primes, beginning with 2, then 3, then 5, then 7, and so on. Table 12.3 illustrates how the prime numbers remain in the set as each nonprime is subtracted.

Program 12.3

```
PROGRAM PRIMEGENERATOR(INPUT, OUTPUT);

    { PURPOSE: TO GENERATE THE PRIME NUMBERS
               BETWEEN 1 AND 100 }

TYPE
    NUMBERS = SET OF 1..100;

VAR
    PRIME : NUMBERS;
    NUM   : INTEGER;
    FIRST : BOOLEAN;

PROCEDURE INITIALIZE (VAR P:NUMBERS; VAR F:BOOLEAN;
                      VAR N:INTEGER);

    BEGIN

        P := [2..100];
        F := TRUE;
        N := 2

    END; { INITIALIZE }

PROCEDURE SIEVE (VAR P : NUMBERS; F : BOOLEAN;
                 N : INTEGER);

    VAR
        COUNT : INTEGER;

    BEGIN

        REPEAT
            IF N IN P
                THEN
                    FOR COUNT := N TO 100 DO
                        IF (COUNT MOD N = 0)
                            THEN IF NOT(F)
                                THEN P := P - [COUNT]
                                ELSE F := FALSE;
            N := N + 1;
            F := TRUE
        UNTIL N = 100

    END; { SIEVE }
```

```
PROCEDURE PRINTOUT (P : NUMBERS);

    VAR
        COUNT : INTEGER;

    BEGIN

        FOR COUNT := 1 TO 100 DO
            IF COUNT IN P
                THEN WRITE(COUNT, ' ');
        WRITELN

    END; { PRINTOUT }

BEGIN { MAIN PROGRAM }

    INITIALIZE(PRIME, FIRST, NUM);
    SIEVE(PRIME, FIRST, NUM);
    PRINTOUT(PRIME)

END.
```

Procedure INITIALIZE initializes the set of prime numbers to [2..100], the BOOLEAN variable F to TRUE, and the first number to be tested to 2. The procedure SIEVE, starts with 2 and determines if 2 is in the set of primes. If 2 is a member of the set, then all numbers less than or equal to 100 that are divisible by 2 are removed from the set of primes by the statement

```
P := P - [COUNT]
```

The next prime is then determined and all multiples of that prime are removed from the set of primes. (Also note in procedure PRINTOUT that the output of the set variable P must be performed indirectly using a loop and the IN operator. Set variables cannot be used in a READ(LN) or WRITE(LN).)

As Program 12.3 demonstrates, variables of a set type can be passed as parameters to a procedure. Variables of a set type can

---

Table 12.3
Set Implementation of
Sieve of Eratosthenes

Given the set

[1, 2, 3, 4, 5, 6, 7, 8, 9, 10, 11, 12, 13, 14, 15, 16, . . .]

Subtract multiples of 2

[1, 2, 3,   5,   7,   9,   11,   13,   15,   . . .]

Subtract multiples of 3

[1, 2, 3,   5,   7,   11,   13,   . . .]

Subtract multiples of 5

[1, 2, 3,   5,   7,   11,   13,   . . .]

Continue through the end of the set

---

also be passed to a function, but cannot be returned as the value of the function.

1. What are the limitations in using sets as parameters?

2. Identify the errors in the following program:

```
PROGRAM TEN (OUTPUT);

VAR
    NUMS : [1..10];
    CNT  : INTEGER;

BEGIN
    FOR CNT := 1 TO 10 DO
        BEGIN
            NUMS := NUMS - CNT;
            WRITELN(NUMS)
        END
END.
```

Lesson 12.4 Programming Tip—Testing

Once a program is designed and written, there is still one important task to perform. The program must be thoroughly tested. If care has been taken at each step in the programming process, few errors will exist. But no matter how confident the programmer is in the final product, complete testing is essential before putting the program to work.

Several aspects of the testing process exist. Each aspect has its own purpose and methodology.

Procedure Testing

Each procedure (and function) in a program must be tested to see that it does what it is supposed to, and that it interacts with other parts of the program as intended. Sometimes this can be done very simply, if the procedure does one thing and interacts little with other parts of the program. More often, a procedure needs to be tested in relation to what it needs to do its job and what it creates for use elsewhere in the program. This may involve writing some code to test the procedure as if it were being used in the program. Some points to look for during this phase of testing follow:

- Test the procedure by using sample scenarios to simulate its intended use. Try to use conditions as close to actual use as possible.
- Determine if the limits (if any) of the procedure can be violated.

- Check for loss of data or production of erroneous data.
- If various hardware setups are possible, check for correct procedure functioning for each configuration. Include testing for any use (reading, writing) of the diskette at this point.
- Check the time needed for the procedure to work, if time is a factor.

Documentation Testing

Check for accuracy of documentation and to see that all features are described fully. Observe the following points:

- Check for contradictions between parts of the documentation.
- Anticipate user questions and address those questions.
- Specifically look for omissions in the documentation.
- Ensure that the documentation is clearly worded and without errors; double-check for misspellings.
- Check to see if the documentation requires that the user have prior knowledge of any terms. Define those terms as necessary.
- Double-check any examples to be sure they are correct.

Destructive Testing

Assuming the program looks good to this point, destructive testing is the time to deliberately try to blow up the operation of the program. This is done by creating error conditions and doing the unexpected; the programmer should, if possible, anticipate user mistakes. Here are a few ideas to help in destructive testing.

- Test for values out of the desired range.
- Test for values not of the expected type.
- Try options that do not appear on menus or other choices for user input.
- Check for wrong diskettes (or no diskettes) in drives.
- Make sure any error messages given in the program are accurate and understandable.

Regression Testing

Regression testing is performed when an error has been found and corrected. At this point, the programmer should make sure the changes made in correcting the error have not caused problems elsewhere in the program. Since the change may not have been part of the original plan, the effects on the rest of the program are unpredictable. Of course, in a large program, repeating every test would probably be too time-consuming. Thus, regression testing should involve several carefully chosen test options. This form of testing cannot be overlooked. One change can cause a chain of errors that will ruin an entire program.

Field Testing

Field testing should take place after the programmer feels comfortable with the operation of the program. Field testing involves getting the program into an actual situation where it will be used with individuals who have no preconceptions concerning the program. A variety of sites should be chosen, as well as a cross section of users with varying backgrounds.

Obviously, testing can be an involved, time-consuming process. The amount of effort and time required, however, is directly related to the effort put into the initial stages of solving the problem. A carefully designed and well-planned solution can greatly decrease the time needed for testing. In addition, much testing of individual procedures can be done as they are developed, increasing the programmer's confidence level in the final product. The programmer has a responsibility to perform all the necessary tests to make sure the program works as intended. Remember, no one wants to commit to using a program and then have it fail at a critical time.

Summary

A Pascal set is a collection of elements of the same ordinal or subrange type. A set identifier must be defined in the TYPE portion or be declared in the variable portion of a Pascal program. An identifier must be declared of that type before it can be assigned any of the set elements. Within the program body this identifier can be assigned to elements of its type. The elements in a set assignment are enclosed in square brackets. Set operations (such as union, intersection, and difference), as well as the relational operators, can be performed on sets.

Sets are useful for error checking and program readability. Greater elegance in programming can be achieved through the use of sets. Relatively few programming languages include this type of implementation.

Key Terms

difference
element
equality
inequality

intersection
membership
set

set operator
subset
union

Answers to Lesson Checks

Lesson 12.1

1. **a.** Legal.
   b. Illegal. The brackets should be replaced by parentheses.
   c. Legal.
   d. Illegal. Since a shortcut definition was used for SHIRTS, the programmer-defined type constants are limited to the set SHIRTS and cannot be included in any other type or set definitions.

2. EVEN := [2,4,6,8,10];
   ODD := [1,3,5,7,9];

Lesson 12.2

1. a. [1..9]
   b. [1,3,5]
   c. [2,4,6,7,8,9]
   d. [1..9]
   e. [8,9]

2. a. TRUE
   b. FALSE
   c. TRUE
   d. TRUE
   e. FALSE

Lesson 12.3

1. A set cannot be returned as the value of a function.

2. No set definition is given for subrange 1..10. Brackets are needed for CNT to remove from NUMS. A set variable cannot be written directly. A corrected version of the program follows:

```
PROGRAM TEN (OUTPUT);

       { CORRECTED VERSION }

TYPE
   ONETOTEN = SET OF 1..10;

VAR
   NUMS : ONETOTEN;
   CNT,
   CNT2 : INTEGER;

BEGIN

   FOR CNT := 1 TO 10 DO
      BEGIN
         NUMS := NUMS - [CNT];
         FOR CNT2 := 1 TO 10 DO
            IF CNT2 IN NUMS
               THEN WRITE(CNT2:3);
         WRITELN
      END

END.
```

Exercises   Set I. Comprehension

For Exercises 1–6, define the set type described in Part **a**, declare the variables listed in Part **b**, and initialize the variables as indicated in Part **c**.

1. a. Define the type: The set of all alphabetic characters, both upper- and lowercase. Use the identifier ALPHABET.

    b. Declare variables: LOWERCASE and UPPERCASE.
    c. Initialize variables: LOWERCASE to the lowercase letters, UPPERCASE to the uppercase letters.

2. **a.** Define the type: The set of integers from 0 to 10. Use the identifier NUMBERS.
    b. Declare variables: EVEN and ODD.
    c. Initialize variables: EVEN to the even integers, ODD to the odd integers.

3. **a.** Define the type: A set of six colors. Use the identifier COLORS.
    b. Declare variables: LIGHT and DARK.
    c. Initialize variables: LIGHT to the empty set, DARK to all possible elements.

4. **a.** Define the type: The set of days in a year, that is, 1 to 366. Use the identifier DAYS.
    b. Declare variables: JANUARY and DECEMBER.
    c. Initialize variables: The first and last 31 days to JANUARY and DECEMBER, respectively.

5. **a.** Define the type: The set of symbols (! through ?). Use the identifier SYMBOLS.
    b. Declare variables: PUNCTUATION, ENDINGS.
    c. Initialize variables: PUNCTUATION to all punctuation (! , . ; : ?), and ENDINGS to the question mark, the period, and the exclamation mark.

6. **a.** Define the type: The set of names DANIELLE, DAVID, MICHELLE, JENNIFER, DAGWOOD, and MICHAEL. Use the identifier NAMES.
    b. Declare variable: DEES.
    c. Initialize variable: DEES to the names beginning with the letter D.

7. Identify the equivalent sets among the following:
    a. ['a'..'z']
    b. ['z'..'a']
    c. []
    d. ['a'..'m', 'n'..'y', 'z']

8. Identify the equivalent sets among the following:
    a. [1, 2, 3]
    b. [1..3]
    c. [3..1]
    d. []
    e. [3, 2, 1]
    f. [3, 1, 2]

9. Evaluate each of the following expressions:
    a. [] + ['A', 'B', 'C']
    b. [] - ['A', 'B', 'C']
    c. ['A', 'B', 'C'] * ['A', 'B', 'C']

10. Evaluate each of the following expressions:
    a. [1..5] + [1..5]
    b. [1..3] - [1..5]
    c. [] * [1..5]

11. Assume appropriate set definitions and declarations have been made, and SET1, SET2, and SET3 have been initialized as follows:

    ```
    SET1 := [1..4];
    SET2 := [2..5];
    SET3 := [1..5];
    ```

    Evaluate each of the following expressions:
    a. SET1 + SET2
    b. SET1 * SET3
    c. SET2 - SET1
    d. SET1 + SET2 * SET3
    e. SET1 - SET2 * []

12. Assume appropriate set definitions and declarations have been made, and SET1, SET2, and SET3 have been initialized as follows:

    ```
    SET1 := [1..20];
    SET2 := [5, 4, 3, 2, 1];
    SET3 := [5];
    ```

    Evaluate each of the following expressions:
    a. SET1 - SET2
    b. SET3 - SET 2
    c. SET1 * SET2
    d. SET2 - SET3
    e. SET2 - SET3 - SET1

13. Evaluate each of the following BOOLEAN expressions using the assignments given in Exercise 11:
    a. SET1 <= SET3
    b. SET3 >= SET2
    c. SET1 - SET2 = SET2 - SET1
    d. SET1 + SET 2 = SET3
    e. SET3 - (SET1 + SET2) = []

14. Evaluate each of the following BOOLEAN expressions using the assignments given in Exercise 12:
    a. SET1 > SET2
    b. SET3 IN SET2
    c. (SET2 * SET3) = SET3
    d. SET2 <> (SET1 * SET3)
    e. SET3 <= SET1

15. Assume LETTER is a set variable whose type consists of the capital letters. Write a set expression using IN for each of the following:
    a. (LETTER = 'A') OR (LETTER = 'B') OR (LETTER = 'C')
    b. (LETTER < 'R') AND (LETTER > 'G')
    c. (LETTER = 'A') OR (LETTER <> ['D'..'Z']) AND (LETTER >= ['B', 'C'])

16. Assume NUM is a set variable whose type consists of the integers from −100 to 100. Write a set expression using IN for each of the following:
    a. (NUM = 5) OR (NUM = 6) OR (NUM = 8)
    b. (NUM > -50) AND (NUM < 50)
    c. (NUM = 2) OR (NUM < 100) AND (NUM > 10)

Set II. Application

17. Write a program to determine if a letter entered by the user is a vowel or a consonant.

18. Write a program that counts the number of consonants and vowels entered by the user and prints the number of each in a table. For example, given input of PASCAL, the program should print

```
LETTER          NUMBER
----------      ------
CONSONANTS        4
VOWELS            2
```

19. Write a program that counts the number of different letters entered by the user and prints the count for each letter in a table. For example, given input of PASCAL, the program should print a table that begins as follows:

```
LETTER   NUMBER
------   ------
   A       2
   B       0
   C       1
   D       0
```

20. Write a program that will allow the user to enter a text passage and which then determines the number and type of punctuation marks present in the passage.

21. Most items of nature can be specified as animal, vegetable, or mineral. First establish the sets for animal, vegetable and mineral. Then write a program to determine if an item entered by the user is a member of one of these sets. If it is, determine whether it is animal, vegetable, or mineral. If the item is not present in any of the sets, then indicate that the item is unknown.

Set III. Synthesis

22. Given the set of colors red, yellow, blue, orange, violet, and green, write a program to determine if a color entered by the user is primary, secondary, or neither. If the color is secondary, the program should give the primary formula for producing that color. Orange, violet, and green are secondary colors, formed in the following manner:

       orange = red + yellow
       violet = red + blue
       green = blue + yellow

Define all the colors to be of type HUES and establish set variables PRIMARY and SECONDARY.

23. Write a program that will find all of the letters that are common to three names entered by the user. Define CHARACTERS to be a set of type CHAR, with ALPHABET as a set variable containing the letters A through Z. The lowercase letters can be included.

24. Create set variables categorizing numbers as to whether they are negative or positive, odd or even, a square, and/or a cube. Write a program to determine if an integer entered by the user belongs in any of these sets. Each set variable should be initialized to the empty set. If the integer belongs to more than one group, it should be added to each appropriate set. When the user has entered 20 numbers, print the members of each set (some may not have any) along with a list of all numbers entered.

Arrays

T he table was a large one, but the three were all crowded together at one corner of it. "No room! No room!" they cried out when they saw Alice coming. "There's plenty of room!" said Alice indignantly, and she sat down in a large arm-chair at one end of the table.

—Lewis Carroll

Overview

Gaining a Perspective

The data types previously discussed allow for the representation of a variety of data values—integers, reals, characters, strings, programmer-defined types, and BOOLEAN values. Several problems arise, however, if there is a need to represent a list of names or a table of numbers. Even if the programmer is willing to create all the individual variables necessary to represent the data, accessing that data in an orderly, easily managed fashion would be nearly impossible. For example, alphabetizing a list of 100 names or searching a table of numbers for a specific value would be a monumental task. Obviously, a programming structure is needed to represent data in a manner that allows for ease of access and manipulation. The most common data structure is an **array.** Arrays allow like data to be grouped under one variable name. Each element of the group is accessed through a label (**subscript** or index), commonly an integer. Thus, retrieving an individual name from a list or switching two numbers in a table becomes nothing more than manipulating the subscripts associated with the actual value(s) in the array. This chapter and the next will explore the implementation of arrays, as well as several applications.

Lesson 13.1   One-Dimensional Arrays

One method for inputting and storing several names in a program would be to write a procedure to read a name. The procedure could be repeatedly called from the main program, as shown in Program 13.1.

Program 13.1

```
PROGRAM READNAMES1(INPUT, OUTPUT);

    { PURPOSE: DATA ENTRY WITHOUT ARRAYS }

VAR
    NAME1,
    NAME2,
    NAME3,
    NAME4,
    NAME5  : STRING;
```

```
PROCEDURE GETNAME(VAR NAME : STRING);

  BEGIN

    WRITE('>');
    READLN(NAME)

  END; { GETNAME }

BEGIN   { MAIN PROGRAM }

  WRITELN('ENTER 5 NAMES');
  GETNAME(NAME1);
  GETNAME(NAME2);
  GETNAME(NAME3);
  GETNAME(NAME4);
  GETNAME(NAME5);
  WRITELN(NAME1,' ',NAME2,' ',NAME3,' ',
          NAME4,' ',NAME5)

END.
```

As the number of names increases, this method of assigning names to variables becomes less desirable. An array structure would be better suited to the task. Array structures allow collections of like data (that is, data of a single type) to be stored in an organized manner. For example, people's names or the test scores of a class can be represented by one variable, with subscripts distinguishing between different values.

Program 13.2 uses the array structure to hold a list of names.

Program 13.2
```
PROGRAM READNAMES2(INPUT, OUTPUT);

  { PURPOSE: TO READ FIVE NAMES USING ARRAYS }

TYPE
  NAMES = ARRAY[1..5] OF STRING;

VAR
  PEOPLE : NAMES;

PROCEDURE GETNAME(VAR NAME : NAMES);

  VAR
    COUNT : INTEGER;

  BEGIN

    WRITELN('ENTER 5 NAMES.');
    FOR COUNT := 1 TO 5 DO
      BEGIN
        WRITE('>');
        READLN(NAME[COUNT])
      END   { FOR }

  END; { GETNAME }
```

```
PROCEDURE PRINTOUT(NAME : NAMES);

   VAR
      COUNT : INTEGER;

   BEGIN

      WRITELN('COUNT':5,'NAME':10);
      FOR COUNT := 1 TO 5 DO
         WRITELN(COUNT:5,NAME[COUNT]:10)

   END; { PRINTOUT }

BEGIN   { MAIN PROGRAM }

   GETNAME(PEOPLE);
   PRINTOUT(PEOPLE)

END.
```

Suppose that in response to the prompt to

`ENTER 5 NAMES.`

the following names were entered:

```
>FRANK
>RON
>KAREN
>PAM
>BUD
```

The output would look like this:

```
COUNT      NAME
    1      FRANK
    2        RON
    3      KAREN
    4        PAM
    5        BUD
```

The memory locations for the array of Program 13.2 are illustrated in Figure 13.1.

Figure 13.1
Contents of Memory
for Array PEOPLE

```
PEOPLE[1] := FRANK
PEOPLE[2] := RON
PEOPLE[3] := KAREN
PEOPLE[4] := PAM
PEOPLE[5] := BUD
```

PEOPLE	
1	FRANK
2	RON
3	KAREN
4	PAM
5	BUD

In Program 13.2, the values for array PEOPLE are stored in a series of memory locations. The retrieval of the entire list of names is much simpler using the array structure. Notice the word TYPE written above the variable declaration. An array is defined as a TYPE, since the programmer must determine the dimensions and data type of the array.

An array identifier, like other Pascal identifiers, must be defined before it is used. The array name is a variable that represents many similar values.

Definition and Declaration of an Array Variable

```
TYPE
    array identifier = ARRAY[lower..upper]
                            OF data type;


VAR
    variable identifier : array identifier;
```

Shortcut Declaration

```
VAR
    variable identifier : ARRAY[lower..upper]
                            OF data type;
```

The lower and upper limits represent the size or **dimension** of the array and establish the range of its subscripts. The subscript type is not limited to integers. It can be any ordered type, including programmer-defined types. The data type of the array can be any of the types covered earlier.

The definition of the array for Program 13.2 can be shortened by using the VAR declaration as follows:

```
VAR
    PEOPLE : ARRAY[1..5] OF STRING;
```

This method is not recommended, however, since the array (without a type definition) could not be used as a parameter in a procedure.

Arrays can be used in a program in several ways. An element of an array can be accessed using an assignment statement. The subscript in brackets, [], specifies a particular element. (In the following examples, PEOPLE and PERSON must be array variables of the same type.)

```
PEOPLE[1] := 'JOHN';
PEOPLE[4] := 'KIM';
PEOPLE[2 + 3] := 'SARA';
PERSON[4] := PEOPLE[5];
PEOPLE[2] := PERSON[4];
```

A WRITELN can be used to print a single element of an array.

```
WRITELN(PEOPLE[4]);
```

To print more than a single element, a FOR loop can be used.

```
FOR COUNT := 1 TO 5 DO
   WRITELN(PEOPLE[COUNT]);
```

An entire array can be assigned to another array of the same type by using an assignment statement with the array variable identifier, as shown in Program 13.3.

Program 13.3

```
PROGRAM ASSIGN(INPUT, OUTPUT);

   { PURPOSE: TO DEMONSTRATE ARRAY ASSIGNMENT }

TYPE
   LETTERS = ARRAY[1..5] OF CHAR;

VAR
   GROUP1,
   GROUP2  : LETTERS;
   COUNT   : INTEGER;

BEGIN
   FOR COUNT := 1 TO 5 DO
      GROUP1[COUNT] := CHR(COUNT + 64);
   GROUP2 := GROUP1
END.
```

In Program 13.3, GROUP1 is assigned the first five letters of the alphabet. Then every element in GROUP2 is assigned the corresponding values stored in GROUP1, as shown in Figure 13.2.

Figure 13.2

Assigning Array
GROUP1 to GROUP2

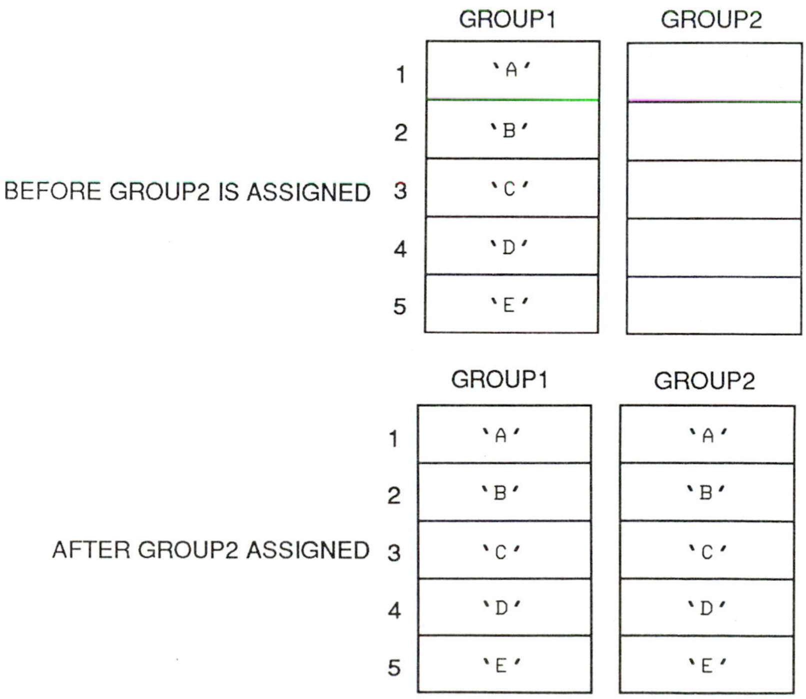

An entire array can be passed to a procedure or function. For example, an output procedure for Program 13.3 could have the following heading:

```
PROCEDURE PRINTOUT(GROUPS : LETTERS);
```

In the main program, the procedure calls would be

```
PRINTOUT(GROUP1);
PRINTOUT(GROUP2);
```

Notice that the array names GROUP1 and GROUP2 are global variables, whereas GROUPS is a local variable of the same type. The array must have a type definition (that is, not the shortcut declaration) if the array is to be used as a parameter.

An array can be passed to a procedure as a value or a variable parameter. Passing an array as a variable parameter saves space, since the memory locations for the array are shared by the procedure and the main program.

Caution: Changes made to the array sent as a variable parameter in the procedure are also made in the main program.

Program 13.4 allows the user to enter some test scores; it then reports the average of the scores, and the lowest and highest score entered.

Program 13.4

```
PROGRAM TESTAVERAGE(INPUT,OUTPUT);

    { PURPOSE: TO ANALYZE TEST SCORES }

CONST
   N = 11;

TYPE
   SCORETYPE = ARRAY[1..N] OF INTEGER;

VAR
   COUNT,
   LARGEST,
   SMALLEST : INTEGER;
   SCORE    : SCORETYPE;
   AVER     : REAL;

PROCEDURE GETSCORES(VAR C:INTEGER; VAR S:SCORETYPE);

   BEGIN
      WRITELN('ENTER SCORES (UP TO 10).');
      WRITELN('ENTER 999 WHEN FINISHED.');
      REPEAT
         C := C + 1;
         WRITE('>');
         READLN(S[C]);
         IF S[C] = 999
            THEN
                C := C - 1
      UNTIL (S[C+1] = 999) OR (C = 10)

   END; { GETSCORES }
```

```
PROCEDURE AVERAGEANDSEARCH(C : INTEGER;
                          VAR LA, SM : INTEGER;
                          S : SCORETYPE;
                          VAR A : REAL);

   VAR
      LOOP,
      SUM  : INTEGER;

   BEGIN

      SUM := 0;
      LA := S[1];    { INITIALIZE LARGE }
      SM := S[1];    { INITIALIZE SMALL }
      FOR LOOP := 1 TO C DO
         BEGIN
            IF S[LOOP] > LA
               THEN LA := S[LOOP];
            IF S[LOOP] < SM
               THEN SM := S[LOOP];
            SUM := SUM + S[LOOP]
         END; { FOR }
      A := SUM/C

   END; { AVERAGEANDSEARCH }

PROCEDURE PRINTOUT(C,LA,SM: INTEGER; S : SCORETYPE;
                   VAR A : REAL);

   VAR
      LOOP : INTEGER;

   BEGIN

      WRITELN;
      WRITE('SCORES: ');
      FOR LOOP := 1 TO C DO
         BEGIN
            WRITE(S[LOOP]);
            IF LOOP < C
               THEN
                  WRITE(',')
         END; { FOR }
      WRITELN;
      WRITELN('AVERAGE.......... ',A:5:2);
      WRITELN('THE LARGEST IS... ',LA);
      WRITELN('THE SMALLEST IS.. ',SM)

   END; { PRINTOUT }

BEGIN { MAIN PROGRAM }

   COUNT := 0;
   GETSCORES(COUNT, SCORE);
   AVERAGEANDSEARCH(COUNT, LARGEST, SMALLEST,
                    SCORE, AVER);
   PRINTOUT(COUNT, LARGEST, SMALLEST, SCORE, AVER)

END.
```

Sample Run

```
ENTER SCORES (UP TO 10).
ENTER 999 WHEN FINISHED.
>72
>49
>98
>63
>999

SCORES: 72,49,98,63
AVERAGE.......... 70.50
THE LARGEST IS... 98
THE SMALLEST IS.. 49
```

Arrays can also use programmer-defined types as either the subscript or the component type of the array. This can add a great deal to the readability of a program. For example, using the names of the days of the week, rather than the numbers 1 to 7, helps to self-document a program. Program 13.5 uses a programmer-defined type for the array subscripts to improve the readability of a program. Using a programmer-defined type as the component type of the array is acceptable; remember, however, that in some Pascal versions, there is no way to directly read or write a programmer-defined type.

Program 13.5

```
PROGRAM TIMECARD(INPUT,OUTPUT);

    { PURPOSE: USE PROGRAMMER-DEFINED TYPES
               TO DETERMINE WEEKLY HOURS WORKED }

TYPE
    DAYTYPE   = (MONDAY,TUESDAY,WEDNESDAY,THURSDAY,
                 FRIDAY,SATURDAY,SUNDAY);

    TIMETYPE = ARRAY[MONDAY..SUNDAY] OF REAL;

VAR
    DAYWORKED   : DAYTYPE;
    HOURSWORKED : TIMETYPE;

PROCEDURE PRINTDAY(DAY : DAYTYPE);

    BEGIN

       CASE DAY OF
          MONDAY    : WRITE('MONDAY':11);
          TUESDAY   : WRITE('TUESDAY':11);
          WEDNESDAY : WRITE('WEDNESDAY':11);
          THURSDAY  : WRITE('THURSDAY':11);
          FRIDAY    : WRITE('FRIDAY':11);
          SATURDAY  : WRITE('SATURDAY':11);
          SUNDAY    : WRITE('SUNDAY':11)
       END { CASE }

    END;  { PRINTDAY }
```

```
PROCEDURE GETHOURS(VAR DHOURS : TIMETYPE);

   VAR
      DAYCOUNT : DAYTYPE;

   BEGIN

      FOR DAYCOUNT := MONDAY TO SUNDAY DO
         BEGIN
            WRITE('ENTER TIME WORKED ON');
            PRINTDAY(DAYCOUNT);
            WRITE(' > ');
            READLN(DHOURS[DAYCOUNT])
         END { FOR }

   END;  { GETHOURS }

PROCEDURE PRINTTIME (DHOURS : TIMETYPE);

   VAR
      DAYCOUNT   : DAYTYPE;
      TOTALHOURS : REAL;

   BEGIN

      TOTALHOURS := 0;
      WRITELN('DAY OF WEEK':11,'HOURS':10);
      WRITELN('----------':11,'-----':10);
      FOR DAYCOUNT := MONDAY TO SUNDAY DO
         BEGIN
            PRINTDAY(DAYCOUNT);
            WRITELN(DHOURS[DAYCOUNT]:10:2);
            TOTALHOURS:=TOTALHOURS+DHOURS[DAYCOUNT]
         END; { FOR }
      WRITELN('----------':11,'------------');
      WRITELN('TOTAL HOURS':11,TOTALHOURS:10:2)

   END; { PRINTTIME }

BEGIN { TIMECARD }

   PAGE(OUTPUT);
   GETHOURS(HOURSWORKED);
   PAGE(OUTPUT);
   GOTOXY(0,5);
   PRINTTIME(HOURSWORKED)

END.
```

Sample Run

```
ENTER TIME WORKED ON    MONDAY > 7.5
ENTER TIME WORKED ON   TUESDAY > 8.5
ENTER TIME WORKED ON WEDNESDAY > 8.0
ENTER TIME WORKED ON  THURSDAY > 8.0
ENTER TIME WORKED ON    FRIDAY > 6.5
ENTER TIME WORKED ON  SATURDAY > 4.0
ENTER TIME WORKED ON    SUNDAY > 0.0
```

```
DAY OF WEEK        HOURS
-----------        -----
     MONDAY         7.50
    TUESDAY         8.50
  WEDNESDAY         8.00
   THURSDAY         8.00
     FRIDAY         6.50
   SATURDAY         4.00
     SUNDAY         0.00
-----------        -----
TOTAL HOURS        42.50
```

With the setup of Program 13.5, an element in the array HOURS-WORKED can be accessed by specifying the day of the week desired. Thus

```
WRITELN(HOURSWORKED[TUESDAY]);
```

clearly means to write the hours that were worked on Tuesday.

Lesson Check 13.1

1. Define and declare a one-dimensional array that will hold 10 integers.

2. Why is the combination of TYPE and VAR preferred over VAR alone in defining arrays?

3. What is wrong with the following procedure? Assume this procedure is to be inserted into Program 13.3.

```
PROCEDURE PRINTOUT (GROUPS:LETTERS);

    VAR
        C : INTEGER;

    BEGIN
        FOR C := 1 TO 5 DO
            WRITELN(GROUPS)
    END;
```

Lesson 13.2   Multidimensional Arrays

Multidimensional arrays can be used to represent a table of data. The information in the table can take on many forms, as long as the data type of the elements is the same. For example, a table associating a musical instrument with the name of the player could be programmed with two one-dimensional arrays, or **parallel arrays.** A more desirable method, however, might be to use a single array to hold all the information.

	1	2
1	JIM	CLARINET
2	SCOTT	FLUTE
3	JUDY	FRENCH HORN
4	SANDY	SAXOPHONE
5	MARGARET	TRUMPET

Storing a person's name with the instrument that person plays is a natural application of a **two-dimensional array.** Here is one way to define this array.

```
TYPE
    ENTRYTYPE = ARRAY[1..5] OF ARRAY[1..2] OF STRING;
```

The array can also be defined by

```
TYPE
    ENTRYTYPE = ARRAY[1..5,1..2] OF STRING;
```

Both methods establish 10 (5 × 2) locations for storing information, although the latter definition is more common. The definition would be followed by a declaration, such as

```
VAR
    ENTRY : ENTRYTYPE;
```

The following statement shows how this array could be entered into memory. The user would enter a name and the corresponding instrument.

```
FOR ROW := 1 TO 5 DO
    FOR COLUMN := 1 TO 2 DO
        READLN(ENTRY[ROW,COLUMN]);
```

For this example,

```
ENTRY[4,1] is SANDY
ENTRY[1,2] is CLARINET
ENTRY[5,2] is TRUMPET
```

The first number controls the row that is to be used, while the second number determines the column (name or instrument).

Two-dimensional arrays are handy for computing results in a table with rows and columns. Program 13.6 requests the input of a word in English and then prints the word in German.

Program 13.6
```
PROGRAM ENGLISHTOGERMAN(INPUT,OUTPUT);

    { PURPOSE: TRANSLATE ENGLISH WORDS TO GERMAN }

TYPE
    WORDTYPE = ARRAY[1..11, 1..2] OF STRING;

VAR
    CHOICE : STRING;
    WORD   : WORDTYPE;

PROCEDURE GETWORDS(VAR W : WORDTYPE);

    VAR
        NUMBER,
        KINDS  : INTEGER;

    BEGIN
        FOR NUMBER := 1 TO 10 DO
            FOR KINDS := 1 TO 2 DO
```

```
                        BEGIN
                           IF KINDS = 1
                              THEN
                                 WRITE('ENGLISH WORD: ')
                              ELSE
                                 WRITE('GERMAN EQUIVALENT: ');
                           READLN(W[NUMBER, KINDS]);
                           WRITELN
                        END { FOR }
            END; { GETWORDS }

   PROCEDURE TRANSLATE(C : STRING; W : WORDTYPE);

      VAR
         NUMBER : INTEGER;

      BEGIN
         NUMBER := 1;
         WHILE (W[NUMBER, 1] <> C) AND (NUMBER <= 10) DO
            NUMBER := NUMBER + 1;
         IF NUMBER = 11
            THEN
               WRITELN('NO KNOWN TRANSLATION.')
            ELSE
               WRITELN('GERMAN: ',W[NUMBER,2])
      END; { TRANSLATE }

   BEGIN { ENGLISHTOGERMAN }

      WRITELN('ENTER 10 ENGLISH WORDS AND THEIR');
      WRITELN('GERMAN EQUIVALENT.');
      GETWORDS(WORD);
      PAGE(OUTPUT);
      WRITELN('ENTER THE ENGLISH WORD YOU WISH TO');
      WRITELN('TRANSLATE TO GERMAN.');
      WRITELN('TYPE ''DONE'' WHEN FINISHED.');
      REPEAT
         WRITELN;
         WRITE('ENGLISH WORD: ');
         READLN(CHOICE);
         IF CHOICE <> 'DONE'
            THEN
               TRANSLATE(CHOICE, WORD)
      UNTIL CHOICE = 'DONE'

   END.
```

Working with the elements of a multidimensional array can occasionally be a bit tricky. Program 13.7 finds the sum of the elements of a matrix, a two-dimensional array of numbers. The example demonstrates how to access the elements efficiently.

Program 13.7

```
PROGRAM MATRIXADD(INPUT,OUTPUT);

      { PURPOSE: CALCULATE SUM OF 3 X 3 MATRIX }

CONST
   R = 3;
   C = 3;
```

```
TYPE
   MATRIXTYPE = ARRAY[1..R, 1..C] OF INTEGER;

VAR
   MATRIX : MATRIXTYPE;
   SUM    : INTEGER;

PROCEDURE MAKEARRAY(VAR M : MATRIXTYPE);

   VAR
      COLUMN,
      ROW     : INTEGER;

   BEGIN

      WRITELN('ENTER ELEMENTS OF 3 BY 3 MATRIX:');
      FOR COLUMN := 1 TO C DO
         FOR ROW := 1 TO R DO
            BEGIN
               WRITE('ELEMENT #');
               WRITE('ROW + 3 * (COLUMN - 1),' > ');
               READLN(M[ROW,COLUMN])
            END { FOR ROW }

   END; { MAKEARRAY }

PROCEDURE SUMARRAY(M:MATRIXTYPE; VAR SUM:INTEGER);

   VAR
      COLUMN,
      ROW     : INTEGER;

   BEGIN

      FOR COLUMN := 1 TO C DO
         FOR ROW := 1 TO R DO
            SUM := SUM + M[ROW,COLUMN]

   END; { SUMARRAY }

PROCEDURE PRINTARRAY(M : MATRIXTYPE; SUM : INTEGER);

   VAR
      COLUMN,
      ROW     : INTEGER;

   BEGIN

      WRITELN;
      WRITELN('THE ARRAY IS:');
      FOR COLUMN := 1 TO C DO
         BEGIN
            FOR ROW := 1 TO R DO
               WRITE(M[ROW,COLUMN],' ');
            WRITELN
         END;
      WRITELN;
      WRITELN('SUM = ',SUM)

   END; { PRINTARRAY }
```

```
BEGIN { MAIN PROGRAM }

    SUM := 0;
    MAKEARRAY(MATRIX);
    SUMARRAY(MATRIX, SUM);
    PRINTARRAY(MATRIX, SUM)

END.
```

Higher-dimensional arrays are also possible by specifying the added dimensions, as in these statements:

```
TYPE
    THREE = ARRAY[1..6,1..4,1..5] OF CHAR;

TYPE
    CUBE = ARRAY[1..3,1..3,1..3] OF INTEGER;
```

An array of type THREE would hold 120 elements ($6 \times 4 \times 5$), and an array of type CUBE would have 27 elements ($3 \times 3 \times 3$).

Another variation available with arrays is a **packed array.** A packed array minimizes the memory requirements for the array. (**Caution:** Packed array variables can be passed to a procedure or function as a value parameter, but not as a variable (VAR) parameter.) The cost of packing an array is a slower compilation time. Consider the following example:

```
TYPE
    CHARRAY1 = ARRAY[0..9] OF CHAR;
    CHARRAY2 = PACKED ARRAY[0..9] OF CHAR;
```

The first array, CHARRAY1, will occupy ten 16-bit locations in memory. This 16-bit location is often called a **word.** Each element (character) occupies one word. Using a packed array, CHARRAY2 requires 8 bits (called a byte) to store each character. Since each 16-bit word can hold two elements, the packed array occupies only five words.

Other packed arrays are possible as follows:

```
TYPE
    NUMBERS = PACKED ARRAY[0..9] OF 0..255;
    BARRAY1 = PACKED ARRAY[0..9] OF BOOLEAN;
    IARRAY  = PACKED ARRAY[0..7] OF 0..3;
    BARRAY2 = PACKED ARRAY[0..3,0..7] OF BOOLEAN;
    PHRASE  = PACKED ARRAY[0..255] OF CHAR;
```

The array NUMBERS would need one byte (8 bits) per element for a total of ten bytes. The array BARRAY1 would require only 1 bit per element—TRUE (1) or FALSE (0). Since BARRAY1 has 10 elements, it needs 10 bits. (This would require two bytes, even though not all the bits would be used.) The elements in the third array (IARRAY) would each be only 2 bits long, since the numbers from 0 to 3 require no more than 2 bits to be represented. (0, 1, 2, and 3 are equivalent to the binary numbers 0, 1, 10, and 11, respectively.) Thus, IARRAY would need 16 bits (two bytes). Multidimensional arrays can also be packed as in BARRAY2, which has 32 elements (4 × 8) and would need 1 bit per element or 32 bits (four bytes). The final example, using a packed array of CHAR, is equivalent to a STRING type definition and would require two hundred and fifty-six bytes.

The savings in memory may not always be exactly what is expected from these examples, but packing any ordinal, subrange, or set type can sometimes save considerable memory.

Lesson Check 13.2

1. Write a type definition for a BOOLEAN array representing the occupied status of squares on a chessboard.

2. What is wrong with the following program segment? Assume correct definitions and declarations, and that GRID contains a table of integers.

```
{ FIND SUM OF EACH ROW }

FOR ACROSS := 1 TO 10 DO
    BEGIN
        SUM := 0;
        FOR DOWN := 1 TO 10 DO
            SUM := SUM + GRID[DOWN,ACROSS];
        WRITELN(SUM)
    END;
```

3. Estimate the memory requirements in bytes for each of the following declarations:

```
LETTERS   = PACKED ARRAY[1..20] OF CHAR;
CONDITION = PACKED ARRAY[1..32] OF BOOLEAN;
NUMBERS   = PACKED ARRAY[1..8] OF 0..3;
```

Lesson 13.3 Manipulating Arrays

Once an array is formed, it can be used in many different ways. A programmer might need to find a specific element in the array, merge two arrays, arrange the array in order, reverse the order of the array, mix the elements in the array, or many other options. In this lesson (and in Chapter 14), several algorithms for use with arrays will be developed. Some are left as exercises.

Reverse

At some time in the programming process, the need may arise to reverse the elements in an array. Assuming the original order is also needed, the reversal can be performed by transforming the array to a new array. Program 13.8 demonstrates such a reversal; for simplicity, our original array contains the numbers 1 to 20.

Program 13.8

```
PROGRAM REVERSAL(OUTPUT);

        { PURPOSE: TO REVERSE ELEMENTS IN AN ARRAY }

CONST
   LIMIT = 20;

TYPE
   NUMBERARRAY = ARRAY[1..LIMIT] OF INTEGER;


VAR
   ORIGINAL,
   REVERSED : NUMBERARRAY;
   COUNT    : INTEGER;


PROCEDURE DEFINEARRAY(VAR CNT : INTEGER;
                      VAR ARRY : NUMBERARRAY);

   BEGIN

      CNT := 0;
      REPEAT
         CNT := CNT + 1;
         ARRY[CNT] := CNT
      UNTIL CNT = LIMIT

   END; { DEFINEARRAY }


PROCEDURE PRINTARRAY(CNT : INTEGER;
                     ARRY : NUMBERARRAY);

   VAR

   BEGIN

      FOR C := 1 TO CNT DO
         WRITE(ARRY[C],' ');
      WRITELN

   END; { PRINTARRAY }


PROCEDURE REVERSEARRAY(CNT : INTEGER;
                       ARRY : NUMBERARRAY;
                       VAR REVER : NUMBERARRAY);

   VAR
      C : INTEGER;

   BEGIN

      FOR C := CNT DOWNTO 1 DO
         REVER[LIMIT - CNT + 1] := ARRY[C]

   END; { REVERSEARRAY }
```

```
BEGIN { REVERSAL }

   DEFINEARRAY(COUNT,ORIGINAL);
   WRITELN('ORIGINAL ARRAY:');
   PRINTARRAY(COUNT,ORIGINAL);
   WRITELN;
   WRITELN('REVERSED ARRAY:');
   REVERSEARRAY(COUNT,ORIGINAL,REVERSED);
   PRINTARRAY(COUNT,REVERSED)

END.
```

If the original array does not need to be remembered, memory can be saved by reversing the array into itself. This is left as an exercise.

Shuffle

Mixing the elements of an array in a random fashion may often be a necessary process in programming. Several methods can be developed to accomplish the shuffling of the elements in an array. Program 13.9 shows one straightforward possibility. The program shuffles by choosing two elements at random and switching them. By doing this a number of times, a fairly thorough mixture can be obtained.

Program 13.9

```
PROGRAM SHUFFLING(INPUT,OUTPUT);

      { PURPOSE: TO SHUFFLE ELEMENTS IN AN ARRAY }

USES
   APPLESTUFF; { FOR RANDOM NUMBER GENERATION }

TYPE
   NUMBERARRAY = ARRAY[1..20] OF INTEGER;

VAR
   NUMARRY : NUMBERARRAY;
   COUNT   : INTEGER;


PROCEDURE DEFINEARRAY(VAR CNT : INTEGER;
                      VAR ARRY : NUMBERARRAY);

   BEGIN

      CNT := 0;
      REPEAT
         CNT := CNT + 1;
         ARRY[CNT] := CNT
      UNTIL CNT = 20

   END; { DEFINEARRAY }
```

```
PROCEDURE PRINTARRAY(CNT : INTEGER;
                     ARRY : NUMBERARRAY);

   VAR
      C : INTEGER;

   BEGIN

      FOR C := 1 TO CNT DO
         WRITE(ARRY[C],' ');
      WRITELN

   END; { PRINTARRAY }


PROCEDURE SHUFFLE(CNT : INTEGER;
                  VAR ARRY : NUMBERARRAY);

   VAR
      C,
      TEMP,
      ELEMENT1,
      ELEMENT2 : INTEGER;

   FUNCTION RND(LOW,HIGH : INTEGER) : INTEGER;

      BEGIN

         RND := RANDOM MOD (HIGH - LOW + 1) + LOW

      END;  { RND }

   BEGIN

      FOR C := 1 TO 50 DO
         BEGIN
            ELEMENT1 := RND(1,CNT);
            ELEMENT2 := RND(1,CNT);
            TEMP := ARRY[ELEMENT1];
            ARRY[ELEMENT1] := ARRY[ELEMENT2];
            ARRY[ELEMENT2] := TEMP
         END { FOR }

   END; { SHUFFLE }


BEGIN { SHUFFLING }

   RANDOMIZE;
   DEFINEARRAY(COUNT,NUMARRY);
   WRITELN('ORIGINAL ARRAY:');
   PRINTARRAY(COUNT,NUMARRY);
   WRITELN;
   WRITELN('SHUFFLED ARRAY:');
   SHUFFLE(COUNT,NUMARRY);
   PRINTARRAY(COUNT,NUMARRY)

END.
```

Queues

Arrays can be used to simulate several structures common to programming, most notably stacks and queues. Stacks were discussed in Chapter 10. A problem to produce a stack using arrays is included in the exercises at the end of this chapter. A **queue** (meaning line) is a structure in which the first element placed in the queue is the first element to be removed, much like a line waiting outside a theater. This rule is known as **FIFO** (First-In First-Out) and can be useful in many programming situations. FIFO is achieved by adding elements to the queue at the rear and removing elements from the queue at the front. Program 13.10 shows the implementation of a queue using an array.

Program 13.10

```
PROGRAM QUEUEARRAY(INPUT,OUTPUT);

     { PURPOSE: USE AN ARRAY TO ILLUSTRATE A QUEUE }

CONST
   QUEUELIMIT = 200;

TYPE
   STRINGARRAY = ARRAY[1..QUEUELIMIT] OF STRING;

VAR
   QUEUE    : STRINGARRAY;
   FRONT,
   REAR     : INTEGER;
   CHOICE   : CHAR;

PROCEDURE INITARRAY(MAX : INTEGER;
                    VAR ARRY : STRINGARRAY);

   VAR
      COUNT : INTEGER;

   BEGIN

      FOR COUNT := 1 TO MAX DO
         ARRY[COUNT] := ''

   END; { INITARRAY }

PROCEDURE ADDELEMENT(VAR RER : INTEGER;
                     VAR ARRY : STRINGARRAY);

   BEGIN

      WRITELN;
      WRITE('ENTER THE ELEMENT : ');
      READLN(ARRY[RER]);
      RER := RER + 1

   END; { ADDELEMENT }
```

```
PROCEDURE REMELEMENT(VAR FRNT : INTEGER;
                     VAR ARRY : STRINGARRAY);

    BEGIN
        FRNT := FRNT + 1
    END; { REMELEMENT }

PROCEDURE PRINTQUEUE(FRNT,RER : INTEGER;
                     ARRY : STRINGARRAY);

    VAR
        C : INTEGER;

    BEGIN
        WRITELN;
        FOR C := FRNT TO RER DO
            WRITE(ARRY[C],' ');
        WRITELN;
        WRITELN;
        WRITE('PRESS RETURN TO CONTINUE ');
        READLN
    END; { PRINTQUEUE }

BEGIN { QUEUEARRAY }

    INITARRAY(QUEUELIMIT,QUEUE);
    FRONT := 1;
    REAR := 1;
    REPEAT
        PAGE(OUTPUT);       { CLEAR SCREEN }
        WRITELN('1. ADD TO QUEUE');
        WRITELN('2. REMOVE FROM QUEUE');
        WRITELN('3. PRINT QUEUE');
        WRITELN('4. END');
        READ(CHOICE);
        WRITELN;
        CASE CHOICE OF
            '1' : IF REAR < QUEUELIMIT
                    THEN
                        ADDELEMENT(REAR,QUEUE)
                    ELSE
                        BEGIN
                            WRITELN;
                            WRITE('CANNOT ADD ');
                            READLN
                        END;
            '2' : IF FRONT < REAR
                    THEN
                        REMELEMENT(FRONT,QUEUE)
                    ELSE
                        BEGIN
                            WRITELN;
                            WRITE('CANNOT REMOVE ');
                            READLN
                        END;
            '3' : PRINTQUEUE(FRONT,REAR,QUEUE)
        END; { CASE }
        WRITELN
    UNTIL CHOICE = '4'

END.
```

This implementation uses a 200-element array in which to store the queue. As additions are made, each element is stored in the appropriate array location and a **pointer** to the rear of the queue is incremented. (A pointer is a variable that refers to a particular element in a list.) When an element is to be removed, a pointer to the front of the queue is incremented, thereby dropping the current front element. This is the simplest implementation and has some drawbacks; for now, however, it will serve to illustrate a queue.

Linear Search

The need to search for an individual element (and its corresponding location) within an array is a common programming task. With the information covered so far, we can perform a simple **linear search,** also known as a **sequential search,** on an array. A linear search can determine if a particular name is in a list, find the specific location of that name, or both.

Program 13.11 performs a linear search on an array of names entered by the user. This program presents the most straightforward method for searching; that is, start at the first element and compare what is being searched for to each element until the search element is found or the end of the list is reached.

Program 13.11

```
PROGRAM LINEARSEARCH(INPUT,OUTPUT);

    { PURPOSE: SEARCH AN ARRAY FOR A
               SPECIFIED ELEMENT }

TYPE
    STRINGARRAY = ARRAY[1..20] OF STRING;

VAR
    STRARRY    : STRINGARRAY;
    COUNT,
    LOCATION   : INTEGER;
    SEARCHKEY  : STRING;
    GOAGAIN    : CHAR;

PROCEDURE GETARRAY(VAR CNT : INTEGER;
                   VAR ARRY : STRINGARRAY);

    BEGIN

        WRITELN('ENTER UP TO 20 NAMES AS PROMPTED.');
        WRITELN('(USE END TO EXIT)');
        CNT := 0;
        REPEAT
            CNT := CNT + 1;
            WRITE('NAME #',CNT,' > ');
            READLN(ARRY[CNT])
        UNTIL ARRY[CNT] = 'END';
        CNT := CNT - 1

    END; { GETARRAY }
```

```
            PROCEDURE PRINTARRAY(CNT : INTEGER;
                             ARRY : STRINGARRAY);

          VAR
             C : INTEGER;

          BEGIN

             FOR C := 1 TO CNT DO
                WRITE(ARRY[C],' ');
             WRITELN

          END; { PRINTARRAY }


       PROCEDURE SEARCH(CNT : INTEGER; ARRY : STRINGARRAY;
                        SKEY : STRING; VAR LOC : INTEGER);

          VAR
             C         : INTEGER;
             FOUND,
             ENDOFARRAY : BOOLEAN;

          BEGIN

             C := 0;
             FOUND := FALSE;
             ENDOFARRAY := FALSE;
             WHILE NOT FOUND AND NOT ENDOFARRAY DO
                BEGIN
                   C := C + 1;
                   IF SKEY = ARRY[C]
                      THEN
                         BEGIN
                            FOUND := TRUE;
                            LOC := C
                         END;
                   IF C = CNT
                      THEN
                         ENDOFARRAY := TRUE
                END { WHILE }

          END; { SEARCH }


       BEGIN { LINEARSEARCH }

          GETARRAY(COUNT,STRARRY);
          WRITELN;
          WRITELN('ORIGINAL ARRAY:');
          PAGE(OUTPUT);        { CLEAR SCREEN }
          PRINTARRAY(COUNT,STRARRY);
          REPEAT
             LOCATION := 0;
             WRITELN;
             WRITE('SEARCH FOR: ');
             READLN(SEARCHKEY);
             SEARCH(COUNT,STRARRY,SEARCHKEY,LOCATION);
```

```
            IF LOCATION <> 0
                THEN
                    BEGIN
                        WRITE(SEARCHKEY,' AT LOCATION ');
                        WRITELN(LOCATION,'.')
                    END
                ELSE
                    WRITELN(SEARCHKEY,' NOT FOUND.');
            WRITELN;
            WRITE('TRY AGAIN?');
            READ(GOAGAIN);
            WRITELN
        UNTIL GOAGAIN = 'N'

END.
```

Sample Run

```
ENTER UP TO 20 NAMES AS PROMPTED.
(USE END TO EXIT)
NAME # 1 > CATHY
NAME # 2 > BEA
NAME # 3 > ALEX
NAME # 4 > ALICE
NAME # 5 > ALBERT
NAME # 6 > FRED
NAME # 7 > SALLY
NAME # 8 > SAM
NAME # 9 > END

ORIGINAL ARRAY:

CATHY BEA ALEX ALICE ALBERT FRED SALLY SAM

SEARCH FOR: FRED
FRED AT LOCATION 6.

TRY AGAIN?Y

SEARCH FOR: BILL
BILL NOT FOUND.

TRY AGAIN?N
```

The search performed by Program 13.11 can actually be accomplished in several ways, with some methods more efficient than others. A detailed discussion of searching and of the efficiency of searches will be included in Chapter 14.

Lesson Check 13.3

1. What is meant by FIFO with respect to a queue?

2. How many search comparisons (probes) would be expected in the worst case (search key found on last try) of a linear search? How many for the best case?

Lesson 13.4 Programming Tip— Program Design

A Detailed Look

The tools for good problem solving have been outlined over the preceding chapters. The programming tips have described a process for solving problems that involves advanced planning, careful implementation, and testing. Following these steps can lead to quality, effective programs. Executing the steps, however, is not as easy as it may seem. An example is necessary to illustrate how each phase of the problem-solving process can be carried out. Here, to demonstrate the process, we begin work on a program to simulate the stock market. This program will be developed in detail over the next few chapters.

The first step is to understand the problem. To do this, the problem should be stated in clear terms and should include a list of specific aspects.

Problem Statement: Simulate the workings of a stock market. Allow buying and selling of stocks over weekly time periods. Maintain information on stocks and players' assets. Features to be included follow:

- Allow up to six players
- Maintain five stocks. Include the ability to expand to cover more stocks.
- Perform weekly computation of changes in stock prices.
- Provide for dividends.
- Provide for stock splits.
- Charge brokerage fees for buying and selling.
- Maintain 52 weeks of information on stocks.
- Allow for a way to review individual stock performance over time.
- Show players' assets.
- Provide for seasonal effects on some stocks.

With this general statement of the problem and the list of specific features desired in the program, the programmer is ready to start the design process. By carefully defining the problem, the next step (program design) is greatly simplified.

Summary

In this chapter, the array structure was introduced as a way of holding lists or tables of information. Elements in an array can be quickly accessed through their subscripts. Arrays are defined under the TYPE heading in the declaration part of the program. Arrays can be of any data type previously introduced, while subscripts of arrays can be any ordinal type. Multidimensional arrays allow the programmer to represent tabular information easily. Arrays can be packed to minimize the memory requirements. A packed array of CHAR is equivalent to the STRING type.

Arrays can be used in a number of ways to accomplish many necessary tasks. Searching an array is made easier by manipulating the respective subscripts of the desired elements. A simple linear search can be performed on a list of elements by starting at the first element and comparing each successive element to the search key until the element is found or the end of the array is reached. Mixing up the elements in an array can be accomplished by using a shuffling algorithm. Several options for shuffling exist. The simplest is to repeat, a number of times, the process of taking two elements at random and switching them. A queue is a special structure that can be represented by an array. A queue follows the FIFO (First-In First-Out) rule. The first element placed in the array must be the first element removed from the array. This structure can be useful in simulating real-life situations, such as cars at a four-way stop light or the "first come, first served" policy of many businesses.

Key Terms

array	one-dimensional	queue
dimension	packed array	sequential search
FIFO	parallel arrays	subscript
linear search	pointer	two-dimensional
multidimensional		

Answers to Lesson Checks

Lesson 13.1

1.
```
TYPE
    TENARRAY = ARRAY[1..10] OF INTEGER;
VAR
    TENS : TENARRAY;
```

2. The type definition is preferred over the shortcut method because the type identifier is needed if the array is to be passed to a procedure or function.

3. The WRITELN statement must include brackets for the array variable to specify which element is to be printed. That is,

```
WRITELN(GROUPS[C])
```

Lesson 13.2

1.
```
TYPE
    OCCUPIED = ARRAY[1..8,1..8] OF BOOLEAN;
```

2. The program segment finds the sum of each column instead of the sum of each row.

3. **a.** Twenty bytes.
   b. Four bytes.
   c. Two bytes.

Lesson 13.3

1. FIFO stands for First-In First-Out. Here it means that the first element to enter a queue is the first to leave it.

2. The number of probes in the worst case would be equal to the number of elements in the array. For the best case, the search key would be found on the first try, so there would be one probe.

Exercises   Set I. Comprehension

1. Write a definition for a one-dimensional REAL array, DECATHLON, that will hold 10 elements, not including the 0 element.

2. Write a definition for a one-dimensional BOOLEAN array, ANSWERS, that will hold exactly 20 elements, including the 0 element.

3. Write a definition for a two-dimensional INTEGER array, TABLE, that will hold exactly 100 elements (10 rows and 10 columns).

4. Write a definition for a 5 × 7 two-dimensional character array, ALPHA.

5. Write a definition for a three-dimensional INTEGER array, BLOCK, that will include five rows, four columns and eight levels.

6. Write a definition for a three-dimensional character array, CHARACTER, that will include four rows, three columns, and two levels.

7. Given this array table,

	0	1	2	3	4	5	6
0	32	33	21	12	24	26	15
1	3	41	40	0	2	12	63
2	2	13	83	94	90	29	20
3	20	72	64	49	4	19	87
4	79	72	49	43	0	2	32
5	10	3	4	21	54	50	0
6	1	10	53	27	35	48	8

define the elements with the following array subscripts:
a. [4,2]
b. [2,4]
c. [0,3]
d. [6,1]
e. [2+4,28−25]
f. [6,3 DIV 3]

8. Using the array table from Exercise 7, give the array subscripts for each of the following values. If there is more than one occurrence of the value, give each set of subscripts.
a. 90
b. 0
c. 35
d. 4
e. 33
f. 63

9. Explain the function of each of the following program segments. Assume in each case that the arrays and variables have been properly declared and that the program segments are independent of each other.

a.
```
N1 := 4;
FOR N2 := 0 TO 9 DO
    WRITE(TABLE[N1,N2]);
```
b.
```
N1 := 2;
FOR N2 := 7 DOWNTO 1 DO
    WRITELN(TABLE[N1,N2]);
```
c.
```
N1 := 1;
FOR N2 := N1 TO 5 DO
    WRITELN(TABLE[N2,N1-1]);
```

10. Explain the function of each of the following program segments. Assume in each case that the arrays and variables have been properly declared and that the program segments are independent of each other.

a.
```
FOR J := 0 TO 5 DO
    FOR K := 0 TO 5 DO
        BOX[J,K] := 0;
```
b.
```
FOR L := 3 TO 9 DO
    FOR M := 2 TO 5 DO
        BOX[L,M] := BOX[L,M] - 1;
```
c.
```
FOR X := 1 TO 10 DO
    FOR Y := 1 TO 10 DO
        IF X/2 = TRUNC(X/2)
            THEN IF Y/2 = TRUNC(Y/2)
                THEN BOX[X,Y] := 'E';
```

11. Give the output for each of the following program segments:

a.
```
FOR J := 1 TO 10 DO
    BEGIN
        NUMBER[J] := J * 2;
        WRITELN(NUMBER[J])
    END;
```
b.
```
FOR J := 0 TO 9 DO
    BEGIN
        NUMBER[J] := 9 - J;
        WRITELN(NUMBER[J])
    END;
```

12. Give the output for each of the following program segments:

a.
```
FOR J := 1 TO 10 DO
    BEGIN
        FOR K := 1 TO J DO
            BEGIN
                A[J,K] := K;
                WRITE(A[J,K])
            END;
        WRITELN
    END;
```
b.
```
FOR L := 1 TO 10 DO
    BEGIN
        FOR M := L DOWNTO 1 DO
            BEGIN
                A[L,M] := L + M;
                WRITE(A[L,M])
            END;
        WRITELN
    END;
```

13. Explain the function of the following program segment:

```
J := 0
REPEAT
   IF TARGET[J] = 100
      THEN BULLSEYE := TRUE;
   J := J + 1
UNTIL BULLSEYE OR (J=20);
```

14. Explain the function of the following program segment. Assume LITE is a BOOLEAN array.

```
FOR X := 1 TO 10 DO
   FOR Y := 1 TO 10 DO
      IF LITE[X,Y]
         THEN LITE[X,Y] := NOT LITE[X,Y];
```

Set II. Application

15. Write a program that will print the following table, along with the total weekly sales of each employee and the total sales for each day.

SALESPERSON	MON	TUE	WED	THU	FRI	SAT
1	48	40	73	120	100	90
2	75	130	90	140	110	85
3	50	72	140	125	106	92
4	108	75	92	152	91	87

16. Write program segments that will initialize a 3 × 3 INTEGER array to each of the following tables, without input from the user.

a. 1 2 3
4 5 6
7 8 9

b. 1 4 7
2 5 8
3 6 9

c. 9 8 7
6 5 4
3 2 1

17. Write a procedure to reverse the order of a one-dimensional array without using another array. The contents of the array should be reversed into itself. For example, given an original array of
4 7 9 2 8 3
the array becomes
3 8 2 9 7 4

Option: Implement this procedure using recursion.

18. Assume a one-dimensional INTEGER array, HOURSWORKED, contains the daily hours worked by an individual for four weeks (20 days). Write a procedure that will search the array and print the day number for each day in which the individual worked more than eight hours.

19. Using the following data, write a program to tabulate election results:

Candidate	Female Vote	Male Vote
Scott	4	2
Sandy	2	3
Kim	1	4

The program should output—in tabular form—the total votes for each candidate, as well as the total female and male votes and the total number of voters.

20. Write a program to determine each of the following for a 5 × 5 REAL array:
    a. The sum of any row.
    b. The sum of any column.
    c. The sum of the diagonals.
    d. The sum of all elements in the array.

    Allow the user to enter the array and specify the option desired, including the specific row or column for options **a** and **b**.

21. Write a program to compute the frequency counts of grades A–F for a test. Assume that test scores correspond to grades in the following manner:

A	90–100
B	80–89
C	70–79
D	60–69
F	0–59

    Allow the user to specify the number of scores and enter each test score. Store the grade frequency in array GRADECOUNT and print the number of A's, B's, C's, D's, and F's, and the percentage of each.

22. Write a program that will determine the frequency of each letter's occurrence in a passage entered by the user. Use an array to hold the counts for each letter A–Z. Allow the user to continue typing until <RETURN> has been pressed.

23. Write a procedure to switch the contents of two one-dimensional character arrays; that is, move the elements from array A to array B and vice versa.

24. Write a procedure to switch the contents of two 10 × 10 INTEGER arrays; that is, move the elements from array A to array B and vice versa. Be sure to keep the rows and columns intact.

25. Write a procedure to shift the contents of three one-dimensional REAL arrays; that is, move the elements from array A to array B, the elements from array B to array C, and the elements from array C to array A.

26. Write a BOOLEAN function, BADDATA, to test an 8 × 12 INTEGER array for errors. Search the array for negative values and return a value of TRUE if any are encountered.

    Option: Implement this function using recursion.

Set III. Synthesis

27. Write a program to produce reversals (mirror images) of a two-dimensional 6 × 6 array. Randomly define the elements of the original array using 0s and 1s. Reverse the array according to the following:

a. In a horizontal reverse,

```
010101              101010
101010              010101
000101   becomes    101000
100001              100001
000000              000000
111011              110111
```

b. In a vertical reverse,

```
010101              111011
101010              000000
000101   becomes    100001
100001              000101
000000              101010
111011              010101
```

c. In a diagonal reverse,

```
010101              110111
101010              000000
000101   becomes    100001
100001              101000
000000              010101
111011              101010
```

In each case, produce the reversal using a separate array so that the original array can be retained.

28. A magic square is a square array of integers such that the sum of elements in each column, row, or diagonal is the same. The square must contain the numbers 1–9 without any repetitions. Write a program that allows the user to input a 3 × 3 array and which will then determine if the array is a magic square.

Option: Write a program that will produce a magic square.

Extension: A magic square can also be a square array of integers such that the product of the elements in each column, row, or diagonal is the same. Repeat Exercise 28, calculating the product instead of the sum.

29. A class of 18 students has been given a test with 10 true-or-false questions. Write a program that will allow the teacher to enter the correct answers into a BOOLEAN array. Use two parallel arrays for the students' ID numbers (INTEGER) and test answers (BOOLEAN). Compute and store the number of correct responses for each student. Print a table displaying the ID numbers and scores.

30. The computer club is holding a raffle to raise money for new computer software. The club is using a computer to store information regarding the raffle. Two one-dimensional arrays are

used to hold each person's name and corresponding raffle number. Assume that 20 raffle tickets will be sold and that the ticket numbers are random integers between 1 and 100, with no duplicates. Write a program to produce an array for the ticket numbers; match the first 20 numbers with the participants' names; and select at random, from those 20, the winning ticket.

31. The Mini-Bucks Lottery Commission needs a program to manage the names, entries, and proceeds of their lottery. The contest consists of five numbers, each ranging from 1 to 20, with no duplicates. A participant pays $1.00 to enter one set of numbers. Winners are determined in the following manner: a participant with five correct numbers wins one-half the proceeds; a participant with four correct numbers wins $5.00; and a participant with three correct numbers wins $1.00. If more than one participant guesses the five numbers correctly, the prize money—one-half the proceeds—is split among those who guessed correctly. The $5.00 and $1.00 prizes are guaranteed regardless of the amount of the proceeds or the number of people with four or three correct numbers.

    Write a program that will allow participants to enter their names and numbers. The program should select the lottery numbers at random, determine if there are any winners, and print the winners' names and the amount won by each. Also, the program should print the total proceeds from the lottery, the total price money paid, and the net profit (or loss).

32. Write a procedure to determine if a tic-tack-toe game is over. To determine whether a player has won, each row, column, and diagonal of the game board (3 × 3 array) must be checked to see if any line of three squares is occupied by the same player. If all squares on the board are occupied, but neither player has won, then a draw occurs. An empty square is represented by a space (' '). Use a character array to send the game board to the procedure. The procedure should return a character value indicating whether or not the game is over and, if so, who the winner is—X, O, or D (for draw). (Use N to indicate that the game is not over.)

33. A prison contains 500 cells. Just for fun, the warden decides to let some prisoners go free, according to the following scheme. He unlocks all 500 cells. Then he starts with cell #2 and turns the key in every other cell. Then he goes back to cell #3 and turns the key in every third cell. He continues this with every cell up to the 500th cell.

    Write a program that will output to the screen or printer how many cells remain open when he is done, and the numbers of those cells. Explain why these particular cells are open. A packed array of BOOLEAN can be used.

34. Write a program using an array to manage a stack that is capable of holding 10 elements. The stack should store names in a Last-In First-Out (LIFO) fashion. Allow the user the option of adding to the stack (PUSH) or taking from the stack (POP). All additions and deletions are done to the top of the stack. A variable (pointer) should be used to keep track of which element in the array represents the top of the stack. Error trapping should be included to check for underflow (an attempt to take an element off the

stack when the stack is empty) and overflow (an attempt to add to the stack when it is full). Include an option to print the entire stack.

35. A maze can be represented in a two-dimensional integer array by four-digit numbers indicating doors and walls. A door is represented by a 0 and a wall is represented by a 1. The first digit gives the status of the element to the north; the second digit, the east; the third digit, the south; and the fourth digit, the west. For example, an array location with the number 1001 indicates that the north and west are blocked by walls, but the east and south are open doorways.

   In the following maze, the location 1,4 (row 1, column 4) would contain 1101. Location 3,2 would contain 1010. Location 2,3 would contain 11 (since leading zeros would not be retained by the computer).

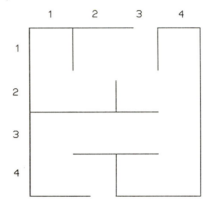

   Write a program to find the solution to a maze entered by the user. Limit the size of the array to 6 × 6. (*Hint:* Recursion may prove helpful in solving this problem.)

   Option: Instead of a two-dimensional INTEGER array, use a three-dimensional BOOLEAN (6 × 6 × 4) array. The four levels would represent the four directions: North, East, South, and West. A wall would be represented by TRUE and a door would be represented by FALSE.

36. The game of Life is a model for birth, survival, and death rates. Using a 20 × 20 board, the status of each square (occupied or empty) can be determined by its neighboring squares. Each square has eight neighbors, except the border squares. For instance, the following figure shows all the squares neighboring the center square.

   Write a program to allow the user to enter the initial generation of organisms into a BOOLEAN array. (A packed array can be used, if desired.) New generations must be stored in a second array and then copied back into the initial array. Each new generation is determined by the following rules:

- Birth. An organism will be born in any empty location that has exactly three occupied neighboring locations.
- Death. An organism with less than two or more than three occupied neighboring locations will die.
- Survival. All other organisms survive to the next generation.

Assume that the area bordering the game board is neutral; that is, it has no effect on the game status and need not be included in calculations.

Allow the user to view each generation and to continue the game for as long as desired or until all organisms have died.

37. Daniel works for a newspaper in the classified advertising section. When someone calls the newspaper to place an ad, he types in the person's message and lets the computer do the typesetting and billing. The newspaper accepts a maximum of 33 characters per line, including spaces. The advertiser is charged $8.00 for three lines or less and $2.50 for each additional line.

Write a program to allow Daniel to enter the ad copy into a character array. The program should determine where spaces exist and should not separate characters that form words. Have the computer print the ad copy with straight left and right margins. In order to obtain straight right margins, some spaces may need to be inserted to spread out the words in a line. To make the line look more evenly spaced, start with the first space and insert one extra space, then move to the next space and insert an extra space, then to the third, and (if necessary) back to the first until the line is exactly 33 characters and the margins are straight. When the advertisement has been formatted, determine the number of lines and compute the amount due.

38. Write a program to find all possible ways to arrange eight queens on a chessboard so that no two queens are threatening to take one another. One possible solution follows:

```
X 0 0 0 0 0 0 0
0 0 0 0 X 0 0 0
0 0 0 0 0 0 0 X
0 0 0 0 0 X 0 0
0 0 X 0 0 0 0 0
0 0 0 0 0 0 X 0
0 X 0 0 0 0 0 0
0 0 0 X 0 0 0 0
```

In order that no two queens should be threatening each other, only one queen can occupy any row, column, or diagonal. The problem can be expanded to work for n queens on an n by n square. Solutions that can be derived symmetrically from other solutions should be eliminated.

39. Write a program to simulate the temperature changes of a rectangular block ($12 \times 8 \times 5$ high) of aluminum. The block lies on a steel plate that is kept at a constant temperature of 200 degrees. The temperature of the air surrounding the block is kept at a constant 70 degrees. Divide the block into 480 elements represented in an array. The program should simulate the

temperature change of the block and check for equilibrium, as defined by a maximum change in the elements. The new temperature of any element is determined by a weighted average of all neighboring temperatures as follows:

- The 6 elements that share a face with the element contribute equally.
- The 12 elements that share an edge contribute 1/4 as much as a face.
- The 8 elements that share a corner contribute 1/8 as much as a face.

Note that the temperature of an element is not used in determining its new temperature.

If equilibrium is reached, report the following:

- The number of passes made.
- The average temperature of the block.
- The high temperature of the elements.
- The low temperature of the elements.
- The 8 temperatures of the $2 \times 2 \times 2$ core elements.
- The 8 temperatures of the corner elements.

Test the program with equilibrium factors of 5, 1, and .5 degrees. The maximum change in any element should be less than this factor for equilibrium to be reached. Report the approximate time for each run.

40. A common problem in computer science is the knight interchange. Two white knights are placed in the bottom corners of a 4×4 board and two black knights are placed in the board's upper corners. Write a program to determine how many moves the knights must make to switch places; that is, until the white knights are in the top corners and the black knights are in the bottom corners. During the moves, no two knights can occupy the same square.

41. Write a program to find all permutations of a group of letters typed in by the user. Recursion is highly recommended for this problem. For n letters, find all ways of arranging them in groups of n. The number of permutations of n items taken n at a time is $n!$ (n factorial). For example, if the input is AB, the output is

AB BA

If the input is ABC, the output is

ABC   ACB   BAC   BCA   CAB   CBA

What is the maximum number of letters that the computer will permute?

Sorting and Searching

... Alice looked all around her at the flowers and the blades of grass, but she could not see anything that looked like the right thing to eat or drink under the circumstances. There was a large mushroom growing near her ... and when she had looked under it, and on both sides of it, and behind it, it occurred to her that she might as well look and see what was on top of it.

—Lewis Carroll

Overview

Sorting
    Bubble Sort
    Selection Sort
    Insertion Sort
    Quicksort
Searching
    Linear Search
    Binary Search
    Two-Stage Search
    Hashing
Programming Tip
    Program Design

Gaining a Perspective

A rrays are the most common structure for holding and manipulating data in the computer. They allow easy, direct access to any element and can be used in many different situations, as illustrated in Chapter 13. When large amounts of data are stored in an array, there are often two things that need to be done with that data, no matter what its nature. The data may need to be placed in some order. Names in a list may need to be alphabetized or grade percentages for a class may need to be listed from highest to lowest to determine grades. Arranging data in a chosen order is called **sorting.** In addition, a particular piece of data may need to be located in a list. For example, a programmer may wish to find a particular entry from a list of cities or find the name of each student receiving an 87 for a test score. Finding a particular entry from a group of data is called **searching.** A simple linear search was presented in Chapter 13. This chapter will look at several options available for sorting and searching arrays.

Lesson 14.1   Sorting

Many kinds of sorts are available to the programmer, each with its own merits. One sort may be easy to write and understand, but slow at performing the task. Another sort may be difficult to follow, but very fast in its execution. Also, the efficiency of a particular sort may increase or decrease with the number of items to be sorted. In the final analysis, after analyzing the requirements of a given situation and the data to be sorted, the programmer must determine the optimum sort.

Bubble Sort

The **bubble sort** is one of the easiest to write, but it is not very efficient for arrays of over 100 elements. Because of its simplicity, a bubble sort is often used on short lists that are nearly in order.

A bubble sort "bubbles" either the smallest or the largest value to the top of the list of values. This value is then fixed in that position and the sort works with the remaining values in the list. For example, suppose the following values are assigned to an array:

56 16 55 8 13 24 5

If the array is to be sorted in ascending order, start by comparing the value in the first position of the array to the value in the second position. If the second value is smaller, switch the two

Figure 14.1
First Pass of
Bubble Sort

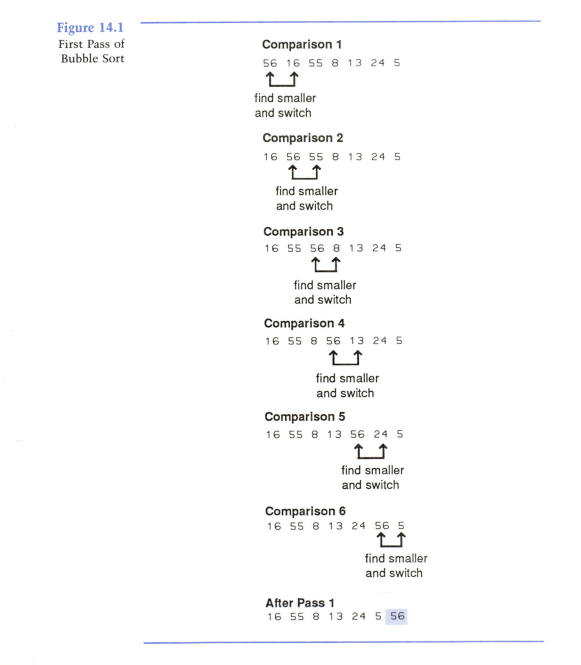

Comparison 1

56 16 55 8 13 24 5

find smaller
and switch

Comparison 2

16 56 55 8 13 24 5

find smaller
and switch

Comparison 3

16 55 56 8 13 24 5

find smaller
and switch

Comparison 4

16 55 8 56 13 24 5

find smaller
and switch

Comparison 5

16 55 8 13 56 24 5

find smaller
and switch

Comparison 6

16 55 8 13 24 56 5

find smaller
and switch

After Pass 1

16 55 8 13 24 5 56

values; otherwise, leave the array in the same order. Now compare the second array element with the third. If the third is smaller, switch the two values. Next compare the third array element with the fourth. If the fourth is smaller, switch the two values. Continuing this process through the array, the largest value ends up in the last position after six comparisons (one less than the number of elements to compare). That last element is in its final spot after this first pass and can be fixed there; it does not need to be compared on any future passes. Figure 14.1 shows the first pass of a bubble sort of the initial array.

Now start the comparing process over. In the second pass (shown in Figure 14.2), the last value does not need to be checked, since it is the largest. The number in the last position is fixed. By the end of the second pass, the next largest number is moved to the next to last position in the list; the last two positions are then fixed.

Figure 14.2
Second Pass of
Bubble Sort

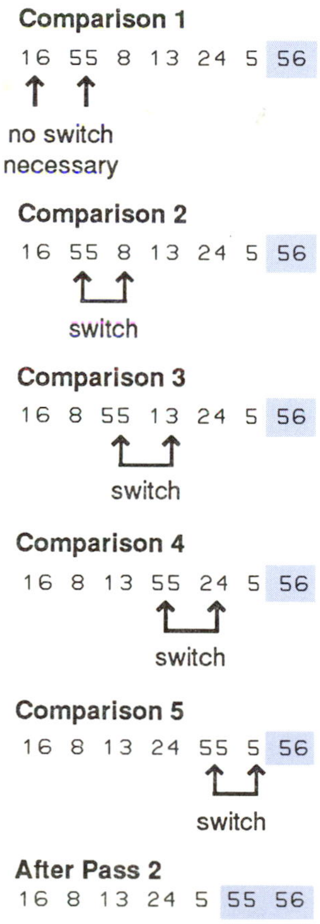

Comparison 1

16 55 8 13 24 5 56

no switch necessary

Comparison 2

16 55 8 13 24 5 56

switch

Comparison 3

16 8 55 13 24 5 56

switch

Comparison 4

16 8 13 55 24 5 56

switch

Comparison 5

16 8 13 24 55 5 56

switch

After Pass 2

16 8 13 24 5 55 56

Figure 14.3
Third Pass of
Bubble Sort

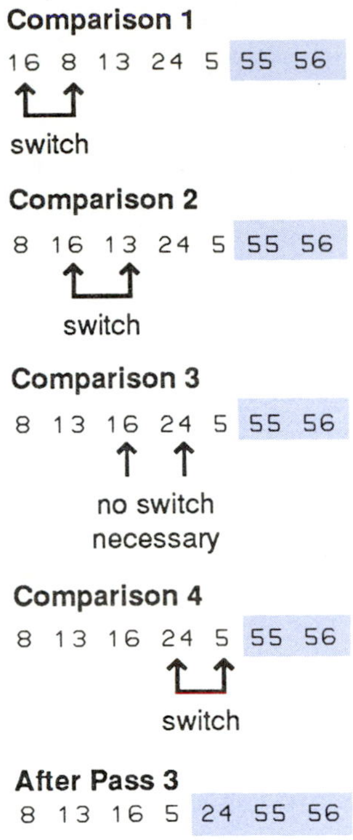

Comparison 1

16 8 13 24 5 55 56
↑ ↑
switch

Comparison 2

8 16 13 24 5 55 56
↑ ↑
switch

Comparison 3

8 13 16 24 5 55 56
↑   ↑
no switch
necessary

Comparison 4

8 13 16 24 5 55 56
↑ ↑
switch

After Pass 3
8 13 16 5 24 55 56

Figure 14.4
Fourth Pass of
Bubble Sort

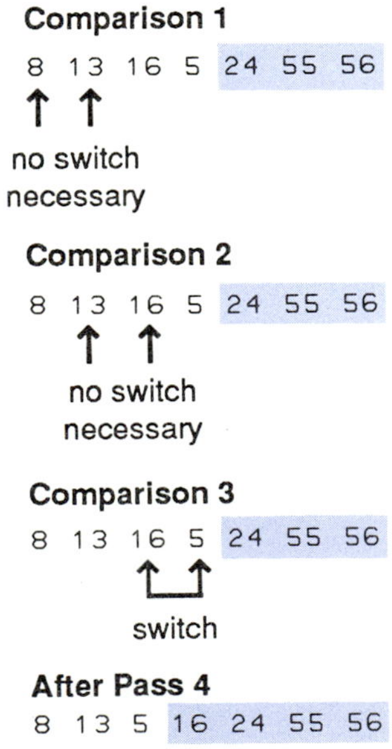

Comparison 1

8 13 16 5 24 55 56
↑ ↑
no switch
necessary

Comparison 2

8 13 16 5 24 55 56
↑ ↑
no switch
necessary

Comparison 3

8 13 16 5 24 55 56
↑ ↑
switch

After Pass 4
8 13 5 16 24 55 56

This pattern continues in the third pass (Figure 14.3), fourth pass (Figure 14.4), fifth pass (Figure 14.5), and sixth pass (Figure 14.6), when the sort is complete. After six passes, the list is

5 8 13 16 24 55 56

Notice that there are seven elements in the list and the number of passes is one less than the number of elements. There are a total of 21 comparisons:

$6 + 5 + 4 + 3 + 2 + 1 = 21$

Program 14.1 is the Pascal implementation of the bubble sort. The sort works equally well on character or numeric data. In this example, words entered by the user are sorted alphabetically.

Figure 14.5
Fifth Pass of
Bubble Sort

Figure 14.6
Sixth Pass of
Bubble Sort

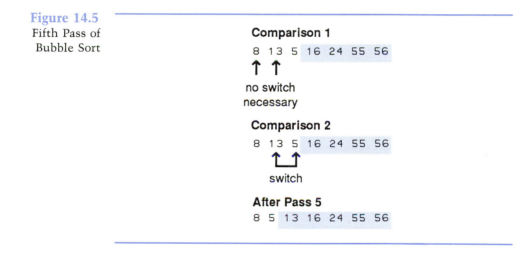

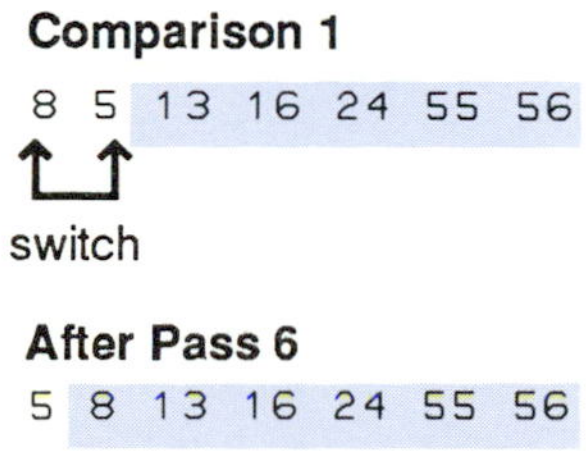

Figure 14.7

Passes of a
Bubble Sort

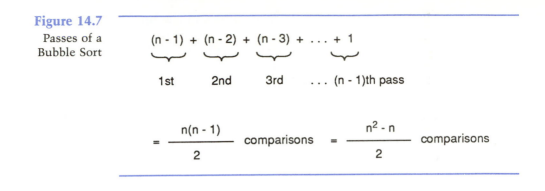

$$(n-1) + (n-2) + (n-3) + \ldots + 1$$

1st   2nd   3rd   ... (n-1)th pass

$$= \frac{n(n-1)}{2} \text{ comparisons} = \frac{n^2-n}{2} \text{ comparisons}$$

Program 14.1

```
PROGRAM BUBBLESORT(INPUT, OUTPUT);

     { PURPOSE: ALPHABETIZE A LIST OF WORDS }

TYPE
    STRING20 = STRING[20]; { LIMIT SAVES MEMORY }
    WORDTYPE = ARRAY[1..30] OF STRING20;

VAR
    WORD  : WORDTYPE;
    COUNT : INTEGER;

PROCEDURE GETVALUES(VAR CNT : INTEGER;
                    VAR W : WORDTYPE);

    VAR
       LOOP : INTEGER;

    BEGIN

       WRITE('ENTER NUMBER OF WORDS TO BE SORTED: ');
       READLN(CNT);
       WRITELN('THERE ARE ',CNT,' WORDS TO SORT.');
       WRITELN('ENTER THE WORDS.');
       FOR LOOP := 1 TO CNT DO
          BEGIN
             WRITE('WORD #',LOOP,' > ');
             READLN(W[LOOP])
          END { FOR }

    END; { GETVALUES }

PROCEDURE SWITCH(VAR FIRST, SECOND : STRING20);

    VAR
       TEMP : STRING20;

    BEGIN

       TEMP := FIRST;
       FIRST := SECOND;
       SECOND := TEMP

    END; { SWITCH }
```

```
PROCEDURE BUBBLE(CNT : INTEGER; VAR W : WORDTYPE);

    VAR
        LAST,
        CURRENT : INTEGER;

    BEGIN

        FOR LAST := CNT-1 DOWNTO 1 DO
            FOR CURRENT := 1 TO LAST DO
                IF W[CURRENT] > W[CURRENT+1]
                    THEN SWITCH(W[CURRENT],W[CURRENT+1])

    END; { BUBBLE }

PROCEDURE PRINTOUT(CNT : INTEGER; W : WORDTYPE);

    VAR
        LOOP : INTEGER;

    BEGIN

        FOR LOOP := 1 TO CNT DO
            WRITELN('  ',W[LOOP])

    END; { PRINTOUT }

BEGIN { MAIN PROGRAM }

    GETVALUES(COUNT, WORD);
    WRITELN;
    WRITELN('BUBBLE SORT RESULTS');
    WRITELN('-------------------');
    BUBBLE(COUNT, WORD);
    PRINTOUT(COUNT, WORD)

END.
```

The bubble sort of Program 14.1 performs $n - 1$ passes, where n is the number of items in the list. For any arbitrary pass m, there are $n - m$ comparisons, as shown in Figure 14.7.

One way to evaluate the effectiveness of a sort is to look at the number of comparisons. In general, a bubble sort could require as many as $(n^2 - n)/2$ comparisons for the worst case. This means that a bubble sort's effectiveness depends on the square of the number of elements (n^2), since n^2 is the dominant term in the expression.

Selection Sort

Like a bubble sort, the **selection sort** is fairly easy to understand. A selection sort generally performs more comparisons and fewer switches than a bubble sort. The nature of the data being sorted should be considered in determining which of these sorts to use.

A selection sort is based on the idea of finding the smallest (or largest, if the data are to be sorted in descending order) element in a list and putting it in the first position of the array by switching it with whatever element is there. That element is then fixed, and the next smallest element is found and moved to the second position. The process continues until the entire array is in order.

Figure 14.8 illustrates this method, given the initial array of

56 16 55 8 13 24 5

The final array is

5 8 13 16 24 55 56

Notice that the selection sort requires $n-1$ passes in a list of n items.

Figure 14.8
Selection Sort

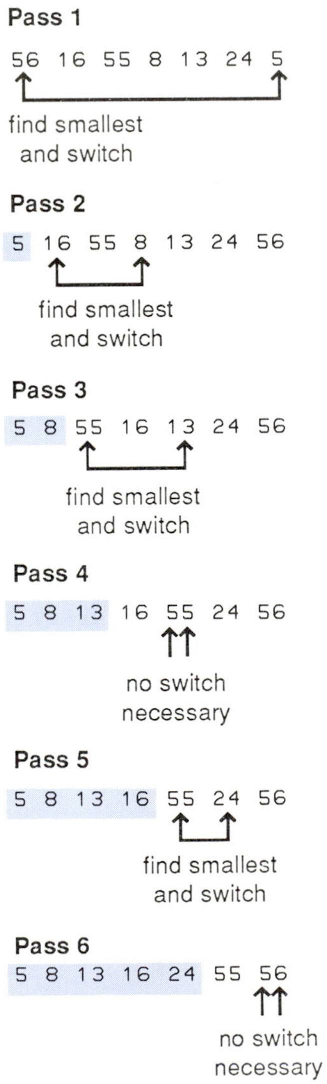

Pass 1

56 16 55 8 13 24 5

find smallest
and switch

Pass 2

5 16 55 8 13 24 56

find smallest
and switch

Pass 3

5 8 55 16 13 24 56

find smallest
and switch

Pass 4

5 8 13 16 55 24 56

no switch
necessary

Pass 5

5 8 13 16 55 24 56

find smallest
and switch

Pass 6

5 8 13 16 24 55 56

no switch
necessary

Program 14.2 gives the Pascal implementation of the selection sort to alphabetize a list of words.

Program 14.2

```
PROGRAM SELECTIONSORT(INPUT, OUTPUT);

    { PURPOSE: ALPHABETIZE USING SELECTION SORT }

TYPE
   STRING20 = STRING[20];
   WORDTYPE = ARRAY[1..30] OF STRING20;

VAR
   WORD  : WORDTYPE;
   COUNT : INTEGER;

PROCEDURE GETVALUES(VAR CNT : INTEGER;
                    VAR W : WORDTYPE);

   VAR
      LOOP : INTEGER;

   BEGIN

      WRITE('ENTER NUMBER OF WORDS TO BE SORTED: ');
      READLN(CNT);
      WRITELN('THERE ARE ', CNT,' WORDS TO SORT.');
      WRITELN('ENTER THE WORDS.');
      FOR LOOP := 1 TO CNT DO
         BEGIN
            WRITE('WORD #',LOOP,' > ');
            READLN(W[LOOP])
         END { FOR }

   END; { GETVALUES }

PROCEDURE SWITCH(VAR FIRST, SECOND : STRING20);

   VAR
      TEMP : STRING20;

   BEGIN

      TEMP := FIRST;
      FIRST := SECOND;
      SECOND := TEMP

   END; { SWITCH }

PROCEDURE SELECT(CNT : INTEGER; VAR W : WORDTYPE);

   VAR
      FIRST,
      CURRENT,
      SMALLEST : INTEGER;
```

```
      BEGIN

        FOR FIRST := 1 TO CNT DO
          BEGIN
            SMALLEST := FIRST;
            FOR CURRENT := FIRST + 1 TO CNT DO
              IF W[CURRENT] < W[SMALLEST]
                THEN SMALLEST := CURRENT;
            SWITCH(W[SMALLEST],W[FIRST])
          END

      END; { SELECT }

  PROCEDURE PRINTOUT(CNT : INTEGER; WRD : WORDTYPE);

      VAR
        LOOP : INTEGER;

      BEGIN

        FOR LOOP := 1 TO CNT DO
          WRITELN('   ',WRD[LOOP])

      END; { PRINTOUT }

  BEGIN { MAIN PROGRAM }

      GETVALUES(COUNT, WORD);
      WRITELN;
      WRITELN('SELECTION SORT RESULTS');
      WRITELN('----------------------');
      WRITELN;
      SELECT(COUNT, WORD);
      PRINTOUT(COUNT, WORD)

  END.
```

The selection sort requires $n - 1$ passes, where n is the number of items to be sorted. There are $n(n - 1)/2$ comparisons, since the outer loop is executed n times and the inner loop is executed $n - 1$ times. A selection sort is similar to a bubble sort in effectiveness. The choice between these two sorts depends on the nature of the data. For small amounts of data that are close to being in order, a bubble sort may be preferred. Neither is a very good choice for large amounts of data.

Insertion Sort

One approach to sorting that is particularly useful for small arrays is to repeatedly insert the next new element into the sequence of previously sorted elements. For example, on the first pass, element one is placed (trivially) in the first position. On the second pass, the second element is placed either before or after the first element according to its appropriate position; on the third pass, the third element is placed either before, between, or after the two sorted elements; and so on. This technique can be especially useful in a situation in which one array must be merged with a second

Figure 14.9
Insertion Sort

	Element Number						
Count	0	1	2	3	4	5	6
initial	-9999	19	16	11	12	15	17
2	-9999	19	16	11	12	15	17
3	-9999	16	19	11	12	15	17
4	-9999	11	16	19	12	15	17
5	-9999	11	12	16	19	15	17
6	-9999	11	12	15	16	19	17
	-9999	11	12	15	16	17	19

ordered array. This process, called an **insertion sort,** can be used to merge the two arrays and maintain the order.

Two processes must take place to accomplish an insertion sort. The location of the element to be stored must be found and the existing elements must to be shifted in order to make room for the new element. These processes can be combined by storing the element in a temporary variable, scanning the list of elements, and shifting those that are greater (or less) than the new element. To simplify the process further, a dummy element (or **flag**) can be stored in position zero to stop the backward scan of the array (see Figure 14.9). Assume an initial array of

19 16 11 12 15 17

Program 14.3 demonstrates the insertion sort on an array of random numbers between 1 and 100.

Program 14.3

```
PROGRAM INSERTSORT(INPUT,OUTPUT);

    { PURPOSE: SORT THE ELEMENTS IN AN ARRAY
               USING AN INSERTION SORT }

USES
    APPLESTUFF;         { FOR RANDOM NUMBER GENERATION }

CONST
    ARRAYSIZE = 20;

TYPE
    NUMBERARRAY = ARRAY[0..ARRAYSIZE] OF INTEGER;

VAR
    NUMBERLIST  : NUMBERARRAY;
    COUNT       : INTEGER;
```

```
FUNCTION RND(LOW,HIGH : INTEGER) : INTEGER;

   BEGIN

      RND := RANDOM MOD (HIGH - LOW + 1) + LOW

   END; { RND }

PROCEDURE DEFINEARRAY(VAR CNT : INTEGER;
                     VAR ARRY : NUMBERARRAY);

   BEGIN

      CNT := 0;
      ARRY[0] := -9999;
      REPEAT
         CNT := CNT + 1;
         ARRY[CNT] := RND(1,100)
      UNTIL CNT = ARRAYSIZE

   END; { DEFINEARRAY }

PROCEDURE PRINTARRAY(CNT : INTEGER;
                     ARRY : NUMBERARRAY);

   VAR
      C : INTEGER;

   BEGIN

      FOR C := 1 TO CNT DO
         WRITE(ARRY[C],' ');
      WRITELN

   END; { PRINTARRAY }

PROCEDURE INSERT(CNT : INTEGER;
                 VAR ARRY : NUMBERARRAY);

   VAR
      COUNTER,
      PREVIOUS,
      TEMP      : INTEGER;

   BEGIN

      FOR COUNTER := 2 TO CNT DO
         BEGIN
            PREVIOUS := COUNTER - 1;
            TEMP := ARRY[COUNTER];
            WHILE TEMP < ARRY[PREVIOUS] DO
               BEGIN
                  ARRY[PREVIOUS+1]:=ARRY[PREVIOUS];
                  PREVIOUS := PREVIOUS - 1
               END;
            ARRY[PREVIOUS + 1] := TEMP
         END

   END; { INSERT }
```

```
BEGIN { INSERTSORT }

    RANDOMIZE;
    DEFINEARRAY(COUNT,NUMBERLIST);
    WRITE('ORIGINAL LIST: ');
    PRINTARRAY(COUNT,NUMBERLIST);
    WRITELN;
    WRITE('SORTED LIST: ');
    INSERT(COUNT,NUMBERLIST);
    PRINTARRAY(COUNT,NUMBERLIST)

END.
```

Quicksort

The idea behind a **quicksort** is to select one of the elements in the list and use it to partition the remaining elements into two groups. One group contains those elements in the list that are less than the partitioning element and the other contains those that are greater. Each group is then sorted by applying the same method recursively. The partitioning can be implemented by choosing the first element as the partitioning element and then simultaneously scanning the elements from left to right and right to left. When two elements are found in the wrong part of the list, they are interchanged, putting them in the correct half of the list. After one complete pass, the partitioning element is placed between the two sublists by interchanging the original partitioning element with the last element in the first list. Then the two sublists are sorted by the same method using recursion.

The quicksort example given in Figure 14.10 uses the first element, 14, as the partitioning element. The left pointer moves towards the right through the list until it encounters an element that is greater than 14, while the right pointer moves towards the left until it encounters an element that is less than 14. When two elements are found that are in the wrong place, they are switched. Then the pointers each continue inward towards each other searching for elements to switch. The switching ends when the pointers cross paths. The partitioning element is then inserted between the two sublists (that is, between the left sublist, with elements less than 14, and the right sublist, with elements greater than 14) by switching places with the last element in the left sublist (5). Figure 14.10 gives the first pass of the quicksort. Each sublist is then partitioned and sorted by its own first element. The process continues with each sublist until the list is sorted.

Program 14.4 shows the quicksort in action (sorting 21 random integers from low to high). The procedure uses F and L to keep track of the first and last element in the list. Two pointers (variables P1 and P2) are used to scan the left and right partitions, respectively, and mark the elements that need to be interchanged. To simplify the process, a flag is stored in location L + 1 (one beyond the end of the list). The flag must be greater than or equal to the largest element in the list.

Figure 14.10
First Pass of Quicksort

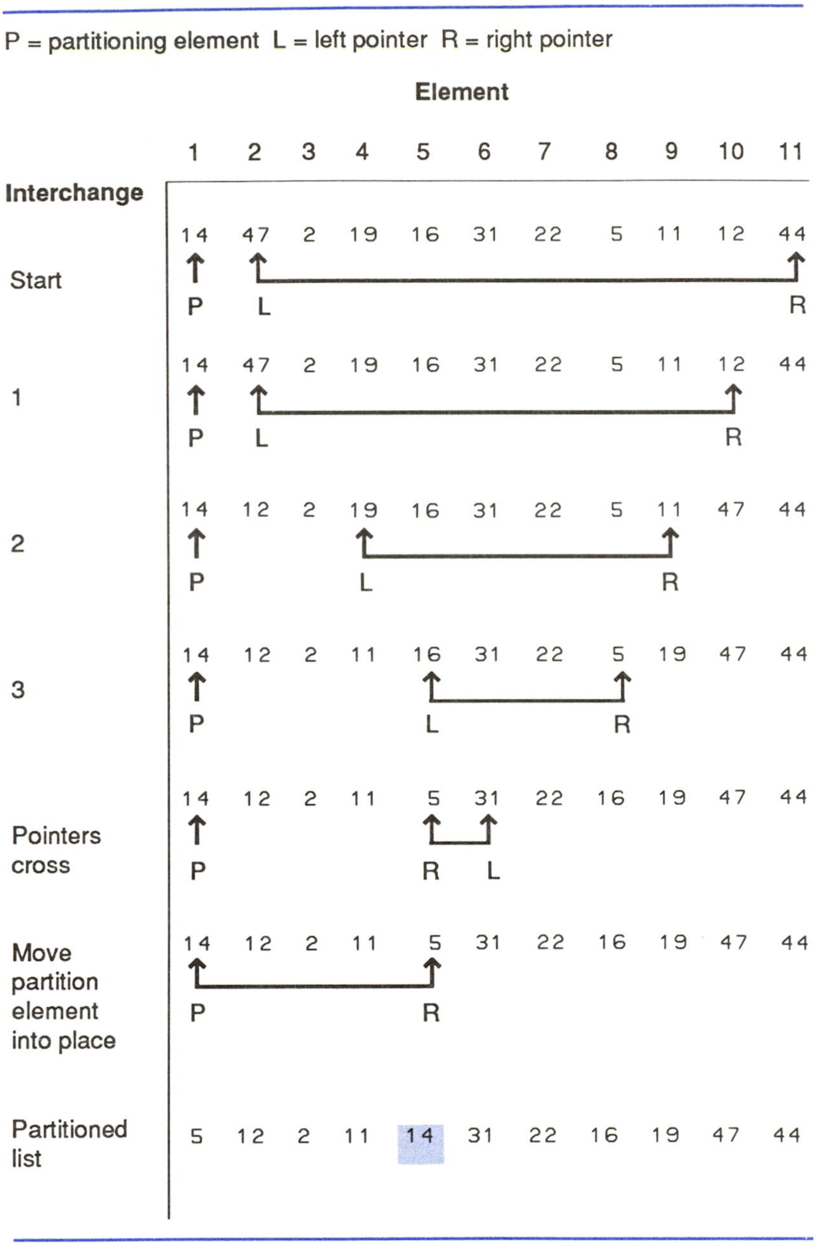

P = partitioning element L = left pointer R = right pointer

Element

	1	2	3	4	5	6	7	8	9	10	11
Interchange											
Start	14	47	2	19	16	31	22	5	11	12	44
	P	L									R
1	14	47	2	19	16	31	22	5	11	12	44
	P	L								R	
2	14	12	2	19	16	31	22	5	11	47	44
	P			L					R		
3	14	12	2	11	16	31	22	5	19	47	44
	P				L			R			
Pointers cross	14	12	2	11	5	31	22	16	19	47	44
	P				R	L					
Move partition element into place	14	12	2	11	5	31	22	16	19	47	44
	P				R						
Partitioned list	5	12	2	11	14	31	22	16	19	47	44

Program 14.4

```
PROGRAM QUICKSORT(INPUT,OUTPUT);

           { PURPOSE : SORT THE ELEMENTS IN AN ARRAY
                       USING A RECURSIVE QUICKSORT }

USES
    APPLESTUFF;      { FOR RANDOM NUMBER GENERATION }

CONST
    ARRAYSIZE = 21;

TYPE
    NUMBERARRAY = ARRAY[1..ARRAYSIZE] OF INTEGER;
```

```
VAR
   NUMBERLIST  : NUMBERARRAY;
   COUNT,
   FIRST,
   LAST         : INTEGER;

FUNCTION RND(LOW,HIGH : INTEGER) : INTEGER;

   BEGIN

      RND := RANDOM MOD (HIGH - LOW + 1) + LOW

   END; { RND }

PROCEDURE DEFINEARRAY(VAR CNT : INTEGER;
                      VAR ARRY : NUMBERARRAY);

   BEGIN

      CNT := 0;
      REPEAT
         CNT := CNT + 1;
         ARRY[CNT] := RND(1,100)
      UNTIL CNT = ARRAYSIZE - 1;
      ARRY[21] := 9999

   END; { DEFINEARRAY }

PROCEDURE PRINTARRAY(CNT : INTEGER;
                     ARRY : NUMBERARRAY);

   VAR
      C : INTEGER;

   BEGIN

      FOR C := 1 TO CNT DO
         WRITE(ARRY[C],' ');
      WRITELN

   END; { PRINTARRAY }

PROCEDURE QUICK(F,L : INTEGER;
                VAR ARRY : NUMBERARRAY);

   VAR
      TEMP,
      P1,
      P2        : INTEGER;

   BEGIN

      IF F < L
         THEN
            BEGIN    { PARTITION THE ELEMENTS }
               P1 := F + 1;
               WHILE ARRY[P1] < ARRY[F] DO
                  P1 := P1 + 1;
               P2 := L;
               WHILE ARRY[P2] > ARRY[F] DO
                  P2 := P2 - 1;
               WHILE P1 < P2 DO
```

```
                         BEGIN
                             TEMP := ARRY[P1];
                             ARRY[P1] := ARRY[P2];
                             ARRY[P2] := TEMP;
                             REPEAT
                                 P1 := P1 + 1
                             UNTIL ARRY[P1] >= ARRY[F];
                             REPEAT
                                 P2 := P2 - 1
                             UNTIL ARRY[P2] <= ARRY[F]
                         END; { WHILE }
                       TEMP := ARRY[F];
                       ARRY[F] := ARRY[P2];
                       ARRY[P2] := TEMP;
                       QUICK(F,P2 - 1,ARRY);
                       QUICK(P2 + 1,L,ARRY)
                   END { IF }

        END; { QUICK }

BEGIN  { QUICKSORT }

    RANDOMIZE;
    DEFINEARRAY(COUNT,NUMBERLIST);
    WRITE('ORIGINAL LIST: ');
    PRINTARRAY(COUNT,NUMBERLIST);
    WRITELN;
    WRITE('SORTED LIST: ');
    FIRST := 1;
    LAST := ARRAYSIZE - 1;
    QUICK(FIRST,LAST,NUMBERLIST);
    PRINTARRAY(COUNT,NUMBERLIST)

END.
```

The quicksort is good for large amounts of data and is generally preferred over the other sorts given in this lesson. One thing can easily be done to make the quicksort even better. Choosing the first element to partition the list is an obvious choice, but may not be the best choice. Ideally, the partitioning element will divide the list into two equal parts. Of course, this cannot be done without significantly slowing down the sort. There is a method, however, that will increase the chance that the partitioning element will be near the middle value of the list. Called the **median-of-three** method, this technique involves taking three elements from the list and choosing the middle (median) value as the partitioning element. The obvious choice for the three values would be the first, middle and last elements. This improvement on the quicksort is left as an exercise.

Lesson Check 14.1

1. Which sort is a good choice for a small list that is already semiordered?

2. Which sort is most useful for merging two arrays?

3. What are some of the differences between a selection sort and a bubble sort?

4. Complete the quicksort example given in Figure 14.10 by showing how each sublist is sorted.

5. What is the median-of-three method with respect to a quicksort?

Lesson 14.2   Searching

As seen in Chapter 13, a simple linear (or sequential) search can be written easily in Pascal. The problem is whether or not the time taken to locate an entry is acceptable. The search presented in Chapter 13 is fine for small amounts of data (fewer than 100 elements). In reality, however, searching is often performed on enormous groups of data, from student records in a school district to Internal Revenue Service files. Large search times could bring a situation involving large amounts of data nearly to a stop. Fortunately, search times can be improved dramatically, especially if the data are in what is called natural order: alphabetic for words and letters, numeric for numbers. As has been seen, obtaining ordered data is not too difficult. Either the data can be maintained in their natural order or the data can be sorted using a number of algorithms presented in the last lesson. This lesson will give several searching techniques that can be used in various programming situations. Unless otherwise indicated in this lesson, the data to be searched are assumed to be in their natural order.

Linear Search

With ordered data, search times can be greatly improved. Even the simple linear (sequential) search can be enhanced. Since the data are in their natural order, each entry is greater than or equal to the previous entry. Thus, a WHILE loop can be used to move quickly through the entries that are less than the item being searched (the search key). A counter is advanced as long as the search key is bigger than the entry pointed to by the counter. Finally, when an entry is found that is not less than the search key, that entry is checked to see if it is equal to the search key. If so, then the search key was found at the location marked by the counter. Otherwise, the search key is not in the list.

Program 14.5 shows the implementation of a linear search on data that is ordered. To store ordered data quickly in an array, a procedure is used to fill an array of 20 elements with the even numbers from 2 to 40. (This will aid in testing the search, since there will be 20 numbers between 1 and 40 that will be found and 20 that will not be found.) To simplify the algorithm, an additional entry is stored in location 21. This entry is larger than the largest entry in the list and is used as a stopping mechanism for the search.

Program 14.5

```
PROGRAM SEARCHDEMO(INPUT,OUTPUT);

       { PURPOSE: SEARCH AN ARRAY FOR A SPECIFIED
         ELEMENT USING A LINEAR SEARCH }

CONST
   ARRAYSIZE = 21;

TYPE
   NUMBERARRAY = ARRAY[1..ARRAYSIZE] OF INTEGER;

VAR
   NUMBERLIST        : NUMBERARRAY;
   NUMBERELEMENTS,
   SEARCHKEY,
   LOCATION          : INTEGER;
   FOUND             : BOOLEAN;

PROCEDURE DEFINEARRAY(VAR CNT : INTEGER;
                      VAR ARRY : NUMBERARRAY);

   BEGIN

      CNT := 0;
      REPEAT
         CNT := CNT + 1;
         ARRY[CNT] := CNT * 2
      UNTIL CNT = ARRAYSIZE - 1;
      ARRY[ARRAYSIZE] := 9999

   END; { DEFINEARRAY }

PROCEDURE PRINTARRAY(CNT : INTEGER;
                     ARRY : NUMBERARRAY);

   VAR
      C : INTEGER;

   BEGIN

      FOR C := 1 TO CNT DO
         WRITE(ARRY[C],' ');
      WRITELN

   END; { PRINTARRAY }

PROCEDURE LINEARSEARCH(KEY : INTEGER;
                       ARRY : NUMBERARRAY;
                       VAR FND : BOOLEAN;
                       VAR LOC : INTEGER);

   VAR
      COUNT    : INTEGER;
```

```
BEGIN

    FND := FALSE;
    COUNT := 1;
    WHILE KEY > ARRY[COUNT] DO
        COUNT := COUNT + 1;
    IF KEY = ARRY[COUNT]
        THEN
            BEGIN
                FND := TRUE;
                LOC := COUNT
            END

END; { LINEARSEARCH }

BEGIN { SEARCHDEMO }

    DEFINEARRAY(NUMBERELEMENTS,NUMBERLIST);
    WRITE('ORIGINAL LIST: ');
    PRINTARRAY(NUMBERELEMENTS,NUMBERLIST);
    WRITELN;
    WRITE('SEARCH KEY: ');
    READLN(SEARCHKEY);
    WRITELN;
    LINEARSEARCH(SEARCHKEY,NUMBERLIST,FOUND,LOCATION);
    IF FOUND
        THEN
            WRITELN(SEARCHKEY,' FOUND AT LOCATION ',
                    LOCATION,'.')
        ELSE
            WRITELN(SEARCHKEY,' NOT FOUND.')

END.
```

An analysis of the time taken to search for an element reveals the effectiveness of the method of searching. By looking at how the search performs in its best case, worst case, and average case, the power of the search algorithm can be determined. For a linear search, the values are

Best Case	Worst Case	Average Case
1	n	$(n + 1)/2$

where n is the number of elements in the array. The best case is 1 since the element searched for could be the first element in the list. The worst case is n since the element could be last. The **order (O)** of a search is an approximation of the effectiveness of an algorithm. For a linear search, the order would be n (written $O(n)$, since n is the dominant term in the expression (making the search time dependent on n).

Binary Search

For large amounts of data, a linear search can be very slow, even when the data are in order. An enormous improvement in search times can be obtained by using a **binary search** on an ordered list. This algorithm determines in which half of the list the search key should be located. This half is then halved again to isolate the search key to one-fourth of the list. The process is repeated until the search key is found or there is no more halving to be done. Figure 14.11 shows a binary search for 19 in a nine-element array. In this search, L represents the low point, M represents the median point, and H represents the high point each time the array is halved. The number being searched for—19—is found at location 8.

Program 14.6 illustrates a binary search on a list of integers. (For simplicity, the program creates a list of the even numbers from 2 to 40.) Two values (LOW and HIGH) are used to keep track of the lowest and highest element number in the segment to be searched. Initially, LOW is 1 and HIGH is 20, since the entire list is to be searched. The middle of the list is then determined (MIDDLE := (LOW + HIGH) DIV 2) and a check is made to see if the search key is below, above, or equal to the element at that position. If the search key is equal to the middle entry, then the search is complete. If the search key is less than the middle element, then HIGH is moved to one position below the middle—halving the search segment. If the search key is greater than the

Figure 14.11

Binary Search

Figure 14.11 Binary Search. 19 is found at location 8.

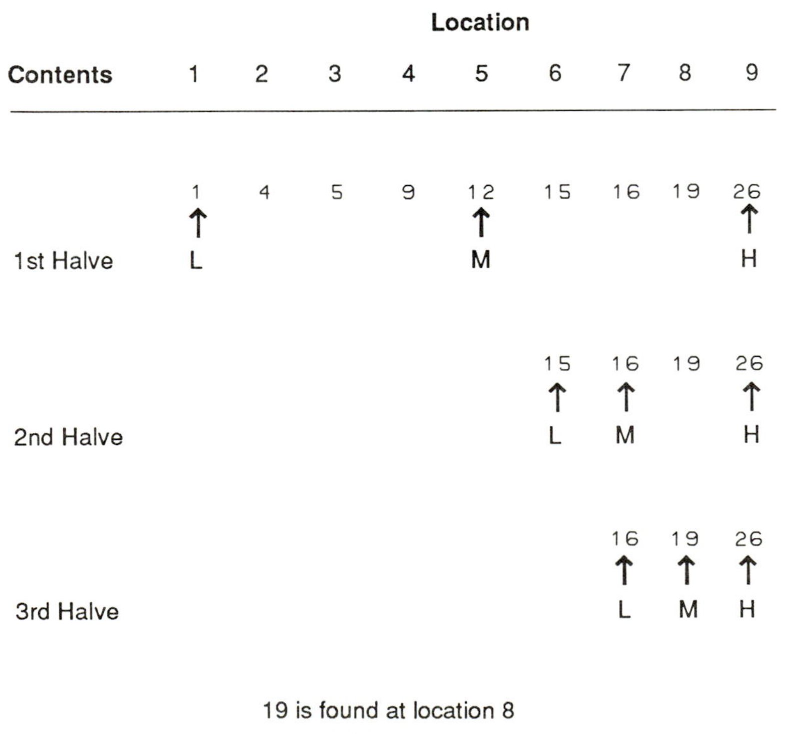

middle element, then LOW is moved to one position above the middle. The search is completed by repeating the process as long as LOW is less than HIGH and the search key is not found.

Program 14.6

```
PROGRAM SEARCHDEMO(INPUT,OUTPUT);

        { PURPOSE: SEARCH AN ARRAY FOR A SPECIFIED
                   ELEMENT USING A BINARY SEARCH  }

CONST
   ARRAYSIZE = 20;

TYPE
   NUMBERARRAY = ARRAY[1..ARRAYSIZE] OF INTEGER;

VAR
   NUMBERLIST       : NUMBERARRAY;
   NUMBERELEMENTS,
   SEARCHKEY,
   LOCATION         : INTEGER;
   FOUND            : BOOLEAN;

PROCEDURE DEFINEARRAY(VAR CNT : INTEGER;
                      VAR ARRY : NUMBERARRAY);

   BEGIN

      CNT := 0;
      REPEAT
        CNT := CNT + 1;
        ARRY[CNT] := CNT * 2
      UNTIL CNT = ARRAYSIZE

   END; { DEFINEARRAY }

PROCEDURE PRINTARRAY(CNT : INTEGER;
                     ARRY : NUMBERARRAY);

   VAR
      C : INTEGER;

   BEGIN

      FOR C := 1 TO CNT DO
        WRITE(ARRY[C],' ');
      WRITELN

   END; { PRINTARRAY }

PROCEDURE BINARYSEARCH(KEY,NUMEL : INTEGER;
                       ARRY : NUMBERARRAY;
                       VAR FND : BOOLEAN;
                       VAR LOC : INTEGER);

   VAR
      LOW,
      HIGH,
      MIDDLE   : INTEGER;
```

```
      BEGIN

         FND := FALSE;
         LOW := 1;
         HIGH := NUMEL;
         WHILE (LOW <= HIGH) AND (NOT FND) DO
            BEGIN
               MIDDLE := (LOW + HIGH) DIV 2;
               IF KEY < ARRY[MIDDLE]
                  THEN
                     HIGH := MIDDLE - 1
                  ELSE
                     IF KEY > ARRY[MIDDLE]
                        THEN
                           LOW := MIDDLE + 1
                        ELSE
                           BEGIN
                              FND := TRUE;
                              LOC := MIDDLE
                           END

            END  { WHILE }

      END; { BINARYSEARCH }

   BEGIN { SEARCHDEMO }

      DEFINEARRAY(NUMBERELEMENTS,NUMBERLIST);
      WRITE('ORIGINAL LIST: ');
      PRINTARRAY(NUMBERELEMENTS,NUMBERLIST);
      WRITELN;
      WRITE('SEARCH KEY: ');
      READLN(SEARCHKEY);
      WRITELN;
      BINARYSEARCH(SEARCHKEY,NUMBERELEMENTS,NUMBERLIST,
                   FOUND,LOCATION);
      IF FOUND
         THEN
            WRITELN(SEARCHKEY,' FOUND AT LOCATION ',
                    LOCATION,'.')
         ELSE
            WRITELN(SEARCHKEY,' NOT FOUND.')

   END.
```

Sample Run:

```
ORIGINAL LIST: 2 4 6 8 10 12 14 16 18 20 22 24 26 28
30 32 34 36 38 40

SEARCH KEY: 36

36 FOUND AT LOCATION 18.
```

In terms of efficiency, a binary search shows great improvement over the linear search. The best case is 1, since the search key could be the middle element in the list. The worst case is $\log_2(n + 1)$. (To see this, take the specific case of a list of 100 elements. By halving the list (using DIV), successive portions are obtained as follows: 50, 25, 12, 6, 3, 1. Thus the maximum number of attempts to find a number in a list of 100 is 7. Note that 2^6 is 64 and 2^7 is 128. In a binary search, the maximum number of tries is equal to the next larger power of two beyond n, or simply $\log_2(n + 1)$.)

Best Case	Worst Case	Average Case
1	$\log_2(n + 1)$	$(1 + 1/n)\log_2(n + 1)$

Thus, a binary search has an order of $\log_2 n$, or $O(\log_2 n)$, since the search time is dependent upon the logarithm of n.

Two-Stage Search

Sometimes the nature of the data is such that the most frequently accessed entries are concentrated in one part of the list. If this is the case, it may be possible to develop an algorithm that will first search the part of the list where the item is most likely to be found, thus improving search times. In particular, if the most frequently searched-for entries are near the front of the list, a **two-stage search** can be designed to take advantage of the arrangement of data.

In Program 14.7, a two-stage search is implemented. The idea is to segment the list starting from the first entry and then check to see if the search key is less than the last entry in the segment. If the search key is less than the last entry, then that segment is searched (using a linear search) for the key. If the search key is not less than the element at the end of the current segment, the process goes on to the next segment.

Choice of a segment length is important. It should be dependent upon the number of items in the list and should divide the list so that the the number of segments is approximately equal to the number of entries in each segment. This can be done easily by taking a segment length equal to the square root of the number of elements in the list. On extremely large sets of data, this type of search can be quite effective. A two-stage search can be improved further by using a binary search with the chosen segment.

Program 14.7

```
PROGRAM SEARCHDEMO(INPUT,OUTPUT);

    { PURPOSE: SEARCH AN ARRAY FOR A SPECIFIED
               ELEMENT USING A TWO-STAGE SEARCH }

USES
    TRANSCEND;          { FOR SQUARE ROOT FUNCTION }

CONST
    ARRAYSIZE = 21;

TYPE
    NUMBERARRAY = ARRAY[1..ARRAYSIZE] OF INTEGER;
```

```
VAR
    NUMBERLIST        : NUMBERARRAY;
    NUMBERELEMENTS,
    SEARCHKEY,
    LOCATION          : INTEGER;
    FOUND             : BOOLEAN;

PROCEDURE DEFINEARRAY(VAR CNT : INTEGER;
                      VAR ARRY : NUMBERARRAY);

    BEGIN

        CNT := 0;
        REPEAT
           CNT := CNT + 1;
           ARRY[CNT] := CNT * 2
        UNTIL CNT = ARRAYSIZE - 1;
        ARRY[ARRAYSIZE] := 9999

    END; { DEFINEARRAY }

PROCEDURE PRINTARRAY(CNT : INTEGER;
                     ARRY : NUMBERARRAY);

    VAR
        C : INTEGER;

    BEGIN

        FOR C := 1 TO CNT DO
           WRITE(ARRY[C],' ');
        WRITELN

    END; { PRINTARRAY ]

PROCEDURE TWOSTAGESEARCH(KEY, NUMEL : INTEGER;
                         ARRY : NUMBERARRAY;
                         VAR FND : BOOLEAN;
                         VAR LOC : INTEGER);

    VAR
        COUNT,
        SEGMENTLENGTH : INTEGER;

    BEGIN

        FND := FALSE;
        SEGMENTLENGTH := ROUND(SQRT(NUMEL));
        COUNT := SEGMENTLENGTH;
        WHILE (COUNT <= NUMEL) AND (NOT FND) DO
           IF KEY <= ARRY[COUNT]
               THEN
                   FND := TRUE          { SEGMENT FOUND }
               ELSE
                   COUNT := COUNT + SEGMENTLENGTH;
        FND := FALSE;
        COUNT := COUNT - SEGMENTLENGTH + 1;
        WHILE KEY > ARRY[COUNT] DO { LINEAR SEARCH }
           COUNT := COUNT + 1;
        IF KEY = ARRY[COUNT]
           THEN
```

```
                    BEGIN
                        FND := TRUE;          { ELEMENT FOUND }
                        LOC := COUNT
                    END

        END; { TWOSTAGESEARCH }

BEGIN { SEARCHDEMO }

    DEFINEARRAY(NUMBERELEMENTS,NUMBERLIST);
    WRITE('ORIGINAL LIST: ');
    PRINTARRAY(NUMBERELEMENTS,NUMBERLIST);
    WRITELN;
    WRITE('SEARCH KEY: ');
    READLN(SEARCHKEY);
    WRITELN;
    TWOSTAGESEARCH(SEARCHKEY,NUMBERELEMENTS,
                   NUMBERLIST,FOUND,LOCATION);
    IF FOUND
        THEN
            WRITELN(SEARCHKEY,' FOUND AT LOCATION ',
                    LOCATION,'.')
        ELSE
            WRITELN(SEARCHKEY,' NOT FOUND.')

END.
```

A two-stage search falls between the linear and binary searches in its effectiveness. Depending on the organization of the data, this may be the search to choose.

Best Case	Worst Case	Average Case
1	n	$(n + 1)/2$

The order of a two-stage search is n, $O(n)$, as in a linear search. However, if the more frequently accessed data items are located near the beginning of the list (which is the natural application for the two-stage search), the order would approach $\sqrt{n}$ (since $\sqrt{n}$ is used as the partitioning factor).

Hashing

If search times are critical, why not devise an algorithm that allows the search key to be found in only one try? The best search would be one that had an order of one; that is, $O(1)$. To accomplish this, the location of an entry must somehow be derived from the entry itself. For example, suppose an array was to contain the names Leanna, Zachary, Albert, Betty, Kerry, and Sue. An entry could be located in one attempt—$O(1)$ searching—by storing each name in the array location equal to the ASCII value of the first letter minus 64. This method for determining the array location is called the hash function for this data, or **hashing.** Leanna would be stored in location 12 (determined by the ASCII value of L—76—minus 64); Zachary, in location 26; Albert, in location 1; and so on. This method works in this situation, since each name starts with a different letter. There are obvious drawbacks, however. The array holding the names must be dimensioned to hold twenty-six entries even though there are only six names to store. More important is the fact that, in most situations, two or more entries would need to be stored in the same location. This is called a **collision** and must be resolved in the final hashing algorithm.

Many methods are employed to write hash functions that avoid collisions. Most are designed to manipulate the binary representation of the characters in the item to be stored. Even with improved hash functions, collisions are inevitable and must be resolved in some way. In this lesson, the method for resolving collisions will be kept simple. In Chapter 17 (when more advanced data structures are available), other options for **collision resolution** will be discussed.

Program 14.8 demonstrates a very simple form of hashing. Names entered by the user are placed in an array location based on the sum of the ASCII values of the characters in the name. For this example, an array that can hold up to 100 entries is used. Thus, the hash function to determine where a particular entry will be stored is the total of the ASCII values MOD 100 + 1. Since the MOD function returns the remainder of the division, the hash function will return values between 1 and 100. A location in the array will be calculated for each entry; however, collisions will undoubtedly occur. Collisions are resolved by placing the colliding element (that is, the element that has collided with an existing element) in the next available (empty) location in the array, using a linear search to find the empty location. For this example, assume that there are fewer than 100 entries to store. The collision resolution will slow down the hashing only slightly and the order of the hashing search is still one, 0(1). (*Note:* Program 14.8 uses the LENGTH function, which returns the length of a string. Strings are discussed in detail in Chapter 19.)

Program 14.8

```
PROGRAM HASHDEMO(INPUT,OUTPUT);

        { PURPOSE: BUILD AN ARRAY OF ELEMENTS
                   USING A HASH FUNCTION }

CONST
   ARRAYSIZE = 20;

TYPE
   NAMEARRAY = ARRAY[1..ARRAYSIZE] OF STRING;

VAR
   NAMES              : NAMEARRAY;
   NUMBERELEMENTS,
   SEARCHKEY,
   LOCATION           : INTEGER;
   FOUND              : BOOLEAN;
   CHOICE             : CHAR;
   ELEMENT            : STRING;
```

```
PROCEDURE INITARRAY(VAR CNT : INTEGER;
                    VAR ARRY : NAMEARRAY);

    BEGIN

        CNT := 0;
        REPEAT
            CNT := CNT + 1;
            ARRY[CNT] := 'EMPTY'
        UNTIL CNT = ARRAYSIZE

    END; { INITARRAY }

PROCEDURE GETELEMENT(VAR EL : STRING);

    BEGIN

        WRITE('ENTER THE NAME: ');
        READLN(EL)

    END; { GETELEMENT }

PROCEDURE PRINTARRAY(CNT : INTEGER;
                     ARRY : NAMEARRAY);

    VAR
        C : INTEGER;

    BEGIN

        WRITELN('CURRENT LIST: ');
        FOR C := 1 TO CNT DO
            WRITE(ARRY[C]:16);
        READLN;
        WRITELN

    END; { PRINTARRAY }

PROCEDURE HASH(KEY : STRING; ARRY : NAMEARRAY;
               VAR LOC : INTEGER);

    VAR
        COUNT,
        TOTAL   : INTEGER;

    PROCEDURE COLLISION(COL : INTEGER;
                        VAR L : INTEGER);

        BEGIN

            WHILE ARRY[COL] <> 'EMPTY' DO
                BEGIN
                    COL := COL + 1;
                    IF COL > ARRAYSIZE
                        THEN
                            COL := 1
                END; { WHILE }
            L := COL

        END; { COLLISION }
```

```
            BEGIN

                TOTAL := 0;
                FOR COUNT := 1 TO LENGTH(KEY) DO
                    TOTAL := TOTAL + ORD(KEY[COUNT]);
                LOC := TOTAL MOD ARRAYSIZE + 1;
                IF ARRY[LOC] <> 'EMPTY'
                    THEN
                        COLLISION(LOC,LOC)

            END; { HASH }

        PROCEDURE FINDELEMENT(KEY : STRING;
                              ARRY : NAMEARRAY;
                              VAR LOC : INTEGER;
                              VAR FND : BOOLEAN);

            VAR
                CHECK,
                COUNT,
                TOTAL    : INTEGER;

            BEGIN

                TOTAL := 0;
                FND := FALSE;
                CHECK := 0;
                FOR COUNT := 1 TO LENGTH(KEY) DO
                    TOTAL := TOTAL + ORD(KEY[COUNT]);
                LOC := TOTAL MOD ARRAYSIZE + 1;
                WHILE (ARRY[LOC] <> KEY) AND
                      (CHECK <= ARRAYSIZE) DO
                    BEGIN
                        CHECK := CHECK + 1;
                        LOC := LOC + 1;
                        IF LOC > ARRAYSIZE
                            THEN
                                LOC := 1
                    END; { WHILE }
                IF CHECK <= ARRAYSIZE
                    THEN
                        FND := TRUE

            END; { FINDELEMENT }

        BEGIN { HASHDEMO }

            INITARRAY(NUMBERELEMENTS,NAMES);
            REPEAT
                PAGE(OUTPUT);
                WRITELN('1. PLACE AN ELEMENT');
                WRITELN('2. FIND AN ELEMENT');
                WRITELN('3. PRINT CURRENT LIST');
                WRITELN('4. END');
                READ(CHOICE);
                WRITELN;
                CASE CHOICE OF
```

```
        '1' : BEGIN
                 GETELEMENT(ELEMENT);
                 HASH(ELEMENT,NAMES,LOCATION);
                 NAMES[LOCATION] := ELEMENT
              END;
        '2' : BEGIN
                 GETELEMENT(ELEMENT);
                 FINDELEMENT(ELEMENT,NAMES,
                             LOCATION,FOUND);
                 WRITE(ELEMENT);
                 IF FOUND
                    THEN
                       BEGIN
                          WRITE(' WAS FOUND AT ');
                          WRITELN(LOCATION,'.')
                       END
                    ELSE
                       WRITELN(' WAS NOT FOUND.');
                 READLN
              END;
        '3' : PRINTARRAY(NUMBERELEMENTS,NAMES)
      END { CASE }
   UNTIL CHOICE = '4'

END.
```

Remember, this is an oversimplified demonstration of hashing; it illustrates the basic concept, but nothing more. More sophisticated hashing functions and methods of collision resolution exist and can greatly enhance hashing as a method for storing and accessing data.

Lesson Check 14.2

1. Give the order (O) of each of the search routines discussed in this chapter. Why are these values significant?

2. When would a two-stage search be preferred over a binary search?

3. Why is $\sqrt{n}$ used for partitioning in a two-stage search?

4. Hashing provides a method for instant recall of an array element. However, collisions can occur if the hash function has not been carefully thought out. What is a collision and how is it avoided?

Lesson 14.3   Programming Tip—Program Design

A Detailed Look

After defining the problem carefully, the next step is to design a solution. This is where the logic diagram comes in handy. While many options exist for program design, this horizontal outline seems to serve the programmer best. Figure 14.12 presents a logic diagram of the stock market problem outlined in Lesson 13.4.

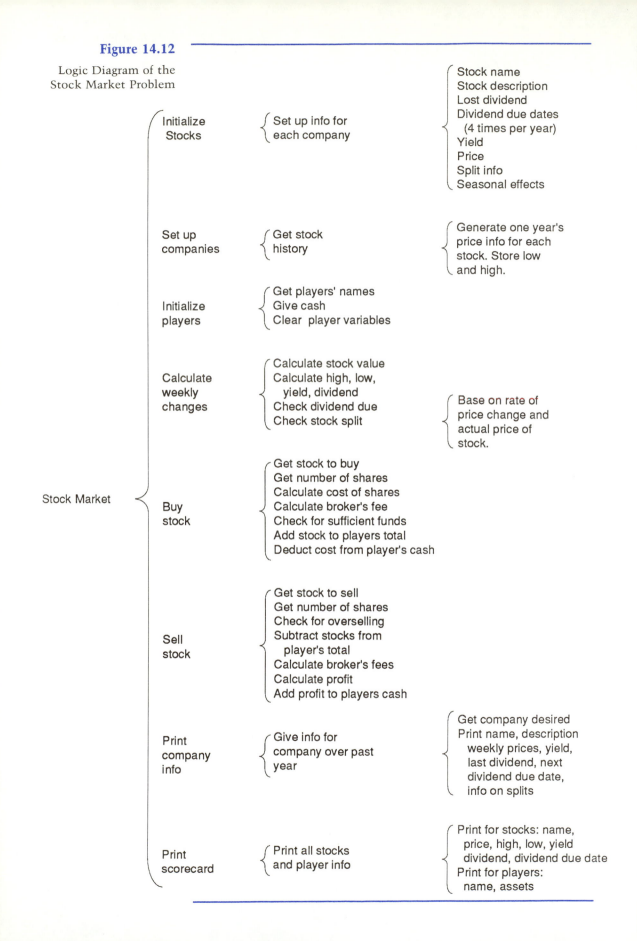

Figure 14.12

Logic Diagram of the
Stock Market Problem

Summary

Two of the most common applications associated with arrays are sorting and searching. Sorting allows the programmer to arrange elements in their natural order. Searching allows the programmer to find a specific element in an array.

Sorting elements in an array can be accomplished in many different ways. Each method of sorting has its own strengths. A bubble sort is one of the easiest to understand and implement. In general, the bubble sort is relatively slow, but works well on small amounts of data or data that are nearly in the correct order. A selection sort is similar to a bubble sort in its effectiveness. A selection sort requires more comparisons and fewer switches than a bubble sort. The nature of the data may determine which sort to choose. Possibly the best sort for small amounts of data is an insertion sort. In an insertion sort, each new element is inserted into the currently sorted list. An insertion sort uses a simple linear search to find the location to insert the new element. The method is particularly suited to merging an array with an ordered array. A quicksort uses a partitioning method to divide the array into two groups of elements: those less than and those greater than the partitioning element. Each of these groups is then partitioned. The process continues until all the elements are in order. Recursion is used in the quicksort to simplify the algorithm and speed up the sort. For arrays of substantial size, the quicksort is far superior to the other sorts in execution time.

Searching an array for a specific element is an essential process in many programs. If the data are ordered (possibly by use of a sort or by maintaining the list in order), search times can be vastly improved. A linear search is still the simplest to implement and is faster for ordered data as opposed to unordered data. For large amounts of data, however, linear searching is far too slow. A binary search can reduce search times dramatically on ordered data. The idea of a binary search is to pick the element in the middle of the list and check to see if the element searched for is less than or greater than the middle element. This reduces the number of elements to search by half. The process is then repeated on the half that may contain the element searched for. By halving each time, the element (if it is in the array) can be found quickly. While a binary search is hard to beat for speed, there are occasions when the size of the array (and nature of the data) may lend itself to a different kind of search algorithm. A two-stage search starts at the beginning of the array and tests segments of the array until the segment in which the element may be found is discovered. A linear or binary search is then performed on that segment. A two-stage search is especially useful if the items being searched for are concentrated near the front of the array.

The ultimate in searching algorithms would be one that could find an element in an array in just one try. Hashing is a method in which each element is stored in a position in the array that is based on the element itself. One way to accomplish this would be to use the ASCII values of the characters in the element. Even with more complex hash functions, collisions are inevitable. Collision resolution is an important part of hashing. One simple method of handling collisions is to store the colliding element in the next empty array location. This can be accomplished by using a linear search, which slows down search times only slightly. Much more efficient hash functions and schemes for collision resolution are possible, as we will see later.

Key Terms

binary search	flag	quicksort
bubble sort	hashing	searching
collision	insertion sort	selection sort
collision	median-of-three	sorting
resolution	order (O)	two-stage search

Answers to Lesson Checks

Lesson 14.1

1. The bubble sort is the best choice in this case.

2. The insertion sort is the best choice in this case.

3. A selection sort usually performs more comparisons and fewer switches than a bubble sort.

4. L = left pointer   P = partitioning element   R = right pointer

Element

1	2	3	4	5	6	7	8	9	10	11
5	12	2	11	14	31	32	16	19	47	44

P↑ L↑→R↑   P↑ L↑→———R↑

| 5 | 2 | 12 | 11 | 14 | 31 | 19 | 16 | 32 | 47 | 44 |

P↑→R↑   P↑———R↑

| 2 | 5 | 12 | 11 | 14 | 16 | 19 | 31 | 32 | 47 | 44 |

PLR   PL↑ R↑   PL↑ R↑   P↑ L↑ R↑

| 2 | 5 | 12 | 11 | 14 | 16 | 19 | 31 | 32 | 47 | 44 |

PR   P↑ R↑   PR   PL↑ R↑

| 2 | 5 | 11 | 12 | 14 | 16 | 19 | 31 | 32 | 47 | 44 |

P↑ R↑

| 2 | 5 | 11 | 12 | 14 | 16 | 19 | 31 | 32 | 44 | 47 |

5. The median-of-three method is a variation of the quicksort algorithm in which these elements (usually the first, middle, and last) of a list are compared before selecting a partitioning element (from among these three values). This method is designed to produce a partitioning element that will divide the list into two equal parts.

Lesson 14.2

1.

Search	Order
Linear search	$O(n)$
Binary search	$O(\log_2(n))$
Two-stage search	$O(n)$
Hash function	$O(1)$

The values are significant because they represent the approximate effectiveness of each search.

2. A two-stage search may be preferred over a binary search when the search element is more likely to be located near the beginning of the list.

3. The square root of n is used for partitioning in a two-stage search because the ideal number of segments should be approximately equal to each segment length itself. For example, for 16 elements, a two-stage search would begin with the first segment containing 4 elements; the search would be of four segments with 4 elements each.

4. A collision occurs when the hash function produces the same location for two elements. Collisions can be minimized by improving the hash function. Collisions can be resolved by moving the colliding element to the next available location.

Exercises   Set I. Comprehension

1. Suppose an array contains the following elements:

   23   12   3   32   33   4

   The array is to be sorted so that the values are in increasing order. Determine the contents of the array after three passes using the
   a. bubble sort.
   b. selection sort.

2. Suppose an array contains the following elements:

   45 -21 12   -9   -3

   The array is to be sorted so that the elements are in decreasing order. Determine the contents of the array after two passes using the
   a. bubble sort.
   b. selection sort.

3. Using the array elements listed in Exercise 1, determine the contents of the array after three passes using the
   a. insertion sort, with array element 0 assigned to −9999.
   b. quicksort.

4. Using the array elements listed in Exercise 2, determine the contents of the array after two passes using the
   a. insertion sort, with array element 0 assigned to −9999.
   b. quicksort.

5. In general, which of the following sorts is the most efficient for large arrays? Which is most efficient for small arrays?
   a. Bubble sort.
   b. Selection sort.
   c. Insertion sort.
   d. Quicksort.

6. Analyze the effectiveness of the insertion sort and compare it to the bubble and selection sorts.

7. Suppose an array contains the following elements:

   ```
   -31  -27   -9   14   17   18   29   30   48
   ```

   Determine the number of comparisons needed to find each element in the array using a binary search. For example, two comparisons are needed to find −9.

8. Suppose an array contains the elements from Exercise 7. Determine the number of comparisons needed to find each element in the array using a two-stage search (with a linear search of the segment).

9. Consider the following list of numbers:

   ```
   27   35   28    3    0    6  12   11   77   65
   ```

   Using the selection sort algorithm (see Figure 14.8), show the results for each pass through the array. Give the total number of comparisons and exchanges.

10. Perform an insertion sort (see Figure 14.9) on the list of numbers given in Exercise 9. Give the total number of comparisons and exchanges.

11. Suppose a program used a hash function that determined the location of a phone number by the sum of its digits. How many collisions would occur using the following list of numbers?

    757-6220, 845-7024, 548-4953, 548-4954, 486-7882,
    838-6724, 503-2272, 476-5304, 929-6042, 650-7716

12. Suppose a program used a hash function that determined the location of a name by the sum of the ASCII values of its first and last letters. How many collisions would occur using each of the following lists of names?
    a. Eddy, Joe, Simon, Travis, Ann, Carla
    b. Jim, Bob, Jack, Jan, Gordon, Carol, Barb
    c. David, Michael, Carrie, Brandon, Daniel

Set II. Application

13. Consider the following:

```
TYPE
    AVEGRADES = ARRAY[1..20,1..2] OF INTEGER;

VAR
    FRESHMAN,
    SOPHOMORE,
    JUNIOR,
    SENIOR     : AVEGRADES;
```

Assume that FRESHMAN, SOPHOMORE, JUNIOR, and SENIOR are ordered arrays (high to low). The first column contains (rounded) student averages and the second column contains the corresponding four-digit student ID numbers. Write a procedure to find the ID number of the students that earned a given average.

14. Consider the following:

```
TYPE
    COURSE = ARRAY[1..50] OF STRING;

VAR
    BIOLOGY,
    MATH,
    ECONOMICS : COURSE;
```

Assume that BIOLOGY, MATH, and ECONOMICS are alphabetically ordered lists of student names. Write a BOOLEAN function to determine if a given name appears in all three arrays.

15. Write a procedure to sort an array from Exercise 13 by student ID number.

16. Write a procedure to append array B to the end of array A. Arrays A and B are one-dimensional INTEGER arrays, each with 10 elements. Store the new array in array C.

17. Write a procedure to insert array B into the last 10 elements of array A. Assume array A is a one-dimensional INTEGER array that can hold 40 elements and that array B is a one-dimensional INTEGER array containing 10 elements.

18. Write a procedure to merge array A with array B. Assume A and B are one-dimensional character arrays of 75 elements each. Array A is in alphabetic order. Create the merged array C, maintaining this order.

19. Write a procedure to randomly merge two INTEGER arrays, A and B. Once the elements from one array have been exhausted, the remaining elements from the other array should be appended to the new array. Assume array A contains 10 elements and array B contains 20 elements.

20. Write a procedure to merge two STRING arrays that are in alphabetical order. The new combined array should maintain the alphabetic ordering of the STRING values. Assume array A contains 75 elements and array B contains 50 elements.

21. Write a program to read a list of students' names and their test scores. Print the list of names in alphabetic order along with each student's test score. Assume the following values:

DONALD, 85
ANN, 79
JOHN, 78
DENNIS, 90
CHUCK, 84
PAM, 98

22. Anne teaches biology to a large group of sophomores. At the beginning of the term, she writes the students' names in her gradebook in alphabetic order, last names first. As the term progresses, eight more students are added to the class, but their names are added to the bottom of the list. When the next term arrives, Anne would like to enter the names again in alphabetical order, including the late students. Write a program to alphabetize the list of student names. Allow Anne to enter the students' names in the form FIRSTNAME LASTNAME. Alphabetize by last names and print the names in the form LASTNAME, FIRSTNAME. Which sorting technique would be most appropriate for this problem? Why?

23. Write a program that generates a list of 50 random integers between 75 and 225, prints the list, sorts it from low to high, and then prints the sorted list.

Set III. Synthesis

24. Write a program that will find the mean, median, and mode of a list of numbers. For example, given the numbers 32, 58, 79, 69, 48, and 79, the mean can be determined by

$$\frac{32 + 58 + 79 + 69 + 48 + 79}{6} = 60.8$$

The median is the value that falls in the middle of a set of values when the values are arranged in order of magnitude. In this case, there is no single middle value, so the two middle values are averaged as follows:

$$\frac{58 + 69}{2} = 63.5$$

The mode is the number appearing the most often in a set of values. Here, the mode is 79.

Extension: Revise the program to check for more than one mode.

25. Write a procedure to sort a gin rummy hand. Assume the 2 × 10 character array contains the cards' values (A, 2, 3, 4, 5, 6, 7, 8, 9, 10, J, Q, K) in the first row and their corresponding suits (C, D, H, S) in the second row. The hand should be sorted so that all cards of the same suit are grouped together in ascending order, with clubs (C) being the first suit; diamonds (D), the second; hearts (H), the third; and spades (S), the fourth. The following array:

K 6 2 A 9 3 A Q 10 2
C D C S H H C C H S

would become:

A 2 Q K 6 3 9 10 A 2
C C C C D H H H S S

26. Write a procedure to search a sorted gin rummy hand from Exercise 25. Allow the user to enter the value and suit of the search card.

27. Write a program to sort a list of birth dates in chronological order. Allow the user to enter up to 30 birth dates in the form MONTHNAME DAYNUMBER YEAR, where MONTHNAME is placed in a one-dimensional STRING array, and DAYNUMBER and YEAR are placed in a two-dimensional INTEGER array.

    Option: Allow the user to enter a person's name along with that person's birth date.

28. Runners in the Tansy Marathon are each assigned a three-digit number (starting at 100) according to their all-time best running time. Write a program to allow the user to enter the runners' names and their corresponding running times in the form HHMMSS (H = hours, M = minutes, S = seconds). Print a list of the runners' names and their assigned numbers in alphabetic order and a list in numeric order.

    Option: Modify the program to allow the user to insert a new runner after the lists have been printed. Renumber the runners and print the new lists.

29. The State Traffic Commission is studying a particular stretch of road. They have placed three speed-checking devices at strategic locations along the road: POINTA, POINTB, and POINTC. A two-dimensional (3 × 300) REAL array, MPH, contains the speeds of cars passing the three checkpoints in a single day. (Assume 300 cars passed each checkpoint and that no cars turned off the road or turned around between checkpoints.) Write a procedure or procedures to perform the following:
    a. Average the three speeds for each car at the checkpoints. Store the average speeds in array AVESPEED.
    b. Sort the speeds in AVESPEED in ascending order. Determine the high, low, and average of all cars, and the median speed for the stretch of road.
    c. Sort the speeds for each checkpoint and determine the high, low, average, and median speed for each location.

A timing device, such as a stopwatch, will be necessary for Exercises 30 and 31.

30. Write a program to test the speed of various sort routines on a common group of data. Create a list of random numbers to be sorted by each routine (using the same list). Test the sort routines on lists of 100, 250, 500, and 1000 items. In order to achieve accurate timings (especially for small amounts of data), each sort routine may need to be placed in a loop and repeated several times on the same unordered data; then the grouped time can be divided

to find an approximate time for that particular amount of data. For example, the bubble sort for 100 items should be placed in a loop and repeated 10 times to allow plenty of time to start and stop the timing device; then the resulting time should be divided by 10.

Each sort should be tested three times on the same data to account for timing inconsistencies and to obtain an average sort time. Record the times in a table similar to the following:

Number of Items

Sort Routine		100	250	500	1000
Bubble	time1				
	time2				
	time3				
	average				
Selection	time1				
	time2				
	time3				
	average				
Insertion	time1				
	time2				
	time3				
	average				
Quicksort	time1				
	time2				
	time3				
	average				

Is any sort faster than the others in all cases?

31. Write a program to test the efficiency of various search routines on a common list of ordered data. Test the search routines on the numbers from 1 to 100, 1 to 250, 1 to 500, and 1 to 1000. Select a random number from each list and have each routine search for the same number. As with Exercise 30, small amounts of data may be difficult to time accurately. These search routines can be placed in a loop to allow plenty of time for starting and stopping the timing device.

Each search should be tested three times on the same list using a different random number. Record the times in a table similar to the one shown in Exercise 30. Use the linear, binary, and two-stage search routines. Is any one of these faster than the others in all cases?

32. Rewrite the quicksort routine (Program 14.4) using the median-of-three method. Examine the first, middle, and last elements, and select the value that falls between the other two values. This median value will be used as the partitioning element.

33. Write a program using a hash function to build a list of 50 phone numbers. Allow the user to enter a name and have the program

print the phone number corresponding to that name. Use the name as the identifying factor in determining the location of the phone number.

34. Write a program to graphically represent the number of comparisons required for each of the following sort methods on an identical group of data:
    a. Bubble sort.
    b. Selection sort.
    c. Insertion sort.
    d. Quicksort.
    e. Median-of-three quicksort.

35. Write a program to graphically represent the number of probes required for each of the following search methods to find a random element in a list of ordered data. Use the same random element for testing each search routine.
    a. Linear search.
    b. Binary search.
    c. Two-stage search.

15 Records

F irst came ten soldiers carrying clubs . . . next the ten courtiers: these were ornamented all over with diamonds. . . . After these came the royal children: there were ten of them . . . all ornamented with hearts. . . .

"And who are these?" said the Queen, pointing to the three gardeners who were lying round the rose-tree; for, you see, as they were lying on their faces, and the pattern on their backs was the same as the rest of the pack, she could not tell whether they were gardeners, or soldiers, or courtiers, or three of her own children.

—Lewis Carroll

Overview

Gaining a Perspective

Humans have long faced the problem of storing information in a manageable form. Maintaining data concerning business clients, keeping transactions for a coin collection, updating inventory; whatever the situation, the common problem of how to organize the information exists. In the case of a coin collection, the owner might want to know the type of coin, its condition, the year and mint mark, the purchase price, date of purchase, and the coin's current value. One approach to organizing the data for each coin might be to use an index card to store the information. This is certainly a logical approach but, until this chapter, not a simple task for the computer. The most probable method would have been to create an array for each characteristic of the coin. Thus, the information for one coin could be accessed by using the common subscript (number of the coin desired) in each of the parallel arrays. This would certainly work, but is extremely awkward (especially as the number of different types of information for each coin increases). Fortunately, Pascal provides an alternative that simplifies the process of storing related information.

A **record** allows grouping of related data items that are of any of the data types covered so far. The record structure closely resembles the index cards that are often used to store information. For the coin collection, each piece of information for a coin is stored in a predefined position of the corresponding record. The record then looks much like an index card containing pertinent information for a coin. A sample index card might look like that shown in Figure 15.1.

Figure 15.1
Coin Collector's Index
Card for Penny

Lincoln Penny

Extra Fine

1909

S

110.00

1978

129.00

The makeup, or definition, of the record would be

Field	Type
Coin	STRING
Condition	CONDITION (PR,BU,AU,XF,VF,F,VG,G)
Year	INTEGER
Mint mark	CHAR
Purchase price	REAL
Purchase date	STRING (could also be a record of month, day, year)
Current value	REAL

The fields in a record can be a variety of types. Simple data types as well as programmer-defined types can be used. A field can consist of another record or an array. A record can also be an element of an array, allowing access to an entire set of information through a single subscript.

Lesson 15.1 Records

Records can be used in any situation where related data must be stored and manipulated. Program Segment 15.1 is an example of a record that might be useful to the owner of a car lot. The record is defined under the TYPE heading at the beginning of a program.

**Program
Segment 15.1**

```
TYPE
    COLORS = (BLUE,BROWN,GREEN,ORANGE,RED,YELLOW);
    CARLOT = RECORD
                MAKE      : STRING[20];
                COLOR     : COLORS;
                YEAR      : 1950..2000;
                WRECK     : BOOLEAN;
                ODOMETER  : INTEGER[7];
                ESTVALUE  : REAL
            END;   { CARLOT }
```

Notice that the record includes a variety of components, or **fields** (positions for storing information). These fields include MAKE, COLOR, YEAR, and so on. Each of these fields is defined as a particular type. Figure 15.2 presents a sketch of this record.

After defining a record, a variable must be declared of this type. In this example, two variable identifiers are declared to be of type CARLOT. Each variable can store information for one used car.

```
VAR
    HONESTJOHNS,
    SMOOTHEDDYS : CARLOT;

{ HONESTJOHNS AND SMOOTHEDDYS ARE USED CAR LOTS. }
```

Figure 15.2
CARLOT Record

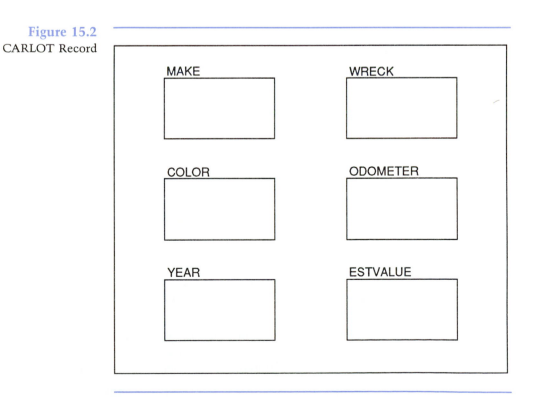

The record identifier is CARLOT. This identifier contains a collection of fields of different types.

```
Record Definition and Declaration of Variables
TYPE
    record identifier = RECORD

                           field identifier : type;
                           field identifier : type;
                           .
                           .
                           .

                        END; { record definition }

VAR
    variable identifier : record identifier;
```

The field identifiers can be of any ordinal data type (that is, INTEGER, CHAR, BOOLEAN, or programmer-defined), REAL, or a structured data type (such as STRING, an array, or a record). An equal sign separates the record identifier and the predefined identifier RECORD. The record definition requires an END statement to denote the end of the list of fields.

Assignments can be made to individual fields of records using **dot notation,** as follows:

```
HONESTJOHNS.MAKE := 'CHEVROLET';

HONESTJOHNS.YEAR := 1984;
```

The form for this notation is to specify the record variable identifier, followed by a period, and then the name of the field desired. (Note that no spaces are allowed between the identifiers and the period.) The period (the "dot" of dot notation) is called the **field selector.** Since a field in a record can itself be a record (**nested record**), more than one period can be used to get to the desired field.

Individual fields of records can be printed using the field selector.

```
WRITELN(HONESTJOHNS.MAKE);
```

This will print the contents of the field MAKE of the record HONESTJOHNS. Again, notice that the first part of the dot notation is the record variable identifier and the last part is a field identifier.

Caution: A common error in an assignment to a field is to use the record type identifier instead of the variable identifier. For example, the following assignment is incorrect:

```
CARLOT.MAKE := 'CHEVROLET'; { ERROR }
```

The fields of a record can also be referenced using the **WITH structure.** Program Segment 15.2 shows how to access an entire record and assign values to all fields of HONESTJOHNS.

Program Segment 15.2

```
WITH HONESTJOHNS DO
    BEGIN

        MAKE := 'CHEVROLET';
        COLOR := BROWN;
        YEAR := 1984;
        WRECK := TRUE;
        ODOMETER := 35000;
        ESTVALUE := 2500

    END; { WITH }
```

This is equivalent to making six assignment statements preceded by "HONESTJOHNS.", as shown in the following:

```
HONESTJOHNS.MAKE := 'CHEVROLET';
HONESTJOHNS.COLOR := BROWN;
HONESTJOHNS.YEAR := 1984;
HONESTJOHNS.WRECK := TRUE;
HONESTJOHNS.ODOMETER := 35000;
HONESTJOHNS.ESTVALUE := 2500;
```

If desired, a portion of the record can be referenced as in Program Segment 15.3. Two fields of the record are given values from the user via READLN.

Caution: For some versions of Pascal, READLN cannot be used directly to assign a value to the field COLOR, a programmer-defined type (see Chapter 11).

Program Segment 15.3

```
WITH HONESTJOHNS DO
    BEGIN
        WRITE('ENTER THE MAKE ');
        READLN(MAKE);
        WRITE('ENTER THE YEAR ');
        READLN(YEAR)
    END; { WITH }
```

This is equivalent to

```
WRITE('ENTER THE MAKE ');
READLN(HONESTJOHNS.MAKE);
WRITE('ENTER THE YEAR ');
READLN(HONESTJOHNS.YEAR);
```

The general form for the WITH command follows:

WITH Form

```
WITH variable identifier DO
    statement;
```

The variable identifier is of a record type and the statement can be any of the statements mentioned in earlier chapters, including a compound statement requiring a BEGIN and END.

An entire record can be assigned to another variable of the same type. For example, suppose HONESTJOHNS is purchased by SMOOTHEDDYS. The entire record of HONESTJOHNS can be assigned to SMOOTHEDDYS in one statement.

```
SMOOTHEDDYS := HONESTJOHNS;
```

Each field in the record SMOOTHEDDYS is assigned the value from the corresponding field in the record HONESTJOHNS.

To summarize, a record can be referenced in any of the following ways:

- Using the field selector or "dot" notation.
- Using the WITH structure.
- Assigning an entire record to another variable identifier of that type.

In the earlier examples, only one record was created for each car lot. In order to create more than one record for HONESTJOHNS and SMOOTHEDDYS, the array structure is used. Program Segment 15.4 establishes an array of CARLOT and allows for up to 50 cars for each lot.

Program Segment 15.4

```
TYPE
    COLORS = (BLUE,BROWN,GREEN,ORANGE,RED,YELLOW);
    CARLOT = RECORD

                MAKE      : STRING[20];
                COLOR     : COLORS;
                YEAR      : 1950..2000;
                WRECK     : BOOLEAN;
                ODOMETER  : INTEGER[7];
                ESTVALUE  : REAL

             END; { CARLOT }

    LOTARRAY = ARRAY[1..50] OF CARLOT;

VAR
    HONESTJOHNS,
    SMOOTHEDDYS : LOTARRAY;
    COUNT,
    PAINT        : INTEGER;
    ANSWER       : CHAR;
```

HONESTJOHNS is now an array of records. (See Figure 15.3) The array definition must follow the record definition, since the array is of the record type. Each record of the array is referenced through a subscript, as shown in Program Segment 15.5. In this example, assignments are made to the fields of each record.

Figure 15.3 Array of CARLOT Records

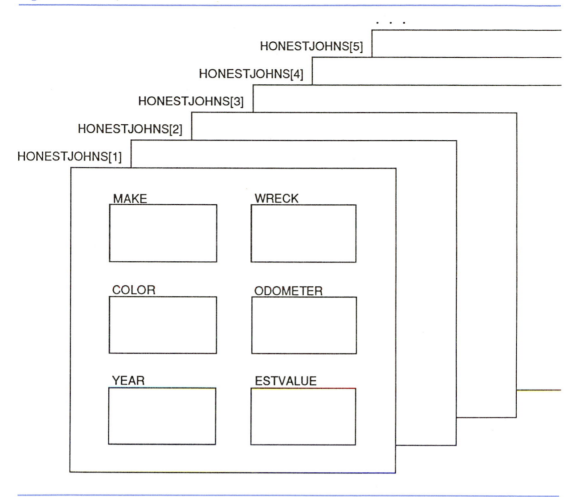

Program
Segment 15.5

```
FOR COUNT := 1 TO 50 DO
   WITH HONESTJOHNS[COUNT] DO
      BEGIN

         WRITE('ENTER THE MAKE: ');
         READLN(MAKE);
         WRITELN('ENTER THE COLOR NUMBER.');
         WRITELN('1=BLUE    3=GREEN   5=RED');
         WRITELN('2=BROWN   4=ORANGE  6=YELLOW');
         READLN(PAINT);
         CASE PAINT OF
            1 : COLOR := BLUE;
            2 : COLOR := BROWN;
            3 : COLOR := GREEN;
            4 : COLOR := ORANGE;
            5 : COLOR := RED;
            6 : COLOR := YELLOW
         END;  { CASE }
```

```
                              WRITE('ENTER THE YEAR: ');
                              READLN(YEAR);
                              WRITE('HAS CAR BEEN IN WRECK? (Y/N) ');
                              READLN(ANSWER);
                              IF ANSWER = 'Y'
                                  THEN WRECK := TRUE
                                  ELSE WRECK := FALSE;
                              WRITE('ENTER ODOMETER READING: ');
                              READLN(ODOMETER);
                              WRITE('ENTER THE ESTIMATED VALUE: ');
                              READLN(ESTVALUE)

                        END; { WITH }
```

The power of an array of records is that different types of related data can be referenced through a single array. Before this, parallel arrays had to be used to store different data types. In the car lot example, the six different fields would have required six parallel arrays.

The cataloging system of a library provides another good example of records. Program Segment 15.6 shows how a record can contain a field of a record type defined earlier—a nested record.

Program Segment 15.6

```
TYPE
    MONTHS = (JANUARY, FEBRUARY, MARCH, APRIL, MAY,
              JUNE, JULY, AUGUST, SEPTEMBER, OCTOBER,
              NOVEMBER, DECEMBER);

    DATE = RECORD

                MONTH : MONTHS;
                DAY   : 1..31;
                YEAR  : 1920..1990

            END; { DATE }

    BOOK = RECORD

                TITLE       : STRING[50];
                AUTHOR      : STRING[20];
                PUBLISHER   : STRING[20];
                CITY        : STRING[20];
                CURRENTDATE : DATE

            END; { BOOK }

VAR
    LIBRARY : BOOK;
```

This library record is shown in Figure 15.4. The library record can be referenced using dot notation,

```
LIBRARY.TITLE := 'PASCAL';
LIBRARY.CURRENTDATE.MONTH := JANUARY;
```

or the WITH structure.

Figure 15.4
Record for Library
Card Catalog

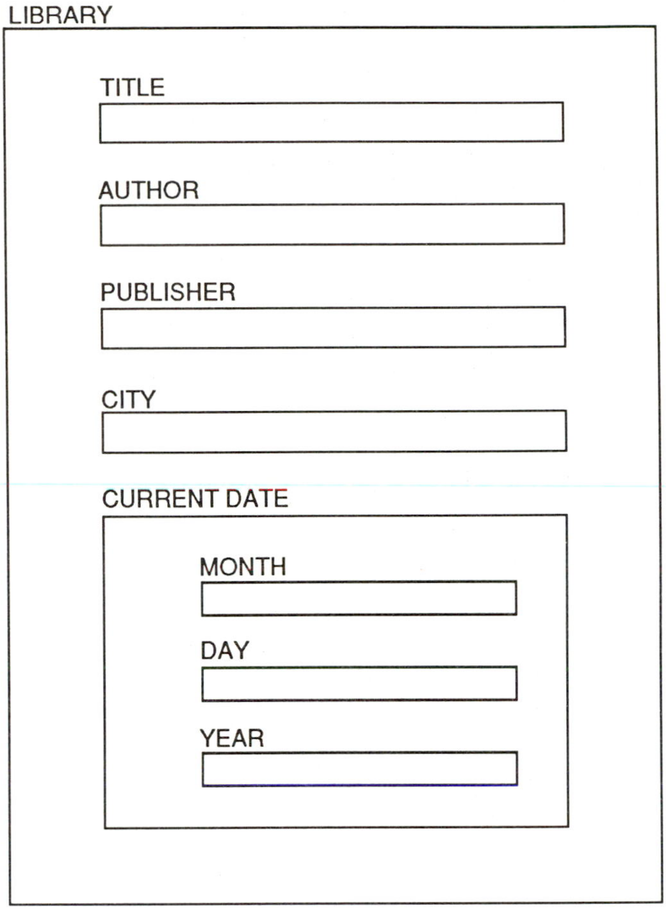

```
WITH LIBRARY DO
    BEGIN

        TITLE := 'PASCAL';
        WITH CURRENTDATE DO
            MONTH := JANUARY

    END; { WITH }
```

An alternative to this method for referencing nested records is

```
WITH LIBRARY, CURRENTDATE DO
    BEGIN

        TITLE := 'PASCAL';
        MONTH := JANUARY

    END; { WITH}
```

In this example, the nesting of the WITH statement is implied. The field identifier CURRENTDATE will be ignored when the assignment is made to LIBRARY.TITLE and used when the assignment to LIBRARY.CURRENTDATE.MONTH is made.

The definition of one record can also occur within another record. The record DATE from Program Segment 15.6 could have been defined within the field CURRENTDATE in record BOOK, as shown in Program Segment 15.7.

Program Segment 15.7

```
TYPE
    MONTHS = (JANUARY, FEBRUARY, MARCH, APRIL, MAY,
             JUNE, JULY, AUGUST, SEPTEMBER, OCTOBER,
             NOVEMBER, DECEMBER);

    BOOK = RECORD

                TITLE      : STRING[50];
                AUTHOR     : STRING[20];
                PUBLISHER  : STRING[20];
                CITY       : STRING[20];
                CURRENTDATE = RECORD
                                MONTH : MONTHS;
                                DAY   : 1..31;
                                YEAR  : 1920..1990
                             END { CURRENTDATE}

         END; { BOOK}
```

The CURRENTDATE field of Program Segment 15.7 can be accessed in the same way as the earlier nested record of Program Segment 15.6.

As in the CARLOT example, arrays can be used to store LIBRARY records. The statement to define the array type would be added after the definition of BOOK.

```
TYPE
    LIBARRAY = ARRAY[1..100] OF BOOK;
```

Then, a variable can be declared to be of type LIBARRAY.

```
VAR
    LIBRARY : LIBARRAY;
```

An array of the library records stored in this manner is shown in Figure 15.5.

A portion of the record can be referenced as shown:

```
LIBRARY[1].TITLE := 'SUNSHINE';
```

Caution: The array subscript must follow directly after the array name. The following statement would be incorrect, since TITLE is a field of array LIBRARY:

```
LIBRARY.TITLE[1] := 'SUNSHINE'; { ERROR }
```

The records for several books can also be accessed through the use of a FOR loop, as demonstrated in Program Segment 15.8.

Figure 15.5 Array of Library Books

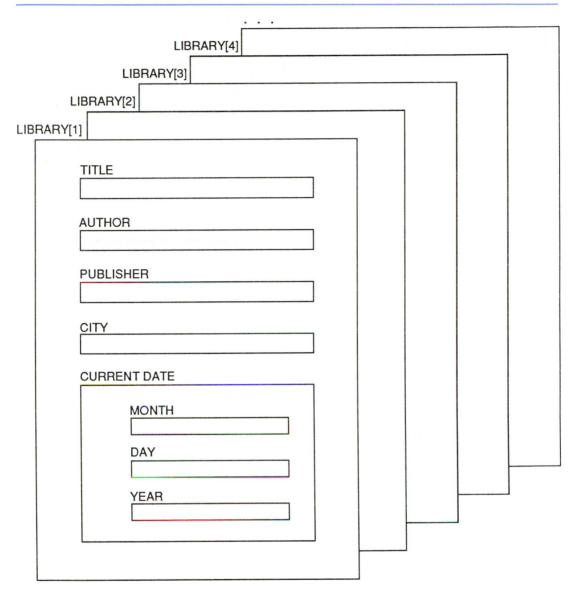

Program Segment 15.8

```
FOR COUNT := 1 TO 50 DO
    WITH LIBRARY[COUNT],CURRENTDATE DO
        BEGIN
            WRITELN('ENTER BOOK TITLE');
            READLN(TITLE);
            WRITELN('ENTER AUTHOR');
            READLN(AUTHOR);
            WRITELN('ENTER PUBLISHER');
            READLN(PUBLISHER);
            WRITELN('ENTER CITY WHERE PUBLISHED');
            READLN(CITY);
            WRITELN('ENTER PUBLICATION MONTH (1-12)');
            READLN(MONNUM);
```

```
                GETMONTH(MONNUM,MONTH);
                    { GET PROGRAMMER-DEFINED TYPE }
                WRITELN('ENTER DAY OF PUBLICATION');
                READLN(DAY);
                WRITELN('ENTER YEAR OF PUBLICATION');
                READLN(YEAR)
            END; { WITH}
```

Lesson Check 15.1

1. Why is an array of records preferred over several parallel arrays?

2. From the following definitions, how would the field COLOR be assigned a value using the dot notation? Using the WITH structure?

```
TYPE
    COLORS = (RED,ORANGE,YELLOW,GREEN,BLUE,PURPLE,
              PINK,WHITE,BLACK);
    JBTYPE = RECORD
                FLAVOR_RATING : 1..10;
                COLOR         : COLORS;
                FLAVOR        : STRING
            END;   { JBTYPE }

VAR
    JELLYBEAN : JBTYPE;
```

3. Identify each of the following assignment statements as valid or invalid. If invalid, explain why. Assume the definitions provided in Program Segment 15.6, and that LIBRARY has been declared of type LIBARRAY as specified in Lesson 15.1.
   a. `LIBRARY[2].TITLE := 'GONE WITH THE WIND';`
   b. `LIBRARY.CITY[3] := 'TAMPA';`
   c. `BOOK[1].AUTHOR := 'EDGAR ALLEN POE';`
   d. `LIBRARY[3].DATE := 5;`
   e. `LIBRARY[9].CURRENTDATE.MONTH := JUNE;`
   f. `LIBRARY[5].AUTHOR := 'U';`

Lesson 15.2   Variant Records

Variant records allow the fields of a record to change (or vary) with differing circumstances. Without the ability to vary the number and type of the fields, a record definition would need to include all possible variable locations, regardless of whether they would need to be used in a given situation. In a large program (or, more particularly, one that uses a large record definition), the memory requirements for all those unused fields would be wasteful. In a variant record, the fields are used only when they are needed, and the unused fields do not reserve any space in memory.

The library example of the previous lesson can be rewritten using variant records. The varying portion could be CURRENTDATE.DAYS—the number of days for each month of the year. Figure 15.6 gives a sketch displaying the variation in the record. The variant record could be defined as in Program Segment 15.9.

Figure 15.6
Book Record with
Variant
CURRENTDATE

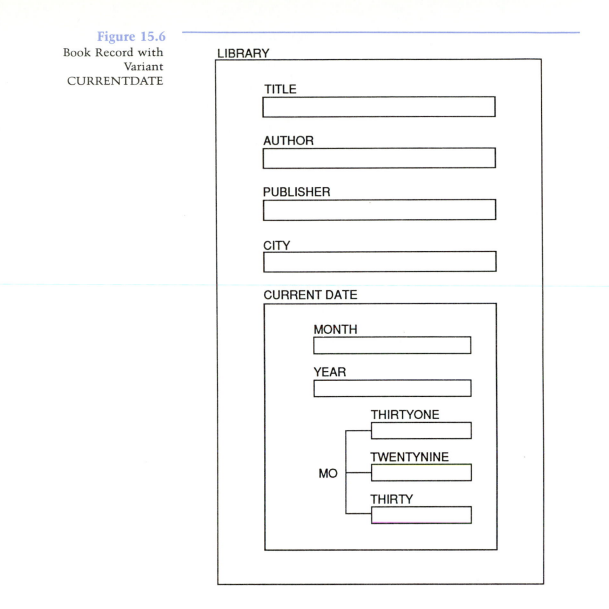

Program
Segment 15.9

```
TYPE
    MONTHS = (JAN, FEB, MAR, APR, MAY, JUN, JUL, AUG,
             SEP, OCT, NOV, DEC);
    BOOK = RECORD

            TITLE     : STRING[50];
            AUTHOR    : STRING[20];
            PUBLISHER : STRING[20];
            CITY      : STRING[20];
```

```
CURRENTDATE = RECORD

    MONTH    : MONTHS;
    YEAR     : 1900..1986;
    CASE MO : MONTHS OF
        JAN, MAR,
        MAY, JUL,
        AUG, OCT,
        DEC       : (THIRTYONE:1..31);
        FEB       : (TWENTYNINE:1..29);
        APR, JUN,
        SEP, NOV : (THIRTY:1..30)

    END { CURRENTDATE AND CASE }

END; { BOOK }

VAR
    LIBRARY : BOOK;
```

These definitions can be used in a program to find the due date of a library book. The program could allow the input of the current date and then determine the due date—taking into consideration the number of days in each month. (Note that February is listed as having 29 days. In that way, February 29 will always be available, even though it will rarely be used.) MO is called the **tag field** and is used to determine which of the variant parts will be used.

The general form for defining a variant record is given in the following:

Variant Record Definition Form

```
TYPE
    record identifier = RECORD

        field identifier : type;
        field identifier : type;
        .
        .
        .
        CASE tagfield : type OF
            constants : (field name : type);
            constants : (field name,
                         field name : type);
            constants : (field name : type;
                         field name : type);
            constants : ()

        END; { RECORD AND CASE }
```

The constants can be one constant or several constants separated by commas. The field name and type for each constant are always enclosed in parentheses. The variant fields can be of any ordinal data type, REAL, or structured data type.

Here are some rules to follow when using variant records.

- A record can contain only one variant portion. (In the example of Program Segment 15.9, the variant portion is MO.) Variant records can, however, be nested, with each level of the nested record possibly containing a variant portion.
- The variant part of a record must follow the invariant (fixed) parts of the record.
- The CASE statement of the variant portion and the record share the same END.
- An empty field in the CASE statement of a variant record is denoted by empty parentheses, as ().

In order to assign a value within a variant record, the particular variant field identifier (constant) must be specified first. For example, to manipulate the field TWENTYNINE of Program Segment 15.9, the month for the variant portion of the record must be accessed (opened).

```
LIBRARY.CURRENTDATE.MO := FEB;
```

Then a value can be assigned to the variable that is defined in that field.

```
LIBRARY.CURRENTDATE.TWENTYNINE := 26;
```

Since the variable TWENTYNINE was defined as a subrange (1..29), an attempt to assign a number greater than 29 to this field would result in an error.

```
LIBRARY.CURRENTDATE.TWENTYNINE := 30; { RANGE ERROR }
```

Caution: Any attempt to assign a value to a variant field before that field has been opened will result in an error message. If a new field of the variant portion is opened, any previously opened field is closed. The following statement opens the field containing JAN:

```
LIBRARY.CURRENTDATE.MO := JAN;
```

For this field, the following assignment can be made:

```
LIBRARY.CURRENTDATE.THIRTYONE := 24;
```

An assignment to LIBRARY.CURRENTDATE.TWENTYNINE cannot be made now because that portion of the variant field is closed when another part is opened.

Program 15.10 uses variant records to vary the possible dimensions needed to compute the area of a circle, square, or rectangle. To find the area of a circle, the radius is needed; for the area of a square, the length of a side must be known; and to find the area of a rectangle, the length and width of the figure are required. (Note that the value for SEESHAPE, a programmer-defined type, cannot be entered directly via READLN in some versions of Pascal and must be assigned in a CASE statement.)

Program 15.10

```
PROGRAM FINDAREA(INPUT, OUTPUT);

CONST
   PI = 3.1416;

TYPE
   SHAPE = (CIRCLE, SQUARE, RECTANGLE);
   SHAPERECORD = RECORD
      CASE SEESHAPE : SHAPE OF
         CIRCLE    : (RADIUS : REAL);
         SQUARE    : (SIDE    : REAL);
         RECTANGLE : (LENGTH,
                         WIDTH : REAL)
      END; { SHAPERECORD/CASE }

VAR
   FIGURE : SHAPERECORD;
   FIG    : CHAR;
   AREA   : REAL;

BEGIN { MAIN PROGRAM }

   WRITELN('ENTER THE NAME OF THE SHAPE.');
   WRITELN('C = CIRCLE, S = SQUARE, R = RECTANGLE');
   READLN(FIG);
   WITH FIGURE DO
      CASE FIG OF

         'C':BEGIN
                SEESHAPE := CIRCLE;
                WRITE('ENTER RADIUS: ');
                READLN(RADIUS);
                AREA := PI * RADIUS * RADIUS;
                WRITELN('FIGURE IS A CIRCLE.');
                WRITELN('AREA IS ', AREA:8:2)
             END; { 'C' }

         'S':BEGIN
                SEESHAPE := SQUARE;
                WRITE('ENTER LENGTH OF A SIDE: ');
                READLN(SIDE);
                AREA := SIDE * SIDE;
                WRITELN('FIGURE IS A SQUARE.');
                WRITELN('AREA IS ', AREA:8:2)
             END; { 'S' }

         'R':BEGIN
                SEESHAPE := RECTANGLE;
                WRITE('ENTER LENGTH AND WIDTH: ');
                READLN(LENGTH, WIDTH);
                AREA := LENGTH * WIDTH;
                WRITELN('FIGURE IS A RECTANGLE.');
                WRITELN('AREA IS ', AREA:8:2)
             END {'R' }

      END { END OF CASE }

END.
```

Lesson
Check
15.2

1. What is the purpose of a variant record?

2. What is a tag field with respect to variant records?

3. Where should the variant portion of a record definition be located?

4. Using the definitions of the library record with variant CURRENTDATE (as shown in Program Segment 15.9), give the two statements necessary to assign a value of 13 to the MAY field.

Lesson 15.3   Programming Tip—Program Design

A Detailed Look: Data Flow Analysis

The logic diagram in Chapter 14 (Figure 14.12) gives a good idea of the programming requirements for the stock market simulation. In fact, the procedures needed are fairly clear after that phase and the tendency might be to start writing procedures at that point. One other step, however, can help make sure the procedures do what they are supposed to do. A data flow analysis will show how parts of the program work together to solve the entire problem. Through a data flow diagram, the interactions among procedures can be checked. Figure 15.7 (see page 418) is the data flow diagram used to analyze the procedures in the stock market simulation. This diagram gives a good idea of the inner workings of the program. There may be a need for a few other small procedures, but these would be a result of expanding one of the main procedures. In addition, the weekly transactions part of this program can be handled in the main program, as will be seen in the next chapter.

Summary

Storing groups of related information can be greatly simplified in Pascal by the use of records. A record is defined in the TYPE portion of the program. Each field in a record can have its own type—either a simple data type or a structured type, including another record. Referencing the fields of a record can be done using the dot notation in which the record name is followed by a period and the specific field desired. The process of referencing several fields of a record can be simplified by using the WITH structure, in which the record variable identifier need be specified only once. The field identifiers are then used like other variables and are associated with the record named. An entire record can be assigned to another record variable of the same type using a single assignment statement. Records can be used with arrays to produce a powerful structure for holding and manipulating information.

Figure 15.7 Data Flow Diagram for Stock Market Simulation

Variant records allow the structure of a record to be altered as conditions change. A CASE statement is used to specify the variant part of the record. The variant portion must be at the end of the record. A record can contain only one variant portion; however, variant records can be nested and each level of the record can contain a variant portion.

Key Terms

dot notation	nested record	variant record
field	record	WITH structure
field selector	tag field	

Answers to **Lesson 15.1**
Lesson Checks

1. An array of records is much more efficient than several parallel arrays for grouping different but related data. This efficiency is due to the fact that a single subscript can be used to access the entire group. For this reason, the readability of a program is vastly improved.

2. ```
JELLYBEAN.COLOR := GREEN;
WITH JELLYBEAN DO
   COLOR := GREEN;
```

3. **a.** Valid.
   **b.** Invalid. The array subscript must follow directly after the array LIBRARY.
   **c.** Invalid. The identifier BOOK is a type identifier and should be replaced with LIBRARY.
   **d.** Invalid. DATE is a type identifier (a record) consisting of the fields MONTH, DAY, and YEAR. DATE should be replaced with one of these fields.
   **e.** Valid.
   **f.** Valid.

**Lesson 15.2**

1. A variant record saves memory by allowing the field variables and their types to vary, depending on the data requirements for a given situation.

2. A tag field is a variable that identifies the field to be used in a variant record.

3. The variant portion of a record definition must follow all the invariant portions.

4. ```
LIBRARY.CURRENTDATE.MO := MAY;
LIBRARY.CURRENTDATE.THIRTYONE := 13;
```

Exercises   **Set I. Comprehension**

Exercises 1–4 use the following definitions and declarations:

```
TYPE
   XTYPE = RECORD
             AFIELD : 'A'..'Z';
             BFIELD : STRING[15];
             CFIELD : REAL;
             DFIELD : INTEGER
           END; { XTYPE }

   YTYPE = RECORD
             AFIELD : 'A'..'Z';
             BFIELD : REAL;
             CFIELD : INTEGER;
             DFIELD : STRING[15]
           END; { YTYPE }
```

```
ZTYPE = RECORD
            MFIELD : 'A'..'Z';
            NFIELD : 0..100
         END; { ZTYPE }

VAR
   QVAR,
   PVAR   : XTYPE;
   JVAR,
   KVAR   : YTYPE;
   SVAR   : INTEGER;
   TVAR   : 'A'..'Z';
   HVAR   : ZTYPE;
```

1. Classify each of the following as valid or invalid statements. For the invalid statements, describe why each is invalid and under what circumstances, if any, the statement could be valid.
   a. QVAR.CFIELD := QVAR.DFIELD;
   b. IF KVAR.DFIELD < 100 THEN KVAR.DFIELD := 100;
   c. JVAR := KVAR;
   d. HVAR.MFIELD := PVAR.AFIELD;
   e. TVAR := JVAR.AFIELD;

2. Classify each of the following as valid or invalid statements. For the invalid statements, describe why each is invalid and under what circumstances, if any, the statement could be valid.
   a. QVAR.AFIELD := PVAR.AFIELD;
   b. IF JVAR.BFIELD >= 10 THEN WRITELN('TRUE');
   c. NFIELD := 45;
   d. QVAR := JVAR;
   e. HVAR := SVAR.NFIELD;

3. Write an assignment statement for each of the following:
   a. Store B and 3 in HVAR.
   b. Transfer the contents of PVAR to QVAR.
   c. Transfer the contents of JVAR to QVAR.
   d. Store SVAR in the proper field of KVAR.
   e. Store the fields of HVAR in the first and last fields of PVAR.

4. Write an assignment statement for each of the following:
   a. Store 5 and 3.2 in QVAR.
   b. Transfer the contents of QVAR to PVAR.
   c. Transfer the contents of PVAR to QVAR.
   d. Store TVAR in the proper field of KVAR.
   e. Store the fields of QVAR in the proper fields of KVAR.

Exercises 5–8 use the following definitions and declarations:

```
TYPE
   LINES = RECORD
               DEGREES : 0..180;
               MINUTES : 0..60;
               SECONDS : 0..60
            END; { LINES }
```

```
LOCATION = RECORD
            LONGITUDE : LINES;
            LONGDIR   : (EAST, WEST);
            LATITUDE  : LINES;
            LATDIR    : (NORTH, SOUTH)
          END; { LOCATION }
VAR
   PLACES : ARRAY[1..100] OF LOCATION;
   COUNT,
   D,
   M,
   S      : INTEGER;
```

5. What does the following program segment do?

```
WITH PLACES[1] DO
   BEGIN
      LONGITUDE.DEGREES := 46;
      LONGITUDE.MINUTES := 10;
      LONGITUDE.SECONDS := 23;
      LONGDIR := WEST
   END; { WITH }
```

6. Identify the errors in the following program segment:

```
FOR COOUNT := 1 TO 10 DO
   WITH PLACES[COUNT] DO
      LONGITUDE.LINES.DEGREES := D;
      LATITUDE := COUNT;
      LOCATION.LATDIR := SOUTH;
      WRITELN(LATITUDE.MINUTES)
   END; { WITH }
```

7. Write an assignment statement to place a value of 35 in the DEGREES field of the last PLACES array location.

8. Write an assignment statement to increment the MINUTES field of location 15 in PLACES by the value of M.

9. Design a record definition and variable declaration for a program concerning the selection of students eligible for scholarships. The student data that might be helpful to a scholarship committee include the following:

   - Student and parent incomes.
   - High-school cumulative grade point average.
   - SAT scores.
   - The prospective college.
   - The college's tuition.
   - Estimated living expenses.

10. Design a record structure for a checking account program. The record should include information used in printing monthly statements of account activity, such as the following:

   - The beginning and ending balances.
   - The number of checks written.
   - The average daily balance.
   - Account overdraft.

Option: Include a variant portion for the type of account and amount of service charge. For example, a premium account might charge a flat monthly fee, while a budget account might charge a small monthly fee plus a charge per check written beyond the monthly allowance of 10 checks.

11. Design a record structure for a medical chart. A patient's chart might consist of the following entries:

    ■ Name, address, and phone number.
    ■ Social Security number.
    ■ Age and sex.
    ■ Name, address, and phone number of employer.
    ■ Name, address, and phone number of relative.
    ■ Name, address, and phone number of insurance company.
    ■ Insurance ID number.
    ■ Allergies (up to five).
    ■ Current medications (up to five).
    ■ Date of last visit.

12. Design a record structure for an automobile insurance company. A client's record might consist of the following entries:

    ■ Name, address, and phone number.
    ■ Social Security number.
    ■ Age and sex.
    ■ Employer name, address, and phone number.
    ■ Type of insurance.
    ■ Driving history.

Set II. Application

13. Given the definitions and declarations for Exercises 5–8, write a procedure to print the elements of PLACES.

14. Given the definitions and declarations for Exercises 5–8, write a BOOLEAN function to search PLACES for a longitude and latitude. Assume that the function argument, TARGET, has been declared to be of type LOCATION.

Exercises 15–18 refer to the CARLOT example from Lesson 15.1.

15. Write a procedure to sort the cars in HONESTJOHNS car lot by their years, oldest to newest.

16. Write a procedure to search HONESTJOHNS inventory of 50 cars for a 1957 red Chevrolet. If the car is available, report the odometer reading, the estimated value, and whether or not it is known to have been in a wreck. Be sure to consider that there may be more than one car matching the description in the inventory. Assume that the cars are listed in order by year, oldest to newest.

17. Write a procedure or procedures to insert or delete a car from HONESTJOHNS inventory. Assume the list of cars is already in order, oldest first. Maintain this order throughout the insertion and deletion process.

18. Notice that the field COLOR of HONESTJOHNS inventory record is a programmer-defined type. Write a procedure to sort the list of cars by their colors in the order given in the type definition.

Exercises 19–22 refer to the coin record example given in the Gaining a Perspective section at the beginning of the chapter.

19. Write a procedure to sort all the coins of a particular denomination by year.

20. Write a procedure to search an array of coin records for a coin with a certain denomination, year, and mint mark. Assume the coins have been sorted by denomination and each denomination group has been sorted by year. If the coin is found, print the condition, purchase price, and current value.

21. Write a procedure to insert or delete a coin in the ordered array.

22. Write a procedure to edit a particular coin record. The procedure should allow the user to view the record and make desired changes.

Set III. Synthesis

23. Write a program to produce an index for diskettes. Use a record structure to hold the name of each program, the category (for example, Games), the amount of memory taken by each program, and the diskette identification number. Allow the user to enter the information for up to 10 diskettes. Print an alphabetized list of program names for each diskette and an alphabetized list of all diskettes. (Include the disk ID number in the printed lists.)

24. Write a program to monitor an airport flight schedule. Design a record structure for the information about each flight; that is, the flight number, its date and time of departure, the number of available seats, the destination, and the date and estimated time of arrival. Allow for up to 10 flights. Enter the necessary flight information and allow the user to obtain ordered printouts (by flight number, time, or destination) and to alter the data as needed.

25. Write a program to schedule a family's daily television viewing. Allow each family member to enter up to five program titles, their starting times, and the length of the features. Provide options for printouts of each family member's list (in order of starting time) and a master list of all TV programs desired. Indicate if there are any time conflicts for two or more programs and allow the user to change entries, if desired.

26. Write a program to process job applications. Allow the user to enter pertinent information about each applicant and to obtain various printouts (alphabetic, by age, and in order of entry). A job application might consist of the following data:

   ■ Date of application.
   ■ Name, address, and phone number.
   ■ Social Security number.
   ■ Age and sex.

- Name, address, and phone number of previous employer.
- Number of years with previous employer.
- Position and salary with previous employer.
- Job title being applied for.

27. Design a record definition for a 52-card poker deck. Write procedures to:
    a. establish a poker deck array.
    b. shuffle the deck.
    c. deal a hand (five cards).
    d. evaluate a hand.

    To evaluate a hand, determine whether it is a flush (all one suit), a straight (five consecutive cards in a row of different suits), a straight flush (five consecutive cards of one suit), four of a kind (same card value), a full house (three of one value and two of another), three of a kind, two pair, or a pair. An ace can be used in a straight at either end of the card values. (For example, A 2 3 4 5 and A K Q J 10 are valid straights, however, 3 2 A K Q is invalid since a straight cannot wrap around.)

    Option: Write the shuffle routine to simulate an actual shuffle. That is, split the deck randomly (roughly in half). Then form a new deck by randomly putting cards from the bottom of the half-decks back into the original array.

28. Complex numbers are numbers of the form

    $$A + Bi$$

    where A is the real part and B is the imaginary part of the number ($i = \sqrt{-1}$). Write a program that will add, subtract, multiply, or divide complex numbers. The program should include a record definition for the complex numbers, with fields for the real and imaginary parts.

16 Files

At this moment the King, who had been for some time busily writing in his note-book, called out "Silence!" and read out from his book "Rule Forty-two. All persons more than a mile high to leave the court." Everybody looked at Alice.

"I'm not a mile high," said Alice. . . . "besides, that's not a regular rule: you invented it just now."

"It's the oldest rule in the book," said the King.

"Then it ought to be Number One," said Alice.

—Lewis Carroll

Overview

Introduction to Files
    Internal and External
    Opening and Closing
    Writing a Text File
    EOF and EOLN
PUT and GET
    File of Records
Random Access of Files
Programming Tip
    Program Design
        Main Program

Gaining a Perspective

Many different methods for storing information in the computer have been introduced to this point, from simple data types (such as INTEGER and CHAR) to data structures (such as arrays and records). A variety of ways to keep values in the computer for later use within a program is available. The problem with all of these methods, however, is that they are **volatile.** That is, the values represented by these variables are lost when the program ends or the power is turned off. Often, the data produced in a program may be needed at a later date, either for use by the same program or for access by other programs. Thus, there is a need for some form of permanent storage to allow data to be saved for later use. **Files** provide just such an option for the programmer. Files allow data of any type (simple data types or structured types) to be stored on diskette (or other storage device) for retrieval at the convenience of the programmer. Without files, many applications of computers would be nearly useless.

Lesson 16.1   Introduction to Files

A file is a sequence of numbers, characters, arrays, or records of the same type. Files allow permanent storage of information on a secondary storage device, such as a disk. The file size is not specified in the program, so the size of the file can grow or shrink as the program is executed; thus, files are often said to be **dynamic.** Figure 16.1 is a sketch of a file whose elements are integers. (EOF marks the end of the file.)

Figure 16.1
INTEGER File

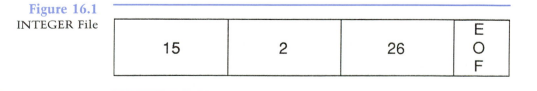

| 15 | 2 | 26 | E O F |

Figure 16.2
File Window

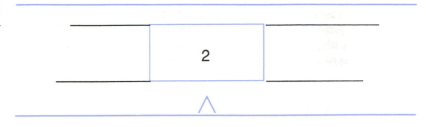

One element of a file can be referenced at a time. The terms **file window** and **file pointer** are used to describe the action of file commands. The file window in Figure 16.2 gives a view of the element that is currently in use or being pointed to.

Writing a Text File

In Pascal, INPUT and OUTPUT are predefined text files. INPUT generally refers to entering data at the keyboard and OUTPUT to the printout on the monitor or the printer.

The subject of this lesson is **text files.** TEXT is a predefined external file. Program 16.1 uses file commands for writing to a text file.

Program 16.1

```
PROGRAM WRITESAMPLE(MESSAGES);

      { PURPOSE: DEMONSTRATE WRITING TO A FILE }

VAR
    SAMPLE : TEXT;


BEGIN   { MAIN PROGRAM }

    REWRITE(SAMPLE,'MYDISK:MESSAGES');
    WRITELN(SAMPLE,'I CAN WRITE MESSAGES TO A FILE.');
    WRITELN(SAMPLE,'I CAN MAKE A BLANK LINE TOO.');
    WRITELN(SAMPLE);
    WRITELN(SAMPLE,'1 + 1 = ',1+1);
    CLOSE(SAMPLE, LOCK)

END.
```

Program 16.1 writes to a text file as shown in Figure 16.3.

Figure 16.3

Contents of Text File
SAMPLE

| I | | C | A | N | | W | R | I | T | E | | . . . | | 1 | | + | | 1 | | = | | 2 | E O F |

As with other external environments, the intent to use a text file should be specified in the program heading. (This is not required in all Pascal versions, but is a good practice.) The file variable should then be declared in a form as follows:

```
PROGRAM program name (file name);

VAR
    file variable : TEXT;
```

For example, a program with a heading of

```
PROGRAM TEST(INPUT, OUTPUT, GRADES);
```

says to expect input from the keyboard, output to a monitor, and the use of a file, GRADES.

A type definition for TEXT can be included, as in

```
TYPE
    TEXT = FILE OF CHAR;    { OPTIONAL }
```

but is not required since TEXT is a predefined file type.

Program 16.1 includes a **REWRITE** statement, which opens a text file to the write mode (enabling the file to be written to). REWRITE is a predefined Pascal procedure that positions the file pointer at the beginning of an empty file and creates an EOF (end-of-file) mark.

```
REWRITE Form

REWRITE(file variable, 'source:file name');
```

The file variable is the identifier declared for the file. The source represents the device where the text will be stored, such as a diskette. The file name is the name under which the file will be stored on that device. The file pointer points to EOF (the end of the file, previously mentioned in Chapter 6) and the file window is empty. EOF marks the beginning of a new file (or the end of an existing file), as shown in Figure 16.4.

Figure 16.4
End-of-File Marker

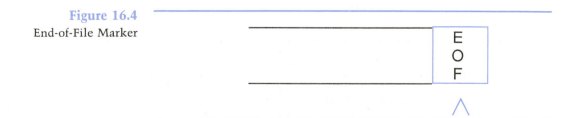

Caution: REWRITE creates a new empty file with the specified file variable, regardless of whether the file has already been created and contains data. Thus, any file previously written using this file variable is destroyed.

A WRITE or WRITELN statement is used to store data on the file. As introduced in Chapter 2, WRITE and WRITELN are predefined Pascal procedures that write information on the screen or to a printer. When a file variable is specified, the information is written to the file and the file pointer is moved ahead one element. (In a new file, the pointer begins at the EOF marker.) In general, the form is

```
WRITE(file variable, values);

or

WRITELN(file variable, values);
```

The file variable is the identifier declared for that file and the values can be characters, strings, numbers (CHAR, STRING, INTEGER, long INTEGER, or REAL), or an expression. (The values can also include field widths.) When WRITELN is used, an end-of-line mark, EOLN, is written after the values in the file.

When finished writing to a file, it should be closed and (usually) locked, as follows:

```
CLOSE Form

CLOSE(file variable, LOCK);
```

CLOSE not only closes the file, but also makes the file pointer undefined. This means that, should the file need to be rewritten later in the program, a new REWRITE statement would be necessary. **LOCK** actually writes the file on the storage device (diskette).

Caution: If a closed file is not locked, then the file is not written to the disk. Unless the file is a temporary program file, it should be locked after each access (writing or reading) to insure that the information is permanently saved.

Reading a Text File

As with input from the keyboard, READ and READLN are also used to obtain information from a text file. Program 16.2 presents an example of reading from a file.

Program 16.2
```
PROGRAM READSAMPLE(OUTPUT, MESSAGES);

    { PURPOSE: DEMONSTRATE INPUT FROM FILE }

VAR
    SAMPLE : TEXT;
    WORDS  : STRING;

BEGIN { MAIN PROGRAM }

    RESET(SAMPLE, 'MYDISK:MESSAGES');
    WHILE NOT EOF(SAMPLE) DO
        BEGIN
            READLN(SAMPLE, WORDS);
            WRITELN(WORDS)
        END; { WHILE }
    CLOSE(SAMPLE, LOCK)

END.
```

To read a text file, the built-in procedure **RESET** is used first to open the file. RESET opens an existing file, enabling the file to be read from (or written to), and positions the file pointer at the beginning of the file. The form of the RESET statement is similar to REWRITE.

> **RESET Form**
>
> ```
> RESET(file variable, 'source:file name');
> ```

Information is read from the file by using the built-in procedure READ or READLN. READ and READLN obtain the next piece of information from the file and advance the file pointer to the next element. In general, the form is

> ```
> READ(file variable, variables);
> ```
> or
> ```
> READLN(file variable, variables);
> ```

Unlike READ, after the last variable listed in a READLN statement is assigned a value, any information remaining in the file line is skipped. READLN is often used for STRING variables to avoid reading blanks at the end of a line.

Using EOF and EOLN

The BOOLEAN function EOF determines whether the current file pointer has reached the last element. When the end-of-file is reached, EOF is TRUE; otherwise, it is FALSE. If EOF is TRUE, the file pointer points to the last element in the file and any operations (such as READ) will be performed on that element.

The BOOLEAN function EOLN (Chapter 6) returns a value of TRUE if the pointer for the text file is at the end of a line. EOLN is always FALSE when the file is first opened and TRUE when it is closed.

The general forms for these BOOLEAN functions follow. (Note that these are not complete statements and must be used as expressions.)

```
EOF(file variable)

EOLN(file variable)
```

Program 16.3 uses both EOF and EOLN to copy the contents of FILEONE to FILETWO. Assume that FILEONE has already been created.

Program 16.3

```
PROGRAM COPYFILE(ONE, TWO);

    { PURPOSE: DEMONSTRATE EOF AND EOLN }

VAR
    FILEONE,
    FILETWO   : TEXT;
    CHARACTER : CHAR;


BEGIN  { MAIN PROGRAM }

    RESET(FILEONE, 'MYDISK:ONE');
    REWRITE(FILETWO, 'MYDISK:TWO');
    WHILE NOT EOF(FILEONE) DO
       BEGIN
          WHILE NOT EOLN(FILEONE) DO
             BEGIN
                READ(FILEONE, CHARACTER);
                WRITE(FILETWO, CHARACTER)
             END; { WHILE NOT EOLN }
          READLN(FILEONE);
          WRITELN(FILETWO)
       END; { WHILE NOT EOF }
    CLOSE(FILETWO, LOCK);
    CLOSE(FILEONE, LOCK)

END.
```

Since FILEONE already exists, it is opened with RESET; FILETWO is created using REWRITE. The first WHILE loop (NOT EOF(FILEONE)) will be executed as long as the file pointer is not at the end of the file. This will insure that all of FILEONE is read. The second WHILE loop (NOT EOLN(FILEONE)) is used to control each line being read. In this inner loop, one character is read from FILEONE and written to FILETWO until the end of the current line in FILEONE is reached. A READLN is then used to move the file pointer in FILEONE to the next line. Similarly, a WRITELN moves the file pointer in FILETWO to the next line for writing. When the transfer is complete, both files are closed and locked. The storage device (diskette) now contains two copies (under different names) of identical files.

Program 16.4 illustrates the use of a file to store INTEGER, REAL, and STRING values, and recall them for use. Remember, a text file can be used for storing any of these simple data types.

Program 16.4

```
PROGRAM SHOWFILES(INPUT, OUTPUT, SAMPLEFILE);

    { PURPOSE: STORE AND RECALL SIMPLE DATA TYPES }

VAR
    SAMPLE : TEXT;

PROCEDURE WRITEFILE;

    { CREATE A FILE }

    VAR
        INT1,
        INT2  : INTEGER;
        REAL1,
        REAL2 : REAL;
        WORD1,
        WORD2 : STRING;

    BEGIN

        REWRITE(SAMPLE, 'MYDISK:SAMPLEFILE');
        WRITE('ENTER TWO INTEGERS: ');
        READLN(INT1, INT2);
        WRITELN(SAMPLE, INT1);
        WRITELN(SAMPLE, INT2);
        WRITE('ENTER TWO REAL NUMBERS: ');
        READLN(REAL1, REAL2);
        WRITELN(SAMPLE, REAL1);
        WRITELN(SAMPLE, REAL2);
        WRITE('ENTER A STRING: ');
        READLN(WORD1);
        WRITE('ENTER A SECOND STRING: ');
        READLN(WORD2);
        WRITELN(SAMPLE, WORD1);
        WRITELN(SAMPLE, WORD2);
        CLOSE(SAMPLE, LOCK)

    END; { WRITEFILE }

PROCEDURE READFILE;

    { READ DATA FROM A FILE }

    VAR
        INT1,
        INT2  : INTEGER;
        REAL1,
        REAL2 : REAL;
        WORD1,
        WORD2 : STRING;
```

```
                    BEGIN

                        RESET(SAMPLE, 'MYDISK:SAMPLEFILE');
                        READLN(SAMPLE, INT1, INT2);
                        READLN(SAMPLE, REAL1, REAL2);
                        READLN(SAMPLE, WORD1);
                        READLN(SAMPLE, WORD2);
                        WRITELN('INTEGERS: ',INT1,' AND ',INT2);
                        WRITELN('REAL NUMBERS: ',REAL1,' AND ',REAL2);
                        WRITELN('WORDS: ',WORD1,' AND ',WORD2);
                        CLOSE(SAMPLE, LOCK)

                    END; { READFILE }

                BEGIN { MAIN PROGRAM }

                    WRITEFILE;
                    READFILE

                END.
```

To summarize, the following steps should be taken when using text files:

- The file variable must be declared to represent the file in the program.
- The file must be opened to be written to or read from.
- The file must be closed to prevent accidental writing to the file.
- The file must be locked in order to save it on the disk.
- The file name(s) should be indicated in parentheses in the program heading.

Lesson Check 16.1

1. How do files differ from data structures such as arrays and records?
2. What is the purpose of REWRITE? What is the purpose of RESET?
3. Why should a file be closed when it is not being written to or read from?
4. How is the BOOLEAN function EOF used in manipulating files? In what ways does it differ from EOLN?

Lesson 16.2   PUT and GET

In addition to WRITE(LN) and READ(LN) for writing to and reading from a file, the built-in procedures **PUT** and **GET** can be used. PUT and GET allow greater flexibility and are used for more complex applications of files, such as storing an entire record.

In order to write to a file using PUT, the file variable must be included in the program heading and the file type must be defined. (The type can be any of the previously mentioned types, except a file or a structured type that contains a file.) Then a file variable is declared.

```
File Definition and Declaration

PROGRAM program name (file name);

TYPE
    type identifier = FILE OF type;

VAR
    file variable : type identifier;
```

Program 16.5 gives an example of using PUT for writing to a file.

Program 16.5

```
PROGRAM WRITEFILE(INPUT, OUTPUT, REAL.DATA);

    { PURPOSE: DEMONSTRATE PUT }

TYPE
    REALFILE = FILE OF REAL;

VAR
    NUMBERS : REALFILE;


BEGIN { MAIN PROGRAM }

    WRITELN('ENTER REAL NUMBERS TO STORE ON A FILE.');
    WRITELN('ENTER 999 WHEN FINISHED.');
    WRITE('>');
    REWRITE(NUMBERS, 'MYDISK:REAL.DATA');
    READLN(NUMBERS^);
    WHILE NUMBERS^ <> 999 DO
        BEGIN
            PUT(NUMBERS);
            WRITE('>');
            READLN(NUMBERS^)
        END; { WHILE }
    CLOSE(NUMBERS, LOCK)

END.
```

Writing a file with PUT requires the REWRITE procedure. The REWRITE statement is typically followed by an assignment or READLN statement. Then, PUT writes the element on the file.

```
PUT Form

REWRITE(file variable,'source:file name');

file variable^ := value;
{ or READLN(file variable^); }
PUT(file variable);
```

After these statements, the value is written to the file. PUT places the value in the location specified by the file pointer and then advances the file pointer to the next position. The file variable∧ represents the current element or component pointed to by the file pointer. (The **caret symbol** (∧) is used to represent the file pointer.) Additional values can be written to the file by using this same sequence of statements, first the assignment and then the PUT. (**Caution:** Do not repeat the REWRITE statement.)

The method for reading a file (assuming the file exists) follows these same steps, except that RESET and GET are used in place of REWRITE and PUT. Program 16.6 gives an example of using GET to read the file created by Program 16.5.

Program 16.6

```
PROGRAM READFILE(OUTPUT, REAL.DATA);

      { PURPOSE: DEMONSTRATE GET }

TYPE
    REALFILE = FILE OF REAL;

VAR
    NUMBERS : REALFILE;

BEGIN { MAIN PROGRAM }

    RESET(NUMBERS, 'MYDISK:REAL.DATA');
    WHILE NOT EOF(NUMBERS) DO
        BEGIN
            WRITELN(NUMBERS^:10:4);
            GET(NUMBERS)
        END; { WHILE }
    CLOSE(NUMBERS, LOCK)

END.
```

RESET prepares the file to be read and positions the pointer at the beginning of the file; the file pointer is then pointing to the first element. The WRITELN statement prints the number that is in the file window (the value pointed to by the file pointer), whereas an assignment statement would place the contents of the file window in the location of the designated variable. The GET statement reads an element of the file and advances the file pointer to the next element. The general form for using GET to read from a file follows:

GET Form

```
RESET(file variable,'source:file name');

variable := file variable^;
{ or WRITELN(file variable^); }
GET(file variable);
```

Program 16.7 brings it all together by storing and recalling the grades for students in a class. Figure 16.5 gives a picture of the file of records.

Program 16.7

```
PROGRAM GRADES(INPUT,OUTPUT,GRADE.DATA);

    { PURPOSE: FILE OF STUDENT RECORDS }

TYPE
    STUDENTRECORD = RECORD
                        NAME  : STRING[30];
                        GRADE : ARRAY[1..4] OF INTEGER
                    END; { STUDENTRECORD }

    FILETYPE = FILE OF STUDENTRECORD;

    ARRYTYPE = ARRAY[1..50] OF STUDENTRECORD;

VAR
    TEMPFILE : FILETYPE;
    STUDENTS : ARRYTYPE;
    COUNT    : INTEGER;


PROCEDURE GETGRADES(VAR CNT : INTEGER;
                    VAR TEMPARRY : ARRYTYPE);

    { FOUR GRADES ARE ENTERED FOR EACH STUDENT }

    VAR
        SCOUNT,
        GCOUNT : INTEGER;

    BEGIN

        WRITE('HOW MANY STUDENTS?');
        READLN(CNT);
        FOR SCOUNT := 1 TO CNT DO
            WITH TEMPARRY[SCOUNT] DO
                BEGIN
                    WRITE('NAME: ');
                    READLN(NAME);
                    FOR GCOUNT := 1 TO 4 DO
                        BEGIN
                            WRITE('GRADE',GCOUNT,': ');
                            READLN(GRADE[GCOUNT])
                        END { FOR }
                END { WITH }

    END; { GETGRADES }

PROCEDURE WRITEGRADES(CNT : INTEGER;
                      TEMPARRY : ARRYTYPE);

    VAR
        SCOUNT : INTEGER;
```

```
            BEGIN

                REWRITE(TEMPFILE,'MYDISK:GRADE.DATA');
                FOR SCOUNT := 1 TO CNT DO
                    BEGIN
                        TEMPFILE^ := TEMPARRY[SCOUNT];
                        PUT(TEMPFILE)
                    END; { FOR }
                CLOSE(TEMPFILE,LOCK)

            END; { WRITEGRADES }

        PROCEDURE READGRADES(VAR CNT : INTEGER;
                             VAR TEMPARRY : ARRYTYPE);

            BEGIN

                RESET(TEMPFILE,'MYDISK:GRADE.DATA');
                CNT := 0;
                WHILE NOT EOF(TEMPFILE) DO
                    BEGIN
                        CNT := CNT + 1;
                        TEMPARRY[CNT] := TEMPFILE^;
                        GET(TEMPFILE)
                    END; { WHILE }
                CLOSE(TEMPFILE,LOCK)

            END; { READGRADES }

        PROCEDURE PRINTGRADES(CNT : INTEGER;
                              TEMPARRY : ARRYTYPE);

            VAR
                SCOUNT : INTEGER;

            BEGIN

                WRITELN('CLASS INFORMATION');
                FOR SCOUNT := 1 TO CNT DO
                    WITH TEMPARRY[SCOUNT] DO
                        BEGIN
                            WRITE('NAME: ');
                            WRITELN(NAME);
                            WRITE('GRADES: ');
                            WRITE(GRADE[1]:6,GRADE[2]:6);
                            WRITELN(GRADE[3]:6,GRADE[4]:6)
                        END { WITH }

            END; { PRINTGRADES }

        BEGIN { GRADES }

            GETGRADES(COUNT,STUDENTS);
            WRITEGRADES(COUNT,STUDENTS);
            READGRADES(COUNT,STUDENTS);
            PRINTGRADES(COUNT,STUDENTS)

        END.
```

Figure 16.5
File of Student Grade
Records

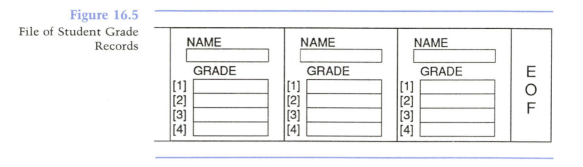

1. What symbol is used with a file variable to designate the value in the file window?

2. What is the purpose of the PUT command? What is the purpose of the GET command?

Lesson 16.3   Random Access of Files

Very often in accessing files, only one element from the file is desired. Reading the entire file into an array just to see one entry is inefficient. Most versions of Pascal provide a procedure that allows **random access,** or access of any entry in a file. **SEEK** allows the program to move the file pointer to any element in the file. (**Caution:** The SEEK command cannot be used with text files.)

SEEK Form

SEEK(*file variable, element number*);

This command changes the file pointer so that the next PUT or GET uses the element specified by the element number. (The elements in files are numbered starting from zero (0).)

Caution: The file window still contains the element that was pointed to by the file pointer prior to the SEEK command. A PUT or GET should be used immediately after the SEEK command in order to bring the new element into the file window and use it.

Program Segment 16.8 shows a procedure that could be used in the GRADES program (Program 16.7) to look at a specific record.

Program
Segment 16.8

```
PROCEDURE GETAGRADE;

    { PURPOSE: DEMONSTRATE RANDOM ACCESS WITH SEEK }

    VAR
        CNT,
        NUM : INTEGER;
```

```
BEGIN

    RESET(TEMPFILE,'MYDISK:GRADE.DATA');
    WRITE('WHICH STUDENT? ');
    READLN(NUM);
    SEEK(TEMPFILE,NUM - 1);
    GET(TEMPFILE);
    WRITELN(TEMPFILE^.NAME);
    FOR CNT := 1 TO 4 DO
        WRITELN(TEMPFILE^.GRADE[CNT]);
    CLOSE(TEMPFILE,LOCK)

END;  { GETAGRADE }
```

The SEEK command moves the file pointer so that it points to the desired record. (NUM − 1 was used to account for the elements being numbered 0,1,2,3, . . . ; the students are assumed to be numbered 1,2,3,4, . . .) The GET command then pulls that record into the file window, allowing the name and grades for that student to be accessed.

In addition, the SEEK command can be used with PUT and GET to replace a record that has been edited. SEEK can be used to locate the desired record and GET can make that record available for editing. After corrections are made, the SEEK command can again be used to position the file pointer and PUT can replace the record. The implementation of a correction procedure for the GRADES program is left as an exercise.

Lesson Check 16.3

1. What is the purpose of the SEEK command? What are the limitations of this method of file access?

2. What is wrong with the following program segment? Assume the definitions of the GRADES program (Program 16.7) and that N is of type INTEGER.

```
N := 5;

{ FIND AND CHECK ELEMENT N OF TEMPFILE }

SEEK(TEMPFILE,N);
IF TEMPFILE^.NAME = 'MARY'
    THEN WRITELN('MARY FOUND AT LOCATION ',N);
```

Lesson 16.4   Programming Tip—Program Design

A Detailed Look: Main Program

The parts of the stock market simulation have been fairly well defined, although the specifics are not written. Now might be a good time to look at a main program that will be used to tie the elements of this program together. A good place to start is the logic diagram from Chapter 14 (Figure 14.12), and the data flow diagram from Chapter 15 (Figure 15.7). From these diagrams, the things that need to be done, as well as a rough idea of the order, can be determined. The tasks that must be accomplished fall into the following categories:

> Setup/Initialization
> > Stock Information
> > One Year's Statistics
> > Player Information
> Transactions
> > Weekly Price Changes
> > Buying Stocks
> > Selling Stocks
> Output of Information
> > Single Company Statistics
> > Overall Statistics for Players and Stocks

The variable declaration and main program for the stock market simulation are shown in Program Segment 16.9.

Program Segment 16.9

```
PROGRAM STOCKMARKET(INPUT,OUTPUT);

USES APPLESTUFF;

CONST
    NUMSTOCK = 5; {CHANGE FOR MORE COMPANIES}

TYPE
    CMPNY = RECORD
                NAME         : STRING[20];
                PRICE        : ARRAY[1..50] OF REAL;
                YIELD        : REAL;
                DESCRIPTION  : STRING;
                NEXTDIV      : 1..4;
                DIVDUE       : ARRAY[1..4] OF INTEGER;
                LASTDIV      : REAL;
                SEASON       : ARRAY[1..10] OF BOOLEAN;
                HIGH         : 1..50;
                LOW          : 1..50;
                SPLITWK      : INTEGER
            END;

    COMPANY = ARRAY[1..NUMSTOCK] OF CMPNY;

    PERSON = RECORD
                NAME   : STRING;
                CASH   : REAL;
                STOCKS : ARRAY[1..NUMSTOCK] OF INTEGER
            END; {PERSON RECORD}

    PEOPLE = ARRAY[1..6] OF PERSON;

VAR
    COMPS      : COMPANY;
    PLAYERS    : PEOPLE;
    WEEK,
    PNUM,
    PTURN      : INTEGER;
    STILLPLAY  : BOOLEAN;
    INKEY      : CHAR;
```

```
BEGIN {MAIN PROGRAM}

    RANDOMIZE;
    PAGE(OUTPUT);
    WRITELN('STOCK MARKET SIMULATION');
    WRITELN('HOW MANY ARE PLAYING, 6 MAX.');
    READLN(PNUM);
    WRITELN('WAIT ... SETTING UP');
    SETUPCOMPS(COMPS);
    INITPPL(PLAYERS);
    STILLPLAY := TRUE;
    WEEK := 1;
    WHILE STILLPLAY DO
        BEGIN
        WKCHANGE(COMPS,PLAYERS,WEEK,COMPS,PLAYERS);
        FOR PTURN := 1 TO PNUM DO
            BEGIN
            WHILE INKEY <> 'E' DO
                BEGIN
                MENU(COMPS,PLAYERS[PTURN],
                        WEEK,INKEY);
                IF INKEY = 'X'
                    THEN STILLPLAY := FALSE;
                IF INKEY = 'B'
                    THEN BUY(COMPS,PLAYERS[PTURN],
                            WEEK,PLAYERS[PTURN]);
                IF INKEY = 'S'
                    THEN SELL(COMPS,PLAYERS[PTURN],
                            WEEK,PLAYERS[PTURN]);
                IF INKEY = 'C'
                    THEN SCOREBOARD(COMPS,PLAYERS,
                                    WEEK);
                IF INKEY = 'L'
                    THEN COMPINFO(COMPS,WEEK)
                END; {IF TURN OVER, GO TO NEXT TURN}
            INKEY := 'Z'
            END;
        WEEK := WEEK + 1;
        IF WEEK > 50
            THEN WEEK := 1;
        IF NOT STILLPLAY
            THEN
                BEGIN
                WRITELN('DO YOU WANT TO QUIT?');
                READ(INKEY);
                IF INKEY <> 'Y'
                    THEN STILLPLAY := TRUE
                END; {CHECK FOR QUITTING}
        INKEY := 'C'
        END; {GO BACK IF NOT QUITTING}
    SCOREBOARD(COMPS,PLAYERS,WEEK)

END.
```

Summary

Files are used for external storage of data. In Pascal, only one
element of a file is accessed at any given time through a file

window. A file pointer indicates which element is currently accessible through the file window. TEXT (a file of CHAR) is a predefined external file used for storing characters or numbers. REWRITE is used to open a new file. RESET opens an existing file. WRITELN (or WRITE) and READLN (or READ) can be used to access text files by specifying the file name inside the parentheses following the command. The BOOLEAN functions EOF and EOLN are used to check for the end of a file and the end of a line in the file, respectively. A file must be closed and locked to make the file permanent.

For more complex file structures, the PUT and GET commands replace WRITELN and READLN for writing to or reading from a file. Using these commands, a file of records can be created. Since the elements of a file are numbered (starting from zero), random access of nontext files is possible using the SEEK procedure. SEEK should be followed by a PUT or GET to access the desired record.

Key Terms

caret symbol	file window	RESET
CLOSE	GET	REWRITE
dynamic	LOCK	SEEK
file	PUT	text file
file pointer	random access	volatile

Answers to Lesson Checks

Lesson 16.1

1. Files are nonvolatile and therefore allow permanent storage of data. In addition, they are dynamic and can grow or shrink as the program requires.

2. REWRITE creates a new file on which to be written. RESET opens an existing file to be read.

3. If the file is not closed, it could be written to or destroyed unintentionally.

4. EOF is used to determine when the end of a file has been reached. EOLN specifies the end of a line of input. There can be several EOLN marks in a single file, but only one EOF.

Lesson 16.2

1. The caret symbol (∧) is used to designate the value in a file window.

2. PUT writes the value in the file window on the file and advances the file pointer. GET reads the value currently in the file window and advances the file pointer.

Lesson 16.3

1. The SEEK command allows random access of a specific element in a file. SEEK cannot be used with text files.

2. The program segment does not include a GET statement immediately following the SEEK command; therefore, the contents

of the file window is the element that was accessed prior to the SEEK command. The program segment will run but will not produce the intended result. The corrected version follows:

```
N := 5;

{ FIND AND CHECK ELEMENT N OF TEMPFILE }

SEEK(TEMPFILE,N);
GET(TEMPFILE);
IF TEMPFILE^.NAME = 'MARY'
    THEN WRITELN('MARY FOUND AT LOCATION ',N);
```

Exercises   Set I. Comprehension

1. Write a program heading for a program FRIENDS and declare the identifier NAMES to be a text file.

2. Write a program heading for a program TOP_TEN and declare the identifier SCORES to be a file of INTEGER.

3. Define a type BOOKFILE to be a file of record BOOKRECORD. Define the identifier DEWEY to be an array of BOOKRECORD with 100 elements. Declare the identifier LIBRARY to be of type BOOKFILE and CARDCATALOG to be of type DEWEY.

4. Define a type CDFILE to be a file of record CDRECORD. Define the identifier ALLCDS to be an array of CDRECORD with 50 elements. Declare the identifier COLLECTION to be of type CDFILE, COMPACTDISC to be of type CDRECORD, and CDARRAY to be of type ALLCDS.

5. Of the following definitions, which are valid? If a definition is invalid, explain why.
   ```
   a. TYPE NUMBERS = FILE OF REAL;
   b. TYPE NUM = RECORD
                       P, S : INTEGER;
                       J    : FILE OF INTEGER
                  END;  { NUM }
   c. TYPE DATA = RECORD
                     CH   : CHAR;
                     FLAG : BOOLEAN
                  END;  { DATA }
           ALPHA = DATA;
   d. TYPE C = RECORD
                   L, M : REAL;
                   Q    : (N, S, E, W)
                END;  { C }
           BETA = FILE OF C;
   e. TYPE WORDS = FILE OF TEXT;
   ```

6. What is the difference between a file window and a file pointer?

7. Consider the following program segment:
   ```
   FOR J := 1 TO 5 DO
      BEGIN
          REWRITE(NUMFILE, 'MYDISK:DATAFILE');
          WRITE(NUMFILE,J*J+J)
      END;
   CLOSE(NUMFILE, LOCK);
   ```

Which of the following indicates the contents of NUMFILE?

a. 30
b. 2   8   20 40 70
c. 2   6   12 20 30
d. 1   4   9 16 25
e. 70
f. 2   8   18 32 50

8. Consider the following program segment:

```
N := 10;
REWRITE(NUMFILE, 'MYDISK:DATAFILE');
WHILE K >= 1 DO
    BEGIN
        K := N DIV 2;
        WRITE(NUMFILE,K);
        N := K
    END;
CLOSE(NUMFILE, LOCK);
```

Which of the following indicates the contents of NUMFILE?

a. 1
b. 0
c. 5   2.5 1.25 0.625
d. 5   2   1   0
e. 0   1   2   5
f. 8

For Exercise 9 and 10, assume the following:

```
PROGRAM NUMS (OUTPUT,DATAFILE);
TYPE
    RFILE = FILE OF REAL;
VAR
    NUMBER : RFILE;
    RVALUE : REAL;
```

9. What would be the result of the following program segment?

```
REWRITE(NUMBER,'MYDISK:DATAFILE');
WRITELN(NUMBER, 52.6);
WRITELN(NUMBER, 45.0);
CLOSE(NUMBER,LOCK);
```

10. What would be the result of the following program segment?

```
RESET(NUMBER,'MYDISK:DATAFILE');
WHILE NOT EOF(NUMBER) DO
    BEGIN
        READLN(NUMBER,RVALUE);
        WRITELN(RVALUE)
    END;
CLOSE(NUMBER,LOCK);
```

11. Assume that prices of furniture are stored in a text file. Each line of the file contains a unique five-digit catalog number, the name of the piece of furniture, and the wholesale and retail price of the piece. The lines in the file are in order by catalog number. All items on a line are separated by spaces. For example,

```
17319 RECLINER 150.00 399.95
18526 SOFA 325.00 749.99
20892 ROCKER 180.00 425.50
```

To compute the markup percentage for an item with catalog number 64329, a program must read

a. the line in the file containing item number 64329, but no other lines.

b. all lines in the file up to and including the lines containing item number 64329, but no other lines.

c. the lines in the file starting with item number 64329 and continuing to the end of the file, but no lines that come before item number 64329.

d. those lines in the file that would be encountered by a binary search for item number 64329, but no other lines.

e. the 64329th line of the file.

f. the entire file.

12. Suppose a program is to record a retail price change for item number 45926 in the text file described in Exercise 11. In order to effect the change, the program must write a line containing the new information and copy

a. all other lines of the file.

b. all lines in the file up to item number 45926, but no other lines.

c. all lines in the file after item number 45926, but no other lines.

d. those lines in the file that would be encountered by a binary search for item number 45926, but no other lines.

e. no other lines of the file.

f. all other lines that contain the same retail price.

Set II. Application

13. Write a procedure that will read a file of integers, INTFILE, sort them into ascending order, and store the sorted file under the same file name.

14. Write a program that will create a text file of at least 25 names and telephone numbers.

15. Write a procedure to alphabetize the file from Exercise 14. Store the new file under a different name.

16. Write a procedure to sort the file from Exercise 14 by phone number. Store the new file under a different name.

17. Write a procedure to search the file from Exercise 15 for a particular name and print the corresponding phone number.

18. Write a procedure that will merge two files of names and telephone numbers (of the type defined in Exercise 14) into a single file. Assume the names in both files are alphabetized. The program should maintain alphabetic order.

19. Write a procedure to append BFILE onto the end of AFILE. Call the new file CFILE. (Assume each is a text file.)

20. Write a procedure that prints the number of times each letter of the alphabet occurs in a given text file.

21. Suppose the text file MODELFILE contains the name, ID number, sex (F/M), hair color, height, weight, and measurements (chest, waist, and hips) for several models working for an agency. A line of the file might look like this:

```
JONES 20453 M BROWN 6.2 190 40 34 36
```

(6.2 for the height means 6 feet, 2 inches)

Write a program segment to search the file and output data on all female models with auburn hair and all male models over six feet tall who weigh 210 pounds or less.

22. Write a procedure to search a text file and count the number of occurrences of a particular character.

23. Write a procedure to alphabetize a file of records containing the information on an electronic bankcard. The record might include the person's name, account number, code number, and expiration date.

24. Given this program segment:

```
PROGRAM MATH (INPUT,OUTPUT,NUMFILE);
TYPE
    INTTYPE = FILE OF INTEGER;
VAR
    NUMBERS : INTTYPE;
```

Write a statement or program segment for each of the following:
a. Open the file to be written.
b. Write five integers to the file.
c. Close the file.
d. Open the file to be read.
e. Read and print the third integer that is in the file.
f. Close the file.

25. Given this program segment:

```
PROGRAM CHEF (INPUT,OUTPUT,RECIPES);
TYPE
    CARD = RECORD
                TITLE,CLASSIFICATION:STRING[20];
                INGREDIENTS : ARRAY[1..30]
                              OF STRING[40];
                DIRECTIONS : STRING
            END;   { CARD }
    CARDFILE = FILE OF CARD;
VAR
    RECIPECARD : CARD;
    COOKBOOK   : CARDFILE;
```

Write a statement or program segment for each of the following:
a. Open the file to be written.
b. Write a recipe for boiled water to the file.
c. Close the file.
d. Open the file to be read.
e. Read and print a recipe for milkshakes from the file.
f. Close the file.

26. Write the correction procedure for the GRADES program (Program Segment 16.8), as described at the end of Lesson 16.3. Use PUT

and GET with the SEEK command to obtain the desired element, make the corrections, and save the information in the appropriate locations in the file.

Set III. Synthesis

27. Write a program that will create a file of address records in order to print address labels. For each address record, allow the user to input a name, street address, city, state, and zip code, and write this information on a file. Allow the user to make changes in the file, add or delete addresses, and obtain printouts of the file.

28. Rewrite the program from Exercise 27 to include options for sorting the list alphabetically according to the last name or numerically according to zip code. Also allow the user to
    a. input a name and have the program search for and print the corresponding address.
    b. input two zip codes and print out all the addresses that are between these zip codes.

29. Write a vocabulary-building program that will allow the teacher to write a file that contains five words, three incorrect definitions for each word, and the correct definition. Write the corresponding program for the student that will read the words and the definitions, output a multiple choice question, allow the student to enter an answer, and compare the student answer to the correct answer. The student should be given two chances for each word.

30. Write a program to maintain the records for a coin or stamp collection. Allow the user to
    a. obtain various printouts, including specific entry records and sorted lists.
    b. search for certain characteristics, such as price or year of issue.
    c. add, delete, or edit entries.

31. Write a program to assist in a track meet. The program should seed (determine each runner's assigned lane according to previous best times) the 100-meter, 200-meter, and 400-meter events. Assume there are eight lanes on the track and eight entrants per event. Runners should be assigned in order of fastest to slowest in lanes 4, 5, 3, 6, 2, 7, 1, and 8. (The runner with the fastest time in an event would be in lane 4; the slowest runner, in lane 8.)

    Allow the user to enter the participants for each event, along with the participants' school name and best times, into a file. Sort the file into three separate, ordered files, one for each event. Print the runners' names next to their assigned lane number for each event. Remember that there may be fewer than eight entrants per event and there may also be dual meets (both men's and women's events).

32. Write a program to maintain information about perspective contributors to a charity. Such information might include the following:

    ▪ Name, address, and phone number.
    ▪ Annual income.

- Number of members in household.
- Whether or not the person is a previous contributor. If so, then list the amount given. (A variant record is optional.)

Allow the user to obtain a printout of any individual record and sorted lists (sorted alphabetically, by income, or by previous contribution; if not a previous contributor, then exclude from this list). Use a menu to allow the user to select an option.

33. Write a program to produce a banner from a word or phrase entered by the user. The program should analyze the input, character by character, and produce a block letter printed sideways for each character. Store the "map" for each character in a file. There are several factors to consider, including how the letters should be formed, what size they should be, how much input should be allowed, and whether it should be punctuated.
    In determining how to form the letters, consider the following:

- Produce the letters using Xs? For example,

```
XXXXXXX
X   X   X
X   X   X
```

- Produce the letters using the character itself? For example,

```
EEEEEEE
E   E   E
E   E   E
```

- What should be the size of the block letters? The example just shown would be very small. Assuming a printer width of 80 characters, perhaps 60 horizontal × 50 vertical would be appropriate. (A more advanced problem would be to make smaller letters but allow for two lines on the banner.) The "lines" of each letter should be more than one character wide so as to be easily read from a distance.
- Should the character input be limited? The program could produce a banner as large as memory allowed (or until the paper ran out).
- Should the banner include punctuation? The program may include or ignore any punctuation; or it may instruct the user to enter input without punctuation.

In addition, the program should include a method for accessing character maps. One obvious solution is to create two-dimensional arrays that represent each character. However, this is a bit tedious and repetitious. Another method might be to design an algorithm around a CASE statement, using codes for different parts of a letter (such as the straight line in letters like B, D, or E) and then associating each character with a set of codes.

34. The goal of an exercise program is often to not only strengthen one's muscles and lung capacity, but also to benefit the heart. A doctor might instruct a patient to exercise 15 minutes a day in an aerobic exercise. An aerobic exercise should maintain a person's heart rate at 70–80 percent of that person's maximum for at least

12 minutes. An individual's training heart rate may be determined by the following formula:

$$RESTRATE + ((MAXRATE - RESTRATE) \times 0.65)$$

where RESTRATE is the person's average pulse for one minute when at rest. MAXRATE is determined by 220 minus the person's age. This is approximately the fastest heart rate the individual can attain and the individual should never exercise at that rate.

Write a program to maintain a log of your exercise and heart rate. Each time you exercise, enter your RESTRATE (it will decrease as you become more fit). Immediately after exercising, check your pulse and enter it into the computer, along with the type of exercise and amount of time. The program should report your ideal training heart rate and determine if your exercise rate is 10 or more beats slower than your training heart rate (meaning that you are not exercising hard enough) or 10 or more beats faster than your rate (meaning that you should slow down).

Allow for the ability to obtain printouts of your progress (include resting and exercise heart rates for each day and the exercises and corresponding time spent). Remember that certain exercises will take longer to achieve the training heart rate than others and that you should not confine yourself to only one type of exercise. For example, walking may require a minimum of 20 minutes to obtain the training heart rate, while jumping jacks may require only 12 minutes.

Option: Include space in the file for your measurements and weight.

35. Write a quiz-builder program to allow a teacher to produce an objective test. The program should use a record definition for each question, and include a variant portion for the question type; that is, true-or-false, multiple choice (character), or short answer (integer, character or string). Allow the user to build the test, save it to a file, make corrections in the file, and print the test.

Option: Include a space in the record for the correct answer.

Linked Lists

Just at this moment Alice felt a very curious sensation, which puzzled her a good deal until she made out what it was: she was beginning to grow larger again, and she thought at first she would get up and leave the court; but on second thoughts she decided to remain where she was as long as there was room for her.

—Lewis Carroll

Overview

Gaining a Perspective

Arrays, sets, and records are examples of **static** data structures; that is, the size of these structures must be predetermined by the programmer. Often only a small percentage of total memory allocated is actually used, which may pose a problem depending on memory requirements and total memory available. In addition, there is often a need to add or remove elements from a structure while maintaining the natural order of the elements. This can be done with static data structures, but excessive shifting of elements can be awkward and time-consuming. Concerns about memory limitations, as well as ease of manipulating the elements of a structure, suggest the need for a data structure that uses memory only as needed and allows for efficient manipulation of its elements. Pascal provides just such a dynamic data structure. (Files, introduced in Chapter 16, give an example of a dynamic data structure.) These structures have the ability to grow and shrink in size as the program executes. That is, they consist of elements that can be created or destroyed during the program's execution. These structures are still limited to available memory, but will use only the memory necessary to store existing information. In addition, manipulations (for instance adding elements and deleting elements) of these structures can be performed with greater efficiency. Dynamic data structures provide programmers with a powerful and versatile tool that can be applied to a variety of programming applications.

Lesson 17.1 Pointers and Lists

A list is a collection of elements of the same type. Arrays are examples of static lists of elements, lists that do not change in size. In this lesson, a dynamic data structure called **linked lists** will be introduced. The elements of a linked list are usually records with at least one additional field that is used to link the records.

The elements of any list are referred to as **nodes.** Each node of a list has a predecessor and a successor. The predecessor of the first element is empty or **NIL,** as is the successor of the last element. (NIL means that the list is empty. Think of it as Nothing In List.) (For example, as shown in Figure 17.1, the predecessor of node 2 is node 1 and the successor of node 2 is node 3.)

The nodes of a list are joined (linked) by **pointers,** which point to an element of the same type. In Figure 17.1, for instance, the pointers point in one direction through the list. A pointer can point to any legal Pascal data type. Here are some examples of pointer definitions.

```
TYPE
    NUMBERPTR = ^INTEGER;
    NAMEPTR   = ^STRING;
```

Pointer variables are then declared as

```
VAR
    NUMBER1,
    NUMBER2 : NUMBERPTR;
    NAME    : NAMEPTR;
```

where NUMBER1 and NUMBER2 point to a location containing an integer and NAME points to a location containing a string.

Pointer Definition and Declaration Form

```
TYPE
    type identifier = ^identifier;

VAR
    identifier : type identifier;
```

Pointers of any type, including a programmer-defined type, can be defined and declared. In the following example, CLASS points to a variable that can store a student's year in high school.

```
TYPE
    CLASSTYPE = (FRESHMAN, SOPHOMORE, JUNIOR, SENIOR);
    CLASSPTR  = ^CLASSTYPE;

VAR
    CLASS : CLASSPTR;
```

For this example, however, there is no way to join one element to another to form a list. The way to accomplish this joining is to use records and make one of the fields in the record a pointer, as in Program Segment 17.1. The pointer can be used to indicate the next element in the list.

Figure 17.1

List of Elements
Linked by Pointers

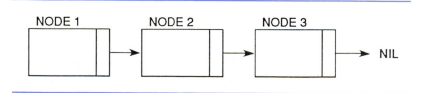

Program Segment 17.1

```
TYPE
   STUDENTPTR = ^STUDENTINFO;
   STUDENTINFO = RECORD

                       NAME  : STRING[20];
                       IDNUM : INTEGER;
                       LINK  : STUDENTPTR

                 END;

VAR
   STPTR1,
   STPTR2,
   LIST    : STUDENTPTR;
```

In the STUDENTINFO record, NAME and IDNUM are data fields and LINK is the link or pointer field. The pointer field ties the records to one another by allowing each element to point to its successor. Notice that STUDENTPTR is declared prior to the record that uses it. By using ∧STUDENTINFO as the data type for STUDENTPTR, the compiler expects the record STUDENT-INFO to be defined later. The general form for defining a pointer in a record follows. (As will be seen later, more than one pointer can be contained in a record.)

Pointer Definition

```
TYPE
   link identifier = ^record identifier;
   record identifier = RECORD
                             identifier:type;
                             identifier:type;
                                     .
                                     .
                                     .
                             identifier:link
                                        identifier
                       END;
VAR
   variable,
   variable : link identifier;
```

As mentioned earlier, lists that use pointers can grow or shrink during the execution of a program. Thus space must be allocated for these variables on demand. This is accomplished by using the predefined procedure **NEW** within the body of the program. The following statements assume the definitions and declarations of Program Segment 17.1.

```
NEW(LIST);
NEW(STPTR1);
NEW(STPTR2);
```

The statement NEW provides one node to which assignments can be made. The node is pointed to by the pointer variable used in the parentheses after the command NEW. NEW only allocates memory for the new node; no assignment is made to the node. (See Figure 17.2.)

Following the NEW statement, any pointers in the node (that is, LINK) should be initialized to the predefined value NIL, as in the following statements. This is used to show that there is nothing in the list beyond the node containing NIL in its pointer field. If the pointers are not initialized to NIL, they will point to erroneous memory locations.

```
LIST^.LINK := NIL;
STPTR1^.LINK := NIL;
STPTR2^.LINK := NIL;
```

The data fields NAME and IDNUM would contain nothing usable at this point since they have not been assigned any values.

Assignments to fields in a node can be done in two ways. One way is a direct assignment statement, as in Program Segment 17.2, and as shown in Figure 17.4.

Program Segment 17.2

```
LIST^.NAME := 'ALBERT';
LIST^.IDNUM := 1297;

STPTR1^.NAME := 'SUSAN';
STPTR1^.IDNUM := 4314;

STPTR2^.NAME := 'ALICE';
STPTR2^.IDNUM := 7826;
```

The notation LIST∧ refers to the node (record) pointed to by the pointer LIST. Since records in dynamic data structures are not numbered (as in arrays), elements in a specific node must be

Figure 17.2

Memory Allocated by NEW Command

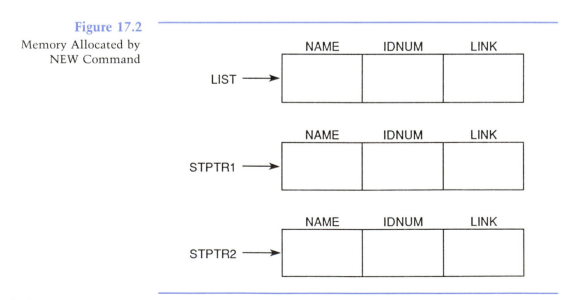

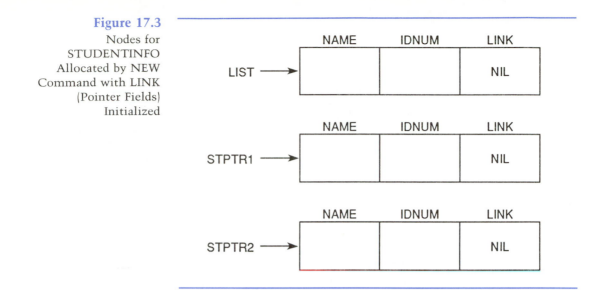

Figure 17.3
Nodes for
STUDENTINFO
Allocated by NEW
Command with LINK
(Pointer Fields)
Initialized

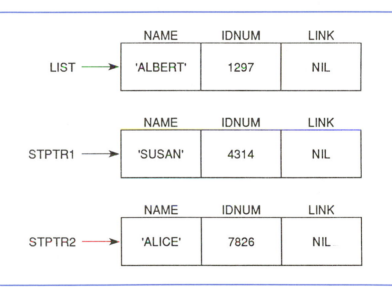

Figure 17.4
Assignment of Values
to Fields in a Node

accessed through the pointer pointing to that node. Thus
LIST∧.NAME refers to the field NAME in the record pointed to
by the pointer LIST. This seems awkward at first, but the easy
manipulation of the list that it allows is more than worth the
shift in thinking.

Another way to assign values to a field is to assign a pointer
to another pointer, as in the following:

```
STPTR1 := STPTR2;
```

As shown in Figure 17.5, assigning STPTR2 to STPTR1 causes
STPTR1 to now point to the node pointed to by STPTR2. Both
pointers now point to the node containing ALICE in its NAME

Figure 17.5
Assigning One Pointer
to Another

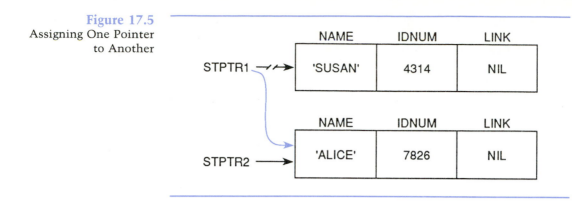

field. The data that were previously pointed to by STPTR1 (the node containing SUSAN) would not be accessible if this assignment were actually made.

The following assignment statement shows a slightly different way of assigning values to the fields in a node. (Assume the values shown in Figure 17.4.)

```
STPTR1^.NAME := STPTR2^.NAME;
```

This assignment does not eliminate the node pointed to by STPTR1. Instead, the content of the NAME field in STPTR2 is copied into the NAME field of STPTR1. (See Figure 17.6.) Remember, STPTR1∧.NAME refers to the NAME data field of STPTR1, whereas STPTR1 refers to the pointer.

Creating a List

The record structure is ideal for creating a list that may need to grow or shrink. Using the record STUDENTINFO, a list of student names and ID numbers can be created (see Program Segment 17.3). This list structure is called a **singly linked list.** The link field of one node points to the next node in the list.

**Program
Segment 17.3**

```
TYPE
    STUDENTPTR = ^STUDENTINFO;
    STUDENTINFO = RECORD

                    NAME  : STRING[20];
                    IDNUM : INTEGER;
                    LINK  : STUDENTPTR

                END;

VAR
    LIST,
    TEMP,
    PTR   : STUDENTPTR;
```

LIST, TEMP, and PTR are variables of type STUDENTPTR that will be used to keep track of the list of student information.

First, the list pointer must be initialized to NIL, since the list is empty at the start. The pointer LIST is used to keep track of the start (first node) of the list.

```
LIST := NIL;
```

Then, NEW is used to create a node for the pointer PTR.

```
NEW(PTR);
```

PTR is used for creating and adding nodes to the list, as shown in Figure 17.7.

Next, values are assigned to the data field and the link field of PTR (see Figure 17.8).

```
PTR^.NAME := 'ALBERT';
PTR^.IDNUM := 1297;
PTR^.LINK := NIL;
```

Finally, the newly-created node is placed in the list by assigning PTR to LIST. As shown in Figure 17.9, the node pointed to by PTR becomes the first node in LIST.

```
LIST := PTR;
```

Other nodes may be added to the list as needed. A common practice is to maintain the list of elements in some natural order. This makes accessing the nodes easier. In the case of student records, an alphabetic arrangement might be desirable. Thus, as new students are added, they should be placed in the correct position alphabetically.

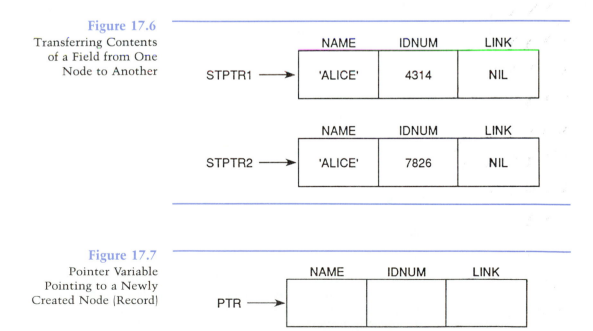

Figure 17.6
Transferring Contents of a Field from One Node to Another

Figure 17.7
Pointer Variable Pointing to a Newly Created Node (Record)

Figure 17.8
Contents of Data
and Link Fields

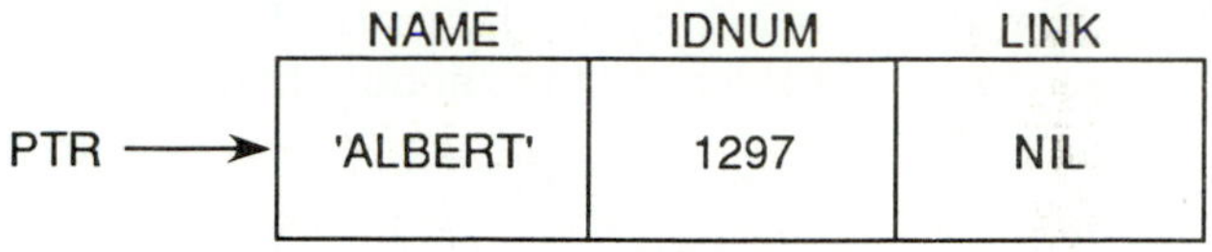

Figure 17.9
Assigning PTR
to LIST

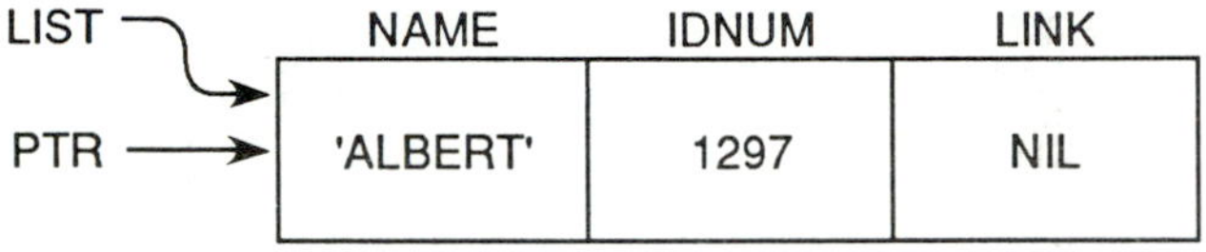

Inserting a Node

The process of inserting a node in a linked list involves looking through the list until the correct position is found. When the position is found, the pointer field in the new node is linked to the node that follows the new node (in some desired order, such as alphabetically). Then the pointer field in the preceding node is changed to point to the new node.

Figure 17.10 shows insertion of a node into a list. (For simplicity, the nodes in this figure are inserted at the end of the list.) Assuming the STUDENTINFO list given in Figure 17.10, the following expressions can be used when examining this list:

Expression	Result
LIST^.NAME	ALBERT
LIST^.IDNUM	1297
LIST^.LINK	Points to node 2
LIST^.LINK^.NAME	BEE
LIST^.LINK^.LINK	Points to node 3
LIST^.LINK^.LINK^.NAME	DENNIS

Program Segment 17.4 can insert a node at the beginning, the middle, or the end of a list (using the definitions provided earlier in Program Segment 17.3). To call procedure INSERT, the following statement should be used:

```
INSERT(NAME,IDNUM,LIST);
```

The procedure receives the new name and ID number, along with the pointer to the list. A new node is created and inserted into the appropriate spot in the list. (The list may or may not contain any nodes initially.)

Figure 17.10 Inserting Nodes into STUDENTINFO List

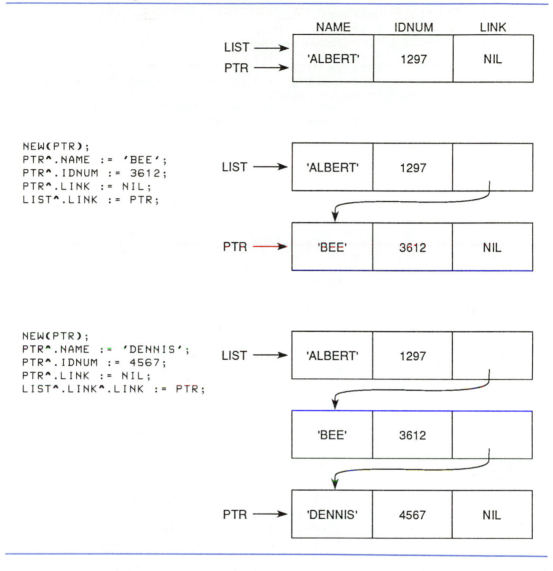

```
NEW(PTR);
PTR^.NAME := 'BEE';
PTR^.IDNUM := 3612;
PTR^.LINK := NIL;
LIST^.LINK := PTR;
```

```
NEW(PTR);
PTR^.NAME := 'DENNIS';
PTR^.IDNUM := 4567;
PTR^.LINK := NIL;
LIST^.LINK^.LINK := PTR;
```

Program Segment 17.4

```
PROCEDURE INSERT(NM:STRING; ID:INTEGER;
                VAR LST:STUDENTPTR);

   { INSERT AND MAINTAIN ALPHABETIC ORDER }

VAR
   FOUND : BOOLEAN;
   BACK,
   TEMP,
   PTR   : STUDENTPTR;
```

```
BEGIN

    NEW(PTR);
    PTR^.NAME  := NM;
    PTR^.IDNUM := ID;
    PTR^.LINK  := NIL;
    BACK := NIL;
    TEMP := LST;  { TEMP IS THE SEARCH POINTER }
    FOUND := FALSE;
    WHILE (NOT FOUND) AND (TEMP <> NIL) DO
        IF TEMP^.NAME > PTR^.NAME
            THEN
                FOUND := TRUE
            ELSE
                BEGIN
                    BACK := TEMP;
                    TEMP := TEMP^.LINK
                    { SEARCH POINTER ADVANCES }
                END;
    PTR^.LINK := TEMP;
    IF BACK = NIL  { INSERT AT FRONT OF LIST }
        THEN LST := PTR
        ELSE BACK^.LINK := PTR

END; { INSERT }
```

For procedure INSERT, a temporary pointer (TEMP) is assigned to the beginning of the list. This search pointer then moves through the list until the correct location for the new element is found. This is done by locating a name that is alphabetically greater than the name in the new node, or by reaching the end of the list (which means the new node belongs at the end). A pointer to the previous node (BACK) is maintained to allow for easy insertion of the new node. When the proper location is found, the pointer of the new node (PTR∧.LINK) is changed to point to the next node. The pointer within the previous node (BACK∧.LINK) is set to PTR to complete the insertion. A provision is included for the special case when the new element belongs at the front of the list (that is, when BACK = NIL).

To summarize, insert or add a node to a list in the following manner:

1. Use the built-in procedure NEW to obtain a new node.
2. Assign a value to the fields in the new node.
3. Find the correct position in the list for the new value.
4. Link the node to the next node in the list.
5. Link the previous node of the list to the new node.

Printing a List

A list can be printed by moving a pointer through the list and checking the current element for NIL. Program Segment 17.5 outputs the elements of LIST.

Program Segment 17.5

```
TEMP := LIST;
WHILE TEMP <> NIL DO
    BEGIN
        WRITELN(TEMP^.NAME);
        WRITELN(TEMP^.IDNUM);
        TEMP := TEMP^.LINK
    END;
```

First, a temporary pointer (TEMP) is assigned to the front of the list. TEMP then moves through the nodes in the list until a node is found that has a LINK field of NIL, indicating no nodes exist beyond that one. The names and ID numbers are written as each node is encountered.

Deleting Nodes

To delete a node, a pointer (TEMP) is moved through the list until the node to be deleted is found (or the end of the list is reached). When the node is found, it is deleted by setting the LINK pointer in the preceding node to the value of the LINK pointer in the node to be deleted. Thus, the node is taken out of the list by being skipped over with pointers (see Figure 17.11). If the first node is to be deleted, the pointer to the front of the list (LIST) is changed to point to the second node in the list (that is, the node pointed to by the LINK field in the first node—LIST∧.LINK).

Program Segment 17.6 deletes a node from the STUDENTINFO list.

Figure 17.11

Deleting BEE from a List

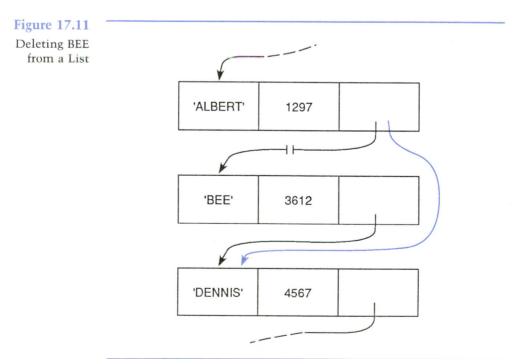

Program Segment 17.6

```
PROCEDURE DELETE(KEY : STRING;
                     VAR LST : STUDENTPTR);

VAR
    TEMP,
    PTR    : STUDENTPTR;

BEGIN
    IF KEY = LST^.NAME
        THEN
            BEGIN
                PTR := LST;
                LST := LST^.LINK
            END { THEN }
        ELSE
            BEGIN
                TEMP := LST;
                WHILE (TEMP^.LINK^.NAME <> KEY) AND
                      (TEMP <> NIL) DO
                    TEMP := TEMP^.LINK;
                PTR := TEMP^.LINK;
                TEMP^.LINK := PTR^.LINK
            END { ELSE }
END; { DELETE }
```

Notice the **chain of pointers** that was used in the DELETE procedure.

```
TEMP^.LINK^.NAME
```

This expression represents the value in the NAME field of the node pointed to by the LINK field of the node TEMP. The use of a chain of pointers allows the program to look beyond the next node.

One problem occurs when deleting nodes. The deleted node is no longer present in the list, but the data for this node still exist in memory and are wasting space. If enough deletions were performed during the execution of a program, all available memory could be used. To remedy this, a pointer (PTR) can be assigned to the deleted node so that the memory allocated to this node can be made available for a new node. Many versions of Pascal provide a built-in procedure, **DISPOSE,** for disposing of unwanted nodes in a dynamic data structure. If available, the DISPOSE command frees memory pointed to by a given pointer. In procedure DELETE, the command DISPOSE(PTR) would be added to clear the memory allocated to the record pointed to by PTR. If the DISPOSE procedure does not exist, a procedure can be written to keep a separate list of available node space. When a new node is to be created, this list of available nodes will be used first. If the list is empty, then the NEW command can be used as usual to create a new node. The implementation of this DISPOSE procedure is left as an exercise.

Figure 17.12
Doubly Linked List

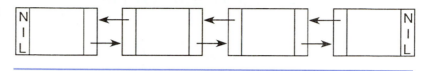

Doubly Linked and Circular Lists

For a **doubly linked list** two link fields are defined; one points to the previous node of the list and one points to the successor. Figure 17.12 illustrates a doubly linked list. The doubly linked list structure provides easier access to nodes in the list than a singly linked list, since a pointer exists to the predecessor and successor of each node. Some applications may call for this structure. The cost, of course, is extra memory to store the added pointer in each node.

Another linked list variation that may be useful is a **circular list.** The last node of this list is linked to the first node, forming a circle. Figure 17.13 illustrates a circular list. Implementations of circular and doubly linked lists are left as exercises.

Lesson Check 17.1

1. How is memory allocated for the nodes of a list?

2. What is the purpose of NIL?

3. What is the difference between PTR∧ and PTR, assuming the following definitions and declarations?

```
TYPE
    RECPTR = ^SAMPLEREC;
    SAMPLEREC = RECORD
                        DATA1    : INTEGER;
                        DATA2    : CHAR;
                        LINKREC  : RECPTR
                    END; { SAMPLEREC }

VAR
    PTR : RECPTR;
```

4. What is a doubly linked list? What are the advantages and disadvantages of this structure?

Figure 17.13 Circular List

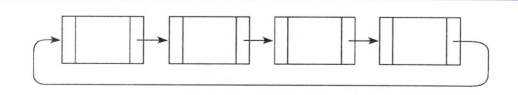

Lesson 17.2   Stacks and Queues

Stacks and queues using arrays were introduced in Chapter 13. These structures lend themselves readily to implementation with linked lists. A stack is a dynamic data structure that accesses elements from one end of a list. The last element entered into a stack is the first element out. (Remember: Stacks operate under the LIFO—Last-In First-Out—principle.) Physical examples of stacks are the entry and exit patterns from an elevator, how dishes are stored in a cupboard, or the way calculations are performed in some calculators (postfix notation). Figure 17.14 is a sketch of a stack. Notice that the pointer to the first element of the stack is called TOP.

The processes for adding to and deleting from a stack are often referred to as **push** and **pop,** respectively. That is, a node can be "pushed" onto the stack (added) or "popped" off (deleted). Figure 17.15 is a sketch of the push process.

Program Segment 17.7 assumes a record definition containing a name (STRING) and a pointer field. The following procedure call would be used:

```
PUSH(NAME,TOP);
```

To push a new node onto a stack, the node is created and its pointer (PTR^.LINK) is set to point at the node that is currently on the top of the stack. The pointer to the top of the stack (TOP) is then set to point at the new node.

The pop process is also fairly straightforward. Figure 17.16 gives a sketch of deleting from the top of a stack. For the corresponding pop procedure (Program Segment 17.8), a check must be made to determine if the stack is already empty before attempting to delete a node.

Figure 17.14

A Stack

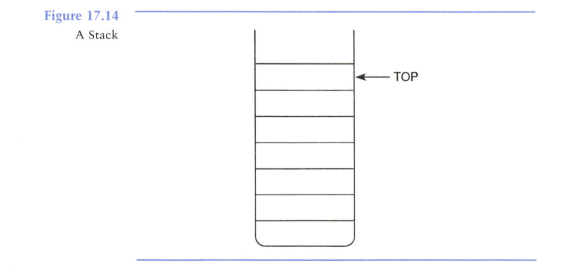

Figure 17.15 Pushing onto a Stack

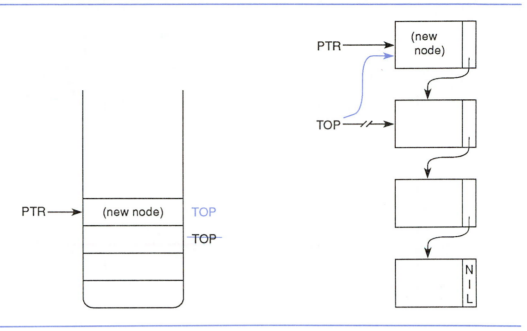

Program Segment 17.7

```
PROCEDURE PUSH(NM : STRING; VAR TOP : STACKPTR);

VAR
    PTR : STACKPTR;

BEGIN
    NEW(PTR);
    PTR^.NAME := NM;   { GET VALUE FOR DATA FIELD }
    PTR^.LINK := TOP;
    TOP := PTR
END;
```

Program Segment 17.8

```
PROCEDURE POP(VAR TOP, PTR : STACKPTR);

BEGIN
    IF TOP <> NIL
        THEN
            BEGIN
                PTR := TOP;
                TOP := TOP^.LINK
            END
        ELSE
            WRITELN('STACK ALREADY EMPTY.')
END;
```

To remove a node, the top pointer is simply set to the next node in the stack by

```
TOP := TOP^.LINK
```

Note that while the node is removed from the stack, it is still occupying memory space. A pointer (PTR) is used to keep track of the deleted node for later use or disposal.

Figure 17.16 Popping from a Stack

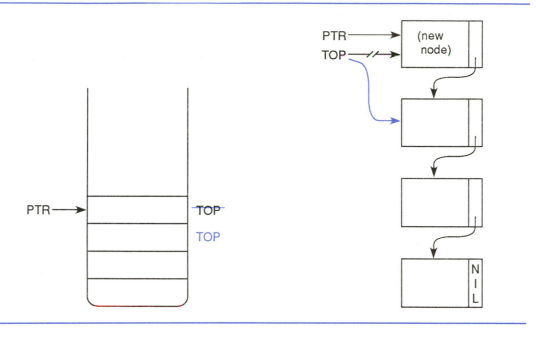

In contrast to a stack, a queue is a dynamic data structure in which elements are entered at one end of the list and are deleted at the other. (Remember: Queues operate under the FIFO—First-In First-Out—principle.) Some physical models of a queue are cars entering and exiting a ferry boat, or people using an escalator. Additions are made at the rear and deletions are made at the front of the list. Pointers are maintained to keep track of the front and rear of the queue. Figure 17.17 is a sketch of this structure.

To add a new node, the pointer field in the last node of the queue is changed to point to the new node and the rear pointer is adjusted accordingly. Figure 17.18 sketches the addition of a node.

Program Segment 17.9 is the corresponding procedure for inserting into a queue. These procedures assume that appropriate definitions and declarations have been made.

Program Segment 17.9

```
PROCEDURE INSERT(NM : STRING;
                 VAR FRONT, REAR: QUEUEPTR);

VAR
    PTR : QUEUEPTR;

BEGIN
    NEW(PTR);
    PTR^.NAME := NM;
    IF REAR = NIL
        THEN BEGIN
                FRONT := PTR;
                REAR := PTR
             END
```

Figure 17.17
A Queue

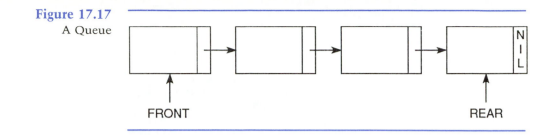

FRONT   REAR

Figure 17.18 Adding onto a Queue

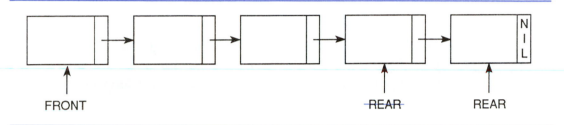

FRONT   REAR   REAR

Figure 17.19 Deleting from a Queue

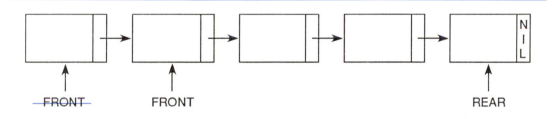

FRONT   FRONT   REAR

```
        ELSE BEGIN
                REAR^.LINK := PTR;
                REAR := PTR
             END
END;
```

Deleting from a queue is also quite simple. The pointer to the front of the queue is merely changed to point to the next node in the queue. Figure 17.19 is a sketch of the delete process. Program Segment 17.10 demonstrates the delete procedure. As with the pop procedure, the queue must be checked to see if it is already empty and a pointer (PTR) is used to keep track of the deleted node.

**Program
Segment 17.10**

```
PROCEDURE DELETE(VAR FRONT, REAR: QUEUEPTR);

VAR
    PTR : QUEUEPTR;
```

```
BEGIN

    IF FRONT <> NIL
        THEN
            BEGIN
                PTR := FRONT;
                FRONT := FRONT^.LINK;
                IF FRONT = NIL
                    THEN REAR := NIL
                        { DELETE LAST ELEMENT IN QUEUE }
            END
        ELSE
            WRITELN('QUEUE ALREADY EMPTY.')

END;
```

Lesson Check 17.2

1. What is the difference between a stack and a queue? Give an example of a physical application of each.

2. What are the purposes of the PUSH (Program Segment 17.7) and POP (Program Segment 17.8) procedures?

Lesson 17.3   Hashing

The concept of hashing was introduced in Chapter 14. Hashing involves a method of storing information to allow instant (or nearly instant) access to the elements of an array. Improvements on this method of searching are possible with linked lists. Two aspects of hashing must be considered: the hash function and collision resolution.

Hash Functions

A hash function calculates the storage location for an element in a data structure. In order to access a particular element, the address is then recalculated and the element is located quickly. Several functions for hashing are possible. A common method involves changing the binary representation of an element into an address. In the examples to follow, the elements to be stored are words. Each letter can be coded as a five-bit binary number (as shown in Table 17.1) derived from the ASCII value of the letter by

```
ORD(LETTER) - ORD('A') + 1
```

Extraction   The extraction technique pulls a few scattered bits from the binary representation of an element and puts those bits together to form an address. Suppose the elements to be stored were the words *FOX, YOUR, THE, IS, RED, HAD,* and *A.* The extraction method could be to take the first two bits and the last bit to form an address. Table 17.2 shows the results.

Table 17.1
Binary and Decimal
Representation of
Alphabet

Letter	Binary	Decimal	Letter	Binary	Decimal
A	00001	1	N	01110	14
B	00010	2	O	01111	15
C	00011	3	P	10000	16
D	00100	4	Q	10001	17
E	00101	5	R	10010	18
F	00110	6	S	10011	19
G	00111	7	T	10100	20
H	01000	8	U	10101	21
I	01001	9	V	10110	22
J	01010	10	W	10111	23
K	01011	11	X	11000	24
L	01100	12	Y	11001	25
M	01101	13	Z	11010	26

Table 17.2
Results of a Hash
Function Based on
Extraction

Word	Binary Form	First Two Bits	Last Bit	Address
FOX	00110 01111 11000	00	0	000 = 0
YOUR	11001 01111 10101 10010	11	0	110 = 6
THE	10100 01000 00101	10	1	101 = 5
IS	01001 10011	01	1	011 = 3
RED	10010 00101 00100	10	0	100 = 4
HAD	01000 00001 00100	01	0	010 = 2
A	00001	00	1	001 = 1

This method works perfectly for these seven words, placing them in array positions 0, 1, . . ., 6. However, if the list contained the words *DOG, BIG, BACK, GUM, BAG, GONE,* and *DIM,* a problem would arise. This hash function would result in an address of 1 for all of the words in the list. Hash functions that produce the same address for many of the elements are said to exhibit **primary clustering.** By itself, extraction is a poor method for hashing since it is based on only a few bits from the binary representation of the element. Better hash functions can be produced by incorporating all of the binary digits.

Compression One method of hashing that uses all of the bits in the element is to compress the binary representation of each character into one number that will be used as the address. This compression technique could be accomplished by simply adding the bits together. XOR, or exclusive-OR (see Chapter 6, Exercise 15) is preferred, however, since it eliminates the need to worry

Table 17.3
XOR Hash Function

THE	10100	XOR	01000	XOR	00101 = 11001 = 25		
FOX	00110	XOR	01111	XOR	11000 = 10001 = 17		
IS	01001	XOR	10011		= 11010 = 26		
RED	10010	XOR	00101	XOR	00100 = 10011 = 19		
A	00001				= 00001 = 1		

about overflow. Using XOR, the address for the word HAD could be computed as

```
01000   XOR   00001   XOR   00100
‾‾‾‾‾‾‾‾‾‾‾‾‾‾‾‾‾‾‾‾
       01001               XOR   00100
       ‾‾‾‾‾‾‾‾‾‾‾‾‾‾‾‾‾‾‾‾‾‾
               01101 = 13   (address)
```

Table 17.3 gives the resulting address for other words using the XOR compression method of hashing.

The biggest problem with compression is that addition and XOR are commutative; that is,

$$(a + b) = (b + a)$$

and

$$(a \text{ XOR } b) = (b \text{ XOR } a)$$

This means that words containing exactly the same letters produce the same hash address even though the letters are in a different order. (PALS, LAPS, and SLAP; or STEAK, STAKE, TAKES, and SKATE are some examples.) A hash function should be designed to break up naturally occurring clusters of elements. One enhancement to compression that can help eliminate these clusters is to rotate the bits in one or more of the segments by varying amounts. Even with this improvement, the best use of compression might be to convert a multiple-letter element into one five-bit binary number for use with other hash functions.

Division   The division hashing method was introduced in Chapter 14. For this technique, the binary representation of the entire element is divided by a carefully selected number. The remainder produced (using MOD) is then used as the address for storing that particular element. In general, the hash function for an element (e) with a binary representation (b) can be written as

$$h(e) = b \text{ MOD } n$$

This makes the hash function very easy to calculate and is based on all the bits of the element. However, the divisor (n) must be chosen with some care. In general, n should be prime or have no small prime factors. This will cut down on naturally occurring clusters and thus minimize collisions. In addition, n must be large enough to produce sufficient addresses to store the maximum number of elements. For example, a hash function to store up to 100 elements might look like the following for the element HAD. In this case, the three binary numbers are joined to create one 15-bit number. This binary number can then be converted to a decimal number. The divisor (101) causes the MOD function to return numbers from 0 to 100, allowing sufficient addresses to store the 100 elements.

HAD   01000 00001 00100 = 8228

$h(\text{HAD}) = 8228 \text{ MOD } 101 = 47$

Thus, HAD would be stored in location 47 of the array.

Using division instead of compression avoids the problem produced by the fact that exclusive-OR is commutative. For example,

PAL   10000 00001 01100

$$2^{14} + 2^5 + 2^3 + 2^2 = 16384 + 32 + 8 + 4 = 16428$$

$$16428 \text{ MOD } 101 = 66$$

LAP   01100 00001 10000

$$2^{13} + 2^{12} + 2^5 + 2^4 = 8192 + 4096 + 32 + 16 = 12336$$

$$12336 \text{ MOD } 101 = 14$$

PAL would be stored in location 66; LAP would be stored in location 14. Had compression been used, both values would have been stored in location 29.

P	10000	01100	L
A	00001	00001	A
L	01100	10000	P
	11101	11101	
	29	29	

Division provides a hash function that is easy to compute, uses all bits of the element, and limits collisions by reducing primary clustering. Other hash functions can be developed; no hash function, however, can be designed to work in all situations. The nature of the elements to be stored, as well as the computer being used, must be considered. Even after great care is taken to design the best possible hash function for a given situation, collisions can still occur and a reliable method of resolving collisions must be developed.

Collision Resolution

In Chapter 14, collisions encountered in a hash function were resolved by using a linear search to find the next available (empty) location in the array. The colliding element was then placed in that location. This method is a form of **linear probing.** For small numbers of elements, where the linear search would be performed relatively quickly, this type of linear probing is adequate. With the availability of linked lists, however, another option may prove more effective.

Chaining   Chaining is a method of **collision resolution** where the calculated hash location in an array contains a pointer to a linked list in which the element (and any elements that collide with it) is stored. Using extraction on the words in Table 17.4, some collisions will occur.

Storage for these elements is shown in Figure 17.20. Notice that elements are stored in linked lists with the original array holding the pointer to the list. If elements collide, they are stored under the same original pointer (location) in a linked list that expands as needed. The elements in the lists can be maintained in order if the need arises.

This type of chaining (called **separate chaining**) stores a **header** (pointer to the start of a linked list) in each array location to separate linked lists for colliding elements. Thus, there is some memory cost.

Lesson Check 17.3

1. What is primary clustering?

2. What are some considerations when developing hash functions?

3. What is meant by linear probing in collision resolution?

Table 17.4
Hash Addresses by Extraction Method

Word	Address
HAD	2
FOX	0
RED	4
A	1
THE	5
DOG	1
BIG	1
DID	0
YOU	7

Figure 17.20
Chaining for Collision
Resolution

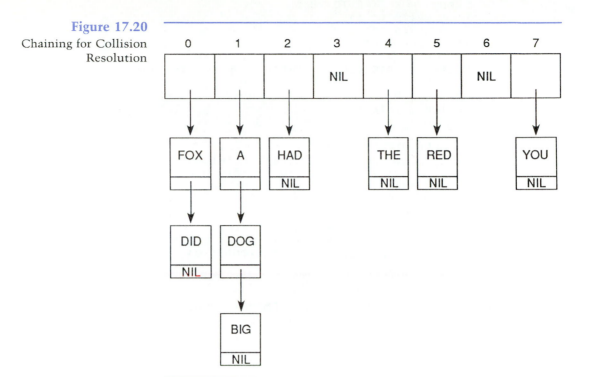

Lesson 17.4 Programming Tip—Program Design

A Detailed Look: Input/Output Procedures

The main program used to drive the stock market simulation was set forth in Lesson 16.4 (Program Segment 16.9). The first thing needed in that program is to do some housekeeping. This includes setting up stocks, establishing one year's worth of stock values, and initializing player information. Also, a menu procedure may be useful as an organizational device. These procedures are included in Program Segment 17.11, along with the printout procedures (which are straightforward). Notice that some local variables are the same as global variables used earlier (Program Segment 16.9). Due to the scope rules of Pascal this does not create any problems—in fact, this illustrates the transportability of procedures. Many of the procedures were written and tested separately before being put together to form the entire program.

Program Segment 17.11

```
PROCEDURE CLEARBOT;

     { CLEAR THE BOTTOM LINE OF TEXT }

   VAR
      XPOS : INTEGER;
```

```
        BEGIN
            GOTOXY(0,23);
            FOR XPOS := 0 TO 78 DO
                WRITE (' ');
            GOTOXY(0,23)
        END; { CLEARBOT }

PROCEDURE STCKDIS (COMPS:COMPANY; WEEK:INTEGER);

    VAR
        STOK : INTEGER;

    BEGIN
        PAGE(OUTPUT);
        WRITELN('NAME':20,'PRICE':10,'HIGH':9,'LOW':9,
                'YIELD':10,'DIV':9,'DIV DUE':12);
        FOR STOK := 1 TO NUMSTOCK DO
            WITH COMPS[STOK] DO
                BEGIN
                    WRITE(NAME:20,PRICE[WEEK]:10:2,PRICE[HIGH]:9:2);
                    WRITE(PRICE[LOW]:9:2,YIELD:10,LASTDIV:9:2);
                    WRITELN(DIVDUE[NEXTDIV]:9)
                END
    END; { STCKDIS }

PROCEDURE SCOREBOARD (COMPS:COMPANY; PLAYERS:PEOPLE;
                        WEEK:INTEGER);

    VAR
        PLA,
        STOK  : INTEGER;
        MONEY : REAL;
        KEY   : STRING;

    BEGIN
        STCKDIS(COMPS,WEEK);
        FOR PLA := 1 TO PNUM DO
            BEGIN
                MONEY := ASSETS(COMPS,PLAYERS[PLA],WEEK);
                WRITELN(PLAYERS[PLA].NAME,'   ',MONEY:15:2);
                MONEY := 0.0
            END; {PLA TO PNUM}
        READLN(KEY)
    END; { SCOREBOARD }

PROCEDURE FIGPRINT(COMPY:CMPNY; XPOS,DISPWK:INTEGER;
                    SCALE,SUB:REAL);

    VAR
        MIDDLE : REAL;
        YPOS   : INTEGER;

    BEGIN
        MIDDLE := COMPY.PRICE[COMPY.HIGH] - SUB/2;
        IF MIDDLE > COMPY.PRICE[DISPWK]
            THEN YPOS:=ROUND((MIDDLE-COMPY.PRICE[DISPWK])
                            /SCALE)
            ELSE YPOS:=ROUND((COMPY.PRICE[DISPWK]-MIDDLE)
                            /SCALE);
        GOTOXY(XPOS,YPOS + 6);
        IF DISPWK = COMPY.SPLITWK
            THEN WRITE('/')
            ELSE WRITE('*')
    END; { FIGPRINT }
```

```
PROCEDURE COMPINFO (COMPS:COMPANY; WEEK:INTEGER);

VAR
    DISPWK,
    XPOS,
    CNUM  : INTEGER;
    SUB,
    SCALE : REAL;
    COMPY : CMPNY;
    KEY   : STRING;

BEGIN
    CLEARBOT;
    WRITE('WHICH COMPANY DO YOU WANT TO LOOK AT?');
    READ(CNUM);
    COMPY := COMPS[CNUM];
    SUB := COMPY.PRICE[COMPY.HIGH] -
           COMPY.PRICE[COMPY.LOW];
    SCALE := SUB/10;
    PAGE(OUTPUT);
    WRITELN('NAME:',COMPY.NAME);
    WRITELN(COMPY.DESCRIPTION);
    FOR XPOS := 1 TO 10 DO
        BEGIN
            GOTOXY(XPOS*5,5);
            WRITE(XPOS*5)
        END;  { PRINT WEEKS ACROSS THE SCREEN }
    XPOS := 0;
    IF WEEK < 2
        THEN
            FOR DISPWK := 50 DOWNTO WEEK DO
                BEGIN
                    FIGPRINT(COMPY,XPOS,DISPWK,
                             SCALE,SUB);
                    XPOS := XPOS + 1
                END
        ELSE  { DISPLAY THE STOCK FLUCTUATIONS }
            BEGIN
                FOR DISPWK := WEEK - 1 DOWNTO 1 DO
                    BEGIN
                        FIGPRINT(COMPY,XPOS,DISPWK,
                                 SCALE,SUB);
                        XPOS := XPOS + 1
                    END; { PARTIAL PRINT OF INFO }
                FOR DISPWK := 50 DOWNTO WEEK DO
                    BEGIN
                        FIGPRINT(COMPY,XPOS,DISPWK,
                                 SCALE,SUB);
                        XPOS := XPOS + 1
                    END { COMPLETE PRINT OF INFO }
            END; { ELSE }
    GOTOXY(0,19);
    WRITELN('YIELD ',COMPY.YIELD:10:2);
    WRITELN('LAST DIVIDEND IN DOLLARS ',
            COMPY.LASTDIV:28:2);
    WRITELN('NEXT DIVIDEND DUE WEEK ',
            COMPY.DIVDUE[COMPY.NEXTDIV]);
    IF COMPY.SPLITWK <> 0
        THEN WRITELN('STOCK SPLIT IN WEEK',
                     COMPY.SPLITWK)
        ELSE WRITELN('STOCK NOT SPLIT IN A YEAR!');
    READLN(KEY)
END; { COMPINFO }
```

```
          PROCEDURE MENU(COMPS:COMPANY; PLAYER:PERSON;
                         WEEK:INTEGER; VAR OUTKEY:CHAR);

      VAR
          STOK:INTEGER;

      BEGIN
          PAGE(OUTPUT);
          WRITELN(PLAYER.NAME,' - YOUR TURN. WEEK',WEEK);
          WRITELN('NAME':21,'PRICE':8,'HIGH':7,'LOW':7,
                  'SHARES':11);
          FOR STOK := 1 TO NUMSTOCK DO
              WITH COMPS[STOK] DO
                  WRITELN(STOK,NAME:20,PRICE[WEEK]:8:2,
                          PRICE[HIGH]:7:2, PRICE[LOW]:7:2,
                          PLAYER.STOCKS[STOK]:11);
          WRITELN('YOU HAVE $',PLAYER.CASH:17:2);
          WRITE('YOU MAY B)UY OR S)ELL STOCKS.');
          WRITELN('L)OOK AT A COMPANY');
          WRITELN('E)ND TURN. C)HECK POINTS. X)IT GAME');
          READLN(OUTKEY)
      END; { MENU }

  PROCEDURE INITSTK(VAR COMPS:COMPANY);

      VAR
          COUNT:1..NUMSTOCK;

      BEGIN
          WITH COMPS[2] DO
              BEGIN
                  NAME := 'FOAM COLA';
                  DESCRIPTION := 'BEVERAGE MANUFACTURER';
                  LASTDIV := 0.25;
                  PRICE[1] := 23;
                  PRICE[2] := 23.5;
                  SEASON[4] := TRUE;
                  SEASON[5] := TRUE;
                  DIVDUE[1] := 10;
                  DIVDUE[2] := 23;
                  DIVDUE[3] := 36;
                  DIVDUE[4] := 48;
                  HIGH := 2;
                  LOW := 1;
                  NEXTDIV := 1
              END; { SET UP STOCK #2 }

          WITH COMPS[3] DO
              BEGIN
                  NAME := 'FIZZ BEVERAGES';
                  DESCRIPTION := 'BEVERAGE MANUFACTURER';
                  LASTDIV := 0.25;
                  PRICE[1] := 10;
                  PRICE[2] := 8.5;
                  SEASON[4] := TRUE;
                  SEASON[5] := TRUE;
                  DIVDUE[1] := 10;
                  DIVDUE[2] := 23;
                  DIVDUE[3] := 36;
                  DIVDUE[4] := 48;
                  HIGH := 1;
                  LOW := 2;
                  NEXTDIV := 1
              END; { SET UP STOCK #3 }
```

```
                    WITH COMPS[1] DO
                        BEGIN
                            NAME := 'MOMCO';
                            DESCRIPTION := 'WORLDWIDE CONGLOMERATE';
                            LASTDIV := 2.25;
                            PRICE[1] := 80;
                            PRICE[2] := 81.5;
                            SEASON[3] := TRUE;
                            SEASON[6] := TRUE;
                            DIVDUE[1] := 10;
                            DIVDUE[2] := 23;
                            DIVDUE[3] := 36;
                            DIVDUE[4] := 48;
                            HIGH := 2;
                            LOW := 1;
                            NEXTDIV := 1
                        END; { SET UP STOCK #1 }

                    WITH COMPS[4] DO
                        BEGIN
                            NAME := 'GERBIL MEDICINES';
                            DESCRIPTION := 'VETERINARY SUPPLIER';
                            LASTDIV := 1.25;
                            PRICE[1] := 35;
                            PRICE[2] := 34.5;
                            SEASON[3] := TRUE;
                            SEASON[4] := TRUE;
                            SEASON[5] := TRUE;
                            SEASON[6] := TRUE;
                            DIVDUE[1] := 10;
                            DIVDUE[2] := 23;
                            DIVDUE[3] := 36;
                            DIVDUE[4] := 48;
                            HIGH := 1;
                            LOW := 2;
                            NEXTDIV := 1
                        END; { SET UP STOCK #4 }

                    WITH COMPS[5] DO
                        BEGIN
                            NAME := 'ORECON';
                            DESCRIPTION := 'WORLDWIDE CONGLOMERATE';
                            LASTDIV := 2.00;
                            PRICE[1] := 50;
                            PRICE[2] := 51.5;
                            SEASON[3] := TRUE;
                            SEASON[6] := TRUE;
                            DIVDUE[1] := 10;
                            DIVDUE[2] := 23;
                            DIVDUE[3] := 36;
                            DIVDUE[4] := 48;
                            HIGH := 2;
                            LOW := 1;
                            NEXTDIV := 1
                        END; { SET UP STOCK #5 }
                    FOR COUNT := 1 TO NUMSTOCK DO
                        COMPS[COUNT].SPLITWK := 0
                END; { INITSTK }
```

```
PROCEDURE SETUPCOMPS(VAR FINCOMP:COMPANY);

    VAR
        COMPS : COMPANY;
        WEEK,
        STOK,
        TEMP  : INTEGER;

    BEGIN
        INITSTK(COMPS);
        FOR STOK := 1 TO NUMSTOCK DO
            BEGIN
                FOR WEEK := 3 TO 50 DO
                    COMPS[STOK].PRICE[WEEK] :=
                    NEWPRICE(COMPS[STOK],WEEK - 1);
                WITH COMPS[STOK] DO
                    BEGIN
                        TEMP := 1;
                        FOR WEEK := 1 TO 50 DO
                            IF PRICE[WEEK] > PRICE[TEMP]
                                THEN TEMP := WEEK;
                        HIGH := TEMP; {HIGH AFTER ONE YEAR}
                        FOR WEEK := 1 TO 50 DO
                            IF PRICE[WEEK] < PRICE[TEMP]
                                THEN TEMP := WEEK;
                        LOW := TEMP {LOW AFTER ONE YEAR}
                    END; { WITH COMPS[STOK] }
                COMPS[STOK].YIELD := COMPS[STOK].PRICE[1]/
                                     COMPS[STOK].LASTDIV
            END; { ONE STOCK IS SET UP }
        FINCOMP := COMPS
    END; { SETUPCOMPS }


PROCEDURE INITPPL(VAR FINPLAY:PEOPLE);

    VAR
        PLAYR,
        STOK    : INTEGER;
        PLAYERS : PEOPLE;
        KEY     : STRING;

    BEGIN
        READLN(KEY);
        FOR PLAYR := 1 TO PNUM DO
            WITH PLAYERS[PLAYR] DO
                BEGIN
                    FOR STOK := 1 TO NUMSTOCK DO
                        STOCKS[STOK] := 0;
                    PAGE(OUTPUT);
                    WRITE('PLAYER #',PLAYR,' NAME: ');
                    READLN(NAME);
                    CASH := 50000.0
                END; { ONE PLAYER }
        FINPLAY := PLAYERS
    END;  { INITPPL }
```

Summary

Linked lists (dynamic data structures) are an alternative to static structures such as arrays. Linked lists keep memory usage to a minimum and are especially useful in the place of **sparse arrays** (that is, arrays with thinly scattered elements). In addition, linked lists make maintaining an ordered list much easier and faster than arrays. Deletions and insertions are performed in a few simple steps.

The elements of a list are called nodes. Nodes are created by the command NEW and are joined (linked) by pointers. In a singly linked list, a pointer points to the front of the list and each node contains a pointer to the next node in the list. A new node is inserted into the list by using a linear search to find its appropriate position. A node may also be deleted in a similar manner. Deleting a node does not free the memory allocated to the node. Many versions of Pascal have a DISPOSE command to restore this wasted memory. If not, a procedure must be written to keep a separate linked list of available nodes. The nodes in this list can then be reused when a new node is needed.

Linked lists can contain more than one pointer in each node. This makes possible a doubly linked list, in which a pointer to the predecessor as well as the successor of a given node is maintained.

Stacks and queues can be implemented easily using linked lists. Stacks store elements in a last-in first-out (LIFO) fashion. A stack of dishes in a cupboard illustrates this method. A queue stores elements in a first-in first-out (FIFO) fashion. A line of people waiting to enter a movie theater is a real-world example of a queue.

Hashing is a method of storing data that allows for nearly immediate access to any element. Hashing can be accomplished by calculating the location in which to store an element from the binary representation of the element itself. Many hash functions exist, including extraction, compression, and division. A good hash function should use all of the bits in the element, be easy to calculate and minimize primary clustering. Regardless of the care taken in designing a hash function, collisions (two elements hashing to the same location) are inevitable. Collision resolution is providing a method to take care of these colliding elements. Linked lists can be used in collision resolution. In separate chaining, a linked list is created for each location calculated by the hash function. When a collision occurs, the colliding element is simply added to the list.

Key Terms

chaining	circular list	compression
chain of pointers	collision resolution	DISPOSE

division	NEW	push
doubly linked list	NIL	separate chaining
extraction	node	singly linked list
header	pointer	sparse array
linear probing	pop	static
linked list	primary clustering	

Answers to
Lesson Checks

Lesson 17.1

1. The NEW command is used to allocate the memory space for a node. NEW simply reserves the space in memory; it does not make any assignments to the node.

2. The predefined value NIL is used to initialize the pointer fields of a linked list. Without this initialization, the pointers would point to meaningless memory locations.

3. The notation PTR∧ refers to the node (a record of type SAMPLEREC) that is pointed to by the pointer PTR. Thus PTR∧ is a record while PTR points to the record.

4. A doubly linked list contains two pointers: one to the predecessor and one to the successor of the node. Applications that involve a lot of forward and backward movement through the list may be simplified by this structure. The disadvantage of this structure is that extra memory is required for the additional pointer field.

Lesson 17.2

1. A stack is a dynamic data structure in which the last element placed in the list is the first element to be removed (LIFO). An example of a stack is the entry and exit pattern of an elevator. In a queue, the first element placed in the list is the first to be removed (FIFO). An example of a queue is the entry and exit pattern of an escalator.

2. The PUSH procedure is used to place a new element onto the top of a stack. The POP procedure is used to remove the top element from the stack.

Lesson 17.3

1. Primary clustering occurs when several elements are given the same address by a hash function; that is, the frequent occurrence of two or more elements being sent to the same location.

2. The nature of the elements to be stored, the relative complexity of the hash function, the method for resolving collisions, and the capabilities of the computer being used are all points to consider when developing a hash function.

3. Linear probing refers to a linear search for the next available location in which to place a colliding element.

Exercises Set I. Comprehension

1. Write a type definition for the record BLOCK which contains a string (NAME), an integer (PHONE), and a pointer (FOLLOW) to the next node in the list.

2. Write a type definition for the record ATOM which contains a string (NAME), an integer (NUMBER), a real (WEIGHT), and two pointers (BEFORE, AFTER) which point to the previous and next nodes.

3. What is wrong with the following type definition?

```
TYPE
   R = RECORD
           FLAG : BOOLEAN;
           J    : INTEGER;
           P    : POINT
       END; { R }
   POINT = ^R;
```

4. What is wrong with the following type definition and declaration?

```
TYPE
   POINT1, POINT2 = ^LIST;
   L = RECORD
           NAME   : STRING;
           NUM    : INTEGER;
           FIRST  : POINT1;
           SECOND : POINT2
       END; { L }

VAR
   P1,
   P2   : POINT1;
```

Use the following to answer Exercises 5–12.

```
TYPE
   POINT = ^LIST;
   LIST = RECORD
             VARA : INTEGER;
             VARB : CHAR;
             NEXT : POINT
          END; { LIST }

VAR
   CURRENT : POINT;
```

5. Which of the following point(s) to a node of the linked structure?
   a. CURRENT^
   b. ^LIST
   c. CURRENT
   d. CURRENT^.NEXT
   e. CURRENT^.VARA
   f. CURRENT^.NEXT^
   g. CURRENT^.NEXT^.NEXT^
   h. CURRENT^.NEXT^.VARA

6. Which of the values from Exercise 5 represent(s) a record or field within a record? One of the values is both a pointer and a field. Identify the value and explain why this is so.

7. Is the following statement valid? Why or why not?

```
NEW(CURRENT^);
```

8. Is the following statement valid? Why or why not?

```
CURRENT := CURRENT^.NEXT;
```

9. Assume the list contains five nodes and CURRENT is pointing to the first node. Write a single statement to make the pointer field in the last node NIL.

10. Assume the list contains at least one node and CURRENT is pointing to the first node. Write the statements necessary to advance the pointer to the last node of the list (whose NEXT is NIL).

11. Suppose the following illustrates the status of a list of three elements:

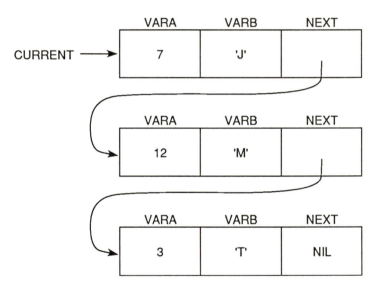

How would it be altered by the execution of this program segment? Assume a call of INCREMENT(CURRENT).

```
PROCEDURE INCREMENT (PTR : POINT);
   BEGIN
      PTR^.VARA := PTR^.VARA + 1;
      PTR^.VARB := SUCC(PTR^.VARB);
      PTR := PTR^.NEXT
   END;
```

12. Suppose the illustration from Exercise 11 is the status of a list of three elements. How would it be altered by the execution of the following segment? Assume a call of INCREMENT(CURRENT).

```
PROCEDURE INCREMENT (VAR PTR : POINT);
   BEGIN
      PTR := PTR^.NEXT;
      PTR^.VARA := PTR^.VARA + 2;
      PTR^.VARB := 'Z';
      PTR := PTR^.NEXT
   END;
```

13. Suppose there are three operations that can be performed, using only one stack and an output list (for storing final results).

    - MOVE the next input to the output list.
    - PUSH the next input onto the stack.
    - POP a value from the stack and move the value to the output list.

    Give each output list for an input list of 7, 4, 1, 3, and 2 using the operations in the following order:
    a. MOVE, PUSH, POP, PUSH, PUSH, POP, POP, MOVE
    b. MOVE, MOVE, MOVE, PUSH, POP, PUSH, POP
    c. PUSH, PUSH, PUSH, MOVE, POP, POP, POP, MOVE

14. Given the stack operations and input list from Exercise 13, which of the following is not a possible output list that could be achieved?
    a. 7 4 1 3 2
    b. 2 3 1 4 7
    c. 4 3 2 1 7
    d. 1 3 2 7 4
    e. 7 4 2 3 1

15. Determine the binary representation (as described in Lesson 17.3) for each of the following.
    a. BOX
    b. TO
    c. FAR
    d. RIDE

16. Determine the binary representation (as described in Lesson 17.3) for each of the following.
    a. FLY
    b. MOON
    c. AWAY
    d. HELLO

17. Using the extraction technique, determine the address for each of the words in Exercises 15 and 16.

18. Using the compression technique, determine the address for each of the words in Exercises 15 and 16.

19. Using the division technique, determine the address for each of the words in Exercise 15. (Use 31 as the divisor.)

20. Using the division technique, determine the address for each of the words in Exercise 16. (Use 17 as the divisor.)

21. Give two words that would produce a collision using the compression technique.

22. Give two words that would produce a collision using the extraction technique.

Set II. Application

23. Write a procedure to transfer a one-dimensional array of records to a linked list of records. Assume the array is in numeric order by ID number, and maintain this order in the linked list.

```
TYPE
   ARRYREC = RECORD
                  IDNUM : INTEGER;
                  NAME  : STRING;
                  SEX   : CHAR
             END; { ARRYREC }
   LISTPTR = ^LISTREC;
   LISTREC = RECORD
                  IDNUM : INTEGER;
                  NAME  : STRING;
                  SEX   : CHAR;
                  NEXT  : LISTPTR
             END; { LISTREC }
```

24. Revise the procedure for Exercise 23 to transfer an unordered array to a ordered linked list (by ID number).

25. Suppose a linked list contains the name and home address of persons invited to a large gathering. Write a function to count the number of people in the list. Assume a record type of REUNION, with a pointer (NEXT) to the next person in the list.

26. Suppose a program has been designed to monitor the list of people attending a presidential debate. Write the procedure to create a file of the attendants' names and political affiliation (Democrat, Republican, and so on). Use a doubly linked list to store the information and maintain the list in alphabetical order. Save the file as DEBATE_FILE. Assume the following record definition:

```
TYPE
   PERSON = ^PEOPLE;
   PEOPLE = RECORD
                  LASTNAME,
                  FIRSTNAME,
                  PARTY      : STRING;
                  ALPHA,
                  OMEGA      : PERSON
             END; { PEOPLE }

VAR
   CURRENTPERSON : PERSON;
```

27. Write a procedure to allow the postmaster to enter a city name and zip code for several cities into a linked list. Maintain the list in alphabetical order and save the information in a file named CITY_FILE. (Assume only one zip code per city.)

28. Write a procedure to read CITY_FILE from Exercise 27 into a linked list. Place the element of the list in numerical order by zip code and store again in a file, this one named ZIP_FILE. (Assume only one zip code per city.)

29. Mandi and Jeni have decided to drive to New York from the West Coast. They wanted to stop in different places, so each decided to take her own car. Each city that they passed through has been entered into a linked list for each woman. The lists have been maintained in alphabetical order. Write a procedure to compare the two lists (one may be longer than the other) and print the cities that both women drove through. Assume the following type definition:

```
TYPE
   DESTINATION = ^TRAVEL;
   TRAVEL = RECORD
              CITY     : STRING;
              NEXT     : DESTINATION
            END; { TRAVEL }
```

30. A high school needs a list of eligible football players that must be excused early on days of away games. Assume two alphabetized linked lists exist, one for all football players, and the other for all students ineligible for extracurricular activities. Write a procedure to compare the lists and produce a new alphabetized linked list of football players that are to be excused early. (If a student's name appears on both lists, then he is not to be excused.)

31. Using the list produced from Exercise 30, write a procedure to produce separate lists for each teacher. Assume a 30-element array contains pointers to a linked list of student names for each teacher. Compare the master list of football players to be excused early with each teacher's student list and create a new list for each teacher containing only those players from his or her own classes that are to be excused.

32. Suppose FIRSTLIST1 and SECONDLIST1 are pointers to the beginning of each of two linked lists. Write a procedure to remove a segment from the first list, up to and including the node pointed to by CURRENT, and put this segment onto the front of the second list. The order of the segment should be maintained.

Set III. Synthesis

33. Write a program to simulate the rotation pattern of a volleyball game. The players rotate to the next position at the beginning of their team's serve. Define a record consisting of the player's name, jersey number, and original position number (1–6). Use a circular list and allow the user to obtain a list of players and their original position numbers at any given point in the game. Also allow for player substitutions of any of the six positions.

34. Write a program to maintain an alphabetical list of student records. Store the information in a file named STUDENT_FILE. The information contained in the record must include student's name, ID number, class, and GPA. The program should include features enabling the user to

   ▪ Add a student.
   ▪ Delete a student.

- Print information for all students.
- Print information for one student.

Option: Develop a hash function for storing the student records.

35. Create a travel log program to be used to record daily information about a trip. This should include destination; miles traveled; and cost of gas, food, and lodging.

    Store the information in a file (TRIP_DATA) and provide the following options for maximum credit:

    - Add a new day to the log.
    - Insert a day.
    - Delete a day.
    - Print the entire trip by day-number.
    - Print a group of days.
    - Print one day by day-number.
    - Print one day by destination.

    Include error handling for bad input and give an option to route output to the printer.

36. A local television station is running a telephone survey on the air. They are requesting that people phone a particular number to vote yes on an issue and another number to vote no. The station wants to eliminate repeat callers so that the results will be as accurate a representation of the audience's feelings as possible. Each caller is asked to give his or her telephone number as a reference. Write a program to store the callers' phone numbers in order in one of two linked lists; that is, either the YES list or the NO list. The program should eliminate duplicate numbers and signal the user of any repeat callers. When the survey is complete, report the total YES votes and the total NO votes.

    Option: Maintain a third list for the duplicate callers so that the user can check this list first for troublemakers.

37. A convention center needs to maximize the use of its facilities. To make the task more efficient, the managers need a program to manipulate their files. The center keeps a record of the following:

    - room number.
    - room type (general purpose, stage/podium, dinner).
    - room capacity (number of chairs).
    - number of electrical outlets.
    - number of tables.
    - cost of one day.

    In addition to the physical aspects of the rooms, the center needs to monitor:

    - reserved dates (up to one year in advance). (Assume that each room is used by no more than one party per day.)
    - the nature of the reservation (for example, business meeting, concert, dinner, political debate, educational seminar).
    - number of security officers needed (if any).

Create a file for the room data. Allow the user to enter new reservations and alter existing reservations. Reservation dates should be maintained in chronological order in a linked list. Available printouts should include the following:

- information for a particular room (by number).
- rooms booked for a certain date.
- dates reserved for a particular room.
- list of room numbers with a particular minimum capacity.
- list of room numbers with a particular maximum cost.
- list of room numbers with a certain minimum number of electrical outlets.

Trees

"In that *direction*," the Cat said, waving its right paw round, "lives a Hatter: and in that *direction*," waving the other paw, "lives a March Hare. Visit either you like."

—Lewis Carroll

Overview

Trees
>   General Tree Structure
>   Terminology of Trees

Binary Trees
>   Traversing a Tree
>>   Postorder
>>   Preorder
>>   Inorder
>>   Level order

Binary Search Trees
>   Formation
>   Traversal

Programming Tip
>   Program Design
>>   Computation Procedures

Gaining a Perspective

A variety of data structures can be designed to fit a given situation. One example would be keeping track of the descendents of a particular individual. Figure 18.1 shows such a chart of family generations.

Representing such a structure in an array would certainly be possible. The representation would be cumbersome, however, and use more memory than necessary. (An array for the data in Figure

Figure 18.1 Chris's Direct Descendants

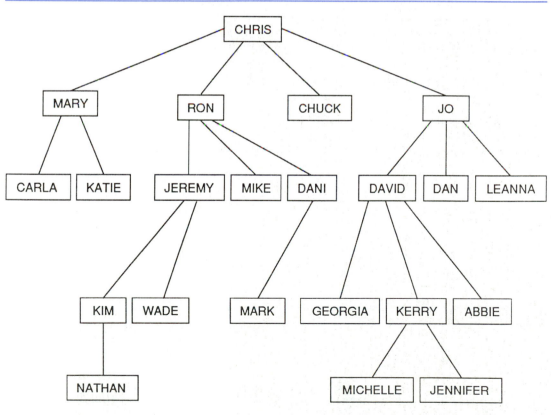

18.1 would require minimum dimensions of 5 rows × 256 columns (assuming space for four children per node), or 1280 locations, only 22 of which would be occupied.) This particular situation lends itself readily to a dynamic data structure. The name of each individual can be stored in a node along with as much information as is desired about the individual. In addition, pointers to all the offspring of an individual could be maintained. (As we saw in Chapter 17, dynamic data structures are not limited to one pointer per node.) A node might look like the one shown in Figure 18.2.

A structure such as that of Figure 18.1 is called a **tree**. The introduction of this data structure opens up various unique possibilities for representing and manipulating data.

Lesson 18.1   Trees

Figure 18.3 shows one convenient way of representing a tree structure. Terminology to describe the structure comes from its resemblance to an actual tree and family relationships. Circles are used to represent each node of the tree. The lines between nodes are referred to as **branches.** Arrows show which nodes are pointed to by a particular node.

The first node (A, in Figure 18.3) is called the **root.** Each node of the tree may or may not point to other nodes. The root is the **parent** of the nodes to which it points; these nodes are called its **children** (**siblings**). Each node, except the root, has a parent (predecessor) and may or may not have children (successors). The pointers between nodes are the branches. Each node can be thought

Figure 18.2
One Node of
Generation Chart

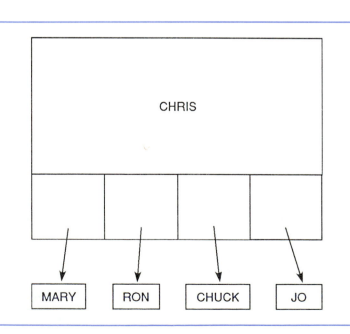

Figure 18.3

Representation of a Tree

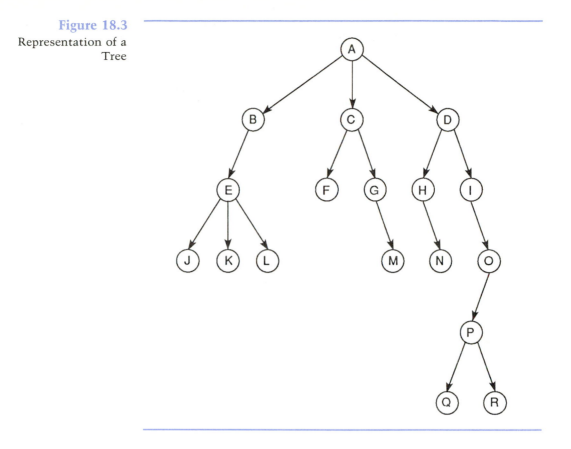

of as a root of its own **subtree** formed by the group of nodes below it. A node that has no children is called a **leaf** (F, J, K, L, M, N, Q, and R). The other nodes (non-leaves) are called **internal nodes.**

The tree structure allows for some interesting possibilities for data manipulation. While a simple linked list can grow and shrink in length, a tree structure accommodates data that expand in two directions—length and width. There are problems, however, with using an unrestricted tree structure; that is, one with an unlimited number of branches from each node. First, the maximum number of branches from a node would have to be determined in advance and memory reserved in each record for storing the pointers. (A record structure for the data in Figure 18.1 would require four pointer fields, even though all four are used together only once.) This is an inefficient use of memory. Second, manipulating the tree would be difficult. For example, searching the tree for a particular node would be messy at best, particularly for a tree whose nodes may contain three, four, five, or more branches each.

Manipulation of a tree structure can be greatly simplified by allowing no more than two pointers from each node. This means that at each node there are only two choices: go to the left or go to the right. Any tree structure can be converted to this binary representation, making it much easier to use. Thus, a general tree is said to have a **natural correspondence** to a binary tree. By rearranging the data in Figure 18.1, a slightly different view of the original tree structure can be given. (See Figure 18.4) Notice that members of the same generation are still given in each row; however, they are left-justified in the new diagram.

By rotating the diagram of Figure 18.4 45 degrees clockwise, a different tree structure is produced, as shown in Figure 18.5. This structure is arranged a little differently than the original generation tree, but the family relationships remain intact. The first child of a person is placed in the left branch, and a brother or sister of that person is placed on the right branch. Since no brothers or sisters were listed for Chris, his right branch is empty. His left branch points to his oldest child, Mary. Mary's right branch points to her brother, Ron, and her left branch points to her older child, Carla. The branches continue downward—to the right for members of the same generation and to the left for each new generation.

Lesson Check 18.1

1. In terms of trees, what is a parent?

2. What types of problems can occur using a tree structure with unlimited branches?

3. What is meant by natural correspondence?

Figure 18.4 Tabular Representation of Chris's Descendants

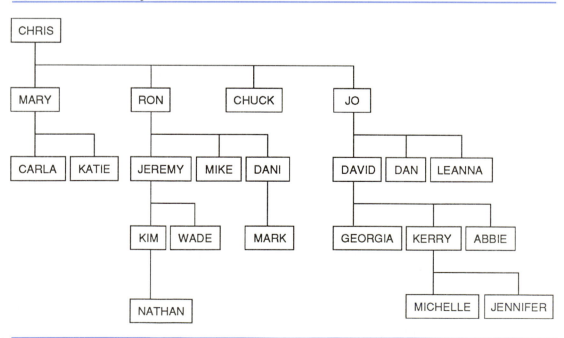

Figure 18.5 Binary Representation of Chris's Descendants

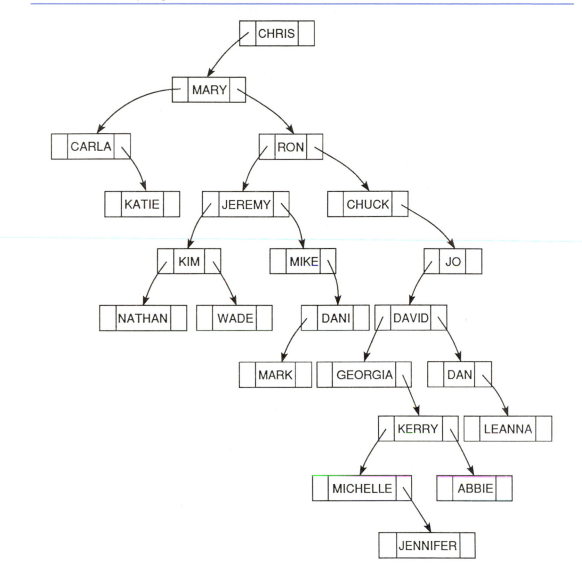

Lesson 18.2 **Binary Trees**

A **binary tree** has no more than two branches from each node, i.e. a left and a right child. Each node contains pointers to its children. Two examples of binary trees follow. Figure 18.6 is called an **extended binary tree.** In it, small boxes are added to the leaves to indicate empty subtrees (NIL pointers). An alternative form of drawing a binary tree is shown in Figure 18.7; in it, the NIL pointers are specified by slash marks within the boxes. Figure

Figure 18.6

Extended Binary Tree

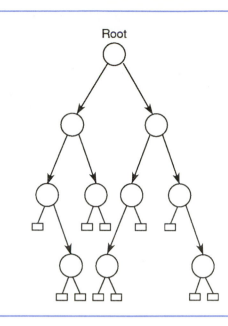

18.7 uses notation similar to that of linked lists, but may be less convenient than Figure 18.6.

Moving through a binary tree and performing a specific task (such as searching for an element) requires a systematic method. This is called traversing the tree (**traversal**) and can be accomplished in a number of ways. As will be seen, recursion lends itself nicely to this process.

One desired operation on a binary tree might be printing the contents of each node of the tree. Here is one set of steps that

Figure 18.7

Alternative Form of Binary Tree

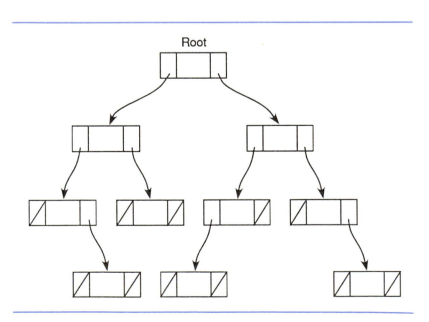

will traverse the tree and print a value (or values) stored in each node.

> **Printing a Binary Tree**
>
> 1. If the current node has a left child, then point to the left child and continue to traverse the tree.
> 2. If the current node has a right child, then point to the right child and continue to traverse the tree.
> 3. Otherwise, print the elements (or perform whatever operation is desired) in the current node.

Step 1 says to go left as long as there is a node to the left. Then, if no node is to the left, Step 2 says to go to the right. Step 3 occurs only after the left and right subtrees have been completely traversed. This is called a **postorder traversal,** since the operation on a given node occurs only after operating on (often called **visiting**) all the nodes below it. These steps can be reworded to correspond more closely to programming instructions. To perform a postorder traversal of a binary tree:

> 1. If the current node's left child is not NIL, then point at the left child and traverse again.
> 2. If the current node's right child is not NIL, then point at the right child and traverse again.
> 3. Otherwise, visit the node.

Figure 18.8 illustrates this technique for traversing a binary tree.

Figure 18.8
Postorder Traversal of a Binary Tree

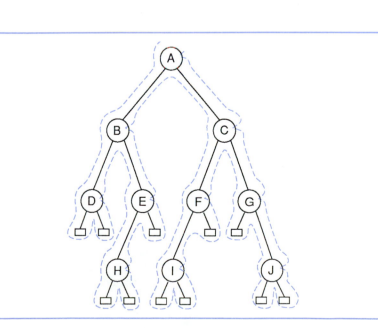

The order in which the nodes would be visited is also indicated. In a postorder traversal, nodes are visited only after going down both branches (subtrees) as far as possible. Notice that the node containing D is the first node visited, since it is the first node to have its left and right branches completely traversed. The next node visited contains H, followed by the node containing E, and so on. The dotted lines indicate the path of the traversal, with each node being visited after its left and right subtrees are traversed. Thus, the last node visited is the root (A).

Implementing this algorithm through recursion will allow backtracking without using backward pointers. Program Segment 18.1 prints the contents of a binary tree using a postorder traversal (sometimes called a **postorder search**).

Program Segment 18.1

```
PROCEDURE PRINTTREE(CURRENT : TREEPOINTER);

    { USE A POSTORDER SEARCH TO VISIT TREE NODES }

    BEGIN

        IF CURRENT^.LEFTCHILD <> NIL
            THEN
                PRINTTREE(CURRENT^.LEFTCHILD);
        IF CURRENT^.RIGHTCHILD <> NIL
            THEN
                PRINTTREE(CURRENT^.RIGHTCHILD);
        WRITELN(CURRENT^.DATA)

    END; { PRINTTREE }
```

In addition to printing the contents of a tree, a postorder search can represent the operation of a calculator. Figure 18.9 shows how arithmetic operations are performed using what is called postfix notation. A postorder search reveals the order of operation of these calculations:

$$A\ B\ C + * D\ E\ F / + -$$

In standard arithmetic notation this would be

$$A * (B + C) - D + E / F$$

Other traversals of a binary tree are possible. Each traversal has its own use depending on the desired order of visiting the nodes. Two that are directly related to the postorder search just discussed are outlined here. To perform a **preorder traversal** of a binary tree:

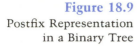

Postfix Representation
in a Binary Tree

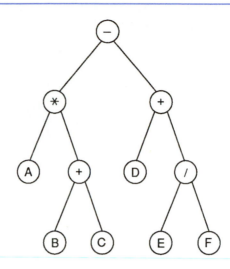

> 1. Visit the node.
> 2. If the left child is not NIL, then point to the left child and traverse again.
> 3. If the right child is not NIL, then point to the right child and traverse again.

To perform an **inorder traversal** of a binary tree:

> 1. If the left child is not NIL, then point to the left child and traverse again.
> 2. Visit the node.
> 3. If the right child is not NIL, then point to the right child and traverse again.

The preorder traversal visits a node before looking at its subtrees; the inorder method traverses the left subtree before visiting the node. One other traversal is worth mentioning here, although it won't be formally discussed. A **level order traversal** visits the nodes by generation (from top to bottom), giving still another way of examining the nodes of a binary tree.

An example may help clarify the differences among these traversing methods. Study the binary tree shown in Figure 18.10. The resulting order of node visits for each type of traversal is shown in the table following the figure.

Figure 18.10

A Binary Tree
Example

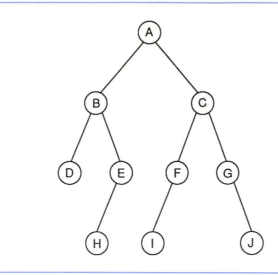

Traversal	Visiting Order
Postorder	D H E B I F J G C A
Preorder	A B D E H C F I G J
Inorder	D B H E A I F C G J
Level order	A B C D E F G H I J

An excellent application of binary trees is in decoding Morse code messages. (See Figure 18.11.) The nodes of the tree consist of the letters of the alphabet arranged according to their Morse code representation. The branches of the tree represent dots (left branch) and dashes (right branch). By moving down the tree to a letter and noting the path (dots and dashes) taken, the Morse code for the letter is obtained. (A Morse code problem is included in the exercises at the end of this chapter.)

Words can be encoded by locating each letter in the diagram of Figure 18.11 and writing down the symbols encountered in the search. For example, SOS is encoded by

$$\begin{array}{ccc} \text{S} & \text{O} & \text{S} \end{array}$$
$$\text{SOS} = \cdots / - - - / \cdots$$

and PASCAL is encoded by

$$\begin{array}{cccccc} \text{P} & \text{A} & \text{S} & \text{C} & \text{A} & \text{L} \end{array}$$
$$\text{PASCAL} = \cdot - - \cdot / \cdot - / \cdots / - \cdot - \cdot / \cdot - / \cdot - \cdot \cdot$$

The tree can also be used for decoding a message. By examining a series of dots and dashes, and traveling left when a dot is encountered or right when a dash is encountered, the path will lead to the appropriate letter. For example,

$$- / \cdots \cdot / \cdot / \cdot$$

Figure 18.11 Morse Code Representation in a Binary Tree

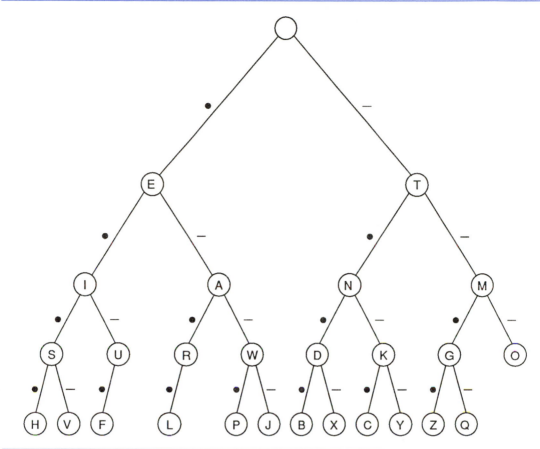

says to go right (T), go left-right-left (R), go left (E), and go left (E). Thus, the decoded message is TREE.

<table>
<tr><td>

*Lesson
Check
18.2*

</td><td>

1. Why is recursion an efficient technique for tree traversals?

2. From the Morse code tree in Figure 18.11, determine the codes for each of the following:
   a. G
   b. T
   c. CAT
   d. DOG
   e. FOX

3. Give the resulting order of visits for an inorder traversal of the Morse code tree.

</td></tr>
</table>

Lesson 18.3   Binary Search Trees

A **binary search tree** is a binary tree in which the inorder traversal of the tree gives the nodes in their natural order (for example, alphabetically). That is, for any node (*n*) in the tree, the element to *n*'s left precedes the element in *n* (through the natural order of the elements) and the element to *n*'s right is a successor of the element in *n*. Figure 18.12 illustrates a binary search tree for a group of letters. The inorder traversal of this tree yields

  A C D F J P R T U V Z

This is the **natural order** of the elements contained in the nodes of the tree.

  Binary search trees allow fast access to the elements, much like the binary search covered in Chapter 14. Alphabetic or numeric data is obviously the most common data to be stored in a binary tree; however, any data that have a natural order can fit into the scheme.

  Figure 18.13 illustrates how a binary search tree is formed when the following numbers are chosen:

  17 25 27 11 15 7 21 19 5 29 23 9

  The key to a binary search tree is in its formation. To build a binary tree, the first element entered would be designated as the root of the tree and the left and right pointers would be NIL. When a new element is entered, it is compared to the root element. If the new element comes before the root element in the natural order, then the new element belongs on the left subtree; otherwise, it belongs on the right subtree. Each new element is placed by comparing it to the elements in the appropriate subtree, moving left or right based on the natural order of the elements. Figure 18.14 shows the development of the binary search tree for the first five numbers.

  To traverse the tree in the natural order of the elements, an inorder traversal is performed. Program 18.2 contains two pro-

Figure 18.12
Binary Search Tree

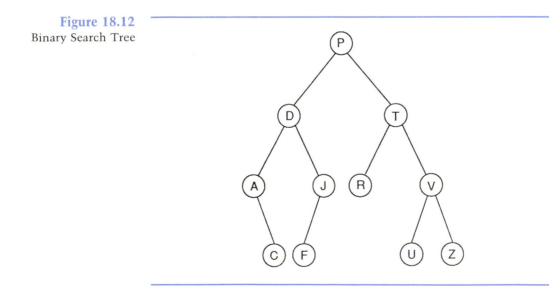

Figure 18.13
Formation of a Binary
Search Tree

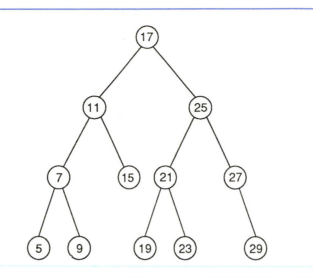

Figure 18.14
Building the Binary
Search Tree

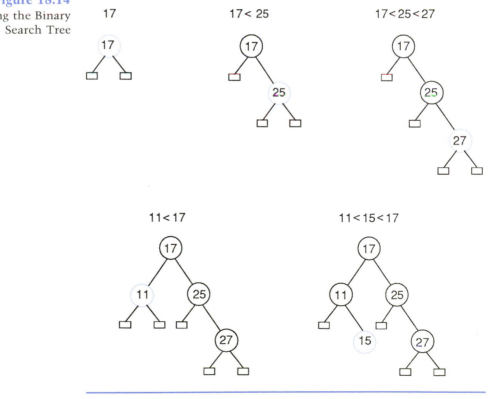

cedures for use with binary search trees. Procedure MAKETREE is used to build the tree as elements are added. A new element is placed in the root if the tree is empty; otherwise, MAKETREE is called recursively using either the left or right pointer (depending on where the new element belongs). Procedure TRAVERSETREE uses an inorder traversal to print the elements of the tree in their natural order.

Program 18.2

```
PROGRAM BINARYTREE(INPUT, OUTPUT);

    { BINARY SEARCH TREE }

TYPE TREEPTR = ^TREE;
     TREE     = RECORD

                    INFO  : INTEGER;
                    LEFT,
                    RIGHT : TREEPTR

                END; { TREE }

VAR
   ROOT  : TREEPTR;
   VALUE : INTEGER;

PROCEDURE MAKETREE(VAL : INTEGER; VAR PTR : TREEPTR);

    BEGIN

       IF PTR = NIL
          THEN
             BEGIN
                NEW(PTR);
                PTR^.INFO  := VAL;
                PTR^.LEFT  := NIL;
                PTR^.RIGHT := NIL
             END
          ELSE
             IF VAL < PTR^.INFO
                THEN
                   MAKETREE(VAL, PTR^.LEFT)
                ELSE
                   MAKETREE(VAL, PTR^.RIGHT)

    END; { MAKETREE }

PROCEDURE TRAVERSETREE(TEMP : TREEPTR);

    BEGIN

       IF TEMP <> NIL
          THEN
             BEGIN
                TRAVERSE(TEMP^.LEFT);
                WRITELN(TEMP^.INFO);
                TRAVERSE(TEMP^.RIGHT)
             END

    END; { TRAVERSETREE }
```

```
BEGIN { BINARYTREE }

    ROOT := NIL;
    WHILE VALUE <> 999 DO
        BEGIN
            WRITELN('ENTER A NUMBER (999 TO END)');
            READLN(VALUE);
            IF VALUE <> 999
                THEN
                    MAKETREE(VALUE,ROOT)
        END;
    WRITELN('THE ELEMENTS OF THE TREE ARE:');
    TRAVERSETREE(ROOT)

END.
```

Lesson Check 18.3

1. What is the difference between a binary tree and a binary search tree?

2. In the process of building a binary search tree for the following list, what would happen upon reaching the second occurrence of the letter G? What about the third occurrence?

    K R G U W B G I S J G E X

Lesson 18.4   Programming Tip—Program Design

A Detailed Look: Computation Procedures

One last aspect of our stock market program remains: the procedures for handling weekly transactions. These include calculating weekly changes (stock prices, dividends, and so on) and the buying and selling of stocks. These procedures are shown in Program Segment 18.3.

Program Segment 18.3

```
FUNCTION ASSETS (COMPYS:COMPANY; PLAYR:PERSON;
                        WEEK:INTEGER):REAL;

    VAR
        STOK : INTEGER;
        TEMP : REAL;

    BEGIN
        TEMP := 0;
        FOR STOK := 1 TO NUMSTOCK DO
            TEMP := TEMP + PLAYR.STOCKS[STOK] *
                    COMPYS[STOK].PRICE[WEEK];
        TEMP := TEMP + PLAYR.CASH;
        ASSETS := TEMP
    END; { ASSETS }

FUNCTION CHKSPLIT(COMPY:CMPNY; WEEK:INTEGER):BOOLEAN;

    VAR
        BASE : INTEGER;
        PERC : REAL;
```

```
            BEGIN
                WITH COMPY DO
                    BEGIN
                        BASE := 0;
                        IF WEEK < 50
                            THEN PERC := (PRICE[WEEK] -
                                        PRICE[WEEK+1])/PRICE[WEEK]
                            ELSE PERC := (PRICE[WEEK] -
                                        PRICE[1])/PRICE[WEEK];
                        IF PERC > 0.3
                            THEN BASE := BASE + 5;
                        IF PRICE[WEEK] > 100
                            THEN BASE := BASE + 10;
                        IF PRICE[WEEK] > 200
                            THEN BASE := BASE + 5
                    END; { BASE ADDITION }
                CHKSPLIT := (RANDOM MOD 101) < BASE;
                IF COMPY.SPLITWK <> 0
                    THEN CHKSPLIT := FALSE
        END; { CHKSPLIT }

    FUNCTION FIND (COMPY:CMPNY; HIGHLOW:BOOLEAN;
                    WEEK:INTEGER):INTEGER;
        VAR
            GUESS,
            TEMP  : INTEGER;

        BEGIN
            IF HIGHLOW
                THEN { FIND HIGH }
                    BEGIN
                        TEMP := COMPY.HIGH;
                        IF COMPY.HIGH = WEEK
                            THEN
                                BEGIN
                                    TEMP := COMPY.LOW;
                                    FOR GUESS := 1 TO 50 DO
                                        IF COMPY.PRICE[GUESS] >
                                            COMPY. PRICE[TEMP]
                                            THEN TEMP := GUESS
                                END { IF HIGH IS NOT OLD HIGH }
                            ELSE
                                IF COMPY.PRICE[WEEK] >=
                                    COMPY.PRICE[COMPY.HIGH]
                                    THEN TEMP := WEEK
                    END { FIND HIGH VALUE }
                ELSE { FIND LOW }
                    BEGIN
                        TEMP := COMPY.LOW;
                        IF COMPY.LOW = WEEK
                            THEN
                                BEGIN
                                    TEMP := COMPY.HIGH;
                                    FOR GUESS := 1 TO 50 DO
                                        IF COMPY.PRICE[GUESS] <
                                            COMPY.PRICE[TEMP]
                                            THEN TEMP := GUESS
                                END { OLD LOW CHANGES }
                            ELSE
                                IF COMPY.PRICE[WEEK] <=
                                    COMPY.PRICE[COMPY.LOW]
                                    THEN TEMP := WEEK
                    END; { FIND THE NEW LOW }
            FIND := TEMP
        END; { FIND }
```

```
FUNCTION NEWPRICE(COMPY:CMPNY; WEEK:INTEGER):REAL;

    VAR
        TIMEYR : INTEGER;
        BASE   : REAL;

    BEGIN
        TIMEYR := WEEK DIV 5;
        IF TIMEYR < 1
            THEN TIMEYR := 1;
        BASE := RANDOM MOD 8 - 4;
        WITH COMPY DO
            BEGIN
                IF SEASON[TIMEYR]
                    { IF GOOD SEASON }
                    THEN BASE := BASE + 0.5;
                IF (DIVDUE[NEXTDIV] - WEEK < 2) AND
                    (DIVDUE[NEXTDIV] - WEEK > 0)
                    { IF DIVIDEND DUE SOON }
                    THEN BASE := BASE + 0.7;
                IF (YIELD > 8) AND (YIELD < 10)
                    { IF YIELD IS GOOD }
                    THEN BASE := BASE + 0.2;
                IF PRICE[HIGH] - PRICE[WEEK] < 2
                    { IF NEARING 50 WEEK HIGH }
                    THEN BASE := BASE - 0.3;
                IF PRICE[WEEK] - PRICE[LOW] < 2
                    { IF NEARING 50 WEEK LOW }
                    THEN BASE := BASE + 0.5;
                IF WEEK = 1
                    THEN
                        IF ABS(PRICE[WEEK] -
                            PRICE[50]/PRICE[WEEK]) > 0.08
                            THEN BASE := BASE - 1
                            ELSE
                    ELSE
                        IF ABS(PRICE[WEEK] -
                            PRICE[WEEK-1])/PRICE[WEEK]>0.08
                            { IF BIG % GAIN }
                            THEN BASE := BASE - 1;
                IF PRICE[WEEK] < 15
                    THEN BASE := BASE * 1.2
                    { BIG CHANGE WITH SMALL PRICES }
            END; { WITH COMPY }
        NEWPRICE := COMPY.PRICE[WEEK] +
                    ((BASE/100) * COMPY.PRICE[WEEK])
    END; { NEWPRICE }

FUNCTION BROKFEES(COMPY:CMPNY; WEEK,NUMBER:INTEGER;
                  BUYSELL:BOOLEAN):REAL;
    VAR
        PERC,
        TEMP : REAL;

    BEGIN
        IF BUYSELL
            THEN PERC := 0.1  { BUYING IS 10% }
            ELSE PERC := 0.08;  { SELLING IS 8% }
        TEMP := PERC * NUMBER;
        BROKFEES := TEMP * COMPY.PRICE[WEEK]
    END; { BROKFEES }
```

```
FUNCTION DIVIDEND(COMPY:CMPNY):REAL;

    VAR
        PRICECH : REAL;
        BASE    : INTEGER;

    BEGIN
        PRICECH:=COMPY.PRICE[WEEK]-COMPY.PRICE[WEEK+1];
        BASE := 1;
        IF (PRICECH > 0) AND
           (PRICECH/COMPY.PRICE[WEEK] < 0.1)
           THEN BASE := 3;
        IF (PRICECH > 0) AND
           (PRICECH/COMPY.PRICE[WEEK] < 0.05)
           THEN BASE := 7;
        BASE := BASE + RANDOM MOD 9;
        DIVIDEND := (BASE/100) * COMPY.PRICE[WEEK]/4
    END; { DIVIDEND }

PROCEDURE BUY(COMPS:COMPANY; PLAYER:PERSON;
             WEEK:INTEGER; VAR OWNER:PERSON);

    VAR
        XPOS,
        STOK,
        NUMBER : INTEGER;
        COST   : REAL;
        ERROR  : STRING;

    BEGIN
        CLEARBOT;
        WRITE('ENTER THE STOCK NUMBER YOU WISH TO BUY:');
        READ(STOK);
        CLEARBOT;
        WRITE(COMPS[STOK].NAME,' COSTS ',
              COMPS[STOK].PRICE[WEEK]:5:2,
              '. HOW MANY DO YOU WANT?');
        READ(NUMBER);
        COST := NUMBER * COMPS[STOK].PRICE[WEEK] +
                BROKFEES(COMPS[STOK],WEEK,NUMBER,TRUE);
        IF PLAYER.CASH - COST > 0
           THEN { PURCHASE IS GOOD }
               BEGIN
                   PLAYER.CASH := PLAYER.CASH - COST;
                   PLAYER.STOCKS[STOK] :=
                       PLAYER.STOCKS[STOK] + NUMBER
               END
           ELSE { NOT ENOUGH CASH }
               BEGIN
                   CLEARBOT;
                   WRITE('INSUFFICIENT FUNDS. YOU ARE ',
                         COST - PLAYER.CASH,
                         ' DOLLARS SHORT.');
                   READLN(ERROR)
               END;
        OWNER := PLAYER
    END; { BUY }
```

```
PROCEDURE SELL(COMPS:COMPANY; PLAYER:PERSON;
               WEEK:INTEGER; VAR FINPLAY:PERSON);

    VAR
        INNUM,
        SOLD  : INTEGER;
        ERROR : STRING;

    BEGIN
        CLEARBOT;
        WRITE('WHICK STOCK DO YOU WANT TO SELL?');
        READ(INNUM);
        IF INNUM > NUMSTOCK
            THEN INNUM := NUMSTOCK;
        CLEARBOT;
        WRITE('YOU OWN ',PLAYER.STOCKS[INNUM]);
        WRITE(' SHARES. SELL HOW MANY?');
        READLN(SOLD);
        IF SOLD > PLAYER.STOCKS[INNUM]
            THEN { UNABLE TO SELL NUMBER OF SHARES }
                BEGIN
                    CLEARBOT;
                    WRITE('SELLING TOO MANY SHARES.');
                    READLN(ERROR)
                END
            ELSE { SELL SHARES }
                BEGIN
                    PLAYER.STOCKS[INNUM] :=
                    PLAYER.STOCKS[INNUM] - SOLD;
                    PLAYER.CASH := PLAYER.CASH + SOLD *
                    COMPS[INNUM].PRICE[WEEK] -
                    BROKFEES(COMPS[INNUM],WEEK,SOLD,FALSE)
                END;
        FINPLAY := PLAYER
    END;  { SELL }

PROCEDURE WKCHANGE(COMPS:COMPANY; PLAYERS:PEOPLE;
                   WEEK:INTEGER; VAR FINCOMPS:COMPANY;
                   VAR FINPLAY:PEOPLE);

    VAR
        STOK,
        PLANUM : INTEGER;
        DIVID  : REAL;
        KEY    : STRING;

    BEGIN
        FOR STOK := 1 TO NUMSTOCK DO
            BEGIN
                IF WEEK = 1
                    THEN COMPS[STOK].PRICE[WEEK] :=
                            NEWPRICE(COMPS[STOK],50)
                    ELSE COMPS[STOK].PRICE[WEEK] :=
                            NEWPRICE(COMPS[STOK],WEEK-1);
                IF WEEK = COMPS[STOK].SPLITWK
                    THEN COMPS[STOK].SPLITWK := 0;
```

```
                    IF CHKSPLIT(COMPS[STOK],WEEK)
                       { CHECK FOR SPLIT }
                       THEN
                          BEGIN
                             FOR PLANUM := 1 TO PNUM DO
                                PLAYERS[PLANUM].STOCKS[STOK]:=
                                PLAYERS[PLANUM].STOCKS[STOK]*2;
                             COMPS[STOK].PRICE[WEEK] :=
                                COMPS[STOK].PRICE[WEEK]/2;
                             COMPS[STOK].SPLITWK := WEEK
                          END;
                    IF COMPS[STOK].DIVDUE[COMPS[STOK].NEXTDIV]
                       = WEEK
                       THEN     { CHECK FOR DIVIDEND }
                          BEGIN
                             DIVID := DIVIDEND(COMPS[STOK]);
                             FOR PLANUM := 1 TO PNUM DO
                                PLAYERS[PLANUM].CASH :=
                                PLAYERS[PLANUM].CASH + (DIVID*
                                PLAYERS[PLANUM].STOCKS[STOK]);
                             COMPS[STOK].LASTDIV := DIVID;
                             IF COMPS[STOK].NEXTDIV + 1 > 4
                                THEN COMPS[STOK].NEXTDIV := 1
                                ELSE COMPS[STOK].NEXTDIV :=
                                   COMPS[STOK].NEXTDIV + 1
                          END;
                    COMPS[STOK].HIGH :=
                       FIND(COMPS[STOK],TRUE,WEEK);
                    COMPS[STOK].LOW :=
                       FIND(COMPS[STOK],FALSE,WEEK);
                    COMPS[STOK].YIELD :=
                       (COMPS[STOK].LASTDIV/
                       COMPS[STOK].PRICE[WEEK]) * 100;
                    IF WEEK = COMPS[STOK].SPLITWK
                       THEN WRITELN(COMPS[STOK].NAME,
                                      ' HAS SPLIT THIS WEEK.')
                 END; { OF THIS STOCK }
              WRITELN('PRESS ANY KEY TO CONTINUE.');
              READLN(KEY);
              FINCOMPS := COMPS;
              FINPLAY := PLAYERS
        END; { WKCHANGE }
```

Summary

Since records can contain more than one pointer, dynamic data
structures other than singly linked lists are possible. In particular,
tree structures present a new approach to representing data. The
first node of a tree is called the root. Pointers from a node point
to the node's children and are called branches. A node with no

children is called a leaf. A tree that allows only two pointers (a left pointer and a right pointer) from each node is known as a binary tree.

A binary tree allows for systematic manipulation of the data stored in its nodes. Traversing a tree refers to moving through the tree and visiting each node. The order that the nodes are visited depends on the type of traversal used (such as preorder, inorder, or postorder). Recursion makes the traversal procedure compact and easy to implement.

Binary search trees are used to speed up locating elements in a tree. The inorder traversal of a binary search tree yields a pattern for accessing the nodes in the natural order of the elements (usually alphabetic or numeric).

Key Terms

binary search tree
binary tree
branches
children
extended binary tree
inorder traversal
internal node

leaf
level order traversal
natural correspondence
natural order
parent
postorder search

postorder traversal
preorder traversal
root
siblings
subtree
traversal
tree
visiting the node

Answers to Lesson Checks

Lesson 18.1

1. A parent is the node that precedes a given node; that is, a node is a parent of its left and right children.

2. A tree structure with three, four, or more branches from any one node would likely result in inefficient use of memory. The maximum number of branches would need to be reserved, even though they may not be needed for a majority of the nodes. Also, manipulating the structure would be cumbersome.

3. The binary tree representation of a general tree is its natural correspondence.

Lesson 18.2

1. Recursion is an efficient method for tree traversals because with it, there is no need to maintain pointers to backtrack through the tree when the end of a subtree has been reached.

2. a. - - ·
   b. -
   c. - - - · / · - / -
   d. - · · / - - - / - - ·
   e. · · - · / - - - / - · · -

3. H S V I F U E L R A P W J B D X N C K Y T Z G Q M O

                              ↑
                             Root

Lesson 18.3

1. A binary tree is a tree with no more than two branches from each node. A binary search tree is a binary tree whose elements are given in their natural order through an inorder traversal.

2. The second G is placed to the right of the first G in the tree, since G is not less than itself. When the third G is encountered, an element (I) has already been placed to the immediate right of the second G, so the third G is placed to the left of I (since G comes before I).

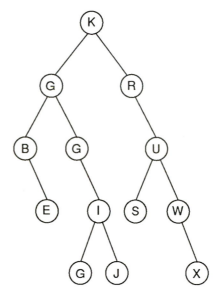

Exercises   Set I. Comprehension

Use the following general tree structure to answer Exercises 1–6.

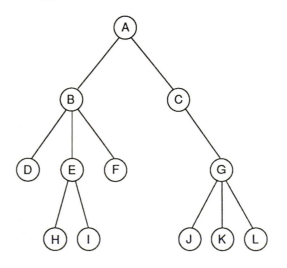

1. The relationship of one node to another is often described using the terminology of lineal charts, or family trees. Describe a cousin and list all the sets of cousins in the tree.

2. Describe an aunt or uncle and list all the aunts or uncles in the tree.

3. Describe the makeup of a node of this tree. How many pointer fields would be needed for the record for each node?

4. What would be the dimensions of an array used to hold the tree information? Would the array be more than 50 percent full?

5. List all the internal nodes of the tree.

6. Redraw the general tree structure as a binary tree.

Use the following binary tree structure to answer Exercises 7–9. Assume that each time a node is visited, its letter is printed.

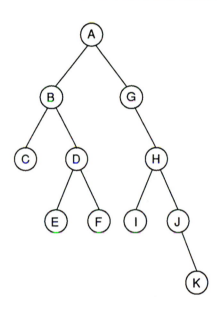

7. Give the result of a postorder traversal of the tree.

8. Give the result of a preorder traversal of the tree.

9. Give the result of an inorder traversal of the tree.

Use the binary tree structure on the following page to answer Exercises 10–12. Assume that each time a node is visited, its letter is printed.

10. Give the result of a postorder traversal of the tree.

11. Give the result of a preorder traversal of the tree.

12. Give the result of an inorder traversal of the tree.

(Binary tree structure for Exercises 10–12).

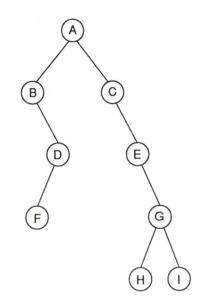

13. Draw a diagram for each binary tree that can be produced with exactly three nodes: A, B, and C. Do not draw diagrams that can be produced by a permutation of the labels A, B, and C. For example, for two nodes—A and B—the possible trees (without permutations) are

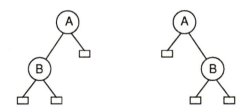

14. Draw a diagram for each binary tree that can be produced with exactly four nodes: A, B, C, and D. Do not draw diagrams that can be produced by a permutation of the labels A, B, C, and D.

15. Draw a binary tree representation of the following expression, as in Figure 18.9.

    $3 + J / 9 - 4 * K$

    A postorder traversal of the tree should yield

    $3 J 9 / + 4 K * -$

16. Draw a binary tree representation of the following expression, as in Figure 18.9.

    $R / (7 - T) + (P + 2) * 4$

    A postorder traversal of the tree should yield

    $R 7 T - / P 2 + 4 * +$

17. Produce a binary search tree for the following input:

    G F A Z K M R

18. Produce a binary search tree for the following input:

    17 43 41 18 2 16 1 8 29

19. Produce a binary search tree for the following words.

    THE QUICK BROWN FOX JUMPED OVER THE LAZY DOG

20. Produce a binary search tree for the following words.

    NOW IS THE TIME FOR ALL GOOD MEN TO COME TO
    THE AID OF THEIR COUNTRY

Set II. Application

21. Write a procedure to perform a preorder traversal of a binary tree.

22. Write a Morse code decoding program as described in Lesson 18.2.
    The program should accept (from the user or a data file) a message
    in Morse code comprised of dots (·) and dashes (−) with words
    separated by a space. It should return the decoded message
    retrieved from a binary tree.

Set III. Synthesis

23. The Animals Game is a two-player game in which one player
    thinks of an animal and the second player tries to guess it. The
    second player is allowed to ask questions concerning the animal;
    however, the questions can only be answered yes or no. The
    second player can continue to ask questions until he or she is able
    to guess the animal or gives up. Write a program to have the
    computer play the Animals Game and "learn" new animals as it
    plays. Use a binary tree to store the animals that the program
    knows. Each node of the tree should contain a question which
    determines the branch, left or right (yes or no), to travel. The
    program should ask the user questions until it has only one guess
    for the animal. If the guess is wrong, the program should ask for
    the name of the animal and a question that will distinguish it
    from the incorrectly guessed animal. (The question should be
    worded so that for the incorrect animal, the answer would be yes,
    and for the new animal, the answer would be no.) A node should
    then be created in the appropriate spot in the tree to store the new
    animal. Files will enhance the program a great deal by allowing
    the program to remember what it has learned from each user. The
    record for a node should consist of

```
MESSAGE : STRING;
CODE    : (QUESTION,ANSWER);
LEFTYES,
RIGHTNO : ANIMALPTR;
```

    The message will be either a question or an answer (hence CODE).
    An answer will be bumped ahead to a new node and replaced by a
    question whenever the answer is incorrect. The trees on the
    following page give an idea of how the tree may progress. (Note:
    The tree must start out with a question and two answers.)

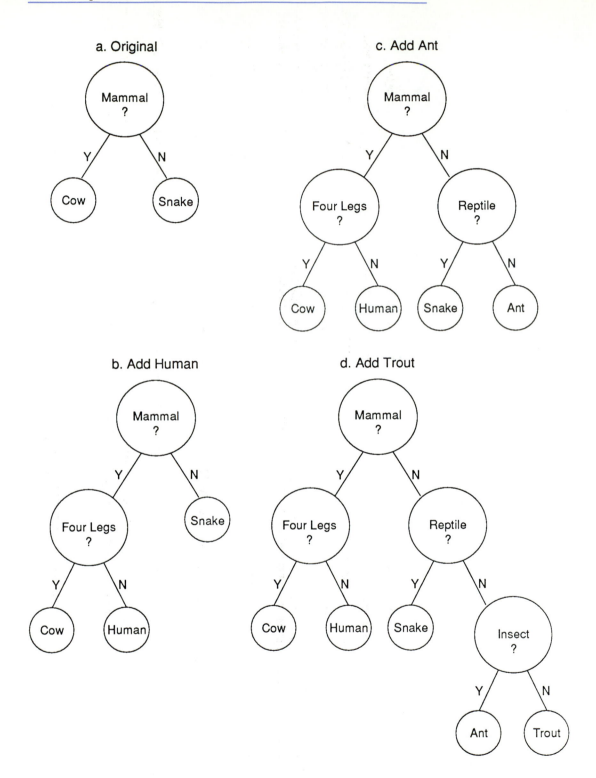

a. Original

b. Add Human

c. Add Ant

d. Add Trout

24. Write a program to store the members of some group (for instance, a club, or class) in a binary search tree by last name. The node should contain several pertinent pieces of data about each individual. The program should allow for the following options:

    - Add an individual to the tree.
    - Print a specified individual.
    - Print all of the names in alphabetic order.

    Other options can be added. A file can be used to retrieve previous information and store new information.

25. Design an algorithm for a level order traversal. Write the procedure.

26. Using the level order traversal from Exercise 25, write a procedure to print a binary tree. For example, the tree from Exercises 10–12 would be printed as

    ```
    A
    B  C
    -  D  -  E
    -  -  F  -  -  -  -  G
    -  -  -  -  -  -  -  -  -  -  -  -  -  -  H  I
    ```

    Each dash represents a NIL pointer.

    Option: Devise a method of printing the tree in a tree-like picture.

27. Write a program to determine the level of a particular node of a binary tree. If the search element is contained in the root, the level would be 0. In the following example, the level of the node containing J is 2:

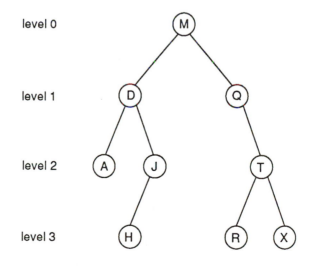

    To test the program, first create an unordered file of integers, and then assemble the binary search tree within the program. The program should print the unordered file, the ordered list, the search element (that is, the integer to be searched for), and the level of the node containing that element.

28. Write a program to determine the height of a binary tree; that is, the maximum level of nodes from the root. For example, the height of the following tree is 5:

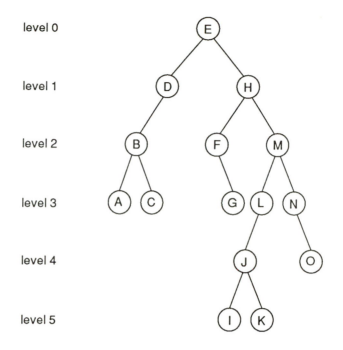

level 0

level 1

level 2

level 3

level 4

level 5

To test the program, first create an unordered file of integers (or use the file from Exercise 27), and then assemble the binary search tree within the program. The program should print the unordered file, the ordered list, and the height of the tree.

29. Suppose a binary search tree of characters has been created which is very unbalanced, as in Example **a**. This can happen when the first element in a list or file is not an appropriate partitioning element (see Chapter 14), or when the list is already semiordered. A search for the node T would require 10 visits. For a list of 20 elements or fewer, 10 visits is very inefficient. A more balanced tree, such as Example **b**, would require only 5 visits to find T. By observing where the median value of a list is located in a tree, an idea of the tree's balance may be given.

    Write a program to find the midpoint of a tree; that is, the median value of its nodes. (The median can be determined as the values are read into the first tree.) Create a new tree with this median as the root. Test the program on the following data:

    3 45 47 35 28 1 6 5 12 49 63 52 67 74 76 89

The program should report the number of elements and the level of the median value. To assure that the balanced tree can be re-created, use a preorder traversal when saving the elements to a file.

a.

b.

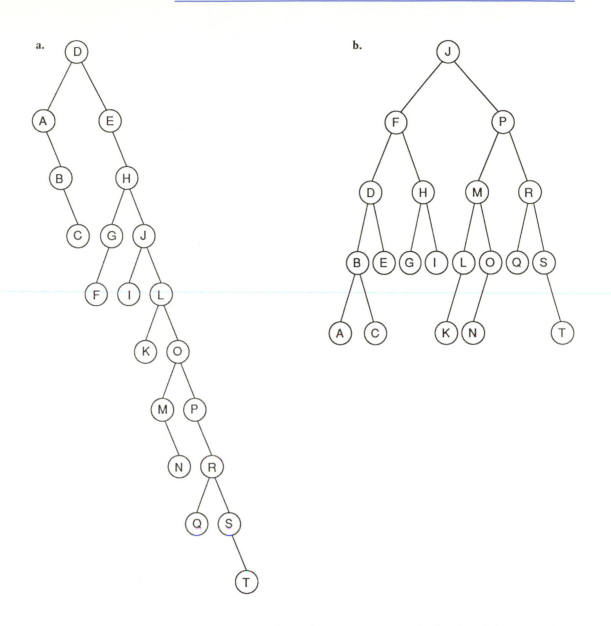

Option: Also have the program report the height of the original tree and the height of the new tree (see Exercise 28).

Extension: Apply the method used for balancing the tree to each of its subtrees. Recursion may simplify this problem.

19 Strings

The Fish-Footman began by producing from under his arm a great letter . . . saying, in a solemn tone, "For the Duchess. An invitation from the Queen to play croquet." The Frog-Footman repeated, in the same solemn tone, only changing the order of the words a little, "From the Queen. An invitation for the Duchess to play croquet."

—Lewis Carroll

Overview

Gaining a Perspective

In Chapter 2, STRING was defined as a data type consisting of a series of characters. STRING variables represent a nonstandard data type; that is, a data type not available in Standard Pascal. In Chapter 13, a packed array of CHAR was introduced as a substitute for STRING. For example, according to the following type definition and variable declaration, the identifier WORD can be assigned a sequence of characters:

```
TYPE
    STRG = PACKED ARRAY[0..80] OF CHAR;

VAR
    WORD : STRG;
```

This definition and declaration is appropriate in Standard Pascal; most Pascal versions, including UCSD, have other options available.

Besides the variable type STRING, there are also special string functions and procedures that allow easy manipulation of strings. For example, numeric data entered from the keyboard as a STRING value can be converted to an INTEGER or REAL value. Thus, the user can enter a dollar amount with the dollar sign, which can then be removed before the string is converted. String functions can also be useful for checking spelling, changing characters to lower- or uppercase, and removing punctuation or spaces in a phrase.

Lesson 19.1 String Functions and Procedures

A variety of built-in functions and procedures are available in UCSD Pascal to manipulate string variables and constants.

The **LENGTH** function finds the number of characters in a given string.

> **LENGTH Form**
>
> `LENGTH(strg)`

The argument *strg* represents a string variable, string constant, or a literal string (string of characters in single quotation marks). The LENGTH function returns a nonnegative integer.

The following program statements illustrate some uses of the LENGTH function. Assume that the variable ALPHA has been declared of type STRING.

```
ALPHA := 'ABCDEFGHIJK';
WRITELN(LENGTH(ALPHA));
WRITELN(LENGTH('HELLO'));
WRITELN(LENGTH(''));
```

The execution of these statements would result in the following integers printed on the screen:

```
11
5
0
```

There are 11 characters in the string ABCDEFGHIJK, 5 characters in HELLO, and 0 characters within the quotation marks (a **null string**).

Program 19.1 uses LENGTH to determine the number of letters in a string entered by the user.

Program 19.1

```
PROGRAM WORDLENGTH(INPUT, OUTPUT);

      { PURPOSE: DEMONSTRATE LENGTH FUNCTION }

VAR
   WORD : STRING;

BEGIN

   WRITE('ENTER A WORD OR PHRASE: ');
   READLN(WORD);
   WRITELN('THE LENGTH OF ',WORD,' IS ',
         LENGTH(WORD),'.')

END.
```

Sample Output

```
ENTER A WORD OR PHRASE: BLAISE PASCAL
THE LENGTH OF BLAISE PASCAL IS 13.
```

The space in the name BLAISE PASCAL is part of the string, and thus included in determining the length.

The **COPY** function returns a portion of a string variable or constant.

COPY Form

```
COPY(strg,start,count)
```

Again, *strg* represents a string variable, string constant, or literal string. The value *start* represents a nonnegative integer corresponding to the position of the first character to be copied, and *count* is a nonnegative integer representing the number of characters to be copied. The function returns the portion of *strg* starting at the character in the *start* position and copying *count* number of characters.

The following example uses the COPY function to copy part of a message. Assume that the variables QUOTE and PARTQUOTE were declared of type STRING.

```
QUOTE := 'WHATEVER IS GOOD';
PARTQUOTE := COPY(QUOTE, 13, 4);
WRITELN(PARTQUOTE);
```

Execution of these statements will print GOOD on the screen. (Copying four characters, beginning with the 13th character (G), results in 'GOOD' being assigned to PARTQUOTE.)

Program 19.2 uses LENGTH and COPY to print a pattern with a word selected by the user.

Program 19.2
```
PROGRAM PATTERN(INPUT, OUTPUT);

VAR
    WORD  : STRING;
    COUNT : INTEGER;

BEGIN

    WRITE('ENTER A WORD: ');
    READLN(WORD);
    FOR COUNT := 1 TO LENGTH(WORD) DO
        WRITELN(COPY(WORD, 1, COUNT))

END.
```

Suppose the user entered the word PASCAL. The following would be printed on the screen:

```
P
PA
PAS
PASC
PASCA
PASCAL
```

In Program 19.2, COUNT is 1 the first time through the loop. Starting in position 1, the first character of the word is printed. The next time COUNT is 2, so the first two characters are printed. This process continues, so that the sixth time through the loop, PASCAL is printed.

Program 19.3 uses LENGTH and COPY to detect palindromes. A palindrome is a word or phrase that is spelled the same way forward and backward. Program 19.3 allows a word to be entered by the user and then finds the length of the word. Next, the program compares the first letter, FIRST, to the last letter, LAST. Then the second letter is compared to the second-to-last letter, and so on. If the corresponding letters are not the same, VALID becomes FALSE and the program indicates that the word is not a palindrome. If a word is spelled the same way forward and backward, VALID remains TRUE and a message will be printed stating that the word is a palindrome.

Program 19.3

```
PROGRAM PALINDROME(INPUT, OUTPUT);

    { PURPOSE: DETERMINE IF A WORD IS A PALINDROME }

VAR
    WORD,
    FIRST,
    LAST     : STRING;
    FINAL,
    LEN,
    POSITION : INTEGER;
    VALID    : BOOLEAN;

BEGIN

    WRITE('ENTER A WORD: ');
    READLN(WORD);
    LEN := LENGTH(WORD);
    FINAL := LEN DIV 2;
    VALID := TRUE;
    POSITION := 1;
    WHILE (POSITION <= FINAL) AND VALID DO
        BEGIN
            FIRST := COPY(WORD, POSITION, 1);
            LAST := COPY(WORD, LEN - POSITION + 1, 1);
            IF FIRST <> LAST
                THEN VALID := FALSE;
            POSITION := POSITION + 1
        END;  { WHILE }
    IF VALID
        THEN WRITELN(WORD,' IS A PALINDROME.')
        ELSE WRITELN(WORD,' IS NOT A PALINDROME.')

END.
```

Two sample runs of Program 19.3 are as follows:

```
ENTER A WORD OR PHRASE: MOM
MOM IS A PALINDROME.

ENTER A WORD OR PHRASE: PAPA
PAPA IS NOT A PALINDROME.
```

CONCAT is a function that concatenates strings (puts strings together).

CONCAT Form

```
CONCAT(s1,s2,...,sn)
```

The arguments, *s1, s2,* through *sn,* represent strings (variable, constant, or literal), each separated by a comma. For example,

```
ONE := 'TO BE';
TWO := ' OR NOT ';
PHRASE := CONCAT(ONE,',',TWO,ONE,
                 ' -- THAT IS THE QUESTION.');
WRITELN(PHRASE);
```

These program statements will print the following phrase:

```
TO BE, OR NOT TO BE -- THAT IS THE QUESTION.
```

Of course, the string variable PHRASE must be declared a minimum length of 44 characters to accommodate each letter of this phrase. (Recall that a string variable can be declared with or without specifying the length. If the length is not specified, the string variable has space for 80 characters.) **Caution:** Care must be taken to insure that the string value returned is not longer than the declared length of the string variable.

Program 19.4 uses both COPY and CONCAT to print a desired set of initials. COPY obtains the first letter of each name and CONCAT puts these letters together. The result is stored in the variable INITIALS.

Program 19.4

```
PROGRAM ABBREVIATE(INPUT, OUTPUT);

    { PURPOSE: USE CONCAT AND COPY TO FIND INITIALS }

VAR
    FIRST,
    MIDDLE,
    LAST,
    INITIALS : STRING;

BEGIN

    WRITE('ENTER FIRST NAME: ');
    READLN(FIRST);
    WRITE('ENTER MIDDLE NAME: ');
    READLN(MIDDLE);
    WRITE('ENTER LAST NAME: ');
    READLN(LAST);
    INITIALS := CONCAT(COPY(FIRST,1,1),
                       COPY(MIDDLE,1,1),
                       COPY(LAST,1,1));
    WRITE('THE INITIALS ARE: ');
    WRITELN(INITIALS)

END.
```

Sample Output

```
ENTER FIRST NAME: JOHN
ENTER MIDDLE NAME: PAUL
ENTER LAST NAME: JONES
THE INITIALS ARE: JPJ
```

Lesson Check 19.1

1. How would a string be simulated in Standard Pascal?

2. What does the string function CONCAT do? Why should this function be used with some caution?

3. What will be printed on the screen after each of the following statements? (Assume WORD is a string variable and has been assigned the value 'CLIMB'.)
   a. `WRITELN(LENGTH('TODAY IS A GREAT DAY'));`
   b. `WRITELN(LENGTH(WORD));`
   c. `WRITELN(COPY(WORD, 1, 2));`
   d. `WRITELN(CONCAT('THE HIGHEST ', WORD));`
   e. `WRITELN(CONCAT('HELLO, ',`
      `      COPY('YOUNG FRIENDS',7,6)));`

Lesson 19.2   More String Maneuvers

In Lesson 19.1, string functions that break apart and put together strings were introduced. In this lesson, string functions or procedures that alter a string, by inserting or deleting characters, as well as a few other functions will be discussed.

The **POS** function locates the position of a string within a larger string.

POS Form

`POS(substrg,strg)`

The *substrg* is a string variable, string constant, or literal string that represents the part of *strg* to be located. The POS function returns a nonnegative integer equal to the starting position of the first occurrence of *substrg* within *strg*. If *substrg* is not found in *strg*, a 0 is returned.

The following program statements use POS to print the location of a word in a phrase:

```
QUOTE := 'PASCAL IS FUN';
PARTQUOTE := 'FUN';
WRITELN(POS(PARTQUOTE, QUOTE));
```

These program statements will print the integer 11, since the string 'FUN' begins at position 11 in QUOTE.

The **DELETE** procedure removes characters from a string.

> **DELETE Form**
>
> `DELETE(strg,start,count);`

The argument *strg* is any string variable (not a string constant or literal), *start* is the position where deletion of characters begins, and *count* is the number of characters to be deleted. DELETE alters the actual contents stored in *strg*. Here are some examples using the DELETE procedure.

```
AGAIN := 'ONE TWO THREE';
DELETE(AGAIN, 5, 3);
WRITELN(AGAIN);
NUMBERS := 'FOUR FIVE SIX';
DELETE(NUMBERS, 10, 3);
WRITELN(NUMBERS);
```

The first DELETE removes 'TWO' from the string AGAIN, since 'TWO' starts at position five and is three characters long. There are two spaces left in string AGAIN between 'ONE' and 'THREE'. The second DELETE removes 'SIX' from NUMBERS, since 'SIX' starts at the tenth position and continues for three characters. The following strings would be printed:

```
ONE   THREE
FOUR FIVE
```

Program 19.5 deletes a vowel from a given phrase using the POS function and the DELETE procedure. The user enters a phrase and the vowel to be deleted, and the program deletes all occurrences of that vowel.

Program 19.5
```
PROGRAM VOWELDELETE(INPUT, OUTPUT);

   { PURPOSE: TO DELETE A VOWEL FROM A PHRASE }

VAR
   PHRASE    : STRING;
   CHECK     : CHAR;
   POSITION  : INTEGER;

BEGIN

   WRITE('ENTER A PHRASE: ');
   READLN(PHRASE);
   REPEAT
      WRITE('ENTER THE VOWEL TO BE DELETED: ');
      READLN(CHECK)
   UNTIL (CHECK IN ['A','E','I','O','U']);
   POSITION := 1;
   WHILE (POSITION <> 0) DO
```

```
      BEGIN
        CASE CHECK OF
           'A' : POSITION := POS('A', PHRASE);
           'E' : POSITION := POS('E', PHRASE);
           'I' : POSITION := POS('I', PHRASE);
           'O' : POSITION := POS('O', PHRASE);
           'U' : POSITION := POS('U', PHRASE)
        END; { CASE }
        DELETE(PHRASE, POSITION, 1)
      END; { WHILE }
    WRITELN('REVISED PHRASE: ', PHRASE)

END.
```

Sample Output

```
ENTER A PHRASE: TO BE OR NOT TO BE
ENTER THE VOWEL TO BE DELETED: O
REVISED PHRASE: T BE R NT T BE
```

The **INSERT** procedure puts characters into a string.

> **INSERT Form**
>
> INSERT(*substrg*,*strg*,*start*);

The argument *substrg* is a string variable, constant, or literal to be inserted into *strg* (a string variable) at position *start*. (Note that *substrg* is inserted before the character located at position *start*.)

The following program statements will delete the string 'WHAT', and then insert 'EVERYTHING':

```
PHRASE := 'WHAT IS IN A NAME';
DELETE(PHRASE, 1, 4);
INSERT('EVERYTHING', PHRASE, 1);
WRITELN(PHRASE);
```

These statements will print

```
EVERYTHING IS IN A NAME
```

Like the DELETE procedure, INSERT changes the contents of the string variable. (**Caution:** Some care must be taken to insure that this string variable can accommodate any characters that may be added.)

The **STR** procedure changes an integer or long integer to a string.

> **STR Form**
>
> STR(*value*,*strg*);

The *value* is an integer or long integer and *strg* represents a string variable. For example, the following statements will transfer the contents of NUMBER to a string variable.

```
NUMBER := 347;
STR(NUMBER,STRG);
WRITELN(STRG);
```

For these statements, STR changes the integer 347 to a string value. After this change, other string procedures and functions can be used with STRG. (Note that the value of NUMBER is not altered.)

Program 19.6 uses the STR procedure to change an integer to a string in order to insert a decimal and a dollar sign.

Program 19.6

```
PROGRAM DOLLAR(INPUT, OUTPUT);

    { PURPOSE: DEMONSTRATE STR AND INSERT PROCEDURES }

VAR
    VALUE : INTEGER;
    STRG  : STRING;

BEGIN

    WRITE('ENTER AN INTEGER: ');
    READLN(VALUE);
    STR(VALUE, STRG);
    INSERT('$', STRG, 1);
    INSERT('.', STRG, LENGTH(STRG) - 1);
    WRITELN('THE DOLLAR AMOUNT IS: ', STRG)

END.
```

Sample Output

```
ENTER AN INTEGER: 347
THE DOLLAR AMOUNT IS: $3.47
```

The first INSERT statement of Program 19.6 places a dollar sign in front of the first character of STRG. Following the execution of this statement, the contents of STRG would be '$347'. The second INSERT statement inserts a decimal point before the third character (4).

Since a string is an array of characters, each letter of a string can be specified using the bracket notation. In the following example, WHAT[1] specifies the first character of the string variable WHAT.

```
WHAT := 'WHAT IS A STAR';
WRITE(WHAT[1]);
WRITE(WHAT[6]);
WRITE(WHAT[7]);
WRITELN(WHAT[2]);
```

These program statements will print:

```
WISH
```

since W is the first character, I is the sixth character, S is the seventh character, and H is the second character of the string variable WHAT.

Program 19.7 uses this bracket notation to print the characters of a string in reverse order.

Program 19.7

```
PROGRAM REVERSE (INPUT, OUTPUT);

    { PURPOSE: DEMONSTRATE BREAKING APART A STRING }

VAR
    WORD  : STRING;
    COUNT : INTEGER;

BEGIN

    WRITE('ENTER A WORD: ');
    READLN(WORD);
    FOR COUNT := LENGTH(WORD) DOWNTO 1 DO
        WRITE(WORD[COUNT]);
    WRITELN

END.
```

Sample Output

```
ENTER A WORD: PASCAL
LACSAP
```

A CHAR value can be assigned to a string variable or a single character substring, as shown in the following statement. Assume that ST is a variable of type STRING and CH is of type CHAR.

```
ST[1] := CH;   { VALID }
```

Of course, a CHAR variable cannot be assigned a STRING value, unless a substring is specified.

```
CH := ST[4];   { VALID }
CH := ST;      { INVALID }
ST := CH;      { INVALID }
```

Lesson Check 19.2

1. Identify the errors in the following statements. Assume correct variable declarations.
   a. POSITION := POS(12,123456);
   b. REMOVE := DELETE(WORD,VOWEL,1);
   c. INSERT('E','FRIGHT',3);
   d. STR(STRGVAR,5919);

2. How can a CHAR value or variable be assigned to a STRING variable?

3. What will be printed by the following program?

```
PROGRAM TEST (INPUT, OUTPUT);

VAR
    PHRASE : STRING;
```

```
BEGIN

    PHRASE := 'TESTING ONE, TWO, THREE';
    WRITELN(POS('ONE',PHRASE));
    DELETE(PHRASE, 8, 4);
    INSERT('O.K. ',PHRASE, 1);
    WRITELN(CONCAT(PHRASE[3], PHRASE[10],
                   PHRASE[20], PHRASE[7]))

END.
```

Summary

String functions and procedures allow easy manipulation of strings. Table 19.1 and Table 19.2 summarize what each function or procedure accomplishes and list the parameters needed.

Table 19.1
String Functions

Function	Parameters	Result
CONCAT	*s1, s2, . . . , sn*	Returns a combined string made up of listed strings (in the specified order).
COPY	*strg, start, count*	Returns a string representing the portion of *strg* beginning at *start* position and copying *count* characters.
LENGTH	*strg*	Returns length of *strg*.
POS	*substrg, strg*	Returns an integer representing the starting position of *substrg* within *strg*.

Table 19.2
String Procedures

Procedure	Parameters	Result
DELETE	*strg, start, count*	Deletes *count* characters of *strg* starting at position *start*.
INSERT	*substrg, strg, start*	Inserts *substrg* into *strg* immediately before position *start*.
STR	*value, strg*	Converts an integer or long integer into a string.

This chapter also described a method for combining STRING and CHAR variables in an assignment statement or expression. This method is as follows:

> *string[count]*
>
> Specifies the character at position *count* in *string*. This allows strings and characters to be used in the same expression without a type conflict.

Key Terms

CONCAT	INSERT	POS
COPY	LENGTH	STR
DELETE	null string	

Answers to Lesson Checks

Lesson 19.1

1. The data type STRING could be simulated by

```
TYPE
    STRING = PACKED ARRAY[0..80] OF CHAR;
```

2. CONCAT takes two or more strings and returns a single combined string. This function should be used with care because a string could be returned that is larger than the declared size of the variable to which it is assigned.

3. **a.** 20
   b. 5
   c. CL
   d. THE HIGHEST CLIMB
   e. HELLO, FRIEND

Lesson 19.2

1. **a.** The arguments of the POS function should be strings.
   b. DELETE is a procedure and cannot be used in an assignment statement.
   c. The substring ('E') cannot be inserted into the string ('FRIGHT') at position 3 since the second argument of the INSERT procedure must be a string variable, not a literal string.
   d. The arguments are in the wrong order.

2. STRING and CHAR variables can be assigned to variables of either type if a single character substring is specified for the string (using the bracket notation). The following examples are valid for the string variable STRGVAR and the character variable CHARVAR:

```
STRGVAR[4] := CHARVAR;
CHARVAR := STRGVAR[27];
IF CHARVAR = STRGVAR[3] THEN ...
STRGVAR := CONCAT(CHARVAR,CHARVAR,STRGVAR[1]);
```

3. The program will print the following:

```
9
KITE
```

Exercises   Set I. Comprehension

For Exercises 1–3, assume that the following assignments have been made:

```
ONE   := 'ABCDEF';
TWO   := 'WXYZ';
THREE := 'ABCDEFWXYZ';
```

1. Find the value of each of the following expressions:
   a. LENGTH(ONE)
   b. POS('B', ONE)
   c. COPY(ONE, 2, 3)
   d. CONCAT(ONE, TWO)
   e. POS('A', CONCAT(THREE, ONE))
   f. POS(ONE, THREE)

2. What is the value of the variable after each of the following statements?
   a. DELETE(THREE, 4, 2);
   b. INSERT('ABC', TWO, 1);

3. Identify the errors in the following program statements:
   a. WRITELN(ONE, CONCAT(ABC, TWO));
   b. INSERT('Y', ONE);
   c. POS(COPY(TWO, 2, 1));

For Exercises 4–6, assume that the following assignments have been made:

```
NUMBERS := '0123456789';
PART1    := '01234';
PART2    := '56789';
```

4. Find the value of each of the following expressions:
   a. LENGTH(NUMBERS)
   b. POS('2', PART1)
   c. COPY(PART2, 1, 5)
   d. CONCAT(PART1, PART2)
   e. POS(PART2, NUMBERS)
   f. POS(PART1, CONCAT(NUMBERS, PART1))

5. What is the value of the variable after each of the following statements?
   a. DELETE(NUMBERS, 5, 5);
   b. INSERT(PART1, PART2, 1);

6. Identify the errors in the following program statements:
   a. VALUE := DELETE(NUMBERS, 1, 2);
   b. WRITELN(POS(NUMBERS, PART1);
   c. CONCAT(LENGTH(PART1), LENGTH(PART2));

7. Assuming the following assignment:

```
NUMBER := 1098;
```

   a. Write a statement that will convert NUMBER to a string, NUMSTRG.
   b. Write a statement that will insert a dollar sign in front of NUMSTRG.
   c. Write a statement that will insert a decimal point two positions from the right in NUMSTRG.

8. Assuming the following assignment:

   ```
   NUM := 2167394;
   ```

   a. Write a statement that will convert NUM to a string, NUMST.
   b. Write a statement that will create a combined string made up of the first, third, fifth, and seventh characters of NUMST and assign this new string to ODDSTRG.
   c. Write a statement that will insert a comma before the second position of ODDSTRG.

Set II. Application

9. Write a program that will print the first word of a sentence entered by the user.

10. Write a program that will print the second word of a sentence entered by the user.

11. Given a letter of the alphabet and a phrase, write a program to determine how many words in the phrase start with that particular letter.

12. Given two strings entered by the user, write a program to determine how many times the second string occurs in the first.

13. Write a program that will print each character of a string on a separate line. For example, given the string 'HAPPY' the program would print

    ```
    H
    A
    P
    P
    Y
    ```

14. Write a program that inserts three exclamation points in the middle of a word.

15. Write a program that will replace all occurrences of a vowel in a string with an asterisk.

16. Write a program that will remove all spaces from a string entered by the user.

17. Write a program that will replace all occurrences of a word in a sentence with another word. Allow the user to enter the search word and the replacement word.

18. Write a program that will check a word entered by the user for correct spelling using the rule "*i* before *e*, except after *c*."

19. Write a program that requests the user's full name and returns the last name (followed by a comma), the first name, and the middle initial. For example, an input of JOHN QUINCY PUBLIC would result in output of

    ```
    PUBLIC, JOHN Q.
    ```

20. Write a program to insert a comma into a number at every thousands position. For example, for an input of 1234567890, the program would print

    ```
    1,234,567,890
    ```

Set III. Synthesis

21. Write a program to find the cost of sending a telegram by determining the number of words in the message. The first 10 words cost 20 cents each, while each additional word costs 15 cents.

22. Telegrams are usually sent using a slash (/) to separate words. Rewrite Exercise 21 to replace each space with a slash.

23. Improve the palindrome program (Program 19.3) to work for phrases (such as, MADAM, I'M ADAM) as well as words. The program should ignore punctuation and spaces, and should print the phrase forward and backward (with punctuation intact).

24. A common coding method is to reverse the alphabet and substitute the corresponding letters. For example, A is substituted for Z; B, for Y; and so on. Write a program that will take a message and encode or decode it according to this scheme.

25. Write a program to count the number of letters in each word of a sentence entered by the user. Find the average number of letters in each word.

26. Write a program that will insert an indefinite article—either *a* or *an*—before a user-entered noun. The indefinite article *a* will be inserted before the noun if the noun begins with a consonant and the indefinite article *an* will be inserted if the noun begins with a vowel.

20 Graphics

" ... What is the use of a book," thought Alice, "without pictures or conversations?"

—Lewis Carroll

Overview

Gaining a Perspective

Built-in graphics procedures and functions are available in many versions of Pascal. The UCSD Pascal graphics package, **Turtlegraphics,** is based on a programming language developed at the Massachusetts Institute of Technology in the Artificial Intelligence Laboratory. Originally, the programming language was a robot demonstration program. The robotic **turtle** could move around on the floor according to the directions it received from the programmer. When it was placed on a piece of paper, the turtle could draw a design using an attached pen. (The pen could be raised and lowered at the programmer's command.) The turtle in UCSD Pascal is, of course, imaginary.

Graphics provide a visual means of interpreting data and illustrating ideas. The graph of a set of data, for example, may provide a clearer picture of the significance of the data than a list or table. Also, many features of Pascal (such as recursion) can be illustrated through graphics.

Lesson 20.1   The Graphics Mode and Commands

Many versions of Pascal provide two types of display: a **text mode** and a **graphics mode.** The text mode is used for printing characters on the screen. The output commands presented in other chapters were text mode commands. The graphics mode is used to place pictures on the screen. In UCSD Pascal, these two modes cannot be used at the same time. Characters are displayed in the graphics mode by drawing images that are similar to text.

Having two display modes is like having two screens. Upon accessing the graphics mode, a **graphics window** (like a shade) is pulled over the text screen. For instance, if a WRITE statement (a text mode command) is executed while in the graphics mode, the output would not be visible on the graphics screen (but would appear on the screen when the user returned to the text mode). Similarly, when returning to the text mode, the graphics design remains on the graphics screen. Text and graphics commands can be executed in either mode, but their results are not actually viewed until the proper mode is accessed.

The graphics mode commands are much different from the text mode commands. Program 20.1 provides a first example of the graphics mode by drawing a square; how this will print on the screen is shown in Figure 20.1.

Program 20.1

```
PROGRAM FIRSTSQUARE(INPUT);

    { PURPOSE: TO DRAW A SQUARE }

USES
    TURTLEGRAPHICS;

PROCEDURE SQUARE;

    BEGIN

        MOVETO(130,100);
        MOVETO(130,130);
        MOVETO(100,130);
        MOVETO(100,100)

    END; { SQUARE }


BEGIN { MAIN PROGRAM }

    INITTURTLE;
    FILLSCREEN(BLUE);
    MOVETO(100,100);
    PENCOLOR(BLACK2);
    SQUARE;
    PENCOLOR(NONE);
    READLN;
    TEXTMODE

END.
```

Figure 20.1

Appearance of Screen
for Program 20.1

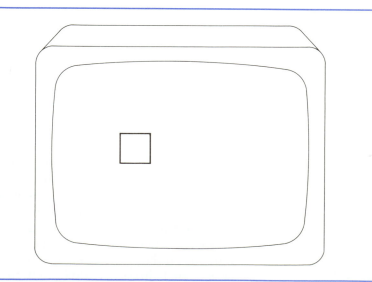

Each statement of Program 20.1 requires a detailed discussion.

UCSD Pascal Turtlegraphics uses procedures that are stored in the SYSTEM.LIBRARY, in which the graphics statements and colors are defined. To use this library, the following statement is included immediately after the program heading:

```
USES
    TURTLEGRAPHICS;
```

The graphics screen has horizontal and vertical components representing points on the screen. When referring to a specific point on the screen, the horizontal component (the X-coordinate) is listed first and the vertical component (the Y-coordinate) is listed second.

```
(horizontal,vertical)
```

As shown in Figure 20.2, the screen is oriented so that the origin is (0,0), the maximum horizontal component is 279, and the maximum vertical component is 191. The initial position of the turtle is (139,95), with an initial direction of east (or to the right). All coordinates are integer values. Real values can be used for the coordinates, but they will be truncated by the computer.

In Program 20.1, the **INITTURTLE** procedure initializes the position and orientation of the turtle, as shown in Figure 20.2. The INITTURTLE procedure performs the following:

1. Sets the graphics mode.
2. Clears the graphics screen.
3. Sets the screen components to maximum (279 horizontal, 191 vertical).
4. Sets the pen color to NONE.
5. Positions the turtle in the center of the screen, facing east.

Figure 20.2

The Graphics Screen and Initial Turtle Position

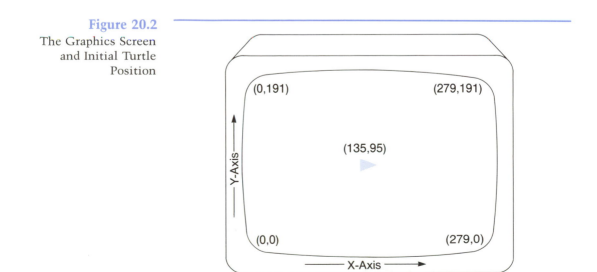

The **PENCOLOR** procedure controls the color of the turtle's pen. Table 20.1 gives the possibilities for PENCOLOR. The choice of color combination is related to what works best on most color televisions. Combinations of WHITE1, BLACK1, GREEN, and/or VIOLET should be used together, while WHITE2, BLACK2, OR-ANGE, and/or BLUE can be used together with good results. The entire screen can be filled with one of these colors by using the **FILLSCREEN** procedure.

FILLSCREEN Form

`FILLSCREEN(color);`

or

`FILLSCREEN(REVERSE);`

The latter statement will fill the screen with the complement of the current screen color. In Program 20.1, for instance, the statements

`FILLSCREEN(BLUE);`

`PENCOLOR(BLACK2);`

change the turtle's pen to black and the background color to blue.

The **MOVETO** procedure of Program 20.1 is one way to move the turtle on the screen. It moves the turtle from its present location (the center of the screen) to the specified point on the screen.

Table 20.1
Options for
PENCOLOR
Procedure

`PENCOLOR(color);`
The value of *color* can be one of the following constants:

Color	Complementary Color
WHITE	BLACK
WHITE1	BLACK1
WHITE2	BLACK2
BLUE	ORANGE
GREEN	VIOLET
ORANGE	BLUE
VIOLET	GREEN

`PENCOLOR(NONE);`
This is equivalent to lifting the pen. If the turtle moves, it will not leave a trace of its path.

`PENCOLOR(REVERSE);`
This changes the pen color to the complement of the current color.

MOVETO Form

`MOVETO(Xcoordinate,Ycoordinate);`

This statement moves the turtle from its present location to the point with coordinates (*Xcoordinate,Ycoordinate*), and leaves a trace of the turtle's path in the current pen color. In the main program of Program 20.1, the turtle is moved to the point (100,100) without drawing a line, since the pen color is NONE initially. (See Figure 20.3.) The MOVETO statements of procedure SQUARE move the turtle to form a square (drawn in black on a blue background) by connecting ordered pairs, from (100,100) to (130,100) to (130,130) to (100,130) and back to (100,100).

The last three statements of Program 20.1 are important for any program that uses graphics. Generally, the turtle characteristics (such as pen color and orientation) should be returned to their original state after a figure is drawn. PENCOLOR(NONE) sets the pen color back to NONE. The READLN, a text mode command, holds the design on the screen until the return key is pressed. Without this statement, the picture would disappear upon executing the TEXTMODE command. (The picture would not remain on the screen long enough for adequate viewing.) **TEXTMODE** returns the computer to the text mode. The graphics design will remain on the graphics screen until INITTURTLE is used. The **GRAFMODE** command can be used to return to the graphics screen without reinitializing (which would erase the picture).

Figure 20.3
Turtle Position after
MOVETO(100,100)

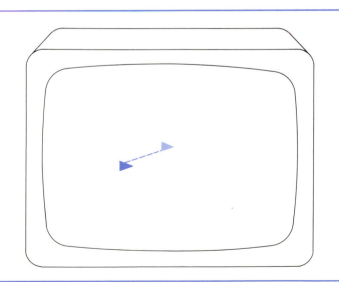

Another method for drawing with the turtle is to use the **TURN** and **MOVE** procedures.

TURN and MOVE Forms

```
TURN(angle);
MOVE(distance);
```

If the angle specified in the TURN procedure is positive, the turtle rotates counterclockwise that many degrees from its present direction. (For a negative angle, the rotation is clockwise.) The angle is an integer that satisfies the following inequality:

$$-359 \leq \text{angle} \leq 359$$

If a smaller or larger value is used for the angle, the computer calculates that angle with respect to a modulus of 360. For example, if the angle is 720, the computer finds

$$720 \text{ MOD } 360 = 0$$

Thus, the angle is zero.

The TURN procedure alone does not draw on the graphics screen; it simply changes the direction the turtle is facing. For example, TURN(60) rotates the turtle 60 degrees counterclockwise, as shown in Figure 20.4.

The MOVE procedure moves the turtle a specified distance (number of dots) in its present direction. If the distance is not within the boundaries of the screen, the turtle will wrap around; that is, it will continue on the opposite edge of the screen. If a pen color has been specified, then MOVE will draw a line.

Program 20.2 gives another version of a square.

Figure 20.4

Rotate Turtle Using TURN

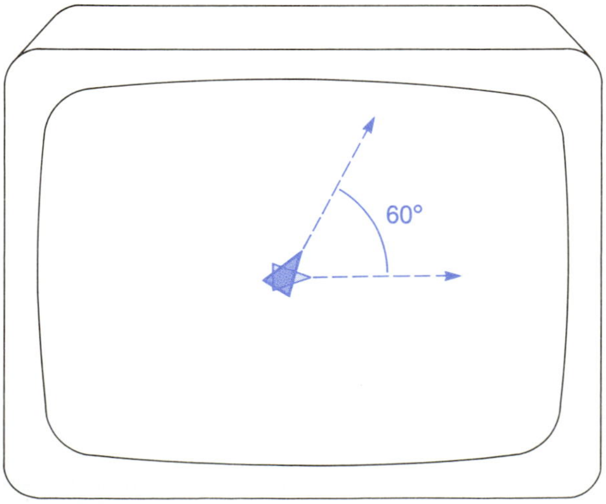

Program 20.2

```
PROGRAM SECONDSQUARE;

    { PURPOSE: TO DRAW A SQUARE }

USES
    TURTLEGRAPHICS;

PROCEDURE SQUARE;

    BEGIN

        MOVE(30);
        TURN(90);
        MOVE(30);
        TURN(90);
        MOVE(30);
        TURN(90);
        MOVE(30);
        TURN(90)

    END; { SQUARE }

BEGIN { MAIN PROGRAM }

    INITTURTLE;
    FILLSCREEN(BLUE);
    MOVETO(100,100);
    PENCOLOR(BLACK2);
    SQUARE;
    PENCOLOR(NONE);
    READLN;
    TEXTMODE

END.
```

Program 20.2 creates the same square as Program 20.1. (See Figure 20.1.) In both programs, notice the use of the statement INIT-TURTLE. INITTURTLE initializes the pen color to NONE, thus allowing a move (MOVETO(100,100)) from the turtle's origin without drawing a line. In Program 20.2, the turtle is returned to its original orientation by the last TURN statement of procedure SQUARE.

Program Segment 20.3 is yet another version of procedure SQUARE. Program Segment 20.3 uses a FOR loop for the repeated statements of Program 20.2.

Program Segment 20.3

```
PROCEDURE SQUARE;

    VAR
        COUNT : INTEGER;

    BEGIN

        FOR COUNT := 1 TO 4 DO
            BEGIN
                MOVE(30);
                TURN(90)
            END

    END; { SQUARE }
```

In both Program 20.2 and Program Segment 20.3, the turtle first moved and then turned. The angle the turtle turned through was the exterior angle of the square. Figure 20.5 shows the turtle forming an equilateral triangle by turning through the exterior angle of the triangle (120 degrees). The program for drawing an equilateral triangle is left as an exercise.

Using the starting point (100,100) of Program 20.3, the square can be pivoted through 360 degrees, as shown in Figure 20.6. Program 20.4 produces the result shown in Figure 20.6.

Program 20.4

```
PROGRAM ROTATESQUARE;

    { PURPOSE: TO ROTATE A SQUARE }

USES
    TURTLEGRAPHICS;

VAR
    ROTATE : INTEGER;

PROCEDURE SQUARE;

    VAR
        COUNT : INTEGER;

    BEGIN

        FOR COUNT := 1 TO 4 DO
            BEGIN
                MOVE(30);
                TURN(90)
            END

    END; { SQUARE }


BEGIN { MAIN PROGRAM }
    INITTURTLE;
    FILLSCREEN(BLUE);
    MOVETO(100,100);
    PENCOLOR(BLACK2);
    FOR ROTATE := 1 TO 18 DO
        BEGIN
            TURN(20);
            SQUARE
        END;
    PENCOLOR(NONE);
    READLN;
    TEXTMODE

END.
```

Notice that in Program 20.4, the product of the limit of the loop and the angle at which each square is drawn is 360 degrees.

Program Segment 20.5 presents another version of the main program, this time using the **TURNTO** procedure.

Figure 20.5
Movement of Turtle
through an Exterior
Angle

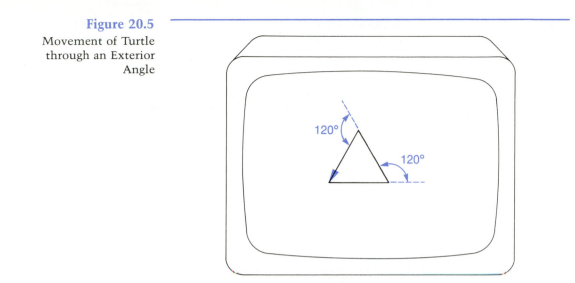

Figure 20.6
Square Pivoting about
a Point

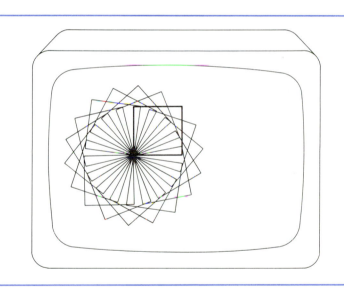

**Program
Segment 20.5**

```
FOR ROTATE := 1 TO 18 DO
   BEGIN
      TURNTO(20 * ROTATE);
      SQUARE
   END;
```

Unlike the TURN procedure, which turns the turtle through an angle relative to its present direction, TURNTO rotates directly to a specific angle, regardless of the turtle's present direction. TURNTO turns the turtle to the integer value indicated in the parentheses (where 0 degrees is east, 90 degrees is north, 180 degrees is west, and 270 degrees is south). The degree measure can be negative or greater than 360 degrees. A positive angle results in a counterclockwise rotation, whereas a negative angle causes the turtle to turn clockwise.

Lesson
Check
20.1

1. What is the purpose of an empty READLN statement following a drawing procedure and before the TEXTMODE command?

2. Identify the graphics command associated with each of the following:
   a. Turns the turtle a given angle relative to its present orientation.
   b. Moves the turtle directly to a location indicated by coordinates.
   c. Switches the screen to the text mode.
   d. Turns the turtle to a specific angle.
   e. Switches the screen to the graphics mode.
   f. Moves the turtle a given distance from its present location.

3. Identify each of the following statements as true or false:
   a. The parameter REVERSE of the statement PENCOLOR(REVERSE) changes the color to the complement of the previous color.
   b. INITTURTLE sets the pen color to black.

Lesson 20.2   Labels and Screen Characteristics

In order to incorporate text with graphics, the procedures **WCHAR** (for characters) and **WSTRING** (for strings) are used, as in Program 20.6. These procedures draw the specified characters at the current position of the turtle. (The turtle position is not altered by WCHAR or WSTRING.) Each character is drawn starting at the lower-left corner. For example, in the following statements,

```
MOVETO(100,100);
WCHAR('A');
```

the lower-left corner of the character 'A' would be placed at the current turtle position (100,100). Figure 20.7 shows a close-up of the graphics screen.

Figure 20.7
Close-up of Graphics
Character

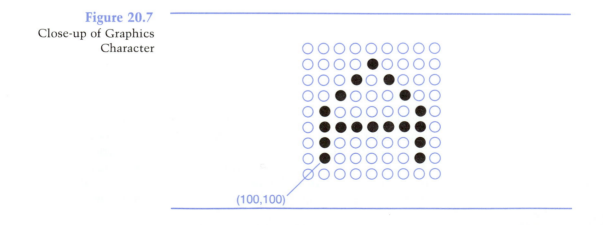

(100,100)

All of the characters are written horizontally on the screen (regardless of the turtle's direction) and are the same size. Characters of varying shapes and sizes can be drawn using the graphics commands, such as MOVE or TURN, to produce additional character sets. (See Programmer's Handbook, Section G.)

Program 20.6

```
PROGRAM DISPLAY;

    { PURPOSE: TO DRAW AND LABEL A SQUARE }

USES
    TURTLEGRAPHICS;

PROCEDURE SQUARE;

    VAR
        COUNT : INTEGER;

    BEGIN

        FOR COUNT := 1 TO 4 DO
            BEGIN
                MOVE(30);
                TURN(90)
            END

    END; { SQUARE }

PROCEDURE LABELSQUARE;

    VAR
        XCOOR,
        YCOOR : INTEGER;

    BEGIN

        XCOOR := TURTLEX;
        YCOOR := TURTLEY;
        PENCOLOR(NONE);
        MOVETO(XCOOR - 5 , YCOOR - 20);
        WSTRING('SQUARE');
        MOVETO(50, 50);
        WSTRING('PRESS RETURN TO CONTINUE.');
        MOVETO(XCOOR, YCOOR)

    END; { LABELSQUARE }

BEGIN { MAIN PROGRAM }

    INITTURTLE;
    MOVETO(100,100);
    PENCOLOR(WHITE);
    SQUARE;
    LABELSQUARE;
    PENCOLOR(NONE);
    READLN;
    TEXTMODE

END.
```

Two integer functions are used in Program 20.6 to find the position of the turtle. **TURTLEX** and **TURTLEY** return the X- and Y-coordinates of the turtle. In procedure LABELSQUARE, the position and orientation of the turtle are stored in variables XCOOR and YCOOR. The turtle is moved to a position below the picture of the square, and the string 'SQUARE' is written. After the labels are completed, the turtle is moved back to its original position.

In addition to TURTLEX and TURTLEY, the integer function **TURTLEANG** can be used to determine the current orientation of the turtle. TURTLEANG returns the direction (absolute angle) of the turtle.

VIEWPORT

The **VIEWPORT** procedure specifies the working size, called the view port, of the graphics screen. (Recall that INITTURTLE initializes the view port to the full-sized screen.)

VIEWPORT Form

`VIEWPORT(left, right, bottom, top);`

The arguments *left, right, bottom,* and *top* represent whole number values that determine the boundaries of the view port. For example,

`VIEWPORT(100,150,40,60);`

means the view port will have a boundary of 100 on the left, 150 on the right, 40 on the bottom, and 60 on top, as shown in Figure 20.8. (Note that the lines indicating boundaries are for ref-

Figure 20.8
Boundaries of
VIEWPORT

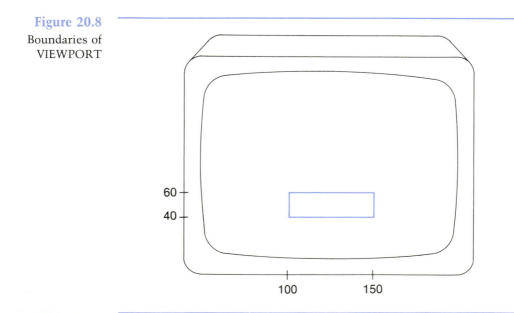

erence only; VIEWPORT does not draw any lines.) By altering the view port in this manner, only the points within (and including) the boundaries can be used. Attempting to draw outside the boundaries will produce no graphics; for example, a line drawn from the center of the view port to a point beyond the boundaries will be seen on the screen only within those boundaries.

Program 20.7 demonstrates one use of VIEWPORT—the creation of a kaleidoscope. The program creates view ports of varying sizes that are defined and quickly changed on the screen, resulting in the appearance of a kaleidoscope.

Program 20.7

```
PROGRAM KALEIDOSCOPE;

    { PURPOSE: TO DEMONSTRATE VIEWPORT }

USES
    TURTLEGRAPHICS;

VAR
    LOOP,
    COUNT : INTEGER;

BEGIN { MAIN PROGRAM }

    INITTURTLE;
    FILLSCREEN(BLUE);
    FOR LOOP := 1 TO 5 DO
        FOR COUNT := 1 TO 45 DO
            BEGIN
                VIEWPORT(6*COUNT, 6*COUNT+10, 0, 191);
                FILLSCREEN(REVERSE);
                VIEWPORT(9, 279, 4*COUNT, 4*COUNT+10);
                FILLSCREEN(REVERSE)
            END;
    READLN;
    TEXTMODE

END.
```

SCREENBIT

The **SCREENBIT** function returns a BOOLEAN value based on the state of a point on the graphics screen.

SCREENBIT Form

SCREENBIT(*Xcoordinate, Ycoordinate*)

If the point specified by the X- and Y-coordinates is black, SCREENBIT returns FALSE; otherwise, SCREENBIT returns TRUE. (Note that SCREENBIT does not indicate the color of the point.) This function can be useful if the programmer wants to draw a line but does not want that line to appear to overlap any other lines.

Lesson Check 20.2

1. Identify each of the following statements as true or false:
   a. The WCHAR and WSTRING procedures are used to draw characters on the graphics screen.
   b. TURTLEX and TURTLEY are integer functions that return the current position of the turtle.
   c. VIEWPORT is a graphics statement that allows the user to view the graphics screen.
   d. SCREENBIT returns the color of a specific point on the screen.

2. Describe the output produced by the following program segment. (Assume procedure SQUARE of Program 20.6.)

```
MOVETO(20,120);
FOR COUNT := 1 TO 5 DO
   BEGIN
      PENCOLOR(WHITE);
      SQUARE;
      PENCOLOR(NONE);
      MOVE(35)
   END;
FOR COUNT := 1 TO 5 DO
   BEGIN
      MOVETO(COUNT * 35 - 3,130);
      WCHAR(CHR(COUNT + 48))
   END;
```

Table 20.2
Summary of Graphics Commands

Command	Description
INITTURTLE	Sets the graphics mode, clears the graphics screen, sets screen to maximum size, sets pen color to none, positions turtle in the center of the screen facing east.
MOVE(*distance*)	Moves the turtle a specified *distance* in the current direction.
MOVETO(*x,y*)	Moves the turtle to the specified (*x,y*) coordinate.
TURN(*angle*)	Rotates the turtle the *angle* specified (0 to 360 degrees) relative to its present direction.
TURNTO(*angle*)	Rotates the turtle directly to the specific *angle*.
TEXTMODE	Changes the mode from graphics to text.
GRAFMODE	Changes the mode from text to graphics.
PENCOLOR(*color*)	Sets the *color* of the turtle's pen.
FILLSCREEN(*color*)	Fills the background.
VIEWPORT(*l,r,b,t*)	Defines a portion of the screen.
TURTLEX	Gives the current X-coordinate of the turtle.
TURTLEY	Gives the current Y-coordinate of the turtle.
TURTLEANG	Gives the current direction of the turtle.
WCHAR(*'c'*)	Outputs a character in the graphics mode.
WSTRING(*'string'*)	Outputs a string in the graphics mode.
SCREENBIT	Indicates the state (black or nonblack) of a point on the screen.

Summary

The graphics procedures and functions used in this chapter can be incorporated into the problems presented in earlier chapters. Table 20.2 presents a summary of these statements.

Key Terms

FILLSCREEN	PENCOLOR	TURTLEANG
GRAFMODE	SCREENBIT	Turtlegraphics
graphics mode	text mode	TURTLEX
graphics window	TEXTMODE	TURTLEY
INITTURTLE	TURN	VIEWPORT
MOVE	TURNTO	WCHAR
MOVETO	turtle	WSTRING

Answers to Lesson Checks

Lesson 20.1

1. The READLN statement is used to hold the graphics design on the screen until the return key is pressed.

2. a. TURN
   b. MOVETO
   c. TEXTMODE
   d. TURNTO
   e. GRAFMODE
   f. MOVE

3. a. True.
   b. False.

Lesson 20.2

1. a. True.
   b. True.
   c. False.
   d. False.

2. The program segment draws five squares across the screen and places a number from 1 to 5 in each.

```
  ┌─────┐  ┌─────┐  ┌─────┐  ┌─────┐  ┌─────┐
  │  1  │  │  2  │  │  3  │  │  4  │  │  5  │
  └─────┘  └─────┘  └─────┘  └─────┘  └─────┘
```

Exercises

Set I. Comprehension

1. Which of the following statements change the coordinates of the turtle? Assume the turtle is at its initial position and orientation as indicated in Figure 20.2.

    a. `MOVETO(139,95);`
    b. `GRAFMODE;`
    c. `TURTLEANG;`
    d. `WRITELN('TURTLE');`

2. Which of the following statements change the orientation of the turtle? Assume the turtle is at (0,0), facing south.
    a. `MOVE(90);`
    b. `INITTURTLE;`
    c. `TURNTO(180);`
    d. `WSTRING('TURTLE');`

For Exercises 3–8, sketch the output of each program segment using approximate lengths. Assume that each segment is preceded by INIT-TURTLE and PENCOLOR(BLUE).

3.
```
MOVE(50);
TURN(90);
MOVE(50);
TURN(45);
```

4.
```
MOVETO(25,25);
TURN(90);
MOVETO(139,25);
TURNTO(0);
```

5.
```
MOVE(75);
TURN(45);
MOVE(50);
TURN(45);
```

6.
```
MOVETO(0,0);
TURNTO(180);
MOVETO(139,95);
TURN(90);
```

7.
```
FOR I := 1 TO 7 DO
    BEGIN
        MOVE(50);
        TURN(I * 360 DIV 7)
    END;
```

8.
```
FOR ROTATE := 1 TO 10 DO
    BEGIN
        MOVE(25);
        TURNTO(ROTATE*36)
    END;
```

9. Write the statements needed to do each of the following:
    a. Change to the graphics mode.
    b. Move the turtle 60 steps.
    c. Turn 90 degrees clockwise.
    d. Change the pen color to blue.
    e. Move to the coordinate (50,50).

10. Write the statements needed to do each of the following:
    a. Face the turtle south.
    b. Draw a line 15 steps long.
    c. Turn the turtle 90 degrees counterclockwise.
    d. Change the pen color to its complement.
    e. Move the turtle to the center of the screen.

11. Write the statements needed to do each of the following:
    a. Establish a 40 × 50 view port in the lower-right corner of the screen.
    b. Face the turtle in the opposite direction.
    c. Change the pen color to none.
    d. Move to the turtle coordinate (65, 0).
    e. Change to the text mode.

12. Write the statements needed to do each of the following:
    a. Establish a view port that is 10 spaces short of the normal screen boundaries on each side.
    b. Turn the turtle 90 degrees clockwise.
    c. Change the color of the background to blue.
    d. Draw a green line 18 steps long.
    e. Hold graphics on the screen.

Set II. Application

13. Write a procedure that will draw an equilateral triangle on the screen. The procedure can be written using recursion.

14. Write a recursive procedure that will draw a square on the screen.

15. Use procedure TRIANGLE from Exercise 13 to make the following designs:

    a.
    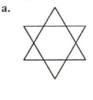

    b.
    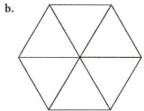

16. Create the following design using the SQUARE procedure from Exercise 14:

    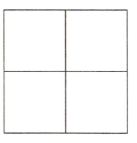

17. Create the following designs using the TRIANGLE and SQUARE procedures from Exercises 13 and 14:

    a.
    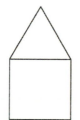

b.

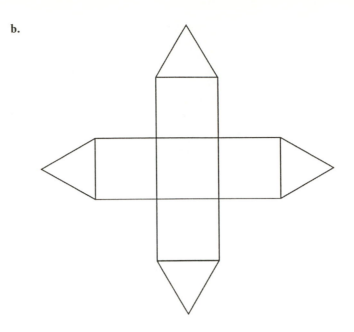

18. Using procedure SQUARE from Exercise 14, write a program to draw the following figure on the screen:

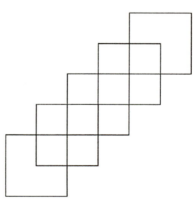

19. Using procedure TRIANGLE from Exercise 13, write a program to draw the following figure on the screen:

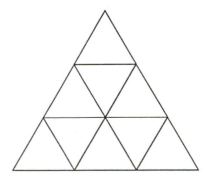

20. Write a program that will output a regular pentagon on the screen and print the string 'PENTAGON' below the picture.

21. Write a program that will output a regular hexagon on the screen and print the string 'HEXAGON' below the picture.

22. Write a program that will output the Cartesian coordinate system and graph the line Y = X as follows:

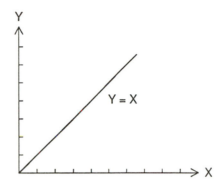

23. A grid used for drawing graphs can be produced using a looping structure. Write a program that will draw a grid of horizontal and vertical lines. Each line of the grid should be 20 spaces from the next line.

24. Write a program using procedures to draw the following figure on the screen. The program should print the string 'MY FLOWER' as indicated. (The main program for this exercise is given on the following page.)

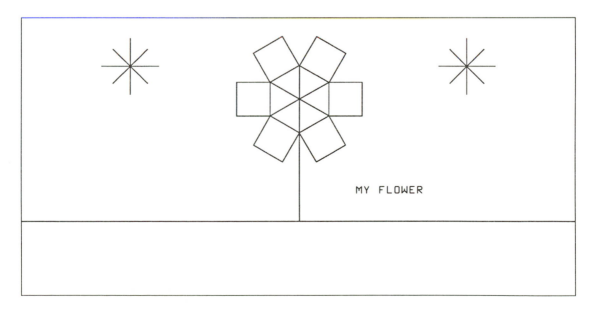

```
BEGIN   { MAIN PROGRAM }

    INITTURTLE;
    BOUNDARY;
    LAWN;
    FLOWER;
    STEM;
    CREATESTAR;
    DRAWSTAR;
    MESSAGE;
    READLN;
    TEXTMODE

END.
```

Set III. Synthesis

25. Create an individualized graphics picture. Use procedures to separate different parts of the picture.

    Option: Include animation in the picture.

26. A regular polygon is a many-sided convex figure with equal sides. For example, a three-sided regular polygon is an equilateral triangle and a four-sided regular polygon is a square. Write a program that will draw a regular polygon with the number of sides selected by the user. Use a looping structure and the expression

    ```
    360 / (number of sides) * (loop variable)
    ```

    as the argument of TURN. If the requested polygon has eight sides or fewer, write its name below it, according to the following table:

Number of Sides	Polygon
3	Equilateral triangle
4	Square
5	Pentagon
6	Hexagon
7	Septagon
8	Octagon

    For polygons with more than 8 sides the form of the name can be n-gon where n is the number of sides.

27. A circle can be thought of as an infinite-sided polygon. By experimenting with Exercise 26, write a procedure that will draw a circle.

28. Write a program that will draw various rectangles using random colors, sizes, and positions on the screen. Use FILLSCREEN and VIEWPORT to color the inside of the rectangles.

29. A cube is a three-dimensional solid with all sides square. Write a program that will simulate a cube centered in the screen and labeled as shown.

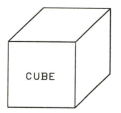

30. Write a program to draw a house with a chimney. Using animation, simulate the smoke rising out of the chimney.

31. Modify procedure TRIANGLE from Exercise 13 to draw three concentric triangles. Concentric means that each triangle is within another triangle.

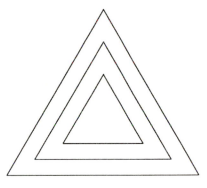

32. A bar graph is a graph that labels a horizontal and vertical axis and specifies data using bars. For example, the following bar graph represents the yearly new car sales of a car lot.

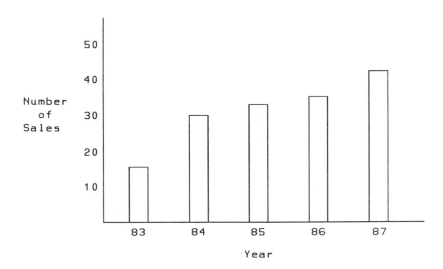

Write a program that will construct bar graphs. Request the labels for the horizontal and vertical axes. Assume that there will be five equally spaced values along both the horizontal and vertical axes.

33. A pie graph consists of a circle divided into pie-shaped pieces. Write a program that will draw a pie graph given the percentage of the pie in each piece. Label the graph and each piece of pie appropriately. The pie graph should be similar to the following:

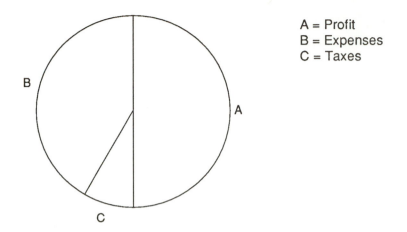

A = Profit
B = Expenses
C = Taxes

34. The simplified floor plan of a typical home follows:

LR	BR1	BR2
DR	KT BA	BR3

Write a program to draw the floor plan and appropriate labels. Use the dimensions provided by the user to compute the area of each room and the total area of the home. Print the areas in the text mode. Allow the user to move between the graphics and text display.

35. Using the axes drawn in Exercise 22, write a program to draw lines. The user will enter a starting point and a slope in the text mode. The starting point is a coordinate (X,Y) and the slope is the vertical change divided by the horizontal change.

36. Create a computerized checkerboard for two players. Draw the board on the screen and allow the players to enter their moves. Show the placement of the pieces and move them according to the players' directions.

Programmer's Handbook

Section A

ASCII and Other Character Sets

ASCII—American
Standard Code for
Information
Interchange

Character (Control Character)		Decimal	Binary	Hexadecimal	Octal
CTRL-@	(NUL)	0	00000000	00	000
CTRL-A	(SOH)	1	00000001	01	001
CTRL-B	(STX)	2	00000010	02	002
CTRL-C	(ETX)	3	00000011	03	003
CTRL-D	(EOT)	4	00000100	04	004
CTRL-E	(ENQ)	5	00000101	05	005
CTRL-F	(ACK)	6	00000110	06	006
CTRL-G	(BEL)	7	00000111	07	007
CTRL-H	(BS)	8	00001000	08	010
CTRL-I	(HT)	9	00001001	09	011
CTRL-J	(LF)	10	00001010	0A	012
CTRL-K	(VT)	11	00001011	0B	013
CTRL-L	(FF)	12	00001100	0C	014
CTRL-M	(CR)	13	00001101	0D	015
CTRL-N	(SO)	14	00001110	0E	016
CTRL-O	(SI)	15	00001111	0F	017
CTRL-P	(DLE)	16	00010000	10	020
CTRL-Q	(DC1)	17	00010001	11	021
CTRL-R	(DC2)	18	00010010	12	022
CTRL-S	(DC3)	19	00010011	13	023
CTRL-T	(DC4)	20	00010100	14	024
CTRL-U	(NAK)	21	00010101	15	025
CTRL-V	(SYN)	22	00010110	16	026
CTRL-W	(ETB)	23	00010111	17	027
CTRL-X	(CAN)	24	00011000	18	030
CTRL-Y	(EM)	25	00011001	19	031
CTRL-Z	(SUB)	26	00011010	1A	032
CTRL-[	(ESC)	27	00011011	1B	033
CTRL-	(FS)	28	00011100	1C	034
CTRL-]	(GS)	29	00011101	1D	035
CTRL-∧	(RS)	30	00011110	1E	036
CTRL-__	(US)	31	00011111	1F	037
SPACE		32	00100000	20	040
!		33	00100001	21	041
"		34	00100010	22	042
#		35	00100011	23	043
$		36	00100100	24	044
%		37	00100101	25	045

Character	Decimal	Binary	Hexadecimal	Octal
&	38	00100110	26	046
'	39	00100111	27	047
(	40	00101000	28	050
)	41	00101001	29	051
*	42	00101010	2A	052
+	43	00101011	2B	053
,	44	00101100	2C	054
−	45	00101101	2D	055
.	46	00101110	2E	056
/	47	00101111	2F	057
0	48	00110000	30	060
1	49	00110001	31	061
2	50	00110010	32	062
3	51	00110011	33	063
4	52	00110100	34	064
5	53	00110101	35	065
6	54	00110110	36	066
7	55	00110111	37	067
8	56	00111000	38	070
9	57	00111001	39	071
:	58	00111010	3A	072
;	59	00111011	3B	073
<	60	00111100	3C	074
=	61	00111101	3D	075
>	62	00111110	3E	076
?	63	00111111	3F	077
@	64	01000000	40	100
A	65	01000001	41	101
B	66	01000010	42	102
C	67	01000011	43	103
D	68	01000100	44	104
E	69	01000101	45	105
F	70	01000110	46	106
G	71	01000111	47	107
H	72	01001000	48	110
I	73	01001001	49	111
J	74	01001010	4A	112
K	75	01001011	4B	113
L	76	01001100	4C	114
M	77	01001101	4D	115
N	78	01001110	4E	116

Character	Decimal	Binary	Hexadecimal	Octal
O	79	01001111	4F	117
P	80	01010000	50	120
Q	81	01010001	51	121
R	82	01010010	52	122
S	83	01010011	53	123
T	84	01010100	54	124
U	85	01010101	55	125
V	86	01010110	56	126
W	87	01010111	57	127
X	88	01011000	58	130
Y	89	01011001	59	131
Z	90	01011010	5A	132
[	91	01011011	5B	133
\	92	01011100	5C	134
]	93	01011101	5D	135
^	94	01011110	5E	136
_	95	01011111	5F	137
`	96	01100000	60	140
a	97	01100001	61	141
b	98	01100010	62	142
c	99	01100011	63	143
d	100	01100100	64	144
e	101	01100101	65	145
f	102	01100110	66	146
g	103	01100111	67	147
h	104	01101000	68	150
i	105	01101001	69	151
j	106	01101010	6A	152
k	107	01101011	6B	153
l	108	01101100	6C	154
m	109	01101101	6D	155
n	110	01101110	6E	156
o	111	01101111	6F	157
p	112	01110000	70	160
q	113	01110001	71	161
r	114	01110010	72	162
s	115	01110011	73	163
t	116	01110100	74	164
u	117	01110101	75	165
v	118	01110110	76	166
w	119	01110111	77	167

Character	Decimal	Binary	Hexadecimal	Octal
x	120	01111000	78	170
y	121	01111001	79	171
z	122	01111010	7A	172
{	123	01111011	7B	173
|	124	01111100	7C	174
}	125	01111101	7D	175
~	126	01111110	7E	176
DEL	127	01111111	7F	177

EBCDIC—Extended Binary Coded Decimal Interchange Code

Character	Binary	Decimal
space	0100 0000	64
	0100 1010	74
.	0100 1011	75
<	0100 1100	76
(	0100 1101	77
+	0100 1110	78
|	0100 1111	79
&	0101 0000	80
!	0101 1010	90
$	0101 1011	91
*	0101 1100	92
)	0101 1101	93
;	0101 1110	94
	0101 1111	95
−	0110 0000	96
/	0110 0001	97
'	0110 1011	107
%	0110 1100	108
_	0110 1101	109
>	0110 1110	110
?	0110 1111	111
:	0111 1010	122
#	0111 1011	123

Character	Binary	Decimal
@	0111 1100	124
'	0111 1101	125
=	0111 1110	126
"	0111 1111	127
a	1000 0001	129
b	1000 0010	130
c	1000 0011	131
d	1000 0100	132
e	1000 0101	133
f	1000 0110	134
g	1000 0111	135
h	1000 1000	136
i	1000 1001	137
j	1001 0001	145
k	1001 0010	146
l	1001 0011	147
m	1001 0100	148
n	1001 0101	149
o	1001 0110	150
p	1001 0111	151
q	1001 1000	152
r	1001 1001	153
s	1010 0010	162
t	1010 0011	163
u	1010 0100	164
v	1010 0101	165
w	1010 0110	166
x	1010 0111	167
y	1010 1000	168
z	1010 1001	169
A	1100 0001	193
B	1100 0010	194
C	1100 0011	195

Character	Binary	Decimal
D	1100 0100	196
E	1100 0101	197
F	1100 0110	198
G	1100 0111	199
H	1100 1000	200
I	1100 1001	201
J	1101 0001	209
K	1101 0010	210
L	1101 0011	211
M	1101 0100	212
N	1101 0101	213
O	1101 0110	214
P	1101 0111	215
Q	1101 1000	216
R	1101 1001	217
S	1110 0010	226
T	1110 0011	227
U	1110 0100	228
V	1110 0101	229
W	1110 0110	230
X	1110 0111	231
Y	1110 1000	232
Z	1110 1001	233
0	1111 0000	240
1	1111 0001	241
2	1111 0010	242
3	1111 0011	243
4	1111 0100	244
5	1111 0101	245
6	1111 0110	246
7	1111 0111	247
8	1111 1000	248
9	1111 1001	249

CDC—Control Data Corporation (ASCII subset)

Character	Binary	Decimal
A	0000 0001	1
B	0000 0010	2
C	0000 0011	3
D	0000 0100	4
E	0000 0101	5
F	0000 0110	6
G	0000 0111	7
H	0000 1000	8
I	0000 1001	9
J	0000 1010	10
K	0000 1011	11
L	0000 1100	12
M	0000 1101	13
N	0000 1110	14
O	0000 1111	15
P	0001 0000	16
Q	0001 0001	17
R	0001 0010	18
S	0001 0011	19
T	0001 0100	20
U	0001 0101	21
V	0001 0110	22
W	0001 0111	23
X	0001 1000	24
Y	0001 1001	25
Z	0001 1010	26
0	0001 1011	27
1	0001 1100	28
2	0001 1101	29
3	0001 1110	30
4	0001 1111	31
5	0010 0000	32

Character	Binary	Decimal
6	0010 0001	33
7	0010 0010	34
8	0010 0011	35
9	0010 0100	36
+	0010 0101	37
−	0010 0110	38
*	0010 0111	39
/	0010 1000	40
(	0010 1001	41
)	0010 1010	42
$	0010 1011	43
=	0010 1100	44
space	0010 1101	45
,	0010 1110	46
.	0010 1111	47
#	0011 0000	48
[	0011 0001	49
]	0011 0010	50
:	0011 0011	51
"	0011 0100	52
−	0011 0101	53
!	0011 0110	54
&	0011 0111	55
'	0011 1000	56
?	0011 1001	57
<	0011 1010	58
>	0011 1011	59
@	0011 1100	60
\	0011 1101	61
∧	0011 1110	62
;	0011 1111	63

Section B BASIC/Pascal Comparisons

For programmers with a background in BASIC, the following comparisons may be useful. Commands not available (indicated here by *n/a*) in a language can usually be simulated in some fashion using other commands.

Description	BASIC	Pascal
Data Types		
Real Numbers	*real*	REAL
Strings of Characters	*string*$	STRING
Integers	*integer*%	INTEGER
Characters		CHAR
Boolean Values		BOOLEAN
Programmer-Defined Ordinal Types		programmer-defined
Operations		
Addition	+	+
Subtraction/Negative	−	−
Multiplication	*	*
Division	/	/
Integer Division	*n/a*	DIV
Modular Division	*n/a*	MOD
Assignment	=	:=
Exponentiation	∧	n/a
Built-in Functions		
ASCII Value of Character	ASC(ST$)	ORD(ST[1])
Character for ASCII Value	CHR$(CH)	CHR(CH)
Absolute Value	ABS	ABS
Arctangent	ATAN	ATAN
Cosine	COS	COS
Sine	SIN	SIN
Tangent	TAN	*n/a*
Exponentiation	EXP	EXP
Natural Log	LOG	LN
Base-10 Log	*n/a*	LOG
Square Root	SQR	SQRT
Square	*n/a*	SQR
Integer Part	INT	TRUNC
Round	*n/a*	ROUND
Random Numbers	RND	RANDOM
		RANDOMIZE

Description	BASIC	Pascal
Sign	SGN	*n/a*
Odd	*n/a*	ODD
End-of-Line	*n/a*	EOLN
End-of-File	*n/a*	EOF

Input

Ncoln User Input

User Input	INPUT NUM,NAME$	READLN (NUM,NAME);
Prompted Input	PRINT "ENTER NUMBER: " INPUT NUM	WRITE('ENTER NUMBER: '); READLN(NUM);

or

INPUT"ENTER NUMBER: ";NUM

Iteration

Definite Iteration

```
FOR CNT=1 TO 10          FOR CNT:=1 TO 10 DO
   (statements)              BEGIN
NEXT CNT                        (statements)
                             END;

FOR CNT=2 TO 10 STEP2    FOR CNT := 1 TO 5 DO
.                            BEGIN
.                               CNT2 := CNT * 2
.                            END;
                         (or simulate with indefinite
                         iteration)

FOR CNT=10 TO 1 STEP-1   FOR CNT := 10 DOWNTO 1 DO
.                            .
.                            .
.                            .
```

Indefinite iteration

```
       n/a               WHILE NUM<10 DO
(must simulate using        (statement)
IF . . . THEN and GOTO)  REPEAT
                            (statement)
                         UNTIL NUM>=10
```

Selection

Two-Way

```
IF NUM<5 THEN            IF NUM<5
   (statement):GOTO 40      THEN
(statement)                    (statement)
                            ELSE
                               (statement)
```

Multiway

```
ON NUM GOTO 1,2,3,4      CASE NUM OF
     or                     1 :statement;
ON NUM GOSUB . . .          2 :statement;
                            3,4:statement
                         END;
```

Description	BASIC	Pascal
Procedures (Subroutines)		
Procedure Call	GOSUB 100	*procedure identifier* *(actual parameters)*;

Procedure Block	100 REM *description of*
	 routine
	
	 (statements)
	
	 RETURN
		PROCEDURE *procedure identifier*
		 (formal parameters);
		 BEGIN
		 (statements)
		 END;

Arrays		
Variable Declaration	DIM NUM(50),NAME$(5)	VAR NUM:ARRAY[0..50] OF REAL; NAME:ARRAY[0..5] OF STRING;
Miscellaneous		
Available Memory	FRE(0)	MEMAVAIL
End of Execution	END	END. (for main program) END; (for compound statement)
Functions	DEF FN R(N)	FUNCTION R(NUM:REAL):REAL; (can be scalar, subrange, or pointer type result)
Unconditional Branch	GOTO 100	GOTO 100 (must be within same block)

Section C Compiler Options

Instructions telling the compiler to perform certain tasks can be embedded in the text file to be compiled. These compiler options are written into a special kind of comment statement and take effect when encountered during compiling. The general form of a compiler option is

```
{$option}

    or

(*$option*)
```

Caution: No spaces are allowed before or after the dollar symbol ($). Several options may be listed in one line, separated by commas; no spaces should be added. A space is allowed in options involving file names or strings, but the file name must be the last item before the end brace (}), as in the following example:

```
{$option1,option2,option3 filename}
```

The following table sets forth the compiler options available in Apple UCSD Pascal.

Option	Description	Comment
C *message*	Places the following message directly into the code file.	Allows copyright or other notice in the code file.
G +	Allows GOTO statements.	See Section U.
G −	Forbids GOTO statements.	Default.
I +	Generates I/O-checking code.	Default.
I −	No I/O checking.	Use with caution.
I *filename*	Includes the indicated source file in compilation.	Useful when file is too large to fit in Editor.
L +	Sends compiled listing to SYSTEM.LST.TEXT on boot disk.	
L −	Makes no compiled listing.	Default.
L *filename*	Sends compiled listing to named file.	*Example:* {$L PRINTER:} For further information, see Programmer's Handbook, Section P.

Option	Description	Comment
N+	Prevents library units from being loaded until activated.	
N−	Loads library units immediately when program runs.	Default.
P	Inserts a page feed into compiled listing immediately before the option.	
Q+	Suppresses screen messages during compilation.	Speeds compile time.
Q−	Sends procedure names and line numbers to CONSOLE:.	Default.
R+	Generates range-checking code.	Default.
R−	No range checking, speeds up program.	Use with caution.
R *procname*	Keeps named procedure loaded while current one is active.	
S+	Puts compiler in swapping mode.	Makes more memory available and slows compiling.
S++	Has compiler do even more swapping.	
S−	Non-swapping mode.	Default.
U+	Compiles user program.	Default.
U−	Compiles system program.	Use with caution (sets R−, G+, and I−).
U *filename*	Specifies name of file for finding library units.	See Programmer's Handbook, Section L.

Section D Diskette Information

Diskette Care

A reasonable amount of caution should be used to protect diskettes. A few moments spent on diskette care may save hours of problems in the future. Here are several recommendations that may provide an ounce of prevention.

- Don't touch exposed surface of diskette.
- Store diskettes in their envelopes and in an appropriate box. Store diskettes in an upright position.
- Store diskettes in dry area, out of direct sunlight. Avoid extremes in temperature.
- Diskettes are sensitive to pressure. Don't bend diskettes. Use only felt-tip pens to write on labels.
- Keep diskettes away from magnets and electrical devices. This includes monitors and some disk drives.
- Keep work area clean. Diskettes will not tolerate dust, eraser particles, or soda.
- Back up all important work on a different diskette and store it in a safe place.

Formatting Pascal Disks

Pascal diskettes must be formatted using a utility program. For Apple UCSD Pascal, the program is called FORMATTER and can be found on the APPLE3 diskette.

One-Drive Setup

Most Pascal operating systems work best with two disk drives; however, one-drive Pascal systems are often possible. Using a single drive will necessitate some diskette swapping. The following diskette arrangement may help to minimize the number of exchanges required. (This setup is for Apple Pascal. Similar arrangements are possible for other systems.)

Boot Disk	Work Disk	Storage
APPLE0:	APPLE0:	STORE:
SYSTEM.PASCAL	SYSTEM.PASCAL	
SYSTEM.MISCINFO	SYSTEM.MISCINFO	
SYSTEM.LIBRARY	SYSTEM.COMPILER	
SYSTEM.CHARSET	SYSTEM.EDITOR	
SYSTEM.SYNTAX	SYSTEM.FILER	
SYSTEM.APPLE	SYSTEM.LIBRARY	
	SYSTEM.CHARSET	
	SYSTEM.SYNTAX	
6/6 files,	8/8 files,	0/0 files<listed/
150 unused,	32 unused,	in-dir>,
150 in largest	32 in largest	6 blocks used,
		274 unused,
		274 in largest

The boot disk and the work disk are given the same volume name. Once the system is booted, the diskettes are exchanged. The work disk has all the required files for programming, plus enough room for a text file of reasonable size. Extra room can be obtained by removing SYSTEM.SYNTAX. This eliminates error messages which would then have to be looked up using the corresponding error number (see Programmer's Handbook, Section E). Also, SYSTEM.LIBRARY can be removed if no library units are needed. Another possibility is to put SYSTEM.FILER on the boot disk. This forces a diskette swap when using the filer, but saves space on the work disk. The storage diskette is used only for storing final versions of programs. Other configurations are certainly possible and may better serve individual needs.

Two-Drive Setup

In addition to APPLE0 for single-drive systems, three other diskettes are used for Apple UCSD Pascal. APPLE1 and APPLE2 are used for a two-drive system (see Programmer's Handbook, Section O); APPLE3 contains demos and utilities. Here is the manner in which these diskettes are normally set up.

APPLE1	APPLE2	APPLE3
SYSTEM.APPLE	SYSTEM.ASSMBLER	SYSTEM.APPLE
SYSTEM.PASCAL	SYSTEM.COMPILER	FORMATTER.CODE
SYSTEM.EDITOR	SYSTEM.LINKER	FORMATTER.DATA
SYSTEM.FILER	LIBMAP.CODE	BINDER.CODE
SYSTEM.LIBRARY	LIBRARY.CODE	LINEFEED.CODE
SYSTEM.MISCINFO	6500.OPCODES	LINEFEED.TEXT
SYSTEM.CHARSET	6500.ERRORS	II40.MISCINFO
SYSTEM.SYNTAX		II80.MISCINFO
SYSTEM.WRK.TEXT		IIE40.MISCINFO
SYSTEM.WRK.CODE		BALANCED.TEXT
		CROSSREF.TEXT
		DISKIO.TEXT
		GRAFCHARS.TEXT
		GRAFDEMO.TEXT
		HAZEL.MISCINFO
		HAZELGOTO.TEXT
		HILBERT.TEXT
		SETUP.CODE
		SPIRODEMO.TEXT
		TREE.TEXT
		128K.APPLE
		128K.PASCAL
10/10 files,	7/7 files,	22/22 files,
63 unused,	96 unused,	6 unused,
63 in largest	96 in largest	6 in largest

Since 63 blocks may not be enough room for a large program text and code file, this setup may occasionally need to be altered. Moving the Filer, Editor, and/or other files to APPLE2 can free some much-needed space on APPLE1.

Section E

Error Messages

Compiler Errors

The following errors may occur during compilation. Many are syntax errors and can be avoided if care is taken during initial writing of the file.

Error Number	Error Message
1	Error in simple type
2	Identifier expected
3	'PROGRAM' expected
4	')' expected
5	':' expected
6	Illegal symbol (maybe a missing or extra ';' on line above)
7	Error in parameter list
8	'OF' expected
9	'(' expected
10	Error in type
11	'[' expected
12	']' expected
13	'END' expected
14	';' expected (possibly on line above)
15	Integer expected
16	'=' expected
17	'BEGIN' expected
18	Error in declaration part
19	Error in field-list
20	' , ' expected
21	' . ' expected
22	'Interface' expected
23	'Implementation' expected
24	'CODE' expected
50	Error in constant
51	' := ' expected
52	'THEN' expected
53	'UNTIL' expected
54	'DO' expected
55	'TO' or 'DOWNTO' expected in FOR statement
58	Error in factor (bad expression)
59	Error in variable

Error Number	Error Message
101	Identifier declared twice
102	Low bound exceeds high bound
103	Identifier is not of the appropriate class
104	Undeclared identifier
105	Sign not allowed
106	Number expected
107	Incompatible subrange types
108	File not allowed here
109	Type must not be real
110	Tagfield type must be scalar or subrange
111	Incompatible with tagfield part
113	Index type must be a scalar or a subrange
114	Base type must not be real
115	Base type must be a scalar or a subrange
117	Unsatisfied forward reference
119	Re-specified parameters not ok for a forward declared procedure
120	Function result type must be scalar, subrange or pointer
121	File value parameter not allowed
122	Result type of forward declared function cannot be re-specified
123	Missing result type in function declaration
125	Error in type of standard procedure parameter
126	Number of parameters does not agree with declaration
128	Result type does not agree with declaration
129	Type conflict of operands
130	Expression is not of set type
131	Only tests on equality are allowed
132	Strict inclusion not allowed
133	File comparison not allowed

Error Number	Error Message
134	Illegal type of operand(s)
135	Type of operand must be boolean
136	Set element type must be scalar or subrange
137	Set element types must be compatible
138	Type of variable is not array
139	Index type is not compatible with the declaration
140	Type of variable is not record
141	Type of variable must be file or pointer
142	Illegal actual parameter
143	Illegal type of loop control variable
144	Illegal type of expression
145	Type conflict
146	Assignment of files not allowed
147	Label type incompatible with selecting expression
148	Subrange bounds must be scalar
149	Index type must not be integer
150	Assignment to standard function is not allowed
152	No such field in this record
154	Actual parameter must be a variable
155	Control variable cannot be formal or non-local
156	Multidefined case label
158	No such variant in this record
159	Real or string tagfields not allowed
160	Previous declaration was not forward
161	Forward declared twice
162	Parameter size must be constant
165	Multidefined label
166	Multideclared label
167	Undeclared label
168	Undefined label
169	Base type of set too large

Error Number	Error Message
175	Actual parameter max string length $<$ formal max length
182	Nested units not allowed
183	External declaration not allowed at this nesting level
184	External declaration not allowed in interface section
185	Segment declaration not allowed in unit
186	Labels not allowed in interface section
187	Attempt to open library unsuccessful
188	Unit not declared in previous uses declaration
189	'Uses' not allowed at this nesting level
190	Unit not in library
191	No private files in unit
192	'Uses' must be in interface section
194	Comment must appear at top of program
195	Unit not importable (interface text not available)
201	Error in real number—digit expected
202	String constant must not exceed source line
203	Integer constant exceeds range
250	Too many scopes of nested identifiers
251	Too many nested procedures or functions
253	Procedure too long
254	Procedure too complex
273	No such unit or segment
277	String too long
301	No case provided for this value

Error Number	Error Message
350	No data segment allocated
352	No code segment allocated
353	Non-intrinsic unit called from intrinsic unit
354	Too many segments for segment dictionary
355	Data segment empty
399	Implementation restriction
400	Illegal character in text
401	Unexpected end of input
402	Error in write to code file, maybe not enough room on disk
403	Error while opening or reading include file
404	Bad open, read, or write to Linker file SYSTEM.INFO
405	Error while reading library
406	Include file not legal in interface nor while including
408	(*$S + *) needed to compile units
409	General Compiler error
500	General Assembler error

Execution Errors

An execution error may occur while a program is running. If so, the error is reported, along with the segment number (S#), procedure number (P#) within the segment, and the byte number (I#) in the procedure where the error occurred. A compiler listing (see Programmer's Handbook, Section P) can help in determining the segment, procedure, and byte.

Error Number	Error Message
0	System error (fatal)
1	Invalid index, value out of range
2	No segment, bad code file

Error Number	Error Message
3	Procedure not present at exit time
4	Stack overflow (available memory exceeded)
5	Integer overflow
6	Divide by zero
7	Invalid memory reference (not used on Apple)
8	User break (CTRL-@ on Apple)
9	System I/O error (fatal)
10	User I/O error
11	Unimplemented instruction
12	Floating point math error (real format, overflow, underflow)
13	String too long
14	Halt, Breakpoint (not used on Apple)
15	Bad block (I/O error #64 on Apple)

Input/Output Errors

When execution error #10 (User I/O error) occurs, the appropriate I/O error message is given.

Error Number	Error Message
0	No error
1	Diskette has bad block (Not used on Apple.)
2	Bad device (volume) number
3	Illegal operation (Ex: attempt to read from printer.)
4	Undefined hardware error (Not used on Apple.)
5	Device is no longer on-line, after successfully starting an operation using that device
6	File is no longer in the diskette directory, after successfully starting an operation using that file
7	Illegal filename (Ex: filename more than 15 characters long.)
8	Insufficient space on specified diskette
9	Specified volume is not on-line
10	Specified file is not in directory of specified volume
11	Attempt to re-write an existing file
12	Attempt to open an already-open file
13	Attempt to access a closed file

Error Number	Error Message
14	Error in reading real or integer (Ex: input character when integer expected.)
15	Characters arriving faster than input buffer can accept them
16	Specified diskette is write-protected
64	Failed to complete a read or write correctly

Section G   Graphics

Turtlegraphics gives the programmer the ability to draw a variety of pictures to enhance programming. For most applications, these line-oriented graphics are fine; on some occasions, however, they are inadequate. Consider a program in which a complicated picture must be drawn at several spots on the screen. Of course, a procedure could be written to draw the picture, using different parameters for directing the location on the screen. This process could be extremely time-consuming, depending on the complexity of the picture. The process would be slowed even more if movement or animation is attempted. Even for a moderately complex picture, the animation would be far too slow to be effective.

DRAWBLOCK Procedure

When using Apple UCSD Pascal, an alternative for these situations is the DRAWBLOCK procedure available through the TURTLEGRAPHICS unit. This procedure allows the programmer to define a picture and then reproduce the picture anywhere on the screen. DRAWBLOCK copies a map (a two-dimensional packed BOOLEAN array) of dots—TRUE for white, FALSE for black—from memory onto the screen. The first and second dimensions of the array are the number of rows and the number of columns, respectively. An entire array, or a portion of the array, can be copied onto the screen at a starting point specified by the programmer. The general form of DRAWBLOCK and an explanation of its parameters follow. (All the parameters, except for the first, are integers.)

```
DRAWBLOCK(source, rowsize, xskip,
          yskip, width, height, xscreen,
          yscreen, mode);
```

- *source* is the variable name (without subscripts) of a two-dimensional packed BOOLEAN array.
- *rowsize* is the number of bytes per row of the array. This can be calculated by

```
2 * ((DOTS + 15) DIV 16)
```

where DOTS is the number of dots per row.
- *xskip* is used to specify a portion (horizontal) of the array. This parameter instructs DRAWBLOCK to ignore the first *xskip* number of dots in the array before copying the picture to the screen.
- *yskip* specifies the number of rows (beginning at the bottom) to pass over before copying the picture to the screen.
- *width* is used with *xskip* to specify the right-hand portion of the array. This parameter instructs the procedure to start

the copy process at *xskip* and continue for *width* number of dots.

- *height* is used with *yskip* to determine the top boundary of the array. The procedure starts at row *yskip* and copies *height* rows upward. Thus, *xskip*, *yskip*, *width*, and *height* form a window to the array and tell what portion of the picture will be transferred to the screen.

- *xscreen* and *yscreen* are the screen coordinates for the lower-left corner of the picture. From this point, *width* and *height* give the dimensions of the window.

- *mode* (from 0 to 15) determines the state of the picture to be copied to the screen. Besides copying the array literally, this parameter can fill the window with white or black (regardless of the array contents), or combine the contents of the array with the current state of the window using logical operators. The following table gives the effect of each value for *mode*; A and S represent the array and screen, respectively.

Mode	Effect
0	Fills the window with black.
1	NOT (A OR S)
2	A AND (NOT S)
3	NOT S
4	(NOT A) AND S
5	NOT A
6	A XOR S
7	NOT(A AND S)
8	A AND S
9	A = S
10	A (Copies array to screen.)
11	A OR (NOT S)
12	S (Screen replaces screen.)
13	(NOT A) OR S
14	A OR S
15	Fills the window with white.

As mentioned earlier, DRAWBLOCK takes a packed BOOLEAN array and treats TRUE as a white dot and FALSE as a black dot. Alternating TRUE and FALSE creates colored areas (TRUE odd dots create odd-numbered colors—green or orange depending on whether the background is BLACK1 or BLACK2). Alternating background colors (for example, BLACK1 versus BLACK2) also alternates between low- and high-numbered colors. Which colors are displayed is related to the manner in which the Apple computer produces color. A little experimentation will show the options available to the programmer.

A program using the DRAWBLOCK procedure to display a playing card at any location on the screen follows:

```
PROGRAM SHAPES(INPUT);

        { PURPOSE: DRAW A PLAYING CARD USING DRAWBLOCK }

USES TURTLEGRAPHICS;

TYPE
    CARDTYPE = PACKED ARRAY[1..41,1..29] OF BOOLEAN;

VAR
    CARD    : CARDTYPE;
    BIT     : BOOLEAN;
    ROW     : INTEGER;

PROCEDURE MAKECARD(VAR BITMAP:CARDTYPE; S:STRING);

    VAR
        J : INTEGER;

    BEGIN
        FOR J := 1 TO LENGTH(S) DO
            BEGIN
                BIT := (S[J] <> ' ');
                BITMAP[ROW,J] := BIT
            END;
        ROW := ROW - 1
    END;

PROCEDURE ACE1;
  BEGIN
    ROW := 41;
    MAKECARD(CARD,'  *************************   ');
    MAKECARD(CARD,'  **************************  ');
    MAKECARD(CARD,'*****************************');
    MAKECARD(CARD,'***          ****************');
    MAKECARD(CARD,'**    ****    ***************');
    MAKECARD(CARD,'**    ****    ***************');
    MAKECARD(CARD,'**            ***************');
    MAKECARD(CARD,'**    ****    ***************');
    MAKECARD(CARD,'**    ****    ***************');
    MAKECARD(CARD,'**    ****    ***************');
    MAKECARD(CARD,'*****************************');
    MAKECARD(CARD,'*****************************');
    MAKECARD(CARD,'*****************************');
    MAKECARD(CARD,'*******  ********************');
    MAKECARD(CARD,'******    *******************');
    MAKECARD(CARD,'*****      ******************');
    MAKECARD(CARD,'****        *****************');
    MAKECARD(CARD,'***          ****************');
    MAKECARD(CARD,'**            ******     *****');
    MAKECARD(CARD,'**            ****  *  *  ***');
    MAKECARD(CARD,'**     *  *    ***    * *   **');
    MAKECARD(CARD,'***   *   *   ****         **');
    MAKECARD(CARD,'*****      ******          **');
    MAKECARD(CARD,'****************          ***');
    MAKECARD(CARD,'*****************          ****');
    MAKECARD(CARD,'******************      *****');
    MAKECARD(CARD,'*******************    ******');
    MAKECARD(CARD,'******************** *******');
    MAKECARD(CARD,'*****************************')
  END;
```

```
PROCEDURE ACE2;

   BEGIN
      MAKECARD(CARD,'*****************************');
      MAKECARD(CARD,'*****************************');
      MAKECARD(CARD,'******************   ****   **');
      MAKECARD(CARD,'******************   ****   **');
      MAKECARD(CARD,'******************   ****   **');
      MAKECARD(CARD,'******************          **');
      MAKECARD(CARD,'******************   ****   **');
      MAKECARD(CARD,'******************   ****   **');
      MAKECARD(CARD,'******************        ***');
      MAKECARD(CARD,'*****************************');
      MAKECARD(CARD,' *************************** ');
      MAKECARD(CARD,'   ***********************   ')
   END;

BEGIN   { MAIN PROGRAM }

   ACE1;
   ACE2;
   INITTURTLE;
   FILLSCREEN(BLACK2);
   DRAWBLOCK(CARD,4,0,0,29,41,70,100,14);
   READLN

END.
```

Storing and Loading Pictures

Occasionally, a programmer may need to store an entire graphics screen on disk and recall it at a later time. The following program shows how a picture on the Apple high-resolution graphics Page1 (abbreviated as HGR Page1) can be stored on disk and recalled. BLOCKREAD and BLOCKWRITE are functions that read and write untyped files (files with no specified data type). They return a number equal to the number of blocks moved. In this program, they are used to transfer bytes between the Apple's memory and a file on disk. An understanding of the program requires some familiarity with where pictures are stored in memory. (HGR Page1 begins at \$2000, or 8192_{10}, and HGR Page 2 begins at \$4000, or 16384_{10}.) The program also involves variant records (Chapter 15) as well as files (Chapter 16). These topics should be mastered before attempting to follow the specifics of the program. However, even with limited knowledge of the inner workings of high-resolution graphics, these procedures can be used (with care) in other programs. (Note that each procedure uses a string function, CONCAT, to produce the appropriate string for writing and reading the file name. See Chapter 19 for more information on string functions.)

```
PROGRAM SCREEN (INPUT, OUTPUT);

    { PURPOSE: STORE/RECALL ENTIRE GRAPHICS SCREEN }

USES TURTLEGRAPHICS;

CONST
   HGRPAGE1 = 8192;

TYPE
   BLOCKRECORD = RECORD
                    CASE B : BOOLEAN OF
                       TRUE  : (INTPART : INTEGER);
                       FALSE : (PRTPART : ^INTEGER)
                    END;  { CASE/RECORD }

VAR
   TEMP      : FILE;     { UNTYPED FILE }
   MEMBLOCK  : BLOCKRECORD;
   FNAME     : STRING;
   TMP       : INTEGER;

PROCEDURE PUTPIC(FILENAME : STRING);

   BEGIN

      FILENAME := CONCAT('MYDISK:',FILENAME,'.PIC');
      MEMBLOCK.INTPART := HGRPAGE1;
      REWRITE(TEMP,FILENAME);
      TMP := BLOCKWRITE(TEMP,MEMBLOCK.PRTPART^,16);
      CLOSE(TEMP,LOCK)

   END;  { PUTPIC }

PROCEDURE GETPIC(FILENAME : STRING);

   BEGIN

      FILENAME := CONCAT('MYDISK:',FILENAME,'.PIC');
      MEMBLOCK.INTPART := HGRPAGE1;
      RESET(TEMP,FILENAME);
      TMP := BLOCKREAD(TEMP,MEMBLOCK.PRTPART^,16);
      CLOSE(TEMP,LOCK)

   END;  { GETPIC }


BEGIN  { MAIN PROGRAM }

   MEMBLOCK.B := FALSE;
   TEXTMODE;
   WRITELN('NAME TO SAVE');
   READLN(FNAME);
   PUTPIC(FNAME);
   READLN;
   INITTURTLE;
   GETPIC(FNAME);
   READLN

END.
```

Section I Implementations

This section addresses some of the differences between UCSD, Standard, and Turbo Pascal.* The following table lists the chapter number or handbook section of this text where additional information on the topic may be found.

Topic	Chapter/Handbook	UCSD Pascal Feature	Standard Pascal Feature	Turbo Pascal Feature
Program Heading	2	External environments are optional.	Not optional.	Program heading is optional.
Screen Output	2	GOTOXY( ) PAGE(OUTPUT)	Not available. Same as UCSD.	Same as UCSD. Use CLRSCR.
Data Types	2	long INTEGER	Not available.	Available in some versions (4.0).
	2	STRING Can specify string length.	Use PACKED ARRAY [ ] OF CHAR;	Must specify string length; for example STRING[5]
Built-in Functions	3	Transcendental functions require statement: USES TRANSCEND;	No additional requirement.	No additional requirement.
	3	PWROFTEN( )	Must use EXP(10*LN(X))	Same as Standard.
	3	ATAN( )	ARCTAN( )	Same as Standard.
	3	LOG( ) (common logarithm)	Not available.	Not available.
FOR Loop	5	Counter has value following exit from loop.	Counter is undefined.	Same as UCSD.
CASE Statement	7	Do not need to list all constants.	Must list all constants.	Same as UCSD.
Procedures/Functions	8–9	Procedures and functions cannot be passed as parameters	Can be passed as value parameters.	Same as UCSD.
Functions	9	Actual and formal parameters of type STRING are not allowed. Must be defined by a type definition.	Strings not available.	Strings can be passed.

*Turbo® Pascal developed by Borland International, Inc.

Topic	Chapter/ Handbook	UCSD Pascal Feature	Standard Pascal Feature	Turbo Pascal Feature
Random Numbers	9	The RANDOMIZE procedure provides a random seed; the RANDOM function generates a random number between 0 and 1, including 0. Requires statement: USES APPLESTUFF;	The programmer must write a special function to generate a random number.	RANDOM function same as UCSD. RANDOM(NUMBER) returns a random number between 0 and NUMBER, including 0.
Recursion	10	No special commands necessary.	Same as UCSD.	Need compiler directive {$A − }
Programmer-Defined Types	11	No readable or printable programmer-defined types.	Same as UCSD.	Same as UCSD.
Arrays	13	Can be packed and unpacked.	Same as UCSD.	Packing occur automatically, so commands do not exist.
Records	15	In some versions, a semicolon is not allowed at the end of the field list.	Semicolon is allowed.	Same as Standard.
		NEW accepts variant records.	Same as UCSD.	NEW will not accept variant records.
Files	16	GET and PUT exist. GET(F) advances file window after transferring record to buffer F∧.	GET and PUT exist. GET advances file window before transfer to buffer.	No GET and PUT. READ and WRITE are extended to handle features of GET and PUT.
		SEEK exists for random access.	Not available.	Same as UCSD.
		File must be closed using CLOSE.	Not available.	Same as UCSD.
		EOF/EOLN different for INTERACTIVE files.	EOF/EOLN same for all file types.	Same as Standard.

Topic	Chapter/ Handbook	UCSD Pascal Feature	Standard Pascal Feature	Turbo Pascal Feature
Linked Lists	17	Use MARK and RELEASE (or programmer procedure).	Use DISPOSE( ).	Same as Standard.
Strings	19	Has many built-in functions and procedures. These functions include COPY, CONCAT, POS, and LENGTH. The procedures include INSERT, DELETE, VAL, and STR.	Use PACKED ARRAY[ ] OF CHAR;	Same as UCSD.
Graphics	20	Turtlegraphics. Has many built-in functions and procedures. Requires statement: USES TURTLEGRAPHICS;	None built-in.	Turtlegraphics and Rectangular Coordinate Graphics.
GOTO/LABEL	G	Control can be altered forward or backward. Must not leave current block.	May leave current block.	Same as UCSD.

The features of Standard Pascal are summarized in *Pascal User Manual and Report* by Kathleen Jensen and Niklaus Wirth (New York: Springer-Verlag, 1978). Standard Pascal is used primarily on mainframe systems. UCSD and Turbo Pascal, on the other hand, were developed for microcomputers. UCSD Pascal includes extensions of Standard Pascal, such as built-in procedures for string manipulation and Turtlegraphics.

Section L Library Units

System Library

In Apple USCD Pascal, the system library stores units that can contain additional commands. APPLESTUFF (Chapter 9), TRANSCEND (Chapter 3), and TURTLEGRAPHICS (Chapter 20 and Programmer's Handbook, Section G) are examples of units stored in the system library. A list of their procedures and functions is given here. Assume the following definitions for the parameter types. (SCREENCOLOR is a type defined in the Turtlegraphics unit.)

```
TYPE
    RSTATTYPE=(RSTATBUSY,RSTATREADY,RSTATOFFLINE);
    RSCHANNEL=(RSOUTPUT,RSINPUT);
    BOOLARRAY=ARRAY[left..right,bottom..top]
                OF BOOLEAN;
```

	Function(F) Procedure(P)	Identifier	Parameters	Function Type
APPLESTUFF	F	PADDLE	SELECT:INTEGER	INTEGER
	F	BUTTON	SELECT:INTEGER	BOOLEAN
	P	TTLOUT	SELECT:INTEGER; DATA:BOOLEAN	Not applicable
	F	KEYPRESS	None	BOOLEAN
	F	RANDOM	None	INTEGER
	P	RANDOMIZE	None	Not applicable
	P	NOTE	PITCH,DURATION: INTEGER	Not applicable
	F	REMSTATUS	CHANNEL: RSCHANNEL	RSTATTYPE
TRANSCEND	F	SIN	X:REAL	REAL
	F	COS	X:REAL	REAL
	F	EXP	X:REAL	REAL
	F	ATAN	X:REAL	REAL
	F	LN	X:REAL	REAL
	F	LOG	X:REAL	REAL
	F	SQRT	X:REAL	REAL
TURTLEGRAPHICS	P	INITTURTLE	None	Not applicable
	P	TURN	ANGLE:INTEGER	Not applicable
	P	TURNTO	ANGLE:INTEGER	Not applicable
	P	MOVE	DIST:INTEGER	Not applicable
	P	MOVETO	X,Y:INTEGER	Not applicable
	P	PENCOLOR	PENMODE: SCREENCOLOR	Not applicable

Function(F) Procedure(P)	Identifier	Parameters	Function Type
P	TEXTMODE	None	Not applicable
P	GRAFMODE	None	Not applicable
P	FILLSCREEN	FILLCOLOR: SCREENCOLOR	Not applicable
P	VIEWPORT	LEFT,RIGHT, BOTTOM,TOP: INTEGER	Not applicable
F	TURTLEX	None	INTEGER
F	TURTLEY	None	INTEGER
F	TURTLEANG	None	INTEGER
F	SCREENBIT	X,Y:INTEGER	BOOLEAN
P	DRAWBLOCK	SOURCE: BOOLARRAY; XSKIP,YSKIP, WIDTH,HEIGHT, XSCREEN,YSCREEN, MODE:INTEGER	Not applicable
P	WCHAR	CH:CHAR	Not applicable
P	WSTRING	STRG:STRING	Not applicable
P	CHARTYPE	MODE:INTEGER	Not applicable

These and other units in the system library can be viewed using the utility LIBMAP.

Library Map

LIBMAP is a utility provided on Apple Pascal system diskettes. It gives a map (list of the contents of units) of a library file. The list can be sent to the console (default), printer, or a text file on diskette. This utility will map the system library or a library that has been customized by a programmer.

Custom Library Units

The Apple Pascal utility LIBRARY allows programmers to install their own commonly used routines in a unit. To do this, the code file must be specially prepared before installing in the library. A library unit is similar to a program in its structure; it consists of a heading and an initialization part. However, a unit also contains interface and implementation sections between the heading and initialization parts.

Unit Heading Form

```
UNIT unitname; INTRINSIC CODE segmentnumber
     DATA segmentnumber;
```

The unit name should be something that will remind the programmer that this unit contains custom routines. This example will use MYSTUFF as the unit name. INTRINSIC refers to the fact that this unit is being installed in the library and will be used without actually inserting the code into the host program code file. The CODE segment number is the segment in the library associated with the unit. The DATA segment number is used if the unit declares variables not contained in functions or procedures. Segment numbers can be between 0 and 31, inclusive. Segments 0 through 6 are reserved for system use. For this example, the heading will be

```
UNIT MYSTUFF; INTRINSIC CODE 14 DATA 15;
```

Swapping should be used when a unit is compiled. Thus, the heading should be preceded by

```
{$S+}
```

The interface part of a unit tells how a host program can communicate with the unit. It is the only portion of the unit visible to program users. The interface declares constants, types, variables, functions, and procedures that can be used by the host program. Procedures and functions are only declared in this part— giving just the name and parameters. For a random number function, the following would be used:

```
FUNCTION RND(HIGH,LOW:INTEGER):INTEGER;
```

For this function, the interface part of the unit would also require APPLESTUFF, the built-in unit that contains the commands for generating random numbers on the Apple.

The implementation part of the unit is where the functions and procedures that were declared in the interface part are actually defined. They are defined without listing the parameters, which were given in the interface part. In addition, any labels, constants, types, variables, procedures, or functions that are to remain private (inaccessible from the host program) are declared in this part.

The initialization part is similar to the BEGIN. . . END block of a main program. The commands in this part will execute automatically before the commands in the host program are executed. This provides a way to set up anything needed by the functions or procedures in the unit. Very often, no such commands are needed; however, a BEGIN . . . END block is still required. A simple example of a ready-to-install unit is given here.

```
{$S+}                { SWAPPING REQUIRED }

UNIT MYSTUFF; INTRINSIC CODE 14 DATA 15;

    INTERFACE                     { PUBLIC }
        USES APPLESTUFF;

        FUNCTION RND(HIGH,LOW : INTEGER): INTEGER;

    IMPLEMENTATION                { PRIVATE }
        FUNCTION RND;
            BEGIN
                RND := RANDOM MOD (HIGH - LOW + 1) + LOW
            END;

BEGIN
        { INITIALIZATION CODE, IF NECESSARY }
END.
```

Installing a Unit

The LIBRARY utility is used to install a prepared unit. The programmer is prompted for information as shown in the following:

Requested information	Example
New library name	*NEW.LIBRARY*
Link code file (source of first units)	*SYSTEM.LIBRARY*
Slot to link (from list of possible units to link)	*0 – 15* = to copy all
Slot to link to (slot in NEW.LIBRARY)	*0 – 31*
New file request	*N*
Link code file	*#5:MYSTUFF*
Slot to link to	*14*
Notice?	*Programmer's own message/copyright*

To use the units in the new library, transfer NEW.LIBRARY to the boot disk and change the new library's name to SYSTEM.LIBRARY. All units (original system units as well as custom units installed by the programmer) are available. To use a unit, the programmer requests that unit in the following manner:

```
program heading;
```

```
USES MYSTUFF;
```

The functions and procedures defined in that unit are now available for use in the host program.

Section M   Music

In order to generate sound in Apple Pascal, the APPLESTUFF unit is used. A special procedure, NOTE, is contained in this unit. NOTE has two parameters that are sent by value: pitch and duration. The pitch is an integer ranging from 0 to 50 and the duration is an integer from 0 to 255. The following program is a short example using the NOTE procedure:

```
PROGRAM THREENOTE;

USES APPLESTUFF;

VAR
    PITCH,
    DURATION : INTEGER;

BEGIN
    NOTE(25,100);
    NOTE(12,255);
    NOTE(6,50)
END.
```

In order to develop personalized songs, a method for translating standard musical scales to NOTE parameters is necessary. The following music scale gives the corresponding pitch for middle C through high C:

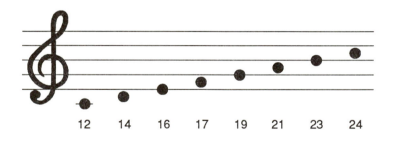

The pitch for sharp notes can also be determined from this scale.

C	C#	D	D#	E	F	F#	G	G#	A	A#	B	C
12	13	14	15	16	17	18	19	20	21	22	23	24

The following example will play all possible pitches:

```
PROGRAM CHROMATICSCALE;

USES APPLESTUFF;

VAR
    PITCH,
    DURATION : INTEGER;
```

```
BEGIN
   DURATION := 100;
   FOR PITCH := 2 TO 48 DO
      NOTE(PITCH,DURATION)
END.
```

Other specifics regarding pitch follow:

- A pitch of 0 gives a rest.
- A pitch of 1 gives a clicking noise.
- A pitch of 2 through 48 yields chromatic scales. The music scale illustrated earlier (of 12 through 24) is one of these scales.

Some standard note durations are given in the following table:

Type of Note	Duration
Whole	255
Dotted half	192
Half	128
Dotted quarter	96
Quarter	64
Dotted eighth	48
Eighth	32
Dotted sixteenth	24
Sixteenth	16
Dotted thirty-second	12
Thirty-second	8
Dotted sixty-fourth	6
Sixty-fourth	4

Section O

Operating System for Apple Pascal

When Apple Pascal is booted (with Version 1.3), the following message appears on the screen:

```
Welcome Apple1, to Apple II Pascal 1.3
Based on UCSD Pascal II.1
Current date is -------
Pascal System size is 64K
Copyright Apple Computer Inc. 1979,1980,1983,1984,1985
Copyright U.C. Regents 1979
```

The Command prompt line

```
COMMAND: F(ile, E(dit, R(un, C(omp, L(ink, X(ecute, A(ssem, ?[1.3]
```

will appear at the top of the screen. For 40-column screens, press <CTRL-A> to see the other half of the screen. This is the command level; selection can be made from among the command options listed.

The Command level can be thought of as the trunk of a tree, with each sublevel (for instance, FILE, EDIT, and RUN) as branches. As shown in Figure O.1, there are also sublevels of these sublevels, which, in the tree analogy, would be represented by leaves. (Note: Depending on the version of Pascal being used, slight differences in appearance may exist.)

Outermost Level Commands

F(ile

Typing F from Command level obtains a level of the sytem called the Filer. The Filer contains commands for saving, reading, moving, and deleting the work file and other disk-related commands.

E(dit

Typing E while at the outermost Command level of the system causes the Editor program to be brought into memory from disk. If a work file is currently stored on the diskette in the boot drive, it is read into the computer; otherwise the Editor asks for the specific text file. While in the Editor, text in the work file, or in any text file, can be created or altered.

R(un

This command causes the code portion of the current work file to be executed. If no such code file is currently stored on the diskette in the boot drive, the Compiler is automatically called in the same manner as described in C(omp. If the compilation requires linkage to separately compiled code, the Linker is au-

Figure O.1   Apple Pascal Command Tree

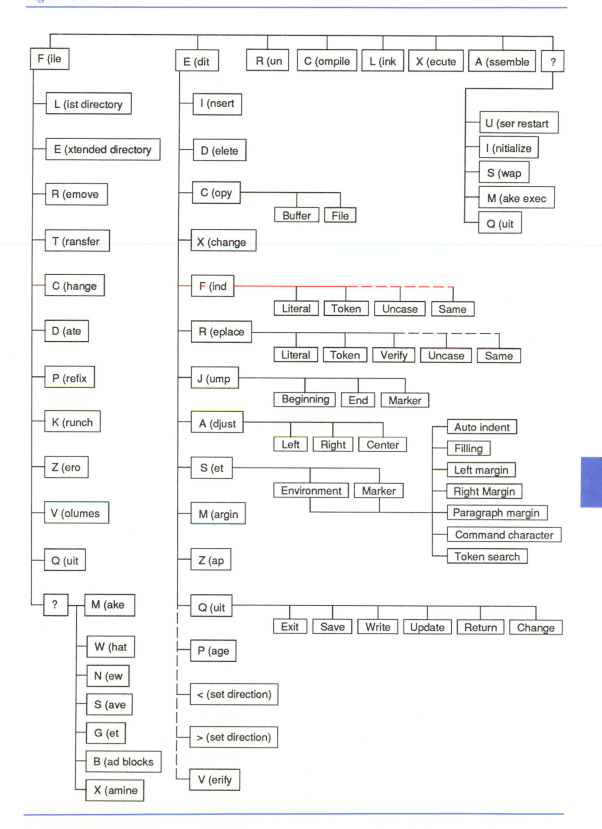

tomatically invoked and uses the file SYSTEM.LIBRARY. After a successful compilation, the program is executed.

C(omp

This command tells the system Compiler to compile the current work file. If there is no work file currently stored on the diskette in the boot drive, the Compiler asks for the specific text file. If a syntax error is detected during compilation, the Compiler stops and displays the error number and the surrounding text of the program. Typing E at this point summons the Editor, placing the cursor near the offending symbol. Or, press the spacebar and the Compiler will continue the compilation. Pressing the escape key, <ESC>, causes the Compiler to stop compiling and return to the Command level. If the compilation is successful (that is, if no compilation errors were encountered), a code file named SYS-TEM.WRK.CODE is saved on the diskette in the boot disk drive and becomes part of the work file.

L(ink

This command starts the system Linker program explicitly, to allow linking routines from libraries other than SYSTEM.LIBRARY.

X(ecute

This command asks for a previously compiled code file. If the file exists, the code file is executed; otherwise the message

NO FILE *xxx*.CODE

is displayed. *Note:* The .CODE suffix on such a file is implicit (do not include the suffix when specifying the file name). If all code necessary to execute the code file has not been linked, the message

MUST L(INK FIRST

is displayed. If the file SYSTEM.LIBRARY is not present or is incomplete, and the code file uses real numbers, then the message

REQUIRED INTRINSICS NOT AVAILABLE

is displayed. X(ecuting programs which have already been compiled (see C(omp) is more convenient than entering the Filer, G(etting the file, Q(uitting the Filer, and then R(unning the program.

A(ssem

This command is similar to C(omp, except the 6502 machine-language Assembler is invoked, rather than the Pascal P-code Compiler.

Utility Programs

There are many utilities needed by users of any operating system. Those not used often enough to deserve placement in the prompt lines are available through the X(ecute command. The sort of utilities which are available are a diskette formatting program, a terminal configuration setup program, library utilities (see Programmer's Handbook, Section L), and a utility to set the screen to 40 columns.

Editor Commands

Cursor

Cursor moves are outlined in the following table. (The number of spaces moved is determined by n.)

Cursor Moves	Action
↓	Moves n lines down.
↑	Moves n lines up.
→	Moves n spaces right.
←	Moves n spaces left.
Spacebar	Moves n spaces in set direction.
CTRL-I	Moves n tab positions in set direction.
RETURN	Moves to start of line that is n lines away, in set direction.
=	Moves to start of latest text found, replaced, or inserted.

Repeat

To repeat a move or command, type the number (n) of desired repetitions before the move or command. (If the repeat factor is indicated by /, the move or command is repeated as many times as possible in the file.) Thus, 7 followed by ↓ moves the cursor down seven lines.

Set Direction

These keys change the direction of P (page), and other movement functions (as shown in the following table), allowing the programmer to move up or down a page quickly.

Key	Action
< , −	All change set direction to backward.
> . +	All change set direction to forward.

Editor Options

The following table outlines frequently used Editor commands:

Command	Action
D	Deletes text.
I	Inserts text from the cursor on.
Q	Leaves the Editor.
X	Exchanges text.
P	Moves one page.
R	Replaces.
A	Adjusts text.
↑	Moves the cursor up.
↓	Moves the cursor down.
→	Moves the cursor right.
←	Moves the cursor left.

Further explanation of these commands and of others used less frequently is provided in the following table:

Command	Action
A(djust	Adjusts indentation of the line the cursor is on. ← and → keys move the line left and right. Moving up with ↑ (or down with ↓) adjusts the line above (or below) by the same amount as the previous line.
C(opy	Copies a diskette file—or what was last inserted, deleted, or zapped—into the file at the position of the cursor.
D(elete	Deletes all text moved over by the cursor. To restore this text, or undelete, back up the cursor.
F(ind	Operates in L(iteral or T(oken mode. Looks in the set direction for the nth occurrence of the

Command	Action
	specified string, which must be typed with delimiters. S means use the same string as before.
I(nsert	Inserts text. Use ← key to backspace over insertion.
J(ump	Jumps to the file's B(eginning or E(nd, or to a previously set M(arker.
M(argin	Starting at the cursor position, adjusts all text between two blank lines to the set margins.
P(age	Moves the cursor n pages in the set direction.
Q(uit	Leaves the Editor. Depending on the version, the programmer can U(pdate the work file, E(xit without updating, W(rite to any diskette file, R(eturn to the Editor, S(ave under the current name, or C(hange to a different file.
R(eplace	Operates in L(iteral or T(oken mode. Looks in the set direction for next occurrence of $<targ>$ string, and replaces it with $<sub>$ string. Continues the number of times indicated by the repeat factor, n. Both string specifications must be typed with delimiters. V(erify option asks for permission to replace. S means use the same $<targ>$ or the same $<sub>$ string as before.
S(et	Sets a M(arker by assigning a string name to the current cursor position. Sets options in the E(nvironment for A(uto-indent, F(illing, M(argins, T(okens, and C(ommand characters.
V(erify	Redisplays the screen with the cursor centered.
X(change	Replaces the character under the cursor with the character typed. Each line must be done separately. Pressing the ← key causes the original character to reappear.
Z(ap	Deletes all text between the current cursor position and what is called the equal position (the start of the latest text found, replaced, or inserted).

Filer Commands

The following table outlines frequently used Filer commands:

Command	Action
G	Gets a file and places it in the work file.
N	Erases the work file.

Command	Action
L	Lists the directions.
T	Transfers files.
R	Removes files from the disk.
S	Saves file on disk.
Q	Exits the Filer.

Further explanation of these commands and of others used less frequently is provided in the following table:

Command	Action
B(ad-blocks	Tests all 280 blocks on the specified diskette to see that information has been recorded consistently. Bad blocks are reported. Use X(amine to fix bad blocks.
C(hange	Renames a diskette or a diskette file.
D(ate	Sets new current date for the system.
E(xtended-directory-list	Shows contents of a diskette, displaying extra information about the files and unused portions.
G(et	Designates a specified diskette file as the work file. The next E(dit, C(ompile, or R(un will use this file.
K(runch	Packs the files on a diskette so that unused portions of the diskette are combined into one area.
L(ist-directory	Shows the contents of a diskette.
M(ake	Creates a diskette directory entry with specified file name. Produces a dummy file on the diskette.
N(ew	Clears the work file, removing all SYSTEM.WRK files from the boot diskette.
P(refix	Changes the current default volume name to the volume name specified.
Q(uit	Leaves the Filer and returns to the outermost command level.
R(emove	Removes the specified file from a diskette's directory.
S(ave	Saves the work file SYSTEM.WRK under the specified file name.
T(ransfer	Transfers information from one file to another file. Can be used to move or save diskette files, copy entire diskettes, or send files to a printer or other device.
V(olumes	Shows the devices and diskettes currently in the system, by volume number and by volume name.

Command	Action
W(hat	Tells the name and state (saved or not) of the work file.
X(amine	Attempts to fix diskette blocks reported bad by the B(ad-blocks command. Marks blocks that can't be fixed.
Z(ero	Erases the directory of a diskette.

Tutorial I. The Editor

In order to enter a program, press E for edit to get into the Edit level. The following message will appear on the screen:

```
Edit what file? (<ret> for new file,
<esc-ret> to exit editor)
-->
```

There are two choices:

- Press <RETURN> to insert a new program.
- Press <ESC> and then press <RETURN> to get back into the Command level.

If READING... appears on the screen, then a program is present in the work file, or SYSTEM.WRK.TEXT. (For this tutorial, the assumption is made that no program exists in the work file.) Press <RETURN>, and a new prompt line appears.

```
>Edit: I(nsrt D(lete C(py X(chng F(nd R(plce J(mp
A(djst S(et M(rgin Z(ap Q(uit
```

In the tree analogy, these options represent leaves. In order to insert new text, press I for insert. A new prompt line appears.

```
>Insert:<Text> <bs> a char, <del> a line,
<ctrlC> accepts, <esc> escapes
```

Now type

```
ABCDEFG
```

There are four options at this level:

- Try the back arrow, ←. What happens? When a typing mistake is observed immediately, use this to make the correction.
- Experiment with <CTRL–X>. This tells the Editor to ignore the entire line being entered.
- Press <CTRL–C> to get back into the Edit level. This directs the Editor to accept the insertion.
- Press <ESC> to destroy all insertions done while in the insert mode, and return to the Edit level.

While in the Edit level, move the cursor using ↑, ↓, ←, and →. Now press I (insert) and enter some text, followed by <CTRL–C>. Next press D (delete) and the following prompt line will appear:

```
>Delete:<moving keys>,<ctrlC>accepts, <esc>escapes
```

Press the spacebar or the → key to delete characters. (The backspace key will reinsert deleted characters.) Then use <CTRL–C> to return to the Edit level and accept the changes.

Clear the work file, deleting all of the text, by pressing D(elete) and the spacebar, starting at the beginning of the text. Move from the Edit level to the Insert mode by pressing I(nsert). Enter the following program:

```
PROGRAM FIRST(OUTUT);

BEGIN
   WRITELN('HELLO')
END.
```

To get back to the Edit level, press <CTRL–C>. Press Q(uit to get out of the Editor. Five options will appear.

```
>QUIT:
    To leave Editor, type
        E(xit to main command line
    To store Text file on disk, type
        W(rite to a new file name
        U(pdate *SYSTEM.WRK.TEXT
    To continue editing, type
        R(eturn to same file
        C(hange to another file
```

Press U(pdate and the system will respond with

```
>Quit:

Writing...

Your file is 62 bytes long.
```

The program has been saved temporarily as SYSTEM. WRK.TEXT on the main disk.

Back at the Command level, press C to compile the program. If the program compiles successfully, the following message will appear:

```
Compiling

Apple Pascal Compiler [1.3]
<  0>..
First {2435 words}
<  3>.
4 lines
Smallest Available space=2435 words
```

Press R(un and the following should appear on the screen:

```
HELLO
```

A shortcut method for C(ompile and R(un would be to simply press R(un. The computer will first compile and then (if compilation is successful) automatically run the program.

Tutorial II.   The Filer

After the program given in Tutorial I. has been entered, compiled, and run, press F to access the Filer. The Filer prompt line will appear.

```
Filer: L(dir E(dir R(em T(rans C(hng D(ate P(refix
K(rnch Z(ero V(ols Q(uit ?
```

Press L(ist-directory to see a directory listing. The following message will appear on the screen:

```
Directory listing of what volume?
```

Enter the name of the main disk. Press L(ist-directory again and enter #4. Press L(ist-directory again and enter #5. (#4 and #5 refer to the volume on-line. Volume #4 is always drive 1 and volume #5, drive 2.) Again press L(ist-directory and enter the name of the storage disk.

Now try a few other functions at the Filer level. To begin, press N(ew. The following message will appear:

```
Throw away current workfile?
```

Press Y and the Filer will indicate that the work file has been cleared. Next, press Q(uit to quit the Filer. This will bring back the Command level.

Tutorial III.   Further Practice with Editor and Filer

Now that the work file is clear, go back into the edit mode and enter another program.

Press E(dit, followed by return, then press I(nsert. Enter the following program, including mistakes:

```
PROGRAM ERRORS(OUTPUT);

BEGIN
   WRITELN('THE ERRORS I WILL MAKE IN THIS PROGRAM');
   WRITELN('WILL BE SPELLING ERRORS');
   WRITLNC'SEE IF YOU CAN FIND ALL OF THEM');
   WRITELNC'SOMETIMES FINDING ERRORS IS DIFFICULT')
ENND.
```

Press <CTRL–C> so that the Editor will accept this insertion. Press Q(uit to quit the Editor, followed by U(pdate. Then press C(ompile and observe how the compiler finds the errors.

```
Compiling...
Apple Pascal Compiler 1.3
<  0>...
ERRORS [2435]
<  3>...
WRITELN('THE ERRORS I WILL MAKE IN THIS PROGRAM');
WRITELN('WILL BE SPELLING ERRORS');
WRITLN <<<<
Line 5, error 104:<sp>(continue),<esc>(terminate),E(dit
```

Notice the three options. Press E(dit to edit the mistake. On top of the screen, the type of error is specified:

```
undeclared identifier Type<sp>
```

This means to press the spacebar. Make the correction by deleting the mistake and then inserting the correction. When the correction is complete, press <CTRL–C> to accept the change and return to the edit level.

Again press Q(uit, U(pdate, and C(ompile. Correct any remaining mistakes in a similar manner. Some mistakes can be corrected by using X(chng.

```
>eXchange: <text>, <bs> a char, <right arrow> copies,
<ctrlC>, <esc>
```

These options are

- ■ Enter text; write the new text over the old.
- ■ Use the back arrow to replace previously exchanged characters.
- ■ Press <ESC> to get back into the Editor and ignore the exchange.
- ■ Press <CTRL–C> to accept the exchange.

When all mistakes have been corrected, and the program has successfully compiled, run the program. The output should be

```
THE ERRORS I WILL MAKE IN THIS PROGRAM
WILL BE SPELLING ERRORS
SEE IF YOU CAN FIND ALL OF THEM
SOMETIMES FINDING ERRORS IS DIFFICULT
```

From the Command level, press F(iler to access the Filer. To save this program on this disk, press S(ave. The following prompt will appear:

```
Save as?
```

Enter the name of the program, as

```
storage disk name:ERRORS
```

Next, press N(ew, followed by Y to clear the work file. The work file is not empty. Press L(ist-directory.

```
Directory Listing of what volume? storage disk name:
```

The program ERRORS.TEXT is stored on the disk. Press G(et to load the program into the work file.

Another handy Filer leaf is T(ransfer. Programs can be transferred to another disk or to the printer. In order to transfer to another disk, first press T.

```
Transfer what file? storage disk name:ERRORS
To where? main disk name:ERRORS
```

The transfer can be verified by checking the directory (L(ist-directory) for *main disk name.*

To transfer a program to the printer, press T(ransfer. The computer will respond with

```
Transfer what file? storage disk name:ERRORS
To where? PRINTER:
```

Section P   Printer Use

This section will show how to obtain two different types of printer listings of Apple Pascal programs. One listing is a printed copy (identical to the program that appears on the screen in the edit mode) and the other is a compiled listing that includes line numbers and errors.

Program Listing

A printed copy of a program may be obtained by accessing the Filer level and pressing T(ransfer. The Filer will respond with

```
Transfer what file?
```

Then enter the name of the program to be printed. For example,

```
Transfer what file? work disk name:filename.TEXT
```

The Filer verifies that *work disk name:* is a disk in one of the drives and that the program is a file on that disk. If so, it responds with

```
TO WHERE?
```

For a listing to the printer, enter

```
PRINTER:
```

or

```
#6
```

(#6 is the volume number of the printer.) If the printer is on and connected properly (in slot 1), a listing of the program will be produced. For example,

```
PROGRAM NUMBERSHAPE(OUTPUT);

    { PURPOSE:  TO DEMONSTRATE NESTED LOOPS }

VAR
    LOOP1,
    LOOP2   : INTEGER;


BEGIN  { MAIN PROGRAM }

    FOR LOOP1 := 1 TO 9 DO
       BEGIN
          FOR LOOP2 := LOOP1 TO 9 DO
             WRITE(LOOP2,' ');
          WRITELN
       END  { FOR LOOP1 }

END.
```

Compiled Listing

To obtain a compiled listing of this program, the following line should be added to the beginning of the program (before the program heading):

```
{$L PRINTER:}
```

This line indicates that the compiled listing should be sent to the printer. The compiled listing includes numbered lines and other specifications. For example,

```
 1  1   1:D      1 {$L PRINTER:}
 2  1   1:D      1 PROGRAM NUMBERSHAPE(OUTPUT);
 3  1   1:D      3
 4  1   1:D      3    { PURPOSE:  TO DEMONSTRATE NESTED LOOPS }
 5  1   1:D      3
 6  1   1:D      3 VAR
 7  1   1:D      3    LOOP1,
 8  1   1:D      3    LOOP2   : INTEGER;
 9  1   1:D      5
10  1   1:D      5
11  1   1:0      0 BEGIN  { MAIN PROGRAM }
12  1   1:0      0
13  1   1:1      0    FOR LOOP1 := 1 TO 9 DO
14  1   1:2     13       BEGIN
15  1   1:3     13          FOR LOOP2 := LOOP1 TO 9 DO
16  1   1:4     24             WRITE(LOOP2,' ');
17  1   1:3     51          WRITELN
18  1   1:2     51       END  { FOR LOOP1 }
19  1   1:2     59
20  1   1:0     59 END.
```

The first column indicates the line number and the second column gives the program level. Notice that the main program and the procedures are numbered in special ways; their meanings follow:

- 1:D indicates that the line belongs to the main program and is a definition or declaration.
- 1:0 indicates that this is the BEGIN or END of the main program.
- 1:1 indicates that this is the first line that is a statement of the main program.

Sending Output to the Printer

A Pascal output device is a form of a text file; therefore, file commands must be used to obtain a printout of the output. To obtain a hard copy of program output, a variable (P) is declared as INTERACTIVE, which is a file of characters (also a text file). INTERACTIVE is a special file feature that is useful with devices such as printers.

```
VAR
    P : INTERACTIVE;
```

Next, in the main program, open a file by using

```
REWRITE(P,'PRINTER:');
```

The printer is activated by relating the file P to the indicated device (the printer). REWRITE is a built-in Pascal procedure that creates a new file and opens this file for input and output to the device.

Now in any line of output, a WRITE or WRITELN statement will write to the printer by using the following formats. WRITE or WRITELN with parameter P indicate that the output will be sent to file P, which (in this case) is the printer.

WRITE or WRITELN Statement Form

```
WRITELN(P,'HELLO');
```

is the form used to print a message.

```
WRITELN(P,variable);
```

is the form used to print the value of a variable.
(This variable may be of type REAL, CHAR, INTEGER, or STRING.)

```
WRITELN(P);
```

is the form used to leave a blank line.

Finally, just before the END statement, the file must be closed.

```
CLOSE(P);
```

The following program gives an example of sending output to the printer:

```
PROGRAM PRINTERTEST(OUTPUT);

    { PURPOSE:  SEND OUTPUT TO PRINTER }

VAR
    STRG : STRING;
    P    : INTERACTIVE;

BEGIN
    REWRITE(P,'PRINTER:');
    WRITELN(P,'THIS PROGRAM WRITES TO THE PRINTER');
    STRG : = 'HELLO THERE';
    WRITELN(P,'IT CAN PRINT THE VALUE OF A VARIABLE');
    WRITELN(P,STRG);   { PRINT VALUE OF VARIABLE }
    WRITELN(P,'IT CAN LEAVE A BLANK LINE');
    WRITELN(P);     { LEAVE BLANK LINE }
    WRITELN(P,'IT CAN COMBINE OUTPUT ON ONE LINE');
    WRITELN(P,'THE VALUE OF STRG IS',STRG); { COMBINATION }
    CLOSE(P)
END.
```

The run of this program produces the following output on the printer:

```
THIS PROGRAM WRITES TO THE PRINTER
IT CAN PRINT THE VALUE OF A VARIABLE
HELLO THERE
IT CAN LEAVE A BLANK LINE

IT CAN COMBINE OUTPUT ON ONE LINE
THE VALUE OF STRG IS HELLO THERE
```

To summarize, send output to a printer by the following steps:

---

1. Add

   ```
   VAR P:INTERACTIVE;
   ```

   to the variable declaration section of the program.

2. Add

   ```
   REWRITE(P,'PRINTER:');
   ```

   to the main program.

3. Modify the WRITE or WRITELNs that are to be sent to the printer.

   ```
   WRITELN(P,'THIS IS SENT TO THE PRINTER');
   ```

4. Close the file.

   ```
   CLOSE(P);
   ```

An easy technique for modifying output statements is to use the replace option in the Editor. If only one replacement is desired, press R in the Edit mode.

```
>Replace[1]: L(it V(fy <targ> <sub> =>
```

Enter /R to replace all occurrences of WRITELN(with WRITELN(P,.

```
>Replace[/]: L(it V(fy <targ> <sub> =>
```

To change only three occurrences, use 3 R.

A number of choices are available in the replace mode, as outlined in the following table:

Command	Action
L(it	This means to change every occurrence or a given number of occurrences of a specific word or part of a word throughout the program. For example, suppose the programmer changed all WRITEs to WRITE(P,. Since WRITE is a part of WRITELN, using L(it would change WRITELN('HI') to WRITE(P,LN('HI'). In other words, if a series of characters contains the word to be changed, those characters will be altered. A literal

Command	Action
	search finds WRITE wherever it occurs. If L(it is not used, then the machine looks for WRITE surrounded by blanks or punctuation.
V(fy	This provides the option of accepting or rejecting each change as it is made.

To specify the change to be made, enter the target (*targ*—one to replace), between slashes, followed by the substitute (*sub*— new version), also between slashes.

```
V /targ//sub/
```

For example,

```
V /ELN(//ELN(P,/
```

will find each occurrence of ELN(and ask if it is to be replaced with ELN(P,. The following appears on the screen:

```
>Replace[/]: <Esc> aborts, 'R' replaces, ' ' doesn't
```

The options follow:

Key	Action
<ESC>	Terminates the entire process.
R	Replaces ELN(with ELN(P,.
Spacebar	Jumps to the next occurence without replacing this particular occurrence.

(To return to the Editor from replace, without making any corrections, press <ESC>.)

Section R

Reserved Words and Predefined Identifiers

Reserved Words

AND	FUNCTION	PROGRAM
ARRAY	GOTO	RECORD
BEGIN	IF	REPEAT
CASE	IMPLEMENTATION	SEGMENT
CONST	IN	SET
DIV	INTERFACE	THEN
DO	LABEL	TO
DOWNTO	MOD	TYPE
ELSE	NIL	UNIT
END	NOT	UNTIL
EXTERNAL	OF	USES
FILE	OR	VAR
FOR	PACKED	WHILE
FORWARD	PROCEDURE	WITH

Predefined Identifiers

The following identifiers have predefined meanings within a Pascal program. If the programmer declares one of these identifiers, the program will run but the original purpose of the identifier will be lost for that program. (In the following tables, the predefined functions are categorized by <b> BOOLEAN, <c> CHAR, <i> INTEGER, <o> ordinal, <r> REAL, and <s> STRING.

Procedures	Functions	Types	Others	
CLOSE	ABS <r>	BOOLEAN	FALSE	(constant)
DELETE	BLOCKREAD <i>	CHAR	INPUT	(file)
EXIT	BLOCKWRITE <i>	INTEGER	KEYBOARD	(file)
FILLCHAR	CHR <c>	INTERACTIVE	MAXINT	(constant)
GET	CONCAT <s>	REAL	OUTPUT	(file)
GOTOXY	COPY <s>	STRING	TRUE	(constant)
HALT	EOF <b>	TEXT		
INSERT	EOLN <b>			
MARK	IORESULT <i>			
MOVELEFT	LENGTH <i>			
MOVERIGHT	MEMAVAIL <i>			
NEW	ODD <b>			
PAGE	ORD <i>			
PUT	POS <i>			
READ	PRED <o>			
READLN	PWROFTEN <r>			
RELEASE	ROUND <i>			
RESET	SCAN <i>			
REWRITE	SIZEOF <i>			
SEEK	SQR <r>			
UNITCLEAR	STR <s>			
UNITREAD	SUCC <o>			
UNITWAIT	TREESEARCH <i>			
UNITWRITE	TRUNC <i>			
WRITE	UNITBUSY <b>			
WRITELN				

Predefined Identifiers for Apple Units

If a library unit has been specified, then the identifiers belonging to that unit are, in effect, reserved words; that is, a compiler error will occur if the programmer attempts to declare an identifier belonging to the unit. If a unit is not being used, the predefined identifiers of that unit are undefined and available for other use by the programmer.

Unit	Procedures	Functions	Type
Applestuff	NOTE RANDOMIZE TTLOUT	BUTTON <i> KEYPRESS <b> PADDLE <i> RANDOM <i>	
Transcend		ATAN <r> COS <r> EXP <r> LN <r> LOG <r> SIN <r> SQRT <r>	
Turtlegraphics	CHARTYPE DRAWBLOCK FILLSCREEN GRAFMODE INITTURTLE MOVE MOVETO PENCOLOR TEXTMODE TURN TURNTO VIEWPORT WCHAR WSTRING	SCREENBIT <b> TURTLEANG <i> TURTLEX <i> TURTLEY <i>	SCREENCOLOR

Section S

Syntax Diagrams

Syntax diagrams are used to illustrate the correct way to write specific statements in Pascal. Their purpose is to help in conceptualizing the structure of the parts of Pascal. The symbols that are used to draw syntax diagrams follow, together with their significance.

OVAL — Reserved word or predefined identifier. The item within this symbol is to be typed exactly as shown.

rectangle — Item that is defined in other syntax diagram, or whose representation is obvious.

○ — Sometimes called a connector, and sometimes a separator, this symbol frequently contains punctuation.

⟶ — Flow of definition sequence.

identifier

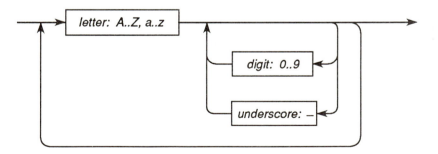

constant

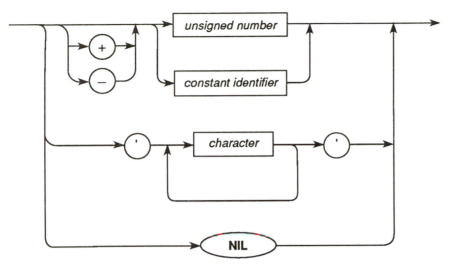

type

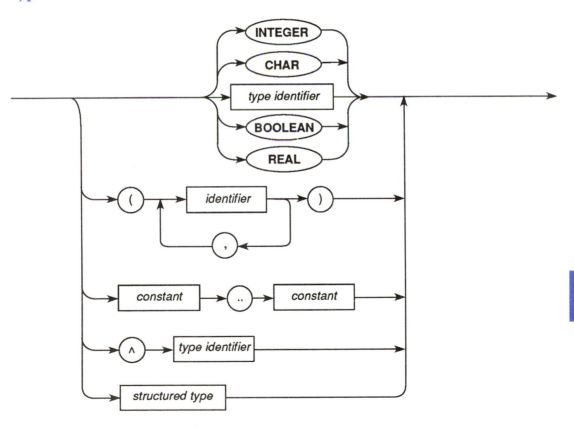

structured type

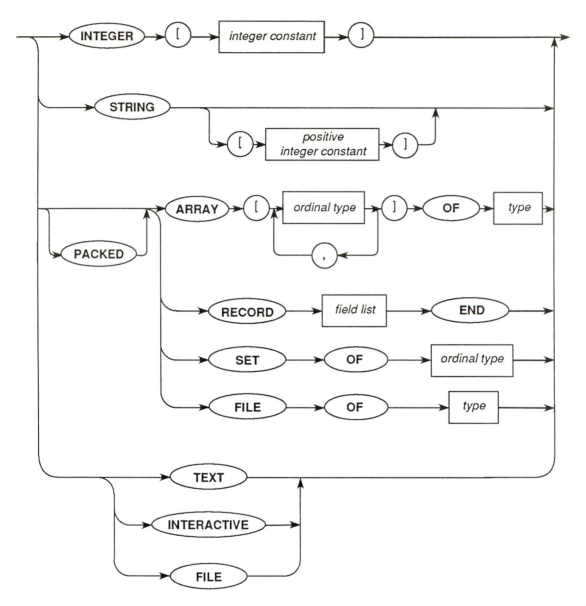

field list

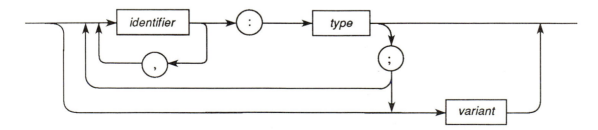

variant

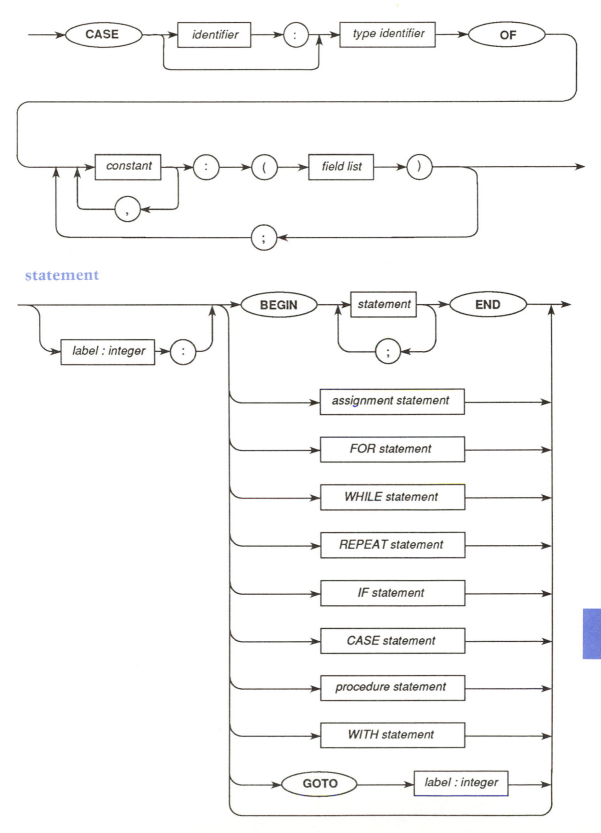

statement

WHILE statement

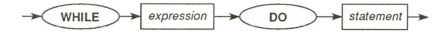

REPEAT statement

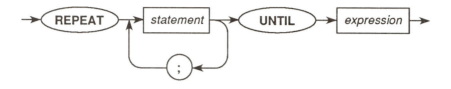

IF statement

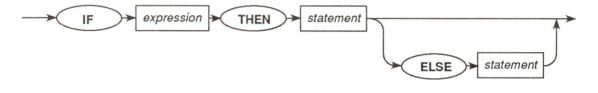

WITH statement

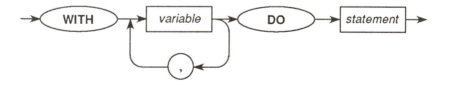

assignment statement

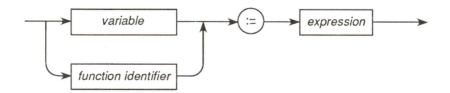

procedure statement

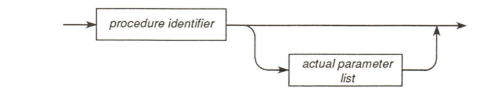

FOR statement

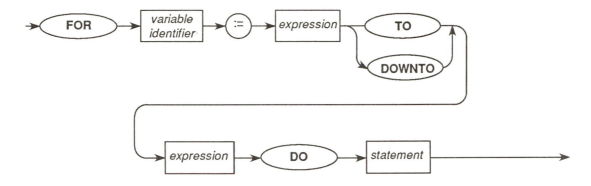

CASE statement

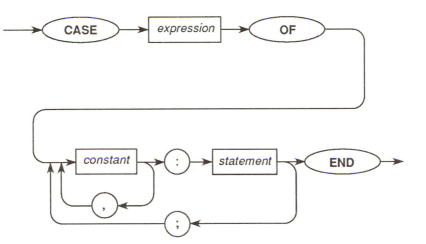

actual parameter list

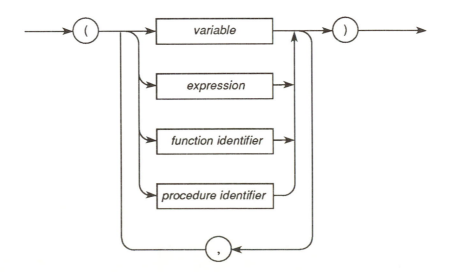

procedure declaration

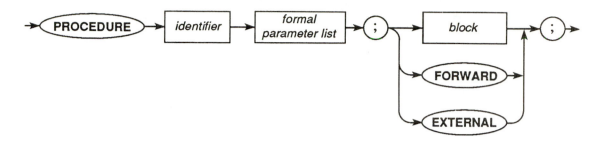

formal parameter list

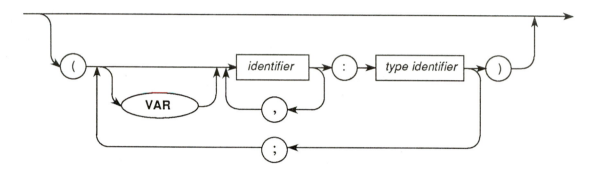

function declaration

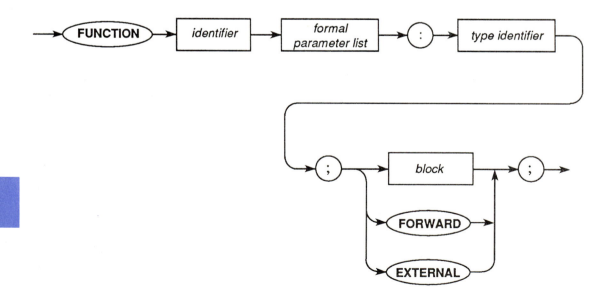

function call

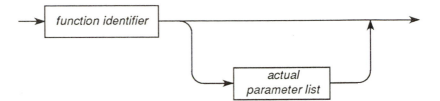

variable

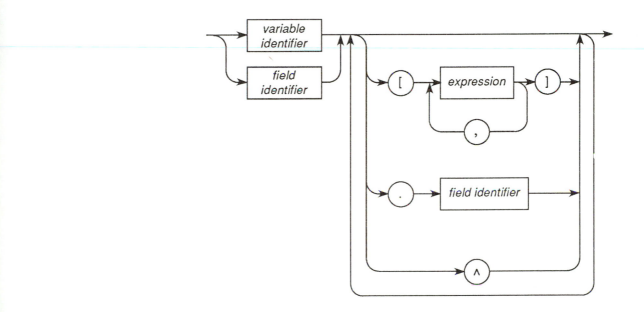

expression

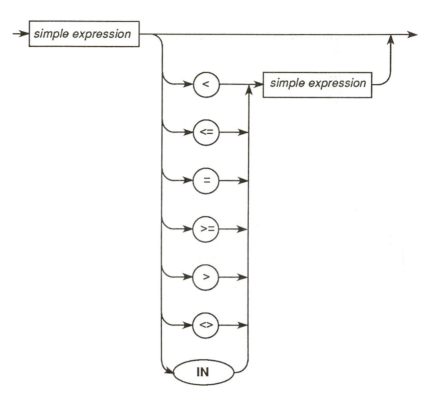

simple expression

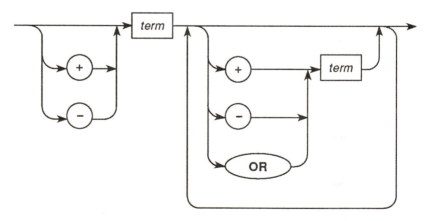

term

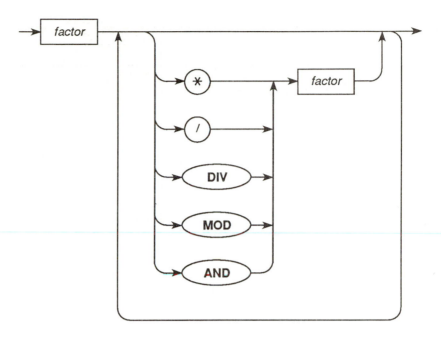

factor

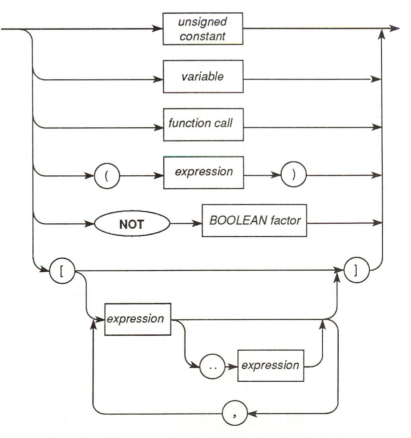

program

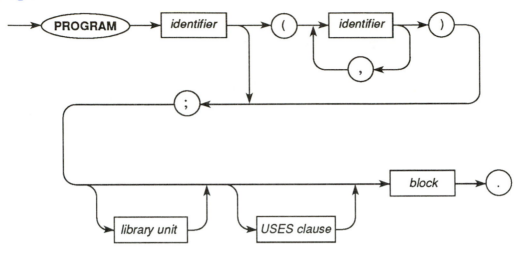

USES clause

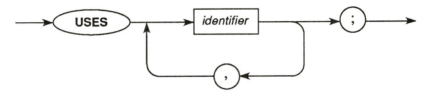

library unit

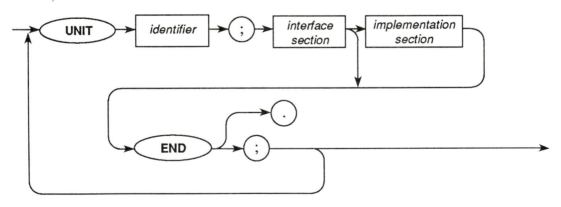

block

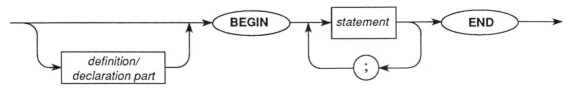

definition/declaration part

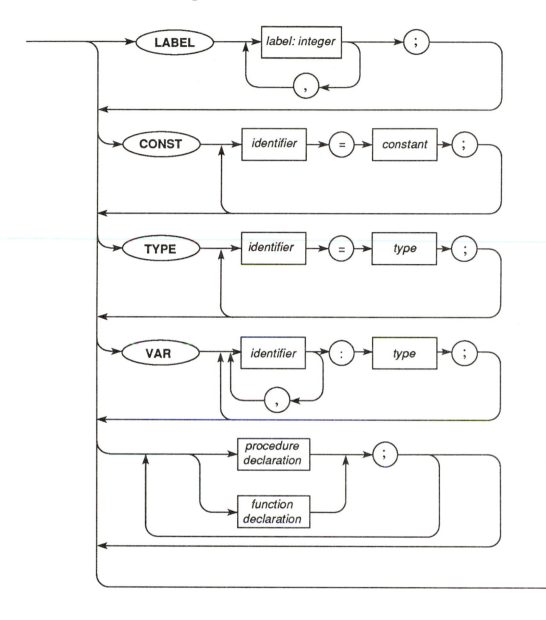

interface section

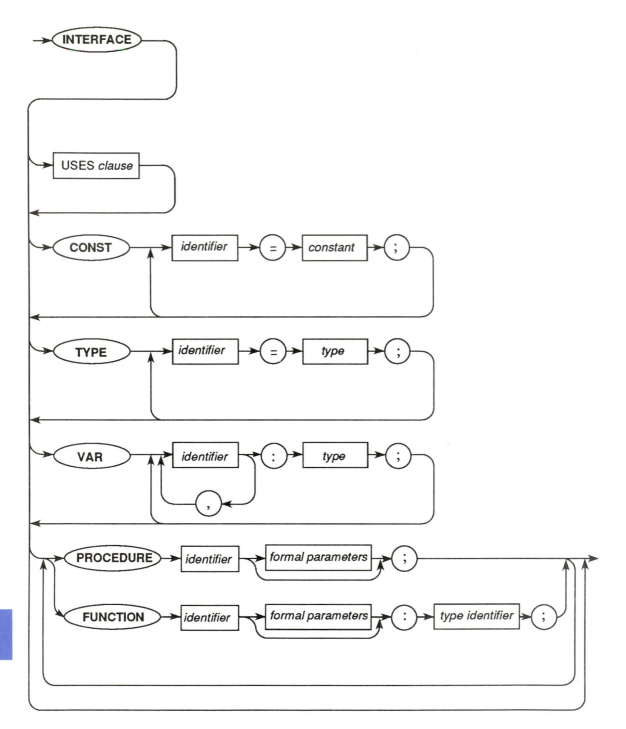

implementation section

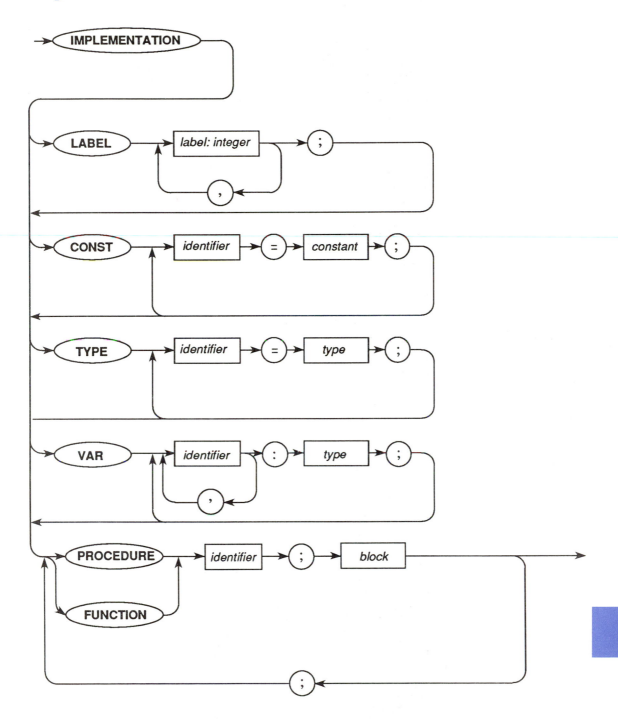

Section U Unconditional Branching

Pascal allows unconditional branching (transfer of control) using the GOTO statement. In UCSD Pascal, the destination of the branch must be within the same program block as the GOTO statement itself. The destination is marked by a label consisting of an unsigned integer of up to four digits (0 to 9999). The label must be declared immediately after the program or procedure heading. The label is separated from the destination statement by a colon. The GOTO compiler option ({$G+}, see Programmer's Handbook, Section C) must be activated to allow use of GOTO.

```
{$G+}
PROGRAM TEST (OUTPUT);

     { PURPOSE: DEMONSTRATE UNCONDITIONAL BRANCHING }

LABEL 3,5;

VAR
   I : INTEGER;

BEGIN  { MAIN PROGRAM }

   I := 1;
3: WRITELN(I,' THIS IS THE FIRST WRITELN.');
   I := I + 1;
   IF I < 6
      THEN GOTO 3
      ELSE GOTO 5;
   WRITELN('THIS LINE WON''T BE PRINTED.');
5: WRITELN(I,' THIS IS THE LAST WRITELN.')

END.
```

Output

```
1 THIS IS THE FIRST WRITELN.
2 THIS IS THE FIRST WRITELN.
3 THIS IS THE FIRST WRITELN.
4 THIS IS THE FIRST WRITELN.
5 THIS IS THE FIRST WRITELN.
6 THIS IS THE LAST WRITELN.
```

Programmers should avoid use of the GOTO statement, especially in early stages of learning Pascal. The readability and flow of a program are hampered by unnecessary branching. GOTO should be used as a last resort.

Section V   Volumes

The Apple Pascal Operating System assigns volume numbers and volume names to the various input/output devices as shown in the following table:

Volume Number	Volume Name	Description of Input/Output Device
#0:		(not used)
#1:	CONSOLE:	Screen and keyboard (echo on input)
#2:	SYSTERM:	Screen and keyboard (no echo on input)
#3:		(not used)
#4:	*diskette name*:	Boot disk drive (slot 6, drive 1)
#5:	*diskette name*:	Second disk drive (slot 6, drive 2)
#6:	PRINTER:	Printer (card in slot 1)
#7:	REMIN:	Remote input (card in slot 2)
#8:	REMOUT:	Remote output (card in slot 2)
#9:	*diskette name*:	Fifth disk drive (slot 4, drive 1)
#10:	*diskette name*:	Sixth disk drive (slot 4, drive 2)
#11:	*diskette name*:	Third disk drive (slot 5, drive 1)
#12:	*diskette name*:	Fourth disk drive (slot 5, drive 2)

Glossary

accumulate   To add specified numbers.

actual parameter   The value (expression) or variable listed in a function or procedure call.

Ada   A high-level computer language, developed in the mid 1970s, named after Ada Byron, Countess of Lovelace.

address   The value (an integer) that the computer uses to reference a memory location.

algebraic function   A function whose argument and result are both numeric and does not require special declaration. For example, ABS(1), SQR(2), and PWROFTEN(3) are algebraic functions.

algorithm   A sequence of steps to solve a given problem.

ALU   The arithmetic/logic unit is a part of the CPU that handles all arithmetic computations and determines the outcome of logic statements or comparisons.

American Standard Code for Information Interchange   *See* ASCII.

applications software   Programs that are written or used by the user, such as a spreadsheet, data base, or word processor.

argument   A value (expression) or variable passed to a function or procedure.

arithmetic/logic unit   *See* ALU.

array   A static structured data type that groups data of the same type by indexing each element; that is, each element of an array is associated with a particular index or subscript.

ASCII   American Standard Code for Information Interchange is a 7-bit numeric code for numbers, letters, and other characters.

assignment statement   A way of assigning values to memory locations.

BASIC   Beginner's All-purpose Symbolic Instruction Code is an easily learned high-level computer language developed at Dartmouth in the mid-1960s.

binary numbers Numbers represented with the digits 0 or 1 (that is, in base-2).

binary search   A way of locating a specific element of an array or list by selecting the middle element and determining if the specific element is in the first half, in the last half, or equal to the middle element. If the element is in a particular half of the list, repeat the searching technique on that half until the element is found. The elements of the list must be in order.

binary search tree A binary tree formed so that the information at any node is greater than its left child and its children, and less than its right child or its children.

binary tree A tree whose nodes can point to at most two children.

bit A Binary digIT.

Boolean algebra The logic of computers, named after George Boole.

Boolean expression An expression with a value of true or false.

bubble sort Sorts a list into ascending (or descending) order by comparing consecutive elements and switching the elements if the first of the consecutive elements is larger (smaller). At most $n - 1$ passes through the entire list may be required to complete this process, where n is the number of elements in the list.

built-in function or procedure A standard function or procedure that is a part of Pascal.

call *See* function call or procedure call.

calling block The portion of the program from which a function call or procedure call occurs.

central processing unit *See* CPU.

child The node pointed to by a branch of a tree.

circular list A list of elements such that all of the elements are linked, and the first element of the list is linked directly to the last element of the list.

COBOL COmmon Business-Oriented Language is a high-level computer language developed to fit the format of business applications that utilize file processing and record keeping.

collating sequence The particular order of the character set used by a specific computer: for example, ASCII.

collision When two or more entries of an array are to be stored in the same location.

collision resolution A programming technique by which collisions are taken care of.

comment A nonexecutable statement that documents a program.

compatible types Variables that are declared of different subranges and that overlap in the values listed in their definition or declaration.

compiler A computer program that converts a high-level computer program into machine language prior to a program's execution.

compound statement A series of Pascal statements grouped together between delimiters, such as BEGIN and END.

computer An information-processing machine that is controlled by a program.

conditional statement A statement that determines the statements that will follow depending on the value of an expression (called a Boolean expression).

constant A memory location (specified by an identifier) that cannot be changed during program execution.

control unit A part of the CPU that interprets each instruction and signals other units when they are needed.

counter A variable used for counting the number of times a series of statements is completed.

CPU The central processing unit is a part of the computer hardware that processes data and executes instructions.

data type The kind of value that can be assigned to a variable.

debug Remove the errors (bugs) from a program.

decrement   Decrease a counter by a certain amount. *See also* increment.

definite iteration   Repeating a task an exact number of times.

delimiters   Identifiers that locate the beginning and end of a group of Pascal statements.

deque   A list in which insertion and deletion are done at both ends.

difference (set)   A set operation such that the difference of set A and set B, A − B, results in all the elements of set A that are not in set B.

dimension   The indices or subscripts of an array.

direct recursion   A procedure or function calling itself.

documentation   Explanations accompanying a program to enhance understanding.

doubly linked list   A linked list whose link fields connect each element to both its predecessor and its successor.

dynamic data type   A structured data type whose size may change while the program is executed.

EBCDIC   Extended Binary Coded Decimal Interchange Code is an 8-bit numeric code some computers use to code numbers, letters, and other characters.

element of a set   A value that is a member of a set.

empty set (null set)   A set that contains no elements.

end recursion   Recursion in which the recursive call is the last statement of the procedure.

E-notation   *See* floating point notation.

Extended Binary Coded Decimal Interchange Code *See* EBCDIC.

extended binary tree   A tree in which boxes have been added that represent the empty subtrees.

field   A component of a record. *See also* record.

field selector   The dot notation used to specify a field of a record. *See also* record.

field width   A way to format output in Pascal that specifies the width of the columns.

FIFO (First-In First-Out)   *See* queue.

file A dynamic structured data type that is made up of a series of elements of the same type.

file pointer   A variable that indicates the particular element being accessed in a file.

file window   An imaginary part of a file that allows a view of the element that is currently in use or being pointed to.

firmware   Programs that are part of the hardware of a computer system.

First-In First-Out (FIFO)   *See* queue.

floating point notation   A way of representing numbers using powers of 10 (also called scientific notation or E-notation).

formal parameter   The variable declared in the parameter listing directly following the procedure identifier in the procedure heading.

FORTRAN   FORmula TRANslator is a high-level computer language used primarily for scientific computations.

FORWARD declaration   A way to announce a function or procedure in advance of its use.

function   A subprogram that performs a specific task for a larger program. The result of a function is usually a single value.

function call   A statement that contains the function name and a list of parameters to be sent to the function.

global identifier   Identifier used in the main program.
graphics mode   The mode that allows graphics pictures to be placed on the screen.

hard copy   Output from a printer.
hardware   The machinery or physical components of the computer.
hashing   A searching technique that allows an element to be located in one try.
hexadecimal numbers   Numbers represented with the digits 0 through 9 and A through F (that is, base-16).
high-level language   A programming language that uses English-like commands.

identical types   Variables declared of the same type.
identifier   Words selected by the Pascal programmer and used in a program.
increment   Increase a counter by a certain amount. *See also* decrement.
indefinite iteration   Repeating a series of statements where the number of times the statements are repeated is determined by one of the series of statements; for instance, REPEAT . . . UNTIL and WHILE . . . DO.
index   *See* subscript.
indirect recursion (mutual)   A procedure that indirectly calls itself; for example, procedure A calls procedure B, which in turn calls procedure A.
infinite loop   A loop that will never stop.
infinite recursion   Recursion with no exit condition.
initialize   Set a memory location to a particular value.
inorder traversal   A way to traverse a binary tree by traversing the left subtree before visiting the node.
insertion sort   A sorting technique that inserts the new element into a sequence of previously sorted elements.
instruction register   A part of the CPU that holds the current instruction.
internal node   All nodes of a binary tree with one or more children.
interpreter   A program that translates a high-level computer program into a machine-readable form when the program is executed.
intersection (set)   A set operation such that set A intersect set B, $A * B$, results in the set containing the elements that set A and set B have in common.
invoke   *See* procedure call.
I/O devices   Input and output devices. *See also* peripheral.
iteration   *See* loop.

Last-In First-Out (LIFO)   *See* stack.
leaf   A node of a tree that has no children.
LIFO (Last-In First-Out)   *See* stack.
limit recursion   Recursion that contains an exit condition.
linear search   A searching technique in which each element from the list is compared to what is being searched for until the element is found.
linked list   A series of values that are linked together, one to the next, by pointers.

LISP   LISt Processing, a high-level computer language developed as a tool for designing artificial intelligence programs.
literal string constant   A string of characters used in a program.
local identifier   An identifier used within a procedure.
logical data type   Variables of type BOOLEAN.
loop   A structure that causes a process to be repeated.
low-level language   A computer language that operates at the machine level.

machine language   A language that is written in binary and that can be understood by the computer.
memory   A part of the computer hardware used for storing information.
memory address register   Holds the addresses of information stored in main memory.
microprocessor   An electrical component of a computer that performs processing functions and stores information on a single chip.
mutual recursion   *See* indirect recursion.

natural order   Increasing order for numbers and alphabetic order for letters.
nested loop   An entire loop occurs with another loop.
nested record   A record definition that is a field of another record.
node   One value of a linked list or tree.
null set   *See* empty set.
null string   A string with no characters; that is ' '.
numeric data type   Variables of type INTEGER, long INTEGER, or REAL.

order of operations   The order in which arithmetic and logical operations are performed when evaluating an expression.
ordinal data type   Variables that have unique values that precede and succeed each element of that type.

parallel arrays   Two or more different arrays that have the same number of subscripts.
parent   A node of a tree that points to other nodes called its children.
Pascal   A high-level computer language written by Niklaus Wirth as a teaching tool. Named for the 17th century French mathematician and philosopher, Blaise Pascal.
pending recursion   A recursive procedure with statements following the recursive call.
peripheral   An external device that communicates with the main computer.
pointer   A device used to represent a position in a list. The pointer is not visible in the program.
postorder traversal   A way to travel through a binary tree that involves traversing the left and right subtrees before visiting the node.
predefined identifier   A word that has been defined previously, but whose meaning may be altered by the programmer.
preorder traversal   A way to travel through a binary tree that involves visiting a node before looking at its subtrees.
procedure   A subprogram that performs a specific task for the calling block.

procedure block The statements that make up the definition of a procedure.

procedure call Reference to a procedure from another portion of the program, sometimes called invoking a procedure.

program A precise set of instructions that tells the computer what steps to perform to solve a particular problem and produce a desired output.

program body The statement portion of a program, not including the definitions and declarations.

program heading The first line of a Pascal program. It includes the word PROGRAM, the program name, and a semicolon. (A list of external environments is optional.)

queue A data structure in which the elements are inserted from one end and deleted from the other end. That is, the first element placed in the queue is the first element removed (this is known as FIFO).

quick sort A recursive sorting technique based on partitioning the data to be sorted into two smaller groups—one containing the elements less than the partitioning element and one containing the elements greater than the partitioning element. The algorithm is then applied to each smaller group.

RAM Random-Access memory is main memory that can be written to and read from.

Random-Access Memory *See* RAM.

Read-Only Memory *See* ROM.

record A data structure that is a collection of related items (*see* fields) that can be treated individually or as a whole.

recursion A process by which a function or procedure calls itself. *See also* infinite recursion.

recursive call A function or procedure call that occurs within that function or procedure.

register A part of the CPU that holds the instructions and data currently being used and stores the intermediate results of all calculations.

reserved word A part of the Pascal language that cannot be used for any other purpose in a program.

ROM Read-Only Memory is main memory that cannot be altered by the programmer.

root The first node of a tree.

scalar type A data type that describes a single quantity (that is, INTEGER, BOOLEAN, CHAR, and REAL).

scope The part or block of a program in which an identifier has meaning.

search The process of locating a particular value in a given list.

selection sort A sorting technique based on the idea of finding the smallest (or largest) element in a list and putting it in the first position of the list by switching it with whatever element is there. That element is frozen and the next largest element is found and moved to the second position. This process continues until the list is sorted.

set A structured data type that consists of elements of the same base type.

set operator The operations of sets are difference, intersection, and union.

siblings Nodes of a tree that have the same parent.

simple data type Variable types BOOLEAN, CHAR, INTEGER, or REAL.

singly linked list A linked list such that each element is linked to its successor, but not its predecessor.

software The programs written for the computer.

sort The process by which the elements of a list are arranged in a particular way.

stack A data structure whose elements are inserted and deleted from one end. That is, the first element placed on the stack is the last element removed (this is known as LIFO).

standard function A function that is a part of, or built-in to, Pascal.

Standard Pascal A version of Pascal developed by the International Standards Organization (ISO).

static data type A data type whose size is fixed at time of compilation.

subrange A way of further specifying an existing type.

subscript The label of an array element.

subset Set B is a subset of set A if all of the elements of set B are in set A.

superset Set B is a superset of set A if all the elements of set A are in set B.

symbolic data type Variables of type CHAR and STRING.

syntax The rules determining valid programming statements.

system configuration A particular arrangement of a computer system.

systems software Programs that are used by other programs, such as operating systems.

tag field The fields of a variant record.

text mode The mode used for printing characters on the screen.

time-sharing An arrangement of a computer system such that many users may share the central processing unit of a computer.

top-down design A programming design technique in which a problem is divided into subtasks and each subtask is further divided and solved until the original problem is solved.

transcendental functions Functions that cannot be written in an algebraic form (for example, SIN, LN, and EXP).

transfer functions Functions that convert certain data types (for example, ORD and CHR).

traversing Traveling through a binary tree in order to perform desired operations on the nodes of the tree (for example, searching for a particular node, printing the nodes in the tree, or adding a node to the tree).

tree A dynamic data structure in which a node, called the root, points to zero or more other nodes, each of which can point to zero or more nodes, and so on.

Turtlegraphics A special graphics package available in many non-standard versions of Pascal.

type *See* data type.

UCSD Pascal A version of Pascal developed at the University of California at San Diego, which allows users to run Pascal programs on microcomputers.

union (set) A set operation such that set A union set B, A + B, consists of all of the elements of both set A and set B.

value parameter A formal parameter that allows the input of values to a procedure. A value parameter is local in scope.

variable A memory location that is specified by an identifier and whose value may be altered within a program.

variable declaration Declaring the name and data type of variables in a program.

variable parameter A formal parameter that allows the input of a variable to a procedure and output of a value from the procedure. A variable parameter is essentially global in scope.

variant record The portion of a record where the data types and number of fields can vary.

Answers to Selected Exercises

Chapter 1

1. d.

3. d.

5. a. Disk Drive
Tape Recorder
  b. Microprocessor
  c. Card Reader
Disk Drive
Keyboard
Modem
Tape Recorder
  d. Disk Drive
Modem
Monitor
Printer
Tape Recorder

7. a. 26
  b. 78
  c. 255

9. a. 11011
  b. 10011000
  c. 1010111

11. a. E3
  b. 53C
  c. F84

13. a. 101011010011
  b. 10101101001110
  c. 101010100000111111111

17. 1. Lay out all socks separately in a row.
  2. Pick up the first sock in the row.
  3. Look through the remaining socks in the row (one at a time) and compare to the first sock.
  4. When a match is found, remove match and first sock from the row.

5. Go back to Step 2. Use the next sock in the row as the first sock.

Chapter 2

1. **a.** Illegal. An identifier cannot begin with a number.
   b. Legal.
   c. Illegal. An identifier cannot contain a space.
   d. Legal.
   e. Legal. However, OUTPUT is a predefined identifier and its intended meaning will be changed.
   f. Illegal. An identifier cannot contain a symbol other than the underscore.
   g. Legal.

3. Identifiers are distinct.

5. **a.** READLN is a predefined identifier.
   b. PROGRAM is a reserved word.
   c. AREA is neither a reserved word nor a predefined identifier.
   d. GOTOXY is a predefined identifier.
   e. END is a reserved word.

7. **a.** A semicolon is missing at the end of the line.
   b. The reserved word BEGIN is used as an identifier.

9. Semicolons are used to separate Pascal statements.

11. **a.** Invalid. Integers do not contain decimal places.
    b. Invalid. Pascal INTEGER values do not contain commas.
    c. Valid.
    d. Valid.

13. **a.** Invalid. A Pascal REAL value must have a number in front of the decimal.
    b. Valid.
    c. Valid.
    d. Valid.

15. **a.** 5854300
    b. .097544
    c. .0004323
    d. -220

17. **a.** 6.30000E4
    b. $-8.98000E6$
    c. $-2.00000E-4$
    d. 1.40000E-6

19. **a.** ```
    VAR
        VALUE : INTEGER;
    ```
    **b.** ```
    VAR
        QUOTIENT : REAL;
    ```
    c. ```
    VAR
        FIRSTNAME : STRING;
    ```
    **d.** ```
    VAR
        SYMBOL : CHAR;
    ```

21. False.

23. a. NUMBER
  b. WORD, LETTER
  c. WORD

25. a. FRACTION
  b. FRACTION, WHOLE
  c. FRACTION, WHOLE

27. There are 13 errors in the program. These include the following:

- Misspelling the word PROGRAM.
- Missing the external environment OUTPUT (or remove ', '). (While this will not produce a compiler error, it is an improper programming practice.)
- Missing a semicolon at the end of the first line of the program.
- The word BEGIN and the variable declaration must be switched.
- In the variable declaration, TITLE should be declared as STRING, not WORD.
- ITEM should be declared as a STRING.
- The user should also be asked to enter the ITEM TO BE SOLD.
- The end quotation marks are missing at the end of the first WRITELN.
- The comma at the end of the READLN should be a semicolon.
- Misspelling the word WRITELN.
- The opening quotation mark is missing ('BUY').
- The semicolons separating parts of the WRITELN should be commas.
- The last END of a program must be followed by a period.

29. Using indentation, meaningful identifiers, and comments can help to clarify the purpose and structure of a program.

31. a. A B   (Spaces in input would be read as characters.)
  b. A D

33. a. _____43.55
  b. _5.33
  c. _6.23_8.65
  d. ____23.5___23.54__23.544
  e. YOU'RE SURE TO WIN!

35.
```
PROGRAM ADDNUMBERS (INPUT, OUTPUT);
     {PURPOSE: TO ADD TWO INTEGERS}
VAR
    NUMBER1,
    NUMBER2  : INTEGER;
BEGIN
    WRITE('ENTER TWO NUMBERS: ');
    READLN(NUMBER1, NUMBER2);
    WRITELN('THE SUM OF ',NUMBER1,' AND ',
            NUMBER2,' IS ',NUMBER1 + NUMBER2)
END.
```

36.
```
PROGRAM MESSAGE (INPUT, OUTPUT);

VAR
    NAME : STRING;
    AGE  : INTEGER;
```

```
      BEGIN
         WRITE('ENTER YOUR NAME: ');
         READLN(NAME);
         WRITE('ENTER YOUR AGE: ');
         READLN(AGE);
         WRITELN(NAME, ', YOU SURE LOOK YOUNG');
         WRITELN('FOR BEING ', AGE, 'YEARS OLD.')
      END.
```

45.
```
PROGRAM GRADEPOINTS (OUTPUT);

      BEGIN
         WRITELN('Student    High-school    College');
         WRITELN('           GPA            GPA');
         WRITELN(1:3, 3.4:14:1, 2.5:12:1);
         WRITELN(2:3, 2.3:14:1, 2.0:12:1);
         WRITELN(3:3, 4.0:14:1, 3.9:12:1);
         WRITELN(4:3, 3.1:14:1, 3.5:12:1)
      END.
```

Chapter 3

1. a. 16
   b. 34
   c. 80
   d. 3
   e. 4
   f. 3

3. a. 5
   b. 7
   c. -11
   d. -9
   e. 0
   f. 5
   g. 2.00000E1
   h. -3.20000E1
   i. 48
   j. 0

5. a. REAL.
   b. INTEGER.
   c. REAL.
   d. INTEGER.
   e. INTEGER.

7. a. 322
   b. 0
   c. 8.00000
   d. 16
   e. 7
   f. 100
   g. 8
   h. 5.00000
   i. 34.8
   j. Q

9. a. 2.37000E1
   b. 31
   c. 1
   d. 4.00000
   e. 2

11. a. X = −5   Y = 5   Z = −1
   b. X = 2   Y = 5   Z = 12
   c. X = 2   Y = 10   Z = −1
   d. X = 2   Y = 5   Z = 2
   e. X = 2   Y = 5   Z = 1.75000

13. a. The = should be :=.
   b. The end parenthesis should precede the first division symbol.
   c. Switch the variable and the expression; that is,
       QUOTIENT := 7 DIV 9;

15 a. (X + Y) / Z
   b. (X + Y) / (W + Z)
   c. X - (Y + W) / (X + Z)

17. a. SQR(A) + SQR(B)
   b. 5 * SQR(A)
   c. EXP(1 / 4 * LN(B))

19. a. C := 1 / 2 * (SQR(A) + SQR(B));
   b. Y := J - SQR(K) + 3;
   c. Z := EXP(3 * LN(R)) + 2 * S * T + W * (D + 5);

21. a. Valid.
   b. Invalid.
   c. Valid.
   d. Valid.
   e. Valid.
   f. Invalid.

23. a. Incorrect.
   b. Incorrect.
   c. Correct.
   d. Incorrect.
   e. Correct.

25. a. B := A - 1;
   b. X := 2 * Y + 4;
   c. C := 3 * B / (C + 4);

27.
```
CONST
    PI = 3.14159;
VAR
    A,
    R    : REAL;

BEGIN
    A := PI * SQR(R);
```

36.
```
PROGRAM CONVERT (INPUT, OUTPUT);
      {PURPOSE: CONVERT FEET TO INCHES}
VAR
    HEIGHT,
    INCHES    : REAL;
```

```
BEGIN
   WRITE('ENTER A HEIGHT IN FEET: ');
   READLN(HEIGHT);
   INCHES := HEIGHT * 12;
   WRITELN(HEIGHT, ' FEET EQUALS ', INCHES)
END.
```

43.
```
PROGRAM BOX (INPUT, OUTPUT);
     {PURPOSE: TO CALCULATE SURFACE AREA AND
                 VOLUME OF A BOX}
VAR
   LENGTH,
   WIDTH,
   DEPTH,
   SURFACEAREA,
   VOLUME        :REAL;

BEGIN
   WRITE('ENTER THE DIMENSIONS OF THE BOX: ');
   READLN(LENGTH, WIDTH, DEPTH);
   SURFACEAREA := 2*(LENGTH*WIDTH + LENGTH*DEPTH
                   + WIDTH*DEPTH);
   VOLUME := LENGTH * WIDTH * DEPTH;
   WRITELN('THE SURFACE AREA OF THE BOX IS ',
           SURFACEAREA,'.');
   WRITELN('THE VOLUME OF THE BOX IS ',VOLUME,'.')
END.
```

Chapter 4

1. c.

3. DANIEL MIGHT HAVE DONE IT
    DAVID DEFINITELY DID IT

5. Z
    B
    A
    Z

7. The structure is not valid. Global variables must be declared before the procedure declaration.

9. Global.
    Local.
    Unknown.
    Unknown.

11. a. True.
    b. True; since there is no call to P5 in P1.
    c. False.

13. c best represents the problem.

21.
```
PROGRAM TICTACKTOE (OUTPUT);
     {PURPOSE: TO DRAW A TIC-TACK-TOE BOARD}
PROCEDURE TWO;

   BEGIN
      WRITELN('   *   *')
   END;
```

```
PROCEDURE LINE;

    BEGIN
        WRITELN('***********')
    END;

BEGIN    { MAIN PROGRAM }

    TWO;
    TWO;
    TWO;
    LINE;
    TWO;
    TWO;
    TWO;
    LINE;
    TWO;
    TWO;
    TWO
END.
```

Chapter 5

1. 111

3. **a** and **c** will print the alphabet in order; **b** and **d** will not.

5. The inner loop (CLOOP) counts from 1 to 5 each time through the middle loop (BLOOP). The middle loop counts from 'A' to 'E' each time through the outer loop (ALOOP).

```
1A1
1A2
1A3
1A4
1A5
1B1
1B2
 .
 .
 .
5E5
```

7. **a.** 50
   b. 81
   c. 3
   d. 31
   e. 3

9. **a.** This segment prints multiples of 3 from 3 through 30.

   b. This segment prints the following:

```
320
419
518
617
 .
 .
 .
203
```

11. ■ The = should be : = in the FOR loop.
    ■ There should not be a semicolon at the end of the FOR loop.
    ■ The two indented assignment statements must be a part of the FOR loop. Use a BEGIN . . . END for this purpose.
    ■ Replace COUNT with ECOUNT in the accumulation statement; that is, SUM := SUM + ECOUNT.

13. PROCESS will be called 105 times.

15. **b** and **d** are necessary.

17. The power consumed and the cost of electricity per unit consumed are the necessary data.

21.
```
PROCEDURE ODD (OUTPUT);

VAR
    COUNT,
    ODDNUMBER : INTEGER;

BEGIN
    FOR COUNT := 1 TO 50 DO
        BEGIN
            ODDNUMBER := 2 * COUNT - 1;
            WRITELN(ODDNUMBER)
        END
END;
```

25. **c.**
```
SUM := 0;
FOR COUNT := 1 TO 100 DO
        SUM := SUM + 1/COUNT;
```

27. **c.**
```
PROGRAM DIAMOND(INPUT,OUTPUT);

VAR
    COLUMN,
    COUNT,
    ROW     : INTEGER;

BEGIN

    FOR ROW := 1 TO 5 DO
        BEGIN
            FOR COUNT := 1 TO 5 - ROW DO
                WRITE(' ');
            FOR COLUMN := 1 TO 2 * ROW - 1 DO
                WRITE('*');
            WRITELN
        END;
    FOR ROW := 4 DOWNTO 1 DO
        BEGIN
            FOR COUNT := 1 TO 5 - ROW DO
                WRITE(' ');
            FOR COLUMN := 1 TO 2 * ROW - 1 DO
                WRITE('*');
            WRITELN
        END

END.
```

Chapter 6

1. **a.** REPEAT.
   b. REPEAT.
   c. NEITHER.

3. **b.**

5. **a.** JUMP <> HIGH
   b. (BANKRUPT < BALANCE) AND (BANKRUPT < 0)
   c. NOT(DONE)

7. **a.** FALSE
   b. TRUE
   c. TRUE

9. **a.** P Q   P OR NOT(Q)
       T T   T
       T F   T
       F T   F
       F F   T
   b. P Q   P AND NOT(Q)
       T T   F
       T F   T
       F T   F
       F F   F
   c. The expression NOT(P AND NOT(P)) is always TRUE.
   d. The expression P OR NOT(P) is always TRUE.

11. **a.** FALSE
    b. TRUE
    c. TRUE

13. Lines 8 and 9 need to be switched.

15. ((A OR B) AND (NOT(A AND B)))

19.
```
COUNT := 1;
REPEAT
   WRITE(COUNT, ' IS ');
   WRITELN(CHR(COUNT));
   COUNT := COUNT + 1
UNTIL COUNT > 25;
```

Chapter 7

1.
```
IF X = 0
   THEN WRITELN('CANNOT DIVIDE BY ZERO');
```

3.
```
IF STUDENT = 'F'
   THEN DORM := 1
   ELSE DORM := 2;
```

5. **a.** POOR
   b. EXCELLENT
   c. O.K.
   d. GOOD

7. Any value of X greater than 304000 will cause PRESSURE to exceed MAX.

9. **a.** FALSE
   b. FALSE
   c. TRUE
   d. TRUE

11. **a.** FALSE
    b. TRUE
    c. TRUE

13. **a.** Valid.
    b. Invalid.
    c. Valid.
    d. Valid.

15. **d**, **f**, and **g**.

17. The WRITE statement will be executed when
    a. X is larger than Y and A is FALSE.
    b. X satisfies the inequality $Y - 1 \leq X \leq Y + 1$.
    c. A is TRUE. If A is FALSE, the WRITE statement will be
       executed if B is TRUE and X is less than Y.

19. ```
2.00000
0.00000
9.00000
1.00000
```

21. ```
CASE I OF
    1 : A := A + 1;
    2 : B := B + 1;
  3,4 : C := C + 1;
    5 : D := D + 1
END; {CASE}
```

23. **a.** ```
IF X IN [1..4]
    THEN CASE X OF . . .
```
    **b.** ```
IF Z IN [1..3,51..53]
    THEN CASE Z OF . . .
```
    c. ```
IF NOT(Y IN [0..10])
    THEN WRITE('TRY AGAIN')
    ELSE CASE Y OF . . .
```

25. ```
IF NOT(G IN ['A', 'B', 'C', 'D', 'F'])
    THEN WRITELN('ERROR ENTERING GRADE')
    ELSE
      CASE G OF
        .
        .
        .
      END; {CASE}
```

27. ```
IF A <= 13
    THEN WRITELN('CHILD')
    ELSE
        IF A < 20
          THEN WRITELN('TEENAGER')
          ELSE
              IF A < 40
                THEN WRITELN('YOUNG ADULT')
                ELSE
                    IF A < 60
                      THEN WRITELN('MIDDLE AGE')
                      ELSE WRITELN('SENIOR');
```
```

```
33. REPEAT
        WRITELN('ENTER A NUMBER BETWEEN 1 AND 7');
        READLN(NUMBER)
    UNTIL NUMBER IN [1..7];
    CASE NUMBER OF
        1 : WRITELN('MONDAY');
        2 : WRITELN('TUESDAY');
        3 : WRITELN('WEDNESDAY');
        4 : WRITELN('THURSDAY');
        5 : WRITELN('FRIDAY');
      6,7 : WRITELN('WEEKEND')
    END; {CASE}


37. PROGRAM ELECTRICBILL (INPUT, OUTPUT);

    VAR
        BILL,
        USAGE:REAL;

    PROCEDURE GETINFO;

        BEGIN
            WRITE('ENTER KILOWATT-HOUR USAGE: ');
            READLN(USAGE)
        END;

    PROCEDURE COMPUTEBILL;

        BEGIN
            IF USAGE <= 300.0
                THEN BILL := 0.04237 * USAGE
                ELSE
                    IF USAGE <= 1200.0
                        THEN BILL := 0.05241 * USAGE
                        ELSE BILL := 0.06113 * USAGE;
            BILL := BILL + 3
        END;

    PROCEDURE PRINTBILL;

        BEGIN
            WRITELN('KILOWATT-HOUR USAGE WAS ',USAGE);
            WRITELN('CHARGE IS ',BILL:6:2)
        END;

    BEGIN    { MAIN PROGRAM }

        GETINFO;
        COMPUTEBILL;
        PRINTBILL

    END.
```

Chapter 8

1. **a.** Global.
   b. Global.
   c. Global.
   d. Local.
   e. Local.

     f. Local.
     g. Local.
     h. Local.
     i. Local.

3. a. Valid.
    b. Invalid.
    c. Invalid.
    d. Valid.
    e. Invalid.
    f. Valid.

5.
```
PROCEDURE FIVE (A : REAL; VAR FLAG : BOOLEAN;
                VAR NUM : INTEGER);
```

7. The output is
```
10
```

9.
- Procedure GETROLL needs a BEGIN...END block.
- The parameter ROLL of procedure GETROLL should be a variable parameter.
- Procedure ADD should have a value parameter (N), a variable parameter (C), and a value parameter (SUM).
- The accumulation statement (SUM := SUM + C;) in procedure ADD should be incremented by N (SUM := SUM + N;).
- In the main program, TOTAL should be initialized to 0 (TOTAL := 0;).

11. The variable S will contain 24, FLAG will be TRUE, Q will be 6, and P will be 10.

15. Procedure TOM could be written as follows:

```
PROCEDURE TOM (PH : INTEGER[7];
                VAR TOTAL1, TOTAL2 : INTEGER);

    BEGIN
      IF TRUNC(PH/10000) = 486
        THEN TOTAL1 := TOTAL1 + 1;
      IF TRUNC(PH/10000) = 487
        THEN TOTAL2 := TOTAL2 + 1
    END;
```

17.
```
PROGRAM AVERAGE (INPUT, OUTPUT);

VAR F,
    L   : INTEGER;
    A   : REAL;

PROCEDURE GETNUMBERS (VAR FIRST, LEN : INTEGER);

    BEGIN
      WRITE('ENTER THE FIRST INTEGER AND ');
      WRITE('THE LENGTH OF THE SEQUENCE: ');
      READLN(FIRST, LEN)
    END;

PROCEDURE COMPUTE (FIRST, LEN : INTEGER;
                    VAR AVERAGE : REAL);

    VAR COUNT,
        SUM    : INTEGER;
```

```
      BEGIN
         SUM := 0;
         FOR COUNT := FIRST TO FIRST + LEN - 1 DO
            SUM := SUM + COUNT;
         AVERAGE := SUM / LEN
      END;

  PROCEDURE PRINTRESULTS (AVERAGE : REAL);

      BEGIN
         WRITELN('THE AVERAGE IS ', AVERAGE)
      END;

  BEGIN   { MAIN PROGRAM }

      GETNUMBERS(F,L);
      COMPUTE(F,L,A);
      PRINTRESULTS(A)

  END.
```

Chapter 9

1. **a.** False. A function returns a value through the function identifier.
   b. False. A function call must occur in an expression, whereas a procedure call is a statement.

3. **a.**
```
FUNCTION P (L, W : REAL) : REAL;
BEGIN
    P := 2 * L + 2 * W
END;
```
   b.
```
FUNCTION A (X,Y,Z : REAL) : REAL;
BEGIN
    A := SQRT(X * X + Y * Y + Z * Z)
END;
```
   c.
```
FUNCTION R (S,T : REAL) : REAL;
BEGIN
    R := 1/S + 1/T
END;
```
   d.
```
FUNCTION A (P,R,T : REAL) : REAL;
BEGIN
    A := P * EXP(T * LN(1 + R))
END;
```

5. **a.** RANDOM MOD 50 + 1
   b. 2 * RANDOM MOD 50 + 2
   c. 5 * RANDOM MOD 41 + 50
   d. 10 * RANDOM MOD 11 - 50

7. **a.**
```
IF RANDOM MOD 2 = 0
   THEN WRITELN('HEADS')
   ELSE WRITELN('TAILS');
```
   b.
```
IF RANDOM MOD 2 = 0
   THEN IF RANDOM MOD 2 = 0
          THEN WRITELN('HEADS, HEADS')
          ELSE WRITELN('HEADS, TAILS')
   ELSE IF RANDOM MOD 2 = 0
          THEN WRITELN('TAILS, HEADS')
          ELSE WRITELN('TAILS, TAILS');
```

```
11. FUNCTION LENGTH (MILES, YARDS, FEET,
                    INCHES : INTEGER) : INTEGER;

    BEGIN
        LENGTH := 5280 * 12 * MILES + 36 * YARDS +
                  12 * FEET + INCHES
    END;

19. PROGRAM SUMPRODUCT (INPUT, OUTPUT);

    USES APPLESTUFF;

    VAR
        L,
        H,
        N1,
        N2,
        S,
        P      : INTEGER;
        ANSWER : CHAR;

    FUNCTION RND(LOW, HIGH : INTEGER) : INTEGER;

    BEGIN
        RND := RANDOM MOD (HIGH - LOW + 1) + LOW
    END;

    PROCEDURE COMPUTE(NUMBER1, NUMBER2 : INTEGER;
                      VAR SUM, PRODUCT : INTEGER);

    BEGIN
        SUM := NUMBER1 + NUMBER2;
        PRODUCT := NUMBER1 * NUMBER2
    END;

    PROCEDURE PRINTRESULTS(NUMBER1, NUMBER2, SUM,
                           PRODUCT : INTEGER);

    BEGIN
        WRITELN('NUMBER1,' + ',NUMBER2,' = ',SUM);
        WRITELN('NUMBER1,' * ',NUMBER2,' = ',PRODUCT)
    END;

    BEGIN   { MAIN PROGRAM }

        REPEAT
            WRITE('RANGE OF RANDOM NUMBERS (LOW,HIGH):');
            READLN(L, H);
            N1 := RND(L, H);
            N2 := RND(L, H);
            COMPUTE(N1, N2, S, P);
            PRINTRESULTS(N1, N2, S, P);
            WRITELN('DO YOU WISH TO CONTINUE (Y/N)?');
            READLN(ANSWER)
        UNTIL ANSWER = 'N'
    END.
```

Chapter 10

1. **a.** F
   b. A
   c. D
   d. E
   e. B
   f. C

3. The recursion that occurs when the numbers from 2 to 500 are summed uses limit-direct-pending recursion to push the numbers on the stack and add them as the recursion is exited.

5. **a.** The recursion used to produce the picture is limit-direct-end recursion.
   b. The recursion used to produce the picture is limit-direct-pending recursion.

7. **a.** 1.00000E1
   b. 5.00000E1
   c. A function call using parameters -1 and 3.0 will result in an overflow error, since the recursion is infinite.

9. The function will be called recursively 40 times (this does not include the initial call from the main program.)

11. **a.** DONE
    b. DONE
       WHAT IS HAPPENING?
    c. DONE
       WHAT IS HAPPENING?
       WHAT IS HAPPENING?
       WHAT IS HAPPENING?
       WHAT IS HAPPENING?
       WHAT IS HAPPENING?

13. ▪ The function heading needs to specify the type of the value to be returned; that is, INTEGER.
    ▪ TRYAGAIN should be TRY.

15.
```
FUNCTION SUM (N : INTEGER) : INTEGER;

BEGIN
   IF N = 1
      THEN SUM := 1
      ELSE SUM := SUM(N - 1) + SQR(2 * N - 1)
END;
```

Chapter 11

1. **a.**
```
TYPE
   MAIN = (SPAGHETTI, STROGANOFF, HAMBURGERS,
           STEW, CHICKEN);
```
   b.
```
TYPE
   PIECES = (PAWN, KNIGHT, BISHOP, ROOK,
             QUEEN, KING);
```
   c.
```
TYPE
   OPERATIONS = (ADD, SUBTRACT, MULTIPLY,
                 DIVIDE);
```

3. a. TYPE
```
        NUMBERS = -20..20;
```
b. TYPE
```
        LETTERS = 'M'..'Z';
```
c. TYPE
```
        FOODS = SPAGHETTI..HAMBURGERS;
```

5. a. Valid.
  b. Invalid. The lower limit must be less than the upper limit.
  c. Valid.
  d. Invalid. Single quotation marks are needed around the characters.
  e. Invalid. Integer overlap.
  f. Valid.
  g. Valid.

7. a. 2
  b. CTRL-A
  c. 65
  d. PEAR
  e. LIME
  f. Undefined.

9. a. True.
  b. True.

11. ▪ In the variable declaration of CONIFER, use a colon instead of the equal sign.
  ▪ FIR is a constant of type TREE and should not be used as a variable name in the procedure heading.
  ▪ The loop counter and the value in the WRITELN statement should be LOOP, not TREE.
  ▪ CASE statements are needed to output the constants of type TREE. (May not be necessary in some versions of Pascal.)

13. a. Compatible.
  b. Neither.
  c. Compatible.
  d. Identical.

19.
```
PROCEDURE FOODCHAIN (FIRST, SECOND : FOODCHAIN);

BEGIN
    IF FIRST < SECOND
        THEN BEGIN
                WRITELN('FIRST IS PREY');
                WRITELN('SECOND IS PREDATOR');
                WRITELN('DISTANCE APART IS ',
                        ORD(SECOND) - ORD(FIRST)
             END
        ELSE BEGIN
                WRITELN('SECOND IS PREY');
                WRITELN('FIRST IS PREDATOR');
                WRITELN('DISTANCE APART IS ',
                        ORD(FIRST) - ORD(SECOND)
             END
END;
```

Chapter 12

1. **a.** TYPE
        ALPHABET = SET OF 'a'..'Z';
    b. VAR
        LOWERCASE,
        UPPERCASE : ALPHABET;
    c. LOWERCASE := ['a'..'z'];
        UPPERCASE := ALPHABET - LOWERCASE;

3. **a.** TYPE
        COLORS = SET OF (RED, WHITE, BLUE, GREEN,
                            YELLOW, PURPLE);
    b. VAR
        LIGHT,
        DARK   : COLORS;
    c. LIGHT := [];
        DARK := [RED,WHITE,BLUE,GREEN,YELLOW,PURPLE];

5. **a.** TYPE
        SYMBOLS = SET OF '!'..'?';
    b. VAR
        PUNCTUATION,
        ENDINGS   : SYMBOLS;
    c. PUNCTUATION := ['!', ',', '.', ';', ':', '?'];
        ENDINGS := ['!', '.', '?'];

7. The sets listed in **b** and **c** are equivalent as are those listed in **a** and **d**.

9. **a.** ['A', 'B', 'C']
    b. []
    c. ['A', 'B', 'C']

11. **a.** [1..5]
    b. [1..4]
    c. [5]
    d. [1..5]
    e. [1..4]

13. **a.** TRUE
    b. TRUE
    c. FALSE
    d. TRUE
    e. TRUE

15. **a.** LETTER IN ['A', 'B', 'C']
    b. LETTER IN ['H'..'Q']
    c. LETTER IN ['A', 'B', 'C']

17. PROGRAM LETTER (INPUT, OUTPUT);

    TYPE
        LETTERS = SET OF 'A'..'Z';

    VAR
        CHARACTER : CHAR;
        ALPHABET,
        VOWELS,   : LETTERS

```
BEGIN
    ALPHABET := ['A'..'Z'];
    VOWELS := ['A', 'E', 'I', 'O', 'U'];
    WRITE('ENTER A LETTER: ');
    READLN(CHARACTER);
    IF CHARACTER IN VOWELS
        THEN WRITELN(CHARACTER, ' IS A VOWEL')
        ELSE WRITELN(CHARACTER, ' IS A CONSONANT')
END.
```

Chapter 13

1. TYPE
     DECATHLON = ARRAY[1..10] OF REAL;

3. TYPE
     TABLE = ARRAY[0..9, 0..9] OF INTEGER;

5. TYPE
     BLOCK = ARRAY[0..4, 0..3, 0..7] OF INTEGER;

7. **a.** 49
    b. 90
    c. 12
    d. 10
    e. 27
    f. 10

9. **a.** The segment prints the contents of row 4, columns 0 to 9.
    b. The segment prints the contents of row 2, columns 7 to 1.
    c. The segment prints the contents of column 0, rows 1 to 5.

11. **a.** 2
       4
       6
       8
       10
       12
       14
       16
       18
       20
    b. 9
       8
       7
       6
       5
       4
       3
       2
       1
       0

13. Checks for a value of 100 in an array of 20 elements. If 100 is found, the BOOLEAN variable BULLSEYE is set to TRUE.

19.
```
PROGRAM ELECTION (INPUT, OUTPUT);

TYPE
    GENDER      = (FEMALE,MALE);
    NAMEARRAY   = ARRAY[1..20] OF STRING[30];
    NUMBERARRAY = ARRAY[FEMALE..MALE,1..20]
                  OF INTEGER;

VAR
    GCANDIDATE  : NAMEARRAY;
    GVOTES      : NUMBERARRAY;
    GCOUNT      : INTEGER;

PROCEDURE GETINFO(VAR CAND  : NAMEARRAY;
                  VAR VOTES : NUMBERARRAY;
                  VAR CNT   : INTEGER);

    VAR
        DONE   : BOOLEAN;
        ANSWER : CHAR;

    BEGIN

        CNT := 0;
        DONE := FALSE;
        WHILE NOT DONE  DO
           BEGIN
              CNT := CNT + 1;
              WRITE('ENTER CANDIDATE NAME: ');
              READLN(CAND[CNT]);
              WRITE('NUMBER OF FEMALE VOTES: ');
              READLN(VOTES[FEMALE,CNT]);
              WRITE('NUMBER OF MALE VOTES: ');
              READLN(VOTES[MALE,CNT]);
              WRITE('DO YOU WISH TO CONTINUE?');
              READLN(ANSWER);
              IF (ANSWER = 'N') OR (CNT = 20)
                 THEN DONE := TRUE
           END  { WHILE }

    END; {  GET INFO }

PROCEDURE PRINTRESULTS(CAND  : NAMEARRAY;
                       VOTES : NUMBERARRAY;
                       CNT   : INTEGER);

    VAR
        LOOP,
        TOTAL,
        TFEMALE,
        TMALE   : INTEGER;
```

```
      BEGIN

          TFEMALE := 0;
          TMALE := 0;
          PAGE(OUTPUT);
          WRITELN;
          WRITELN('CANDIDATE':10,'FEMALE':10,
                  'MALE':10,'TOTAL':10);
          FOR LOOP := 1 TO CNT DO
             BEGIN
                 TFEMALE := TFEMALE+VOTES[FEMALE,LOOP];
                 TMALE := TMALE + VOTES[MALE,LOOP];
                 TOTAL := VOTES[FEMALE,LOOP] +
                          VOTES[MALE,LOOP];
                 WRITELN(CAND[LOOP]:10,
                          VOTES[FEMALE,LOOP]:10,
                          VOTES[MALE,LOOP]:10,
                          TOTAL:10);
             END;
          WRITELN(TFEMALE:20,TMALE:10,
                  TFEMALE + TMALE:10)

      END; { PRINTRESULTS}

   BEGIN { MAIN PROGRAM }

      GETINFO(GCANDIDATE,GVOTES,GCOUNT);
      PRINTRESULTS(GCANDIDATE,GVOTES,GCOUNT)

   END.
```

23.
```
   PROCEDURE SWITCH (VAR A, B : CHARACTERARRAY;
                     LIMIT : INTEGER);

   VAR
      COUNT : INTEGER;
      TEMP  : CHAR;

   BEGIN
      FOR COUNT := 1 TO LIMIT DO
         BEGIN
             TEMP := A[COUNT];
             A[COUNT] := B[COUNT];
             B[COUNT] := TEMP
         END
   END;
```

Chapter 14

1. **a.** 12   3 23 32   4 33
     3 12 23   4 32 33
     3 12   4 23 32 33
   b. 3 12 23 32 33   4
     3   4 23 32 33 12
     3   4 12 32 33 23

3. **a.** −9999 23 12   3 32 33 4
     −9999 12 23   3 32 33 4
     −9999   3 12 23 32 33 4

b. 4 12   3 23 33 32
       4   3 12 23 32 33
       3   4 12 23 32 33

5. Quicksort is most efficient for large arrays. Insertion sort is most efficient for small arrays.

7.
Number	Comparisons Needed
−31	Four
−27	Three
14	Three
17	One
18	Three
29	Two
30	Three
48	Four

9.
Pass 1:	0	35	28	3	27	6	12	11	77	65
Pass 2:	0	3	28	35	27	6	12	11	77	65
Pass 3:	0	3	6	35	27	28	12	11	77	65
Pass 4:	0	3	6	11	27	28	12	35	77	65
Pass 5:	0	3	6	11	12	28	27	35	77	65
Pass 6:	0	3	6	11	12	27	28	35	77	65
Pass 7:	0	3	6	11	12	27	28	35	77	65
Pass 8:	0	3	6	11	12	27	28	35	77	65
Pass 9:	0	3	6	11	12	27	28	35	65	77

Comparisons = 45
Exchanges = 9

11. Three collisions would occur.

17.
```
PROCEDURE INSERT (VAR A, B : NUMBERARRAY);

BEGIN
   FOR LOOP := 31 TO 40 DO
      A[LOOP] := B[LOOP - 30]
END;
```

21.
```
PROGRAM SORT (INPUT, OUTPUT);

TYPE
   NAMEARRAY = ARRAY[1..30] OF STRING;
   SCOREARRAY = ARRAY[1..30] OF INTEGER;

VAR
   GNAME:    : NAMEARRAY;
   GSCORE    : SCOREARRAY;
   GNUMBER   : INTEGER;

PROCEDURE GETNAMES (VAR NAME : NAMEARRAY;
                    VAR SCORE : SCOREARRAY;
                    VAR NUMBER : INTEGER);
VAR
   COUNT : INTEGER;
```

```
BEGIN
    WRITE('ENTER NUMBER OF NAMES TO BE SORTED: ');
    READLN(NUMBER);
    WRITELN('ENTER STUDENT''S NAME, PRESS RETURN');
    WRITELN('THEN ENTER HIS OR HER SCORE.');
    FOR COUNT := 1 TO NUMBER DO
        READLN(NAME[COUNT], SCORE[COUNT])
END;

PROCEDURE SWITCH (VAR FIRSTNAME,
                      SECONDNAME : STRING;
                      VAR FIRSTSCORE,
                      SECONDSCORE : INTEGER);

VAR
    TEMPNAME  : STRING;
    TEMPSCORE : INTEGER;

BEGIN
    TEMPNAME := FIRSTNAME;
    TEMPSCORE := FIRSTSCORE;
    FIRSTNAME := SECONDNAME;
    FIRSTSCORE := SECONDSCORE;
    SECONDNAME := TEMPNAME;
    SECONDSCORE := TEMPSCORE
END;

PROCEDURE BUBBLE (VAR NAME : NAMEARRAY;
                      VAR SCORE : SCOREARRAY;
                      NUMBER : INTEGER);

VAR
    LAST,
    CURRENT  : INTEGER;

BEGIN
    FOR LAST := NUMBER - 1 DOWNTO 1
        FOR CURRENT := 1 TO NUMBER - LAST DO
            IF NAME[CURRENT] > NAME[CURRENT + 1]
                THEN SWITCH(NAME[CURRENT],
                            NAME[CURRENT+1],
                            SCORE[CURRENT],
                            SCORE[CURRENT + 1])
END;

PROCEDURE PRINTRESULTS (NAME : NAMEARRAY;
                            SCORE : SCOREARRAY;
                            NUMBER :INTEGER);

VAR
    LOOP : INTEGER;

BEGIN
    FOR LOOP := 1 TO NUMBER DO
        WRITELN(NAME[LOOP],' ', SCORE[LOOP])
END;
```

```
BEGIN   { MAIN PROGRAM }

   GETNAMES(GNAME, GSCORE, GNUMBER);
   BUBBLE(GNAME, GSCORE, GNUMBER);
   PRINTRESULTS(GNAME, GSCORE, GNUMBER)

END.
```

Chapter 15

1. **a.** Valid.
   b. Invalid. DFIELD is a string, not a number.
   c. Valid.
   d. Valid.
   e. Valid.

3. **a.**
```
HVAR.MFIELD := 'B';
HVAR.NFIELD := 3;
```
   b. `QVAR := PVAR;`
   c.
```
QVAR.AFIELD := JVAR.AFIELD;
QVAR.BFIELD := JVAR.DFIELD;
QVAR.CFIELD := JVAR.BFIELD;
QVAR.DFIELD := JVAR.CFIELD;
```
   d. `KVAR.CFIELD := SVAR;`
   e.
```
PVAR.AFIELD := HVAR.MFIELD;
PVAR.DFIELD := HVAR.NFIELD;
```

5. The program segment assigns a longitude (measurement and direction) to the first array element of PLACES.

7. `PLACES[100].LONGITUDE.DEGREES := 35;`

9.
```
TYPE
    STUDENTDATA = RECORD
        STUDENTNAME   : STRING[30];
        STUDENTINCOME : REAL;
        PARENTINCOME  : REAL;
        GRADEPOINT    : REAL;
        SATMATH       : INTEGER;
        SATVERBAL     : INTEGER;
        COLLEGE       : STRING[20];
        TUITION       : REAL;
        EXPENSES      : REAL
    END;   { STUDENTDATA }
```

11.
```
TYPE
    DIRECTORY = RECORD
        NAME    : STRING[20];
        ADDRESS : STRING[50];
        PHONE   : STRING[20]
    END;

    DATE = RECORD
        MONTH : (JANUARY,FEBRUARY,MARCH,APRIL,
                 MAY,JUNE,JULY,AUGUST,SEPTEMBER,
                 OCTOBER,NOVEMBER,DECEMBER);
        DAY   : 1..31;
        YEAR  : 1987..1995
    END;
```

```
MEDICALCHART = RECORD
    PATIENT    : DIRECTORY;
    SSNUM      : STRING[11];
    AGE        : INTEGER;
    SEX        : (FEMALE, MALE);
    EMPLOYER   : DIRECTORY;
    RELATIVE   : DIRECTORY;
    INSURANC   : DIRECTORY;
    INSUR      : INTEGER;
    ALLERGIES  : ARRAY[1..5] OF STRING[20];
    CURRENTMED : ARRAY[1..5] OF STRING[20];
    LASTVISIT  : DATE
END;
```

Chapter 16

1.
```
PROGRAM FRIENDS(INPUT,OUTPUT,NAMES.DATA);
   { NAMES.DATA IS EXTERNAL FILE NAME }
VAR NAMES : TEXT;
```

3.
```
TYPE
   BOOKRECORD = RECORD
                  .
                  .
                  .
                END;  { BOOKRECORD }
   BOOKFILE = FILE OF BOOKRECORD;
   DEWEY = ARRAY[1..100] OF BOOKRECORD;
VAR
   LIBRARY     : BOOKFILE;
   CARDCATALOG : DEWEY;
```

5. **a.** Valid
   b. Invalid. RECORD cannot contain a FILE.
   c. Valid.
   d. Valid.
   e. Valid. However, WORDS will not be treated as a standard TEXT file. More appropriate would be

   ```
   TYPE WORDS = TEXT;
   ```

7. **a** indicates the contents of NUMFILE.

9. The file would contain

52.6	45.0	EOF

11. **b** is correct.

14.
```
PROGRAM NAMES (INPUT,OUTPUT,NAME.DATA);

VAR
   TEMPFILE : TEXT;
   NAME,
   PHONE : STRING;
```

```
BEGIN
   REWRITE(TEMPFILE,'MYDISK:NAME.DATA');
   WRITELN('USE ''END'' FOR NAME WHEN DONE.');
   REPEAT
      WRITE('NAME: ');
      READLN(NAME);
      WRITE('TELEPHONE: ');
      READLN(PHONE);
      IF NAME <> 'END'
         THEN
            BEGIN
               WRITELN(TEMPFILE,NAME);
               WRITELN(TEMPFILE,PHONE)
            END
   UNTIL NAME = 'END';
   CLOSE(TEMPFILE,LOCK)
END.
```

Chapter 17

1.
```
TYPE
   BLOCKPOINT = ^BLOCK;
   BLOCK = RECORD
              NAME   : STRING;
              PHONE  : INTEGER;
              FOLLOW : BLOCKPOINT
           END;  { BLOCK RECORD }
```

3. The definition of POINT should come before the record definition R.

5. **c** and **d** point to a node of the linked structure.

7. Invalid. The value in parentheses should be the pointer CURRENT. The notation CURRENT∧ represents the node pointed to by CURRENT.

9. `CURRENT^.NEXT^.NEXT^.NEXT^.NEXT^.NEXT := NIL;`

11.

13. **a.** 7 4 3 1 2
     b. 7 4 1 3 2
     c. 3 1 4 7 2

15. **a.** BOX   00010 01111 11000
    b. TO   10100 01111
    c. FAR   00110 00001 10010
    d. RIDE   10010 01001 00100 00101

17. The following addresses pertain to the words in Exercise 15:
    a. BOX   000 = 0
    b. TO   101 = 5
    c. FAR   000 = 0
    d. RIDE   101 = 5

19. **a.** BOX   00010 01111 11000 = 2552
                                2552 MOD 31 = 10
    b. TO   10100 01111 = 655
                                655 MOD 31 = 4
    c. FAR   00110 00001 10010 = 6194
                                6194 MOD 31 = 25
    d. RIDE   10010 01001 00100 00101 = 599173
                                599173 MOD 31 = 5

21. The answers to this exercise will vary; one example is DROP and PROD.

25. { TYPE PTR = ^REUNION }

```
FUNCTION COUNTPEOPLE (FRONT : PTR); INTEGER;

   VAR
      COUNT : INTEGER;
      TEMP  : PTR;

   BEGIN
      COUNT := 0;
      TEMP  := FRONT;
      WHILE TEMP <> NIL DO
         BEGIN
            COUNT := COUNT + 1;
            TEMP := TEMP^.NEXT
         END;
      COUNTPEOPLE := COUNT
   END;
```

Chapter 18

1. D, E, and F are first cousins of G.
   H and I are second cousins of G.
   J, K, and L are second cousins of D, E, and F.
   H and I are third cousins of J, K, and L.

3. Three pointer fields would be needed since the maximum number of branches from a node is three.

5. A, B, E, C, and G are the internal nodes.

7. C E F D B I K J H G A

9. C B E D F A G I H J K

11. A B D F C E G H I

13.

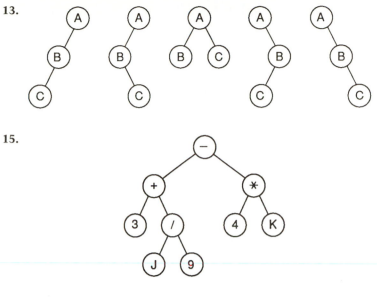

15.

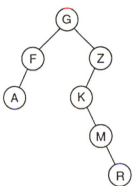

17.

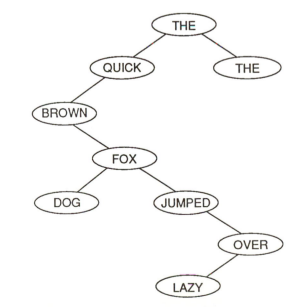

19.

Chapter 19

1. **a.** 6
   b. 2
   c. BCD
   d. ´ABCDEFWXYZ
   e. 1
   f. 1

3. **a.** Need single quotation marks around ABC.
   b. Need to specify the position in the string where the letter is to be inserted.
   c. Need to specify another string as an argument.

5. **a.** 01239
   b. 0123456789

7. **a.** NUMSTRG := STRG(NUMBER);
   b. INSERT('$', NUMSTRG, 1);
   c. INSERT('.', NUMSTRG, LEN(NUMSTRG) - 1);

11.
```
PROGRAM COUNTLETTERS (INPUT, OUTPUT);

VAR
    PHRASE,
    LETTER : STRING;
    P,
    NUMBER : INTEGER;

BEGIN
    P := 1;
    NUMBER := 0;
    WRITE('ENTER A PHRASE: ');
    READLN(PHRASE);
    WRITE('ENTER LETTER TO COUNT IN PHRASE: ');
    READLN(LETTER);
    WHILE P <= LENGTH(PHRASE) DO
        BEGIN
            IF COPY(PHRASE, P, 1) = LETTER
                THEN
                    IF (COPY(PHRASE, P-1,1) = ' ') OR
                       ((POS(LETTER,PHRASE) = 1) AND
                       (P = 1))
                    THEN NUMBER := NUMBER + 1;
            P := P + 1
        END;
    WRITELN('THE NUMBER OF TIMES THE LETTER');
    WRITELN('APPEARS AT THE BEGINNING OF A WORD');
    WRITELN('IN THE PHRASE IS ', NUMBER,'.')
END.
```

15.
```
PROGRAM VOWEL (INPUT, OUTPUT);

VAR
    LET,
    WORD : STRING;
    POSITION : INTEGER;
```

```
BEGIN
    WRITE('ENTER A WORD: ');
    READLN(WORD);
    POSITION := 1;
    WHILE POSITION <= LENGTH(WORD) DO
        BEGIN
            LET := COPY(WORD, POSITION, 1);
            IF (LET IN ['A','E','I','O','U')
                THEN
                    BEGIN
                        INSERT('*', WORD, POSITION);
                        DELETE(WORD, POSITION + 1, 1)
                    END;
            POSITION := POSITION + 1
        END;
    WRITELN('THE NEW WORD IS ', WORD,'.')
END.
```

Chapter 20

1. **a** changes the coordinates.

3.

5.

7.

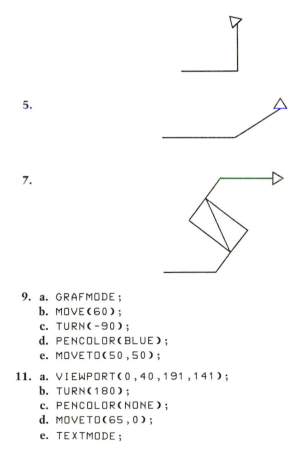

9. **a.** GRAFMODE;
    b. MOVE(60);
    c. TURN(-90);
    d. PENCOLOR(BLUE);
    e. MOVETO(50,50);

11. **a.** VIEWPORT(0,40,191,141);
    b. TURN(180);
    c. PENCOLOR(NONE);
    d. MOVETO(65,0);
    e. TEXTMODE;

```
13. { ASSUME PROCEDURE CALL OF POLYGON(3) }

    PROCEDURE POLYGON (SIDE : INTEGER);

    BEGIN
       IF SIDE > 0
          THEN
             BEGIN
                MOVE(50);
                TURN(120);
                POLYGON(SIDE - 1)
             END
    END;
```

Index